THE COMPARATIVE HERMENEUTICS OF RABBINIC JUDAISM

VOLUME FOUR

SEDER QODOSHIM

THE COMPARATIVE HERMENEUTICS OF RABBINIC JUDAISM

Volume Four

Seder Qodoshim

Jacob Neusner

Academic Studies in the History of Judaism
Global Publications, Binghamton University
2000

Copyright © 2000 by Jacob Neusner

All rights reserved. No portion of this publication may be duplicated in any way without the expressed written consent of the publisher, except in the form of brief excerpts of quotations for the purposes of review.

Library of Congress Cataloging-in-Publication Data

Jacob Neusner, *The Comparative Hermeneutics of Rabbinic Judaism. Volume 1V. Seder Qodosim*

1. Hermeneutics   2. Judaic Studies   3. Religious Studies
4. Zebahim   5. Menahot   6. Temurah

ISBN 1-586840-13-4

Published by Academic Studies in the History of Judaism
Distributed by Global Publications
Binghamton University, State University of New York
Binghamton, New York, USA 13902-6000
Phone: (607) 777-4495. Fax: 777-6132
E-mail: pmorewed@binghamton.edu
http://ssips.binghamton.edu

ACADEMIC STUDIES IN THE HISTORY OF JUDAISM

Editor-in-Chief

Jacob Neusner
Bard College

Editorial Committee

Alan J. Avery-Peck, *College of the Holy Cross*

Bruce D. Chilton, *Bard College*

William Scott Green, *University of Rochester*

James Strange, *University of South Florida*

TABLE OF CONTENTS

PREFACE   xi

1. **TRACTATE ZEBAHIM**   1

   I. The Definition of the Category-Formation, Zebahim-Menahot   1
   II. The Foundations of the Halakhic Category-Formations   16
   III. The Exposition of the Components of the Given Category-Formation by the Mishnah-Tosefta-Yerushalmi-Bavli   21
   IV. Documentary Traits   113
        A. The Mishnah and the Tosefta   113
        B. The Bavli   113
   V. The Hermeneutics of Zebahim   113
        A. What Fuses the Halakhic Data into a Category-Formation?   113
        B. The Activity of the Category-Formation   120
        C. The Consistency of the Category-Formation   130
        D. The Generativity of the Category-Formation   130

2. **TRACTATE MENAHOT**   139

   I. The Definition of the Category-Formation   139
   II. The Foundations of the Halakhic Category-Formations   141
   III. The Exposition of the Components of the Given Category-Formation by the Mishnah-Tosefta-Yerushalmi-Bavli   142
   IV. Documentary Traits   226
        A. The Mishnah and the Tosefta   226
        B. The Bavli   226
   V. The Hermeneutics of Menahot   226
        A. What Fuses the Halakhic Data into a Category-Formation?   226
        B. The Activity of the Category-Formation   231
        C. The Consistency of the Category-Formation   236
        D. The Generativity of the Category-Formation   236

3. **TRACTATE HULLIN**   241

   I. The Definition of the Category-Formation   241
   II. The Foundations of the Halakhic Category-Formation   247
   III. The Exposition of the Components of the Given Category-Formation by the Mishnah-Tosefta-Yerushalmi-Bavli   248
   IV. Documentary Traits   286
        A. The Mishnah and the Tosefta   286
        B. The Bavli   286

		V.	The Hermeneutics of Hullin	287
			A. What Fuses the Halakhic Data into a Category-Formation?	287
			B. The Activity of the Category-Formation	289
			C. The Consistency of the Category-Formation	292
			D. The Generativity of the Category-Formation	292

4. TRACTATE BEKHOROT — 295

    I. The Definition of the Category-Formation — 295
    II. The Foundations of the Halakhic Category-Formation — 299
    III. The Exposition of the Components of the Given Category-Formation by the Mishnah-Tosefta-Yerushalmi-Bavli — 301
    IV. Documentary Traits — 343
        A. The Mishnah and the Tosefta — 343
        B. The Bavli — 344
    V. The Hermeneutics of Bekhorot — 344
        A. What Fuses the Halakhic Data into a Category-Formation? — 344
        B. The Activity of the Category-Formation — 345
        C. The Consistency of the Category-Formation — 348
        D. The Generativity of the Category-Formation — 349

5. TRACTATE ARAKHIN — 351

    I. The Definition of the Category-Formation — 351
    II. The Foundations of the Halakhic Category-Formation — 359
    III. The Exposition of the Components of the Given Category-Formation by the Mishnah-Tosefta-Yerushalmi-Bavli — 360
    IV. Documentary Traits — 392
        A. The Mishnah and the Tosefta — 392
        B. The Bavli — 392
        C. The Aggadah and the Halakhah in the Bavli — 392
    V. The Hermeneutics of Arakhin — 397
        A. What Fuses the Halakhic Data into a Category-Formation? — 397
        B. The Activity of the Category-Formation — 400
        C. The Consistency of the Category-Formation — 404
        D. The Generativity of the Category-Formation — 404

6. TRACTATE TEMURAH — 407

    I. The Definition of the Category-Formation — 407
    II. The Foundations of the Halakhic Category-Formation — 415
    III. The Exposition of the Components of the Given Category-Formation by the Mishnah-Tosefta-Yerushalmi-Bavli — 415
    IV. Documentary Traits — 442

		A.	The Mishnah and the Tosefta	442
		B.	The Bavli	442
	V.	The Hermeneutics of Temurah	442
		A.	What Fuses the Halakhic Data into a Category-Formation?	442
		B.	The Activity of the Category-Formation	445
		C.	The Consistency of the Category-Formation	450
		D.	The Generativity of the Category-Formation	450

7. TRACTATE KERITOT   451

	I.	The Definition of the Category-Formation	451
	II.	The Foundations of the Halakhic Category-Formation	456
	III.	The Exposition of the Components of the Given Category-Formation by the Mishnah-Tosefta-Yerushalmi-Bavli	457
	IV.	Documentary Traits	475
		A.	The Mishnah and the Tosefta	475
		B.	The Bavli	475
		C.	The Aggadah and the Halakhah in the Bavli	475
	V.	The Hermeneutics of Keritot	480
		A.	What Fuses the Halakhic Data into a Category-Formation?	480
		B.	The Activity of the Category-Formation	481
		C.	The Consistency of the Category-Formation	483
		D.	The Generativity of the Category-Formation	483

8. TRACTATE MEILAH   485

	I.	The Definition of the Category-Formation	485
	II.	The Foundations of the Halakhic Category-Formation	490
	III.	The Exposition of the Components of the Given Category-Formation by the Mishnah-Tosefta-Yerushalmi-Bavli	490
	IV.	Documentary Traits	514
		A.	The Mishnah and the Tosefta	514
		B.	The Bavli	514
	V.	The Hermeneutics of Meilah	514
		A.	What Fuses the Halakhic Data into a Category-Formation?	514
		B.	The Activity of the Category-Formation	515
		C.	The Consistency of the Category-Formation	518
		D.	The Generativity of the Category-Formation	519

PREFACE

A distinguished historian of religion once said, "The history of religions is the exegesis of exegesis." In a profound sense, that judgment animates an entire field of learning. In this project in the history of religions, I undertake an inductive account, through systematic inquiry into data, of the hermeneutics of the principal documents of Rabbinic Judaism. I ask whether a theory of interpretation guides the sages in their exposition of the topics, the category-formations, of Rabbinic Judaism in the documents that expound those formations. As the title means to suggest, my answer is, a hermeneutics of comparison and contrast governs the selection of data and the interpretation thereof for the entire corpus of category-formations of the Halakhah. The rest of this project serves to spell out the meaning and effect of that sentence. Hence "comparative hermeneutics" here bears the primary meaning, "a hermeneutics of analogical-contrastive analysis."

These documents fall into two classes, Halakhic, normative for behavior and Aggadic, normative — if in a different way — for belief. I use the word "hermeneutics" to refer to the process of interpretation — selection and interpretation of data, their systematization, rationalization, configuration and representation — that guides thought about all of the native categories of the Halakhah, their configuration and their articulation. Rather than beginning with the whole — the Halakhah, or the Halakhah as represented by the Mishnah — I work, as is my way, from the parts, bottom up. I find my way back from details of the Halakhic documents to their exegetical program, and thence — from the exegesis — to the rules of interpretation that govern the document's presentation of all topics. Finally, within the framework of the documentary theory of the Rabbinic corpus that I have spelled out, I undertake the comparison and contrast of the rules of interpretation realized in the respective documents (so far as these vary, as they do occasionally). That is what I mean, in the present context, by the comparative hermeneutics of the Rabbinic Judaism: the rules for interpreting the topics that all together comprise the Halakhah, the norms of actuality, of that Judaism.

The goal of this study is to define the main lines of that process, the hermeneutics of the Halakhah, as that hermeneutics governs the formation of native-categories out of a mass of data, some deriving from Scripture, some from natural reason, and further guides the interpretation and articulation of each of those native-categories.[1] A subsidiary goal is comparative, namely, an effort to identify evidence of variation within the hermeneutics of the native-categories as these categories are set forth in the successive documents of the Halakhah, from the Mishnah, ca. 200, which is primary, to the Tosefta, ca. 300, Yerushalmi, ca. 400, and Bavli, ca. 600. Here, therefore, we deal with the hermeneutics of the Halakhic documents, within a very particular framework: the native-categories of the Halakhah. We analyze the topical framework within which the Halakhic compilations conduct their discourse, the entire Halakhah being organized by subject matter and within logic comprised by two components. First, the organizing logic imputes coherence to the requirements of topical exposition. Second, the logic insists, within the concrete case, abstract principles are to be encapsulated. Specifically, in this protracted exercise I identify the theory of how a given topic is to be interpreted, specifically moving backward from exegesis of cases to hermeneutics of topics, that is, from the evidence of the consequent exegesis that gives actuality to that theory backward to the theory of interpretation itself. Since Rabbinic Judaism in its normative corpus comes to us in four documents, the Mishnah, the Tosefta, the Yerushalmi (Talmud of the Land of Israel), and the Bavli (Talmud of Babylonia), documentary hermeneutics enters in. Therefore I further compare and contrast the theory of presenting a given topic that dictated the character of the one document with the theory that governed in another of the cognate writings of Judaism.

Succinctly to explain the actual program of research at hand, I parse the title of the project as a whole. First comes the key word, "hermeneutics." In the present context, dealing with a religion realized in a textual community, what issue falls into the category of hermeneutics, the theory of interpretation of a received document? The hermeneutics of a religion of a textual commu-

---

[1] I stress, I deal with hermeneutics, not exegesis, the technology of problem-solving. That distinction is standard and need not detain us. A considerable body of literature on what the authors call "hermeneutics" that deals with rules for the exegesis of Scripture, comparable to Graeco-Roman rules of rhetoric on interpreting mythic or legal writings, plays no role in my inquiry. I do not regard as problems of hermeneutics, but only as exercises of exegesis, the relationship between a verse of Scripture and the explanation of that verse of Scripture by Rabbinic exegetes. Using "hermeneutics" for the rules by which the Torah is expounded (hammiddot shehattorah nidreshet bahen) errs. Those rules are exegetical in classification, and not hermeneutical; they propound no large-scale theory of mediation and interpretation of a received corpus, only ad hoc rules for concrete cases, and a very different matter. Exegetics can go forward (if in an intellectual coarse manner) without theology; hermeneutics forms a chapter in theology. But, we cannot forget hermeneutics is the father of exegetics properly executed.

nity governs how a given topic is going to be expounded by the cognate texts of that community. To begin with, the hermeneutics determines the category-formations of that textual community, by which I mean, how random data fall into classifications and form coherent compositions. Hermeneutics in guiding the formation of organizing categories thereby defines the rules of coherence. It guides reading the received and Holy Scriptures. It defines the laws that dictate questions that will be raised and those that will not be raised. Hermeneutics here forms the theory that guides the formulation and transmission of tradition from generation to generation.

How do I conceive hermeneutics to relate to the detailed work of exegesis? Common usage suffices: hermeneutics forms the governing process of interpreting data, mediating chaos into order, and exegesis takes up the consequent, episodic challenges to harmonious reason, coherence, cogency. First comes the theory of interpretation, then its application to specific problems. Accordingly, hermeneutics defines the exegetical task, that is, the work of dealing with detail in a consistent, rational manner. That is because hermeneutics identifies what, within a received piece of writing, requires attention, framing problems for exegetical inquiry in a particular setting. Defining rationality, hermeneutics explains the coherence of the bits and pieces of the writing.

But that is not the direction of this project, which starts with small things and aims at a few large generalizations. I know how to move only from the patient sifting of large aggregates of textual data to the patterns and constructions that inhere therein. In the present context, as is always my way, I progress from detail to generalization. That is to say, I progress from the results of a process of exegetics to what I conceive to form the generative hermeneutics, from the manner of the exegesis of details to the guiding hermeneutics of the whole.

This I do in an encompassing framework, reading first the documents — the Mishnah, Tosefta, Yerushalmi, and Bavli — in sequence, then the entire corpus of authoritative writings viewed whole. And that brings us to the second key word of the title: what of the "comparative" exercise? Here, if "hermeneutics" derives from the theory of exposition of a given topic that sustains the successive writings of the authoritative Rabbinic sages of late antiquity, "comparative hermeneutics" concerns itself with the logical next step. That is, the comparison and contrast of the respective theories of the exposition of a single program of topics in cognate documents. How a given topic is expounded, the issues people deem to inhere therein and to require exposition — description, analysis, and interpretation — these rules of interpretation in particular terms embody the general theory of how to make sense of a received, determinate tradition, that is, the Torah or "Judaism."

What of the religion under discussion? "Rabbinic Judaism" refers to the Judaic religious system — way of life, world view, realized by a determinate "Israel" — portrayed, for the present purpose, solely by the Rabbinic documents of the classical age, the first six centuries of the Common Era. Now, as a matter of fact, these documents not only come to us with a vast exegetical literature. They themselves constitute an exercise of exegesis as well: they systematically mediate between a corpus of information, deriving from various sources encompassing Scripture in particular, and the formulation of law in expository, not exegetical, form by the Mishnah and the Tosefta. So far as the history of religions is the exegesis of exegesis, this is a project at the very heart of the history of religions as that discipline takes up the Judaic problematic in its larger enterprise.

Having used such grandiose language, I had best specify what is at stake. What, exactly, do I promise to do in producing the information required for this inquiry? After much labor over many topics, I offer a few generalizations about how any given topic is likely to be expounded in a given document, and what characterizes the theory of interpretation characteristic of the respective documents. Some may reasonably think that that is a rather modest result for a formidable effort, and I concur. But it is more than we have now. More to the point, along with everyone who has studied from start to finish all of the documents treated here (and there are not many), I have formed some impressions. Now I seek to transform general impressions into specific knowledge.

So to conclude: I present a systematic comparison of Mishnah-Tosefta-Yerushalmi-Bavli on how each document determines what it wants to know, and say, about a shared agendum of specified subjects. What may we expect the Mishnah to do with its topic? What then does the Tosefta want to accomplish in the presentation of the same topic, whether in dialogue with the Mishnah or not (that is an autonomous question)? When the Yerushalmi takes up the same topic, what interests its framers? Finally, how does the Bavli recapitulate the subject, and what are the traits of its mind in addressing a common heritage? I do not know a systematic account of these matters, and that is what I am trying to achieve. For the mighty labor may produce modest results, but very solid ones: we know how Rabbinic Judaism worked out its theory of interpreting the topical program, the corpus of native-categories, that encompass and impose rationality upon the vast corpus of details that all together comprise the norms of that Judaism: the hermeneutics of the Halakhic sector.

What must follow, as is now self-evident, is an account of the hermeneutics of the Aggadic sector — not the (theoretical) theology, which I have proposed, but the hermeneutics. But that account depends upon a theory of what, exactly, comprises the set of category-formations of the Aggadah that correspond to those of the Halakhah. More accurately, I still puzzle on how to define those category-formations to begin with. In my *Theology of the Oral Torah: Revealing the Justice of God* I allowed the generative logic I brought to the problem — the inner dialectics of monotheism — to dictate the large constructions of which in my account the system is comprised; but that is my logic, not logic teased out of the sources. I also do not know the criteria that would designate a category-formation as such; the Halakhic ones are primary to the texts, e.g., tractate this, tractate that. When it comes to Aggadah, by contrast, the category-formations that hold the whole together and organize its data do not match the lines of documents or their subdivisions. As I do this work, I have some tentative hypotheses in mind concerning the foundations of the Aggadic category-formations: their very definitions and boundaries. But much more thought on the category-formations of the Halakhah is required before I shall find myself prepared to take up that much more difficult question.

It remains to acknowledge the support for my research which comes from Bard College, where I hold the position of Research Professor of Religion and Theology. I received exceedingly valuable and challenging comments on this project from Professor Günter Stemberger, University of Vienna, Professor Ithamar Gruenwald, Tel Aviv University, Professor David Aaron, Hebrew Union College-Jewish Institute of Religion, Cincinnati, Professor Robert Berchman, Dowling College, and Professor William Scott Green, Dean of the University of Rochester. My thanks go to them, as well as to my colleagues at Bard, with whom I have discussed these problems over time.

JACOB NEUSNER
BARD COLLEGE

1.
TRACTATE ZEBAHIM

I. THE DEFINITION OF THE CATEGORY-FORMATION, ZEBAHIM-MENAHOT

Israel relates to God in a blood-rite mediated by the priesthood, an interchange that takes place above the Land, in the Temple, at the Land's highest point. Through offerings of meat, grain, wine, oil, and incense, Israel atones for sin and seeks to win God's favor, as, in the Torah, God had declared that he may be propitiated. There on the altar Israel, jointly and severally, presents corporate and individual, obligatory and votive offerings. Then the priests toss onto the altar drops of blood gathered from the beast and burn up on the fires of the altar those parts of the sacrificial beast that a given classification of offering yields; or they take and offer up a handful of meal-offering for the same purpose. The smoke ascends to Heaven, a pleasing savor to God, bearing the message of Israel's conciliation with God's will. In the native category-formations, Zebahim and its companion, Menahot, we find a systematic exposition of the issues deemed urgent, the generative principles that govern Israel's meeting with God. All these are realized principally in details, made manifest through perspicacious exposition of those details. Of the three necessary components that comprise the category-formation,

[1] the particular hermeneutics of the category-formation(s),
[2] the facts supplied by Scripture or tradition, and
[3] the working out of a generic hermeneutics of the Halakhah, the first forms the center of interest.

The particular hermeneutics of Zebahim and the matching Menahot is what imparts specificity and supplies the source of intellectual energy that animates the category-formation viewed whole. It concerns the power of intentionality to effect or disrupt the rite of expiation. But the generic hermeneutics shows itself at its most effective, and the Halakhah encompassed within this category-formation provides a remarkably clear picture of the working of the generic hermeneutics.

[1] The generic hermeneutics requires no attention in this context. It is the aspect of comparative hermeneutics that defines the grounds for comparison, the mode of thought characteristic of all category-formations of the Halakhah. It suffices to say that the generic hermeneutics of the Halakhah raises familiar issues of mixtures and confusion of categories, rules of precedence, potentiality and actuality, interstitiality, and the like. The reprise of the

Halakhah suffices to define the generic hermeneutics' impact upon the present category formation, which is profound and definitive.

[2] As to Scripture's contribution, Zebahim encompasses four bodies of rules, most of them addressing issues not taken up in Scripture but precipitated by Scripture's account of matters and actualized in Scripture's detailed laws. The Written Torah supplies the hard facts that the category-formation systematizes, in which the category-formation finds indicative traits susceptible to ordering. Out of, but in line with, the elaborate account of the Written Torah, the category-formation identifies its own concerns. While Scripture at Leviticus and Deuteronomy does not differentiate among the locations at which the altar is located (anywhere or in one place only, respectively), the category-formation of the category-formation systematizes information on the same matter and deals with the diverse rules governing sacrifices at the several locations at which Israel made offerings prior to the building of the Temple. Much of the enterprise of the category-formation proves to be one of generalization upon, and systematization of, Scripture's facts. Were we engaged by the question of how the category-formation responds to that Scripture, we should find here the exemplary cases for defining the pattern of that response.

[3] What of the particular hermeneutics? As I shall demonstrate now, the hermeneutics particular to Zebahim and to its companion, Menahot, presents a fully-exposed theory of the role of intentionality in the sacrificial cult, an issue not explicitly addressed in the Written Torah's treatment of the same subject but (plausibly) deemed implicit therein. Therein, I find the animating hermeneutics of the category-formations, Zebahim and Menahot. It centers upon sorting out whose attitude shapes the outcome of the rite. The intentionality of which category of participant, concerning which matters, in what context, and for what purpose — these form the motivating concerns that impart to the category-formation its distinctive program. The data that are chosen, the way they are interpreted — these respond to that program.

These general remarks carry us to the particular task at hand, which is to identify the species and proceed to speculate about the genus of which it is part. We begin with a brief outline of the category-formation, Zebahim:[1]

---

[1] In this volume I use the word "sacrifier," perhaps not entirely familiar to all readers. The word, as distinct from "sacrificer," refers to the one who benefits from the presentation of the offering, e.g., who achieves atonement or expiation through the beast or the meal-offering that is presented. This is by contrast to "the sacrificer," the one who actually carries out the physical action, e.g., of tossing the blood on the altar or the handful of meal-offering into the altar fires, the priest.

I. IMPROPER INTENTION AND INVALIDATING THE ACT OF SACRIFICE
   A. The Priority of Correct Intentionality for the Sin Offering
   B. Improper Rites that Invalidate all offerings
   C. Improper Intentionality and the invalidation of all offerings
   D. The Priority of Correct Intentionality for the Sin Offering
   E. Improper Rites that Invalidate all offerings
   F. Improper Intentionality and the invalidation of all offerings

II. THE RULES OF SACRIFICE OF BEASTS AND FOWL
   A. Beasts
   B. Fowl

III. THE RULES OF THE BLOOD-OFFERING ON THE ALTAR
   A. Disposing of Sacrificial Portions or Blood that Derive from Diverse Sacrifice and Have Been Confused
   B. The Altar Sanctifies What Is Appropriate to It, but Not What Is Not Appropriate to It
   C. Precedence in Use of the Altar
   D. Blood of a Sin-offering that Spurts onto a Garment: "Whatever Touches the Flesh Shall be Holy, and when any of its blood is sprinkling on a garment, you shall wash that on which it was sprinkled in a holy place. And the earthen vessel in which it is boiled shall be broken; but if it is boiled in a Bronze vessel, it shall be scoured and rinsed in water" (Lev. 6:27-28)
   E. The Division among the Eligible Priests of the Meat and Hides of Sacrificial Animals

IV. THE PROPER LOCATION OF THE ALTAR AND THE ACT OF SACRIFICE PERFORMED THEREON

Now my opening observation on the role of Scripture, the generic hermeneutics, and the particular hermeneutics of the category-formation takes on weight. Scripture provides a formidable corpus of rules about the sacrifice of beasts and fowl, each such sacrifice serving to expiate a given classification of inadvertent sin or to accomplish some other purpose. Turning first to the topic — the selection of pertinent facts — we note that the category-formation clearly has chosen to homogenize all animate offerings — birds and beasts — and to present the rules that govern them all. The topic is (I) sacrifice on the altar of the Temple in Jerusalem, the sub-topic is, (II) beasts and fowl, with special reference to (III) the disposition of the blood and meat of animal- or bird-sacrifices. But the facts that are selected, effecting the homogenization of animate offerings under a few encompassing rules, do not signal either the results of analogical-contrastive analysis or the consequent hermeneutical principles for interpreting the chosen data.

To approach the work of reconstructing the analogical-contrastive analysis that I think has produced the Halakhic category-formations, Zebahim and Menahot, we now proceed to identify comparable species and the genus that they comprise. We first turn to what is clearly the other species of the common genus. If the genus is, offerings on the altar in Jerusalem, and the species at hand is, animate offerings, then the corresponding species must be, inanimate offerings, and that immediately requires us to compare the program of the category-formation, Zebahim, with that of its topical counterpart, Menahot, on meal-offerings. We see that they coincide on all that matters and differ only as to particulars.

ZEBAHIM	MENAHOT

I. IMPROPER INTENTION AND INVALIDATING THE ACT OF SACRIFICE
  A. The Priority of Correct Intentionality for the Sin Offering
  B. Improper Rites that Invalidate all offerings
  C. The power of improper Intentionality in the invalidation of all offerings
  D. The Priority of Correct Intentionality for the Sin Offering
  E. Improper Rites that Invalidate all offerings
  F. Improper Intentionality and performances of rites improperly in the invalidation of all offerings
II. THE RULES OF SACRIFICE OF BEASTS AND FOWL
  A. Beasts
  B. Fowl
III. THE SPECIAL RULES OF THE BLOOD-OFFERINGS ON THE ALTAR
  A. Disposing of Sacrificial Portions or Blood that Derive from Diverse Sacrifice and Have Been Confused
  B. The Altar Sanctifies What Is
	I. IMPROPER INTENTION AND INVALIDATING THE ACT OF SACRIFICE (REPRISE OF ZEBAHIM)
	  A. ImproperIntention
	  B. And Invalidating the Act of Sacrifice
	  B. Other Rules of Invalidation of Meal-Offerings
	II. THE PROPER PREPARATION OF MEAL-OFFERINGS
	  A. General Rules
	  B. The Meal-Offering that Accompanies the Thank-Offering
	  C. Sources of Flour, Oil, and Wine Used for the Meal-Offering
	  D. Measuring the Materials Used for the Offering
	III. SPECIAL MEAL-OFFERINGS. THE 'OMER
	V. PARTICULAR PROBLEMS OF INANIMATE OFFERIGS: VOWS IN CONNECTION WITH MEAL-OFFERINGS

Appropriate to It, but Not What Is Not Appropriate to It C. Precedence in Use of the Altar D. Blood of a Sin-offering that Spurts onto a Garment: "Whatever Touches the Flesh Shall be Holy, and when any of its blood is sprinkling on a garment, you shall wash that on which it was sprinkled in a holy place. And the earthen vessel in which it is boiled shall be broken; but if it is boiled in a Bronze vessel, it shall be scoured and rinsed in water" (Lev. 6:27-28) E. The Division among the Eligible Priests of the Meat and Hides of Sacrificial Animals IV. PARTICULAR PROBLEMS OF ANIMATE OFFERINGS: THE PROPER LOCATION OF THE ALTAR AND THE ACT OF SACRIFICE PERFORMED THEREON	

Menahot at the points of the particular hermeneutics matches Zebahim, citing its critical compositions verbatim and changing only the operative language, so a single pattern governs both category-formations. That pattern is more than topical, it is substantive. The matched category-formations move from the abnormal to the normal, from how the offering is ruined to how it is properly carried out. Both begin with long exercises on the role of improper intentionality in rendering the offering null, whether animate or inanimate. And then both proceed on their respective paths, dealing with facts particular to the animate or the inanimate offering, as the case requires. Such a pattern, dealing with abnormal, then normal transactions, with the abnormal pervaded by issues of intentionality, is entirely familiar from the Babas. Indeed, we address the counterpart to the Babas, with their attention first to abnormal transactions, to which intentionality forms the critical variable in assessing responsibility, then to normal ones, to which intentionality pertains only marginally if at all.[2]

---

[2] I am satisfied to note that parallel. I do not contend that in the deep structure

How to account for the particular hermeneutics of Zebahim-Menahot? Since I claim to replicate the thought-processes of analogical-contrastive analysis that generate the hermeneutics of the Halakhic category-formations, my task is to propose the specifics of that process that has yielded the present category-formation(s). For that purpose I require a genus that will encompass Zebahim-Menahot and some other specie(s) as well: a species that is sufficiently alike to sustain analogy, and sufficiently unlike for the purposes of contrast. I turn immediately to establish the analogy I conceive to be in play, the genus that precipitates the contrast and effects the identification of species.

How then to proceed? To identify the hermeneutical crux in both Zebahim and Menahot, so defining the two category-formations so far as the particular hermeneutics effects that definition, we have to stand back and ask a question of the species, Zebahim and Menahot, seen together as a genus. It is, do Zebahim and Menahot themselves combine to form a species of a still more encompassing genus? The point at which they unite and form a common genus — the critical consideration of the power of intentionality to effect or disrupt the activities at the altar, as I have just now shown — answers that question. Where a particular hermeneutics — not supplied by Scripture, not imposed by the generic hermeneutics of the category-formation — comes into operation in both category-formations jointly, it concerns the affect, upon the transaction, of intentionality. In due course in the reprise of the Halakhah I shall amply show that that is so. Specifically, at issue for both category-formations, the two species of the genus before us, is the power of intentionality to transform the material facts of the offering and deprive the offering — whether animate or inanimate — of the power to expiate sin. Intentionality, not actuality, governs — explicitly so. That is where the two category-formations not only intersect but overlap: the role of intentionality in the before-the-fact validation or invalidation of offerings. Indeed Menahot in fact repeats word for word the opening rules of Zebahim, on intentionality and animal sacrifices, only substituting "meal-offering" for "sacrifice," as the case requires.

In line with the homogenizing interest of the category-formation, the rule is encompassing: all offerings are subject to disqualification by reason of improper intentionality. That is stated in so many words at M. Zebahim 2:2 and its counterpart, M. Menahot 1:3. The importance of the underlined language will become clear in a moment.

---

of the Halakhic sector is a preference for the self-evidence of the ordering, abnormal/normal, intentionality-effective/intentionality-null.

> *He who slaughters the animal offering* [intending] to toss its blood outside [of the Temple court], (1) or part of its blood outside, to burn its sacrificial portions outside, (2) or part of its sacrificial portions outside, to eat its meat outside (3) or an olive's bulk of its meat outside, or to eat an olive's bulk of the skin of the fat tail outside — it is invalid. But punishment by extirpation does not apply to it [e.g., in the case of the priest who eats thereof]. *[Supply: He who slaughters the animal offering*, intending] to toss its blood on the next day, (1) or part of its blood on the next day, to burn its sacrificial portions on the next day, (2) or part of its sacrificial portions on the next day, to eat its meat on the next day, (3) or part of its meat on the next day, or an olive's bulk of the skin of the fat tail on the next day — it is refuse. And they [who eat it, even at the proper time] are liable on its account to punishment by extirpation.
>
> M. Zebahim 2:2

> *He who takes up the handful of meal-offering* [with the improper intention] to eat its residue outside, or an olive's bulk of its residue outside, to burn a handful thereof outside, or an olive's bulk of a handful thereof outside, or to burn its frankincense outside — it is invalid. But extirpation does not apply to it. *[If he takes up the handful of meal-offering* with the improper intention] to eat its residue on the next day, or an olive's bulk of its residue on the next day, to burn a handful thereof on the next day, or an olive's bulk of a handful thereof on the next day, or to burn its frankincense on the next day, it is refuse. And they are liable to extirpation on its account.
>
> M. Menahot 1:3

That is to say, the tossing of the blood of the animal offering, the taking up of the handful of the meal-offering — both mark the climax of their respective presentations, and in both cases, that is the moment of expiation. That is the case, whatever else the animal or meal has been designated to accomplish (e.g., thank-offering, peace-offering, and the like). So much for the formation of the species into a genus. But that genus is a species of yet another, and what might that be?

So much for the actuality of the analogy, but what about the contrastive component of the process? Clearly, we need a corresponding species to form the counterpart within a common genus. Specifically, since the two species of offerings, animate and inanimate, form a genus, offerings spoiled by improper intentionality, we have to ask, to what encompassing genus does the species, "offerings spoiled by improper intentionality," belong? We have now to identify the genus that will encompass both the species, Zebahim-and-Menahot, and its opposed counterpart: expiation where intentionality counts (in any aspect of activity), expiation where it does not count (in any way at all). To answer that question, logic requires us to ask, what category-formation shares with Zebahim-and-Menahot the same outcome, atonement, but differs as to the matter of intentionality? We require a species of media of atonement that effect their teleology whether or not an improper attitude or expression of intentionality (on the part of any player) has taken effect.

The source of the answer has already been signaled by M. Zebahim 2:2 = M. Menahot 1:3, at the underlined language. The answer locates itself in the critical moment of the transaction. The transformative moment, the point at which intentionality makes all the difference, takes place with the act that effects expiation *eo ipse*. So the formulation of intentionality that accompanies the act of the tossing of the blood onto the altar or the taking of the handful of meal for the altar-fires, respectively defines the critical moment at which incorrect intentionality disrupts the expiatory process. So the right question is, is there an act of expiation of sin or crime to which at the critical moment of expiation the intentionality of the actor is irrelevant? And do we know an act of expiation that so far as intentionality is concerned works *ex opere operato*? The path to the answer to our question about a genus to accommodate both the animal- and the meal-offering as well as some other medium of expiation or atonement now opens wide before us.

For we know full well how else — besides the animal- or meal-offering — the sinner or criminal achieves atonement, specifically, through an action and transaction to which intentionality is null. The answer now is obvious. The sinner or criminal attains expiation, also, through the media of atonement afforded by corporal or capital punishment, e.g., the penalties catalogued in Sanhedrin-Makkot, Shebuot, Horayot, and Keritot. To these penalties the attitude of the participants — the court, the criminal or sinner as he is flogged or put to death, and the one who inflicts the penalty — scarcely pertains. The crime or sin is atoned for, so that the criminal or sinner may now look forward to a portion of the world to come, without regard to the matter of intentionality or attitude, which at no point in Sanhedrin-Makkot, Shebuot, Horayot, or Keritot, is invoked — or in the Halakhah, even imagined — as a criterion relevant to the effect of the action.

To state the matter simply, [1] flogging remits the penalty of extirpation, and [2] the attitude of the person who administers the flogging has no bearing upon the effect of the flogging as an atoning transaction. The Mishnah's statement of the Halakhah is explicit on the first point at M. 3:15 and leaves no doubt on the second by what it does not say:

[A] And a reader reads: "If You will not observe to do . . . the Lord will have your stripes pronounced, and the stripes of your seed" (Dt. 28:58ff.) (and he goes back to the beginning of the passage). "And you will observe the words of this covenant" (Dt. 29:9), and he finishes with, "But he is full of compassion and forgave their iniquity" (Ps. 78:38), and he goes back to the beginning of the passage.
[B] And if the victim dies under the hand of the one who does the flogging, the latter is exempt from punishment.
[C] [But if] he added even a single stripe and the victim died, Lo, this one goes into exile on his account.
M. Makkot 3:14

[A] "All those who are liable to extirpation who have been flogged are exempt from their liability to extirpation,"
[B] As it is said, "And your brother seem vile to you" (Dt. 25:3) —
[C] "Once he has been flogged, Lo, he is tantamount to your brother," the words of R. Hananiah b. Gamaliel.
M. Makkot 3:15

M. 3:15 places flogging into the same genus as Zebahim-Menahot, media for the expiation of sin or crime. M. 3:14 leaves no possibility for the intrusion of disqualifying intentionality. It states the correct attitude by citing the pertinent verses of Scripture — but does not say, "and if they omitted the reading...," or suggest that the attitude, either the one who administers the flogging or the one who receives it registers. It goes without saying that descriptions of the administration of the death penalty follow suit. To state matters simply, if the felon or sinner about to be put to death does not say, "May my death atone for all my sins," his death nonetheless takes effect. He does not have to confess, though he is encouraged to do so, because, whether he does or does not, the same result follows. Through his death in expiation of his sins or crimes, he gains his portion in the world to come. Death speaks plainly, without the mediation of the attitude that accompanies its advent. But when it comes to an offering, the intrusion of the wrong intentionality at the moment of expiation disrupts the transaction.

Now to the upshot: we may define the common genus that encompasses Zebahim and Menahot and Sanhedrin-Makkot and related category-formations. The genus is, "ways by which the sinner or criminal establishes a right relationship with God and so may hope to rise from the grave, stand in judgment, and acquire a portion in the world to come." That outcome is reached through a variety of media of expiation and atonement.[3] The sizable genus, "diverse media for atoning for sin or crime," then for the present purpose is comprised by the two species, [1] media to which intentionality of the empowered actor, the priest, is critical, the animal- and meal-offerings, Zebahim and Menahot, and [2] media of expiation that attain their purpose whatever the attitude of the empowered actor(s) *("ex opere operato")*, to which intentionality is tangential or irrelevant altogether. The latter media then are represented by capital or corporal punishment. Succinctly to state the result: the genus, "media of expiation or atonement," which is to say, the genus of means of expiation and atonement, of removing obstacles to the world to come, divides into [1] media of the altar and [2] media of the courts whether Heavenly or earthly that inflict corporal and capital punishment.

Focusing upon the altar, the category-formation thus lays matters out in its way, which is to say, we begin (as in the Babas!) with a process of speciation of a hither-to-undefined genus: media for expiation and atonement to which intentionality is critical. To begin with, we then discern two distinct classifications of offering for atonement and expiation, [A] those in which the intentionality that has sanctified a particular beast to expiate a particular sin or carry out a particular cultic obligation — the sin- and Passover-offerings — and [B] all other offerings. But when we deal, in due course, with the details, we shall realize, the Halakhic repertoire commences with what is preliminary and only then leads us to what is primary, which is, the kinds of intentionality that invalidate all offerings on the altar, whether animate or inanimate.

M. Zebahim 2:3=M. Menahot 1:3 states matters with the Mishnah's usual sharpness:

> Whoever slaughters, or receives [the blood], or conveys [the blood], or sprinkles [the blood] [intending] to eat something which is usually eaten [meat], [or] to burn something which is usually burned [entrails], outside of its proper place [which is, the Temple court for Most Holy Things, the walled city of Jerusalem for Lesser Holy Things] — it is invalid [and the meat may not be eaten]. And extirpation does not apply to it. [Supply: Whoever slaughters, or receives the blood, or conveys the blood, or sprinkles (the blood), intending to eat something which is usually eaten, to burn something which is usually burned] outside of its proper time — it is refuse. And they are liable on its account to extirpation [even if despite their declared intention,

---

[3] I do not differentiate expiation and atonement, in the present context they bear the same meaning, because they produce a common result. But I readily concede they are not the same thing. They represent distinct categories within a common category-formation.

they actually eat the meat within the time limit].

M. Zebahim 2:3

So we come right to the point: intentionality in the category-formation before us represents no abstraction but a concrete plan. Intentionality takes effect before the act that it concerns and without regard to whether the intended act is realized. That is amazing, because it accords to intentionality affective power even if unrealized in actuality.

Whose intentionality bears such weighty power, and why? The attitude of the priest in performing the act of sacrifice — killing the beast, collecting the blood, conveying it to the altar, and tossing it on the altar — toward what he is going to have to do later on in the full realization of the rite has an immediate bearing upon the specified, critical actions when he carries them out. What he wills to do later on takes effect here and now. Then for intentionality universally to invalidate offerings on the altar, it must concern one of two matters. These are the intention [1] later on to eat the priest's portion at the improper time or [2] later on to do the priest's duty to burn what is to be disposed of in the improper place. Intentionality affects matters before the fact, as to the time or the place of a subsequent action, matters over which the priest alone bears full power.

The rule accords to the priest's intentionality a palpability and immediacy that transform the future into a power in the here and now. What the priest has not done and may not do but merely plans to do makes all the difference. So we must ask, why should intentionality for a future action that may or may not be carried out so drastically take effect at the moment of the critical actions of the rite in particular concerning those two subsequent actions in the rite, the time for the consumption of the offering by the priests, the place for the disposition of the offering by the priests? Why, in actions done now, does how the priest plans matters for later on, change everything, and what accounts for the remarkable power of transformation that is accorded to the intangible of the priest's will? And how come, does the priest take up a mediating position in the transaction of expiation?

To begin to answer these questions, which carry us into the very heart of the hermeneutics of Zebahim and Menahot and all of the many offerings that their general rules govern, we must first ask, what is excluded in this remarkably narrow construction imposed upon the affective dimensions of intentionality? The obvious answer, made explicit by the category-formation is, the intentionality of the person who has brought the animal to begin with. That is the sacrifier, the person who has designated the beast and presented it to the priests to offer to God and (in most though not all classifications of offering) to eat for himself as well, and perhaps (in some classifications) to provide meat for himself and his family. That exclusion of the sacrifier's intentionality is made explicit at M. Zebahim 4:6:

> For it is a condition imposed by the court, that intentionality follows only [the mind and will and attitude of] the one who carries out the act [not the owner; and the officiant does not have to specify the six considerations at all. If he acts in commendable silence, that suffices].
>
> M. Zebahim 4:6

And T. Zebahim 5:13 improves upon the matter:

> For [if] the one who slaughters the animal has the intention of making the offering as a sin-offering, and the owner has the intention of making the offering as a burnt-offering, [or if] the one who slaughters has the intention of making the offering as a burnt-offering, and the owner has the intention of making the offering as a sin-offering — under all circumstances all things follow only after [the intention of] the one who performs the act of sacrifice.
>
> T. Zebahim 5:13

The upshot is simple. When it comes to the power of intentionality before the fact to produce material, actual consequences in the process of securing expiation or atonement without regard to the facts later on, the attitude of the priest registers, that of the sacrifier does not. We may forthwith account for the exclusion of the intentionality of the sacrifier. His position in the transaction is no different from that of the felon or criminal who is flogged or executed: the correct medium of expiation suffices to atone for the sin and produces that reconciliation that will lead to life eternal. The deed done right suffices; the felon or criminal atones willy-nilly. Corporate Israel has wiped out wickedness from its midst and restored the person who did the act to its midst; to that transformation intentionality is null.

Then to whom do we compare and contrast the priest? It is to the court that inflicts the flogging or death penalty, whichever court of the system (among those described at Sanhedrin Chapters One through Three) is involved. The rite of expiation of sin or crime performed by the priest and the counterpart rite performed by the court, produce the same effect, but the priest's attitude registers at the critical point and the court's members' attitudes do not. The upshot is clear, and the answer to our questions begins to emerge. The hermeneutics of Zebahim and Menahot compares and contrasts the power of the priest's intentionality with that of those counterparts in the courts, on earth and in Heaven, who effect atonement and expiation for other sins or crimes than those covered by meat- or meal-offerings. What is at stake in the Halakhic category-formations, Menahot and Zebahim, but not in Sanhedrin-Makkot, Shebuot, Horayot, and Keritot, therefore, is the role of the intentionality of the priest in charge of the rite, not of the judges, nor of the sacrificer who presents the beast or the meal for the atonement of his sin or crime. That carries us to the heart of the matter.

The priest must intend at the very act of slaughter to toss the blood within the span of time in which the death of the beast as an act of expiation has taken place, which is to say, by sundown of the day on which the beast has died. He must, at that same moment of slaughter, intend to burn the sacrificial portions within the whole place, where it belongs. Whatever he does later on in time or elsewhere in space, his heart at that moment must be pure of improper intentionality. Why then? Because what matters is that the officiating priest impose the intentionality upon the offering — beast, or meal — at the very moment that his act takes effect — slaughtering for the blood, taking up the handful — that the cult requires to expiate the sin or crime for which the beast is presented and atone therefor. Why the priest, the sacrificer, and not the Israelite, e.g., the householder, the sacrifier? The issue is defined in so many words: when he does the deed, the priest must conform, in his attitude, to the occasion and the context, taking the life of the beast or the handful of the meal in accord with the purpose the Torah has set forth, planning to dispose of the meat or the meal in accord with the correct conditions. His action is critical to the act of transformation, not only the act of the sacrifier in presenting the offering, because he is the one who takes the life of the animal-offering (or does the corresponding deed in the meal-offering), and not the sacrifier. The priest becomes party to the transaction in a way in which the one who flogs or who inflicts the death penalty does not.

That his intentionality govern means, the priest in the present context is the mediator, the principal, and he is the actor — the one whose intentionality animates the transaction. That role forms the counterpart to the householder's in the designation of the beast as holy for a particular purpose and a specified classification of sacrifice; then the householder's intentionality is what has transformed the status of the beast or the meal. The priest cannot sanctify the beast belonging to the householder, only the expressed will of the householder can do that. The householder cannot desecrate the beast through an improper act of will, only the priest can do that. The attitude of each registers at the point, in the transaction, over which each exercises sole power. Where intentionality makes all the difference, then, whose intentionality registers, and in what context? The answer leads us to the end of this effort to identify the particular hermeneutics of Zebahim and Menahot. The intentionality of the priest makes the difference, in the Temple, specifically at the very moment at which the priest undertakes those actions that he alone can do, and to which he alone gives effect by his attitude of the instant. And the actions that he alone can do are the ones that effect the transaction with God: atone for sin through blood, so that the life of the beast substitutes for the life of the one who has (unintentionally) sinned.

Why, then, does the priest's intentionality and not that of the sacrifier register? It is all a matter of context. The sacrifier's attitude does count in sanctifying the animal for its purpose; the priest cannot sanctify the beast belonging to the householder for expiating the sin of the householder. That to which the householder's power extends is indeed subject to his intentionality. He controls the selection for sanctification of the beast, the purpose for which he has designated. Then, if the purpose of his selection must match the purpose of the priest's disposition of the beast — an animal designated as a sin- or Passover-offering must be presented as a sin- or Passover-offering and for no other purpose, as both tractates say at the outset — his intentionality registers even at the heart of the sacrificial rite. But if the householder designates the beast as a thank-offering and the priest offers the beast as a peace-offering, no consequence results. Then the intentionality of the sacrifier is null. So the same thing is said of many things, and the category-formation encompasses the intentionality of the householder, the sacrifier, as much as that of the priest, and in proper proportion.

Only the comparison and contrast with the other species of the same genus endows, places that observation into meaningful context. As we realize, the sins for which the blood-rite atones are those of inadvertence, not of deliberation:

> A. For those [thirty-six transgressions] are people liable, for deliberately doing them, to the punishment of extirpation,
> B. And for accidentally doing them, to the bringing of a sin offering,
> C. And for not being certain of whether or not one has done them, to a suspensive guilt offering [Lev. 5:17]
>
> M. Keritot 1:2

By contrast, the death penalty expiates sins done deliberately, intentionally, and knowingly. So correct intentionality at the moment of expiation confirms the rite's message, which is, the sin or crime was done inadvertently, not as an act of rebellion against God's will. The priest's intentionality matters because at the moment that submission to God's will is the issue, he is in charge; and he stands for the sponsor of the rite, the sacrifier, and embodies in his correct attitude, the sincere will of the penitent sacrifier to do God's will in God's own way. It is a complex transaction, because the correct attitude of more than a single party registers: the intentionality of the one who inadvertently sinned, and discovering what he has done, has sanctified a beast to atone for the sin; the intentionality of the priest who will kill the beast and substitute its blood for the blood of the sacrifier.

So if we ask, what is the genus, speciated into Zebahim-Menahot, on the one side, and Sanhedrin-Makkot, Shebuot, Horayot, and Keritot, on the other? The answer now is blatant. The genus is comprised of category-formations that bear in common the power to atone for or expiate sin or crime. It breaks down into two species, one in which intentionality effects the expiation or atonement, one in which intentionality is irrelevant. The difference is, in the one, the agency of a particular class of Israel is required, the priest having been assigned the task by God, and in the other, any Israelite is perfectly well qualified to carry out the task, that is, inflict the flogging or the death penalty. That is with the proviso that, the Halakhah takes for granted, a court of sages will have declared the man guilty of the specified sin or crime and imposed the pertinent sanction. Then the court acts for God just as the priest acts for God. I take for granted, the court's intentionality is not made an issue because everyone knows — as the concluding statements of Horayot make clear — that the sages may be relied upon to realize the proper intentionality and act out of the right attitude. I cannot point to a single saying or story in the entire Halakhic corpus that conceives otherwise.

A final comparison is in order. Why the priest's intentionality matters but the court's does not raise the ultimate question, which established facts served to answer. The priest is qualified in his person, by genealogy, the court merely by learning. The priest is integral to the rite of expiation; only he can carry out the rites. Any Israelite can sit on the court, inflict a flogging, impose one of the four media of the death penalty. A system engaged by issues of attitude, then, will find in the priest, the sole medium for integrating considerations of intentionality into the category-formation, "the rites of expiation and atonement;" it is the only entry-point at which the differentiating variable, intentionality, can come to bear. So the particular hermeneutics of Zebahim-Menahot selects its data and interprets them by asking of a particular corpus of data, a general question: where does attitude make a difference, and whose attitude in particular registers? Then there is no alternative to the answer, at the very act that effects the purpose of the rite — the act that expiates sin and attains atonement — the accompanying attitude registers. And the person whose attitude counts, is the only one whose attitude can count, and that is the priest. And the object of intentionality — when the priests' portion of the offering is eaten, where the rest will be disposed of — is equally integral to the activity at hand. So a generative hermeneutics of right attitude yields the particular hermeneutics that makes of Zebahim-Menahot more than a compilation of inert data — much more. The priest stands for the Israelite for all the obvious reasons that the Torah has set forth, and his intentionality defines the matter, showing in the case at hand, Israel's remorse at its inadvertent, not willful or rebellious violation of God's will.

To conclude: the particular hermeneutics of Zebahim and Menahot then focuses upon the character of improper intentionality and its power. That is, what distinguishes the category-formations from others of their genus, the speciation that endows those category-formations with consequence. Where the facts of Scripture or the generic hermeneutics of the Halakhah are formed into constructions that transcend those facts and make of them into something more than a reprise and a recapitulation, — that is to say, where hermeneutics becomes actual, imposes a layer of meaning upon inert information — it is the consequence of the particular hermeneutics of the category-formation, Zebahim, that realizes the results of the thought-processes of analogical-contrastive analysis that I have recapitulated here: systematic, sequential reflection upon where intentionality registers, whose intentionality counts, and the context and occasion on which, to begin with, intentionality makes a difference. All else, in the category-formations before us, represents an execution here, of the generic hermeneutics of the category-formation, systematically working through facts supplied by Scripture or tradition.

II. THE FOUNDATIONS OF THE HALAKHIC CATEGORY-FORMATIONS

What, in general, we must know to begin the work, therefore, are these established facts? Scripture provides many of the facts subject to interpretation by the particular hermeneutics of the present category-formation. Animal offerings may derive from cattle, sheep, goats, turtledoves and young pigeons. There are four classes of public or votive offerings: burnt-offerings, sin-offerings, guilt-offerings, and peace-offerings, differentiated as indicated in Scripture. Three individual or offerings are the Passover, the firstling, and tithe of cattle, dealt with elsewhere. Public offerings are presented either as burnt-offerings or sin-offerings, the former yielding nothing for the priests, the latter producing meat for the priests. Congregational offerings are as follows: daily whole offerings, additional offerings for the Sabbath, New Moon, and Festivals; the he-goat for a sin-offering on the Day of Atonement. Individuals present these offerings: the firstling, the tithe, the Passover offering, and the festal offering (Hagigah) classified as a peace offering; the pilgrimage offering, a burnt-offering; the proselyte's offering; the vow- or free-willing offering, presented either as a burnt-offering or a peace-offering, and so on. As we shall see in detail, therefore, the Halakhah sometimes amplifies, but oftentimes complements the rules of the Written Torah, which, self-evidently, are everywhere taken for granted. But so far as the category-formation makes of Scripture's facts a construction of its own, it is in response to that program of interpretation just now outlined.

Of the issues that predominate in the category-formation — especially the role of intentionality in linking God and Israel — Scripture knows little or nothing. But wherever they can, the Halakhah's sages find in Scripture, the starting point for their own systematic reflection. For its part, Scripture's governing provisions for animal offerings are set forth at the following passages:

> The Lord called to Moses and spoke with him from the tent of meeting, saying, "Speak to the people of Israel and say to them, 'When any man of you brings an offering to the Lord, you shall bring your offering of cattle from the herd or from the flock. If his offering is a burnt offering from the herd, he shall offer a male without blemish; he shall offer it at the door of the tent of meeting that he may be accepted before the Lord; he shall lay his hand upon the head of the burnt offering, and it shall be accepted for him to make atonement for him. Then he shall kill the bull before the Lord, and Aaron's sons the priests shall present the blood and throw the blood round about against the altar that is at the door of the tent of meeting. And he shall flay the burnt offering and cut it into pieces, and the sons of Aaron the priest shall put fire on the altar and lay wood in order upon the fire, and Aaron's sons the priests shall lay the pieces, the head and the fat, in order upon the wood that is on the fire on the altar; but its entrails and its legs he shall wash with water. And the priest shall burn the whole on the altar as a burnt offering, an offering by fire, a pleasing odor to the Lord.'"
>
> Lev. 1:1-9

> "If his offering to the Lord is a burnt offering of birds, then he shall bring his offering of turtledoves or of young pigeons. And the priest shall bring it to the altar and wring off its head and burn it on the altar; and its blood shall be drained out on the side of the altar; and he shall take away its crop with the feathers and cast it beside the altar on the east side in the place for ashes; he shall tear it by its wings, but shall not divide it asunder. And the priest shall burn it on the altar, upon the wood that is on the fire; it is a burnt offering, an offering by fire, a pleasing odor to the Lord."
>
> Lev. 1:14-17

> "If a man's offering is a sacrifice of peace offering, if he offers an animal from the herd, male or female, he shall offer it without blemish before the Lord. And he shall lay his hand upon the head of

his offering and kill it at the door of the tent of meeting; and Aaron's sons, the priests shall throw the blood against the altar round about. And from the sacrifice of the peace offering, as an offering by fire to the Lord, he shall offer the fat covering, the entrails, and all the fat that is on the entrails, and the two kidneys with the fat that is on them at the loins, and the appendage of the liver which he shall take away with the kidneys. Then Aaron's sons shall burn it on the altar upon the burnt offering, which is upon the wood on the fire; it is an offering by fire, a pleasing odor to the Lord."

Lev. 3:1-5

"If any one of the common people sins unwittingly, in doing any one of the things that the Lord has commanded not to be done and is guilty, when the sin that he has committed is made known to him, he shall bring for his offering a goat, a female without blemish, for his sin that he has committed. And he shall lay his hand on the head of the sin offering and kill the sin offering in the place of burnt offering. And the priest shall take some of its blood with his finger and put it on the horns of the altar of burnt offering and pour out the rest of its blood at the base of the altar. And all its fat, he shall remove, as the fat is removed from the peace offerings, and the priest shall burn it upon the altar for a pleasing odor to the Lord, and the priest shall make atonement for him and he shall be forgiven."

Lev. 4:27-31

"Whatever touches the flesh shall be holy, and when any of its blood is sprinkling on a garment, you shall wash that on which it was sprinkled in a holy place. And the earthen vessel in which it is boiled shall be broken; but if it is boiled in a Bronze vessel, it shall be scoured and rinsed in water."

Lev. 6:27-28

"This is the law of the guilt offering. It is most holy; in the place where they kill the burnt offering, they shall kill the guilt offering, and its blood shall be thrown on the altar round about. And all its fat shall be offered, the fat tail, the fat that covers the entrails, the two kidneys with the fat that is on them at the loins, and the appendage of the liver that he shall take away with the kidneys; the priest shall burn them on the altar as an offering by fire to the Lord; it is a guilt offering. Every male among the priests may eat of it; it shall be eaten in a holy place; it is most holy. The guilt offering is like the sin offering, there is one law for them; the priest who makes atonement with it shall have it."

Lev. 7:1-7

> "If any man of the house of Israel, kills an ox or a lamb or a goat in the camp or kills it outside the camp and does not bring it to the door of the tent of meeting, to offer it as a gift to the Lord before the tabernacle of the Lord, blood-guilt shall be imputed to that man. This is to the end that the people of Israel may bring their sacrifices that they slay in the open field, that they may bring them to the Lord, to the priest at the door of the tent of meeting, and slay them as sacrifices of peace-offerings to the Lord; and the priest shall sprinkle the blood on the altar of the Lord at the door of the tent of meeting."
>
> Lev. 17:3ff.

The Priestly Code organizes information within its governing categories, just as does the Halakhah; these categories go over the same topics, but each focuses facts in its own way. That familiar fact requires no elaboration.

Given the importance, I have assigned to the matters of refuse and remnant as the hermeneutical crux of the category-formation, we must wonder how the later sages find in Scripture the foundations for the rule at hand. A sizable passage comes to its climax in one among several demonstrations, a small part of which suffices for our purpose:

> Q. *Rather, said Raba, "The entire rule derives from the protracted statement. For it is written,* 'And if any of the meat be at all eaten on the third day...it shall be an abomination' (Lev. 7:18) — using the intensive form, Scripture refers to two acts of eating, one the consumption by man, the other, consumption by the altar [thus burning of the sacrificial portions on the altar-fires]. 'Of the sacrifice of his peace offerings' — just as improper intentionality concerning parts of the peace offering may impose the status of refuse, and improper intentionality concerning parts of the pace offering may be given the status of refuse, so in sacrifices where there are parts that can impose on the whole, the status of refuse and parts that can be rendered subject to the status of refuse, so the law of refuse pertains. [Freedman, *Zebahim, ad loc.*: the blood of the peace offering is the medium through which the status of refuse is effected, that is, if an improper intentionality is expressed during one of the acts of service connected with the blood, the meat and the parts that are to be burned are, thereby, given the status of refuse. Just as this is so in the case of the pace offering, so does the law of refuse operate in the case of all sacrifices of this, the same can be said. This excludes the meal-offerings of priests and of the anointed priest and of the drink offerings.] 'Third' refers then to an intentionality to eat the meat after a specified span of time. 'It shall not be accepted' means, as the acceptance of the valid sacrifice so is that of the invalid; and as the acceptance of the

valid sacrifice, means that all of the parts that permit the meat to be eaten by the priest must be offered up, so the acceptance of the invalid one means that all of the parts the correct disposition of which permit the offering to be eaten by the priests likewise are to be offered. 'Him that offers'" — it becomes unfit in offering, but it does not become unfit through the actual act of being eaten on the third day [hence sacrifice becomes refuse through an illegitimate intention; for it becomes unfit only when it is actually being offered, if the priest at that moment intends later on to eat the meat on the third day; but if there was no illegitimate intention at the actual moment of offer, yet the priest actually ate the meat on the third day, the meat does not retrospectively become refuse (Freedman)]. 'It' means that Scripture speaks of the sacrifice and not the priest. 'It shall not be imputed' [29A] means that other aspects of intentionality must not be confused therein [so the animal becomes refuse only if the intention pertains to eating it after the right time was the only intention; but if the priest expressed any other disqualifying intentionality that would disqualify the offering without rendering it refuse, the one intentionality negates the other]. '...refuse...' this refers to the intention of eating the meat outside of the proper time. 'It shall be' teaches that they combine with each other [both improper aspects of intentionality combine together and so if he intended eating half as much as an olive's bulk after the proper time and half outside of the proper place, the intentionality affecting each half is effective in that it joins with the other half to invalidate the offering]. 'And the soul that eats of it:' one but not two, and which is it? It is the intention of eating it after the proper time, for the meaning of 'iniquity' derives from the sense that pertains with regard to left-over meat of the offering, since it is subject to the same rules as to time and the high places."

Bavli Zebahim 2:2 II:2 Q/28b-29a

It would carry us far afield to review the prior demonstrations and the criticism to which each is subjected. We need not, then, be detained by the possibility that Scripture has explicitly articulated the rule; the character of the proof suffices to suggest otherwise. It suffices to conclude, Scripture has supplied many facts, but sages have discovered the generative hermeneutics, and I contend, it was through a process of autonomous reason within the logic of analogical-contrastive analysis, I have attempted to recapitulate, or, more truly, reconstruct on my own. In the reprise that follows, we shall find ample occasion to note the contribution of the third component of any category-formation of the Halakhah, the generic hermeneutics.

III. THE EXPOSITION OF THE COMPONENTS OF THE GIVEN CATEGORY-FORMATION BY THE MISHNAH-TOSEFTA-YERUSHALMI-BAVLI

I. IMPROPER INTENTION AND INVALIDATING THE ACT OF SACRIFICE:

    A. *THE PRIORITY OF CORRECT INTENTIONALITY FOR THE SIN-OFFERING AND THE PASSOVER-OFFERING*

    M. 1:1 All animal offerings that were slaughtered not for their own name are valid [so that the blood is tossed, the entrails burned], but they do not go to the owner's credit in fulfillment of an obligation, except for the Passover and the sin offering — the Passover at its appointed time [the afternoon of the fourteenth of Nisan], and the sin offering of any time. R. Eliezer says, "Also: the guilt offering. The Passover at its appointed time, and the sin offering and the guilt offering at any time." Said R. Eliezer, "The sin offering comes on account of sin, and the guilt offering comes on account of sin. Just as the sin offering is unfit [if it is offered under some classification other than that originally designated [not for its own name = "under some other name"], so the guilt offering is unfit if offered under some classification other than that originally designated [not for its own name = "under some other name"]."

    T. 1:1 R. Joshua says, "All animal offerings which were slaughtered not for their own name are valid, but they do not go to their owner's credit in fulfillment of an obligation, except for the Passover and the sin-offering — the Passover at its appointed time, and the sin-offering at any time." R. Eliezer says, "Also: the guilt-offering. The Passover at its appointed time, and the sin-offering and the guilt-offering at any time." R. Eliezer says, "The sin-offering comes on account of sin, and the guilt-offering comes on account of guilt. Just as the sin-offering is invalid if it is not for its own name, so the guilt-offering is invalid if it is not for its own name [= M. 1:1F-J]." Said to him R. Joshua, "No. If you have said so concerning the sin-offering, the blood of which is placed above [the red line on the altar], on which account if one slaughtered it, not for its own name, it is invalid, will you say so of a guilt-offering, the blood of which is placed below, on which account if one slaughtered it, not for its own name, it is valid?" Said to him R. Eliezer, "The Passover will prove [my case]. For its blood is placed below [the red line], and if one slaughtered it, not for its own name, it is invalid. So, I encompass the guilt-offering, the blood of which is placed below. If one slaughtered it, not for its own name, it is invalid." Said to him R. Joshua, "No. If you have said so in the case of the Passover, to which applies a fixed time, so that if one slaughtered it not for its own name, it is invalid, will you say so concerning the guilt-offering, to which does not apply a fixed time, so that if one slaughtered it not for its own name, it is valid?" Said to him R. Eliezer, "The sin-offering will prove the matter. For it is not subject to a fixed time, and if one slaughtered it, not for its own name, it is invalid. So I encompass [under the rule] the guilt-offering, which is not subject to a fixed time. If one slaughtered it, not for its own name, it [too] should be deemed invalid." Said to him R. Joshua, "We have come full circle." R. Eliezer says, 'It is a sin-offering' (Lev. 5:9). And 'It is a guilt-offering' (Lev. 5:19). Just as the sin-offering is invalid when it is offered, not for its own name, so a guilt-offering is invalid, not offered in its own name." Said to him R. Joshua, "Concerning the sin-offering, it says, 'And he shall kill it for a sin-offering' (Lev. 4:33), [meaning] that its slaughter must be in the name of the sin-offering. In the case of the Passover, it says, 'It is the sacrifice of the Passover to the Lord' (Ex. 12:27), [meaning] that its sacrifice must be in the name of the Passover. But in the case of guilt-offering, it [says], 'It is a guilt-offering' (Lev. 5:19) only in connection with the burning of the fat. 'It' itself — even though one has not offered up the fat, is valid."

T. 1:2 A guilt-offering [which requires a lamb] of the first year, for which one brought [a lamb] of the second year, and one [requiring a lamb] of the second year for which one brought [a lamb] of the first year, or one which one slaughtered before the time [had arrived] for the owner [to offer them] — their appearance is allowed to become rotten, and they are taken out to the place of burning.

T. 1:3 The burnt-offering of a Nazir, the burnt-offering of a woman after childbirth, and the burnt-offering of a *mesora'* which one slaughtered at the age of twelve months and one day, or which one slaughtered before the time [had arrived] for the owner [to offer them] — ascend to the altar and require drink-offerings. But they do not go to their owner's credit in fulfillment of an obligation. This is the general principle of the matter: Whatever does not invalidate a free-will burnt-offering does not invalidate an obligatory burnt-offering. And whatever invalidates a sin-offering, invalidates guilt-offering, except for the guilt-offering which one slaughtered not for its own name.

B. 1:1-2 II.2/8B AS TO A BEAST DESIGNATED FOR THE PASSOVER OFFERING, AT THE TIME AT WHICH IT IS SUPPOSED TO BE OFFERED [MIDDAY ON THE FOURTEENTH OF NISAN UNTIL NIGHTFALL], IF THE BEAST IS SLAUGHTERED FOR THE PURPOSE FOR WHICH IT WAS ORIGINALLY DESIGNATED, IT IS VALID, AND IF NOT SLAUGHTERED FOR THE PURPOSE FOR WHICH IT WAS ORIGINALLY DESIGNATED, IT IS INVALID. AS TO THE REST OF THE YEAR [A BEAST THAT IS DESIGNATED AS A PASSOVER OFFERING] THAT IS OFFERED FOR THE PURPOSE FOR WHICH IT

HAS BEEN DESIGNATED IS INVALID, BUT IF IT IS NOT OFFERED FOR THE PURPOSE FOR WHICH IT HAS BEEN DESIGNATED, IT IS VALID.

M. 1:2 R. Yosé b. Honi says, "Those [other offerings] which are slaughtered for the sake of the Passover and for the sake of the sin offering are invalid." R. Simeon, brother of Azariah, says, "[If] one slaughtered them for the sake of that which is higher than they, they are valid. [If one slaughtered them] for the sake of that which is lower than they ["But if under the name of a lower grade"], they are invalid. How so? Most Holy Things which one slaughtered for the sake of Lesser Holy Things are invalid. Lesser Holy Things which one slaughtered for the sake of Most Holy Things are valid. The firstling and tithe which one slaughtered for the sake of peace offerings are valid, and peace offerings which one slaughtered for the sake of a firstling, [or] for the sake of tithe, are invalid."

M. 1:3 The beast that was designated as a sacrifice for the Passover which one slaughtered on the morning of the fourteenth [of Nisan] under some classification other than that for which it was originally designated — R. Joshua declares valid, as if it were slaughtered on the thirteenth [of Nisan]. Ben Beterah declares invalid, as if it were slaughtered at twilight [of the fourteenth]. Said Simeon ben Azzai, "I have received a tradition from the seventy-two elder[s], on the day on which they seated R. Eleazar b. Azariah in session, that: all animal offerings which are eaten, which were slaughtered not for the purpose for which they were originally designated are fit, but they do not go to the owner's credit in fulfillment of an obligation, except for the Passover and the sin offering." And Ben Azzai [thereby] added only the burnt offering. But sages did not agree with him.

M. 1:4 The animal designated as a Passover and the sin offering which one slaughtered not for the purpose for which the beast was originally designated — the blood [of which] one received, conveyed, or tossed not for the purpose for which the beast was originally designated — or for the purpose for which the beast was originally designated and also not for the purpose for which the beast was originally designated — or not for the purpose for which the beast was originally designated and also for the purpose for which the beast was originally designated — are unfit. How [does one do it] for the purpose for which the beast was originally designated and also not for the purpose for which the beast was originally designated? For the sake of the Passover [at its time] and for the sake of peace offerings. ...not for the purpose for which the beast was originally designated and also for the purpose for which the beast was originally designated? For the sake of peace offerings and for the sake of the Passover. For an animal offering is made unfit [by improper intention or deed] in four respects: (1) in slaughtering, and (2) in receiving [the blood], and (3) in conveying [the blood], and (4) in tossing [the blood]. R. Simeon declares fit in the case of [improperly] conveying [the blood]. For R. Simeon did say, "It is not possible [to prepare an animal offering] without slaughtering, and without receiving [the blood] and without tossing [the blood]. But it is possible [to make an animal offering] without conveying [the blood]. One slaughters [the animal] at the side of the altar and [forthwith, without conveying the blood at all] tosses [the blood onto the altar]." R. Eleazar says, "He who conveys [the blood] — [if he does so] in a situation in which he has to convey [the blood], [the wrong] intention renders invalid [the act of sacrifice]. [If he does so] in a situation in which he does not have to convey [the blood], the [wrong] intention does not render [the act of sacrifice] invalid."

T. 1:4 Sheep of the community['s offering] which one slaughtered in the name of sheep and which turned out to be rams go to the credit of the community in the name of rams. Rams of the community['s offering] which one slaughtered in the name of rams and which turned out to be sheep go to the credit of the community as sheep. And the remainder ascend to the altar and require drink-offerings. [If] one slaughtered it in its own name but pinched its neck not for its own name, it is valid, for it already has been rendered valid by [correct] slaughter [= M. Zeb 1:4]. [If this was done with improper intention to eat or offer up the sacrifice] outside its proper place, it is invalid, but the penalty of extirpation does not apply to it. [If this was done with improper intention to do so] outside of its proper time, it is deemed piggul, and the penalty of extirpation does apply to it. [If this was done with improper intention to do so] outside its proper time and place, it is invalid, and the penalty of extirpation does not apply to it. And R. Simeon declares valid in the case of conveying, [= M. Zeb. 1:4L]. So, too in respect to [improper intention to do the rite] outside its proper time and place.

T. 1:5 Said R. Simeon, "R. Yosé BeRibbi came across me in Sidon and said to me, 'The case of conveying which Meir did declare invalid — what is [the rule in your view]?' I said to him, 'For my part I declare it fit.' He said to me, 'For what reason?' I said to him, 'Because it is not possible to carry out the sacrifice without slaughtering, or without receiving the blood, or without tossing the blood, but it is possible [to do so] without conveying [the blood]. [If] one slaughtered it at the side of the altar or on top of the altar [it is not necessary to convey the blood at all] [= M. Zeb. 1:4M].'" R. Eliezer says, "Every case of conveying the blood which is required for the act of sacrifice has the capacity to invalidate the act of sacrifice, and every case of conveying the blood which is not required for the act of sacrifice does not have the capacity to invalidate the act of sacrifice [= M. Zeb. 1:40-P]. What is the case of conveying the blood which is not required for the act of sacrifice? [If] one slaughtered it and received the blood to go and toss it on the altar, and at the moment of conveying it he gave [improper] thought to it — this is a case of conveying which is required for the act of sacrifice. But [if] he slaughtered [the animal] and received the blood to go and leave it in some other place, and at the time of conveying it, he gave thought to it — this is a case of conveying which is not required for the act of sacrifice."

An animal is declared holy for a particular purpose, and that classifies the animal ("in its own name"). If the priest declares at the moment of sacrifice that he offers the beast in another category than the designated one, the offering remains valid; the owner still owes an offering for the purpose for which he originally designated the beast. But that is not the rule for the sin-offering and the Passover. The animal designated as a sin-offering atones for a specified sin, and if it is not offered by the priest as a sin-offering, it does not atone at all. The beast designated as a Passover, when offered on the afternoon of the fourteenth of Nisan, must be presented as a Passover, and the details are beautifully clarified by the Tosefta.

B. *IMPROPER RITES THAT INVALIDATE ALL OFFERINGS*

M. 2:1 All animal offerings, the blood of which was received by (1) a non-priest, (2) [a priest] mourning his next of kin, (3) a [priest who was] in the status of one who had immersed on that selfsame day and was awaiting sunset to complete the rites of purification [tebul yom], (4) [a priest] lacking proper priestly garments, (5) a [priest] whose atonement is not yet complete, (6) a [priest] whose hands and feet are not washed, (7) [an] uncircumcised [priest], (8) an unclean priest, (9) [a priest] who was sitting down, (10) [a priest] standing on utensils, on a beast, on the feet of his fellow, — he has rendered it invalid. [If] he received it in his left hand, he has rendered [the sacrifice] invalid. R. Simeon declares valid. [If] it [the blood] was poured onto the floor and one [then] collected it, it is invalid. [If] one [a priest who was fit, by contrast to M. 3:1E] sprinkled it [the blood] on the ramp, not by the [altar] base [but rather on the southeast corner, which had no base] — [if] one sprinkled those [drops of blood] which are to be sprinkled below [the red line around the altar], above [the red line around the altar], and those which are to be sprinkled above [the red line around the altar], below [the red line around the altar], those which are to be sprinkled inside [that is, the inner altar], outside [on the outer altar], and those which are to be sprinkled outside [on the outer altar], inside [that is, the inner altar] — it is invalid. And punishment by extirpation does not apply to it [for him who eats thereof, because of M. 2:3J].

T. 1:5 And so did R. Eliezer say, "Even if one of his feet was on the pavement, it is invalid." [If] one foot was on the pavement and one foot was on the brick, one foot on the pavement and one foot on the utensil — if one should remove the utensil and he should be able to stand on his own, it is fit, and if not, it is unfit. [If] the receiving was in his right hand and in his left simultaneously, it is unfit. And R. Simeon declares fit. And if his left hand was supporting his right hand, all agree that it is fit.

T. 1:6 R. Simeon did say, "Any action concerning which hand is stated requires the right hand, and any action concerning which hand is not stated does not require the right hand. And any concerning which finger is not stated does not require the right [one] [M. Zeb. 2:1B-C]." R. Eleazer b. R. Simeon says, "Any action concerning which placing by hand is stated — [if] one switched [hands] during the act of placing, it is unfit. [If he did so] during the act of receiving [the blood], it is fit. And any concerning which receiving by hand is stated — if one switched [hands] during the act of receiving, it is unfit. [If he did so] during the act of placing, it is fit."

T. 1:7 [If] the priest received [the blood], [if] a suitable [priest] received the blood, [if a suitable priest] received the blood in his right hand, [if a suitable priest] received the blood in a utensil used for the sacred service, it is valid. [If] a non-priest received the blood, [if] an unfit [priest] received the blood, [if] he received the blood in his left hand, [if] he received the blood in an ordinary [unconsecrated] utensil, it is unfit [M. Zeb. 2:1A]. [If] the suitable [priest] received the blood but the unsuitable [priest] tossed it, [if] the unsuitable priest received the blood and the suitable priest tossed it, it is invalid.

T. 1:8 Expounded R. Aqiba, "How do we know that the receiving of the blood should only be done by an unblemished priest and with a vestment used for the service? Scripture says, 'And the sons of Aaron shall present the blood [and toss the blood round about against the altar' (Lev. 1:5). Might one think that this refers to tossing the blood? When it says, 'And they shall toss it,' this clearly refers to tossing the blood. Accordingly, 'And [they] shall present', refers only to receiving the blood. [Scripture], therefore, joins receiving to tossing. Just as tossing must be done by an unblemished priest and with a vestment used for the service, so are conveying the blood [and] receiving the blood [to be done] by an unblemished priest and with a vestment used for the service. And elsewhere, it says, 'And you shall anoint them to serve as priest to him' (Ex. 40:15). Just as priest stated elsewhere refers to an unblemished priest and a vestment used for the service, so priest stated here refers to an unblemished priest and a vestment used for the service." Said to him R. Tarfon, "Aqiba, how long are you going to rake up and bring against me [senseless rubbish]? May I bury my sons if I have not heard a distinction between receiving the blood and tossing it on the altar. But you treat as equivalent receiving the blood and tossing it on the altar!" He said to him, "Will you permit me to state before you what you have taught me?" He said to him, "State it." He said to him, "In respect to receiving the blood, the law has not treated intention as tantamount to action. But in respect to sprinkling the blood on the altar, the law has treated intention as tantamount to action. He who receives the blood [with the intention of eating the flesh] outside [the courtyard] is free [of liability to extirpation]. But he who sprinkles the blood [with the intention of doing so] outside [the courtyard] liable. [If] unfit [men — laymen or drunken priests] received it, they are not liable on its account, but [if] unfit [men] tossed it, they are liable on its account." He said to him, "By the Temple service! You have not strayed either right or left. I heard [the rule] but was unable to explain it, and you expound it and bring into conformity to the law [both aspects of the rule]. Lo, whoever leaves you is as if he leaves life."

T. 1:9 As to [receiving and sprinkling] the blood of the red cow offered as a purification-sacrifice — one slaughters [the cow] with the right hand and receives the blood with the left and then sprinkles the blood with his right finger, and if he switched [any of the foregoing to the opposite hand], it is unfit. R. Judah says, "With the right hand did he slaughter [the red cow], and he put the knife down before him, or to this one who stands at his right hand. He receives the blood with his right hand and empties it out with his left. He sprinkles with his right finger, and if he switched it, it is unfit [= T. Parah 3:10]." The acts of tossing the blood of the red cow which he carried out not for their own name, or which were not properly aimed, or one of which was omitted, or [if the officiating priest] dipped his finger once but sprinkled two times, or dipped his finger two times but sprinkled one time only — Lo, these are unfit [= T. Par. 4:2]. The acts of sprinkling the blood of the sacrifice of the *mesora'*, which one carried out not for their own name, or which were not properly aimed, or one of which was omitted, or [if] he dipped his finger one time and sprinkled twice, or dipped his finger twice and sprinkled one time — Lo, these are valid.

T. 1:10 [As to] the blood of the guilt-offering of the *mesora'* — one received the blood with his right hand and poured it out with his left, sprinkled with his right finger. And if he switched [any of the forenamed], it is unfit. [If] he emptied from his left hand to his right and poured into his left and went and sprinkled with his right, it is invalid. And the reason that it is invalid is not that he switched, but that the log was lacking even so little as a drop [of its contents].

T. 1:11 The blood of all [animals which] is to be tossed above [the red line] which one tossed [not] in accord with their proper manner, or which missed [the proper location], Lo, these are valid. The blood of all [animals which] is to be tossed below [the red line] which one did not toss in accord with their proper manner, or which missed the base — Lo, these are invalid [M. Zeb. 2:1F-G]. The blood of all [animals which] is to be tossed above [the red line] does one receive in a utensil and toss with a utensil, and if he tossed by hand, it is unfit. The blood of all [animals which] is to be tossed below [the red line] does one toss by hand. If one tossed with a utensil, it is unfit. The log of oil of a *mesora'* one receives with his right hand and places into his left, and he tosses it with his right finger. And if he switches, it is invalid. But in the case of the fowl, the law is not so. But in the case of the burnt-offering of fowl, one wrings out the blood by itself. And in the case of the sin-offering of a fowl, one sprinkles and wrings out the blood by itself. In the case of all of them in which he received with a utensil and sprinkled by hand, [received] by hand and sprinkled with a utensil, Lo, these are invalid. As to the burning of the fat and limbs and wood, which one placed on top of the fires, whether [he did so] by hand or by a utensil, whether with the right hand or the left, Lo, these are valid.

T. 1:12 The handful [of meal-offering] and the incense-offering and the meal-offering of priests and the meal-offering of the anointed priest and the meal-offering offered with the drink-offerings, which one sanctified in a utensil and set on the fire, whether by hand or with a utensil — Lo, these are valid. The wine which one offered as a libation in a qisvah- [measure] and which one [then] poured into a hin-measure is valid. [If one did so] by hand or with an unconsecrated utensil, it is invalid. All the same are the drink-offering of water and the drink-offering of wine, which one poured out as a libation, whether into a hin-measure, or into a bowl, or into a qisvah-measure, or into a siphon — Lo, these are valid.

B. 2:1A-C IV.2/18A-B IF THE PRIESTLY GARMENTS TRAILED ON THE FLOOR OR DID NOT REACH THE FLOOR, IF THEY WERE THREADBARE, AND A PRIEST OFFICIATED WHILE WEARING THEM, HIS ACT OF SERVICE IS VALID. IF HE PUT ON TWO PAIRS OF PANTS, TWO GIRDLES, IF ONE GARMENT WAS LACKING, OR IF THERE WAS ONE TOO MANY, OR IF HE HAD A BANDAGE ON A WOUND IN HIS BODY, OR IF HIS GARMENTS WERE SMEARED OR TORN, AND HE PERFORMED AN ACT OF SERVICE, HIS ACT OF SERVICE IS INVALID.

B. 2:1D I.9.26A MOST HOLY THINGS ARE TO BE SLAUGHTERED ON THE NORTH SIDE OF THE TEMPLE COURT AND THEIR BLOOD IS TO BE RECEIVED IN UTENSILS OF SERVICE ON THE NORTH SIDE OF THE TEMPLE COURT. IF THE PRIEST

STOOD IN THE SOUTHERN PART OF THE COURT AND STRETCHED OUT HIS HAND INTO THE NORTH AND SLAUGHTERED THE BEAST, HIS ACT OF SLAUGHTER IS VALID. IF HE RECEIVED THE BLOOD IN SUCH A POSTURE, IT IS INVALID. IF HE POKED HIS HEAD AND THE GREATER PART OF HIS BODY INTO THAT SPACE, IT IS AS THOUGH THE WHOLE OF THE PRIEST HAD ENTERED THAT SPACE. IF IN ITS DEATH THROES THE BEAST STRUGGLED AND WENT INTO THE SOUTHERN PRECINCT AND THEN RETURNED TO THE NORTH, IT REMAINS VALID. AS TO LESSER HOLY THINGS, THEY ARE TO BE SLAUGHTERED ANYWHERE WITHIN THE TEMPLE COURT AND THEIR BLOOD IS TO BE RECEIVED IN UTENSILS OF SERVICE ANYWHERE WITHIN THE TEMPLE COURT. IF THE PRIEST STOOD OUTSIDE OF THE COURT AND STRETCHED OUT HIS HAND WITHIN THE TEMPLE COURT AND SLAUGHTERED THE BEAST, HIS ACT OF SLAUGHTER IS VALID. IF HE RECEIVED THE BLOOD IN SUCH A POSTURE, IT IS INVALID. IF HE POKED HIS HEAD AND THE GREATER PART OF HIS BODY INTO THAT SPACE, IT IS AS THOUGH THE WHOLE OF THE PRIEST HAD NOT ENTERED THAT SPACE. IF IN ITS DEATH THROES, THE BEAST STRUGGLED AND WENT OUTSIDE AND THEN RETURNED TO THE INSIDE SPACE OF THE COURTYARD, IT IS INVALID.

Before we turn to improper intentionality that invalidates all offerings, we take up those persons and deeds that can spoil the procedure. While a priest is not required for slaughtering the animal, a priest alone can toss the blood and carry out the other parts of the blood-rite. A non-priest or an unsuited priest cannot do these rites, and if he does, he spoils the procedure and the beast is invalid. A priest who does not assume the correct posture, who is seated or not standing on the ground, invalidates the rite.

C. *IMPROPER INTENTIONALITY AND THE INVALIDATION OF ALL OFFERINGS*

M. 2:2 He who slaughters the animal offering [intending] to toss its blood outside [of the Temple court], (1) or part of its blood outside, to burn its sacrificial portions outside, (1) or part of its sacrificial portions outside, to eat its meat outside (1) or an olive's bulk of its meat outside, or to eat an olive's bulk of the skin of the fat tail outside — it is invalid. But punishment by extirpation does not apply to it [e.g., in the case of the priest who eats thereof]. [Supply: He who slaughters the animal offering, intending] to toss its blood on the next day, (1) or part of its blood on the next day, to burn its sacrificial portions on the next day, (1) or part of its sacrificial portions on the next day, to eat its meat on

the next day, (1) or part of its meat on the next day, or an olive's bulk of the skin of the fat tail on the next day — it is refuse. And they [who eat it, even at the proper time] are liable on its account to punishment by extirpation.

T. 2:1 He who slaughters the animal-offering [intending] to toss its blood outside [of the Temple court], or part of its blood outside, to burn its sacrificial portions outside, or an olive's bulk of its sacrificial portions outside, to eat of its flesh outside or an olive's bulk of its flesh outside — it is invalid. And punishment by extirpation does not apply to it. [= M. Zeb. 2:2A-G]. And so you rule in the case of uncircumcised [priests] [and] unclean [priests]. How so? He who slaughters the Passover on condition that uncircumcised or unclean [priests] toss its blood outside, [or] part of its blood outside or on condition that uncircumcised or unclean [priests] burn its sacrificial portions outside, or an olive's bulk of its sacrificial portions outside, on condition that uncircumcised priests or unclean priests eat its flesh outside, or an olive's bulk of its flesh outside — it is invalid. And punishment by extirpation does not apply to it. [He who slaughters the animal-offering intending] to toss its blood the next day, or part of its blood the next day, to burn its sacrificial portions the next day, or an olive's bulk of its sacrificial portions the next day, to eat its flesh the next day, or an olive's bulk of its flesh the next day — it is refuse. And they are liable on its account to punishment by extirpation [= M. Zeb. 2:2H-N]. And so you rule in the case of uncircumcised [priests] and unclean [priests]. How so? He who slaughters the Passover on condition that uncircumcised or unclean [priests] toss its blood on the next day, or part of its blood on the next day, on condition that uncircumcised or unclean [priests] burn its flesh on the next day, or an olive's bulk of its flesh on the next day — it is refuse. And they are liable on its account for extirpation.

T. 2:2 He who slaughters the burnt-offering [intending] to toss its blood outside, or part of its blood outside, to eat its flesh outside, or an olive's bulk of its flesh outside — it is invalid. And extirpation does not apply to it. And so do you rule in the case of uncircumcised or unclean [priests]? [If one does so intending to carry out the listed acts] on the next day, it is refuse. And they are liable on its account for extirpation. And so do you rule in the case of uncircumcised or unclean [priests]?

T. 2:3 He who slaughters the animal-sacrifice [intending] to eat an olive's bulk of the skin of the fat tail outside of its proper place [M. Zeb. 2:2E] — it is unfit. And the penalty of extirpation does not apply to it [If he does so intending to eat an olive's bulk of the skin of the fat tail] outside of its proper time, it is refuse. And they are liable on its account for extirpation. R. Eleazar b. Judah of Eiblayim says in the name of R. Simeon and so did R. Simeon b. Judah of Kefar Akkum say in the name of R. Simeon, "All the same are the skin of the fat tail and the skin of the head and of the tender calf and the skin of the hooves in the case of small cattle, and everything which is eaten, because the skin is equivalent to the flesh. [If one slaughters the animal intending to eat any of the afore-named items] outside of their proper time, it is unfit. And extirpation does not apply to it. [If he does so intending to eat any of them] outside of its proper time, it is refuse. And they are liable on its account for extirpation."

M. 2:3 This is the general rule: Whoever slaughters, or receives [the blood], or conveys [the blood], or sprinkles [the blood] [intending] to eat something which is usually eaten [meat], [or] to burn something which is usually burned [entrails], outside of its proper place [which is, the Temple court for Most Holy Things, the walled city of Jerusalem for Lesser Holy Things] — it is invalid [and the meat may not be eaten]. And extirpation does not apply to it. [Supply: Whoever slaughters, or receives the blood, or conveys the blood, or sprinkles (the blood), intending to eat something which is usually eaten, to burn something which is usually burned] outside of its proper time — it is refuse. And they are liable on its account to extirpation [even if despite their declared intention, they actually eat the meat within the time limit]. And [the foregoing rule applies] on condition that what renders the offering permissible [the blood, which permits the sacrificial portions to be burned on the altar and the meat to be eaten by the priest or owner, that is, the proper sprinkling or tossing of the blood] is offered in accord with its requirement.

T. 2:16 He who slaughters the animal-sacrifice [intending] to eat its sacrificial portions and to burn its flesh, to eat something which is not usually eaten, to burn something which is not usually burned — it is valid [= M. Zeb. 2:3C]. And R. Judah declares invalid. Rabbi said, "R. Eliezer declares invalid. And R. Joshua declares valid." Said to them R. Judah, "Now, if he left the blood for the next day, he does not invalidate [the sacrifice]" — and sages say, "This and that are valid" — accordingly you have nothing, which invalidates a sacrifice except improper intention concerning eating, burning, and tossing the blood."

T. 2:17 Said Rabbi, "One time we were in session before R. Eleazar. And Issi the Babylonian [also] was in session before him. And he [Issi] was much beloved by him [Eleazar]. He said to him, 'Rabbi, He who slaughters the animal-sacrifice [intending] to eat its sacrificial parts and to burn its flesh — what is the law?' He said to him, 'It is valid. But R. Eliezer declares invalid, and R Joshua declares valid.' He said to him, 'Repeat the ruling for me.' And he repeated it for him. At the time of the afternoon-offering he came to him. He said to him, 'Repeat the matter to me.' And he repeated it to him. The next day he said to him, 'Repeat the matter to me.' And he repeated it to him. He said to him, 'What is this, Issi?' He said to him, 'It seems that our traditions did not correspond.' He said to him, 'Yes, Rabbi. But R. Judah repeated the tradition to us: It is invalid. And I went full circle among all my colleagues, and I found no colleague to agree with me. I thought that it might be an error in the hand of Rabbi. Now that you have told me a ruling in the name of R. Eliezer, you have restored to me what I lost.' His eyes filled up with tears, and he said, 'Happy are you, O righteous men, for you cherish the Torah, thereby carrying out that which Scripture says, Oh, how I love thy law! It is my meditation all the day (Ps. 119:97).' Lo, since Judah is the disciple of Ilai, and Ilai is the disciple of Eliezer, therefore, he repeats the teaching of R. Eliezer."

M. 2:4 How is "what renders the offering permissible offered in accord with its requirement"? [If] one slaughtered in silence [lacking improper intent], [but] received [the blood] and conveyed [the blood] and sprinkled [the blood] [intending to eat or burn the flesh] outside of its proper time, or [if one] slaughtered [intending to eat or burn the flesh] outside of the proper time, received [the blood] and conveyed [the blood] and sprinkled [the blood] in silence [lacking improper intent] , or [if he] slaughtered, received [the blood], and conveyed [the blood] and sprinkled [the blood] [intending to eat or burn the flesh] outside of its proper time — this is a case in which what renders the offering permissible is offered in accord with its requirement. How is "what renders the offering permissible not offered in accord with its requirement"? [If] one slaughtered [intending to eat or burn the flesh] outside of its place, received [the blood] and conveyed [the blood] and tossed [the blood] [intending to eat or burn the flesh] outside of its time, or [if] one slaughtered [intending to eat or burn the flesh] outside its proper time, received [the blood] and conveyed [the blood] and tossed [the blood] [intending to eat or burn the flesh] outside of its place, or [if one] slaughtered, received [the blood] and conveyed [the blood] and tossed [the blood] [intending to eat or burn the flesh] outside of its place — the Passover and the sin offering which one slaughtered not for their own name [that is, the beast was designated as a Passover or a sin offering but was slaughtered for some purpose other than that for which it originally had been designated] — [the blood of which] one [also] received and conveyed and tossed [intending to eat or burn the flesh] outside of their proper time, or which one slaughtered [intending to eat or burn the flesh] outside of their proper time, [and the blood of which] one received and conveyed and tossed not for their own name [that is, the beast was designated as a Passover or a sin offering but was slaughtered for some purpose other than that for which it had been designated] — or which one slaughtered, received, and conveyed and tossed not for their own name [that is, the beast was designated as a Passover or a sin offering but was slaughtered for some purpose other than that for which it had been designated] — this is a case in which what renders the offering permissible is not offered in accord with its requirement.

M. 2:5 [Supply: If a man slaughtered an animal offering and received, conveyed, and tossed the blood intending] — to eat an olive's bulk outside [the proper place] and an olive's bulk on the next day [at an improper time], an olive's bulk on the next day and an olive's bulk outside, half an olive's bulk outside and half an olive's bulk on the next day, half an olive's bulk on the next day and half an olive's bulk outside — it is unfit. But extirpation does not apply to it. Said R. Judah, "This is the general rule: if the [improper] intention concerning time came before the [improper] intention concerning the place, it is refuse, and they are liable on its account for extirpation. And if the [improper] intention concerning the place came before the [improper] intention concerning the time, it is invalid. And extirpation does not apply to him." And sages say, "This and that are invalid. And extirpation does not apply to him." [If one intends] to eat half an olive's bulk and to burn half an olive's bulk, the offering is valid. For eating and burning are not joined together.

T. 2:4 All animal-sacrifices, which one sacrificed not for their own name, [the blood of which] one received, and conveyed, and tossed [intending to eat the flesh] outside of their proper time, or which he sacrificed [with intention to eat the flesh] outside of their proper time, [or the blood of which] one received, and conveyed, and tossed not for their own name, are refuse. And they are liable on their account for extirpation. And [the fore-going rule applies] on condition that what renders the offering permissible is offered in accord with its requirement [= M. Zeb. 2:3J].

T. 2:5 How is what renders the offering permissible offered in accord with its requirement? [If] one slaughtered in silence, received, and conveyed, and tossed the blood [intending to eat the flesh] outside of its proper time, or slaughtered [intending to do so] outside of its proper time, received, and conveyed, and tossed the blood in silence [M. Zeb. 2:4A-D], or slaughtered, received, and conveyed, and tossed the blood in silence — this is a case in which what renders the offering permissible, is offered in accord with its requirement [M. Zeb. 2:4F].

T. 2:6 How is what renders the offering permissible, not offered in accord with its requirement? [If] one slaughtered [intending to eat or burn the flesh] outside of its place, received, conveyed, and tossed the blood [intending to eat the flesh] outside its proper time, or if one slaughtered [intending to eat or burn the flesh] outside of its proper time, and received, conveyed and tossed the blood [intending to do so] outside of its proper place, or if one slaughtered and received, and conveyed, and tossed the blood [intending to eat the flesh] outside of its proper place [M. Zeb. 2:4G-J] — whether the improper intention concerning time came before the improper intention concerning place, or whether the improper intention concerning place came before the improper intention concerning time, it is invalid. And extirpation does not apply to it. R. Judah says, "Even in this case, [if] the improper thought concerning time came before the improper thought concerning the place, it is refuse, and they are liable on its account for extirpation. [But if] the improper intention concerning the place came before the improper intention concerning the time, it is invalid. And extirpation does not apply to it [M. Zeb 2:5H-I]. What is a case in which the improper intention concerning place came before the improper intention concerning the time? If one slaughtered [intending to eat the flesh] outside of its proper place, then received, conveyed, and tossed the blood [with the improper intention to eat the flesh] outside of its proper time — [this is a case in which the improper intention concerning the place came before the improper intention concerning time]."

T. 2:7 [Continuing the foregoing:] "What is a case in which the improper intention concerning place came before the improper intention concerning time? [If] one slaughtered [intending to eat the flesh] outside of its proper place, then received, conveyed, and tossed the blood [with the improper intention to eat the flesh] outside of its proper time [this is a case in which the improper intention concerning place came before the improper intention concerning time]."

T. 2:8 The Passover and the sin-offering, which one slaughtered not for their own name, are invalid. And the penalty of extirpation does not apply to it, because that which renders the offering permissible has not been offered in accord with its requirement.

T. 2:9 He who slaughters the animal-sacrifice [intending] to eat its flesh outside, to burn its sacrificial portions on the next day, to eat its flesh on the next day, to burn its sacrificial portions outside, whether the improper intention concerning time came before the improper intention concerning place, or whether the improper intention concerning place came before the improper intention concerning time — it is invalid. And extirpation does not apply to it. R. Judah says, "Even in this case, [if] the improper intention concerning time came before the improper intention concerning place, it is refuse. And they are liable on its account for extirpation. [If] the improper intention concerning place came before the improper intention concerning time, it is invalid. And extirpation does not apply to it [= M. Zeb. 2:5H-I]."

T. 2:10 All animal-sacrifices which one slaughtered [intending to eat their flesh] outside of their time, or the blood of which unfit priests received and threw in silence, or the blood of which was kept over night and they [then] tossed it in silence, or the blood of which went forth outside of the veils and they threw it in silence — even [if the blood was thrown] with intention of eating the flesh outside of the proper time — it is unfit. And extirpation does not apply to it.

T. 2:11 He who slaughters the animal-sacrifice [intending] to eat an olive's bulk of its flesh outside and an olive's bulk of its flesh inside to burn an olive's bulk of its sacrificial parts outside and an olive's bulk inside, it is unfit. And extirpation does not apply to it. [If he did so intending] to eat an olive's bulk of its flesh on the same day and an olive's bulk on the next day to burn an olive's bulk of its sacrificial parts on the same day and olive's bulk on the next day — it is refuse. And they are liable on its account for extirpation.

T. 2:12 He who slaughters the animal-sacrifice [intending] to eat a half olive's bulk of its flesh outside and a half olive's bulk of its flesh inside, to burn a half olive's bulk of its sacrificial parts outside and a half olive's bulk inside — it is valid. And so with respect to [intention to do so on] the next day [= time], it is valid. He who slaughters the animal-sacrifice [intending] to eat an olive's bulk of its flesh on the same day and an olive's bulk on the next day, to burn an olive's bulk of its sacrificial parts on the same day and an olive's bulk on the next day, whether the improper intention concerning time came before the improper intention concerning place, or whether the improper intention concerning place came before the improper intention concerning time, it is invalid. And extirpation does not apply to it. R. Judah says, "Even in this case, [if] the improper intention concerning time came before the improper intention concerning place, it is refuse. And they are liable on its account for extirpation. [If] the improper intention concerning place came before the improper intention concerning time, it is invalid. And extirpation does not apply to it [= M. Zeb. 2:5H-I]."

T. 2:13 He who slaughters the animal-sacrifice [intending] to eat a half-olive's bulk of its flesh outside [and] to burn a half olive's bulk of its sacrificial parts outside, to eat a half olive's bulk of its flesh the next day, [and] to burn a half olive's bulk of its sacrificial parts on the next day — it is valid. For burning and eating do not join together [= M. Zeb. 2:5L]. But eating [with one sort of improper intention] and eating [with another], burning [with one sort of improper intention] and burning [with another] do join together. How so? He who slaughters the animal-sacrifice [intending] to eat an olive's bulk of its flesh outside and an olive bulk of its flesh on the next day to burn an olive's bulk of its sacrificial parts outside, and to burn an olive's bulk of its sacrificial parts on the next day — it is invalid. And extirpation does not apply to it. For eating [with one sort of improper intention] and eating [with another], burning [with one sort of improper intention] and burning [with another] do join together.

T. 2:14 He who slaughters the animal-sacrifice on condition to eat a half olive's bulk of its flesh on the next day, and at the time of tossing the blood, gave further thought to burn a half olive's bulk of its sacrificial parts on the next day — it is refuse. And they are liable on its account to extirpation. For slaughtering [the animal] and tossing the blood to join together.

T. 2:15 He who slaughters the animal-sacrifice [intending] to burn less than an olive's bulk of its sacrificial parts on the next day — it is valid. For less than an olive's bulk does not impart the status of refuse or invalidate [the sacrifice] under any circumstances.

M. 3:1 All unfit people [e.g., the ten listed at M. 2:1A] who [in behalf of the Temple cult] slaughtered [an animal designated for a sacrifice] — their act of slaughter is valid. For an act of slaughter [in general, not in the cult] is valid [when done] by non-priests, women, slaves, and unclean men — even in the case of [their slaughtering] Most Holy Things. And [this is so] on condition that the unclean people do not touch the meat. Therefore, they [who are listed above also have the power to] invalidate [the offering they have slaughtered] by improper intention [in the act of slaughtering]. But all of them [who are unfit] who received the blood [intending to eat the meat] outside its proper time or outside its proper place, if the lifeblood [suitable for tossing] still remained [in the beast, that is, the blood which gushes at the moment of death] — a fit person should go and [with proper intention] receive [it].

T. 3:1 All animal-sacrifices which one slaughtered not for their own name, Lo, they are valid [= M. Zeb. I:1A]. Therefore, if one gave thought concerning them [to eat their flesh] outside of its proper place, it is invalid. And extirpation does not apply to it. [If one gave thought to them to eat their flesh] outside of its proper time, it is refuse. And they are liable on its account for extirpation. All sacrifices which one of those who are unfit slaughtered — Lo, they are valid. Therefore, if he gave thought to it [to it eat] outside of its proper place, it is invalid. And extirpation does not apply to it. [On the other hand, if he gave thought to it to eat it] outside its proper time, it is refuse. And they are liable to extirpation on its account. How so? He who slaughters the animal-sacrifice on condition that uncircumcised or unclean [priests] toss its blood, on condition that uncircumcised or unclean [priests] burn its sacrificial parts, on condition that uncircumcised or unclean [priests] eat its flesh — it is valid. Therefore, if he gave improper thought to it [to eat it] outside of its proper place, it is invalid. And extirpation does not apply to it. [If it was so that they eat it] outside its proper time, it is refuse. And they are liable to extirpation on its account.

T. 3:2 [If] the priest received [the blood], [if] the fit [priest] received [the blood], [if] he [a fit person] received it in his right hand, [if] he received it in a sacred vestment, it [the receiving of the blood] is valid. Therefore, if he gave thought [during the act of receiving the blood, to burn the sacrificial portions] outside of its proper place, it is unfit. And extirpation does not apply to it. [If he gave thought, during the act of receiving the blood, to eat the flesh] outside of its proper time, it is refuse, and they are liable to extirpation on its account. [If] he gave thought to toss those [drops of blood] which are to be tossed below, above, or those which are to be tossed above, below, those which are to be tossed inside, outside, or those which are to be tossed outside, inside, it is valid [since, in accord with M. Zeb. 3:6, improper thought is effective only concerning place or time]. Therefore, if he gave thought concerning it [during the tossing, to burn the sacrificial part] outside of its place, it is invalid. And extirpation does not apply to it. [If he gave thought, during the tossing, to eat the flesh] outside of its proper time, it is refuse, and they are liable on its account to extirpation [M. Zeb. 3:1].

T. 3:3 All animal-sacrifices, the blood of which one of those unfit received, Lo, they are invalid. Therefore, if he [an unfit person] gave thought concerning them [during the receiving of the blood, to eat the flesh or burn the sacrificial part] whether outside the proper time or outside the proper place — the law of refuse does not apply to it.

T. 3:4 The Passover and the sin-offering which one slaughtered not for their own name, — Lo, they are invalid. Therefore, if one gave thought to them [during the act of slaughter, to eat the flesh or to burn the sacrificial parts] outside its proper place or outside its proper time — the law of refuse does not apply to it. All the same are the Passover and the sin-offering [on the one side], and any one of the animal-sacrifices the blood of which is collected by a non-priest, a priest in mourning, a Tebul Yom, a priest lacking proper garments, [a priest] lacking completion of rites of atonement, [a priest] whose hands and feet have not been washed, an uncircumcised [priest], an unclean [priest], [a priest] who is sitting down, [a priest] who is standing on utensils, on cattle, on the feet of his fellow — it is unfit [=M. Zeb. 2:1]. Therefore, if [any one of these] gave thought to it [during the act of collecting the blood, to eat the flesh or to burn the sacrificial part] whether outside its proper time or outside its proper place — the law of refuse does not apply to it. [If] a non-priest received [the blood], [if] an unfit person received the blood, [if] he received in his left hand, if he received [the blood] in an unconsecrated utensil, it is invalid. Therefore, if [one of these] gave thought to it [during the act of receiving the blood, to eat the flesh or to burn the sacrificial part] outside of its proper time or outside its proper place, the law of refuse does not apply to it.

T. 3:5 [If] one tossed those [drops of blood] which are to be tossed outside, inside, or those which are to be tossed inside, outside, it is invalid. Therefore, if [during the act of improper tossing by a fit person], he gave thought to it [to eat the flesh or to burn the sacrificial part] outside of its proper time or outside of its proper place, the law of refuse does not apply to it. This is the general principle [which has been expressed in the foregoing examples]: The animal-sacrifice is invalidated by only four actions: (1) by the act of slaughter, (2) by the acting of collecting [the blood] in a utensil, (3) by the act of conveying, and (4) by the act of tossing [the blood on the altar]. Added to them are the Passover and the sin-offering (5) which one slaughtered not for their own name. And added to them is (6) the Passover, which may be invalidated by the intention of uncircumcised and unclean priests.

M. 3:2 [If] a fit person received [the blood] and handed it over to an unfit person, [without conveying it] he [the unfit one] should return it to the fit person. [If] he received the blood in his right hand and put it into his left, he should return it to his right hand. [If] he received it in a sacred utensil and put it into an unconsecrated utensil, he should put it back into a sacred utensil. [If after the blood was received in a utensil], it poured from the utensil onto the pavement and one gathered it up, it is valid. [If] he [who was unfit] tossed it on the ramp, not against the foundation [of the altar], [if] he tossed those which are to be tossed below, above, or those which are to be tossed above, below, those which are to be tossed inside, outside, or those which are to be tossed outside, inside, if the lifeblood still remained in the beast, a suitable person should go and receive it [and repeat the sprinklings] [= M. 3:1G-H].

T. 3:6 All animal-sacrifices [slaughtered by two priests] which the first priest slaughtered in silence [without improper intent], and which the second priest [slaughtered with the improper intention to eat the flesh] outside of its proper time, even though this one slaughtered in silence and [then] tossed the blood [properly] — it is invalid. The Passover and the sin-offering [slaughtered by two priests] which the first [priest] slaughtered in their own name, and the second priest not in their own name, even though this one slaughtered in their own name and [then] tossed the blood [properly] — it is invalid. This is the general principle of the matter: Every [sacrifice] which is invalidated by improper intention, whether it was by the improper intention of the first or whether it is the improper intention of the last, is invalid. Even though there is life-blood [remaining] in another cup, it is invalid. And any [sacrifice] which is invalidated by an improper deed whether the first priest had an improper thought or the last priest had an improper thought, is invalid. If [however] there is another cup [of valid blood], a valid priest should go and receive it. [If] a non-priest received [the blood], [if] an unfit person received the blood, if he received it in his left hand, if he received it in unconsecrated vestments, it is invalid. [But] if there is another cup of blood, a valid person should go and receive it in another cup. [If] he tossed these [drops of blood] which are to be tossed below, above, or those which are to be tossed above, below, those which are to be tossed inside, outside, or those which are to be tossed outside, inside, it is invalid. And if there is life-blood in another cup, a fit person should go and receive it.

M. 3:3 He who slaughters the animal sacrifice [intending] to eat something which is not usually eaten, to burn something which is not usually burned — [the offering nonetheless] is valid. R. Eliezer declares invalid. [If he does so intending] to eat something which is usually eaten, or to burn something which is usually burned, but the intentionally concerned [in volume] less than an olive's bulk of meat, [the offering] is valid. [If he does so] intending to eat a half-olive's bulk, and to burn a half-olive's bulk [in an improper manner], it is valid. For eating and burning do not join together.

M. 3:4 He who slaughters the animal offering [intending] to eat an olive's bulk of (1) the hide, (2) the grease, (3) the sediment [jelly], (4) the flayed-off meat [offal], (5) the bones, (6) the tendons, (7) the hooves, (8) the horns, outside of the proper time or outside of the proper place — it is valid. And they are not liable on their account for violation of the laws of refuse, remnant, or uncleanness.

M. 3:5 He who slaughters [female] consecrated animals [intending] to eat the foetus or the afterbirth outside [the proper place or time] has not rendered the sacrifice refuse [for these are not usually eaten]. He who wrings the necks of turtledoves inside [intending] to eat their eggs outside [the proper place or time] has not rendered the sacrifice refuse. [As to] the milk of [female] consecrated beasts and the eggs of turtledoves [which are not integral to the body of the sacrifice] — they are not liable on their account in respect to the laws of refuse, remnant, and uncleanness.

B. 3:3-3:5 I.1/35A SAID R. ELEAZAR, "IF THE PRIEST EXPRESSED AN INTENTIONALITY THAT WOULD CLASSIFY THE OFFERING AS REFUSE IN REGARD TO THE ANIMAL THAT IS BEING SACRIFICED, THEN THE STATUS OF THE FOETUS IS THE SAME AND IT IS DEEMED REFUSE. BUT IF THE PRIEST EXPRESSED AN INTENTIONALITY THAT WOULD CLASSIFY THE OFFERING AS REFUSE IN REGARD TO THE FOETUS INSIDE THE

ANIMAL THAT IS BEING SACRIFICED, THEN THE STATUS OF THE MOTHER IS NOT THE SAME AND IT IS NOT DEEMED REFUSE. IF THE PRIEST EXPRESSED AN INTENTIONALITY THAT WOULD CLASSIFY THE OFFERING AS REFUSE IN REGARD TO THE OFFAL, THEN THE STATUS OF THE CROP IS THE SAME AND IT IS DEEMED REFUSE. BUT IF THE PRIEST EXPRESSED AN INTENTIONALITY THAT WOULD CLASSIFY THE OFFERING AS REFUSE IN REGARD TO THE CROP, THEN THE STATUS OF THE OFFAL IS NOT THE SAME AND IT IS NOT DEEMED REFUSE. IF THE PRIEST EXPRESSED AN INTENTIONALITY THAT WOULD CLASSIFY THE OFFERING AS REFUSE IN REGARD TO THE PARTS THAT ARE TO BE BURNED ON THE ALTAR, THEN THE STATUS OF THE BULLOCKS IS THE SAME AND IT IS DEEMED REFUSE. BUT IF THE PRIEST EXPRESSED AN INTENTIONALITY THAT WOULD CLASSIFY THE OFFERING AS REFUSE IN REGARD TO THE BULLOCKS, THEN THE STATUS OF THE PARTS THAT ARE TO BE BURNED ON THE ALTAR IS NOT THE SAME AND IT IS NOT DEEMED REFUSE."

M. 3:6 [If] one slaughtered it [an animal sacrifice] on condition of leaving over its blood [and not to toss it] or its sacrificial parts [and not to offer them up] for the next day, or to take them outside — R. Judah declares invalid [as would be the case if the officiant actually did so]. And sages declare valid. [If] he slaughtered it on condition [that he intended] (1) to sprinkle it on the ramp, not at the foundation [of the altar] [M. 2:11], (2) to sprinkle those which are to be sprinkled below, above, (3) or those which are to be sprinkled above, below, (4) those which are to be sprinkled inside, outside (5) or those which are to be sprinkled outside, inside — (1) that unclean people eat it, (2) that unclean people offer it up, (3) that uncircumcised priests eat it, (4) that uncircumcised priests offer it up, (1) to break the bones of the Passover [Ex. 12:9], (2) or to eat of it while it is raw [Ex. 12:46], (3) to mix its blood with the blood of unfit beasts — it is valid. For improper intention invalidates only in respect to [eating the meat or burning the sacrificial parts] outside its proper place or outside its proper time, and, in respect to the Passover and the sin offering, [improper intention invalidates when this involves slaughtering them] not for their own name [not for the purpose for which the beast was originally designated as a Holy Thing].

T. 3:7 There are things (I) which render [a sacrifice] refuse, but are [themselves] not rendered refuse, [An illegitimate intention in regard to these things renders the sacrifice refuse, but they do not become refuse themselves.] (II) are [themselves] rendered refuse, but do not render [a sacrifice] refuse, (III) both render [the sacrifice] refuse and [themselves] are rendered refuse. (IV) neither render [the sacrifice] refuse nor are [themselves] rendered refuse. What are the things which (I) render [the sacrifice] refuse, but are not themselves rendered refuse? (I) Slaughtering [the animal] and (2) receiving and (3) conveying the blood. How so? [If] the priest slaughtered [the animal] and received and conveyed [the blood] on condition of burning the sacrificial parts on the next day, Lo, these render [the sacrifice] refuse. How are they not rendered refuse? [If the priest] slaughtered [the animal] on condition of receiving, and received the blood on condition of conveying [it], on the next day, Lo, these are not rendered refuse. What are those which (II) are [themselves] rendered refuse, but do not render [the sacrifice] refuse? (1) The remnants of the blood, and (2) the burning of the sacrificial parts, and (3) the eating of the flesh. How so? [If] one pours out the remnants of the blood on condition of burning the sacrificial parts and of eating the flesh on the next day, Lo, these are rendered refuse. How do they not render [the sacrifice] refuse? [If] one poured out the remnants of the blood on condition of burning the sacrificial parts, and burned the sacrificial parts on condition of eating the flesh, on the next day — Lo, these do not render [the sacrifice] refuse.

T. 3:8 Tossing [the blood] renders [the sacrifice] refuse and itself is rendered refuse (III). How is it [itself] rendered refuse? [If] one slaughtered the animal and received the blood and conveyed it on condition of tossing the blood on the next day, Lo, this is rendered refuse. How does it render [the sacrifice] refuse? [If] one tossed the blood on condition of pouring out the remnants of the blood, or of burning the sacrificial parts, or of eating the flesh, on the next day, Lo, this imparts the status of refuse to the animal-sacrifice.

T. 3:9 T. What are the things which (IV) do not impart the status of refuse and [themselves] are not made refuse? (I) The bones (2) the tendons, (3) the horns, (4) the hooves, (5) the hair of the head of lambs, (6) the hair of the beard of he-goats, (7) the eggs of turtledoves, (8) the crop of fowl, (9) the skin, (10) the limb, (11) the flayed off flesh, (12) the foetus, and (13) the afterbirth. All of these do not impart the status of refuse [to the animal-sacrifice], either [in respect to improper intention to eat the flesh] outside of its time or [in respect to improper intention to burn the sacrificial parts] outside of its proper place, nor does improper intention invalidate in its case on account of refuse [that is, they are not rendered refuse on their own account]. And he who offers it outside is free of liability.

M. 4:1 The House of Shammai say, "In the case of any [offering, the tossings of the blood of which] are to be placed on the outer altar, if [on the outer altar] one [properly] tossed one tossing [of blood], has effected atonement [=M. 5:3-8]. But in the case of the sin offering, two tossings [properly tossed on the outer altar are required to effect atonement]." And the House of Hillel say, "Even in the case of a sin offering, the tossing [of the blood of

which] was properly placed [in the case of] one placing, has effected atonement." Therefore, if one placed the first [tossing of the blood[in the proper manner [in silence], but the second [articulately intending to eat the flesh or burn the sacrificial portion] outside of its proper time, [the offering is valid and] it has effected atonement. [The first placing of the blood sufficed.] [If] one placed the first [intending to eat the flesh or burn the sacrificial portion] outside its proper time, and the second outside its proper place [= M. 2:4], the offering is refuse [that which permits the offering to be eaten having been offered in accord with its requirement], and they are liable on its account for extirpation.

M. 4:2 In the case of any [animal offering, the tossings of the blood of which] are to be placed on the inner altar, if one omitted one of the acts of tossing of blood, the offering has not effected atonement [=M. 5:1-2]. Therefore, if one tossed all of them in the proper manner, but one of them not in its proper manner, it is invalid. But extirpation does not apply to it. [One application of the blood does not suffice to make the sacrifice fit. A sacrifice cannot be made into refuse through an act of service that is incomplete in itself to make the sacrifice fit].

T. 4:1 R. Eliezer says, "If there is no blood, there is no flesh. And even though there is no flesh, there is blood." R. Joshua says, "If there is no blood, there is no flesh. If there is no flesh, there is no blood." How so? [If] the blood is made unclean, or [if] it is poured out, or [if] it went outside of the veils, [as to] the flesh, its appearance is allowed to decay, and it goes forth to the place of burning. [If] the flesh is made unclean or rendered invalid or goes out beyond the veils — R. Eliezer says, "One may toss the blood." R. Joshua says, "One may not toss the blood." But if one tossed the blood, whether inadvertently or deliberately, R. Joshua concedes that it is accepted.

T. 4:2 R. Joshua says, "Lo, it [Scripture] states, 'And you shall offer your burnt offerings, the flesh and the blood' (Deut. 12:27) — if there is no blood, there is no flesh. If there is no flesh, there is no blood." Said to him R. Eliezer, "Lo, it says, 'And the blood of your sacrifices shall be poured out against the altar of the Lord your God' (Deut. 12:27) — even though there is no blood. How do I interpret the flesh and the blood [of the same Scripture cited at A]? Scripture joins flesh to blood. Just as blood is [offered] by being tossed [on the altar], so flesh [is offered] by being tossed on the altar. Might one think that one tosses [the flesh] but [neatly] piles up [the meat on the altar]? Scripture says, 'And the priest shall arrange them' (Lev. 1:12) — he tosses and arranges [them], but he does not toss [them] and pile [them up on the altar]."

T. 4:3 R. Joshua says, "All the sacrifices which are mentioned in the Torah, of which there remained an olive's bulk of flesh and an olive's bulk of fat — [the priest] sprinkles the blood on its account. [If there remained] a half olive's bulk of flesh or a half olive's bulk of fat, he does not toss the blood on its account. And in the case of a burnt-offering, even if there is a half olive's bulk of flesh or a half olive's bulk of fat, one tosses the blood on its account, because all of it is suitable for burning. And in the case of a meal-offering, if there [did not] remain of the sacrifice a half olive's bulk of meat or a half olive's bulk of fat, even if the whole meal-offering in its entirety remains available, one does not sprinkle the blood on its account. As to the Passover, if there is an olive's bulk for each and every [participant], one tosses [the blood] and if not, one does not toss the blood."

T. 4:4 [If] one slaughtered in silence [without improper intention], and [the blood] went forth outside the veils, and one tossed it in silence, Lo, this is as it was [valid]. [In such a case] they subject the flesh of Holy Things, to the laws of sacrilege, but they do not subject to the laws of sacrilege the sacrificial parts of Lesser Holy Things. And they are not liable on their account because of [transgressing the law of] remnant or because of [transgressing the law of] uncleanness. [If, however] the blood was made unclean and one tossed it in silence [without improper intention], they do not subject to the laws of sacrilege the flesh of Most Holy Things. But, they do subject to the laws of sacrilege the sacrificial parts of Lesser Holy Things. And they are liable on their account because of [transgressing the laws of] remnant and uncleanness. For the high priest's front plate effects atonement on account of that which is unclean, but it does not effect atonement either on account of that which is kept overnight or on account of that which goes forth [beyond the veil].

T. 4:5 [If] one slaughtered in silence, and the flesh went outside the veils and [then] one tossed the blood in silence — R. Eliezer says, "Lo, it is as it was. They subject to the laws of sacrilege the flesh of Most Holy Things, but they do not subject to the laws of sacrilege the sacrificial parts of Lesser Holy Things, and they are not liable on their account because of [transgression of the laws of] remnant and uncleanness." R. Aqiba says, "The high priest's front plate appeases for that which goes forth [beyond the veils]. [Therefore], they do not subject to the laws of sacrilege the flesh of Most Holy Things, but they do subject to the laws of sacrilege the sacrificial parts of Lesser Holy Things, and they are liable on their account because of [transgression of the laws of] remnant and uncleanness." [If] the flesh is made unclean, and one [then] tossed the blood in silence, all agree that they do not subject to the laws of sacrilege the flesh of Most Holy Things. But they do subject to the laws of sacrilege the sacrificial parts of Lesser Holy Things, and they are liable on their account because of [transgression of the laws of] remnant and because of [transgression of the laws of] uncleanness. For the high priest's plate effects atonement on account of that which is made unclean but not for that which remains overnight or for that which goes forth [beyond the veils].

T. 4:6 [If] one slaughtered in silence, and the blood went outside of the veils, and one tossed it [intending to eat the flesh] outside of its proper time, or [if] one slaughtered [the sacrifice, intending to eat the flesh] outside of its proper time, and the blood went outside of the veils, and one tossed it [intending to eat the flesh] outside of its proper time, Lo, this is as it was. They subject to the laws of sacrilege the flesh of Most Holy Things, but they do not subject to the laws of sacrilege the sacrificial parts of Lesser Holy Things. And they are [not] liable on their account because of [transgression of the laws of] refuse.

T. 4:7 [If] the blood was made unclean, and one tossed it [intending to eat the flesh of the sacrifice] outside of its proper time, still do they subject to the laws of sacrilege the flesh of Most Holy Things. But they do not subject to the laws of sacrilege the sacrificial parts of Lesser Holy Things. But they are liable on their account because of [transgression of the laws of] refuse. For the high priest's plate effects atonement for that which is unclean, but it does not effect atonement either for that which is kept overnight or for that which goes forth [beyond the veils].

T. 4:8 [If] one slaughtered in silence, and the flesh went forth outside of the veils, and one [then] tossed the blood [with the intention to eat the flesh] outside of its proper time, or one slaughtered [intending to eat the flesh] outside its proper time, and the flesh went outside of the veils, and one tossed the blood in silence, or [if] one slaughtered [the animal, intending to eat the flesh] outside of its proper time, and the flesh went outside of the veils, and one [then] tossed the blood in silence, or [if] one slaughtered [the animal, intending to eat the flesh] outside of its proper time, and the flesh went outside of the veils, and one tossed the blood [intending to eat the flesh] outside of its proper time — R. Eliezer says, "Lo, it is as it was. They subject to the laws of sacrilege the flesh of Most Holy Things, but they do not subject to the laws of sacrilege, the sacrificial parts of Lesser Holy Things. And they are not liable on their account because of [transgressions of the laws of] refuse." R. Aqiba says, "The High priest's plate effects atonement for that which goes forth. Still, do they subject to the laws of sacrilege, the flesh of Most Holy Things, but they do not subject to the laws of sacrilege the sacrificial parts of Lesser Holy Things. But they are liable on their account because of [transgression of the laws of] refuse." [If] the flesh is made unclean, and one tossed the blood [intending to eat the flesh] outside of its proper time, all agree that still do they subject the laws of sacrilege, the flesh of Most

Holy Things, and they do not subject to the laws of sacrilege the sacrificial parts of Lesser Holy Things. But they are not liable on their account because of [transgression of the laws of] refuse. For the high priest's plate effects atonement for that which is unclean, and the high priest's plate does not effect atonement either for that which remains overnight or for that which goes forth [beyond the veils].

T. 4:9 R. Eliezer b. Jacob says, "[This is] one rule of the lenient rulings of the House of Shammai and the stringent rulings of the House of Hillel:" The House of Shammai say, 'Two [proper acts of] placing the blood validate and render subject to the laws of refuse in the case of a sin-offering and one proper act of placing the blood in the case of all [other] sacrifices.' And the House of Hillel say, 'All the same are the sin-offering and all [other] sacrifices: One [proper act of] tossing the blood validates and renders subject to the laws of refuse'" [=M. 4:1B-C]. How so? [If] one placed [tossed] the blood one time in silence and the blood was poured out — The House of Shammai declare invalid. And the House of Hillel declare valid [if] one placed two in silence, and the blood [then] was poured out all agree that it is valid. [If one placed the blood] one time [with the intent of eating the flesh] outside of its proper time, and the blood was poured out. The House of Shammai say, 'It is invalid, and extirpation does not apply to it.' And the House of Hillel say, 'It is refuse, and they are liable to extirpation on its account.' [If one placed the blood] twice [with the intention of eating the flesh outside of its proper time], and the blood was poured out, all agree that it is refuse. "[If one placed the blood] one time [with the intention of eating the flesh] outside of its proper time, and one time [with the intention of eating the flesh] outside of its proper place — The House of Shammai say, 'It is invalid. And extirpation does not apply to it.' And the House of Hillel say, 'It is refuse. And they are liable on its account for extirpation.' Under what circumstances? In the case of a sin-offering. But in the case of all other offerings, [if] one placed [the blood] one time in silence, and [then] the blood was poured out, all agree that it is valid. [If one placed the blood] one time [intending to eat the flesh] outside of its proper time, and the blood was poured out, all agree that it is refuse. [If one placed the blood] one time [intending to eat the flesh] outside of its proper time and [intending to eat the flesh] outside of its proper place, it is invalid. And they are not liable to extirpation on its account. Under what circumstances? With respect to [the] tossing [of the blood]. But with respect to slaughtering, and receiving, and conveying [the blood], whether one gave thought to it concerning the first or whether one gave thought to it concerning the last, even with reference to the remnants of the blood, [if one gave thought to eating the flesh] outside of its proper place, it is invalid, and extirpation does not apply to it, [and if one gave thought to eating its flesh] outside of its proper time, it is refuse, and they are liable on its account to extirpation." Under what circumstances? With reference to the drops of blood which are to be placed outside, on the outer altar. But with respect to the drops of blood which are to be placed inside, on the inner altar. For example, the forty-eight [sprinklings of blood] of the Day of Atonement, and the eleven [sprinklings of blood] of the bullock of the community, and the eleven [sprinklings of blood] of the bullock of the anointed priest, whether with reference to slaughtering, or receiving the blood, or conveying the blood, whether he gave thought [only] to the last, or whether he gave thought to the first, even [if he gave thought to eating the flesh] outside of its proper place in the case of [only] one of them, it is invalid, and extirpation does not apply to it. [If he gave thought to eating the flesh] outside of its proper time, it is refuse, and they are liable on its account to extirpation," the words of R. Meir. And sages say, "[The laws of] refuse do not [apply at all to sacrifices which are slaughtered on the] inner [altar]."

Now we come to the particular hermeneutics of the category-formation, Zebahim. If at the four critical acts of the blood rite — slaughtering the animal, collecting the blood of the carotid artery, conveying the blood to the altar, and sprinkling the blood on the altar — one forms the intention of tossing the blood outside of the Temple court or eating the meat outside, the beast is spoiled, but if a priest inadvertently eats the meat, he is not subject to extirpation. If the improper intention concerned doing so the next day, that is to say, when the occasion for the presentation of the offering has passed with sundown, the animal is classified as refuse, and eating it inadvertently involves the penalty of extirpation. In both instances, what one actually does is not at issue, only what one intends in advance to do; if one, having formed the improper intention, actually tosses the blood on the altar or eats the meat in the right place or does the deeds within the valid span of time, the offering remains null. The Tosefta expands the range of the rule but not its principle. M. 2:3 bears the qualification that improper intentionality takes effect only if the deed of tossing the blood is properly done ("offered in accord with its requirement"). Then the offering is validated and the improper intentionality affects an otherwise validly-sacrificed beast. But if the blood-rite is improperly carried out, then the prior, improper intentionality, has affected a null-beast. To put it differently, for the improper intentionality to take effect, the acts of the blood rite must afterward be correctly carried out, thus subjecting the beast to the prior intentionality. Then, if the priest tosses the blood and eats the meat at the right place or at the right time, that initial, invalidating intentionality carries in its wake the invalidation of which we have spoken. This matter is beautifully expounded by M. 2:4f. and its accompanying Tosefta-passages. The latter raise a variety of interstitial issues, e.g., at T. 2:11-13. The intentionality of a person who to begin with has no power to conduct the blood-rite, has no affect upon the rite that he performs. Then the entire matter concerns intangibilities.

D. THE LAW OF REFUSE AND THE MATTER OF IMPROPER INTENTIONALITY

M. 4:3 These are things on account of which they are not liable because of [transgression of the law of] refuse [if the offering itself is refuse, the following are not affected, so if the priest took a handful intending to eat the residue the next day, the entire offering is refuse, but there is no liability for eating the handful itself. The status of refuse applies only to what is subject to eating only through a valid rite performed at some other aspect of the sacrifice, for instance, the rest of the meal-offering is ordinarily permitted to be eaten when the handful is taken out, but the handful itself is not permitted through anything else; the same is so of incense, frankincense, and the rest]: (1) the handful [Lev. 2:1-2], (2) and the frankincense [Lev. 2:1-2], (3) and the incense offering [Ex. 30:7-8], (4) and the meal-offering of the priests [Lev. 6:16], (5) and the meal-offering of the anointed priest [Lev. 6:15], (6) and the meal-offering [which accompanies] the drink offerings [Num. 15:2ff.], (7) and the blood. (8) "And drink offerings which come by themselves [but not those which come with a sacrifice, vs. No. 6]," the words of R. Meir (9) And sages say, "Also: those which come along with a beast. [=No. 6. Meir's view is that the blood of the sacrifices permits the drink offering to the altar. Sages point out that the drink offering may come later (=Meir, G.)]. As to (10) the log of oil of the *mesora'* [person afflicted with the skin ailment] [Lev. 14:10] — R. Simeon says, "They are not liable on its account because of [transgression of the law of] refuse [if the guilt offering is made refuse]." And R. Meir says, "They are liable on its account because of [violation of the laws of] refuse [if the guilt offering is made refuse]. For the blood of the guilt offering, renders it permitted [for offering or eating], and on account of whatever has that which renders the offering permissible [for offering or eating], whether for man or for the altar, are they liable because of [transgression of the law of] refuse?"

M. 4:4 (1) The whole offering — its blood renders permissible its flesh for the altar, and its hide for the priests. (2) The whole offering of fowl — its blood renders permissible its flesh for the altar (3) The sin offering of fowl — its blood renders permissible its flesh for the priests [Lev. 5:9]. (4) Bullocks which are to be burned and (5) he-goats which are to be burned — their blood renders it permissible to offer their sacrificial portions. R. Simeon says, "Any [offering, the blood of which is] not [sprinkled] on the outer altar, as in the case of peace offerings — they are not liable on its account because of [transgression of the laws of] refuse."

T. 5:1 "The drink-offerings which come along with a beast [= M. Zeb. 4:3E] — they are liable on their account to the laws of refuse, because the blood of the sacrifice [is what] permits them [to be eaten, when it is properly offered up]," the words of R. Meir. And sages say, "They are not liable on their account because of the laws of refuse, for a man may bring his sacrifice today, and his drink-offerings after twenty days." Said to them. R. Meir, "Also I for my part only stated the rule in reference to the case in which one has sanctified it in a utensil." They said to him, "Even though one has sanctified it in a proper utensil, one can transfer them to another sacrifice."

T. 5:2 "The log of oil of the *mesora'* [= M. Zeb. 4:3D] — "they are liable on its account because of the laws of refuse, for the blood of the guilt-offering [is required to] permit [the application of the oil to the places on the body of the *mesora'* on which the oil is to be placed]," the words of R. Meir [= M. Zeb. 4:3D, F]. And sages say, "They are not liable on its account because of the laws of refuse, because a man brings his guilt offering today and his log of oil twenty days later." Said to them R. Meir, "Also 1, for my part, stated the rule only at the time that he has sanctified it in a utensil." They said to him, "Even though he has sanctified it in a utensil, he can transfer it to the guilt-offering of another *mesora'*." R. Simeon says, "The incense-offering and frankincense — if they are not suitable for eating [the priests' use] they are not liable on their account because of transgression of the laws of refuse, remnant, and uncleanness."

T. 5:3 R. Simeon did rule, "The power of the altar is greater than the power of the priests, and the power of the priests [is greater] than the power of the altar. The power of the altar is greater in the case of the handful and the frankincense and the meal-offering of the priests and the meal-offering of the anointed priest and the meal-offering which comes along with drink-offerings, and the burnt-offering of fowl, for priests have no portion in them whatsoever. Greater is the power of the priests in the case of the two loaves of bread, and the show-bread, and of the remnants of the meal-offerings,] and the sin-offering of fowl, for the altar has no part in them whatsoever [M. Men. 5:3]. Greater is the power of the priests than the power of the Israelites, and the power of the Israelites than the power of the priests. Greater is the power of the priests in the case of Most Holy Things and of the firstling, for the Israelites have no part in them whatsoever. Greater is the power of the Israelites in the case of the tithe of the beast and of the Passover, for the priests have no part in them whatsoever."

T. 5:4 "Bullocks which are to be burned and he-goats which are to be burned, once one has slaughtered them and tossed their blood, are subject to the laws of sacrilege, and they are liable on their account because of transgression of the laws of refuse," the words of R. Meir. And sages say, "They are liable because of transgression of the laws of refuse only on account of something which is equivalent to peace-offerings, the blood of which is placed on the outer altar." Said R. Simeon, "This law did R. Aqiba state to me, 'They are liable on account of transgression of the laws of refuse only for something which is like peace-offerings and the blood of which is placed on the outer altar.'" R. Eleazer says in the name of R. Yosé, "[If one had an intention which imposes the status of] refuse concerning [an action] which is done in their connection on the inner [altar], he has not imposed upon them the status of refuse." How so? "[If] one slaughtered and received the blood on condition of tossing the blood on the next day, he has not imposed the status of refuse. For it is an intention [formed] outside concerning an action which is done inside."

T. 5:5 He who tosses the blood on condition of burning the sacrificial parts on the next day has not imposed the status of refuse. For it is a thought inside pertinent to something which is done outside. But if he slaughtered, received the blood, and conveyed the blood on condition of pouring out the remnants of the blood and of burning the sacrificial parts on the next day, he has imposed the status of refuse. For it is a thought outside pertinent to something which is done outside.

M. 4:5 As to Holy Things presented by gentiles — "they are not liable on their account because of [transgression of the laws of] refuse, remnant, and uncleanness. And he who slaughters them outside [the courtyard] is free of liability," the words of R. Meir. R. Yosé declares one liable [for refuse, remnant, uncleanness, and slaughter outside the courtyard]. Things on account of which they [priests who express an inappropriate intentionality or do an improper deed] are not liable because of [transgression of the laws of] refuse [=M. 3:4-5, 4:3], on their account are they [nonetheless] liable because of [transgression of the laws of] remnant, because of [transgression of the laws of] uncleanness, except for the blood [M. 4:3A7]. R. Simeon says, "[This is the rule] for something which is usually eaten. But [in the case of something not usually eaten], for example, wood, and frankincense, and the incense offering, they are not liable on their account because of [transgression of the laws of] uncleanness." And sages say, "Also: something which is not usually eaten — they are liable because of uncleanness."] [The affect of the laws of uncleanness is not solely upon food.]

T. 5:6 "[As to] the Holy Things of a gentile, they are not liable on their account because of transgression of the laws of remnant and uncleanness [M. Zeb. 4:5A]. And [while] they do not derive benefit [from them], (and) they are not subject to the laws of sacrilege in their regard, and they do not impart the status of a substitute, [to animals designated in their stead]. But they do require drink offerings," the words of R. Simeon. Said R. Yosé, "I deem [the law] in the case of all of them to be stringent." Under what circumstances? In the case of Holy Things offered on the altar. But in the case of Holy Things brought for the upkeep of the Temple-house, R. Simeon concedes that they are subject to the laws of sacrilege in their regard. (And) things on account of which they are not liable because of transgression of the laws of refuse, (and) they are liable on their account because of the transgression of the laws of remnant and because of transgression of the laws of uncleanness [M. Zeb. 4:5D]. It is not possible [simultaneously] to invoke the laws of refuse and of remnant and of uncleanness with reference to a single sacrifice. For they are liable on their account because of transgression of the laws of refuse and remnant and uncleanness only after the tossing of the drops of blood.

T. 5:7 A more strict rule applies in the case of refuse than in the case of remnant and uncleanness, and [a more strict rule applies] in the case of remnant and uncleanness than applies in the case of refuse. For the law of refuse applies through [improper] intention [alone, without action] and applies [even] before the tossing of the drops of blood. And if part of the sacrifice becomes refuse, the whole sacrifice is deemed refuse, which is not the case in regard to the rules of remnant and uncleanness. And more strict is the rule in regard to remnant and uncleanness. For [only] things for which they are not liable on account of refuse are they liable on account of remnant and uncleanness. As to remnant — they are liable on its account both because of remnant and because of uncleanness, which is not the case with respect to refuse. [Something can be invalid as remnant and on account of uncleanness. But it cannot be invalid as refuse, and also because of violation of the rules governing remnant and uncleanness.]

T. 5:8 A more strict rule applies in the case of refuse and of remnant than applies in the case of uncleanness, and [a more strict rule applies] in the case of uncleanness than in the case of refuse and of remnant. For [violation of the laws of] refuse and remnant [imposes the requirement to bring a sacrifice] through a single spell of inadvertence, but [violation of the law of] uncleanness [imposes the requirement to bring a sacrifice only in the case of] two spells of inadvertence. Refuse and remnant [require a sin-offering, which is] of fixed value while uncleanness [requires] a sacrifice of variable value. [Sacrifices which have been subjected to] refuse and remnant are never released from their status, but [sacrifices which are subject to] uncleanness [are released from that] status [in that unclean sacrifices, in the case of the Passover, are offered and eaten].

T. 5:9 More strict is the rule in the case of uncleanness. For uncleanness applies to first fruits, heave-offering, and tithes, and applies after the sprinkling of the drops of blood. And if part of the limb is made unclean, the whole of it is deemed unclean, which is not the case for refuse and remnant.

T. 5:10 More strict is the rule which applies to uncleanness, than that which applies to something which goes forth [beyond its boundaries, e.g., the veil, the Temple court, or Jerusalem], and [more strict is the rule] which applies to that which goes forth than [the rule] which applies to uncleanness. For the rule of uncleanness applies to Most Holy Things and Lesser Holy Things and to Holy Things in the provinces [as well, e.g., to heave-offering], which is not the case for [the prohibition for] that which goes forth [beyond its boundaries].

T. 5:11 More strict is the rule which applies to that which goes forth. For that which goes forth is never released from its status. And the high priest's plate does not effect atonement on its account, [neither of] which is the case for that which is unclean.

T. 5:12 Concerning what sort of unclean [person] did they speak? Concerning an unclean person who ate clean flesh or concerning unclean flesh. But a clean person who ate unclean flesh, and he who eats Holy Things before the sprinkling of the drops of blood [on the altar], and [he who eats] of the burnt-offering and the sacrificial parts, whether before or after the sprinkling of the drops of blood — Lo, this one is smitten forty times [because of eating before the meat is rendered permissible (D) or because of eating which may not be eaten at all (E)] The sum of the matter is this: They are liable for a sacrifice only in connection with transgression of the laws of refuse, remnant, and uncleanness.

M. 4:6 For the sake of six things is the animal offering sacrificed: (1) for the sake of the animal offering, (2) for the sake of the one who sacrifices it, (3) for the sake of the Lord, (4) for the sake of the altar fires, (5) for the sake of the odor, (6) for the sake of the pleasing smell. And as to the sin offering and the guilt offering, for the sake of the sin [expiated thereby]. Said R. Yosé, "Even if one who was not [mindful] in his heart [that he performed the various rites] for the sake of any one of all of these correct points of intentionality, [but slaughtered without specifying that he did so with these things properly in mind] — it is valid. For it is a condition imposed by the court, that intentionality follows only [the mind and will and attitude of] the one who carries out the act [not the owner; and the officiant does not have to specify the six considerations at all. If he acts in commendable silence, that suffices]."

T. 5:13 For the sake of six things, is the animal-offering sacrificed. For the sake of the animal-offering, for the sake of the one who sacrifices it, for the sake of the animal-offering [read: the Lord], for the sake of the sin, for the sake of the altar-f res, for the sake of the sweet-savor. And in the case of the sin-offering and guilt-offering, for the sake of the sin [expiated thereby]. Said R. Yosé, "Even one who was not mindful in his heart for the sake of one of all of these — it is valid. For it is a condition imposed by the court that intention governing the status of the sacrifice follows only after [the intention of] the one who carries out the act" [=M. Zeb. 4:6A-C]. Under all circumstances all things follow only after [the intention of] the one who performs the act of slaughter. For [if] the one who slaughters the animal has the intention of making the offering as a sin-offering, and the owner has the intention of making the offering as a burnt-offering, [or if] the one who slaughters has the intention of making the offering as a burnt-offering, and the owner has the intention of making the offering as a sin-offering — under all circumstances, all things follow only after [the intention of] the one who performs the act of sacrifice.

The matter of intentionality, as regards, the imposition of the status of refuse now is spelled out. What we have at M. 4:3 is a refinement of the matter. The status applies only what is subject to eating via a valid rite, as already explained. A further refinement takes up the matter of Holy Things presented by gentiles (e.g., free-will offerings). The Tosefta at T. 5:7f. conducts one of its fine exercises of comparison and contrast of cognate categories, here, refuse, remnant, and uncleanness, then extending the matter beyond the triplet. The only important Halakhic statement comes at M. 4:6, which specifies the foci of intentionality: the pertinent objects of one's attitude.

II. THE RULES OF SACRIFICE OF BEASTS AND FOWL

A. *BEASTS*

M. 5:1 What is the place [in which the act of sacrifice] of animal offerings [takes place]? Most Holy Things [the whole offering, sin offering, and guilt offering] — the act of slaughtering them is carried out at the north [side of the altar]. The bullock and the he-goat of the Day of Atonement — the act slaughtering them is at the north. And the receiving of their blood is carried out in a utensil of service, at the north [side of the altar]. And their blood requires sprinkling over the space between the bars [of the ark], and on the veil, and on the golden altar. One act of placing of their [blood] [if improperly done] impairs [atonement]. And the remnants of the blood did one pour out at the western base of the outer altar. [But] if he did not place [the remnants of their blood at the stated location], he did not impair [atonement].

T. 6:1 What is [the area to be defined as] the northern [side] of the altar, which is valid for slaughtering Most Holy Things? "[From] the wall of the northern side of the altar to the northern wall of the courtyard, along the face of the entire altar. And this encompasses thirty-two cubits," the words of R. Meir. R. Eliezer b. R. Simeon adds [the area] from opposite [the space] between the entrance-hall to the altar, up to the area opposite the knives' room [the place in the Temple where the slaughtering knives were kept]. And this encompasses twenty-two cubits. And Rabbi adds the area in which Israelites have the right to go, eleven cubits in breadth, and eighty-seven in length, and the area in which priests have the right to go, eleven in breadth and one hundred eighty-seven in length, from the surrounding enclosure of the northern wall to the eastern wall of the courtyard. And just as the slaughtering is in the north, so is the receiving of the blood in the north.

T. 6:2 [If a priest] was standing in the south and stretched his hand out in the northern direction and slaughtered [the animal and received the blood]. It is as if, his entire body had entered [the appropriate area, and] the act of slaughtering is valid. But if he received the blood [in such a manner], it is invalid. [If] he poked his head and the greater part of his body into the northern area and slaughtered [the animal and received the blood], it is as if his entire body had entered [that area, and the act of slaughtering is valid]. A struggling animal which writhed out into the southern area and which one pushed back into the northern area — it is valid[ly slaughtered].

M. 5:2 Bullocks which are to be burned and he-goats which are to be burned — the act of slaughtering them is at the north [side of the altar]. And the receiving of their blood is in a utensil of service at the north. And their blood requires sprinkling on the veil and on the golden altar. [The improper sprinkling of] one act of placing of their [blood] impairs [atonement]. The remnants of their blood did one pour out on the western base of the outer altar. If he did not place [the remnants of the blood at the stated location], he did not impair [atonement]. These and those are burned in the ash pit.

T. 6:3 Lesser Holy Things — their slaughtering is [to take place] inside [the Temple court], and the receiving of their blood [also] is inside [the Temple court]. [If] one slaughtered [a sacrifice of Lesser Holy Things] inside and received the blood outside, [or if one slaughtered a sacrifice of Lesser Holy Things] outside and received the blood inside, it is invalid. [The sacrifice of Lesser Holy Things is valid only] if he will slaughter [the animal] inside and receive the blood inside.

T. 6:4 [If the priest] was standing outside and stretched his hand inside and slaughtered the animal, it is valid. But if he received the blood [in this manner], it is invalid.

T. 6:5 [If] he poked his head and the greater part of his body inside and slaughtered [the animal], it is invalid, as if he had not poked his entire body [inside]. [If] a struggling animal went out into the outer area [beyond the courtyard], and one brought it back inside, it is invalid.

T. 6:6 And just as the act of slaughter takes place by day, so does the receiving of the blood take place by day. [If] he slaughtered by day and received the blood by night, [slaughtered] by night and received the blood by day, it is invalid. [The rite] is valid only when one will slaughter by day and receive the blood by day.

T. 6:7 [In the case of] bullocks which are to be burned and he-goats which are to be burned, once he slaughtered and received their blood, he entered and stood between the golden altar and the candelabrum. The altar was further inside than he. He dipped [his finger] and sprinkled [blood] seven times toward the House of the Holy of Holies. For each and every act of sprinkling, there was an act of dipping. [If] he placed the blood on the horn of the altar on either side, it is valid. [If he did so] from the horn toward the inside, it is invalid.

T. 6:8 [If] he changed [the order] of placing on the horns, it is invalid. [If] he left out of the acts of placing the blood even one, it is invalid. He went out and poured the remnants of the blood on the western base of the outer altar. And [that of] the outer altar did he pour on the southern base of the [altar]. R. Simeon says, "These and those [are to be poured out] on the western base."

T. 6:9 These and those mix together in the gutter and flow out to the Qidron brook and are sold to gardeners for fertilizer. "And the laws of sacrilege apply to them," the words of R. Meir and R. Simeon. And sages say, "The laws of sacrilege do not apply to blood."

M. 5:3 As to sin offerings of the community and of the individual — what are the sin offerings of the community? He-goats [offered for] new moons and for festivals — the act of slaughtering them is to be carried out at the north side of the altar. And receiving their blood is to be done in a utensil of service at the north. And their blood requires four acts of placing on the four horns [corners of the outer altar] — How so? [The officiating priest] went up on the ramp, and went around the circuit, and went around to the southeastern corner, the northeastern corner, the northwestern corner, the southwestern corner. The remnants of the blood, he poured out on the southern base. And they are eaten inside the veils [that is, in the courtyard] by males of the priesthood, and [cooked for food] in any [manner of cooking] food [roasting or boiling], for a day and night, up to midnight.

T. 6:10 The sin-offering of the community and the individual — how was the placing of their [drops of] blood done? [The priest] went up on the ramp and went around the circuit and came to the southeastern horn [=M. Zeb. 5:3G]. He dipped the index finger of his right-hand, placing his larger finger on either side [of the bowl, to support it], and applies it with a downward movement against the edge of the horn of the altar, until the blood on his finger was used up. [If] he put blood on the horn on either side, it is valid. [But if he did so] on the inner side of the horn, it is invalid. [If] he altered the manner of placing the blood on the horns, it is invalid. [If] he left out even one of any of the acts of placing the blood, it is invalid. As to the remnants of the blood, he poured them out, and he goes down to the southern base [to do so]. R. Yosé b. R. Judah and R. Eliezer b. R. Simeon say, "In his place did he stand and pour them out onto the southern base."

T. 6:11 The base went around the surface of the entire altar from the north to the western side, a cubit [in breadth] by a cubit [in depth], [and] a handbreadth toward the east. But it consumes at the southern side of the altar one cubit, and on the eastern side of the altar, one cubit. And at the southeastern horn, southward and eastward, there was no base. But the red line was in the middle of the altar. From it downward, was a space of five cubits, from it and upward was a space of five cubits. "For all the drops of blood which were to be placed below the line were valid if placed from the red line and downward, and all the drops of blood which are to be placed upward are valid, if they are located from the red line and upward," the words of R. Meir. And sages say, "Under what circumstances? In the case of the burnt-offering of fowl. But in the case of the sin-offering of cattle, they did place the drops of blood only on the horn." The foundation had cavities like two slender snouts, through which the blood flowed down and was mixed together in the gutter and went forth to Qidron brook. And it was sold for fertilizer. And the laws of sacrilege apply to it [T. Zeb. 6:9B].

M. 5:4 The burnt offering is classified as Most Holy Things. The act of slaughtering is carried out at the north side of the altar. And the receiving of its blood is done in a utensil of service at the north. And its blood requires two acts of placing which are [divided at the corner into] four. And it requires flaying, and cutting into pieces, and [being] wholly [burned] on the altar fires.

T. 6:12 The burnt-offering [M. Zeb. 5:4], the substitute of the burnt-offering, the peace-offerings of the community, the guilt-offerings [M. Zeb. 5:5], the thank-offerings, rams and peace-offerings, the ram of the Nazir [M. Zeb. 5:6] and peace-offerings, the peace-offerings which come on account of Passover, the eleventh which is of the tithe [M. Bekh. 9:8], and the Passover past its time — how is the placing of the blood of all of these carried out? [The priest] comes to the northeastern corner and places blood on the eastern side [of the corner], to the [south] western corner and places blood on the southwestern side. R. Nehemiah and R. Eliezer b. Jacob say, "He comes to the northeastern corner and placed blood on the eastern side, to the northwestern corner and places the blood on the western side thereof."

T. 6:13 R. Simeon of Mispah did repeat [the following tradition] concerning the daily burnt-offering: "He came to the northeastern corner and placed blood to the northeast, to the [south] western corner, and placed blood on the western side, [then] (to the southwestern corner and) he places blood on the southern side." [If] he placed on each corner on either side, it is valid. But if he placed the blood on the inner side of the horn, it is invalid.

T. 6:14 [If he] changed the order of the placing of the blood on the several horns, [if] he left out the acts of placing of the blood [one application], or [if] he placed the blood on only one of the horns, it is valid. The remnants of the blood, did he pour out below.

T. 6:15 The firstling and the tithe of cattle and the Passover — he poured out [the drops of blood] in one act of pouring, against the base. [If] he poured them out not against the base, Lo, these [several offerings] are valid.

M. 5:5 Peace offerings of the congregation and guilt offerings — What are guilt offerings? (1) The guilt offering for false dealing, and (2) the guilt offering for acts of sacrilege, and (3) the guilt offering [because of intercourse with] a betrothed bondwoman, and (4) the guilt offering of a Nazir, and (5) the guilt offering of the *mesora'* [one afflicted with the skin ailment], and (6) the suspensive guilt offering — the act of slaughtering them is done at the north [side of the altar]. And the receiving of their blood is carried out with a utensil of service at the north. And their blood requires two acts of placing, which are four. And they are eaten [only] inside the veils, by males of the priesthood, and [cooked for food] in any [manner of cooking] food, for a day and a night, up to midnight.

M. 5:6 The thanksgiving offering and the ram of the Nazirite are classified as Lesser Holy Things. The act of slaughtering them may be performed in any place in the courtyard. And their blood requires two acts of placing, which are four. And they are eaten throughout the city [of Jerusalem], by any person, [cooked for food] in any [manner of cooking] food, for a day and a night, up to midnight. That which is raised up from them [the breast and thigh, as heave offering] follows their rule, except that which is raised up from them [as heave offering] is eaten [only] by priests, by their wives, children and slaves.

M. 5:7 Peace offerings are classified as Lesser Holy Things. The act of slaughtering them may be carried out in any place in the courtyard. And their blood requires two acts of placing which are four. And they are eaten throughout the city, by any person, [cooked for food] in any [manner of cooking] food, for two days and one [intervening] night. That which is raised up from them [the breast and thigh, as heave offering] follows their rule, except that which is raised up from them [as heave offering] is eaten by priests, by their wives, children, and slaves.

M. 5:8 The firstling and tithe [of cattle] and Passover are classified as Lesser Holy Things. The act of slaughtering them is to be done in any place in the courtyard. And their blood requires a single act of placing, provided that one places [the blood] at the base [on the part of the altar that has a base under it]. [The law] imposed a difference on their manner of eating. [The firstling and tithe of cattle, which are subject to a rule different from that governing the eating of the Passover]: The firstling is eaten by priests. And tithe [of cattle] by any person. And they are eaten throughout the city [cooked for food] in any [manner of cooking] food, for two days and one [intervening] night. The Passover is eaten only at night. And it is eaten only up to midnight. And it is eaten only by those that were assigned to it. And it is eaten only roasted.

T. 6:16 Where is the act of eating of all of them [carried out]? The sin-offering, the guilt-offering, the peace-offerings of the community, the sin-offering of fowl, the suspensive guilt offering and the log of oil of the *mesora'*, the two breads, the show-bread, the remnants of the meal — all of them are Most Holy Things and are eaten within the veils. And they are eaten by the males of the priesthood, [prepared] in any manner of cooking, for a day and a night, up to midnight [M. Zeb. 5:5F]. And they are not liable on their account because of remnant. And intention [to eat them at the wrong time] does not invalidate them on account of refuse [unless said intention is to eat them] from the time of the appearance of the morning star. All the same are perfect animals and blemished animals so far as division [M. Zeb. 12:12] is concerned.

T. 6:17 The firstling, that which is taken up from the thank-offering, and the ram of the Nazir, are eaten by men and women and man-servants and maidservants. This is the principle: Whoever [in a priest's household] eats heave-offerings, eats these, and whoever does not eat heave-offerings, does not eat these.

T. 6:18 The peace-offerings, the tithes, and the eleventh, which is of tithe [of cattle (M. Bekh. 9:8)] are eaten for two days and one night, during the day [of slaughter], the night thereof, and the day thereafter. Once it gets dark [on the day thereafter], they are liable on their account because of remnant. And intention [to eat at the wrong time] invalidates in their case on account of refuse. And their burning takes place only by day. And [while] in all cases, the day follows the night, as to the eating of Holy Things, the night follows after the day.

M. 6:1 Most Holy Things, [supposed to be slaughtered at the north side of the altar,] that one slaughtered on top of the altar — R. Yosé says, "They are as if they were slaughtered at the north [side of the altar]." R. Yosé b. R. Judah says, "From the midpoint [above] the altar to the north is deemed equivalent to the north, from the midpoint [above] the altar to the south is deemed equivalent to the south." Meal-offerings were taken in hand in any place in the courtyard, and [the residue] was eaten within the veils by males of the priesthood, [cooked] in any manner of preparing food, for that day and the [following night] down to midnight.

T. 7:1 R. Yosé says, "The whole altar [is deemed] north, as it is said, 'And he shall kill it on the north side of the altar before the Lord' (Lev. 1:11)." R. Yosé b. R. Judah says, "From the midway point of the altar and to the north [is deemed] north, and from the midway point and outward [is deemed] south," [M. Zeb. 6:1A-C]. And so did R. Yosé b. R. Judah say, "Two small doors were in the house of knives, open to the west, eight cubits above the ground, so that the [entire] courtyard should be valid for the eating of Most Holy Things and for the slaughtering of Lesser Holy Things, even the area behind the Mercy Seat, as it is said, 'And he shall kill it at the door of the tent of Meeting' (Lev. 3:2)."

T. 7:2 The meal-offerings were taken in hand in any place in the courtyard [= M. Zeb. 6:1D] — even on top of the altar.

From the systematic exposition of the data chosen and interpreted by the particular hermeneutics of the category-formation, Zebahim, we move on to the presentation of required, but systemically-inert information deriving from Scripture or tradition. The starting point addresses the location at the altar of various animal offerings and other locative issues comparably hierarchized. A single pattern governs throughout. While the Tosefta refines matters and introduces a secondary and derivative range of questions, it does not materially reshape the category-formation.

B.   FOWL

M. 6:2 The sin offering of fowl was prepared [its neck wrung, its blood tossed] at the southwestern corner [of the altar]. [If it was prepared] in any place [in the courtyard, however,] it was valid. But this was its [usual] place. And three purposes did the space of that [southwestern] corner serve below [the red line around the altar], and three above: Below [the red line was sprinkled the blood of] (1) the sin offering of fowl, and (2) the bringing near [of meal-offerings (M. Men. 5:5)], and (3) [for pouring out] the remnants of the blood [M. 5:3]. Above [the red line at the southwestern horn were poured out]: (1) [for] the water offering [M. Suk. 4:9], and (2) [for] the wine offering, and (3) [for] the burnt offering of fowl, when it [the burnt offering of fowl] was [too] abundant at the east.

M. 6:3 Whoever goes up to the altar goes up on the right [east side] and makes a circuit and goes down on the left, except for the one who goes up for these three things [=M. 6:2E], rightward.

T. 7:7 All who go up to the altar, go up at the east and go down at the west, [go up] at the right and go down at the left, except for [those who go up to the southwestern corner, in connection with] the libation of water and wine and the burnt-offering of fowl, who go up at the west and go down at the west, [go up] at the right and go down at the right, [M. Zeb. 6:3].

B. 6:2-3 II.1/63B-64A IF THE PRIEST PINCHED THE NECK OF THE BIRD OFFERING ANYWHERE AT THE ALTAR, IT IS VALID. IF HE SPRINKLED THE BLOOD ON ANY PART OF THE ALTAR, IT IS VALID. IF HE SPRINKLED THE BLOOD, BUT DID NOT DRAIN IT OUT, IT IS VALID, SO LONG AS HE PUTS SOME OF THE GUSHING BLOOD BELOW THE RED LINE ON THE ALTAR. IF THE PRIEST PINCHED THE NECK OF THE BIRD OFFERING ANY WHERE AT THE ALTAR, IT IS VALID. IF HE SPRINKLED THE BLOOD ON ANY PART OF THE ALTAR, IT IS VALID. [FOR] IF HE SPRINKLED AND DID NOT DRAIN THE BLOOD, IT IS VALID [SO IT IS VALID EVEN IF HE OMITTED DRAINING THE BLOOD, AND, THEREFORE, IT IS CERTAINLY VALID WHEN HE DRAINS IT ANYWHERE BY THE ALTAR], SO LONG AS HE PUTS SOME OF THE GUSHING BLOOD BELOW THE RED LINE ON THE ALTAR.

M. 6:4 The sin offering of fowl — how was it prepared? [The priest] would pinch off its head close by its neck. But he does not divide [the head from the body]. And [holding onto the bird], he sprinkles its blood on the wall of the altar. The remnants of its blood, he would drain out on the base [below the red line, as at M. 6:2D]. The altar owns only its blood, but the whole [rest] of [the carcass] belongs to the priests.

M. 6:5 The burnt offering of fowl — how was it prepared? [The priest] went up on the ramp and went around the circuit. He came to the southeastern cornet. He would wring off its head from its neck and divide [the head from the body]. And he drained off its blood onto the wall of the altar. He took the head and pressed the place where it was severed against the altar. And he dried it with salt and tossed it on the altar fires [Lev. 2:13]. He came to the body and removed the crop and the plumage and the intestines which come out with it. And he threw them on the place of the ashes. He slit [the body] open [at the wings] but did not divide it. But if he divided it, it is valid. And he dried it with salt and tossed it on the altar fires.

M. 6:6 [If] he did not remove the crop or the plumage or the intestines which go out with it and did not salt it — anything which he did in a different way after he had drained out its blood — it is valid. [If] he divided [the head from the body] in the case of a sin offering [of fowl] but did not divide [them] in the case of burnt offering [of fowl], [since this is before the rite of draining of the blood of the body], he has rendered it invalid. [If] he drained off the blood of the head but did not drain off the blood of the body, it is invalid. [If] he drained off the blood of the body but did not drain off the blood of the head, it is valid.

T. 7:3 All the same are the sin-offering of fowl and the burnt-offering of fowl: they derive from unconsecrated birds, [are offered] by day, and [are slaughtered] by the right hand.

T. 7:4 How does he wring the neck of the sin-offering of fowl [M. Zeb. 6:4]? He puts its two wings in his two fingers, and its two legs in his two fingers, and he would stretch its neck out on his fingers. He would wring [pinch] its neck with his fingernail at its shoulder. And he does not divide [the head from the neck]. And he sprinkles its blood on the wall of the altar [M. Zeb. 6:4]. And just as slaughtering [requires the severing of] one or the greater part of one [organ of the throat, the gullet or windpipe], so wringing the neck [requires the severing of] one or the greater part of one.

T. 7:5 R. Eliezer b. R. Simeon says, "A sin-offering of fowl, of which one wrung the neck properly, and [which] he divided, is valid [M. Zeb. 6:6D]. [If] he wrung the neck anywhere in the courtyard, it is valid [M. Zeb. 6:2B]. [If] he drained out the blood anywhere on the altar, it is valid. [If] he sprinkled the blood, but did not drain it out, it is valid [M. Zeb. 6:4D], provided that he place some of the blood of the soul from it below [the red line], toward the foundation [M. Zeb. 6:4D]. And if it was valid, it was eaten by the priests [M. Zeb. 6:4F], but if not, he tosses it on the ash."

T. 7:6 R. Ishmael b. R. Yohanan b. Beroqah says, "There was a window at the west of the ramp, and it was called hollow [rebukah], in which they throw the invalid sin-offering of fowl, so that its appearance deteriorates [there], and it goes forth to the place of burning."

T. 7:8 Just as one wrings the neck in the case of the sin-offering of fowl, so he wrings the neck in the case of the burnt-offering of fowl [M. Zeb. 6:5]. But in the case of the burnt-offering of fowl, one would divide [the head from the neck] and drain out the blood onto the wall of the altar [M. Zeb. 6: 5D-E]. [If] one drained out the blood from the head, it is invalid. [If he did so] from the body, it is valid [M. Zeb. 6:6E-F].

T. 7:9 [If] one drained out blood on the ramp or on the horn or on the foundation, it is invalid. [If] one did it from the place at which he was standing and upward by a cubit, it is valid. [If one did it] from the place at which he was standing and downward by a cubit, it is valid. R. Simeon and R. Yohanan ben Beroqah say, "It was done on top of the altar."

T. 7:10 Abba Yosé ben Dosai says, "As to the craws, he would toss them on the ash [M. Zeb. 6:5H-I]." He came to the body. He slit it open by hand but not by a knife. Whether he slit it open by hand or whether he slit it open by a knife, it did not divide [the head from the neck] or divided [the head from the neck], but did not slit it open, it is as if he did not slit it open [M. Zeb. 6:5J]. [If] he salted it, but did not dry it, or dried it but did not salt it, it is valid [M. Zeb. 6:5G-L]. This is the general principle: All the changes which he effected by hand before the draining of its blood — it is invalid. [And those effected] after the draining of its blood — it is valid [M. Zeb. 6:6A].

T. 8:18 [If] he severed the head at once — [if] he received [the blood] from the head, it is invalid. [If he received the blood] from the body, it is valid [M. Zeb. 6:6E-F].

M. 6:7 The sin offering of fowl, [the neck] of which he wrung not for its own name [but rather under some classification other than that for which the animal was originally designated as holy], the blood of which he drained not for its own name, or [one of which he did] for its name and [one] not for its own name, or [one of which he did] not for its own name and [one] for its own name — [In the case of] the burnt offering of fowl, it is valid, with the proviso that it has not gone to the credit of its owner. All the same [in the following aspects] are the sin offering of fowl and the burnt offering of fowl, — [the heads] of which he wrung off, and the blood of which he drained out — [with the intention] (1) to eat something which is usually eaten, (2) to burn something which is usually burned, outside of its proper place — it is invalid. And extirpation does not apply to it. [If] he wrung off the head or drained the blood] with the intention of eating what is to be eaten

or of burning what is to be burned outside of its proper time, it is refuse, and they are liable on its account for extirpation, with the proviso that which renders the offering permissible, is offered in accord with its requirement. How is that which renders the offering permissible, offered in accord with its requirement? [If] he wrung the neck in silence, and drained the blood [intending to eat what is to be eaten or to burn what is to be burned] outside of its proper time, or [if] he wrung the neck [intending to eat what is to be eaten or to burn what is to be burned] outside of its proper time, and drained off the blood in silence, or [if he] wrung the neck and drained off the blood [articulately intending to eat the flesh or burn the sacrificial parts] outside of its proper place — this is [what is meant by a case in which] that which renders the offering permissible, has been offered in accord with its requirement. How is that which renders the offering permissible, not offered in accord with its requirement? [If] he wrung the neck [with the intention of eating the flesh or offering the sacrificial parts] outside of its proper place, and he [then] drained off the blood [intending to eat the flesh or offer the sacrificial parts] outside of its proper time, or [if] he wrung the neck [intending to eat the flesh] outside of its proper time, and drained off the blood [intending to eat the flesh or to burn the sacrificial parts] outside of its proper place [intending to eat what is to be eaten or to burn what is to be burned] outside of its proper time, or [if] he wrung the neck and drained off the blood [intending to eat the flesh] outside of its proper place — the sin offering of fowl, [the neck of which] one wrung not for its own name, and the blood of which one drained off [intending to eat the flesh or to offer up the sacrificial parts] outside of its proper time — or the neck of which one wrung [intending to eat the flesh or to burn the sacrificial parts] outside of its proper time, and the blood of which one drained off not for its own name — or the neck of which one wrung and the blood of which one drained off not for its own name -- this is a case in which, that which renders the offering permissible has not been offered in accord with its requirement. [If one did any of these things intending] to eat an olive's bulk outside and an olive's bulk on the next day, an olive's bulk on the next day and an olive's bulk outside, a half-olive's bulk outside and a half-olive's bulk on the next day, a half-olive's bulk on the next day and a half-olive's bulk outside -- it is unfit. And extirpation does not apply to it. Said R. Judah, "This is the general rule: If the [improper] intention concerning time came before the [improper] intention concerning place, it is refuse, and they are liable on its account to extirpation. But if the [improper] intention concerning place came before the [improper] intention concerning time, it is invalid and extirpation does not apply to it." And sages say, "This [case] and that are invalid, and extirpation does not apply to it." [If one intended] to eat a half-olive's bulk and to offer up a half-olive's bulk, it is valid. For eating and offering up, do not join together.

T. 7:11 A sin-offering of fowl, the neck of which one wrung [intending] to sprinkle its blood outside, or part of its blood outside [intending] to eat its flesh outside, or an olive's bulk of its flesh outside — is invalid. And extirpation does not apply to it [T. Zeb. 2:2].

T. 7:12 A burnt-offering of fowl, the neck of which one wrung [intending] to sprinkle its blood outside or part of its blood outside. To eat its flesh outside or an olive's bulk of its flesh outside — is refuse, and they are liable on its account to extirpation [T. Zeb. 2:3]. This is the general principle: Whoever wrings the neck and sprinkles the blood in the case of the sin-offering of fowl, [and] whoever wrings the neck and drains the blood in the case of burnt-offering of fowl, [intending] to eat something which is usually eaten or, Lo, burn something which is usually burned — outside of its place — it is invalid, and extirpation does not apply to it. [And if his intention in these regards is to do so] outside of its proper time, it is refuse, and they are liable on its account to extirpation, with the proviso that which renders the offering permissible is offered in accord with its requirement [M. Zeb. 6:7A-J].

T. 7:13 How is that which renders the offering permissible offered in accord with its requirement? [If] one wrung the neck in silence and [then] drained the blood [intending to eat that which is eaten or to burn that which is burned] outside of C [or if] one wrung the neck and drained the blood in silence [with no improper intention, in which that which renders the offering permitted has been offered in accord with its requirement [M. Zeb. 6:7K-O, T. Zeb. 2:5].

T. 7:14 How is that which renders the offering permissible not offered in accord with its requirement? [If] one wrung the neck intending to eat the flesh or burn the parts outside of its proper place and drained out the blood [intending to eat the flesh or burn the sacrificial parts] outside of its time, or if one wrung the neck [intending to eat the flesh or burn the parts outside of its proper time and then drained the blood [intending to eat the flesh or burn the parts] outside of its place [M. Zeb. 6:7P-S] or [if] one both wrung the neck and drained off the blood [intending to eat the flesh or burn the parts] outside of its place whether the [improper] intention concerning time came before the improper intention concerning place, or whether the improper intention concerning place came before the improper intention concerning time, it is invalid, and extirpation does not apply to it. R. Judah says, "If the improper intention concerning time came before the improper intention concerning place, it is refuse, and they are liable on its account of extirpation. But if the improper intention concerning place came before the improper intention concerning time, it is invalid, and extirpation does not apply to it [M. Zeb. 6:7AA-BB, T. Zeb. 2:6]." How does improper intention concerning time come before improper intention concerning place? [If] one wrung the neck intending to eat the flesh or burn the parts outside of the proper time and drained off the blood [intending to eat the flesh or burn the parts] outside of its proper place. How does improper intention concerning place come before improper intention concerning time? [If] one wrung the neck [intending to eat the flesh or burn the parts] outside of its place and then drained off the blood [intending to eat the flesh or burn the parts] outside of its proper time [T. Zeb. 2:7].

T. 7:15 The sin-offering of fowl, the neck of which one wrung not for its own sake [as a sin-offering], is unfit, and extirpation does not apply to it, because that which renders the offering permissible has not been offered in accord with its requirement [T. Zeb. 2:8]. This is the summary-principle of the matter: Whatever rules of refuse apply to the sin-offering of a beast, apply to a sin-offering of fowl, and whatever rules of refuse apply to the burnt-offering of a beast, apply to a burnt-offering of fowl.

M. 7:1 A bird that one designated to serve as sin offering of fowl, which one prepared below [the red line], (1) [that is to say, properly], in accord with the rites of the sin offering [M. 6:4], (2) in the classification ["name"] of the sin offering, [obviously] is valid. [If one prepared a bird designated to serve as a sin offering of fowl] (1) in accord with the rites of the sin offering, (2) but in the classification ["for the name"] of a burnt offering [M. 6:7] — (1) [or] in accord with the rites of the burnt offering [below the line, M. 6:5], (2) but in the classification ["for the name"] of a sin offering — (1) [or] in accord with the rites of the burnt offering, but in the classification ["for the name"] of a burnt offering, it is invalid. [If] one prepared it above [the red line instead of below, but, otherwise,] in accord with the rites of either of them, it [in all events] is invalid.

M. 7:2 The burnt offering of fowl, which one prepared above [the red line], (1) in accord with the rites of the burnt offering, (2) but in the classification ["for the name"] of the burnt offering, is valid. [If one prepared it] (1) in accord with the rites of the burnt offering, (2) in the classification ["for the name"] of the sin offering, it is valid, except that it does not go to the owner's credit [in fulfillment of an obligation]. [If he did so] (1) in accord with the rites of the sin offering under the classification ["for the name"] of a burnt offering, [or] (1) in accord with the rites of the sin offering, (2) in the classification ["for the name"] of the burnt offering, (1) in accord with the rites of the sin offering, (2) in the classification ["for the name"] of the sin offering, it is invalid. [If] he prepared it below [the red line] in accord with the rites of either of them, it is invalid.

M. 7:3 And all of them [which are invalid] do not impart uncleanness in the gullet. [The carrion of clean fowl imparts uncleanness to the one who is eating it when it is located in the gullet, so that the person eating it becomes a Father of uncleanness. The birds have been properly slaughtered, so they are invalid as sacrifices, but they are not deemed carrion.] And the laws of sacrilege apply to them, except in the case of the sin offering of the fowl which one prepared below in accord with the rites of the sin offering for the name of the sin offering [which may be eaten by the priest].

M. 7:4 The bird designated as burnt offering of fowl, which one prepared below [instead of above], in accord with the rites of the sin offering, for the sake of the sin offering — R. Eliezer says, "The laws of sacrilege apply to it." R. Joshua says, "The laws of sacrilege do not apply to it." Said R. Eliezer, "Now if the sin offering, to which the laws of sacrilege do not apply [when one prepared it] in the classification for which the beast was originally designated ["for its own name"] [M. 7:3C], is subject to the laws of sacrilege when one did it not in the classification for which the beast was originally designated [for the sake of some other name (lit. "when he changed its name")], the burnt offering, to which the laws of sacrilege do apply [when one offered it] in the classification for which the beast was originally designated [for its own name], when one did it not in the classification for which the beast was originally designated [for the sake of some other name] ["when he changed its name"] — is it not logical that the laws of sacrilege should [continue to] apply to it?" Said to him R. Joshua, "No. If you have so stated the rule in the case of the sin offering, in which case the beast originally designated as a sin offering has been offered up as a burnt offering ["the name of which one has changed to the name of the burnt offering"], [that is because] one indeed has offered the beast in the classification to which the laws of sacrilege apply in any event ["changed its name to that of something to which the laws of sacrilege apply"]. But will you so state the rule in the case of the burnt offering, in which case an animal originally designated as a burnt offering is now offered in the classification of sin offering [the name of which one changed to the name of the sin offering]? For indeed he has classified the beast in a classification that did not originally apply [changed its name] to that of classification of offering to which the laws of sacrilege do not apply." Said to him R. Eliezer, "Now, behold — Most Holy Things which one slaughtered at the southern [side of the altar, instead of the northern side], and slaughtered in the classification ["for the name"] of Lesser Holy Things [e.g., peace offerings], will prove the case. For one indeed has offered the beast in a classification that did not initially apply ["changed their name"] to that classification of offering to which the laws of sacrilege do not apply, [for said law applies only to the sacrificial portions], yet the laws of sacrilege do apply to them. So you should not be surprised concerning the burnt offering. For even though one offered a beast originally designated as a burnt offering ["changed its name"] to the classification of something to which the laws of sacrilege do not apply, the laws of sacrilege should most certainly apply to it." Said to him R. Joshua, "No. If you have so stated the rule in connection with Most Holy Things, which one slaughtered at the southern side of the altar and slaughtered for the sake of Lesser Holy Things, [that is because] he indeed has offered the beast in a classification other than that for which it was originally designated ["changed their name"], specifically, a classification in which there is both what is forbidden [the sacrificial portions of Lesser Holy Things are forbidden under the law of sacrilege] and what is permitted [their flesh is permitted]. But will you say so concerning the beast originally designated as a burnt offering, the classification ["name"] of which one has changed for that of something which is wholly permitted [the classification of offering in the case of a sin offering, which is entirely given over to the priest, M. 6:4]?"

T. 7:16 The burnt-offering of fowl which one prepared above [the red line around the altar] [in accord with] the rites of the sin-offering for the sake of the sin-offering — R. Eliezer says, "The laws of sacrilege apply to it." R. Joshua says, "The laws of sacrilege do not apply to it." Said R. Eliezer, "Now [in the case of] the sin-offering, the laws sacrilege do not apply to it [when it is prepared] in its own name. Yet, if one changed its name [offered it for some other purpose], the laws of sacrilege do apply to it. [Likewise], the burnt-offering, to which the laws of sacrilege do apply [when one offered it] for its own name, when one changed its name, is it not logical that the laws of sacrilege should apply to it?"

T. 7:17 Said to him R. Joshua, "No. If you have so stated the rule in the case °S the sin-offering, the name of which one changed to that of the burnt-offering, [that is because] he has indeed changed its name to that of something which is subject to the laws of sacrilege. "[But] will you say so in the case of the burnt-offering, the name of which one has changed to that of the sin-offering? For indeed he has changed its name to that of something to which the laws of sacrilege do not apply."

T. 7:18 Said to him R. Eliezer, "Lo, he who slaughters Most Holy Things at the northern side of the altar for the sake of peace-offerings will prove my case." For Lo, he has changed its name for that of something to which the laws of sacrilege do not apply, yet the laws of sacrilege apply to them. "Do not be surprised about this case, for even though he changed its name to that of something to which the laws of sacrilege do not apply, the laws of sacrilege should apply to it."

T. 7:19 Said to him R. Joshua, "No. If you have so stated the rule in connection with Most Holy Things slaughtered at the north for the sake of peace-offerings, [the reason is] that even though he changed their name, he has not changed their place." "Will you say so in this case, in which he has changed its name and changed it place?"

T. 7:20 Said to him R. Eliezer, "Lo, he who slaughters a burnt-offering of cattle at the southern [side of the altar] for the sake of a guilt-offering will prove it." "For he has changed its name and changed its place, yet the laws of sacrilege do apply to it. So you should not be surprised concerning it, for even though he changed its name and changed its place, the laws of sacrilege should apply to it." Said to him R. Joshua, "No. If you have so stated the rule in the case of the one who slaughters burnt-offering of cattle at the southern side of the altar for the sake of a guilt-offering, for even though he changed its name and changed its place, he has not changed the conduct of its rites, and he has changed [it for] something, part of which is subject to the laws of sacrilege. But will you state the rule in this case, in which he has changed its name and changed its place, changed the conduct of its rites, and changed it for something to [even] part of which the laws of sacrilege do not apply?"

M. 7:5 (1) [If] one pinched the neck with his left hand or at night, (2) [if he] slaughtered unconsecrated [birds] inside [the Temple courtyard] or Holy Things [consecrated birds] outside — they do not impart uncleanness of the gullet [M. 7:3A]. (1) [If] one pinched the neck with a knife [not with his fingernail, as is required], (2) [if] he pinched the neck of unconsecrated [birds] inside the Temple courtyard, or of Holy Things outside [instead of inside the courtyard, where consecrated fowl alone are properly killed by pinching the neck] — [if he pinched the neck of] (1) turtledoves whose time had not yet come [to serve as sacrifices], (2) and young pigeons whose time had passed [for serving as sacrifices], (3) or [a blemished bird, e.g.,] whose wing had dried up, (4) or whose eye was blinded, (4) or whose eye was blinded, (5) or whose leg was cut off [which are not suitable for sacrifices] — [the meat of the bird is deemed carrion and, therefore] imparts uncleanness of the gullet. This is the encompassing principle: Any [bird] which became invalid [while] in the sanctuary [subject to the rites of sacrifice] does not impart uncleanness of the gullet [for the pinching itself is valid to remove the carcass from the category of carrion]. [If] it did not become invalid [while] in the sanctuary [subject to the cultic processes], it does impart uncleanness of the gullet. And all those [people who are] invalid [listed at M. 2:1], who pinched the neck of a bird — their act of pinching the neck is invalid [so far as the cult is concerned]. But [the carcasses of the birds whose necks they have pinched] do not impart uncleanness of the gullet [since the aspect of the killing of the bird that has led to its classification as invalid has to do with the cultic processes, but not with the act of pinching or the character of the bird itself].

M. 7:6 [If] one pinched off the neck and [the bird] turned out to be terefah — R. Meir says, "It does not impart uncleanness of the gullet [since slaughtering a beast is wholly equivalent to pinching the neck of a bird]." R. Judah says, "It does impart uncleanness of the gullet." [Birds and beasts in no way are comparable; neither slaughtering an unconsecrated clean bird nor pinching the neck of a consecrated one will exempt from uncleanness a bird which turns out to be terefah.] Said R. Meir, "It is an argument a fortiori [that it does not impart uncleanness of the gullet.] Now, if in the case of the carrion of a beast, which imparts uncleanness through contact and through carrying, proper slaughter renders clean from its uncleanness that which was terefah, [in the case of] the carrion of fowl, which does not impart uncleanness through contact and through carrying, it should logically follow that its proper slaughter should render clean from its uncleanness that which was terefah. Just as we find that its proper slaughter [in the case of a bird or beast] renders it valid for eating and renders it clean from its uncleanness in the case of terefah, so proper pinching of the neck, which renders it valid for eating, should render it clean from its uncleanness in the case of terefah." R. Yosé says, "It is sufficient that it [the slaughtering of the bird] be equivalent to the carrion of a beast: its [a beast's or a bird's] slaughtering renders clean [what is terefah], but the pinching of the neck [of a bird does] not [render clean what is terefah]."

T. 7.21 The sin-offering of fowl, which comes on account of doubt, imparts uncleanness as a matter of doubt and imparts uncleanness of the gullet.

T. 7:22 [A fowl] which has been subjected to bestiality, one which is set aside [for idolatrous purposes] and one which has been worshipped [for idolatrous purposes], the harlot's hire and the price of a dog, and [a fowl] which is lacking distinctive sexual traits and one which exhibits the sexual traits of male and female impart uncleanness of the gullet. R. Eliezer says, "The [fowl] lacking distinctive sexual traits and that which exhibits both male and female sexual traits, do not impart uncleanness of the gullet, for every place at which male is said removes from consideration that which is lacking distinctive sexual traits and that which exhibits both male and female sexual traits."

T. 7:23 [If] an outsider pinched [the neck of a consecrated bird in the sanctuary], or one who is invalid pinched [the neck], they do impart uncleanness of the gullet [M. Zeb. 7:5]. That which has become refuse and that which is left over [after the proper time of eating] do not impart uncleanness of the gullet, because that act which renders them invalid is not in the sanctuary [but takes place only after the rite of sacrifice is complete]. This is the general principle. Any [bird] which became invalid in the sanctuary [does not] impart uncleanness of the gullet. [If] the invalidity was not in the sanctuary, they do impart uncleanness of the gullet [= M. 7:5L-M].

We proceed from animal- to bird-offerings, reviewing the same program of locative and other questions. The points of differentiation from the procedures for animal offerings (e.g., M. 6:7) and consequent interstitial issues (e.g., at M. 7:1-4) are well framed.

III. THE RULES OF THE BLOOD-OFFERING ON THE ALTAR

The rules of the blood-offering on the altar present a systematic repertoire of the workings of the generic hermeneutics of the Halakhah, a beautifully crafted, systematic exposition of how, in the context of Zebahim, some of the Halakhah's most characteristic hermeneutical concerns play themselves out. Mixtures, the teleology of things (the taxonomic power of intrinsic traits), problems of hierarchization (as intrinsic traits resolve those problems) — these three fundamental components of the generic hermeneutics are fully propounded, each case serving as an example, all cases inviting generalization and extension. I cannot claim that III A, B, and C are situated side by side by reason of an intent to take up a distinctive component of the hermeneutics of the present category-formation — the generic component — in the way in which unit I is devoted to the particular hermeneutics. That seems to me unlikely, because units IV and V do not conform, and it is self-evident, the topical principle of organization predominates. But the subdivision represented by III A, B, and C certainly forms a handbook of the generic hermeneutics and should be appreciated as such. It is more than a small gem of a composite, it is intellectually incandescent.

> A. DISPOSING OF SACRIFICIAL PORTIONS OR BLOOD THAT DERIVE FROM DIVERSE SACRIFICE AND HAVE BEEN CONFUSED
> **M. 8:1 All [animals that had been designated for the purpose of] offerings that were mixed up with (1) sin offerings that had been left to die [M. Tem. 2:2] or (2) an ox sentenced to be**

stoned — even one [sin offering left to die] in ten thousand [suitable animal offerings] — let all of them be left to die. [If] they [animals designated for use as offerings] were mixed up with (1) an ox upon which a sin was committed, or [71A] (2) [an ox] which had been found guilty of killing a man on the evidence of a single witness or on the evidence of the owner, (1) with an ox which had sexual relations with a human, or (2) with an ox with which a human had sexual relations, or (3) with an ox which had been set aside [for idolatry (M. Tem. 6:1)], or (4) with an ox which had been worshipped, or (5) with an ox which had served as a harlot's hire, or (6) with an ox which had served as the price of a dog, or (7) with an ox which was crossbred, [71B] or (8) with an ox which was terefah, or (9) with an ox born from the side — let them [any of those beasts that had been confused in this way] pasture until they suffer a blemish [since one of them is a valid consecrated beast], and [then] be sold, and let [the owner] bring [another sacrifice, purchased] with the proceeds of the best of them of that kind [that had been mixed up with the invalid beasts]. [If] they were mixed up with unblemished unconsecrated beasts, the unconsecrated beasts are to be sold to those who require that particular kind [of sacrifice].

M. 8:2 Consecrated beasts [belonging to several owners, which were mixed up] with [other] consecrated beasts of the same kind [of offering, so that while all the beasts in the lot have been designated for the same purpose, we still do not know to whom in particular the several beasts belong] — this one is offered for the sake of one [among the owners] and that one is offered for the sake of one [among the owners]. Consecrated beasts [which were mixed up] with other consecrated beasts [e.g., burnt offerings and peace offerings], not of the same kind [of offerings] [and which, therefore, are offered with different rites, e.g., different numbers of acts of sprinkling blood, rules of consuming the flesh, and the like] — let them pasture until they suffer a blemish, and [then] be sold [separately], and let [the owner] bring with the proceeds of the best of them [a sacrifice] [e.g., peace offerings] of that kind, and let him lose [make up] the [added] difference from his own property. [If] they were mixed up with a firstling or with tithe [of cattle] — let them pasture until they suffer a blemish, and be eaten as a firstling [by priests] and as tithe [by ordinary folk] [but not slaughtered in the public market or sold by weight]. All can be mixed up [without the possibility of discerning an animal for one sacrifice from that for another], except a sin offering, [which is female or which is a male goat], with a guilt offering, [which is a male sheep or ram].

T. 8:1 All animal sacrifices which were mixed up — they and

their offspring and their substitutes — let them pasture until they suffer a blemish, and [then] be sold, and let the owner bring [another sacrifice] with the price of the best of them from one kind, and with the proceeds of the best of them from that kind, and let him make up the difference from his own property [M. Zeb. T. 8:2B-D].

T. 8:2 [If] they were mixed up with an ox, which has had sexual relations with a human, or with an ox with which a human has had sexual relations, with an ox which had been set aside for idolatry, or with an ox which had been worshipped, with an ox which had served as a harlot's hire, or with an ox which had served as the price of a dog, with an ox which was cross-bred, or with an ox which was terefah, or with an ox born from the side, let them pasture until they suffer a blemish, and [then] be sold, and let the owner] bring [another sacrifice, purchased] with the proceeds of the best among them of that same kind [that had been mixed up with the invalid beasts]. And the rest [of the oxen] are deemed unconsecrated beasts [and available for ordinary use] [M. Zeb. 8:1E-F]. [If] they were mixed up with unblemished unconsecrated beasts, let him consecrate them for the sake of that kind of sacrifice [which had been mixed up with them] [M. Zeb. 8:1G]. [If] they were mixed up with [other] animal-sacrifices, [if] one of them died, let him bring [an animal] in its stead from another source and make a condition concerning it. [If] the proceeds [of the sale of animal-sacrifices] were mixed up, Lo, this one purchases with them three beasts, whether from one source or from three sources, and render profane the proceeds of a sin-offering by means of a sin-offering, and the proceeds of a burnt-offering by means of a burnt-offering, and the proceeds of peace-offerings by means of peace-offerings. And they give [the now-deconsecrated coins] to the owners [of the respective offerings]. But one should not give them to the owners until he will have rendered profane [the proceeds of the sale of the animal-sacrifices] by means of all of them [the newly-purchased beasts].

M. 8:3 A guilt offering that was mixed up with peace offerings — let them pasture until they suffer a blemish [M. 8:2]. R. Simeon says, "Both of them are slaughtered at the north [as is required for a guilt offering, [M. 5:5] and are eaten in accord with the rules governing the more stringent of them" [as a guilt offering, inside the courtyard, by male priests for a day and a night]. They said to him, "They do not bring Holy Things to the status of invalidity." [If] pieces [of meat of one offering] were mixed up with pieces [of meat of other offerings] — Most Holy Things with Lesser Holy Things [e.g., pieces of a sin offering or a guilt offering with pieces of a thank offering], things which are to be eaten on one day with things, which are to be eaten on two days [e.g., pieces of a thank offering and those of peace offerings] — they are eaten in accord with the rules governing the more stringent of them.

T. 8:3 A burnt-offering which was mixed up with any one of all other kinds of offerings — let them pasture until they suffer a blemish and [then] be sold, and let [the owner] purchase with the proceeds of the best of them [another] animal-offering, and with the proceeds of the best of them [another] burnt-offering. [If] his animal-sacrifice already had been offered, let him purchase with its proceeds another animal-offering. [If] his burnt-offering already had been offered, let him bring with its proceeds another burnt-offering.

T. 8:4 A sin-offering which was mixed up with any one of all other kinds of offerings — let them pasture until they suffer a blemish and [then] be sold, and let [the owner] purchase with the proceeds of the best of them [another] animal-offering, and with the proceeds of the best of them a sin-offering. [If] the animal-offering already had been sold, let him bring with its proceeds another animal-offering. [If] his sin-offering already had been offered, both of them are left to die.

T. 8:5 A guilt-offering which was mixed up with any one of all other kinds of offerings — let them pasture until they suffer a blemish, and [then] be sold, and let [the owner] purchase with the proceeds of the best of them an animal-offering, and with the proceeds of the best of them a guilt-offering. [If] his animal-offering had already been offered, let him bring with its proceeds another animal-offering. [If] his guilt-offering had already been offered, both of them fall to [the category of] free-will-offerings.

T. 8:6 The coins [set aside for] a sin-offering and the coins [set aside for] a guilt-offering which were mixed up with each other — let [the owner] purchase with them two beasts, whether from one source or from two sources. And let the owner render unconsecrated the funds of the sin-offering in exchange for the sin-offering, and the funds of the guilt-offering in exchange for the guilt-offering. [If] his sin-offering had already been offered, let him bring to the Dead Sea [the coins set aside for the purchase of a sin-offering] [If] his guilt-offering already had been offered, let [the money set aside therefore] fall to [the Temple Treasury for] a free-will offering.

T. 8:7 A thank-offering which was mixed up with its substitute — let both of them be offered, and let [the priest] wave the bread with them.

T. 8:8 A thank-offering which was mixed up with one of all other kinds of animal-offerings — let them pasture until they suffer a blemish, and let [the owner] sell [them], and bring with the proceeds of the best of them an animal-offering, and with the proceeds of the best of them a thank-offering. [If] his animal-offering already had been offered, let him bring with its proceeds another animal-offering. [If] the thank-offering already had been offered, let him bring with its proceeds another thank-offering.

T. 8:9 Peace-offerings which were mixed up with one of all other kinds of animal-offerings — let them pasture until they suffer a blemish, and let [the owner] sell them, and bring with the proceeds of the best of them an animal-offering, and with proceeds of the best of them peace-offerings. [If] the peace-offerings already had been offered, let him bring with its value other peace-offerings.

T. 8:10 Peace-offerings which were mixed up with peace-offerings which come on account of the Passover — let them pasture until they suffer a blemish, and let [the owner] sell them and bring with the proceeds of the best of them peace-offerings. And let him eat [them] during a period of a day and a night — until midnight. And with the proceeds of the best of them [let him purchase] other peace-offerings. And let him eat [them] during a period of two days and one night.

T. 8:11 Ben Azzai says, "Peace-offerings" which come on account of the Passover — Lo, they are deemed equivalent to the Passover in every respect, "except that they are eaten for one day and a night."

T. 8:12 A firstling which was mixed up with a Passover — let both of them pasture until they suffer a blemish. And they eat [them] as a firstling. R. Simeon says, "This one is slaughtered for the sake of one thing, and this one is slaughtered for the sake of one thing. And both of them are eaten as a Passover, and by those who are counted in the eating of the Passover."

T. 8:13 Tithe of cattle which was mixed up with a Passover — let both of them pasture until they suffer a blemish and be sold as tithe of cattle. R. Simeon says, "This one is slaughtered for the sake of one thing, and that one is slaughtered for the sake of one thing. And both of them are eaten as a Passover and by those who are counted in the eating of the Passover."

T. 8:14 The firstling and tithe of cattle which were mixed together — R. Simeon says, "This one is slaughtered for the sake of one thing, and that one is slaughtered for the sake of one thing. And both of them are eaten as one, because the placing of their blood is subject to the same rule." But sages did not agree with R. Simeon, because he thereby, brings Holy Things to the status of invalidity [M. Zeb. 8:3C]. Under what circumstances? When they were mixed together while alive. But when already-slaughtered animals were mixed up, let them be eaten in accord with the rules governing the eating of the more stringent of them. [If] they were mixed up with animals unfit to be Holy Things or with unconsecrated animals which were slaughtered in the courtyard, let their appearance be spoiled [and then] let [them] go forth to the place of burning.

T. 8:15 A thank-offering which was mixed up with the ram of a Nazir — both of them are offered, and [the priest] waves the bread with them.

M. 8:4 The limbs of a sin offering which were mixed up with the limbs of a burnt offering — R. Eliezer says, "Let him place [them all] above [the altar fires]. And I regard the meat of the sin offering [which is] on top [of the fires] as if it were wood." And sages say, "Let their appearance be spoiled, and let them then go out to the place of burning [as remnant, not as mere fuel]."

T. 8:15 Said R. Judah, "Sages concur with R. Eliezer in the case of limbs of animal-offerings which were mixed up with limbs of a burnt-offering, that they should be offered up [M. Zeb. 8:4]. R. Eliezer concurs with sages that [if] they were mixed up with an animal which had intercourse with a human and an animal with which a human has had intercourse, with an animal set aside for idolatrous worship and an animal which had been worshipped, with the hire of a harlot and the price of a dog, and with a crossbred animal, and with a terefah-animal, and with an animal born from the side — their appearance should be spoiled and they should go forth to the place of burning. Concerning what did they differ? Concerning a case in which the limbs of a blemished animal were mixed up with the limbs of an unblemished animal. For R. Eliezer says, 'Let them be offered up. And I regard the parts belonging to the blemished animal which are mixed up with those belonging to an unblemished animal as if they were wood.' And sages say, 'Let their appearance be spoiled, and let them go forth to the place of burning.'"

M. 8:5 Limbs [of burnt offerings] which were mixed with the limbs of blemished beasts [which are not offered] — R. Eliezer says, "If the head of one of them was [inadvertently] offered, let all the heads be offered [in the assumption that the one which already has been offered is the one that was blemished]. [If] the leg of one of them [had been offered], let all the legs be offered [in the same assumption]." And sages say, "Even if all of them except one had inadvertently] been offered, let it go forth to the place of burning [since that one may be the blemished one]."

M. 8:6 Blood which was mixed with water, if it [the mixture] has the appearance of blood, is valid. [If] it was mixed in wine, they regard it as if it were water [and if the mixture is blood-color, it is valid]. [If] it [blood of Holy Things] was mixed with the blood of a beast or with the blood of fowl [which were unconsecrated], they regard it as if it were water. R. Judah says, "Blood [under any circumstances] does not annul blood."

T. 8:16 Blood which was mixed up with water — they regard it as if it were wine. [If] it was mixed up with wine, they regard it as if it were water [M. Zeb. 8:6C-D].

T. 8:17 [If] it was mixed up with the blood of a beast or with the blood of a wild animal, they regard it as if it were wine mixed up with water [M. Zeb. 8:6E]: if its appearance is annulled, it is invalid, and if not, it is valid. R. Judah says in the name of Rabban Gamaliel, "Blood does not annul blood [M. Zeb. 8:6F]." You have nothing which effects atonement except for the blood of life alone, as it is said, 'For the life of the flesh is in the blood; and I have given it for you upon the altar to make atonement for your souls; for it is the blood that makes atonement, by reason of the life' (Lev. 17:11). What is 'the blood of life'? [It is the blood which issues] so long as it gushes. And [what is] blood which exuded after death? It is any which does not gush.

M. 8:7 [If] it was mixed with the blood of unfit [offerings], let it be poured out into the gutter. [If it was mixed] with blood which exuded after death, let it be poured out into the gutter. R. Eliezer declares [it] valid. If the priest did not pay mind to it and placed [the blood on the altar], [the offering in the end] is valid.

T. 8:19 [If] it was mixed up with the blood of invalid beasts, let it be poured out into the gutter [M. Zeb. 8:7A]. Or [if it was mixed up with] blood which exuded after death [M. Zeb. 8:7B] — they tell him not to place [it on the altar], but if he placed [it on the altar], they regard it as if it were wine mixed with water: if its appearance is annulled, it is invalid, and if not, it is valid. R. Eliezer declares valid in the case of blood which issued after death [M. Zeb. 8:7C].

M. 8:8 Blood of unblemished animals [which was mixed] with the blood of blemished animals — let it be poured out into the gutter. A cup [of one kind of blood which was confused] with cups [containing another kind of blood] — R. Eliezer says, "[If] one cup was offered, let all the cups be offered." And sages say, "Even if all of them except one had been offered, let it [the remaining one] be poured out into the gutter."

T. 8:20 [If blood] was mixed up with [blood of] a beast which has had intercourse with a human or a beast with which a human has had intercourse, with a beast set aside for idolatrous worship or with a beast which had been worshipped, with the hire of a harlot, with the price of a dog, with a cross-bred beast, and with a beast which turned out to be terefah. And with one which had gone forth from the side — whether it was a cup confused with [other] cup[s] or [the different kinds of blood] were stirred together — let it be poured forth into the gutter. [If] one cup [was mixed up with] a hundred cups [M. Zeb. 8:8] — R. Eliezer says, "If one cup had been offered, let all the cups be offered." And sages say, "Even if all of them except for one had been offered up, let it be poured out into the gutter." R. Judah says, "R. Eliezer and sages did not dispute concerning blood of a burnt-offering which was mixed with the blood of [other] offerings, that they [all the cups] should be offered. [Nor did they dispute] concerning that which was mixed up with [the blood of] a beast which had intercourse with a human, or with a beast with which a human has had intercourse, with a beast set aside for idolatrous worship, or with one which had been worshipped, with a beast which had served as the hire of a harlot or as the price of a dog, whether a cup [was confused] with other cups or [all the blood was] together — blood of a blemished animal, whether stirred together or whether one cup was mixed with a hundred cups — that it should be poured out into the gutter. Concerning what did they dispute? Concerning a case in which the blood of a blemished animal was mixed together with the blood of an unblemished animal. For R. Eliezer says, 'Let them be offered up together. And I regard the blood of the blemished animal mixed up with the blood of an unblemished animal as if it were water.' And sages say, 'Let it be poured out into the gutter.'"

M. 8:9 [Blood] which was to be sprinkled below [e.g., of a burnt offering] which was mixed up with [blood] which is to be sprinkled above [e.g., of a sin offering, as at M. 5:3] — R. Eliezer says, "Let him [the priest] sprinkle it [first] above [the red line in four acts of sprinkling]. And I regard [the blood which is to be sprinkled] below [that has been sprinkled] above as if it were water. And [then] let him go and sprinkle [blood one time] below [the line as well. The remnants of blood of a sin offering in any case are poured out at the base, so M. 5:3]." And sages say, "Let them be poured out into the gutter." But if [the priest] did not pay mind to it [inquire about it] and placed [the blood on the altar], [the offering] is valid.

T. 8:21 Drops of blood which are to be tossed below which were mixed up with drops of blood which are to be tossed above — R. Eliezer says, "Let them be tossed above." And sages say, "Let them be poured out into the gutter" [M. Zeb. 8:9]. [If] one tossed them below and did not inquire — R. Eliezer says, "Let him [also] place them above." And sages say, "Let him pour them out into the gutter. But the ones tossed below have gone to his credit." [If] he placed them above and did not inquire, these and those agree that he should go and place them [below]. [If he placed them] below [and did not inquire], these and those agree that they have not gone to his credit.

M. 8:10 [Blood] which is to be tossed in a single act of tossing which was mixed up with [blood] which is to be tossed in a single act of tossing — let them be tossed in a single act of tossing [below the red line]. [Blood] which is to be tossed in four acts of tossing [which was mixed up with] blood which is to be tossed in four acts of tossing — let them be tossed in four acts of tossing [below the red line]. [Blood] which is to be tossed in four acts of tossing [which was mixed up] with blood which is to be tossed in one act of tossing — R. Eliezer says, "Let them be tossed in four acts of tossing." R. Joshua says, "Let them be tossed in a single act of tossing." Said to him R. Eliezer, "And Lo, he transgresses the rule against diminishing [the required acts of tossing, so Dt. 4:2]." Said to him R. Joshua, "And lo, he transgresses the rule against adding [to the required acts of tossing — Dt. 4:2]." Said to him R. Eliezer, "The prohibition against adding is stated only in connection with the act in itself." Said to him R. Joshua, "The prohibition against diminishing is stated only in connection with the act in itself." And further did R. Joshua say, "When you placed [the blood four times], you transgressed the prohibition against adding, and you did the deed with your own hand, and when you did not sprinkle [four times], you transgressed against the prohibition against diminishing, but [at least] you did not do the deed with your own hand."

T. 8:22 [The blood of] a sin-offering of an individual which was mixed up [with the blood of the sin-offering of an individual], [the blood of the sin-offering of the community which was mixed up [with the blood of the sin-offering of the community], [the blood of] the sin-offering of an individual [and the blood of the sin-offering of] the community which were mixed up — and so with thank-offerings, and so with burnt-offerings, and so with peace-offerings — one executes four acts of sprinkling from each one of them. And if he executed four acts of sprinkling from [a mixture of] all of them, he has fulfilled his obligation. Under what circumstances? When they were mixed together while alive. But when they were mixed together when already slaughtered, he executes four acts of placing from all of them. And if he executed a single act of placing from all of them, he has fulfilled his obligation. R. Meir says, "We regard the act of placing: If it should be divided and there should be sufficient for an act of placing for each and every one of them, [he then has fulfilled his obligation]" [M. Zeb. 8:10].

T. 8:23 [Blood] which is to be tossed in a single act of tossing which was mixed up with blood which is to be tossed in a single act of tossing — let them be tossed in a single act of tossing. Blood which is to be tossed in four acts of tossing [which was mixed up with] blood which is to be tossed in four acts of tossing — let them be tossed in four acts of tossing. [If blood] which is to be tossed in four acts of tossing [was mixed up] with blood which is to be tossed in one act of tossing — R. Eliezer says, "Let them be tossed in four acts of tossing." R. Joshua says, "Let them be tossed in a single act of tossing." Said R. Eliezer, "Lo, he transgresses the rule against diminishing [the required acts of tossing, Deut. 4:2]." Said R. Joshua, "Lo, he transgresses the rule against adding [to the required acts of tossing]." Said R. Eliezer, "'You shall not add' is said only concerning the act by itself, but you do add to it when it is involved with other actions." Said R. Joshua, "You shall not diminish is said only concerning the act by itself, but you do diminish from it when it is involved with other actions." Said R. Eliezer, "The matter is still suspended. Who shall settle it?" Said to him R. Joshua, "I shall settle the matter. When I do it with my own hand, I turn out to transgress a negative commandment, and Lo, it is by my own hand. But when I leave it as it is, I turn out to transgress a negative commandment, but it is not by my own hand" [M. Zeb. 8: 10E-L].

M. 8:11 [Blood] that is to be placed on the inside altar [M. 5:1-2] that is mixed up with blood that is to be placed on the outside altar — let it be poured out into the gutter. [If the priest without paying mind] placed the blood outside and then went and placed it inside, it is valid. [If he placed it] inside and then went and placed it outside — R. Aqiba declares invalid [the sacrifice on the outer altar]. And sages declare valid. For R. Aqiba did say, "All drops of blood [that should have been sprinkled outside] but are brought inside the sanctuary to effect atonement are invalid." And sages say, "[This applies] to the sin offering alone [which is invalidated by being brought inside before the blood is tossed on the outer altar]." R. Eliezer says, "[It also applies] to the guilt offering, since it says, 'As is the sin offering, so is the guilt offering' (Lev. 7:7)."

T. 8:24 Blood which is to be placed inside which is mixed up with blood which is to be placed outside, let it be poured out into the gutter [M. Zeb. 8:11A-B]. [If] he placed it outside, not having inquired, let him go and place it inside, and those which he placed outside go to his credit. [If] he placed it inside, not having inquired, these and those do not go to his credit — except for that which is mixed up with [the blood of] a sin-offering, for a sin-offering, the blood of which is brought inside, is invalid [M. Zeb. 8:1 ID, F, H]. R. Eliezer says, "Also, the guilt-offering, as it is said, as is the sin-offering, so is the guilt-offering (Lev. 7:7)" [M. Zeb. 8:11I].

M. 8:12 A sin offering [sacrificed in the courtyard], the blood of which one received in two cups — one of them went forth [outside the courtyard] — the one that remained inside, is valid [and so is the sin offering]. [If] one of them went inside [into the inner sanctum, where the inner altar was located, and so was invalidated, M. 8:11G-H] — R. Yosé the Galilean declares the one that remained outside [in the courtyard] to be valid. And sages declare it invalid. Said R. Yosé the Galilean, "Now if in a situation in which improper intention renders the rite invalid, namely, in connection with [the intention to sprinkle the blood] outside [the Temple court] [= M. 2:2], [the law of M. 8:12A-C] has not treated that which remains as equivalent to that which goes forth, in a situation in which intention does not render the rite invalid, [namely, in connection with the intention to sprinkle the blood (= M. 3:6)] inside [the Temple court], is it not logical that we should not treat that which remains as equivalent to that which enters in?" "[If] it was taken inside to make atonement, even though he did not make atonement, it is invalid," the words of R. Eliezer. R. Simeon says, "[It does not become invalid] until it makes atonement." R. Judah says, "If he brought it in inadvertently [even if he tossed the blood], it is valid." [As to] all kinds of invalid blood which were placed on the altar — the frontlet does not effect acceptance except for the unclean [blood in the mixture]. For the frontlet effects acceptance for that which is unclean. But it does not effect atonement for that which goes forth.

T. 8:25 A sin-offering, the blood of which one received in two cups, [if] one of them was made unclean, or was poured out, or went inside the veils, or was tossed below [the red line], Lo, its fellow remains valid. There is an argument, a fortiori, concerning those [which remain] inside [the veils], that, if one of them went outside [the veils], its fellow should not be invalid. And logic teaches as follows: Now if in a situation in which intention [to carry the blood] outside invalidates [the rite], the blood which [actually] is taken outside does not invalidate the blood which [remains] is inside a situation in which intention [to take the blood] inside [into the sanctuary (Hekhal)] does not invalidate the blood which remains – [inside the courtyard] — is it not logical that the blood which is taken inside should not invalidate the blood which remains outside? Scripture therefore states thus: "Its blood has not been brought into the inner part of the sanctuary" (Lev. 10:18).

T. 8:26 [If] it was brought inside, it is valid. [If] it went outside, it is invalid. Flesh of Holy Things which was brought inside is valid. And logic requires that it be invalid: Now, if in a situation in which blood which is outside has not invalidated blood which is inside, shall we declare invalid meat which goes outside? In a case in which blood which is taken inside has invalidated blood which is outside, is it not logical that we should declare invalid [also] meat which is taken there? Scripture says, "And meat in the field which is torn by beasts you shall not eat" (Ex. 22:31).

T. 8:27 [If] it is brought inside, its fellow is deemed refuse. [If] it is taken outside, its fellow is deemed valid. [If] a priest received the blood, if one who is suitable received the blood, if he received the blood in his right hand, if he received the blood in a consecrated utensil, its fellow is valid, for this one is suitable to be offered inside.

T. 8:28 [If] an outsider received the blood, [if] an invalid person received the blood, [if] he received the blood in his left hand, [if] he received the blood in an unconsecrated utensil, its fellow is invalid, for this one is not suitable to be offered inside. [If a bird] in writhing went inside and one put it back, it is valid. A sin-offering of fowl which in writhing went inside and which one put back [outside] is valid.

T. 8:29 A sin-offering, the blood of which one received in four cups — if one placed blood from all four of them on the four corners of the altar — all of them are poured out on the foundation. But if he placed blood from only one of them in four acts of placing, that one is poured out onto the foundation, and the rest of them are poured out into the gutter. R. Eliezer b. R. Simeon says, "Even if he placed blood from only one of them in four acts of placing, all of them are poured out onto the foundation." This is the general principle which governs the matter: (I) Any blood which is poured out onto the foundation — (and) its blood necessitates washing [Lev. 6:20], and improper intention, therewith, invalidates on account of refuse, and he who takes it outside is liable. (2) Any blood which is poured into the gutter — its blood does not necessitate washing, and improper intention therewith does not invalidate it on account of refuse, and he who takes it outside is free [of liability to punishment].

The program of topical and generic-hermeneutical presentation of the category-formation accounts for this sub-division. The topic is, the blood-offering and its conduct. The generic-hermeneutical program involves cases of mixture, confusion and doubt, an ideal opportunity for the exposition of interstitiality: the conflict of equally-valid rules and how it is resolved. M. 8:1 begins with the basic principles: confusion of diverse beasts with animals that must be left to die means all animals that are mixed up must be left to die; the ones under the death sentence impart their status to all others. But there are other sorts of mixtures and other means of resolving the confusion as well, as M. 8:2ff show. That the issues transcend the cases is shown, especially, at M. 8:10ff. None of these matters has anything to do with the particular hermeneutics of Zebahim.

B. THE ALTAR SANCTIFIES WHAT IS APPROPRIATE TO IT, BUT
    NOT WHAT IS NOT APPROPRIATE TO IT

M. 9:1 The altar sanctifies that which is appropriate to it. [If something is placed on the altar that is suitable for the altar, it is not to be removed.] R. Joshua says, "Whatever is appropriate to [not the altar but] the altar fires, if it has gone up [onto the fires], should not go down, since it is said, 'This is the burnt offering — that which goes up on the hearth on the altar' (Lev. 6:9): just as the burnt offering, which is appropriate to the altar fires, if it has gone up, should not go down, so whatever is appropriate to the altar fires, if it has gone up, should not go down." Rabban Gamaliel says, "Whatever is appropriate to the altar, if it has gone up, should not go down, as it is said, 'This is the burnt offering on the hearth on the altar' (Lev. 6:2): just as the burnt offering, which is appropriate to the altar, if it has gone up, should not go down, so whatever is appropriate to the altar, if it has gone up, should not go down." The difference between the opinion of Rabban Gamaliel and the opinion of R. Joshua is only the blood and the drink offerings. For Rabban Gamaliel says, "They should not [having been placed on the altar] go down." And R. Joshua says, "They should go down." R. Simeon says, "[If] (1) the animal sacrifice is valid and the drink offerings invalid, (2) the drink offerings valid and the animal sacrifice invalid, [or] even if (3) this and that are invalid — the animal sacrifice should not go down, but the drink offerings should go down."

T. 9:1 The difference between the opinion of Rabban Gamaliel and the opinion of R. Joshua is only the blood and the drink-offerings [M. Zeb. 9:10]. As to the blood: In accord with the opinion of Rabban Gamaliel, one tosses it onto the fires. As to the drink-offering: One puts it into cups.

M. 9:2 And what are those things, which if they have gone up, should not go down? That which remains overnight, and that which is unclean, and that which goes forth [from its proper bounds], and that which is slaughtered [with the intention to burn the sacrificial parts or to eat the flesh] outside of its proper time or outside of its proper place, and that the blood of which unfit people [M. 2:1] have received or tossed. R. Judah says, "(1) That which is slaughtered by night, and (2) that, the blood of which has been poured out, and (3) that, the blood of which has gone forth beyond the veils — if it has gone up, should go down." R. Simeon says, "It should not go down. For the cause of its invalidity [took place] in the [sanctuary]." For R. Simeon did say, "Anything, the cause of the invalidity of which [took place] in the sanctuary — the sanctuary accepts it [so that it should not be removed from the altar]. [If] its invalidity did not [take place] in the sanctuary, the sanctuary does not accept it [and it should be removed from the altar]."

M. 9:3 What are those things, the invalidity of which did not [take place] in the sanctuary? (1) The animal which has had sexual relations with a human, and (2) the animal with which a human had sexual relations; and (3) that which is set aside for idolatrous worship, and (4) that which actually is worshipped; and (5) the hire of a harlot, and (6) the price of a dog; and (7) the crossbred animal; and (8) the animal which turned out to be terefah, and (9) that which goes out by the side, and (10) animals which are blemished. R. Aqiba declares valid in the case of animals which are blemished. [Thus if they have gone up, they should not go down.] R. Hananiah, Prefect of the Priests, says, "Father did reject animals which had been blemished [even] from on top of the altar."

T. 9:2 The Passover and the sin-offering which one slaughtered not for their own name and which went up onto the altar, Lo, these should not go down. All animal-offerings which went up onto the altar and are found to be invalid, Lo, these do not go down.

T. 9:3 The bones, sinews, horns, and hooves which have gone up onto the altar and which are found to be invalid, Lo, these do not go down.

T. 9:4 A dam and its offspring [slaughtered on the same day] which have gone up onto the altar should go down. For the altar sanctifies only that which is appropriate to it.

T. 9:5 The beast which has had sexual relations with a human and the beast with which a human has had sexual relations, that which is set aside for idolatrous worship and that which has been worshipped, the hire of a harlot and the price of a dog, the cross-bred beast, the beast which turned out to be terefah, and that which goes forth from the side which have gone up onto the altar should go down, because their invalidity has not [taken place] in the sanctuary [M. Zeb. 9:3A-B]. This is the general principle: Any animal, the invalidity of which has taken place in the sanctuary — the sanctuary receives it. If its invalidity has not taken place in the sanctuary — the sanctuary does not receive it [M. 9:2D]. Except for a blemished animal. For R. Simeon says in the name of R. Aqiba, "A blemished specimen in the case of fowl is valid." R. Hanina, Prefect of the Priests, says, "Father did reject animals which had been blemished from being sacrificed" [M. Zeb. 9:2E]. On what account did they say, that which remains overnight and that which goes forth [beyond the veils] and that which is unclean which went up onto the altar should not go down [M. Zeb. 9:2A]? Because that which is left overnight is valid. And peace-offerings and that which goes forth [beyond the veils] are valid in the case of a high place. And that which is unclean is valid in the case of a communal offering.

M. 9:4 Just as, if they have gone up, they should not go down, so if they have gone down, they should not [once more] go up. But all of them [M. 9:2A] which have gone up alive to the top of the altar should go down. A burnt offering which went up alive to the top of the altar should go down. [If] one did slaughter it on top of the altar, [however] he should then flay and divide it in its place [where it lies, on top of the altar].

T. 9:7 A burnt-offering which has gone up onto the altar and turned out to be invalid — one should burn it on its hide.

T. 9:8 Limbs which remained overnight in the courtyard are subject to the laws of sacrilege the whole night. Those which are on the ramp [and] those which are on top of the altar are subject to the laws of sacrilege perpetually. Just as, if they have gone up, they should not go down, so if they have gone down, they should not go up. And if they have gone up, they should go down [M. 9:4]. The handful which one placed on the fires — the residue is permitted. Limbs which one has placed on the fires — the flesh is permitted.

T. 9:9 That which is refuse, remnant, and unclean which one placed on top of the altar — they are [not] liable on their account because of the transgression of the laws of refuse, remnant, and uncleanness. An already-slaughtered burnt-offering which went up onto the altar or which went up alive and which one slaughtered — Lo, one flays and cuts it up, and he brings down the blood and tosses it below. He brings down the parts which are offered and rinses them in water and goes and offers them up. And he brings down the hide for the priests and goes and burns the whole.

T. 9:10 Animal-offerings which already had been slaughtered which went up onto the altar — Lo, this one should flay and cut them up and bring down the blood and toss it below [the red line]. He brings down the parts which are offered and washes them in water and goes and offers them up. And he brings down the hide and the flesh for the owners. Then he goes and offers up the remainder. [If] they were brought up alive, he brings them down and slaughters them below. You have nothing which is sanctified by the outer altar except for that which is appropriate to it.

M. 9:5 What are those things which, [even] if they have gone up, should go down [being removed from the altar because they are not offered at all and, therefore, are not appropriate to the altar]? (1) The meat [that constitutes the share of the priests] of Most Holy Things [sin offerings and guilt offerings] and the meat [that constitutes the share of the priests] of Lesser Holy Things [e.g., peace offerings], (2) and the excess of the sheaf of first barley that is presented from Passover through Pentecost [the *omer*], (3) and the two loaves [of Pentecost] and the show bread

[Lev. 24:5-19], (4) and the residue of meal-offerings, (5) and the incense offering [that has been erroneously placed on the outer, rather than the inner altar to which it is appropriate]. But the (1) wool on the heads of lambs, (2) the hair of the beard of goats, (3) the bones, (4) the sinews, (5) the horns, and (6) the hooves, when they are attached [to the flesh], should go up [onto the altar], as it is said, "And the priest shall burn the whole upon the altar" (Lev. 1:9). [If] they are separated [from the corpus of the offering, however], they should not go up, as it is said, "And you shall offer your burnt offerings, the flesh and the blood" (Dt. 12:27).

T. 9:6 The handful and the frankincense, the meal-offerings of priests, and the meal-offering of the anointed priest, and the meal-offering which goes along with the drink-offerings which have gone up on the altar and turned out to be invalid — Lo, these do not go down [M. Zeb. 9:2]. But the incense which went up onto the altar should go down [M. Zeb. 9:5A(5)], for the altar sanctifies only that which is appropriate to it [M. Zeb. 9:1A].

M. 9:6 And any of them which burst from off the altar — one should not put them back. And so [is the rule for] a coal which burst from off the altar. Limbs which burst from off the altar, [if this was] before midnight — one should put them back, and the laws of sacrilege apply to them. [If they burst] after midnight, one should not put them back, but the laws of sacrilege still do not apply to them.

M. 9:7 Just as the altar sanctifies that which is appropriate to it, so the ramp sanctifies. Just as the altar and the ramp sanctify that which is appropriate to them, so utensils [Ex. 30:28-29] sanctify [that which is appropriate to them]. Utensils for liquids [blood, wine, oil, water] sanctify liquid; and measures for drystuffs [the tenth of the *ephah* and half *issaron* measures] sanctify that which is dry. Utensils for liquids do not sanctify that which is dry, and measures for drystuffs do not sanctify that which is liquid. Holy utensils which are perforated, if they perform their former function as they did when they were whole, sanctify. And if not, they do not effect sanctification. And all of them effect sanctification [of what is contained in them] only [when they are located] in the sanctuary [courtyard].

T. 9:11 Utensils for liquids sanctify liquid, and a measure for drystuffs sanctifies that which is dry. Utensils for fluids do not sanctify drystuffs, and a measure for drystuffs does not sanctify liquid [M. Zeb. 9:7B-C]. It sanctifies only when it is full. It sanctifies only within [the Temple court [M. Zeb. 9:7F]. [If] they were perforated or damaged [and then] plastered over, if they carry out their former function, which they performed when they were whole, they sanctify, and if not, they do not sanctify [M. Zeb. 9:7E].

The power of a component of the rite to affect the rite depends upon its carrying out its assignment — teleology governs effects — finds its counterpart in other aspects of the Halakhah. For example, on the Sabbath, considerations of the normal use or function of an object enter into the assessment of whether or not the object may be utilized on the Sabbath, and in connection with priestly rations, priests must use the priestly rations for the natural purpose that inheres in them, e.g., food is for eating, not for burning — these are comparable expressions of the teleological principle that governs here. That principle then requires nuanced application here. Sanctification is a status, not a condition, so the power of the altar or the fires of the altar encompasses only what is suited to the altar or the fires, and what is unsuited or inappropriate, violating the teleology thereof, is unaffected by the altar or the fires. Since the principle comes to concrete expression in diverse areas of the Halakhah, it must be classified as a component of the generic hermeneutics of the Halakhah, not the particular hermeneutics of Zebahim. The exposition of the case, M. 9:1ff could not be more systematic or carefully crafted. Indeed, if I had to choose one, among the many, truly perfect exhibitions of the Halakhic power of clear and cogent exposition, this would present itself as a leading candidate for balance, proportion, clarity, and comprehensiveness: all possibilities are covered, but no absurdities.

C. *PRECEDENCE IN USE OF THE ALTAR*

M. 10:1 Whatever is [offered] more often than its fellow takes precedence over its fellow: (1) Daily whole offerings take precedence over additional offerings. (2) The additional offerings of the Sabbath take precedence over the additional offerings of the new moon. (3) The additional offerings of the new moon take precedence over the additional offerings of the New Year [which also is a new moon], since it is said, "In addition to the morning burnt offering which is for a daily whole offering you will prepare these" (Num. 28:23).

M. 10:2 And whatever is more holy than its fellow takes precedence over its fellow: (1) The blood of the sin offering takes precedence over the blood of the burnt offering, because it makes atonement [for a sin]. (2) The limbs of the burnt offering take precedence over the sacrificial parts of a sin offering, because they are wholly given over to the fires [to be burned up]. (3) The sin offering takes precedence over the guilt offering, because its blood is placed on the four corners [of an altar] and on the foundation. (4) The guilt offering takes precedence over the thank offering and the ram of the Nazir, because it is Most Holy Things. (5) The thank offering and the ram of the Nazir take precedence over peace offerings, because they are eaten for one day [unlike peace offerings which are eaten for two days] and require bread [Lev. 7:12-13]. The peace offerings take precedence over the firstling, because they require [two placings which are] four placings [of blood], and laying of hands, and drink offerings, and waving of the breast and thigh.

M. 10:3 (7) The firstling takes precedence over tithe of cattle, because it is sanctified from the womb, and it is eaten [only] by priests. (8) The tithe of cattle takes precedence over fowl [even though the latter falls within Most Holy Things], because it is an animal sacrifice [killed with a knife, unlike fowl], and there pertain to it [traits that classify an offering as] Most Holy Things: its blood and its sacrificial parts [which are placed on the altar].

M. 10:4 (9) Fowl take precedence over meal-offerings, because they fall [within the class] of [that which produces] blood [for atonement]. The meal-offering of a sinner [Lev. 5:13] takes precedence over the free will meal-offering, because it comes on account of sin. The sin offering of fowl takes precedence over the burnt offering of fowl, and so [too it takes precedence over the burnt offering] when [the two birds] are dedicated [for an offering, Lev. 5:7].

T. 10:1 Whatever is [offered] more often than its fellow takes precedence over its fellow [M. Zeb. 10:1A]. And whatever is more holy than its fellow takes precedence over its fellow [M. Zeb. 10:2A].

T. 10:2 [If] the bullock of the anointed priest and the bullock of the congregation stand [awaiting sacrifice], the bullock of the anointed priest takes precedence over the bullock of the congregation in all aspects of its rite, because the anointed priest effects atonement, but the congregation is subject to atonement. It is better that that which effects atonement take precedence over that for which atonement is effected, as it is said, "And he shall atone for himself and for his house and for the whole congregation of Israel" (Lev. 16:17). A bullock which comes in connection with any of the commandments takes precedence over the goats offered in behalf of the congregation, and the goats offered in behalf of the congregation take precedence over the goat of the Nasi, and the goat of the Nasi takes precedence over the she-goat of an individual, and the she-goat of an individual takes precedence over the ewe of an individual.

T. 10:3 The thank-offering takes precedence over the ram of the Nazir, because the thank-offering requires four kinds of bread, but the ram of the Nazir requires only two kinds of bread. Tithe of cattle takes precedence over fowl [M. Zeb. 10:3B]. Said R. Simeon, "Now is not tithe of cattle Lesser Holy Things, while fowl are Most Holy Things? [If] Lesser Holy Things take precedence over Most Holy Things, then one must conclude that there are in connection with tithe of cattle sacrificial parts [belonging to the status of] Most Holy

Things, which is not the case for fowl."

T. 10:4 The sin-offering of fowl takes precedence over the burnt-offering of fowl [when the two are] offered up [and also] when the two are designated [for their respective purposes] [M. Zeb. 10:4E-F]. One should not say, "This one is for my burnt-offering and that one for my sin-offering," but one says, "This one is for my sin-offering, and that one is for my burnt-offering." The sin-offering of fowl of a woman who has given birth takes precedence over her sheep. The meal-offering of a man takes precedence over the meal-offering of a woman. The meal-offering of wheat takes precedence over the meal-offering of barley. The meal-offering takes precedence over wine. And wine takes precedence over oil. And oil takes precedence over salt. And salt takes precedence over wood. And wood takes precedence over anything else.

T. 10:5 Bullocks take precedence over rams, and rams take precedence over sheep. Under what circumstances? When they come simultaneously. But that which comes first is offered first, and that which comes last is offered last. Show-bread takes precedence over the two loaves.

T. 10:6 When he divides them up on Pentecost, he says, "Here is unleavened bread for you, here is leavened bread for you, here is unleavened bread for you, here is leavened bread for you." Abba Saul says, "The two loaves take precedence over the show bread. When he divides them up on Pentecost, he says, 'Here is leavened bread for you, here is unleavened bread for you, here is leavened bread for you, here is unleavened bread for you.' For the two loaves are more precious." Just as this takes precedence over that when they are offered up, so this takes precedence over that when they are eaten [M. Zeb. 10:6A]. [Most] Holy Things take precedence over Lesser Holy Things.

M. 10:5 All sin offerings which are [mentioned] in the Torah take precedence over guilt offerings [listed at M. 5:5 = M. 10:2A3], except for the guilt offering of the person afflicted by the skin ailment of Lev. 13, because [in line with Lev. 14] it comes to render [him] fit [to enter the Temple and eat Holy Things]. All guilt offerings which are [mentioned] in the Torah come from animals in their second year and must be two shekels in value, except for the guilt offering of the Nazir and the guilt offering of the person afflicted with the skin ailment, which are offered in their first year and do not have to be two shekels in value.

M. 10:6 Just as they [the above-mentioned offerings, more holy than some other, M. 10:2-4] "take precedence in being offered up, so they take precedence in being eaten. Peace offerings of yesterday and peace offerings of today — those of yesterday take precedence, peace offerings of yesterday and a sin offering and a guilt offering of today — those of yesterday take precedence," the words of R. Meir. And sages say, "The sin offering takes precedence, because it is Most Holy Things."

T. 10:7 Those sacrifices which are eaten for one day take precedence over those sacrifices which are eaten for two days. The peace-offerings sacrificed yesterday take precedence over the sin-offering and the guilt-offering of today [M. Zeb. 10:6C]. R. Simeon says, "The sin-offering and the guilt-offering of today take precedence over those of yesterday." And in the case of all of them, the priests are permitted to vary the manner of eating them [M. Zeb. 10:7A]. "In the case of meal-offering, [they are allowed] to stir them in water and to remove their oil. And to put into them unconsecrated spices for spices of heave-offering," the words of R. Simeon. R. Meir says, "Unconsecrated spices but not spices of heave-offering, so that he not bring it to the state of invalidity [M. Zeb. 10:7B-C], nor to the condition by which he limits that which may be eaten" [M. Zeb. 8:3].

M. 10:7 And in the case of all of them [which are eaten], the priests are permitted to vary the manner of eating them: "to eat them (1) roasted, (2) seethed, or (3) cooked. And to put in them unconsecrated spices or spices of heave offering," the words of R. Simeon, R. Meir says, "He should not put into them spices of heave offering, so that he not bring heave offering to the state of invalidity."

M. 10:8 Said R. Simeon, "If you have seen oil spread about in the Temple court [divided up among the priests], you do not have to ask, 'What is it?' For [one may take for granted that] it is the residue of the meal-offering wafers of Israelites or of the log of oil of a person healed of the skin ailment. If you have seen oil put on top of the altar fires, you do not have to ask, 'What is it?' But it is the residue of the meal-offering wafers of priests or the meal-offering of the anointed priest." For: they do not offer oil as a freewill offering. R. Tarfon says, "They do offer oil as a freewill offering."

T. 10:8 [Similarly:] they do not cook a sin-offering or a guilt-offering with that which is separated from a thank-offering, nor the ram of a Nazir with tithe of cattle [or] with that which is separated from peace-offerings, for one [thereby] diminishes [the number of those who] eat them and the time during which they may be eaten. Nor [should one cook] peace-offerings of yesterday with the sin-offering or the guilt-offering of today because one diminishes [the number of those who] eat them, and the place in which they may be eaten, and the time in which they may be eaten. But the sin-offering and guilt-offering are cooked with one another, and the thank-offering and the ram of the Nazir are cooked with one another, and the firstling and that which is separated from peace-offerings are cooked with one another, because all of them are [respectively] subject to the same rule.

The generic hermeneutics proceeds to its next issue, problems of precedence. Here the case announces its generalization: Whatever is offered more often than its fellow takes precedence over its fellow; and whatever is more holy than its fellow takes precedence over its fellow. Then illustrative cases drive the point home. Further hierarchical issues follow, each explaining itself in context.

D. *BLOOD OF A SIN-OFFERING THAT SPURTS ONTO A GARMENT: "WHATEVER TOUCHES THE FLESH SHALL BE HOLY, AND WHEN ANY OF ITS BLOOD IS SPRINKLING ON A GARMENT, YOU SHALL WASH THAT ON WHICH IT WAS SPRINKLED IN A HOLY PLACE. AND THE EARTHEN VESSEL IN WHICH IT IS BOILED SHALL BE BROKEN; BUT IF IT IS BOILED IN A BRONZE VESSEL, IT SHALL BE SCOURED AND RINSED IN WATER" (LEV. 6:27-28)*

M. 11:1 The blood of a sin offering which splattered on the garment — Lo, this [garment] requires washing. Even though Scripture speaks only about [sin offerings] that are eaten, as it is said, "In a holy place will it be eaten" (Lev. 6:26), [nonetheless], all the same in requiring washing are that which is eaten and that [the blood of which must be brought to the] inner area, as it is said, "The law of the sin offering" (Lev. 6:25) — one law for all sin offerings.

M. 11:2 An invalid sin offering — its blood [that had spurted on a garment] does not require washing, (1) whether it had a moment of validity [for tossing the blood] or (2) it did not have a moment of validity [having been invalidated before the receiving of the blood]. What is the sort which had a moment of validity? That which remained overnight or which was made unclean or which went forth [beyond the veils] [since prior to these events, the offering had been entirely valid]. And what is the sort which did not have a moment of validity? That which was slaughtered [with the intention to eat the meat or to toss the blood] outside its proper time or outside its proper place, and that [the blood of] which unfit people received, or the blood of which [unfit people] tossed.

M. 11:3 [If] the blood spurted [directly] from the neck [of the slaughtered beast] onto the garment [and was not received in a pot, being invalid for sprinkling on the altar], it does not require washing. [If the blood spurted] from the horn or from the foundation [of the altar], it does not require washing. [If] it was poured onto the pavement and one gathered it up [and then it spurted onto a garment], it does not require washing. That [sort of blood] which requires washing is only the blood which has been received in a utensil and is suitable for sprinkling [on the altar]. "[If blood] spurted onto the hide before it was flayed, it does not require washing. [If it spurted onto the hide] after it was flayed, it does require washing," the words of R. Judah, and R. Eleazar says, "Also: [if it spurted onto the hide] after it was flayed, it does not require washing." Only (1) the place [on which] the blood has fallen, and (2) something which is susceptible to receive uncleanness, and (3) something suitable for washing require washing.

T. 10:9 All the same are sin-offerings [the blood of which is tossed] outside and sin-offerings [the blood of which is tossed] inside in respect to washing [garments on which a drop of blood of a sin-offering has spurted (M. Zeb. 11:1)], as it is said, "The law of the sin-offering" (Lev. 6:25) — one law for all sin-offerings [M. Zeb. 11:1D]. As to the sin-offering of fowl, its blood does not require washing. An invalid sin-offering — its blood does not require washing [M. Zeb. 11:2A]. [If] it [a sin-offering] had a moment of validity and then was made invalid, its blood does require washing," the words of R. Jacob. R. Simeon says, "Even though it had a moment of validity and then was made invalid, its blood does not require washing." [If] one put the blood on the horn [of the altar] and on the ramp and on the foundation, it [blood which spurts] does not require [washing] [M. Zeb. 11:3A-C]. [If] [the blood] spurted from his hand when he sprinkles it on the ladle, one scrapes it off, and it is clean.

T. 10:10 "[If] it spurted onto the hide before it was flayed, it does not require washing. [If this happened] after it was flayed, it does require washing," the words of R. Judah and R. Eleazar says, "R. Eliezer says, 'Even [if the blood of a sin-offering spurted onto a hide] after it was flayed, lit does not require washing] [M. Zeb. 11:3E-F].'" Only that requires washing which is the [actual] place [on which] the blood [actually has fallen,] something which is suitable to receive uncleanness, and something which is suitable for washing [M. Zeb. 11:3G]. Where does one wash it? Inside [the courtyard]. [If] it went outside [the courtyard], one brings it inside and washes it.

M. 11:4 The same are the cloth and the sackcloth and the hide: they require washing. And the washing must be in a holy place [Lev. 6:20]. And the breaking of earthenware utensils [in which a sin offering is cooked] is [to be] in a holy place. And the scouring and rinsing in the case of a copper utensil [are to be] in a holy place. In this matter the [rule] is more strict in the case of the sin offering than in the case of Most Holy Things.

M. 11:5 A garment which went forth outside of the veils is brought back, and one washes it in a holy place. [If] it was made unclean [while] outside of the veils, one tears it, and it is brought back, and one washes it in a holy place. An earthenware utensil which went forth outside of the veils is brought back, and one breaks it in a holy place. [If] it was made unclean outside of the veils, one makes a hole in it, and it is brought back, and one breaks it in a holy place.

M. 11:6 A copper utensil which went forth outside of the veils is brought back, and one scours it and rinses it in a holy place. [If] it was made unclean outside of the veils, one breaks it down, and it is brought back and one scours and rinses it in a holy place.

T. 10:12 Utensils made of dried dung and utensils made of stone and utensils made of earth do not require scouring and rinsing, but [only] washing up [M. Zeb. 11:3G]. Earthenware utensils require only breaking. Where does he break it? Inside [the courtyard]. [If] it went outside, one brings it back inside and breaks it [M. Zeb. 11:5C-D].

M. 11:7 All the same are one in which one has cooked and one into which one has poured boiling [stew], [and] all the same are one [used] for Most Holy Things [e.g., a sin offering or a guilt offering] and one for Lesser Holy Things [e.g., peace offerings]: they require scouring and rinsing. R. Simeon says, "Those used for Lesser Holy Things do not require scouring and rinsing." R. Tarfon says, "If one cooked in it from the beginning of the festival, he cooks therein throughout the festival." And sages say, "At the end of the time [which is permissible] for eating [the offering], [the pot is subject to] scouring and rinsing." Scouring [is done] as is the scouring of a cup. And rinsing [is done as is] the rinsing of a cup [on the outside]. Scouring is done with hot water, and rinsing is done with cold water. And the spit and the grill [used for a sin offering] does one put into scalding water.

T. 10.11 R. Simeon says, "Those used for Lesser Holy Things do not require scouring and rinsing [M. Zeb. 11:7C]." "But they do require washing out, because [of the possibility that that which is more holy has] imparted [its] flavor." [Utensils used for the cooking of the meat of] invalid sheep do not require scouring and rinsing. R. Jacob says, "[If] they had a moment of validity and became invalid, they do [delete: not] require scouring and rinsing." R. Simeon says, "Even though they had a moment of validity and then became invalid, they do not require scouring and rinsing."

T. 10:13 R. Tarfon says, "[If] one cooked in it at the beginning of the festival, one cooks in it throughout the festival [M. Zeb. 11:7D]. After the festival it does not require scouring and rinsing." Said R. Nathan, "R. Tarfon stated this rule only in connection with Lesser Holy Things alone." Where does one scour and rinse them? Inside [the courtyard]. [If] it went forth, one brings them back and scours and rinses them inside. [If] they were made unclean outside, one renders them clean and brings them back and then scours and rinses them inside [M. Zeb. 11:6B].

T. 10:14 How is their scouring and rinsing [done]? In the place in which [what is cooked in] them is eaten [there are done] their scouring and their rinsing. At [the end of the] time [which is permissible] for eating [the offering cooked in them], [the pot is subject to] scouring and rinsing [M. Zeb. 11:7B].

M. 11:8 [If] one cooked in it Holy Things and unconsecrated food, or Most Holy Things and Lesser Holy Things, if they were [sufficient] to impart flavor, Lo, that [the rule of which is] less [stringent] is eaten in accord with [that the rule of which] is the more stringent [thus applying to the more holy things]. And [if they do not impart flavor] they do [not] require scouring and rinsing, and [if the invalid proportion of the mixture does not impart flavor], they do not invalidate merely by having made contact. An [unfit] wafer which touched [another] wafer, or a piece of meat [which touched] another piece of meat — not the whole of the wafer or the whole of the piece(s) [of meat] is prohibited. Prohibited is only the place which absorbed [that which is forbidden].

T. 10:14 [If] one cooked in it [a pot] Most Holy Things, one scours and rinses [at the time at which it no longer is permitted to eat] Most Holy Things [M. Zeb. 11:8B]. [If one cooked in it] Lesser Holy Things, one scours and rinses [the pot at the time at which it no longer is permitted to eat] Lesser Holy Things. [If] one cooked in it Most Holy Things and Lesser Holy Things, one scours and rinses [the pot at the time at which it no longer is permitted to eat] the more strict of the two. [If] one rinsed but did not scour, scoured but did not rinse, one should eat [what is left in the pot] in accord with the rule governing the more stringent of the two of them.

T. 10:15 A strict rule applies to [blood for] sprinkling [which spurts onto a garment] which does not apply to scouring and rinsing, and [a strict rule applies] to scouring and rinsing which does not apply to [blood used for] sprinkling [which spurts onto a garment]. For [the law concerning the splattering of blood used for] sprinkling applies to sin-offerings which are offered on the inner altar and applies before the [actual] sprinkling of the blood, which is not the case with scouring and rinsing. The strict rule which applies to scouring and rinsing is that scouring and rinsing apply to Most Holy Things and to Lesser Holy Things. And if only part of a utensil is used for cooking, the whole utensil requires scouring and rinsing, which is not the case with [blood used for] sprinkling [which spurts onto a garment].

Scripture's facts are subjected to the generic hermeneutics of the Halakhah: exposition. The Halakhah takes up familiar interstitial problems, e.g., M. 11:2ff., M. 11:8, and interstitial cases, e.g., M. 11:5f., of various kinds, e.g., what if the blood that spurted is not of the status of which Scripture speaks, does it require washing? As usual, the Tosefta refines and improves, thus at T. 10:9 the Tosefta homogenizes what the Mishnah has differentiated.

E. *THE DIVISION AMONG THE ELIGIBLE PRIESTS OF THE MEAT AND HIDES OF SACRIFICIAL ANIMALS*

M. 12:1 (1) A priest who has immersed and awaits sunset to complete his purification rite [= a tebul-yom] and one whose atonement is not yet complete do not share in Holy Things, eating them in the evening. (2) a priest who has suffered a bereavement may touch [Holy Things] but does not make offerings and does not share [in Holy Things], eating them in the evening. (3) Blemished [priests], whether suffering permanent blemishes or temporary blemishes, share and eat [in Holy Things in the evening], but they do not offer up [sacrifices]. (1) And whoever is not fit for the [sacrificial] service does not share in the meat. (2) And whoever does not have [a portion of] the meat has no portion in the hides [Lev. 7:8], even [a priest who is] unclean at the time of the tossing of the blood but clean at the time of the burning of the fat does not share in the meat, as it is said, "He among the sons of Aaron who offers the blood of peace offerings and fat shall have the right thigh for a portion" (Lev. 7:33).

T. 11:1 A priest who mourns his next of kin is not permitted to bring animal-offerings all seven days [of the period of mourning] [M. Zeb. 12:1B]. All the same are sacrifices which are suitable to come as a freewill-offering and sacrifices which are not suitable to come as a freewill-offering, even wine, even wood, and even frankincense, as it is said, Peace-offerings [Lev. 3:6: And if his offering for a sacrifice of peace-offerings]. R. Simeon says, "Peace-offerings [are so-called because] all are at peace in them: Part of them are for the altar, and part of them for the priests, and part of them for the owner."

T. 11:2 The animal-sacrifices of thank-offering — Lo, this is a thankoffering under all circumstances, as it is said, "He who brings a thank-offering as his sacrifice honors me; to him who orders his way aright, I will show the salvation of God" (Ps. 50:23).

T. 11:3 "A high priest offers [sacrifices] while he is a mourner, but does not eat [the flesh of the sacrifice]," the words of R. Meir [M. Zeb. 12:1B]. R. Judah says, "That entire day." R. Simeon says, "He finishes the act of sacrifice for which he is responsible and goes forth." But an ordinary priest who was standing and making an offering and suffered a bereavement leaves off the act of sacrifice for which he is responsible and goes forth. Therefore, if he tossed the blood or burned the incense for the act of sacrifice which he has carried out, Lo, these [actions] are invalid.

T. 11:6 The adult [priest] takes a share, even though he is blemished [M. Zeb. 12:1C]. The minor [priest] does not take a share, even though he is unblemished. When is a minor fit to take a share of the Holy Things of the sanctuary? When he will produce two pubic hairs. But they do not bring him near [to participate in] the sacrificial service until his 'beard' is full. Rabbi says, "I say, Until he will be twenty-years old and thereafter: They appointed the Levites from twenty years old and upward, to have the oversight of the work of the house of the Lord (Ezra 3:8)."

M. 12:2 Of any [burnt offering], the meat of which the altar has not acquired [e.g., which was invalidated before the blood was tossed] — the priests do not acquire a right to the hide, as it is said, "A man's burnt offering" (Lev. 7:8) — a burnt offering which has been burned to the credit of a man. A burnt offering which was slaughtered for some purpose other than that for which the beast was originally designated ["not for its own name"], even though it has not gone for the credit of the owner — its hide belongs to the priests [because the altar has acquired its meat]. All the same are the burnt offering of a man and the burnt offering of a woman — their hides belong to the priests.

T. 11:4 All sin-offerings, the blood of which is taken inside — the priests have no right to any part of them at all [M. Zeb. 12:2A]. But the blood and the sacrificial parts belong to the altar. And the hide and the flesh go out to the place of burning [M. Zeb. 12:2B]. Where do they burn them? In the great place of ashes outside of Jerusalem and to the north of Jerusalem, outside of the three camps. And they did not burn them whole, but they would chop them up on their hide like pieces of burnt-offerings.

T. 11:5 The priests do not take a share of meat instead of [some other] meat, or of fowl instead of [some other] fowl, of meat instead of fowl, of fowl instead of meal-offerings, or meal-offerings instead of [other] meal-offerings, as it is said, "And every cereal offering, mixed with oil or dry, shall be for all the sons of Aaron, one as well as another" (Lev. 7:10).

T. 11:8 [If] one slaughtered it [with the intention of burning the sacrificial parts or eating the meat] outside of its proper time or outside of its proper place since the altar has not acquired its meat, the priests do not acquire its hide [M. Zeb. 12:2A-B]. "A burnt-offering which is sanctified — its hide does not belong to the priests," the words of R. Judah. And sages say, "Its hide belongs to the priests." R. Yosé b. R. Judah adds, "Even that of proselytes, women, and slaves, as it is said, 'The sin-offering of a man' (Lev. 7:8) — excluding these." They said to him, "Has it not already been stated, 'And the priest who offers any man's burnt-offering shall have for himself the skin of the burnt-offering which he has offered' (Lev. 7:8) — If so, why has it been said, 'The burnt-offering of a man'? But: a burnt-offering which has gone up for a man's credit — its hide belongs to the priests. And that which has not gone up to a man's credit — its hide does not belong to the priests."

M. 12:3 The hides of Lesser Holy Things belong to the owner, and the hides of Most Holy Things belong to the priests. And [this proposition is supported by] an argument *a fortiori:* now if the burnt offering, the meat of which does not belong to the priests, produces a hide that belongs to them, Most Holy Things, the meat of which does belong to the priests, all the more so should produce hides which belong to them. The altar itself does not prove the contrary, because it has no portion in the hide under any circumstances.

T. 11:7 The burnt-offering belongs wholly to the Most High, but its hide belongs to the priests. Most Holy Things: The blood and sacrificial parts belong to the altar, and the meat and hide to the priests. Lesser Holy Things: The blood and sacrificial parts belong to the altar, and the hide and meat belong to the owner. This is the general principle: Whoever has a share in the meat has a share in the hides. Whoever does not have a share in the meat does not have a share in the hides [M. Zeb. 12:1E], except for the burnt-offering, concerning which Scripture explicitly supplied the rule: "And the priest who offers any man's burnt-offering shall have for himself the hide of the burnt-offering which he has offered" (Lev. 7:8).

M. 12:4 All Holy Things [burnt offering, sin offering, guilt offering] which suffered an invalidity before they were flayed — their hides do not belong to the priests. [If an invalidity was incurred] after they were flayed, their hides belong to the priests. Said R. Hananiah, Prefect of the Priests, "In all my days I never saw a hide taken out to the place of burning." Said R. Aqiba, "From his statement we learn: 'he who flays the firstling [which was blemished and slaughtered] [that is, it was disqualified even before flaying] and it turns out to be terefah — the priests make use of its hide.'" And sages say, "We have not seen is no proof. But: It goes forth to the place of burning."

T. 11:9 [If] one slaughtered it and did not flay it and did not have time to toss the blood before the blood was made unclean, or [if] one slaughtered it and flayed it, and did not have time to toss the blood before the blood was made unclean — the blood is [not] tossed, and the hide and meat are prohibited [M. Zeb. 12:4A]. If the blood is tossed, the hide and the flesh are permitted.

T. 11:10 [If] one slaughtered it and did not flay it and did not have time to toss the blood before the sacrifice was made unclean, the hide is prohibited. [If] one slaughtered it and flayed it, and the sacrifice (hide) was made unclean, and afterward one tossed the blood, the hide is permitted, the words of Rabbi. R. [Eleazar b. R.] Simeon says, "The hide is prohibited."

T. 11:11 [If] one slaughtered it and did not flay it, tossed the blood, and afterward the sacrifice was made unclean, the hide is prohibited. R. Eleazar b. R. Simeon says, "Let him flay the hide from the meat." [If] one slaughtered it and flayed it, tossed the blood, and afterward the sacrifice was made unclean, all agree that the hide is permitted.

T. 11:12 [If] one slaughtered it and did not flay it and did not have time to toss the blood before the blood went forth [beyond the veils], or [if] one slaughtered it and flayed it and did not have time to toss the blood before the blood went forth [beyond the veils], the blood is [not] to be tossed. The hide and the flesh are prohibited. And even though the blood is tossed, the hide and meat are prohibited. [If] one slaughtered it and did not flay it, and did not have time to toss the blood until the sacrifice went forth (remained overnight), the hide is prohibited.

T. 11:13 [If] one slaughtered it and flayed it and the sacrifice went outside [the veils] and afterward one tossed the blood, the hide is permitted, the words of Rabbi. R. Eleazar b. R. Simeon says, "The hide is prohibited." [If] one slaughtered it and did not flay it and tossed the blood and afterward the sacrifice went outside [the veils], the hide is prohibited, the words of Rabbi. R. Eleazar b. R. Simeon says, "Let him flay the hide with the meat." [If] one slaughtered it and flayed it and tossed the blood and afterward the sacrifice went forth [beyond the veils], all agree that the hide is permitted.

T. 11:14 [If] one slaughtered it and did not flay it and did not have time to toss the blood before the blood went forth [beyond the veils] or [if] one slaughtered it and flayed it and did not have time to toss the blood before the blood was kept overnight, the blood is [not] to be tossed. The hide and the flesh are prohibited. And even though the blood is tossed, the hide and the meat are prohibited. [If] one slaughtered it and did not flay it and did not have time to toss the blood before the sacrifice was kept overnight, the hide is prohibited. [If] one slaughtered it and did not flay it and the sacrifice remained overnight, and afterward one tossed the blood, it is prohibited, the words of Rabbi. R. Eleazar b. R. Simeon says, "Let him flay the hide from the flesh." [If] one slaughtered it and flayed it and tossed the blood and afterward the sacrifice remained overnight, all agree that the hide is permitted.

T. 11:15 Rabbi says, "The blood effects appeasement for the hide by itself [that is, when it already has been flayed from the meat]. When it is with the meat, [however, that is, before it is flayed] [if] an invalidity occurs in it, whether before the tossing of the blood or after the tossing of the blood, lo, it follows its [the meat's] status." R. Eleazar b. R. Simeon says, "The blood does not effect atonement for the hide by itself [that is, even when it has been flayed from the meat]. When it is with the meat [before flaying], [if] the blood has been tossed [properly] for it, it has been accepted for one moment. Therefore, if an invalidity occurs in it, even after the tossing of the blood, let him flay the hide from the meat [and make full use of it.]"

T. 11:16 At first they would bring in the hides of Holy Things to the chamber of the Bet Happarwah and would divide them in the evening among all the priestly families of that day. But the powerful men of the priesthood would come and grab them by force. They ordained that they should divide them on Fridays among each and every watch. But still did the powerful men of the priesthood come and grab them by force. The owners, thereupon, went and sanctified them to heaven.

T. 11:17 Abba Saul says, "Poles of sycamore were in Jericho, and strong men take them. They went and sanctified them [to heaven]." They said, "The owners sanctified to heaven only poles of sycamore alone."

M. 12:5 Bullocks which are to be burned and goats which are to be burned [M. 5:1-2, Lev. 4:3, 13-14, 16:9, Num. 15:24], when they are [valid and therefore] to be burned in accord with their requirement [and have not been invalidated], are burned in the place of ashes. And they [who burn them] impart uncleanness to [their] clothing [Lev. 16:28]. And if they are [invalid and therefore] not burned in accord with their requirement, they are burned in the Temple precincts. And they do not impart uncleanness to the clothing [of the one who handles them and burns them].

M. 12:6 They would carry them on poles. [If] the foremost [bearers] went outside the wall, and the latter did not [yet] go outside the wall, the former impart uncleanness to clothing, and the latter do not impart uncleanness to clothing-until they [actually] go forth. [If] both went forth, these and those impart uncleanness to clothing. R. Simeon says, "These and those [who are to burn the bullocks or goats] do not impart uncleanness to clothing until [they actually do the burning so that] the flame will take hold of their [the carcasses] greater part." [When] the meat has been wholly burned [to ashes], the one who burns it no longer imparts uncleanness to clothing [which he wears].

T. 11:18 Bullocks which are to be burned and goats which are to be burned, when they are burned in accord with their requirement, are burned in the place of ashes. And they [who burn them] impart uncleanness to [their] clothing. And if they are not burned in accord with their requirement they are burned in the Bet Habbirah. And they do not impart uncleanness to clothing [M. Zeb. 12:5]. R. Yosé the Galilean says, "In the great house of ashes did they burn them — even with straw, even with stubble even with chips. And even if the fire has caught only the greater part of it, Lo, these are valid [that is, the rite of burning is deemed suitably begun]" [M. Zeb. 12:6F].

Another free-standing component carries us to the issue of how to define those priests that share the task of consuming, along with God, the meat of the Holy Things. Forthwith, interstitiality — not valid now, but valid later on, not valid to participate in the work now, but valid later on, as against not valid at all, neither now nor later — defines the active considerations. Then, again, M. 12:2, 4, if the altar has not acquired the offering, the priests do not acquire the hide.

IV. THE PROPER LOCATION OF THE ALTAR AND THE ACT OF SACRIFICE PERFORMED THEREON

A. *OFFERINGS OUTSIDE OF THE TEMPLE COURTYARD AND LIABILITY THEREFOR*

M. 13:1 He who outside [the Temple courtyard] [both] slaughters [Holy Things] and offers up [Holy Things] is liable [on both counts, namely:] for the act of slaughtering and is liable for the act of offering up. R. Yosé the Galilean says, "[If] inside [the Temple courtyard] he slaughtered [the animal], but outside [the Temple courtyard] he offered it up, he is liable. [If] he both slaughtered outside and offered up outside, he is free [of liability for the offering up]. For he has offered up outside only something which [in any event] is invalid. [Having been slaughtered outside, it could not have been offered inside anyhow]." They said to him, "Also: He who slaughters inside and offers up outside, since he took it outside, has invalidated it [and so too consistency would require]."

T. 12:1 Rabbi says, "There is a difference between [the case of one] who slaughters inside and offers up outside and [that of one] who slaughters outside and offers up outside. For he who slaughters inside and offers up outside — it [the offering] had a moment of validity. But he who slaughters outside and offers up outside — it [the offering] never had a moment of validity." R. Eleazar b. R. Simeon says, "There is a difference between [the case of one] who slaughters inside and offers up outside and [the case of one] who slaughters outside and offers up outside. For he who slaughters inside and offers up outside — the sanctuary accepts it. He who slaughters outside and offers up outside — the sanctuary does not accept it" [M. Zeb. 13:1].

M. 13:2 An unclean person who ate either unclean Holy Things or clean Holy Things, is liable. R. Yosé the Galilean says, "An unclean person who ate clean [Holy Things] is liable. But an unclean person who ate unclean [Holy Things] is free [of liability]. For he ate only something [of Holy Things] which [in any event] is unclean." They said to him, "Also: The unclean person who ate clean [Holy Things], since he touched it, has rendered it unclean." And a clean person who ate unclean [Holy Things] is free of liability on that count, for he is liable only on account of the contamination of the body.

M. 13:3 A more strict rule applies to slaughtering [animals designated as Holy Things outside of the Temple] than to offering up [offerings outside of the Temple], and to offering up [offerings outside of the Temple] than to slaughtering. More strict is [the rule which applies] in the case of slaughtering [animals designated as Holy Things outside of the Temple]: For one who slaughters [animals designated as Holy Things outside of the Temple] [in behalf of] an ordinary person [instead of God!] is liable. But one who offers up [offerings outside of the Temple] for [the use, e.g., the eating] of an ordinary person is free. More strict is [the rule which applies] in the case of offering up [offerings outside of the Temple]: two who took hold of a knife and slaughtered [with it] are free of liability. [If] they took hold of a limb and offered it up, they are liable. "[If] one offered up [offerings outside of the Temple] and went and offered up [again] [offerings outside of the Temple] and went and offered up [again] [offerings outside of the Temple], he is liable [to bring a sin offering] for each and every act of offering up [offerings outside of the Temple]," the words of R. Simeon. R. Yosé says, "He is liable only for one [act of offering up] [offerings outside of the Temple]." And he is liable only when he will offer up on the top of the altar [which he has built outside]. R. Simeon says, "Even if he offered up on a rock or on a stone, he is liable."

T. 12:1 It is not possible for one to slaughter after another has slaughtered [the same animal], but there can be a case in which one offers up after another has offered up [parts of the same animal] [M. Zeb. 13:3C-D].

T. 12:2 [If] two slaughtered it, they are free. [If] two offered it up, they are liable. [If] one offered it up and went and offered it up again, he is liable for each and every act of offering up. The words of R. Simeon. R. Yosé says, "He is liable only for one [such action] [M.

Zeb. I 3:3H-1]. And one is liable only if he will build an altar and arrange [the wood]," the words of R. Yosé and R. Simeon says, "Even if he offered it up on a stone or on a rock, he is liable" [M. Zeb. 13:3K].

M. 13:4 All the same are valid Holy Things and invalid Holy Things, the invalidation of which took place inside the sanctuary [M. 9:2], and which one offered up outside — the one who does so is liable. He who offers up as much as an olive's bulk of flesh of a burnt offering and of the sacrificial parts outside [the courtyard] is liable. (1) The handful, and (2) the frankincense, and (3) the incense, and (4) the meal-offering of priests, and (5) the meal-offering of the anointed priest, and (6) the meal-offering which goes along with drink offerings, an olive's bulk of one of which one offered up outside of the Temple — he is liable. R. Eleazar declares him free of liability, until he offers up the entire [volume of the meal-offering]. And all of them which one offered up inside, and of which one left as residue an olive's bulk, which one offered up outside — he is liable. And all of them which lacked any [of the requisite] amount at all, which one offered up outside — he is free [of liability, since offering them inside is invalid in any event].

T. 12:3 A burnt-offering, the burnt-offering of fowl, the fat, the handful of the meal-offering the frankincense, the meal-offering of priests, the meal-offering of the anointed priest, and the meal-offering which goes along with drink-offerings, an olive's bulk of one of which one has offered up outside — he is liable. R. Eleazar declares free until he will offer up the entire quantity [M. Zeb. 13:4D-E]. R. Eleazar agrees that if he offered up [most of the stated item] inside and left an olive's bulk over as residue and offered it up outside, that he is liable [M. Zeb. 13:4F], for so it is appropriate to be offered inside [M. Zeb. 13:8C].

T. 12:7 The burnt-offering, the burnt-offering of fowl, the fat, the handful [of meal-offering], the frankincense, the meal-offering of priests, the meal-offering of the anointed priest, and the meal-offering which comes with drink-offerings, a half-olive's bulk of any one of which one has offered up [outside] — he is free [M. Zeb. 13:4D].

B. 13:4D-H, 13:5A/109B HE WHO BURNS UP AN OLIVE'S BULK OF INCENSE OUTSIDE OF THE TEMPLE IS LIABLE; IF HE BURNED HALF OF WHAT WAS ACTUALLY THE REQUISITE VOLUME OF INCENSE PRESENTED DAILY, MORNING AND EVENING, HE IS NOT LIABLE.

M. 13:5 He who offers up Holy Things and their [unsevered] sacrificial parts outside is liable. A meal-offering from which the handful had not been taken, which one offered up outside — he is free of liability. [If] he took up the handful and put back the handful, and he offered it up outside, he is liable.

M. 13:6 The handful and the frankincense, one of the two of which one offered up outside — he is liable [since either one alone is suitable for offering inside on its own]. R. Eleazar declares free of liability unless he offers up the second [as well, M. 13:4E]. [If he offered up] one inside [first] and one outside [afterward], he is liable. Two dishes of frankincense, one of which one offered outside-he is liable. R. Eleazar declares exempt unless he offers up the second. [If he offered up] one inside [first] and [then] one outside [afterward], he is liable. He who tosses [even only] part of the blood [on an altar] outside [of the Temple] is liable. R. Eleazar says, "Also: he who offers the water libation of the Festival [of Sukkot] on the festival [on an altar] outside [of the Temple] is liable." R. Nehemiah says, "The residue of the blood [of sin offerings of the inner altar (M. 5:1-3)] which one offered up [on an altar] outside [of the Temple] — he is liable."

T. 12:4 The handful and the frankincense one of which one offered outside — he is liable. And R. Eleazar declares free [until he will offer] the second. R. Eleazar agrees that if he offered up one inside and left its fellow and offered it up outside, that he is liable [M. Zeb. 13:6A-C] for so it is appropriate to be offered inside.

T. 12:5 Two dishes of frankincense, one of which one offered outside — he is liable. R. Eleazar declares free, until he will offer the second [as well]. R. Eleazar agrees that if he offered up one of them inside and left its fellow and offered it up outside, that he is liable [M. Zeb. 13:6D-F], for so it is appropriate to be offered inside. R. Eleazar agrees in the case of the handful of the meal-offering of a sinner and the frankincense given as a thank-offering which one offered up outside, that he is liable, for so it is appropriate to be offered inside.

T. 12:6 He who offers as a libation three logs of wine outside is liable. R. Eleazar b. R. Simeon says, "Unless he sanctifies it in a utensil, he is free of liability. Once he has sanctified it in a utensil, he is liable." He who pours out as a libation three logs of water on the Festival [of Sukkot] outside is liable. [If he does so] on the other days of the year, he is free. R. Eleazar says, "Even in the case of the Festival, if [the jug] was filled for the sake of the festival, he is liable. But if not, he is exempt" [M. Zeb. 13:6H].

T. 12:7 And he who pours out as a libation outside [the Temple] less than three logs of water, [or] less than three logs of wine is free. R. Nehemiah says, "The residue of the blood — they are liable on their account [if they have sprinkled it] outside" [M. Zeb. 13:6]. Said R. Jacob, "And are they not merely the residue [minor details] of the commandment? How are people liable for [not properly performing] the residue of the commandment?" Said R. Nehemiah, "The burning of the fats will prove the matter For they are the residue of the commandment, and people are liable on their account [for burning them] outside." Said to him R. Jacob, "Even though they are the residue of the commandment, they [derive in importance from] the beginning of the sacrificial act."

M. 13:7 He who pinches the neck of fowl inside the Temple and offered it up outside the Temple is liable [since pinching the neck is the valid means of slaughtering the bird for sacrificial purposes, and that was correctly done]. **[If] he pinched the neck outside the Temple and offered it up outside the Temple, he is free.** [Pinching the neck is done only to kill the bird as a sacrifice; since this was done outside of the Temple, it is null.] **He who slaughters fowl inside the Temple and offered it up outside the Temple is free. [If] he slaughtered it outside the Temple and offered it up outside the Temple, he is liable. It turns out that the way of rendering it suitable** [=killing the bird as a sacrifice, by pinching the neck] **inside the Temple is that which frees it from penalty outside the Temple, and the way of rendering it suitable outside the Temple** [=slaughter for eating unconsecrated fowl] **is that which frees it from penalty inside the Temple. R. Simeon says, "Any act for which they are liable [when it is done] outside the Temple, for the like act are they liable [when it is done] inside the Temple and when one offered it up outside the Temple, except for him who slaughters inside the Temple and offers up [the bird offering] outside the Temple."**

T. 12:8 A sin-offering of fowl which is brought on account of doubt and which one offered up outside — they are liable on its account [to bring] a suspensive guilt-offering. A suspensive guilt-offering which is brought on account of doubt — [if] they offered it up outside, they are liable on its account [to bring] a sin-offering.

M. 13:8 A sin offering, the blood of which one received in a single cup, and [the blood of which] one [first] placed [on an altar] outside, and then placed [on an altar] inside, [or placed] [on an altar] inside and then placed [on an altar] outside — he is liable, for all of it is suitable to come [to be placed on the altar] inside. [If] one received its blood in two cups, and placed [the blood of] both of them [on an altar] inside, he is free. [If he placed] the blood of both of them [on an altar] outside, he is liable. [If he placed the blood of] one of them [on an altar] inside and [then placed the blood of] one of them [on an altar] outside, he is free [for the latter no longer is suitable to come inside]. **[If he placed the blood of] one of them [on an altar] outside and [then] one of them [on an altar] inside, he is liable for that which he has placed [on an altar] outside, but the one [the blood of which he then**

placed] [on an altar] inside effects atonement. To what is the matter to be likened? To him who separates his sin offering, and it was lost, and he separated another in its place, and afterward the first one turned up, so that, lo, both of them are now available [and he may slaughter either of them]. [If] he slaughtered both of them [on an altar] inside, he [obviously] is free [of liability]. [If] he slaughtered both of them [on an altar] outside, he [obviously] is liable. [If he slaughtered] one [on an altar] inside and one [on an altar] outside, he is free. [If he slaughtered] one [on an altar] outside and the other [on an altar] inside, he is liable for the one [the blood of which he placed] he has placed [on an altar] outside, but the one which he sacrifices [on an altar] inside effects atonement. Just as [the sprinkling of] its blood renders its meat free [from the law of sacrilege], so it renders the meat of its fellow free.

T. 12:9 A burnt-offering, the blood of which one received in a single cup [if] he placed the blood inside and went and placed the blood outside and went and placed the blood inside — he is liable [for the one placed outside], for all of it is suitable to be brought inside. [If] he received its blood in two cups [and] placed [the blood of both of them inside, he is free. [If he placed the blood of] both of them outside, he is liable. [If he placed the blood of one of them inside and [the blood of the] other outside, he is free [M. Zeb. 13:8B-F]. [If he placed] one outside and one inside, (if) the one placed on the inner altar has effected atonement. He is liable for that which [he has placed] outside [M. Zeb. 13:8G,H]. To what is the matter comparable? To one who has set aside his sin-offering. It was lost, Then he went and set aside another in its place. And afterward the first was found.

T. 12:10 [If] he slaughtered both of them inside he is free. [If he slaughtered] both of them outside, he is liable. [If he slaughtered] one inside and one outside [or] one outside and one inside, that which he has slaughtered inside has effected atonement. He is liable for that which he has slaughtered outside [M. Zeb. 13:8I-K]. [If] he slaughtered it, and Lo, the blood is located in [two] cups [if] he put [the blood of] both of them inside, he is free. [If he put the blood of] both of them outside, [or] one of them inside and one of them outside, he is free. [If he put] one of them outside and one of them inside, [if] the one which he put inside has effected atonement. He is liable [for that placed outside].

T. 12:11 The offspring of a sin-offering and the substitute of a sin-offering and a sin-offering, the owner of which died — [he who] offers them up outside is free. [If] the owner [had already] effected atonement, or [if] it became superannuated, or [if] it was lost and then found before its owner effected atonement, [he who offers them up outside] is liable. [If this happens] after the owner has effected atonement, he is free.

M. 14:1 [On account of] a [red] cow for purification [ashes] [Num. 19:9] that one burned outside of its pit — and so: a goat to be sent forth that one offered outside of the Temple — he is free, as it is said, "To the door of the tent of meeting he did not bring it" (Lev.17:4) — For whatever is not appropriate to come to the door of the tent of meeting they are not liable [if such a classification of offering is carried out outside of the Temple].

M. 14:2 (1) The animal which had sexual relations with a human, and (2) the animal with which a human had sexual relations, and (3) the animal set aside for idolatrous worship, and (4) the animal which had been worshipped, and (5) the animal used for the hire of a harlot, and (6) the animal used to pay for a dog, and (7) the crossbred animal, and (8) the animal which turns out to be terefah, and (9) the animal which went forth from the side [M. 8:1], which one offered outside — he is free, as it is said, "Before the altar of the Lord" (Lev. 17:4) — Whatever is not appropriate [to come] before the altar of the Lord — they are not liable on its account. Blemished animals, whether permanently blemished or temporarily blemished, which one offered outside — he is free. R. Simeon says, "Permanently blemished animals [which one offered outside] — he is free. But temporarily blemished animals [which one offered outside] — they transgress a negative commandment [Dt. 12:8, 13]." Turtledoves whose time had not yet come and young pigeons whose time had passed, which one offered outside — he is free. R. Simeon says, "Pigeons whose time had passed [which he offered up outside) — he is free, Turtledoves whose time had not yet come [which he offered up out-side] — [they transgress] a negative commandment." (1) It and its offspring [Lev. 22:28: And whether the mother is a cow or a ewe, you shall not kill both her and her young in one day], and that (2) [within seven days of birth, Ex. 22:29] whose time [to be offered] had not yet come [which one offered outside] — he is free. R. Simeon says, "Lo, this one has transgressed a negative commandment." For R. Simeon did say, "Whatever is appropriate to come at a later time, Lo, this one has transgressed a negative commandment, but extirpation does not apply to it." And sages say, "Whatever is not subject to extirpation is not subject to a negative commandment."

T. 12:12 Bullocks which are to be burned and goats which are to be burned which one offered up outside — he is free [M. Zeb. 14:1A]. A dam and its offspring [Ex. 22:29] which one offered outside — he is liable for the first and free [of liability] on account of the second. R. Simeon says, "To the second a negative commandment applies [which he has transgressed, and he, therefore, is liable on that account]" [M. Zeb. 14:2N-P].

M. 14:3 [An animal] whose time had not yet come — whether in itself or in respect to its owner. What is an offering whose time had not yet come in respect to its owner? The Zab, and the Zabah, and the woman who has given birth, and the person afflicted with the skin ailment, who [during their time of counting clean days] offered their sin offering and [solely in the case of the person afflicted with the skin ailment of Lev. 13] — their guilt offering outside are free [since the offerings serve neither to fulfill an obligation nor to be counted as a thank offering]. [If they offered] their burnt offerings and [in the case of the Nazirite] their peace offering outside, they are liable. He who offers up (1) part of the flesh of a sin offering, (2) part of the flesh of a guilt offering, (3) part of the flesh of Most Holy Things, (4) part of the flesh of Lesser Holy Things, (5) the residue of the omer, and the two breads, and the showbread, and (6) the residue of meal-offerings [all of which are eaten by the priests, not offered on the altar] — he who (1) pours out [oil over the meal-offering], he who (2) mixes [meal with the oil], he who (3) breaks [meal-offering cakes] into pieces, he who (4) salts [meal-offering], he who (5) waves [it], he who (6) brings it near [opposite the southwest corner of the altar], he who (7) arranges [the bread on table], he who (8) trims the lamps, he who (9) takes the handful, he who (10) receives the blood [none of which actions completes the sacrificial rite] — outside — is free. They are not liable on its account either (1) because of being alien [not being priest], or (2) because of uncleanness, or (3) because of lacking the proper vestments, or (4) because of having unwashed hands and feet.

T. 12:13 A burnt-offering [and one] whose time had not come in itself [M. Zeb. 14:2N(2)] — [if it was a sacrifice whose time had not yet come] in itself, he is free of obligation. [And if it was an offering whose time had not yet come] in respect to the owner he is liable. R. Simeon says, "[In the case of one whose time had not yet come] in itself, he is subject to a negative commandment." A sin-offering [and one] whose time had not yet come, whether in respect to itself or in respect to the owner — [he who offers up either of the forenamed] is free. R. Simeon says, "Lo, this one is subject to a negative commandment" [M. 14:3A-D].

T. 12:14 He who takes a handful [of meal-offering and he who receives its [an animal-sacrifice's] blood outside is free of liability [M. 14:3F(9-10)]. This is the general principle: Any action which is done on account of the sacrificial rite and which [produces something] suitable for offering inside — on its account are they liable [if they do it] outside. And any action which is not done on account of the sacrificial rite and which does not [produce something] suitable for offering inside — on its account are they not liable [if they do it] outside. o. R. Eleazar b. R. Simeon says, "Also: Anything which is done on account of the sacrificial rite and appropriate to be offered inside [if] a non-priest did a like action inside, he is liable, except for him who slaughters" [M. Zeb. 13:7].

T. 12:15 A priest who performed a sacrificial act while unclean [and] in the status of a Tebul Yom, and lacking proper priestly vestments, and lacking the completion of the rites of atonement, and with unwashed hands and feet, is liable only for one [penalty if at one and the same time he transgressed all of the afore-listed prohibitions].

T. 12:16 A non-priest who performed a sacrificial act while unclean [and] in the status of a Tebul Yom, lacking priestly vestments, and lacking the completion of the rites of atonement, and with unwashed hands and feet [also] is liable only for one [penalty].

T. 12:17 And these are the ones who are subject to the death-penalty: He who eats untithed food, and a non-priest who ate heave-offering, and an unclean priest who ate clean heave-offering, and a non-priest, one in the status of Tebul Yom, one lacking priestly vestments, one whose rites of atonement were not yet complete, and one with unwashed hands and feet, and those with unkempt hair, and those who were drunk, who served [at the altar] — all of them are subject to the death-penalty. But an uncircumcised [priest] and a priest in mourning, and one who was sitting down [while at the altar], Lo, these are subject to warning. "A blemished priest [who performed a sacrificial rite] is subject to the death penalty," the words of Rabbi. And sages say, "He is subject to the penalty for transgressing a negative commandment." He who deliberately carried out an act of sacrilege — Rabbi says, "He is subject to the death-penalty." And sages say, "He is subject to the penalty for transgressing a negative commandment."

T. 12:18 And these are actions on account of which they are liable to the death-penalty: [If] one tossed the blood in the innermost altar or, in the case of fowl he who drains the blood and offers up [the sacrificial parts] on the altar — he who pours out as a libation three logs of water or three logs of wine outside — Lo, these are liable to the death-penalty. But he who takes up the handful [of the meal-offering] and he who receives and conveys [the blood] — [if] the non-priest received, or the invalid person received [the blood] [or if] one received the blood in the left hand, [or if] one received the blood in an unconsecrated utensil, [or if one] put the drops of blood which are to be sprinkled below [the red line], above it, and those which are to be sprinkled above [the red line], below it, [or if one sprinkled] those which are to be sprinkled inside, outside, or those which are to be sprinkled outside inside, or [if] one slaughtered [with the intention of eating the meat or burning the sacrificial parts] outside of their proper time or outside of their proper place, the Passover and the sin-offering which one slaughtered not for their own names — Lo, these are subject to the penalty for transgressing a negative commandment.

The generic hermeneutics governs: the rule and its subdivisions, and how the variations in the cases are sorted out thereby. M. 13:3 provides a fine example of those subdivisions: slaughtering outside as against offering up outside the Temple, and the hierarchization of those subsets. So, too we find at M. 13:4 Holy Things, whether valid or invalid, that were invalidated inside the Temple and then offered up outside. Liability is incurred on both counts. What is suitable for offering inside on its own, even when mixed with something else suitable for offering inside on its own, carries liability for being offered outside, "since either one alone may be offered inside on its own" (M. 13:6). The best case is at M. 13:7 (with its formal counterpart at M. 13:8), which introduces the variables, fowl/neck-pinching/inside/outside, with the explicit result fully articulated, lest we lose our way: It turns out that the way of rendering it suitable [=killing the bird as a sacrifice, by pinching the neck] inside the Temple is that which frees it from penalty outside the Temple, and the way of rendering it suitable outside the Temple. What we have is yet another triumph of the generic hermeneutics.

B. *LOCATIONS OF THE ALTAR AND PROCEDURES AND RITES THAT PERTAINED THERETO*

M. 14:4 Before the tabernacle was set up, (1) the high places were permitted, and (2) [the sacrificial] service [was done by] the first born [Num. 3:12-13, 8:1618]. When the tabernacle was set up, (1) the high places were prohibited, and (2) the [sacrificial] service [was done by] priests. Most Holy Things were eaten within the veils, Lesser Holy Things [were eaten] throughout the camp of Israel.

M. 14:5 They came to Gilgal. The high places were permitted. Most Holy Things were eaten within the veils, Lesser Holy Things, anywhere.

M. 14:6 They came to Shilo. The high places were prohibited. (1) There was no roof beam there, but below was a house of stone, and hangings above it, and (2) it was "the resting place" [Dt. 12:9]. Most Holy Things were eaten within the veils, Lesser Holy Things and second tithe [were eaten] in any place within sight [of Shilo].

M. 14:7 They came to Nob and Gibeon. The high places were permitted. Most Holy Things were eaten within the veils, Lesser Holy Things, in all the towns of Israel.

M. 14:8 They came to Jerusalem. The high places were prohibited. And they never again were permitted. And it was "the inheritance" [Dt. 12:9]. Most Holy Things were eaten within the veils, Lesser Holy Things and second tithe within the wall.

T. 13:1 Before the tabernacle was set up, the high places were permitted What did they [then] sacrifice? Cattle, beasts, and fowl, large and small, male and female, unblemished and blemished, clean, but not unclean. Everything was offered as a burnt-offering and required flaying and chopping up. The gentile at this time are permitted to do so.

T. 13:2 Before the tabernacle was set up, the high places were permitted, and the [sacrificial] service was done by first-born sons. When the tabernacle was set up, the high places were prohibited, and the [sacrificial] service was valid only [when done] by priests [M. Zeb. 14: 4A-B].

T. 13:3 Most Holy Things were eaten within the veils, Lesser Holy Things throughout the camps of Israel [M. Zeb. 14:4C]. He who puts [a sacrifice] on the altar when it is disassembled, or when the wind has raised the veil, has done nothing. [If he did so] at the time of journeying, Holy Things are invalidated. And as to the unclean, each one keeps separate within his designated area.

T. 13:4 They came to Gilgal. The high places were permitted. Most Holy Things were eaten within the veils, Lesser Holy Things, anywhere [M. Zeb. 14:5], the words of R. Judah. R. Simeon says, "In any place within sight [of the tabernacle]." What is the meaning of within sight? [A place from which] one sees without an intervening obstacle.

T. 13:5 They came to Nob and to Gibeon. The high places were permitted. Most Holy Things were eaten within the veils, and Lesser Holy Things any place [M. Zeb. 14:7] outside the veils, the words of R. Judah and R. Simeon says, "Any place in sight." What is the meaning of within sight? [A place from which] one sees without an intervening obstacle.

T. 13:6 The days of the tent of meeting which was in the wilderness were forty [years] less one, and in Gilgal, fourteen years, and in Shiloh, three hundred and seventy years less one and in Nob and Gibeon, fifty-seven. In the Eternal House, four hundred and ten years from the time that it was built the first time, four hundred and twenty years from the time that it was built the last time.

T. 13:20 "What is 'the rest' [Deut. 12:9]? This is Shiloh [M. Zeb. 14:6C]. And 'the inheritance'? This is Jerusalem [M. Zeb. 14:8D], as it is said, 'For you have not come as yet to the rest and to the inheritance' (Deut. 12:9). And it says, 'My inheritance is to me a painted bird' (Jer. 12:9). And it says, 'My inheritance was to me as a lion in the forest' (Jer. 12:8)," the words of R. Judah. R. Simeon says, "'Inheritance' refers to Shiloh. 'Rest' refers to Jerusalem. As it says, 'The Lord has chosen Zion. This is my resting place forever.

There I shall dwell, because I have desired it' (Ps. 132:13, 14)."

M. 14:9 All the Holy Things which one sanctified at the time of the prohibition of the high places and offered at the time of the prohibition of high places outside — Lo, these are subject to the transgression of a positive commandment and a negative commandment, and they are liable on their account to extirpation [for sacrificing outside the designated place, Lev. 17:8-9, M. 13:lA]. [If] one sanctified them at the time of the permission of high places and offered them up at the time of the prohibition of high places, Lo, these are subject to transgression of a positive commandment and to a negative commandment, but they are not liable on their account to extirpation [since if the offerings had been sacrificed when they were sanctified, there should have been no violation]. [If] one sanctified them at the time of the prohibition of high places and offered them up at the time of the permission of high places, Lo, these are subject to transgression of a positive commandment, but they are not subject to a negative commandment at all.

T. 13:7 Four general principles did R. Simeon teach in connection with Holy Things: "Whatever they have sanctified at the time of the prohibition [of high places] — he who offers it up outside [on a high place] is liable on account of a positive commandment and liable on account of a negative commandment and liable for extirpation [M. Zeb. 14:9A-B]. Whatever they have sanctified at the time of the permission [of high places] and slaughtered at the time of [their] prohibition — he who offers it up outside is liable for the transgression of an affirmative commandment and liable for the transgression of a negative commandment and free of the penalty of extirpation [M. Zeb. 14:9C]. Whatever they have sanctified at the time of the prohibition [of high places] and slaughtered at the time of their permission is liable for the transgression of a positive commandment and free of liability for the transgression of a negative commandment and free of the punishment of extirpation [M. Zeb. 14:9D-E]. Whatever they have sanctified at the time of the permission [of high places] and slaughtered at the time of permission is free of liability for the transgression of a positive commandment and free of liability for the transgression of a negative commandment and free of liability to extirpation. And Holy Things which they sanctified on a great high place and sacrificed on a small high place [fall into the foregoing category]." What is that sort of case in which they have sanctified [animals] at the time of the prohibition of high places and slaughtered at the time of the prohibition of high places [M. Zeb. 14:9A = B above]? Holy Things which they have sanctified for the tabernacle are to be offered in the tabernacle. Those which they have sanctified for Shiloh [are to be offered] in [Those which they have sanctified in the time of] the eternal house are to be offered in the eternal house. Therefore, he who offers them up outside is liable for the transgression of a positive commandment and liable for the transgression of a negative commandment and liable for extirpation [M. Zeb. 14:9B].

T. 13:8 What is the case in which they sanctified in the time of the permission [of high places] and slaughtered in the time of the prohibition of high places [= M. Zeb. 14:9C, T. 13:7C]. Holy Things which they sanctified are to be offered in the tabernacle, [thus:] [Holy Things which they sanctified to be offered] in Gilgal, and they came to Shiloh, are to be offered in Shiloh. [Holy Things which they sanctified to be offered] in Nob and in Gibeon [in both of which there was a tabernacle], and they came to the [eternal] house before the eternal tabernacle was set up, and then the eternal tabernacle was set up are to be offered in the eternal house. Therefore, he who offers it up outside is liable for the transgression of a positive commandment and liable for the transgression of a negative commandment and free of the penalty of extirpation [M. Zeb. 14:9C].

T. 13:9 What is the case in which they sanctified in the time of the prohibition of high places and slaughtered [the sacrifice] in the time of the permission [of high places] [M. Zeb. 14:9D = T. Zeb. 13:7D]? Holy Things which were sanctified in the time of the tabernacle, (when) they came to Gilgal, are to be offered up in Gilgal. [Holy Things which they sanctified in the time] of Shiloh when they came to Nob and Gibeon are to be offered up in Nob and in Gibeon. Therefore, he who offers them up outside is liable for the transgression of a positive commandment and free of liability for the transgression of a negative commandment [M. Zeb. 14:9E], and free of liability to extirpation [T. Zeb. 13:7D].

T. 13:10 What is the case in which they sanctified at the time of the permission of high places and slaughtered at the time of the permission of high places [T. Zeb. 13:7E]? Holy Things which they sanctified in Gilgal may be offered up in Gilgal. [If they were sanctified in] Nob and Gibeon, let them be offered up in Nob and in Gibeon. Therefore, he who offers them up outside, is free [of liability for transgression] of a positive commandment and free of liability for the transgression of a negative commandment and free of liability to extirpation [T. Zeb. 13:9E].

M. 14:10 These are the Holy Things offered in the tabernacle [of Gilgal, Nob, and Gibeon: Holy Things which were sanctified for the tabernacle]. Offerings of the congregation are offered in the tabernacle. Offerings of the individual [are offered] on a high place. Offerings of the individual which were sanctified for the tabernacle are to be offered in the tabernacle. And if one offered them up on a high place, he is free. What is the difference between the high place of an individual and the high place of the

community? (1) Laying on of hands, and (2) slaughtering at the north [of the altar], and (3) placing [of the blood] round about [the altar], and (4) waving, and (5) bringing near. R. Judah says, "There is no meal-offering on a high place [but there is in the tabernacle]" and (1) the priestly service, and (2) the wearing of garments of ministry, and (3) the use of utensils of ministry, and (4) the sweet-smelling savor and (5) the dividing line for the [tossing of various kinds of] blood, and (6) the rule concerning the washing of hands and feet. But the matters of time, and remnant, and uncleanness are applicable both here and there [by contrast to M. 14:3F-I].

T. 13:11 All are fit to offer a sacrifice on a high place even proselytes, even women, and even freed slaves.

T. 13:12 Whatever is subject to a vow or a freewill-offering is offered on the high place of an individual. Whatever is not subject to a vow or a freewill-offering is not offered on the high place of an individual, the words of R. Meir. And sages say, "Offered on the high place of an individual are only a burnt-offering and peace-offerings alone."

T. 13:13 As to the high place of an individual, there are no drink-offerings, the words of R. Meir. And sages say, "It requires drink-offerings." R. Judah says, "Anything which the community and the individual offer up in the tent of meeting which is in the wilderness do they offer up in the tent of meeting which is in Gilgal." [Continued at T. 13:14.]

T. 13:14 The only difference between the situation prevailing at the time of the tent of meeting which was in the wilderness and that at the time of the tent of meeting which was in Gilgal is that in the wilderness, there was no permission for high places [elsewhere], while in Gilgal there was permission for high places [elsewhere]. [Continued at T. 13:15.]

T. 13:15 [In the case of one who has] his high place on the top of his roof, the individual offers, thereon, only a burnt-offering and peace-offerings alone. And sages say, "Anything which the community offers in the tent of meeting which was in the wilderness do they offer in the tent of meeting which is in Gilgal. In both cases the individual offers on it only a burnt-offering and peace-offerings alone." R. Judah says, "Also the community offered in the tent of meeting which was in the wilderness only that which was assigned to it by the Torah alone."

T. 13:16 And so did R. Simeon say, "He who slaughters the Passover on the high place of an individual and offered it outside at the time of the prohibition of the high place — it is prohibited." [If he does so] at the time of the permission of a high place, it is permitted, as it is said, "You shall not be able to slaughter the Passover" (Deut.

16:8). Might one think that also on the other days of the year [the prohibition applies]? Scripture says, "In one of your gates" — "At the time that the Israelites are gathered together in one place." One must say: "This is at the time of the festival."

T. 13:17 These are the differences between the great high place and the small high place: The horn and the ramp and the foundation [are to be found] at the great high place. There are no horn, ramp, and foundation in the small high place. A laver and a basin are found in a great high place. A laver and a basin are not found in a small high place. The breast and thigh belong to the priests in a great high place. The breast and the thigh belong to the owner in a small high place. The hide of a burnt-offering belongs to the priests in a great high place. The hide of a burnt-offering belongs to the owner in a small high place. [The improper intention to burn the sacrificial parts] outside of the proper place applies in the great high place. [The improper intention to burn the sacrificial parts] outside of the proper place does not apply [at all in the small high place].

T. 13:18 In these respects are the great high place and the small high place equivalent: Slaughtering applies in the great high place. Slaughtering applies in the small high place. Flaying the hide and chopping up the parts apply in the great high place. Flaying the hide and chopping up the parts apply in the small high place. [The disposition of the] blood renders the offering permitted, renders it valid, or renders it refuse in a great high place. [The disposition of the] blood renders the offering permitted, renders it valid, or renders it refuse in a small high place. A blemish invalidates an offering in a great high place. A blemish invalidates an offering in a small high place. [The improper intention to eat the meat] outside of its proper time applies in the great high place. [The improper intention to eat the meat] outside of its proper time applies in a small high place.

T. 13:19 What is the case of a great high place? At the time that a high place is prohibited, the tent of meeting is stretched out in the normal way. The ark is not placed there. What is the case of a small high place? At the time of the permission of a high place, a man makes a high place at the door of his courtyard or at the door of his garden. He offers up a sacrifice on it, he and his son and his daughter and his man-servant and his maid-servant.

The complex of information provided by Scripture on where offerings were legitimately presented, with what rites, by personnel of what classification, and under what conditions is classified and systematized, yet another exercise of the generic hermeneutics. And not only does the Mishnah powerfully illustrate its basic mode of analyzing and ordering facts in intelligible patterns, but the Tosefta too, in the present case embodies its finest intellectual procedures, e.g., at T. 13:7. I do not believe any category-formation is better served by the generic hermeneutics than is Zebahim. And yet, having said that, I also maintain the category-formation accomplishes its entire task in the opening unit. Without the Halakhah but with Scripture's facts in hand, we should have found possible the replication of the main body of the Halakhah. But without the particular hermeneutics embodied in the opening unit, we should never have attained that theory of the interplay between action and intentionality that the present category-formation embodies and instantiates in so dense and subtle a manner.

IV. DOCUMENTARY TRAITS

A. THE MISHNAH AND THE TOSEFTA

The Tosefta's contribution is massive but subordinate; the category-formation remains stable throughout.

B. THE BAVLI

The Bavli's contribution focuses on matters of detail and refinement. But the repertoire cited above scarcely hints at the sophistication of its exegesis of the Halakhah.

V. THE HERMENEUTICS OF ZEBAHIM

A. WHAT FUSES THE HALAKHIC DATA INTO A CATEGORY-FORMATION?

The data of Scripture, the outcome of the generic hermeneutics, and the particular hermeneutics of Zebahim produce a sustained, coherent statement. How does the whole hold together, forming a whole that exceeds the sum of the parts? The answer is, the particular hermeneutics fuses the initial component of the composite into a cogent statement, the generic hermeneutics impart energy and variety to the rest of the exposition, and the facts of Scripture and tradition provide the wherewithal.

The heart of the matter is that the blood-rite forms the center of the transaction between Israel and God at the altar, and the one consideration that governs in all classifications of animal offerings is the validity of the priest's attitude, at the moment of the taking of life, toward two critical components of the rite later on. That is shown in the answer to the question. At what point is the offering validated, so that the disposition of the animal bears consequences? It is when the blood has been properly sprinkled or tossed. Then the offering is "permissible," meaning, the blood is burned on the altar and so the meat is eaten by the priest and (where appropriate) the Israelite sacrifier. When the rite is performed properly with the correct intentionality, it accomplishes its goals (it is "valid"). When the rite is performed by the proper gestures and actions but by the priest's attitude classified incorrectly, it is invalid. The category-formation bears no messages concerning the meaning of the blood-rite, only the conditions that are required for its effective accomplishment. The particular hermeneutics of the category-formation then takes as its problem an issue on which the Written Torah makes no statement within the framework of normative prescriptions. But Scripture makes an elaborate statement indeed within the setting of narrative of exemplary events and transactions from the beginning to the end.

Let us come right to the critical question: Why does the attitude of the officiating priest bear so heavily on the matter? Here the category-formation shows its power. To find the answer, we take the classic case of how intentionality invalidates a deed. What we see is that what one intends before the fact governs the status of the act itself, and even though one performs the act correctly and ultimately acts in accord with the law, the initial intentionality and not the ultimate deed still dictates the outcome. I can think of no more powerful way of stating that what one intends in advance, and not what one does in fact, determines the result of a transaction. Before us then is the extreme position: the intentionality that motivates an action, not what is really done, governs. The way this is said is not complicated. It involves a rule about the priest's consuming the meat of the offering that he presents and how, at the moment of slaughter (encompassing the other phases of the blood rite) he intends to eat that meat: when and where. Specifically, the meat of the offerings that the priests receive must be eaten by them within a specific span of time, two nights and the intervening day. If the priest when slaughtering the beast (or wringing the neck of a bird) says that he will eat the meat later on, that very act of intentionality suffices to render the act of slaughter one of abomination, and the status of the offering is determined — without any action whatsoever on the priest's part.

Now we see what it means to evaluate what happens solely by reference to what one intends to make happen: not what one actually does after the fact, but what one is thinking in advance of it. The rule is framed in terms of not what the priest does but what he is thinking of doing later on: He who slaughters the animal offering intending to toss its blood outside of the Temple court, to burn its sacrificial portions outside, to eat its meat outside, or to eat an olive's bulk of the skin of the fat tail outside — it is invalid. He who slaughters the animal offering, intending to toss its blood on the next day, to burn its sacrificial portions on the next day, to eat its meat on the next day, or an olive's bulk of the skin of the fat tail on the next day — it is refuse. And that is without regard to the actual deed of the priest. If he after the fact of the declared intention, he did the deed at the correct time or place, it changes nothing. With such remarkable power over the status of the beast that the mere intention to eat the meat outside of its proper time or to dispose of it outside of the proper place suffices to ruin the offering, the priest's intentionality in connection with immediate, concrete actions in other aspects of the offering will make a massive difference as well.

What about the transaction of the priest in behalf of the sacrifier? Here too, the action is evaluated by the initiating intention, not the ultimate deed, so that even if all the rites are correctly carried out, if the priest does not do them with the right attitude, the sacrifier loses out. This is expressed in the formulation that follows. If a beast, designated as sanctified by its own for a particular classification of offering, is actually slaughtered for a purpose other than that for which it was originally designated, what is the result? If the officiating priest does not carry out the intention of the Israelite who purchased and sanctified the beast, the offering remains valid; the blood is collected, conveyed to the altar, and tossed there. So far as the beast is concerned, the act of sanctification is irrevocable. So far as the householder is concerned, his obligation has not yet been carried out; he must present another animal to accomplish his purpose, e.g., to present a sin-offering or carry out a vow. There are two exceptions to this rule. If on the afternoon of the fourteenth of Nisan an Israelite's animal, designated to serve as a Passover offering, is offered for some other purpose, e.g., as peace-offerings, it is null. So too an animal designated as a sin-offering must be presented for that purpose and for no other. In both cases, the specificity of the occasion — the Passover, the sin — takes over; the animal that has been mis-classified by the priest is lost.

The upshot is, attitude or intention takes priority in the validation of the rite over actualities of deed. This is expressed — to go over what is by now familiar — in the following way. A bird that one designated to serve as sin offering of fowl which one prepared below the red line, (1) that is to say, properly, in accord with the rites of the sin offering, (2) in the classification "name" of the sin offering, obviously is valid. What does it take to invalidate the rite? If one did the actions correctly but classified the transaction improperly, that is, had the wrong intention, it is invalid. If one prepared a bird designated to serve as a sin offering of fowl (1) in accord with the rites of the sin offering, (2) but in the classification ("for the name") of a burnt offering — (1) or in accord with the rites of the burnt offering below the line, (2) but in the classification ("for the name") of a sin offering — (1) or in accord with the rites of the burnt offering, but in the classification ("for the name") of a burnt offering, it is invalid. If one prepared it above the red line instead of below, but, otherwise, in accord with the rites of either of them, it in all events is invalid. It would be difficult to state more forcefully that the right attitude governs, taking priority, even, over right action, so that if things are done correctly but with improper intentionality, the rite is null.

Why in the end does the particular hermeneutics lay its entire stress on intentionality, and what outcome for Israel's relationship with God do we discern? The answer carries us back to the original definition of the category-formation: the dynamics of the expiatory transaction derives from the active intentionality. Several parties participate. The Israelite has the power to change the status of a beast from secular to sacred, and this he does by an act of will: "Lo, I will that that beast be sanctified to serve as a sin-offering for the sin that I inadvertently committed." He designates a beast as sacred, specifying the purpose of the act of sanctification. So the entire process of presenting personal offerings (as distinct from the public ones) depends upon the act of will effected by the individual Israelite. And since the rites are carried out at the critical turnings by the priest, his attitude that governs his activities likewise must register. So the category-formation portrays the cult as the stage on which Israel — priest and Israelite alike — work out in concrete actions the results of their interior reflections. It is not surprising, then, that when the priest is dealt into the transaction, it is where his act of will registers as well. We should not miss the difference. The sacrifier-Israelite inaugurates the process, the sacrificer-priest concludes it; the former does so by a positive act of intentionality, the latter does so by refraining from a negative one.

Since, as with the daily whole-offerings of all Israel all together, the rite is time and again represented as an exercise in expiation of sin, even though a variety of offerings serves another purpose altogether (e.g. celebration, thanksgiving, and the like), we do well to recall the principal (but not sole) occasion for individual participation, as we saw at M. Ker. 1:2, cited above. The cult (e.g., the sin-offering and the guilt-offering) expiates sin when the sin is inadvertent; deliberate sin is expiated through the sacrifice of years, ("extirpation") or all, of life in the death penalty. Then the entire transaction at the altar, so far as the expiation of sin forms the center, concerns those actions that one did not intend to carry out but nonetheless has done. The intentionality governing the deed therefore proves decisive, and we may not find surprising the focus upon attitude accompanying the action of sacrifice. The offering demonstrates the right attitude of the sacrifier and (it goes without saying) the sacrificer.

Just as the offering expiates an inadvertent sin, so the attitude that motivates the sacrifier (and, correspondingly, the priest too) will define matters: "it is for this particular sin, that I did not mean to do, that I have deliberately designated as holy that particular beast." An unintentional, sinful act then provokes an intentional act of expiation. Then what God follows with close anticipation is how this act of will is realized — confirmed in actuality; that occasion of acute *advertence* is what concludes the transaction begun inadvertently. And that means in the concrete arrangements of the cult, how the actions of the priest conform in the priest's intentionality to the original act of sanctification brought about by the Israelite's intentionality. The entire relationship between Israel and God works itself out as a match of the intentions of the several parties, each of them qualified to form an independent act of will, all of them conforming to bring about the successful result, the expiation of sin or the fulfillment of commitment. The Israelite attains atonement and reconciliation with God only when, after an unintended violation of the Torah, he demonstrates that, in giving something back (whether a costly beast, whether a bird of no account), he subordinates his will to that of God. We find matched acts of willful and deliberate subordination — the priest's to the Israelite's, the Israelite's to God's.

The sequence of acts in conformity with the will of another having been worked out, God then accepts the actions that come about by reason of right attitude and responds by accepting the blood-offering as an act of propitiation and atonement, on the one side, or of fulfillment of obligation, on the other. What is required in a valid act of fulfillment of the Israelite's act of consecration is uniform conformity of deed to will. When it comes to characterizing Israel's relationship with God, what counts, then, is that God follows this sequence of steps, this process leading the beast from the secular herd to the sacred altar, its blood turned into the reagent to wash away the inadvertent sin of the sacrifier. Everyone must concur in sequence, the sacrifier, the sacrificer, and God in confirmation to the correct intention of both. It is as though God wished to set up a system carefully to monitor the will of successive participants in the process, each exposing for God's inspection the contents of his hearts.

Then when is a beast sanctified with such specificity as to be lost by the priest's contradictory intentionality? It is when either the time or the circumstance intervenes and so defines the status as to sanctification of the beast as to render the beast useless for all other purposes. For the Passover-offering in particular, the time is the eve of the Passover, when the lamb designated for the Passover offering must be offered up under that designation and no other. Any other time, the same lamb may serve as peace-offerings. So the time makes all the difference in avoiding confusion as to the intent of the sacrifier. The other consideration — the circumstance — appeals to much weightier concerns, confirming what has already been said about why intentionality registers in so weighty a way. The circumstance is the inadvertent commission of a particular sin. The beast designated as the sin-offering for a given sin can serve to expiate no other. It is the demonstration of correct intention — the good will, not the rebellious will — that the offering embodies. The correlation of the sin-offering with the inadvertent sin is expressed in the following way:

> [If] it is a matter of doubt whether or not one has sinned, he brings a suspensive guilt-offering [M. Ker. 4:1, 2A-B]. [If] he has sinned, but is not certain what particular sin he has committed, he brings a sin-offering. [If] he has sinned and is informed of the character of his sin but he as or gotten what sin he has committed, Lo, this one brings a sin-offering [M. Ker. 4:2C-D], and it is slaughtered for the sake of whichever [sin he has committed] and it is eaten. Then he goes and brings a sin-offering for that sin of which he is informed, and it is slaughtered for the sake of whatever [particular sin he has done] and it [too] is eaten.
>
> Tosefta Keritot 2:4

A very particular occasion then has precipitated the act of will involved in designating the beast as a sin-offering, and that same purpose must govern throughout.

In both cases, then, the act of sanctification takes on a particularity that drastically limits options in case of priestly error. The reason for the latter — the sin-offering — is self-evident. God permits the man who has inadvertently sinned to atone for the sin he did not mean to commit or even know at the time knew that he was committing. Once he finds out what he has done, he wishes to show the true state of his will, and that is through the sin-offering. The offering then is linked to that action and no other. Sin is particular, concrete, and delimited — an action, not a condition. And so is the intention to be made manifest: that act I did not intend to commit, shown by this act, which I fully will.

That negative rule — the sin-offering and Passover are invalidated if the priest's intentionality does not conform to the occasion (the will of the sacrifier) or the time (the afternoon of the fourteenth of Nisan, when the Passover offering is obligatory) — yields a striking, positive result. It is that God pays exceedingly close attention to the act of will exercised by both the sacrifier and the sacrificer, responding to what is in the heart of each in assessing the effect of the act viewed whole. Then the activity that yields the event — the sacrifier's selection of the beast, designation of its purpose in an act of consecration, his presentation to the priest with the sacrifier's laying on of hands, then the priest's cutting of the beast's throat and collection of its blood, conveyance of its blood to the altar and the splattering of its blood thereon — all of these activities must be uniformly animated by the initial intention of the Israelite, and the continuation of the program by the priest is at issue. It would be difficult to formulate a more concrete and far-reaching statement that God pays the closest possible attention to the Israelite's will than the rule at hand. The offerings at the altar accomplish their goal because God attentively engages with, responds to, the Israelite's and the priest's intentionality. God will respond, the Halakhah takes for granted, and accord atonement, register the fulfillment of an obligation for example, only when these coincide: the will of the sacrifier, the will of the sacrificer.

But an important qualification enters here, in two parts. When, in particular, does intentionality register? First, if a person may validly perform an action within the sacrificial rite, e.g., slaughter the animal, then his or her intentionality registers. But if an unfit person collects the blood, the action is null, and so too the intention of such a person in connection with that action is null. So we discern a close correspondence of opposites, a tight logic that governs the whole. What matters — intentionality at the critical points — is all that matters. Second, going over the same ground in a different way, intentionality must concern what is legitimate to begin with. He who slaughters the animal sacrifice intending to eat something which is not usually eaten, to burn something which is not usually burned — the offering nonetheless is valid. God monitors the normal and legitimate; there improper intentionality proves affective. But God does not take account of attitudes in procedures that to begin with are null. And there is a third point not to be missed: when it comes to actions, God takes the lenient view that an act improperly performed can and should be corrected; if properly performed at the end, the rite is not ruined. The entire construction of the law reinforces the centrality of intentionality in relationship to legitimacy: an improper attitude toward that which one may properly do makes its mark. The act must match the intention, but if the intention is correct, the improper act, brought into line, cannot spoil the procedure.

If, as we now realize, questions of intentionality are raised by the particular hermeneutics, the generic kind makes its contribution as well. It registers in the compositions that concern rules for the regulation of the altar? These go over five distinct issues, as we have seen: disposing of sacrificial portions or blood that derive from diverse classes of sacrifices and have been confused; what the altar sanctifies, which is what is appropriate to it, but not what is not appropriate to it; precedence in use of the altar; blood of a sin-offering that spurts onto a garment; and the division among the eligible priests of the meat and hides of sacrificial animals. Of these five matters three yield encompassing generalizations, the other two producing ad hoc rules that articulate the Written Torah's details. The program of the category-formation aims at sorting out confusion in a practical, rational way. If animals are confused, so that some may be suitable for the altar, some not, we wait until a blemish disqualifies the beasts and sell them, using the proceeds for the altar. A correct but practical solution resolves the matter, the sanctity imparted to the beast by the act of consecration not indelibly affecting the animal; it is relative to the animal's own suitability for its purpose. The value is consecrated, the body of the animal not.

So too, the altar sanctifies what is appropriate to it but has no affect upon what is not appropriate to it. Sanctification does not inhere in the altar, such that mere contact with the altar transforms what touches the altar into something permanently sacred. And along these same lines, perfectly rational considerations govern questions of precedence. In all three instances of the disposition of "the sacred," we find sanctity not an inherent trait but one that depends upon circumstance and suitability. The full meaning of these important components of the category-formation emerges only when we consider the Written Torah's judgment of the same matter, which is stated at Ex. 29:37: "the altar shall be most holy; whatever touches the altar shall become holy." That Halakhah significantly qualifies that statement, adding the language "that is appropriate" to the phrase, "whatever touches...." The issue is whether sanctification is indelible or stipulative.

Schismatic opinion holds that what is sanctified in the sanctuary is indelibly sanctified so is not removed from the altar. If, then, the cause of invalidation for the altar took place in the sanctuary, the sanctuary accepts the thing in any event and it is not removed from the altar. If its invalidity did not take place in the sanctuary, the sanctuary does not accept it and it should be removed from the altar. But that position concerning sanctification by being assigned to a named sage as against "sages" is labeled as not normative, and consequently the category-formation underscores the logic of its generative position, which is, sanctification affects status, not substance.

Then we must ask, does not the Land sanctify? Does not the city sanctify? Does not the altar sanctify? We know that all three do have that power, to take one case, produce designated as second tithe is sanctified upon entry within the walls of Jerusalem. So introducing the principle of appropriateness qualifies what we should have anticipated would represent an absolute condition. Since Scripture explicitly declares the altar itself to be not only holy but capable of imparting holiness to whatever touches it, we cannot miss the drastic way in which the category-formation mediates the meaning of sanctification. It is now not a condition but a transaction, subject to variables and stipulations; it is no longer locative and place-bound, nor, indeed, is it utopian (the altar is unique and singular, where it is and no where else, as Deuteronomy has made the fact). Fusing the category-formation, the Halakhah draws upon diverse intellectual resources to produce a coherent statement.

B. THE ACTIVITY OF THE CATEGORY-FORMATION

We come now to the specificities of the category-formation, which show how it acts not to differentiate but to homogenize. The question that preoccupies the framers is this: what rules apply to *all* classes of offerings on the altar? Where Scripture differentiates, as we have seen, and then compares and contrasts, the category-formation homogenizes, subjects diverse classes of offerings to a single body of governing principles. The starting point should not be missed. While Scripture presents the transaction that takes place at the altar by classifying types of offerings, e.g., the burnt-offering, sin-offering, guilt-offering, peace offerings, firstling, tithe of cattle, and the Passover, the category-formation forms its own classifications, setting forth rules that apply to all (or most) classes of offerings throughout. So the category-formation systematizes by identifying the four cultic acts that, properly performed by the priest, render any and every animal-sacrifice suitable for yielding parts for the altar fires and parts for the priests' consumption. These are the act of slaughtering the beast, the act of collecting the blood in a utensil of service from the neck of the beast, the act of bringing the blood to the altar, and the act of tossing drops of blood on the altar. These four acts pertain to all classifications of offerings of beasts. To all classifications of offerings of fowl two apply: pinching the head of the bird from the body and draining the blood out onto the altar. Since priests eat part of the offering, rules governing how they prepare and eat their portion.

INTENTIONALITY IN THE SACRIFICIAL SYSTEM: If the category-formation aims at systematization of the already-systematic presentation of the same topic in the Written Torah, still the focus of the work that transcends mere systematization remains to be identified. Where the category-formation contributes more than the systematization and hierarchization of received facts of Scripture, it, predictably, pursues problems of the interplay between the Israelite's, the priest's, and God's will and plan for the blood-rite in any particular circumstance. The one donates, the other delivers, the offering. What each party has in mind in the exchange must coincide with the thought of the other. The action bears consequence by reason of the attitude that animates it. And here, the Israelite and the priest must concur on the meaning of what is done; then the message intended by the action may register. Much of the efficacy of the rites depends upon the harmonies of intentionality that animate the participants in the offering. And then God concurs.

At what points, in connection with what specific actions, does the intentionality of the donor and the priest register? The category-formation makes its statement solely through its cases, and here, by what it says, it also eliminates many possibilities. The offering is offered for six purposes, and the priest acting in behalf of the donor must have in mind the proper attitude concerning all six. The attitude of the officiating priest governs, and if the priest expresses no improper attitude, that suffices to validate the offering on these points. For the sake of six things, is the animal offering sacrificed? That is to say, the officiating priest has to have in mind the particular offering at hand, offering a burnt-offering as a burnt-offering and not as peace-offerings. The one who sacrifices it is the donor of the animal, who benefits, e.g., from the expiation. The intent must be for God, not for an idol (!). The intent must be to roast the meat on the fire of the altar, not at any other location. One must intend an odor to ascend from the roast. And in the case of the sin- or guilt-offering, the particular sin that is expiated must be in mind. As to the particular actions at which these six aspects of intentionality must conform, they involve these deeds: cutting the pertinent organs, collecting the blood in a bowl, conveying the blood to the altar, and tossing the blood on the altar.

The priest is required for preparation of an offering; a non-priest cannot carry out the critical procedures of the blood-rite. An invalid priest likewise spoils the rite by his participation, e.g., one who was unclean, improperly dressed, and the like. But if the status of the priest weighs heavily on the rite, the attitude of the priest carries still greater consequence. Specifically, as just now noted, four processes integral to the rite, killing the beast, collecting the blood, conveying the blood to the altar, and tossing the blood on the altar, must be carried out by the officiating priest in accord with the intentionality of the *sacrifier* — the person who benefits from the offering, as distinct from the sacrificer, the priest who carries out the offering. There must be an accord between the will of the sacrifier in designating the beast and the will of the sacrificer in carrying out the rite. Should the priest declare that he carries out the action for some purpose other than the designated one, e.g., conveying the blood of a lamb for the purpose of peace-offerings when it is the fourteenth of Nisan and the beast has been designated for a Passover, the rite is spoiled.

Here the initial designation is indelible and the animal that has been destined for the specified purpose may then serve no other. If an animal sanctified as a Passover- or sin-offering is slaughtered for some other purpose, it too is unfit. This principle of specificity is broadened by the generalization that follows: If one slaughtered them for the sake of that which is higher than they, they are valid. If one slaughtered them for the sake of that which is lower than they But if under the name of a lower grade, they are invalid. How so? Most Holy Things which one slaughtered for the sake of Lesser Holy Things are invalid. Lesser Holy Things which one slaughtered for the sake of Most Holy Things are valid. The firstling and tithe which one slaughtered for the sake of peace offerings are valid, and peace offerings which one slaughtered for the sake of a firstling, or for the sake of tithe, are invalid.

While intentionality bears, also, upon the effectiveness of the rite, there are limits, and these show us the boundaries of the rite, indicating what, in the entire procedure, bears consequence. What matters is the blood-rite, that alone. Much else can go wrong and not matter. So long as the blood is properly tossed, the rest of the sacrifice may be burned or eaten, as the case requires. If this is done properly and the sacrifice is not spoiled by some other invalidating element before the tossing of the blood, then the liability to extirpation applies. The intentionality that prevails at that point dictates the classification of the act. This is expressed in the following language: How is what renders the offering permissible offered in accord with its requirement? If one slaughtered in silence lacking improper intent, but received the blood and conveyed the blood and sprinkled the blood intending to eat or burn the flesh outside of its proper time, or if one slaughtered intending to eat or burn the flesh outside of the proper time, received the blood and conveyed the blood and sprinkled the blood in silence lacking improper intent, or if he slaughtered, received the blood, and conveyed the blood and sprinkled the blood intending to eat or burn the flesh outside of its proper time — this is a case in which what renders the offering permissible is offered in accord with its requirement. In the foregoing case, then, the blood rite has not been invalidated. How is what renders the offering permissible not offered in accord with its requirement? If one slaughtered intending to eat or burn the flesh outside of its place, received the blood and conveyed the blood and tossed the blood intending to eat or burn the flesh outside of its time, or if one slaughtered intending to eat or burn the flesh outside its proper time, received the blood and conveyed the blood and tossed the blood intending to eat or burn the flesh outside of its place, or if one slaughtered, received the blood and conveyed the blood and tossed the blood intending to eat or burn the flesh outside of its place — this is a case in which what renders the offering permissible is not offered in accord with its requirement.

Intentionality invalidates only if what is subject to improper intention concerns eating the meat or burning the sacrificial parts outside its proper place or outside its proper time, and, in respect to the Passover and the sin offering, improper intention invalidates when this involves slaughtering them not for their own name not for the purpose for which the beast was originally designated as a Holy Thing. The details present their own surprises, once more underscoring the narrow definition of the range at which intentionality registers. If he slaughtered it on condition that he intended (1) to sprinkle it on the ramp, not at the foundation of the altar, (2) to sprinkle those which are to be sprinkled below, above, (3) or those which are to be sprinkled above, below, (4) those which are to be sprinkled inside, outside (5) or those which are to be sprinkled outside, inside — (1) that unclean people eat it, (2) that unclean people offer it up, (3) that uncircumcised priests eat it, (4) that uncircumcised priests offer it up, (1) to break the bones of the Passover Ex. 12:9, (2) or to eat of it while it is raw, (3) to mix its blood with the blood of unfit beasts — it is valid. Furthermore, the intentionality that invalidates must concern the routine and ordinary. If one forms an improper intentionality that departs from the norm, that idiosyncratic plan has no consequences. He who slaughters the animal sacrifice intending to eat something which is not usually eaten, to burn something which is not usually burned — the offering nonetheless is valid. He who slaughters female consecrated animals intending to eat the foetus or the afterbirth outside the proper place or time has not rendered the sacrifice refuse for these are not usually eaten. So at stake is the blood-rite in relationship to the altar. That is the focus of God's concern — "for the blood is the life" — and that is the point at which man's attitude registers as well. But, it goes without saying, in confirming these facts of Scripture — upon which no comment here is required — the category-formation in no way innovates. It makes its contribution by investigating questions not raised in the Written Torah but provoked thereby.

WHO MAY PARTICIPATE IN THE CULT, AND WITH WHAT EFFECT: If the intentionality of an Israelite, not only a priest, affects the status of the offering, then we may not find surprising that the participation of Israelites, not only priests, finds a valid role. Outsiders to the priesthood may not participate in the blood-rite itself, so their intentionality, should they do so, has no consequences. But anyone may slaughter the animal, if not collect the blood in a bowl. And it follows that the improper intentionality at the moment of doing the action of non-priests, even women, slaves, and unclean men who engage in the act of slaughter, may also affect the offering. But outsiders to the priesthood may not receive the blood, and hence, their intentionality in connection with an action in that regard has no affect upon the acceptability of the offering.

Sages treat in a lenient way the intervention of unfit parties into the activities of the rite. What happens if an unfit person participates? The answer is, the procedure is corrected and is not invalidated. The attitude of the unfit person cannot register, so his action is merely dismissed, replaced by the right person. If a fit person received the blood and handed it over to an unfit person, without conveying it, the unfit one should return it to the fit person. If the priest received the blood in his right hand and put it into his left, he should return it to his right hand. If he received it in a sacred utensil and put it into an unconsecrated utensil, he should put it back into a sacred utensil. If he who was unfit tossed it on the ramp, not against the foundation of the altar, if he tossed those which are to be tossed below, above, or those which are to be tossed above, below, those which are to be tossed inside, outside, or those which are to be tossed outside, inside, if the lifeblood still remained in the beast, a suitable person should go and receive it and repeat the sprinklings. The upshot may be stated simply. Deed on its own bears limited consequences; improper intentionality at the crucial turnings invalidates the rite, even where no action confirms the incorrect attitude. A final detail on its own makes the main point. If after the blood was received in a utensil, it poured from the utensil onto the pavement and one gathered it up, it is valid. I cannot think of a more eloquent way of saying, "the holy" does not inhere in the substance, but sanctification forms a transaction, validated by adherence to rules. We shall return to this point presently.

OFFERING UP BEASTS AND FOWL: The category-formation hierarchizes the offerings by reference to the indicators of priority supplied by Scripture itself. The Written Torah differentiates one offering from another, as we noted earlier. The category-formation sets forth rules governing them all. That is why the Halakhah, but not Scripture, produces a native-category, Zebahim, sacrifices, and no native-categories such as Scripture defines, "the burnt-offering," "the sin- or purification-offering," "the peace-offering," make their appearance in the Halakhic repertoire. Indeed, we do have Halakhic category-formations pertaining to only two particular rites: the procedures for the Day of Atonement (Yoma), and the one for the festival offering (Hagigah). There, in these category-formations, sages do not go over the ground covered here. The category-formation of Zebahim encompasses also the rites treated in Yoma and in Hagigah; distinctive statements pertinent to those categories emerge from the topical program followed therein, as we have already seen in the pertinent passages.

The results of hierarchization here strike me as inert. Different parts of the altar serve for offerings of various classifications. The northern side of the altar served for Most Holy Things. The Temple court sufficed for Lesser Holy Things. As to the location for eating them, in the case of the former they had to be eaten only by male priests "inside the veils," that is, within the Temple-courtyard area, while in the case of the latter, the meat might be eaten anywhere in the city, by the priests and their families in the case of the thank-offering, by those registered with the offering in the case of the Passover. If a substantive problematics frames the inquiry of the category-formation, I cannot define what it might have been. Whatever issues inhered in Scripture's schematization of matters do not emerge in the presentation that is before us. In my view, that is because at issue is the protocol of proper action — how the priest kills the beast or bird, where he sprinkles the blood, how he disposes of the carcass. These are matters of fact and at no point do the variables of intention enter in (except as they apply throughout, without differentiation, to all offerings). So we may say, where the category-formation takes up its generative problematics, there it will pursue in general terms problems that affect all types of offerings; where that problematics does not shape issues for analysis, that is, where specific offerings and the concrete activities in their regard are concerned, there the category-formation contributes little more than a systematic reprise of established facts. The category-formation emerges as a generalizing and systematizing enterprise. But the dynamic of that category-formation derives from the generative myth, which concerns itself with the contention between God's and man's, then Israel's, will.

THE RULES OF THE ALTAR: The category-formation here focuses upon solving problems of confusion, responding to the generic hermeneutics of the category-formation. This is in three aspects. First, once we have classified offerings and produced the blood-rite for them, what happens when the products of the offering — meat, blood — are confused with those of some other, e.g., animals designated for a given purpose confused with animals classified in some other way? Second, what if the altar receives an appropriate offering at the wrong time or for the wrong purpose, e.g., an animal that is ordinarily offered up, but not for the purpose that it is at a given instance asked to serve? Third, how do we sort out claims to priority in the hierarchy of sanctification, that is, confusion as to precedence?

CONFUSION: When it comes to the confusion of animals that have been sanctified for diverse purposes, or animals that include both sanctified and secular beasts, we take up a practical problem. Here, therefore, practical considerations take over. On the one hand, consecrated beasts have to be treated as holy. On the other hand, they cannot serve the purpose for which they have been designated, since we do not know what that purpose is for any given beast. Hence we sell the beasts and so redeem them, and use the proceeds for the purchase of a suitable offering. To do so, we must wait until the consecrated beasts (whichever they were) are no longer suitable for an offering; then they are redeemed: let them any of those beasts that had been confused in this way pasture until they suffer a blemish since one of them is a valid consecrated beast, and then be sold, and let the owner bring another sacrifice, purchased with the proceeds of the best of them of that kind that had been mixed up with the invalid beasts. If they were mixed up with unblemished unconsecrated beasts, the unconsecrated beasts are to be sold to those who require that particular kind of sacrifice.

Where consecrated beasts belonging to several owners are mixed up with others of the same class, the procedure that is set forth proves even simpler: Consecrated beasts belonging to several owners, which were mixed up with other consecrated beasts of the same kind of offering, so that while all the beasts in the lot have been designated for the same purpose, we still do not know to whom in particular the several beasts belong — this one is offered for the sake of one among the owners and that one is offered for the sake of one among the owners.

MIS-LOCATION: What happens when the priests place on the altar something that, at a given moment, does not belong there, or that does not belong there at all? The Halakhah takes for granted that the altar does not *ex opere operato* sanctify whatever touches it. The status of sanctification is just that — a status, not an intrinsic trait. What is appropriate to the altar, e.g., a lamb or a handful of grain, is left there. The potentiality for sanctification is actualized by the placement on the altar. What cannot potentially be sanctified, e.g., a wild beast, or, in this context, one that is set on the altar while not yet slaughtered, is simply removed, unaffected as it is by the sanctity of the altar. And what we say of the altar pertains, also, to other locations and objects that impart the status of sanctification to what is situated on or in them: Just as the altar sanctifies that which is appropriate to it, so the ramp sanctifies. Just as the altar and the ramp sanctify that which is appropriate to them, so utensils Ex. 30:28-29, sanctify that which is appropriate to them. Utensils for liquids blood, wine, oil, water sanctify liquid; and measures for drystuffs the tenth of the *ephah* and half *issaron* measures sanctify that which is dry. Utensils for liquids do not sanctify that which is dry, and measures for drystuffs do not sanctify that which is liquid.

What are those things which, even if they have gone up, should go down being removed from the altar because they are not offered at all and, therefore, are not appropriate to the altar? (1) The meat that constitutes the share of the priests of Most Holy Things sin offerings and guilt offerings and the meat that constitutes the share of the priests of Lesser Holy Things e.g., peace offerings, (2) and the excess of the sheaf of first barley that is presented from Passover through Pentecost the *omer*, (3) and the two loaves of Pentecost and the show bread (Lev. 24:5-19), (4) and the residue of meal-offerings, (5) and the incense offering that has been erroneously placed on the outer, rather than the inner altar to which it is appropriate.

Whether the criterion for appropriateness is the altar or the fire is subject to dispute, but the principle is established. What is encompassed in the rule that the altar takes over whatever is put there that can at the right time or in the right circumstance appropriately be put there? That which remains overnight, and that which is unclean, and that which goes forth from its proper bounds, and that which is slaughtered with the intention to burn the sacrificial parts or to eat the flesh outside of its proper time or outside of its proper place, and that the blood of which unfit people have received or tossed. Simeon's position, differentiating the location of the event that invalidated the offering, stresses that if invalidation took place in the sanctuary, the sanctified beast remains on the altar; if the event took place outside the sanctuary, it should be removed from the altar. Such events include the following: What are those things, the invalidity of which did not take place in the sanctuary? (1) The animal which has had sexual relations with a human, and (2) the animal with which a human had sexual relations; and (3) that which is set aside for idolatrous worship, and (4) that which actually is worshipped; and (5) the hire of a harlot, and (6) the price of a dog. If, on the other hand, when the beast reached the sanctuary, it was valid, entry into the sanctuary indelibly changes its character and sanctifies it. That is not the normative view, but it underscores what is at stake.

PRECEDENCE: This brings us, third, to precedence and priority among classes of sanctified things: which is holier than which else? In a system animated by the principles of natural history, we find predictable the mode of answering the question. Sages identify the traits, inherent in the various candidates for precedence, that differentiate the one from the other, and, further, they then hierarchize those traits. The available facts then leave no quandaries whatsoever.

Sages, first, assign priority to the offering that is more frequent: Whatever is offered more often than its fellow takes precedence over its fellow: (1) Daily whole offerings take precedence over additional offerings. (2) The additional offerings of the Sabbath take precedence over the additional offerings of the new moon. They, second, invoke the established hierarchization of offerings, e.g., Most Holy Things, Lesser Holy Things, and logically assign precedence to the higher in the ladder, even identifying the indicative traits that validate their decision: And whatever is more holy than its fellow takes precedence over its fellow: (1) The blood of the sin offering takes precedence over the blood of the burnt offering, because it makes atonement for a sin. (2) The limbs of the burnt offering take precedence over the sacrificial parts of a sin offering, because they are wholly given over to the fires to be burned up. (3) The sin offering takes precedence over the guilt offering, because its blood is placed on the four corners of an altar and on the foundation. (4) The guilt offering takes precedence over the thank offering and the ram of the Nazir, because it is Most Holy Things. (5) The thank offering and the ram of the Nazir take precedence over peace offerings, because they are eaten for one day unlike peace offerings which are eaten for two days and require bread Lev. 7:12-13. The peace offerings take precedence over the firstling, because they require two placings which are four placings of blood, and laying of hands, and drink offerings, and waving of the breast and thigh. What we see, then, is that sages systematize available facts, following the logic they find implicit in those facts, which they articulate. The indicative traits fall into two main categories, the formal rules of procedure, the substantive considerations of motivation in making the offerings. The systematization, as we shall see, yielded fundamental judgments on why the blood-rite matters and what it accomplishes. Then the hierarchization of the diverse rites carried the systematic message overall, as we shall see in the next section.

BLOOD THAT SPURTS: When we come to the category-formation that amplifies Lev. 6:27-28, washing a garment on which blood of a sin-offering spurts, scouring and rinsing a utensil in which the sin-offering is cooked, the category-formation contributes clarification. The first is, the requirement pertains to a valid, not an invalid sin-offering: An invalid sin offering — its blood that had spurted on a garment does not require washing, (1) whether it had a moment of validity for tossing the blood or (2) it did not have a moment of validity having been invalidated before the receiving of the blood. So too the blood must spurt not directly from the opened vein but from the bowl in which it is received and thereby consecrated: If the blood spurted directly from the neck of the slaughtered beast onto the garment and was not received in a pot, being invalid for sprinkling on the altar, it does not require washing. If the blood spurted from the horn or from the foundation of the altar, it does not require washing. What is implicit is this: the designation of the beast as a sin-offering, slaughtering it as a sin-offering — these do not indelibly affect the carcass and its blood. Only the successful realization of the rite transforms the blood into an effective substance, such that Scripture's requirement pertains. But the substantive trait of the sin-offering — its power of expiation — by analogy imposes the law on all offerings that serve the same purpose: All the same are one in which one has cooked and one into which one has poured boiling stew, and all the same are one used for Most Holy Things e.g., a sin offering or a guilt offering and one for Lesser Holy Things e.g., peace offerings: they require scouring and rinsing. The upshot is, the formal considerations recede in importance, the substantive ones are highlighted.

THE LOCATION OF THE ALTAR AND HOW IT MAKES A DIFFERENCE: Lev. 17:3 as sages read it states that slaughter must take place in the Temple, and the Halakhah takes as fact that at issue is only Holy Things; slaughter for secular purposes takes place anywhere. The Halakhic definition of what is prohibited outside of the Temple then is simple: what is prohibited outside of the Temple is an action in connection with slaughter that, if done in the Temple, would be valid. What is holy in the Temple is forbidden outside; if something in the Temple is null, then the same act outside is not liable. That is expressed in the principle underlying the following case: A sin offering, the blood of which one received in a single cup, and the blood of which one first placed on an altar outside, and then placed on an altar inside, or placed on an altar inside and then placed on an altar outside — he is liable, for all of it is suitable to come to be placed on the altar inside. If one received its blood in two cups, and placed the blood of both of them on an altar inside, he is free. If he placed the blood of both of them on an altar outside, he is liable. The same principle is expressed in a different way in this language: On account of a red cow for purification ashes Num. 19:9 that one burned outside of its pit — and so: a goat to be sent forth that one offered outside of the Temple — he is free, as it is said, "To the door of the tent of meeting he did not bring it" (Lev.17:4) — For whatever is not appropriate to come to the door of the tent of meeting they are not liable if such a classification of offering is carried out outside of the Temple. Thus one is liable when the whole of a given substance or action is suitable for the Temple; whatever is not suitable "to come to the door of the Tent of meeting" does not produce liability if done outside. The basic principle is articulated in diverse, complex ways, but retains its simplicity throughout. So much for the localization of the cult and the differentiation of that locus from the world outside.

What about Jerusalem as the unique focus of cultic activity? Two issues define matters, the status of high places, the location for the eating of the priests' and Israelites' share of the offering. The tabernacle, in its day, functioned as does the Temple, limiting the location of sacrifice, requiring the priests to officiate, differentiating the area walled off ("within the veils") from the rest of the Israelite camp, deemed the counterpart, later on, to Jerusalem. This same focus on where the offerings might be eaten registers through the later settings. At each point, the area "within the veils" is where Most Holy Things had to be eaten. But where is "Jerusalem"? The answer is, anywhere Israel is located (for Gilgal); anywhere in sight of the place (for Shilo), in all the towns of Israel (for Nob and Gibeon). That pattern correlates with the status of high places; when the Lesser Holy Things might be eaten wherever Israel was located, high places were permitted; when they might be eaten only within sight of the holy place, the high places were forbidden. And that reaches its permanent conclusion with Jerusalem: Most Holy Things within the veils, Lesser Holy Things within the wall of the city; and the location of Israel no longer makes a difference.

C. THE CONSISTENCY OF THE CATEGORY-FORMATION

I see no point at which the category-formation encompasses inconsistent components or produces rules out of phase with the generative logic of the whole.

D. THE GENERATIVITY OF THE CATEGORY-FORMATION

The category-formation, Zebahim, expands its logical limits partly through exclusions, principles and issues that gain no entry. The category-formation generates the disenchantment of the altar, the desacralization of the persons and substances that are engaged, opening the way to the advent of a revolutionary conception. It is that at issue is not the rite of reconciliation but the act and attitude of reconciliation. And in due course, under different circumstances, the Aggadah would reach the conclusion, "We have another means of atonement, like that one, and what is it? Deeds of loving kindness." How, specifically, does that thought-process get underway within the Halakhah that would in its logical unfolding come to such a remarkable conclusion? The answer lies in what is spread before us in the explicit norms of the Halakhah: what the altar represents within Zebahim is merely the place at which a given transaction can take place, the only place where, under proper conditions and stipulations, God and Israel meet for the purpose at hand. It is holy because of what circumstance and occasion, not because of its intrinsic quality or character: "...sanctifies what is appropriate...." That represents a remarkably generative component of the category-formation, once that flows logically from the particular hermeneutics of Zebahim, with its stress on the relativities effected by attitude, right and wrong, without regard to the actualities of the rite.

We recall that elsewhere in the Halakhah, it is the intersection of Israel, the people, with the Land of Israel that brings about the activation of processes of sanctification that inhere therein — again, a transaction and an occasion, not a process that functions *ex opere operando*. When the Israelite farmer, who possesses the Land, expresses his intentionality to make use of the produce, then God's interest is aroused in the produce of the Land that he, God, owns. A gentile farmer of the Land of Israel does not produce the same effect. So "the sacred" does not inhere in the untithed crop or even in the portion of the crop removed for the priestly ration or heave-offering. The altar then corresponds to the Land, each in its context setting the stage for an encounter that can take place only there and nowhere else. But neither the altar nor the Land plays a part in the meeting; the Land requires the presence of Israel, the altar, of the priest. The walls of the City encompass second tithe; entry within them means the produce cannot then be removed from the City. But the walls do not impart the status of sanctification to the produce; the farmer has done so by designating it as second tithe. These and numerous other details of the law make the same point as to what takes place in the transaction of sanctification, when Israel relates to God: it is the realization of what is potentially present by reason of forces extrinsic to the setting, but intrinsic to God's and Israel's very being. And that, I hardly need specify, is what is common to them: the freedom to choose, the autonomy of the will, in Israel's case, obedience freely proffered.

What is at stake is the insistence of the normative Halakhah that, while the altar alone serves as the nexus of Heaven and earth, not even the altar embodies let alone transmits what is intrinsically holy. What can become holy realizes its potential upon the altar: the right place, the right time, confirmed by the right intentionality. Then some things are relative to others, and location, time, and attitude all together coincide: then the potential sanctity becomes actual, then alone. We cannot speak in the Halakhic framework of "the Holy," only the status of holiness, which depends upon meeting specified conditions and turns out to be relative and stipulative.

If sanctification represents a classification, the wherewithal of a transaction, not a condition, then we should anticipate other indications of that same fact. And so we find in the unfolding of the Halakhah of our present category-formation. Raising the question of priority or precedence among classes of Holy Things presupposes that "the Sacred" is not uniform and inherent, homogenizing whatever is affected thereby. It differentiates and itself is differentiated. But throughout the category-formation, start to finish, no supernatural intervention is required to determine priority among differentiated Holy Things. Again we cannot speak of "the Sacred," but only the status of sanctification, with its appropriate consequences. The entire transaction underscores the relative and stipulative character of sanctification and denies its absoluteness. Here too, precedence is assigned for fundamentally neutral and extrinsic reasons, not by appeal to the substantive and intrinsic character of what is sanctified. But when we identify the governing criteria for priority among Holy Things, we find our way deep into conceptions of Israel's relationship to God. Here, we encounter the truly generative qualities of the present category-formation: its power to hierarchize even "the sacred." And, in context of a pervasive power of intentionality to transform actuality into consequence or inconsequence, that represents a logic of disenchantment.

If I had to identify the basis for the differentiation of "the sacred" into its classes and the hierarchization of those classes — the mode of natural history that drives sages' thought throughout — it is the identification of indicative taxonomic traits, with the implicit conviction that, once we know how classes are formed, on the same basis of such differentiation we also know how they are ranked. Where the reason for the ranking is self-evidence — frequency, for instance, in the theory that what God wants more often God values more — sages do not find it necessary to articulate matters. But where the indicative mark of differentiation is not self-evident, sages tell us their reasoning, and the "because-" clauses of M. 10:2ff. open the window onto their inner thinking. These are the governing considerations in the Mishnah's formulation of the Halakhah:

(1) Because it makes atonement for a sin.
(2) Because they are wholly given over to the fires to be burned up.
(3) Because its blood is placed on the four corners of an altar and on the foundation.

(4) Because it is most holy things.
(5) Because they are eaten for one day unlike peace offerings which are eaten for two days and require bread (Lev. 7:12-13).
(6) Because they require two placings which are four placings of blood, and laying of hands, and drink offerings, and waving of the breast and thigh.
(7) Because it is sanctified from the womb, and it is eaten only by priests.
(8) Because it is an animal sacrifice killed with a knife, unlike fowl, and there pertain to it traits that classify an offering as most holy things
(9) Because they fall within the class of that which produces blood for atonement.
(10) Because it comes on account of sin.

The corresponding passage of the Tosefta amplifies the matter on its own:

(1) Because it makes atonement for a sin.
(2) Because they are wholly given over to the fires to be burned up.
(3) Because its blood is placed on the four corners of an altar and on the foundation.
(4) Because it is Most Holy Things.
(5) Because they are eaten for one day unlike peace offerings which are eaten for two days and require bread (Lev. 7:12-13).
(6) Because they require two placings which are four placings of blood, and laying of hands, and drink offerings, and waving of the breast and thigh.
(7) Because it is sanctified from the womb, and it is eaten only by priests.
(8) Because it is an animal sacrifice killed with a knife, unlike fowl, and there pertain to it traits that classify an offering as Most Holy Things.
(9) Because they fall within the class of that which produces blood for atonement.
(10) Because it comes on account of sin.

The governing considerations fall into these groups:

(1) Sin and atonement (1, 9, 10)
(2) Wholly consumed on the fires (2)
(3) More elaborate blood-rite (3, 6)
(4) Designated as Most Holy Things by Scripture (4)

(5) Strict rule governing the eating of the priests' portion (5, 7)
(6) Beast over fowl = more elaborate over cheaper (8)
(7) Sanctified by nature or circumstance rather than by human decision (7)

The indicative traits that mark one classification of sanctification as holier than another then derive from circumstance and context.

Then what makes the difference above all? On the one side, the circumstantial rules of the altar govern, e.g., which offering belongs wholly to God, which not; which has the more elaborate blood-rite, the stricter rule governing the priests' disposition of their portion of the offering, and the like; or Scripture's own designation. What is wholly consumed on the fires wholly belongs to God, so T. 11:7: The burnt-offering belongs wholly to the Most High, but its hide belongs to the priests. Most Holy Things: The blood and sacrificial parts belong to the altar, and the meat and hide to the priests. Lesser Holy Things: The blood and sacrificial parts belong to the altar, and the hide and meat belong to the owner. This is the general principle: Whoever has a share in the meat has a share in the hides. Whoever does not have a share in the meat does not have a share in the hides (M. Zeb. 12:1E), except for the burnt-offering, concerning which Scripture explicitly supplied the rule: "And the priest who offers any man's burnt-offering shall have for himself the hide of the burnt-offering which he has offered" (Lev. 7:8). On the other side, the motivation behind the offering dictates priority. This is expressed in the blanket-rule, M. 10:5: All sin offerings which are mentioned in the Torah take precedence over guilt offerings, except for the guilt offering of the person afflicted by the skin ailment of Lev. 13, because in line with Lev. 14 it comes to render him fit to enter the Temple and eat Holy Things.

This same emphasis upon the substantive purpose of the blood-rite, which is the atonement of sin, emerges in the Halakhic treatment of the requirement to scour utensils used for cooking the sin-offering's meat (Lev. 6:28). The analogy provided by the type of offering, the one that atones for sin, then governs. And the (now-predictable) Halakhic result is clearly stated: All the same are one in which one has cooked and one into which one has poured boiling stew, and all the same are one used for Most Holy Things e.g., a sin offering or a guilt offering and one for Lesser Holy Things e.g., peace offerings: they require scouring and rinsing. Since much of Halakhic thought in the formative age follows analogical lines of development, we cannot find surprising the sages' extension of the requirement to all offerings of the same classification.

This brings us to the correlation of activity and location in reference to the cult. Scripture recorded enlandised loci of the cult outside of Jerusalem,

Shiloh, Nob, Gibeon, for example, all of these facts required sorting out and systematization. And in doing so, the Halakhah not only regularized and harmonized the narratives. It also drew out what the narratives left implicit — a further mark of the generativity of the category-formation. The first point that the category-formation in its generative mode registers by reference to localization carefully differentiates between two like actions, the act of slaughter of a beast or a bird. If it is done outside of the Temple in the manner in which it is done in the Temple, it is a culpable act; the sanctity of the Temple has been violated by the transfer outside of the Temple of an action particular to the blood-rite. If it is done inside of the Temple in the manner in which it is done outside of the Temple, it is not culpable; nothing has happened. So the Temple serves as the mirror-image of the world: what serves in the situation of sanctification is null outside, and vice versa. The Halakhah expresses this in the following language: He who pinches the neck of fowl inside the Temple and offered it up outside the Temple is liable since pinching the neck is the valid means of slaughtering the bird for sacrificial purposes, and that was correctly done. If he pinched the neck outside the Temple and offered it up outside the Temple, he is free. Pinching the neck is done only to kill the bird as a sacrifice; since this was done outside of the Temple, it is null. He who slaughters fowl inside the Temple and offered it up outside the Temple is free. If he slaughtered it outside the Temple and offered it up outside the Temple, he is liable. It turns out that the way of rendering it suitable (= killing the bird as a sacrifice, by pinching the neck) inside the Temple is that which frees it from penalty outside the Temple, and the way of rendering it suitable outside the Temple (= slaughter for eating unconsecrated fowl) is that which frees it from penalty inside the Temple.

Along these same lines, if one offers up outside of the Temple an animal that cannot serve as an offering, e.g., one that has had sexual relations with a human being, the offer is null. That the Halakhah mediates between the conflicting instructions in this regard of Leviticus and Deuteronomy is self-evident; that it makes a statement of its own is equally obvious. And what the Halakhah registers is that where Israel meets God, in God's abode, actions that in Israel's domain make a difference do not matter in God's, and vice versa. So just as time forms a critical variable — the Passover offered not for its own name on the eve of Passover, as distinct from the same offered at any other time — the location of an action dictates the classification of that action.

When it comes to the status of Jerusalem, it goes without saying, the Halakhah sets forth in its terms the familiar position that the Temple stands on the highest hill of the highest place in the Land of Israel. Here again we deal with the interplay of space and time: when the cult is located in a given place, then the following rules pertain. That underscores all the more decisively the change that took place with the establishment of the Temple (and its reconstruction). Before Jerusalem and its Temple, the location of Israel within the Land served to consecrate a locus for cultic liturgy: wherever Israel was living, "in all the towns of Israel," and the like. Then the high places would serve; Israel the people endowed with sanctity the land on which it was situated. Once Jerusalem was established and the Temple built, the location of Israel no longer registered. The category-formation could not make a more explicit statement of that fact, nor would Deuteronomy permit any other. God having taken up residence, nothing more could take place other than the restoration of Israel to the Land and God to his abode as well. With its recapitulation of the Written Torah's presentation of matters, the Halakhah makes explicit the critical factor that will bring about the restoration, which turns out to be the same power that in the offerings on the altar brings about expiation and reconciliation: the realization in actuality of the required intention, which only Israel has the power to bring into being.

To conclude: the blood-rite and all the elaborate arrangements of a spatial and material character round about it are represented, time and again, as essentially a medium for atoning for sin; that is explicitly why the daily whole-offerings are required in the formulation of the category-formation, Tamid. Whatever other motivations animate God's commandments concerning the sacrificial cult, the main one, the governing one, repeatedly is, atonement for sin. And here, in the Halakhic recapitulation of Scripture's norms and narratives, it is the *only* variable that transcends fixed rules, meaning, it is the only effective variable. Atonement for sin alone appeals to other than established procedures, hence the distinction that makes the significant difference. It is not only the Halakhah, but also the Aggadah, that takes the view of the blood-rite: it is principally an act of atonement for sin, and when the rite was brought to an end, another medium of atonement had to be identified:

A. One time after the destruction of the Temple Rabban Yohanan ben Zakkai was going forth from Jerusalem, with R. Joshua following after him. He saw the house of the sanctuary lying in ruins.

B. R. Joshua said, "Woe is us for this place which lies in ruins, the place in which the sins of Israel used to come to atonement."

C. He said to him, "My son, do not be distressed. We have another mode of atonement, which is like atonement through sacrifice, and what is that? It is deeds of loving kindness.

D. "For so it is said, 'For I desire mercy and not sacrifice, and the knowledge of God rather than burnt offerings' (Hos. 6:6)."

The Fathers According to Rabbi Nathan IV.V.2

In this context, we find that the Halakhah and Aggadah match in finding the governing variable in hierarchizing cultic activities not only the formal but also the substantive, not only the ordering by the strict character of the rules pertinent to one but not so much to another act of service but also the ordering by appeal to the purpose of the entire exercise. And that revolutionary recognition simply represents the next stage in the logic of the category-formation, the particular hermeneutics of which makes actuality depend upon, relative to, attitude and intentionality. So a remarkably tight logic has dictated the course of the Halakhah to its climax in the Aggadah.

2.
TRACTATE MENAHOT

I. THE DEFINITION OF THE CATEGORY-FORMATION

The category-formation, Menahot, Meal-Offerings, addresses a particular problem by reason of its comparability to its companion, Zebahim. The generative hermeneutics is embodied in the question of how more than a single category of creation — inanimate as well as animate, in this case — accomplishes one and the same task. Scripture is clear that animal offerings atone. It is equally explicit that, where necessitated by reason of poverty, so do vegetable offerings, meal-offerings in particular. But otherwise Scripture carefully delineates and distinguishes the product of the herd and flock from the produce of the orchard and field. For example Moses prohibits the wearing of garments made from wool together with those made from linen, in the theory that what derives from beasts should not be mixed with what derives from the field. And yet, when it comes to atonement, the expiation of sin, Scripture is equally clear that an offering of the one serves equally well as an offering of the other.

Here is where the generic hermeneutics of the Halakhah accomplishes the task defined by the particular hermeneutics of a category-formation. The way in which the Halakhah sorts out matters defines the critical focus of the analysis here, and the solution, the specification of rules that apply to both distinct categories of offering such as to yield a common result, proves characteristic of the Halakhic system throughout. So what is achieved through the ordering of facts, most of them provided by Scripture, vastly transcends the mere recapitulation, within an encompassing and rational framework, of familiar data. Through the very work of regularization and rationalization, comparison and contrast, imposing upon meal-offerings the rules that govern animal offerings, the Halakhah solves a critical problem. It is one that we might classify as a problem of an ontological character: how animal and vegetable, distinct categories of creation, yield the same consequence.

How is the task carried out? The Torah specifies numerous offerings of grain, wheat or barley, and these serve diverse occasions. The Halakhah homogenizes these. It indeed affords recognition only to two distinct grain offerings — the offering of the first barley of the new agricultural season, from the advent of the full moon of Nisan through Pentecost, called the 'omer, and the two loaves and show bread placed on the altar at Pentecost. All of the other diverse meal-offerings are encompassed within a common set of rules. These impose their own modes of differentiation, in place of Scripture's. To review the program of the category-formation:

I. IMPROPER INTENTION AND INVALIDATING THE ACT OF
   SACRIFICE (REPRISE OF ZEBAHIM)

   A. Improper Intention and Invalidating the Act of Sacrifice
   B. Other Rules of Invalidation of Meal-Offerings

II. THE PROPER PREPARATION OF MEAL-OFFERINGS

   A. General Rules
   B. The Meal-Offering that Accompanies the Thank-Offering
   C. Sources of Flour, Oil, and Wine Used for the Meal-Offering
   D. Measuring the Materials Used for the Offering

III. SPECIAL MEAL-OFFERINGS

   A. The 'Omer

IV. VOWS IN CONNECTION WITH MEAL-OFFERINGS

This outline has already made possible the definition of the category-formation, Menahot, in the setting of Zebahim. Where the two intersect, at the opening unit, we find the definition of the category-formation of Menahot as much as of Zebahim. The remainder of the category-formation is comprised by exercises of generic hermeneutics (some) and the systematization of received facts of Scripture and tradition (many).

The Halakhah in the exposition of the category-formation proceeds from general rules for all meal-offerings comparable to those pertaining to animal offerings, to the special rules and problems that differentiate one from another. First of all, the Halakhah sets forth rules for meal-offerings of all categories and classifications, however prepared, for whatever purpose. Then it turns to general rules for the presentation of meal-offerings, e.g., the source for the grain, oil, and wine, the character of the measuring cups that are used for them all, and the like. It turns, third, to the special public offerings, the 'omer and the counterparts for Pentecost. At the end, the Halakhah reviews the language that is used for vows for votive offerings, and how that language is to be interpreted. I cannot conceive of an argument in behalf of Menahot as comparable in intellectual vitality to Zebahim, but when, in the Halakhic setting, I am not able to see more in a fact than the fact itself, I blame myself.

II. THE FOUNDATIONS OF THE HALAKHIC CATEGORY-FORMATIONS

Five classes of votive cereal offerings are specified: [1] a meal-offering of fine flour, a meal-offering baked in the oven in two forms, [2] cakes and [3] wafers, [4] a meal-offering made in a griddle and [5] a meal-offering made in a pan. All are subject to the same governing regulations: a tenth ephah of fine flour and a log of oil. The principal pertinent verses are these:

> "When any one brings a cereal offering as an offering to the Lord, his offerings shall be of fine flour; he shall pour oil upon it and put frankincense on it and bring it to Aaron's sons the priests. And he shall take from it a handful of the fine flour and oil with all of its frankincense, and the priest shall burn this as its memorial portion upon the altar, an offering by fire, a pleasing odor to the Lord. And what is left of the cereal offering shall be for Aaron and his sons; it is a most holy part of the offerings by fire to the Lord. When you bring a cereal offering baked in the oven as an offering, it shall be unleavened cakes of fine flour mixed with oil, or unleavened wafers spread with oil. And if your offering is a cereal offering baked on a griddle, it shall be fine flour unleavened, mixed with oil; you shall break it in pieces and pour oil on it; it is a cereal offering. And if your offering is a cereal offering cooked in a pan, it shall be made of fine flour with oil. And you shall bring the cereal offering that is made of these things to the Lord, and when it is presented to the priest, he shall bring it to the altar. And the priest shall take from the cereal offering its memorial portion and burn this on the altar, an offering by fire, a pleasing odor to the Lord. And what is left of the cereal offering shall be for Aaron and his sons; it is a most holy part of the offerings by fire to the Lord. No cereal offering which you bring to the Lord shall be made with leaven; for you shall burn no leaven nor any honey as an offering by fire to the Lord. As an offering of first fruits you may bring them to the Lord, but they shall not be offered on the altar for a pleasing odor. You shall season all your cereal offerings with salt; you shall not let the salt of the covenant with your God be lacking from your cereal offering; with all your offerings you shall offer salt."
>
> Leviticus 2:1-13

> "This is the law of the cereal offering. The sons of Aaron shall offer it before the Lord in front of the altar. And one shall take from it a handful of the fine flour of the cereal offering with its oil and all the frankincense which is on the cereal offering and burn this as its memorial portion on the altar, a pleasing odor to the Lord. And the rest of it Aaron and his sons shall eat; it shall be eaten unleavened in a

holy place; in the court of the tent of meeting they shall eat it. It shall not be baked with leaven. I have given it as their portion of my offerings by fire; it is a thing most holy, like the sin offering and the built offering. Every male among the children of Aaron may eat of it, as decreed for ever throughout your generations, from the Lord's offerings by fire; whoever touches them shall become holy."

Leviticus 6:7-11/14-18

"And every cereal offering baked in the oven and all that is prepared on a pan or a griddle shall belong to the priest who offers it. And every cereal offering mixed with oil or dry shall be for all the sons of Aaron, one as well as another."

Leviticus 7:9-10

Obligatory meal-offerings, in addition, include these: the meal-offering of a poor sinner by reason of the sins specified at Lev. 5:11-13, the meal-offering of jealousy, presented by the woman accused of adultery (Num. 5:15), the meal-offering of the anointed priest or the cakes of the high priest presented every day (Lev. 6:13-16), and the meal-offering brought with drink offerings along with whole offerings of peace-offerings brought by reason of vows or as votive offerings (Num. 15:2-16), with daily whole offerings and additional offerings (Num. 28:5ff), with the whole offering of a bullock (Num. 15:24), with the offerings of a Nazirite (Num. 6:15), with the offerings of the 'omer (first barley) and with the two loaves of show-bread (Lev. 23:13, 18), with the offerings of the person healed of the skin ailment (Lev. 14:10), with the two loaves and the show bread (Lev. 23:15-17, 24:5-9) and so on. What we see is how in insisting on the cogency of its topic, the Halakhic category-formation defies the diversity of the data that Scripture provides.

III. THE EXPOSITION OF THE COMPONENTS OF THE GIVEN CATEGORY-FORMATION BY THE MISHNAH-TOSEFTA-YERUSHALMI-BAVLI

I. IMPROPER INTENTION AND INVALIDATING THE ACT OF SACRIFICE (REPRISE OF ZEBAHIM)

A. *IMPROPER INTENTION AND INVALIDATING THE ACT OF SACRIFICE*

M. 1:1 All meal-offerings from which the handful was taken not for the purpose for which the meal-offering was originally designated ["not for their own name"] are valid [for offering up, and, in the case of the residue, for the priests' eating]. But they have not gone to their owner's credit in fulfillment of an obligation, except for the meal-offering of a sinner and the meal-offering of jealousy [of a suspected adulteress] [which, if improperly designated for a purpose other than that for which originally designated, are invalid]. The meal-offering of a sinner and the meal-offering of a suspected adulteress (1) from which the handful was taken not for the purpose for which the meal-offering was originally designated ["not for their own name"], (2) [or which] one put into a utensil, and (3) conveyed and (4) offered up not for the purpose for which the meal-offering was originally designated ["not for their own name"], or for the purpose for which the meal was originally designated ["for its own name"] and not for the purpose for which the meal-offering was originally designated ["not for their own name"], or not for the purpose for which the meal-offering was originally designated ["not for their own name"] and for the purpose for which the meal was originally designated ["for its own name"], are invalid. How so [in a case of doing one of the afore-listed actions] is it or for the purpose for which the meal was originally designated ["for its own name"] and not for the purpose for which the meal-offering was originally designated ["not for their own name"]? [If one did one action] (1) for the sake of the meal-offering of a sinner and (2) [another action] for the sake of a freewill meal-offering. Or [how do we define a case of doing one of the afore-listed actions] or not for the purpose for which the meal-offering was originally designated ["not for their own name"] and for the purpose for which the meal was originally designated ["for its own name"] For the sake of (2) a freewill meal-offering and for the sake of (1) the meal-offering of a sinner.

T. 1:1 R. Simeon says, "All meal-offerings, from which the handful was taken not for their own name are valid. And they do go to their owner's credit in fulfillment of an obligation [M. Men. 1:1A-B]. For meal-offerings are not comparable to animal-sacrifices. [For if the priest takes a handful from meal-offering prepared] on a griddle [and refers to it as one prepared] in a pan, the rites pertaining to it [in any case] indicate that [he is dealing with one prepared] on a griddle. [If he is dealing with] a dry meal-offering and [refers to it as one] mixed with oil, [this is of no consequence because] the rites pertaining to it indicate that [he is dealing with] a dry one. But in the case of animal sacrifices, there is only one rite for all of them, and one mode of slaughter for all of them."

T. 1:2 A strict rule applies to slaughtering [an animal-sacrifice] which does not apply to taking up the handful of meal-offering, and [a strict rule applies] to taking up a handful of meal-offering which does not apply to slaughtering [an animal-sacrifice]. For slaughtering an animal has an established place at the north of the altar, and has an established place at the neck [of the animal], and applies to all animals which are offered, and renders prohibited unconsecrated animals [which are slaughtered] inside the Temple courtyard, and Holy Things [which are slaughtered] out side the Temple courtyard, and they are liable for doing it outside — which is not the case of taking up a handful of meal-offering. A strict rule which applies to taking up a handful, of meal-offering, for taking up the handful of meal-offering requires a priest [to do the rite] and vestments of priestly service, which is not the case for slaughtering an animal. Taking up a handful of meal-offering is done with a utensil, but as to slaughtering, [it may be done] even with the pointed tip of a reed.

T. 1:3 A strict rule applies to slaughtering which does not apply to pinching the neck of fowl, and to pinching the neck which does not apply to slaughtering. For slaughtering overrides the [prohibitions of] the Sabbath and [the rules concerning] uncleanness, and applies to public as to private [rites]. It requires a utensil. And it requires [location at] the northern side of the altar, which is not the case for pinching the neck of fowl. A more strict rule applies to pinching the neck, for pinching the neck of fowl requires [that the act be done by] a valid priest, which is not the case for slaughtering.

T. 1:4 A strict rule applies to taking the handful of meal-offering which does not apply to pinching the neck of a bird, and to the pinching of the neck of a bird which does not apply to the taking of the handful of meal-offering. For taking the handful of meal-offering overrides [the prohibitions of] the Sabbath, and overrides [the considerations of] uncleanness and applies to public as to private rites, and requires a utensil, which is not the case of pinching the neck of fowl. More strict is the rule governing pinching the neck of fowl, for pinching the neck of fowl is subject to a fixed place on the neck, and applies to all offerings, which is not the case of taking up the handful of meal-offering.

M. 1:2 All the same are the meal-offering of a sinner and of all [other sorts of] meal-offerings, the handful of which was taken by (1) a non-priest, (2) a priest mourning his next of kin, (3) a priest who is in the status of one who has immersed on the self-same day and awaits sunset to complete the rite of purification [a tebul-yom], (4) a priest lacking proper priestly vestments, (5) a priest whose rites of atonement had not yet been completed, (6) a priest whose hands and feet had not been washed, (7) an uncircumcised priest, (8) an unclean priest, (9) a priest who was seated, (10) a priest who was standing on utensils, on a beast, on the feet of his fellow — he has rendered [it] invalid. [If] he took the handful with his left hand, he has rendered [it] invalid. Ben Beterah says, "Let him put it back, and go and take up a handful in his right hand." [If] he took a handful and there came up in his hand a pebble or a grain of salt or a grain of frankincense, it [the pebble, etc.] has rendered [it] invalid. For they have said, "The handful which is too much or which is too little is invalid." What is a case of a [handful] which is too much? [A case in which] one took an overflowing handful. And one which is too little? [A case in which] one took up a handful with his fingertips. What does one do? He stretches out his fingertips over the palm of his hand.

T. 1:5 R. Eliezer says, "Even if one of his feet is on the pavement and one of his feet is on a brick, one of his feet on the pavement and one of his feet on utensils if the utensil should be removed and he should be able to stand by himself, it is valid. And if not, it is invalid" [M. Men. 1:2A10 = T. Zeb. 1:5].

T. 1:6 One unclean with corpse-uncleanness and one whose atonement has not yet been completed and a Tebul Yom [M. Men. 1:2A, 3] — the [priestly] frontlet does not effect atonement for the uncleanness of the body [of the aforementioned priests]. For what does the [priestly] frontlet effect atonement? For the uncleanness of the blood and of the handful of meal-offering and for the drink-offerings.

T. 1:7 One who was lacking the priestly vestments [M. Men. 1:2A4] — a High Priest serves in eight garments, and an ordinary priest in four. And if a High Priest serves in four and an ordinary priest in eight and carried out his rite, it is invalid. [If] one carried out a rite requiring golden garments in white ones, or one requiring white ones in golden ones, his rite of service is invalid.

T. 1:8 [If the priestly garments] trailed [on the floor] or did not reach [the floor] or were threadbare, and he performed the rite [in them], his rite of service is valid. [If] he wore two pairs of trousers or two undergarments or two sashes, or if they were torn, or if one of them was missing, or if [a priest] put a poultice on his skin under his garments and carried out a rite of service, his rite of service is invalid.

T. 1:9 A priest whose hands and feet were not washed [M. Men. 1:2A6] — how so? One washes [sanctifying] his hands and feet, with a utensil of service, inside. [If] he washed his hands and feet with a utensil of service outside, or with an unconsecrated utensil inside, or if he immersed in cave-water and carried out a rite of service, his rite of service is invalid.

T. 1:10 How does one wash [sanctify]? He puts his right hand on his right foot, his left hand on his left foot, he rubs and rinses, rubs and rinses. R. Judah says, "Even if his two hands were on top of one another he washes them [in that position]." They said to him, "It is not possible to make certain of the matter."

T. 1:11 Priests who did not immerse and did not wash their hands and feet — and so too a high priest who immersed but did not wash his hands and feet — between one rite of service and the next or between donning one set of garments and another, and who performed a rite of service — [their] rite of service is valid. But priests who did not immerse and did not wash their hands and feet [at all], and so too a high priest who immersed but did not wash his hands and feet in the morning — and who performed a rite of sacrifice — [their] rite of sacrifice is invalid.

T. 1:12 All the same are a high priest and an ordinary priest who served in the morning with unwashed hands and feet — Lo, these are liable to the death-penalty, as it is said, "When they come to the tent of meeting, they shall wash in water and so not die" (Ex. 30:19).

T. 1:13 [If a priest] was standing and making offerings all night, at dawn he requires washing of hands and feet. Rabbi says, "The passing of the night does not invalidate in the case of the washing of hands and feet." R. Eleazar b. R. Simeon says, "Even if he interrupts in the rite of sacrifice three days, the passage of the night does not invalidate in the case of washing hands and feet."

T. 1:14 [If a priest] sat down on the pavement [M. Men. 1:2A9], it is invalid, as it is said, "To stand to serve" (Deut. 18:4). [If a priest] stood on a brick [M. Men. 1:2A10], it is invalid, as it is said, "Like all his brothers, the Levites" (Deut. 18:2).

T. 1:15 If one took the handful of meal-offering in his left hand, it is invalid. Ben Beterah says, "Let him put it back and go and take up a handful of meal-offering in his right hand" [M. Men. 1:2C-D]. Said R. Eleazar b. R. Simeon, "So did R. Judah ben Betera say in connection with all those who are invalid [to serve as priests]." R. Yosé b. Yasin and R. Judah the baker say, "Under what circumstances? At a time that he has not yet sanctified the handful of meal-offering in a utensil. But if he has already sanctified this handful of meal-offering in a utensil, all agree that he should not repeat [the action]." Rabbi says, "One way or the other, let him put it back, for a utensil does not effect the sanctification of the handful of meal-offering which has not been taken up from its container."

T. 1:16 What is the order of meal-offerings? One would bring it from home in a silver or a golden utensil. He put it into a utensil of service and sanctified it in a utensil of service and put its oil and its frankincense on it. He went in [to the courtyard] and offered it up at the southeastern corner of the altar, at the southern side of the corner. He puts it on the altar and that suffices. Then he removes its frankincense from one side and takes up a handful of meal-offering from the place at which the oil is located and puts it into a utensil of service and sanctifies it in a utensil of service. Then he gathers the frankincense and puts it on top of it. And he raises it onto the altar and salts it and puts it onto the altar fires. And the residue do they give to the priests.

T. 1:17 The priests are permitted to put into the residue of meal-offerings wine, olive-oil, and honey, but are prohibited from allowing it to ferment. What does he do? He stretches out his fingers over the palm of his hand [M. Men. 1:2K-L], and the pieces does he level from above to below [B. Men. 11 a: He must level it with his thumb on top and with his little finger below]. [If] he put in too much oil or put in too little oil, put in too much flour or put in too little flour, it is invalid. [If] he put in too much incense, it is valid [M. Men. 1:3A]. If he put in too little incense, even two grains, it is valid," the words of R. Judah. R. Simeon says, "The handful of meal-offering and the frankincense which lack any amount at all are invalid." All the same are the meal-offering of Israelites and the meal-offerings of priests, but the meal-offering of priests is entirely burned on the fire:, of the altar, as it says, "And the whole meal-offering of the priest will be entirely consumed. It will not be eaten" (Lev. 6:16).

M. 1:3 [If] he put in too much of its oil [M. 9:3] or put in too little oil or put in too little frankincense [M. 13:3], it is invalid. He who takes up the handful of meal-offering [with the improper intention] to eat its residue outside, or an olive's bulk of its residue outside, to burn a handful thereof outside, or an olive's bulk of a handful thereof outside, or to burn its frankincense outside — it is invalid. But extirpation does not apply to it. [If he takes up the handful of meal-offering with the improper intention] to eat its residue on the next day, or an olive's bulk of its residue on the next day, to burn a handful thereof on the next day, or an olive's bulk of a handful thereof on the next day, or to burn its frankincense on the next day, it is refuse. And they are liable to extirpation on its account. This is the general principle: [In] every [case in which] one (1) takes the handful of meal-offering, or (2) puts it into a utensil, or (3) conveys it, or (4) offers it up, [with the improper intention] to eat something which is usually eaten [the residue] or to offer up something which is usually offered up [the meal-offering — outside of its proper place, it is invalid. But extirpation does not apply to it. [If one does so with the improper intention to eat the residue or to offer up the meal-offering] outside of its proper time, it is refuse. And they are liable on its account to extirpation. [And the foregoing rule applies] on condition that that which renders the offering permissible is offered in accord with its requirement. How is that which renders the offering permissible offered in accord with its requirement? [If] one took the handful in silence [without improper intention] and put it into the utensil and conveyed and offered it up [with the improper intention to do so] outside of its proper time, or [if] one took the handful of meal-offering [with the improper intention of eating that which is eaten or offering up that which is offered up] outside of its proper time, and [then] put it into a utensil and conveyed and offered it up in silence [without improper intention], or [if] one took the handful and put it into a utensil and conveyed and offered it up [with the improper intention to eat that which is eaten or to burn that which is burned] outside of its proper time [only] — this is a case in which that which renders the offering permissible is offered up in accord with its requirement.

M. 1:4 How is that which renders the offering permissible not offered in accord with its requirement? [If] one took the handful [with the improper intention of eating that which is eaten or burning that which is burned] outside of its proper place, and [then] put it into a utensil and conveyed and offered it up [with the improper intention of eating that which is eaten or burning that which is burned] outside of its proper time, or [if] one took the handful [with the improper intention of eating or burning] outside of its proper time, and [then] put it into a utensil and conveyed and offered it up [with the improper intention of eating or burning] outside of its proper place, or [if] one took the handful and put it into a utensil and conveyed and offered it up [with the improper intention of eating or burning] outside of its proper place [in addition to time] — [and likewise] the meal-offering of a sinner and the meal-offering of a suspected adulteress of which one took the handful not for their own name, and put into the utensil and conveyed and offered up [with the improper intention of eating or burning] outside of their proper time, or [if] one took the handful [with improper intention to eat or burn] outside of their proper time, and [then] placed [it] into the utensil and conveyed and offered it up not for their own name, or [if] one took the handful and put it into a utensil and conveyed and offered it up not for their own name [at all] — this is a case in which that which renders the offering permissible has not been offered up in accord with its requirement. If one did so to eat an olive's bulk outside and an olive's bulk on the next day, an olive's bulk on the next day and an olive's bulk outside, a half-olive's bulk outside and a half-olive's bulk on the next day, a half-olive's bulk on the next day and a half-olive's bulk outside — it is invalid. But extirpation does not apply to it. Said R. Judah, "This is the general rule: If the improper intention concerning time came before the improper intention concerning place, it is refuse. And they are liable on its account to extirpation. But if the improper intention concerning place came before the improper intention concerning time, it is invalid. But extirpation does not apply to it." And sages say, "Both this and that are invalid. But extirpation does not apply to it." [If one took up the handful with the improper intention to eat a half-olive's bulk and to offer up a half-olive's bulk [at the wrong time or in the wrong place], it is invalid. For [improper intention concerning] eating and [improper intention concerning] offering up do

not join together.

T. 2:1 He who takes a handful of meal-offering [with the improper intention, while doing so] to eat its residue outside, or an olive's bulk of its residue outside, to offer up its handful outside, or an olive's bulk of its handful outside, to offer up its frankincense outside, or an olive's bulk of its frankincense outside — it is invalid. And extirpation does not apply to it. [If he does so with the improper intention, at the time of the deed] to eat its residue on the next day, or an olive's bulk of its residue on the next day, to offer up its handful on the next day, or an olive's bulk of its handful on the next day, to offer up its frankincense, or an olive's bulk of its frankincense on the next day, it is refuse. And they are liable on its account to the penalty of extirpation [M. Men. 1:3B-M].

T. 2:2 All meal-offerings of which one took a handful not for their own name, conveyed and offered up [with the improper intention of eating the residue or burning the meal-offering] outside of their proper time or of which one took a handful [with the improper intention of eating the residue or burning the meal-offering] outside of their proper time, and conveyed and offered up not for their own name — [these are] refuse. And they are liable on its account for extirpation. [And the foregoing rule applies] on condition that that which renders the offering permitted has been offered up in accord with its requirement [M. Men. 1:3S].

T. 2:3 How is that which renders the offering permitted offered in accord with its requirement? [If] one took the handful in silence [without improper intention] and put it into a utensil and conveyed it [to the altar] and offered it up [with the improper intention, at any one of these acts, of eating the residue or burning the offering] outside of its proper time, or [if] one took the handful [with improper intention concerning eating or offering] outside of its proper time, and put it into a utensil and covered it and offered it up in silence [M. Men. 1:3T-V], or [if] one took the handful and put it into the utensil and conveyed it and offered it up in silence [T. Zeb. 2:5] — this is a case in which that which renders the offering permitted has been offered in accord with its requirement [M. Men. 1:3X].

T. 2:4 How is that which renders the offering permitted not offered in accord with its requirement? [If] one took the handful with improper intention concerning eating or offering it up] outside of its proper time and put it into the utensil and conveyed it and offered it up [with improper intention concerning eating or offering up] outside of its proper time, or [if] one took the handful [with improper intention] concerning time and put it into a utensil and conveyed and offered it up [with improper intention concerning] its place [M. Men. 1:4C], or [if] one took the handful and put it into a utensil and conveyed it and offered it up [with improper intention concerning] its proper place [M.

Men. 1:4D]. Whether the improper intention concerning time came before the improper intention concerning place, or whether the improper intention concerning place came before the improper intention concerning time, it is invalid. But extirpation does not apply to it [T. Zeb. 2:6]. R. Judah says, "Even in this case: [If] improper intention concerning time came before improper intention concerning place, it is deemed refuse. And they are liable on its account to extirpation. [If] improper intention concerning place came before improper intention concerning time, it is invalid. And extirpation does not apply to it" [M. Men. 1:4N].

T. 2:5 How does the improper intention concerning time come before improper intention concerning place? [If] he took the handful [with improper intention to eat the residue or burn the meal-offering] outside of its proper time, and then put it into a utensil and conveyed it and offered it up [with the improper intention to eat the residue or offer up the meal-offering] outside of its proper place. How does the improper intention concerning place come before improper intention concerning time? If he took the handful [with improper intention to eat the residue, etc.,] outside of its proper place, and then he put it into a utensil and conveyed it and offered it up [with the improper intention to eat it, etc.] outside of its proper time [T. Zeb. 2:6-7].

T. 2:6 The meal-offering of a sinner and the meal-offering of jealousy [of the woman accused of adultery], of which one took the handful not for their own name — it is invalid. And extirpation does not apply to it, because that which renders the offering permitted has not been offered in accord with its requirement [T. Zeb. 2:8].

T. 2:7 He who takes the handful of meal-offering [with the improper intention] to eat its residue outside, to offer up its handful on the next day to eat its residue on the next day, to offer up its handful outside — whether the improper intention concerning time came before the improper intention concerning place, or whether the improper intention concerning place came before the improper intention concerning time — it is invalid. And extirpation does not apply to it [vs. M. Men. 2:1 B]. R. Judah says, "Also in this case. [If] the improper intention concerning the time came before the improper intention concerning place, it is refuse. And they are liable on its account to extirpation. [But if] the improper intention concerning place came before the improper intention concerning time, it is invalid. And extirpation does not apply to it" [= T. Zeb. 2:9].

T. 2:8 All meal-offerings of which one took the handful [with the improper intention to eat the residue] outside of their proper time or of which unfit people took the handful and which they offered up in silence, or the handful of which was kept overnight and which they [then] burned in silence [without improper intention] or the handful of which went out beyond the veils and which one [then] offered up in silence — [even if one had the improper intention to eat the residue] outside of its proper time — it is invalid. And extirpation does not apply to it [= T. Zeb. 2:10].

T. 2:9 He who takes the handful of meal-offering [with the improper intention] to eat its residue an olive's bulk on that day, and an olive's bulk on the next day — to offer up its handful — an olive's bulk outside and an olive's bulk inside — it is invalid. And extirpation does not apply to it. [If he did so] to eat its residue an olive's bulk outside and an olive's bulk inside — to offer up its handful — an olive's bulk that day, and an olive's bulk the next day — it is refuse, and they are liable on its account to extirpation [= T. Zeb. 2:11].

T. 2:10 He who takes the handful of meal-offering [with the improper intention] to eat its residue, a half olive's bulk outside and a half olive's bulk inside — to offer up its handful, a half olive's bulk outside and a half olive's bulk inside — it is valid. And so with respect [to improper intention regarding doing these things] on the next day, it is valid [T. Zeb. 2:12].

T. 2:11 He who takes the handful of meal-offering [with the improper intention] to eat its residue — an olive's bulk outside, and a half olive's bulk inside, whether the improper intention concerning time came before the improper intention concerning place, or whether the improper intention concerning place came before the improper intention concerning time — It is invalid. And extirpation does not apply to it R. Judah says, "Also in this case: [if] the improper intention concerning time came before the improper intention concerning place, it is refuse and they are liable on its account to extirpation. [But if] the improper intention concerning place came before the improper intention concerning time, it is refuse. But extirpation does not apply to it" [= T. Zeb. 2:12].

T. 2:12 He who takes the handful of the meal-offering [with the improper Intention] to eat of its residue, a half olive's bulk outside — and to offer up of its handful, a half olive's bulk outside — to eat, of its residue, a half olive's bulk on the next day, and to offer up of its handful a half olive's bulk on the next day — to eat of its remnant a half olive's bulk outside — and to offer up of its handful a half olive's bulk on the next day — it is valid. For the act of taking the handful of the meal-offering and the act of offering up [the handful] do not join together with one another. But one act of taking the handful of meal-offering does join together with another such act, and one act of offering up the meal-offering does join together with another such act [= T. Zeb. 2:13].

T. 2:13 How so? He who takes a handful of meal-offering [with the improper intention] to eat of its residue an olive's bulk outside, and an olive's bulk on the next day, to offer up of its meal-offering a half olive's bulk outside and a half olive's bulk on the next day — it is invalid, and extirpation does not apply to it. For one act of taking a handful of meal-offering and another such act, or one act of offering up the meal-offering and another such act, do join together with one another [= T. Zeb. 2:13].

T. 2:14 He who takes a handful of meal-offering [with the improper intention] to eat of its residue a half olive's bulk on the next day, [and] at the time of the offering up, he [then] gave thought further more to offer up of its handful of meal-offering a half olive's bulk on the it is refuse, and they are liable on its account to extirpation. For an act of taking the handful of meal-offering and an act of offering it up do join together with one another to impart the status of refuse.

T. 2:15 He who takes the handful of meal-offering [with the intention] to offer of the handful a half-olive's bulk on the next day — it is valid. For less than an olive's bulk does not impart the status of refuse or invalidate under any circumstances.

T. 2:16 He who takes a handful of meal-offering [with the improper intention] to eat the handful of meal-offering itself and to offer up its residue — to eat something which is not usually eaten and to offer up something which is not usually offered up — it is valid [M. Men. 3:1]. And R. Judah declares invalid. [If one does so] to leave the handful of meal-offering and its residue for the next day, or to take them outside [the courtyard] — it is valid. And R. Judah declares invalid. R. Eleazar says, "R. Eliezer declares invalid, and R. Joshua declares valid." Said to him R. Judah, "Now if one left the handful for the next day he does not render it invalid." And sages say, "This and this are valid. You have nothing which is invalid except improper intention concerning taking the handful and offering it up alone."

M. 2:1 He who takes the handful of meal-offering [with the improper intention] to eat its residue or to burn its handful on the next day — R. Yosé agrees in this case that it [the sacrifice] is refuse and they who eat it are liable on its account to extirpation [= M. 1:3]. [If he does so with the improper intention] to burn its frankincense on the next day, R. Yosé says, "It [the sacrifice] is invalid. And extirpation does not apply to it." And sages say, "It is refuse. And they are liable on its account to extirpation." They said to him, "What is the difference between this case [of the meal-offerings and frankincense] and the animal sacrifice?" He said to them, "The animal sacrifice — its blood and its flesh and its sacrificial parts are [of] one [genre]. But the frankincense is not from the meal-offering [which is flour]."

M. 2:2 [If] he slaughtered two lambs [Lev. 23:19, the peace offering at Shabuot], [with the improper intention] to eat one of the loaves [that accompany that rite] on the next day [after the festival] — [If] he burned the two dishes [of frankincense, with the improper intention to eat one of the rows [on the next day] — R. Yosé says, "That particular loaf or that particular row to which he gave thought [improperly to eat on the next day] is refuse. And they are liable on its account to extirpation. But the second [loaf of bread or row] is invalid. And extirpation does not apply to it." And sages say, "Both this and that are refuse, and they are liable on its account to extirpation." [If before the tossing of the blood or burning of the incense,] one of the loaves or one of the rows was made unclean, R. Judah says, "Both of them go out to the place of burning. For an offering made in behalf of the congregation is not to be divided." And sages say, "The unclean [remains] subject to its uncleanness, but the clean one may be eaten."

T. 3:1 He who slaughters two lambs, [intending] to eat one of the loaves of bread on the next day, [or] who offers up two dishes of frankincense, [intending] to eat one of the rows on the next day — "It is refuse, and they are liable on its account to extirpation," the words of R. Meir [= sages, M. Men. 2:2E]. And sages say, "This one [concerning which he formed the improper intention] is refuse, and they are liable on its account to extirpation. But the second ,is invalid, and extirpation does not apply to it" [= Yosé, M. Men. 2:2C-D].

T. 3:2 Two dishes of frankincense, one of which was made unclean — let it be offered in a state of uncleanness, and its fellow in a state of cleanness. R. Judah says, "The offering of the congregation is not divided [= M. Men. 2:2H], but let both of them be offered in a state of uncleanness."

T. 3:3 The handful and the frankincense, one of which was made unclean — let both of them go out to the place of burning.

T. 3:4 If one was offering two loaves of bread and they became unclean in his hand, they say to him, "Be smart and shut up."

T. 3:5 [If] one was offering up two rows [of bread] and they became unclean in his hand, they say to him, "Be smart and shut up." [If] he was offering two dishes of frankincense and they became unclean in his hand, they say to him, "Be smart and shut up." [If] he was offering the meal-offering of priests and the meal-offering of the anointed priest, and they became unclean in his hand, they say to him "Be smart and shut up."

T. 3:6 [If] he was offering the meal-offering of bullocks and lambs and they became unclean in his hand, one says, "Let them bring another in its stead." [If] there was there only that one, they say to him, "Be smart and shut up."

T. 3:7 "If he was offering the 'omer and it was made unclean, they say, 'Let them bring another in its stead.' If there is only that one, they say to him, 'Be smart and shut up,'" the words of R. Eleazar b. R. Simeon. Rabbi says, "One way or the other, they say to him, 'Be smart and shut up,' for the 'omer which they reaped not in accord with its requirement 15 Invalid."

M. 2:3 [An improper intentionality concerning] the thank-offering makes the bread [brought along with the thank-offering, Lev. 7:13, M. 7:1] refuse, but [an improper intentionality concerning] the bread does not make the thank-offering refuse. How so? He who slaughters the thank-offering [with the improper intention] to eat of it on the next day — it and the bread are made refuse. [If he does so with the improper intention] to eat of the bread on the next day, the bread is made refuse, but the thank-offering is not made refuse. [Improper intentionality concerning] the lambs make the bread [Lev. 23:19, 20, M. 2:2] refuse, but [improper intentionality concerning] the bread does not make the lambs refuse. How so? He who slaughters the lambs [with the improper intention] to eat of them on the next day — they and the bread are made refuse. [If he does so with the improper intention] to eat of the bread on the next day, the bread is made refuse, but the lambs are not made refuse.

M. 2:4 [Improper intentionality concerning] the animal sacrifice makes the drink offerings refuse, ("once they have been sanctified in a utensil," the words of R. Meir) — but [improper intentionality concerning] the drink offerings do not make the animal sacrifice refuse. How so? He who slaughters the animal sacrifice [with the improper intention] to eat of it on the next day — it and its drink offerings are made refuse. [If he does so with the improper intention] to offer up part of the drink offerings on the next day, the drink offerings are made refuse, but the animal sacrifice is not made refuse.

T. 3:8 "The thank-offering is essential to, and imparts the status of refuse upon, the bread, but the bread is essential to, and does not impart the status of refuse upon, the thank-offering [M. Men. 2:3A]. Lambs are essential to, and impart the status of refuse upon, the bread, but the bread is essential to, and does not impart the status of refuse upon, the lambs [M. Men. 2:3G]. The animal-sacrifice imparts the status of refuse to the drink-offerings once they have been sanctified in a utensil," the words of R. Meir. But the drink-offerings do not impart the status of refuse upon the animal-sacrifice [= M. Men. 2:4A-C].

M. 2:5 [If one formed an improper intention, such that he has] (1) made refuse the handful [of meal for the meal-offering] but not the frankincense, (2) the frankincense but not the handful — R. Meir says, "It is refuse, and they are liable on its account to extirpation." And sages say, "Extirpation does not apply to it, until [through improper intention to eat or offer up the whole outside the proper time] he will render refuse the whole of that which renders the offering permissible [for the priests to eat]." But sages concur with R. Meir in the case of the meal-offering of a sinner and the meal-offering of a woman accused of adultery [neither of which is accompanied by incense], that if one has imparted the status of refuse to the handful [of the meal-offering], it is refuse, and they are liable to extirpation on its account. For it is [solely] the handful [of meal-offering] which renders the offering permissible. [If] one slaughtered one of the lambs [with the improper intention] to eat the two loaves on the next day, [or if he] burned one of the two dishes [of frankincense, with the improper intention] to eat both rows on the next day — R. Meir says, "It is refuse, and they are liable on its account to extirpation." And sages say, "It is not refuse until one will impart the status of refuse to the whole of that which renders the sacrifice permissible." [If] he slaughtered one of the lambs [with the improper intention] to eat of it on the next day, it is refuse, but its fellow is valid. [If he slaughtered one lamb intending] to eat its fellow on the next day, both are valid.

T. 3:9 "[If] one took the handful in silence [without improper intention] and when he came to the act of offering it up, offered up the handful in silence, but the frankincense [with the improper intention to dispose of it] outside of its proper time — "It is refuse, and they are liable on its account to extirpation," the words of R. Meir. And sages say, "Extirpation does not apply to it until one will impose the status of refuse on the entirety of that which renders the offering permitted to be eaten" [= M. Men. 2:5B-C]. When does the opinion of R. Meir pertain? At the time that he will offer up that which permits the offering to be eaten in accord with its requirement. But if it was kept overnight or invalidated or went forth beyond the veils or unfit people offered up one of them, even with the improper intention to dispose of it outside of its proper time, it is invalid. And extirpation does not apply to it.

T. 3:10 [If] one offered up one of them, even [with the improper intention to eat what is eaten or to offer up what is offered up] outside of its proper time, he has rendered it invalid, and extirpation does not apply to it. [If] he offered up one of them today, on condition to offer up its fellow on the next day, all [Meir, sages] agree that it is refuse, and they are liable to extirpation on its account.

T. 3:11 "Two dishes of frankincense, the first of which one offered up in silence, and the second of which one offered up with improper intention [to dispose of the sacrifice] outside of its proper time — it is refuse, and they are liable on its account to extirpation," the words of R. Meir. And sages say, "Extirpation applies to it only if one will impose the status of refuse on the whole of that which renders the offering permissible to be eaten." When do the words of R. Meir apply? At the time that the second has been in accord with its requirement. But if it was kept overnight or invalidated or went out beyond the veils, or [if] invalid people offered up one of them — even with the improper intention to dispose of the sacrifice outside of its proper time — it is invalid, and extirpation does not apply to it. [If] one offered up one of them on condition to offer up part of its fellow on the next day, all agree that it is refuse, and they are liable on its account to extirpation.

T. 3:12 "The two lambs of the festival, the first of which one slaughtered in silence, and the second of which one slaughtered with the intention of eating outside its proper time" — "it is refuse, and they are liable on its account to extirpation," the words of R. Meir. And sages say, "Extirpation applies to it only if one will impart the status of refuse to the entirety of that which permits the offering to be eaten." When does the opinion of R. Meir apply? At such time that the second will be offered in accord with its extirpation. But [if] it was kept overnight or invalidated or went forth beyond the veils, or [If] one of those who was invalid slaughtered and tossed the blood even with the improper intention to eat the meat and burn the sacrificial parts outside of its proper time, it is invalid, and extirpation does not apply to it.

T. 3:13 [If] one slaughtered one of them today on condition of eating its fellow on the next day, all agree that it is valid [=M. Men. 2:5M]. For the lamb does not impart to its fellow the status of refuse or invalidate its fellow under any circumstances.

M. 3:1 He who takes the handful of meal-offering [with the improper intention] to eat something [e.g., the handful, the frankincense] which is not usually eaten, to offer up something [e.g., the residue] which is not usually offered up, it is valid. R. Eliezer declares [the offering] invalid. [If one does so with the improper intention] to eat something which is usually eaten, to offer up something which is usually offered up, [in a volume] less than an olive's bulk — it is valid. [If he does so with the improper intention] to eat a half-olive's bulk and to offer up a half-olive's bulk — it is valid. For eating and offering up do not join together.

The category-formation, Menahot, simply replicates the points of its counterpart, Zebahim, making the necessary changes required by the subject-matter, e.g., at M. 1:3. But the issue of intentionality is framed within a single pattern, which imposes a verbatim identity on the two category-formations, M. 1:3-4, M. 2:1-2. Here is where the category-formation twice accomplishes its goal of homogenization: first, of Menahot with Zebahim, but second, of all classifications of meal-offerings among themselves. The latter task defines the program of the next sub-set of the Halakhah.

B. OTHER RULES OF INVALIDATION OF MEAL-OFFERINGS

M. 3:2 [If] one (1) did not pour [oil over the fine flour], (2) did not mingle [the oil with unleavened cakes], (3) did not break up [the meal-offering prepared in a baking pan], (4) did not salt it, (5) did not wave it [if such is required, as in the case of the meal-offering of the 'omer and of the woman accused of adultery], (6) did not bring it near [M. 5:5-6] — or [if] he broke it up into big pieces or did not anoint it [with oil after baking (M. 6:3)] — [the meal-offerings so prepared] are valid. [If] its handful [of meal-offering] was mixed with the handful of its fellow [meal-offering] — (1) with the meal-offering of priests, (2) with the meal-offering of the anointed priest, (3) with the meal-offerings brought with drink offerings [M. 6:2] — it is valid. R. Judah says, "In the case of [mixture with] the meal-offering of the anointed priest or with the meal-offering brought with drink offerings, it is invalid. For in the case of one, its mixture is thick [M. 3:3], and in the case of the others, its mixture is thin [M. 9:4], and each absorbs from the other." [One handful will have absorbed too much oil, the other has been diluted and now has too little oil.]

T. 5:6 The Torah has imposed a more stringent rule in connection with intention in respect to animal-sacrifice than in respect to their actual deeds [rites] concerning them [and it also has imposed a more stringent rule in connection with] the actual deed in respect to an animal-sacrifice than [in connection with] intention pertaining to them. How [is the rule of] intention pertaining to animal-sacrifices [more strict] than [the rule governing] actual deeds concerning them? (1) He who slaughters the animal sacrifice [with the improper intention] to toss its blood outside of the proper place or part of its blood outside, to offer up its sacrificial parts outside or part of its sacrificial parts out side, to eat its flesh outside or part of its flesh outside, he has invalidated it. And extirpation does not apply to it [M. Zeb. 2:2, T. Zeb. 2:1]. But if he actually did so [tossed the blood, etc., outside], it is not invalid. (2) [If he slaughtered the animal with the improper intention] to toss its blood on the next day, or part of its blood on the next day, to offer up its sacrificial parts on the next day or an olive's bulk of its sacrificial parts on the next day, to eat its flesh on the next day or an olive's bulk of its flesh on the next day, it is refuse, and they are liable on its account to extirpation. But if he actually did so, it is not deemed refuse.

T. 5:7 (3)He who takes a handful of meal-offering [with the improper intention] to eat its residue outside, or an olive's bulk of its residue outside to offer up its handful outside, or an olive's bulk of its handful outside, to burn its frankincense outside or an olive's bulk of its frankincense outside — it is invalid. But extirpation does not apply to it. And if he actually did so, it is not invalid. (4) [He who takes a handful of meal-offering with the improper intention] to eat its residue on the next day, or an olive's bulk of its residue on the next day, to offer up its handful on the next day, or an olive's bulk of its handful on the next day, to burn its frankincense on the next day, or an olive's bulk of its frankincense on the next day, it is refuse. And they are liable on its account to extirpation. And if he actually did so, it is not deemed refuse.

T. 5:8 How so [has the Torah imposed a more stringent rule in connection with] rites of the animal-sacrifice than in connection with intention concerning them? (1) He who slaughters the animal-sacrifice on condition that uncircumcised [priests] and unclean [priests] toss its blood, on condition that uncircumcised and unclean priests offer up its sacrificial parts, on condition that uncircumcised priests eat its flesh, it is valid. But if he actually did so, Lo, this is invalid. (2) [If] one [slaughtered the animal, with the intention of] tossing the drops of blood which are to be placed below, above, and the drops of blood which are to be placed above, below, those which are to be placed inside, outside, and those which are to be placed outside, inside, it is valid. But if he actually did so, Lo, this is invalid.

T. 5:9 (3) He who slaughters a sin-offering [intending] to bring its blood inside [to the inner altar] — it is valid. A sin-offering, the blood of which one has actually brought inside — even any amount at all — is invalid. (4) He who takes the handful of meal-offering [intending] to offer up of its handful less than an olive's bulk on the next day — it is valid. The handful [of meal-offering] which was lacking any amount at all [of its requisite volume] is invalid.

T. 5:10 All meal-offerings of which one took the handful not for them. Therefore, if one gave thought to it [to offer it up] outside of its proper place, it is invalid. And extirpation does not apply to it. [If he did so with the improper intention to offer it up] outside of its proper time, it is refuse. And they are liable on its account to extirpation.

T. 5:11 [If] a priest took the handful, [if] a valid priest took the handful, [if] he took the handful in his right hand, [if] he took the handful in a consecrated utensil, it is valid. Therefore, if he gave thought to it [to offer it up] outside of its proper place, he has invalidated it. And extirpation does not apply to it. [If he took the handful with the improper intention to offer it up] outside of its proper time, it is refuse, and they are liable to extirpation on its account.

T. 5:12 [If] a valid [priest] took the handful but gave it to an invalid one he should return it to the valid priest and it is valid. [If it was] in the hand of an invalid person and he gave thought to it [to offer it up] whether outside of its proper time or outside of its proper place, the matter of refuse does not apply to it. [If it was] in the hand of a valid person and he gave thought to it [to offer it up] outside of its proper time, it is invalid, and extirpation does not apply to it. [If he gave thought to it to offer it up] outside of its proper time, it is refuse, and they are liable on its account to extirpation.

T. 5:13 "[If] one took the handful with his right hand and put it into his left hand, he should put it back into his right hand, and it is valid. [If it was] in his left hand and he gave thought to it [to offer it up] whether outside of its proper time or outside of its proper place, it is not subject to the matter of refuse. [If it was] in his right hand and he gave thought to it [to offer it up] outside of its proper place, it is invalid. And extirpation does not apply to it. [If it was in his right hand and he gave thought to it, offer it up] outside of its proper time, it is refuse, and they are liable to extirpation on its account."

T. 5:14 "[If] he took the handful with a consecrated utensil and put it into an unconsecrated utensil, let him put it back into a consecrated utensil, and it is valid. [If it was] in an unconsecrated utensil and he gave thought to it [to offer it up] whether outside of its proper time or outside of its proper place, the matter of refuse does not apply to it. [If it was] in a consecrated utensil and he gave thought to it [to offer it up] outside of its proper place, it is invalid. And extirpation does not apply to it. "[If he gave thought to it to offer it up] outside of its proper time, it is refuse. And they are liable on its account to extirpation," the words of R. Eleazar b. R. Simeon. And sages say, "[If] a valid person took the handful and gave it to an invalid person, his act of handing it over has rendered it invalid. [If] he took the handful in a consecrated utensil and put it into an unconsecrated utensil, his act of putting it [into the unconsecrated utensil] has invalidated it.

T. 5:15 "[If] one took the handful in his right hand and put it into his left hand, his act of putting [it into his left hand] has invalidated it. But he who takes the handful from an unconsecrated utensil and puts it into a consecrated utensil — [if] before he put in its oil and frankincense, he gave thought to it [to offer it up] whether outside of its proper time or outside of its proper place, it is invalid. And extirpation does not apply to it [If] after he put in its oil and its frankincense, he gave thought to it [to offer it up] outside of its proper place, it is invalid. And extirpation does not apply to it. [If he gave thought to offer it up] outside of its proper time it is refuse, and they are liable on its account to extirpation." [If] he took the handful for [meal-offering which is offered] outside and went inside, let him go and take the handful [inside], and it is valid. [If he took the handful] outside and gave thought to it, [to offer it up] whether outside of its proper time or outside of its proper place, it is not subject to the matter of refuse. [If he took the handful] inside and gave thought to it [to offer it up] outside its proper place, it is invalid. And extirpation does not apply to it. [If he did so inside and gave thought to it, to offer it up] outside of its proper time, it is refuse, and they are liable on its account to extirpation.

T. 5:16 [If] the handful [of meal-offering] was scattered on the pavement he should go and gather it up, and it is valid. [If] before he gathered it up, he gave thought to it [to offer it up] whether outside of its proper time or outside of its proper place, it is not subject to the matter of refuse. [If] after he gathered it up, he gave thought to it [to offer it up] out side of its proper time, it is invalid. And extirpation does not apply to it. [If he gave thought, after gathering it up, to offer up the handful] outside of its proper time, it is refuse, and they are liable on its account to extirpation.

T. 5:17 The meal-offering of a sinner and the meal-offering of jealousy [of a woman accused of adultery] upon which one put frankincense, and from which one collected the frankincense, are valid. [If] before one has gathered up the frankincense, one gave thought to it [to offer it up] whether outside of its proper time or outside of its proper place, the matter of refuse does not apply to it. [If] after one has gathered up the frankincense he gave thought to it [to offer it up] outside of its proper place, it is invalid. And extirpation does not apply to it. [If he gave thought, after gathering it up, to offer it up] outside of its proper time, it is refuse, and they are liable on its account to extirpation.

T. 5:18 All meal-offerings which were waved but not brought near, [or] which were brought near but not waved, [or on which one] poured oil but which one did not stir, which one stirred but [on which] one did not pour oil, which one broke into pieces but did not salt, salted but did not break into pieces — it is valid [M. Men. 3:2]. Therefore, if one gave thought to it [to offer it up] outside of its proper place, it is invalid. And extirpation does not apply to it. [If one gave thought to it, to offer it up] outside of its proper time, it is refuse. And they are liable on its account to extirpation. Therefore, [if] one offered up the handful by itself and the frankincense by itself, or one offered up the handful by itself two times, it is valid. Therefore, if one gave thought to it [to offer it up] outside of its proper place, it is invalid. And extirpation does not apply to it. [If he gave thought to it, to offer it up] outside of its proper time, it is refuse, and they are liable on its account to extirpation. This is the general principle: meal-offerings are invalidated only in respect to four actions: (1) the taking of the handful, (2) and the conveying [of the handful], and (3) the placing of the handful into the utensil, and (4) the offering up. In addition to them: the meal-offering of the sinner and the meal-offering of jealousy [of the woman accused of adultery], from which one took the handful not for their own name — Lo, these are invalid. Therefore, if one gave thought to it [to offer it up] whether outside of its proper time or outside of its proper place, the matter of refuse does not apply to it [at all].

T. 5:19 All the same are the meal-offering of the sinner and all meal-offerings, from which the handful was taken by a non-priest, a priest in mourning, a priest who was a Tebul Yom, a priest who has lacking in the proper vestments, a priest whose rites of atonement had not yet been completed, a priest with unwashed hands and feet, an uncircumcised priest, an unclean priest, a priest who was sitting down, a priest who was standing on utensils or on a beast or on the foot of his fellow — it is invalid [M. Men. 1:2]. [If, therefore] one gave thought to it [to offer it up] whether outside of its proper time or outside of its proper place, the matter of refuse does not apply to it.

T. 5:20 [If] the handful was overflowing, or [if] one took the handful and there came up in his hand a pebble or a grain of salt or a grain of frankincense [M. Men. 1:2E], it is invalid. Therefore, [if] he gave thought to it [to offer it up] whether outside of its proper time or outside of its proper place, the matter of refuse does not apply to it.

T. 5:21 [If] a non-priest took the handful, it is invalid. [If] he took the handful with his left hand, took the handful in an unconsecrated utensil, it is invalid. Therefore, if he gave thought to it [to offer it up] whether outside of its proper time or outside of its proper place, the matter of refuse does not apply to it. [If] he put in too much oil or put in too little oil, put in too much flour or put in too little flour, it is invalid [M. Men. 1:3]. Therefore, if he gave thought to it [to offer it up] whether outside of its proper time or outside of its proper place, the matter of refuse does not apply to it.

T. 5:22 If one took the handful not from the place of the oil or not from the place of the frankincense, or [if] one did not put in it frankincense — even many amount at all — it is invalid. Therefore, if he gave thought to it [to offer it up], whether outside of its proper time or outside of its proper place, the matter of refuse does not apply to it.

T. 5:23 The meal-offering of a sinner and the meal-offering of jealousy [of a woman accused of adultery] on which one put oil is invalid [M. Men. 5:3]. Therefore, if he gave thought to it [to offer it up] whether outside of its proper time or outside of its proper place, the matter of refuse does not apply to it.

T. 5:24 [If] one took it in a utensil or put on it [oil in a utensil (M. Men. 5:4)], it is valid. Therefore, if he gave thought to it [to offer it up] outside of its proper place, it is invalid. And extirpation does not apply to it. [If he gave thought to it, to offer it up] outside of its proper time, it is refuse. And they are liable on its account to extirpation. This is the general principle: The matter of refuse applies only to something which is suitable for the cult and in a place which is suitable to the cult [compare T. Zeb. 3:1-5].

T. 6:1 These are [the items] which require salt: (1) The limbs of the burnt-offering, (2) the sacrificial parts of Most Holy Things, (3) the sacrificial parts of Lesser Holy Things, (4) the handful [of meal-offering], (5) frankincense, (6) the meal-offering of priests, (7) the meal-offering of the anointed priest, and (8) the burnt-offering of fowl. But (1) blood, (2) wine, (3) wood, and (4) incense do not require salt.

T. 6:2 In three locations was the salt placed: (1) in the salt-chamber, (2) on the ramp, and (3) at the head of the altar, at the southwestern corner.

T. 6:3 With the salt which was in the hewn-stone chamber did they salt the hides. With that which was on the ramp did they salt the limbs. With that which was at the head of the altar at the southwestern corner did they salt the invalid [better: sacrificial] parts of Most Holy Things and the sacrificial parts of Lesser Holy Things, the handful, and the frankincense, the meal-offering of priests, and the meal-offering of the anointed priest, and the burnt-offering of fowl.

T. 6:4 As to the salt which is on the ramp and on the altar: they do not derive benefit therefrom, but the laws of sacrilege do not apply to it. And as to that which is on the limbs: The laws of sacrilege apply to the whole of it. How do they salt the limbs? They would put them on the salt and go and turn them over.

T. 6:5 And these are those things to which the laws of sacrilege apply the entire night: (1) The limbs of the burnt-offering, (2) the sacrificial parts of Most Holy Things, (3) the sacrificial parts of Lesser Holy Things, (4) the meal-offering which goes along with drink-offerings [supply:] brought by themselves, and (5) the burnt-offering of fowl. But [as to] the handful and the frankincense and the meal-offering of priests and the meal-offering of the anointed priest — the laws of sacrilege do not apply to them all night long. This is the general rule: To anything, of which that which renders the offering permissible is offered that day, the laws of sacrilege apply all night long. To anything, of which that which renders the offering permissible is not offered that day, the laws of sacrilege do not apply all night long. What does one do? He puts it on the altar at sunset. They continue to be consumed all night.

T. 6:6 He who offers up an olive's bulk of the two loaves in the rite or outside, Lo, this one is liable, as it is said, "As an offering of first fruits you may bring them to the Lord, but they shall not be offered on the altar [for a pleasing odor]" (Lev. 2:1 2).

T. 6:7 All the same are the altar and the ramp. Therefore, he who [there] offers up part of the flesh of the sin-offering and part of the flesh of the guilt-offering, part of the flesh of Most Holy Things and the flesh of Lesser Holy Things — it is permitted.

T. 6:8 The 'omer and the two loaves of bread and the residue of meal-offerings of leaven or of honey — [he who brings offerings made of these] transgresses a negative commandment, as it is said, "For you shall burn no leaven nor any honey [as an offering by fire to the Lord]" (Lev. 2:11).

T. 6:9 He who permits the meal-offering to leaven [M. Men. 5:1] — all the same are the valid and the invalid one — transgresses a negative commandment, as it is said, "No meal-offering which you shall bring to the Lord shall be made with leaven" (Lev. 2:11).

M. 3:3 **Two meal-offerings from neither one of which the handful had been taken and which [having fallen into a single utensil] were mixed up together — if one can take the handful from this one by itself and from that one by itself, [both] are valid. And if not, they are invalid. The handful [taken from a meal-offering] which was mixed up with a meal-offering from which the handful had not been taken — he should not offer it [the mixture] up. And if he offered it up, this one from which the handful had been taken goes to the credit of its owner. And this one from which the handful had not been taken does not go to the credit of its owner. [If] its handful was mixed up with its residue, or with the residue of its fellow, he should not offer it up. But if he offered it up, it goes to the credit of the owner. [If] the handful was made unclean and one [nonetheless] offered it up, the priest's frontlet effects acceptance. [If] it went forth [beyond the veils] and one offered it up, the priest's frontlet does not effect acceptance. For the priest's frontlet effects acceptance for that which is unclean, but it does not effect acceptance for that which goes forth beyond the veils [M. Zeb. 8:12].**

T. 4:1 A meal-offering from which the handful had not been taken which was mixed up with a meal-offering from which the handful had been taken — if one can take the handful by itself from this one from which the handful had not been taken, it is valid. And if not, it is invalid. But he should offer up the handful of the first [in any event] [= M. Men. 3:3E-G].

T. 4:2 The handful [of meal-offering] which was mixed up with the residue [= M. Men. 3:3H] — Lo, this should not be offered. And if it was offered, it is valid [M. Men. 3:3I]. R. Eliezer says, "It should be offered [to begin with]." [If] it was mixed up with the residue of another meal-offering, or with the meal-offering from which a handful had not been taken, Lo, this should not be offered. And if it is offered, it is valid. R. Eliezer says, "It should be offered" [M. Zeb. 8:4-6]. [If] it was mixed with the meal-offering of priests or with the meal-offering of an anointed priest or with the meal-offering which is brought with drink-offerings [= M. Men. 3:2E], and so a meal-offering of priests, and so a meal-offering of an anointed priest, and a meal-offering brought with drink-offerings which were mixed up with one another — Lo, these should be offered [M. Men. 3:2F]. And not only so, but furthermore two priests bring their meal-offerings in a single utensil and offer them up on the altar, because the whole of it [the two meal-offerings, in any case] is wholly consumed by the [altar] fires.

T. 4:3 [If] it was mixed up with the meal-offerings of bullocks, rams, and sheep, Lo, these are to be offered up. R. Judah says, "They are not to be offered up, because in the case ° this one, its mixture is thick, and in the case of the other, its mixture is thin, and they absorb one from the other [M. Men. 3:2H]."

T. 4:4 Dry [meal-offering] which was mixed up with one soaked in oil — Lo, this one should be offered up. R. Judah says, "It should not be offered up, because it [the dry] absorbs from it [the one soaked in oil]."

B. 3:3J-L I.1/25A "AND AARON SHALL BEAR THE INIQUITY OF THE HOLY THINGS" (EX. 28:38) [THE HIGH PRIEST'S HEAD PLATE ATONES FOR FAULTS IN CONNECTION WITH THE OFFERING] — AND WHAT IS THE INIQUITY FOR WHICH THE HEAD PLATE ATONES? IF YOU SHOULD SAY THAT IT IS FOR THE SIN OF MAKING THE OFFERING REFUSE, LO, IT IS STATED TO THE CONTRARY, "IT SHALL NOT BE ACCEPTED" (LEV. 19:7). IF YOU SAY, IT IS THE SIN OF LEAVING THE MEAT OVER BEYOND THE PROPER TIME, LO, IT IS STATED, "NEITHER SHALL IT BE IMPUTED TO HIM" (LEV. 7:18). LO, IT CAN BEAR THE INIQUITY ONLY FOR THE SIN OF UNCLEANNESS, FOR THAT IS REMITTED FROM THE PREVAILING PROHIBITION WHEN IT COMES TO THE OFFERING OF THE COMMUNITY.

M. 3:4 [If before the handful was offered up] its residue was made unclean, [if] its residue was burned, [if] its residue was lost, in accord with the reasoning of R. Eliezer, it is valid, and in accord with the reasoning of R. Joshua, it is invalid. [If the meal-offering] was not in a utensil of service, it is invalid. R. Simeon declares valid. [If] one offered up its handful two times [that is, by halves], it is valid.

T. 4:5 Said R. Yosé, "I prefer the opinion of R. Eliezer, who stated, 'If there is no handful [of meal-offering], there is no residue. [But] even though there is no residue, there is a handful,' to the opinion of R. Joshua, who stated, 'If there is no handful, there is no residue, if there is no residue, there is no handful'" [M. Men. 3:4B].

T. 4:6 [If] the handful is made unclean or invalidated or taken outside the veils, [as to the] residue — its appearance is left to rot, and it is taken to the place of burning. [If] the residue is made unclean or invalidated or taken outside the veils — R. Eliezer says, "Let the handful be offered up." And R. Joshua says, "It is not to be offered up." And if it is offered up, whether inadvertently or intentionally, R. Joshua agrees that it is accepted [M. Men. 3:4B].

T. 4:7 Residue which was found to be lacking — [if this was] before the handful was offered, is invalid. [If this was] after the handful was offered, it is valid [M. Men. 3:4A]. Cakes of a meal-offering of an Israelite which were found to be lacking before the handful was offered are invalid. [If found to be lacking] after the handful was offered, they are valid. Loaves which accompany a thank-offering and cakes of a Nazir which were found to be lacking before the blood of the sacrifice was tossed are invalid. [If they were found to be lacking] after the blood of the sacrifice was tossed, they are valid. The two loaves which were found to be lacking before the blood of the lambs was tossed, are invalid. [If they were found to be lacking] after the blood of the lambs was tossed, they are valid.

T. 4:8 Two rows which were found to be lacking before the dishes of frankincense were offered up, are invalid. [If they were found to be lacking] after the dishes of frankincense were offered up, they are valid. But drink-offerings brought with a beast which were found to be lacking, whether this was after the animal-sacrifice was offered or before the animal-sacrifice was offered, are valid. For they may bring other drink-offerings to take their place [in any event].

T. 4:9 [If] one took the handful in silence [without improper intent], and the handful went forth beyond the veils, and one offered it up in silence, Lo, this is as it was. The laws of sacrilege apply to the residue. But they are not liable on their account because of violation of the laws of remnant and uncleanness. [If] the handful was made unclean and one offered it up in silence, the laws of sacrilege do not apply to the residue. But they are liable on their account because of violation of the laws of remnant and uncleanness. For the priestly frontlet effects acceptance for that which is unclean. But the priestly frontlet does not effect acceptance for that which is allowed to remain overnight or for that which goes forth beyond the veils [M. Men. 3:3L].

T. 4:10 [If] one took the handful in silence and the residue was taken outside of the veils and one offered up the handful in silence R. Eliezer says, "Lo this is as it was. The laws of sacrilege apply to the remnants, but they are not liable on their account because of violation of the laws of remnant and uncleanness." R. Aqiba says, "The priestly frontlet effects acceptance for that which goes forth. And the laws of sacrilege do not apply to the residue, but they are liable on their account because of violation of the laws of remnant and uncleanness."

T. 4:11 [If] the residue was made unclean and one offered up the handful in silence, all agree that the laws of sacrilege do not apply to it, but they are liable on their account for violation of the laws of remnant and uncleanness. For the priestly frontlet effects acceptance for that which is unclean but the priestly frontlet does not effect acceptance either for what remains overnight or for that which goes forth beyond the veils.

T. 4:12 [If] one took the handful in silence and the handful went forth beyond the veils, and one offered it up [with improper intention to eat the residue] outside of its proper time, or [if] one took the handful [with the improper intention to eat the residue or offer the handful] outside of its proper time and the handful went forth outside the veils, and one [then] offered it up in silence, or [if] one took the handful [with the improper intention to eat the residue or to burn the handful] outside of its proper time, and it went forth beyond the veils, and one [then] offered it up [with the improper intention to eat the residue] outside of its proper time, the laws of sacrilege apply to the residue, but they are not liable on its account because of violation of the laws of refuse.

T. 4:13 [If] the handful was made unclean and one offered it up [with improper intention to eat the residue] outside of its proper time, still do the laws of sacrilege apply to the residue, and they are liable on their account because of violation of the laws of refuse. For the priestly frontlet effects acceptance for that which is unclean, but the priestly frontlet does not effect acceptance for that which remains overnight or for that which goes forth beyond the veils.

T. 4:14 [If] one took the handful in silence and the residue went forth beyond the veils and one offered up the handful [with the improper intention to eat the residue] outside of its proper time, or [if] one took the handful [with the improper intention to eat the residue or to offer up the handful] outside of its proper time, and the residue went forth beyond the veils, and one offered up the handful in silence or [if] one took the handful [with the improper intention to eat the residue or to offer up the handful] outside of its proper time, and the residue went forth beyond the veils, and one offered up the handful [with the improper intention to eat the residue] outside of its proper time R. Eliezer says, "Lo, this is as it was. The laws of sacrilege apply to the residue, but they are not liable on their account because of violation of the laws of refuse." R. Aqiba says, "The priestly frontlet effects atonement for that which goes forth beyond the veils. Still do the laws of sacrilege apply to the residue, and they are liable on their account because of violation of the laws of refuse." [If] the residue is made unclean and one offered up the handful [with the improper intention to eat the residue] outside of its proper time, all agree that still do the laws of sacrilege apply to the residue, and they are liable on their account because of violation of the laws of refuse. For the priestly frontlet effects acceptance for that which is unclean, but it does not effect acceptance either for that which remains overnight or for that which goes forth beyond the veils.

T. 4:15 The two loaves which went forth beyond the veils and the blood of the lambs was tossed [with the improper intention to eat is to be eaten] outside of its proper time — R. Eliezer says, "They are not liable on account of this bread because of violation of the laws of refuse." R. Aqiba says, "They are liable on account of this bread because of violation of the laws of refuse" And sages say, "The handful requires [that it be put into] a utensil of service" [M. Men. 3:4C]. How so? One takes the handful from a utensil of service and puts it into a utensil of service and sanctifies it in a utensil of service. And if he did not sanctify it in a utensil of service, he has invalidated. R. Eleazar b. R. Simeon says, "Even if he took the handful from a utensil of service and salted it and put it on the fires, it is valid."

M. 3:5 (1) The handful [of meal-offering]: [the absence of] the smaller part of it impairs the validity of the greater part of it [= M. 1:2]. (2) The tenth [of the ephah]: [the absence of] the smaller part of it impairs the validity of the greater part of it. (3) Wine: [the absence of] the smaller part of it impairs the validity of the greater part of it [Num. 15:5; 7:10]. (4) Oil: [the absence of] the smaller part of it impairs the validity of the greater part of it. (1) Flour and oil impair the validity of one another. [If one is invalidated, the other is as well.] (2) The handful of meal-offering and frankincense impair the validity of one another.

M. 3:6 (3) The two goats of Yom Kippur impair the validity of one another. (4) The two lambs of Aseret [Pentecost/Shabuot] impair the validity of one another. (5) The two loaves of bread impair the validity of one another (6) The two rows [of showbread] impair the validity of one another. (7) The two dishes [of frankincense] impair the validity of one another. (8) The rows [of showbread] and the dishes [of incense] impair the validity of one another. (1) The two kinds [of cakes] which pertain to [the offering of] the Nazirite, (2) the three [kinds used for] the red cow, (3) the four [kinds used in connection with] the thank-offering, (4) the four [kinds] which are in the lulab [Lev. 23:40], (5) the four kinds used for the person afflicted with the skin ailment impair the validity of one another. The seven sprinklings of blood of the red cow impair the validity of one another. (1) The seven sprinklings of blood between the bars [on the Day of Atonement], and (2) those which are on the veil [of the Holy of Holies], and (3) those which are on the golden altar impair the validity of one another [M. Zeb. 5:1].

M. 3:7 (1) The seven branches of the candlestick [Ex. 25:31-32] impair the validity of one another. And its seven lamps impair the validity of one another. (2) The two portions [of Scripture] in the mezuzah [Dt. 6:4-9, 11, 13-21] impair the validity of one another, and even [the shape of] one letter impairs their validity. (3) The four portions [of Scripture] which are in prayerbox [tefillin] [Dt. 6:4A, 11:13-21, Ex. 13:1-10, 11-16] impair the validity of one another, and even [the shape of] one letter impairs their validity. The four fringes impair the validity of one another, for the four of them constitute a single commandment. R. Ishmael says, "The four of them constitute four distinct commandments [so they do not impair the validity of one another]."

T. 5:1 The two lambs of 'Asseret, [Pentecost] impair the validity of one another [M. Men. 3:6B]. [If] one of them died, or escaped, or turned out to be terefah, let [the owner] purchase a mate for the second. [If] one slaughtered one of them for its properly designated purpose, let the owner purchase a mate for the second. [If] both of them were slaughtered not for their own name, let him bring two [others] as at the outset and wave the bread with them. What is the rule as to sprinkling the blood? On the festival let it be sprinkled, and it [the sacrifice] is permitted for eating. And as to the Sabbath, it should not be tossed, and it is permitted for enjoyment. And if one has tossed the blood, whether inadvertently or intentionally, the meat may be eaten, and the sacrificial parts are to be offered up at the end of the Sabbath.

T. 5:2 He who [on the Sabbath] slaughters two sin-offerings for the community and requires only one of them is liable for the last. [He who slaughters] two burnt-offerings for the community and requires only one of them, is liable for the last. The sin-offering of the community which one slaughtered on the Sabbath not for its own name, Lo, this one is liable. [If] he offered up the sacrificial parts, Lo, this one is liable.

T. 5:3 The burnt-offering of the community which one slaughtered on the Sabbath not for its own name, lo, this one is liable. But let him offer up the sacrificial parts in the evening. The sin-offering of an individual and the burnt-offering of an individual which one slaughtered on the Sabbath for their own name, and the blood of which one tossed for their own name, lo, this one is liable. But they have gone to their owner's credit in fulfillment of an obligation.

T. 6:10 The cakes of the meal-offering of an Israelite, impair the validity of one another. And their smaller part impairs the validity of their greater part [M. Men. 3:5A — B]. The loaves of a thank-offering and the cakes of a Nazir, impair the validity of one another. And their smaller part impairs the validity of their greater part. The bullock does not impair the validity of the he-goat, and the he-goat does not impair the validity of the bullock. All the acts of sprinkling the blood on the inner altar for example, the forty-eight [such acts] of the Day of Atonement, the eleven [acts of sprinkling of the blood of] the bullock of the congregation, and the eleven of the bullock of the anointed priest impair the validity of one another. And their smaller number [obviously] impairs the validity of their larger number.

T. 6:11 The seven acts of sprinkling the blood of the red cow impair the validity of one another [M. Men. 3:6M]. The seven acts of sprinkling the blood in the case of the *mesora'* impair the validity of one another. The two birds [to be brought by the *mesora'*] impair the validity of one another [M. Men. 3:6K]. The stones of the house afflicted with a nega' and its wood and its dirt impair the validity of one another. The cedar wood and hyssop and red stuff [burned with the red cow] impair the validity of one another [M. Men. 3:6H]. The blue and purple crimson and white linen [Ex. 28:5-6] impair the validity of one another. The eight garments of the high priest, impair the validity of one another. The four garments of the ordinary priest, impair the validity of one another. The onyx stones and the stones for setting [Ex. 25:7] impair the validity of one another. The [letters of the] writing which is on them [Ex. 28:11] impairs the validity of one another. The spices of the incense and the spices of the anointing oil impair the validity of one another. And their smaller part impairs the validity of their larger part. The seven lamps of the candelabrum impair the validity of one another and its seven lights impair the validity of one another [M. Men. 3:7A]. Its cups, its capitals, and its flowers [Ex. 25:31] impair the validity of one another. The horn, the ramp, the foundation, and the square impair the validity of one another. R. Yosé b. R. Judah says, "Also the circuit."

T. 6:12 The measure of the altar, whether as to its length or breadth, does not impose invalidity. But its size impairs their validity. And the table and the candelabrum and the altars impair the validity of one another. R. Simeon b. Eleazar says, "Priests, Levites, and Israelites impair the validity of the sacrifice." The [three clauses of] blessing of the priests impair the validity of one another. The blessings of the high priest impair the validity of one another. The blessings of fasts impair the validity of one another. The blessings of the New Year impair the validity of one another. Blessings impair the validity of one another. The teqi'ot-sounds of the Shofar impair the validity of one another. The blessings and the teqi'ot-sounds of the Shofar impair the validity of one another. The blessing of the Hallel, the words of praise, and prayer, impair the validity of one another. The tefillin of the hand and of the head, impair the validity of one another [vs. M. Men. 4:1B]. If one has only one of them, he should put it on.

M. 4:1 The [absence of] blue [in the fringes, Num. 15:38, M. 3:7] does not impair the validity of the white, and the [absence of] white does not impair the validity of the blue. (2) The [absence of] the box containing prayer-parchments [tefillah] for the hand does not impair the validity of that for the head, and that for the head does not impair the validity of that for the hand. (3) The [absence of] flour and the oil [which accompany drink offerings] does not impair the validity of the wine, and the [absence of] wine does not impair their validity. (4) The [omission of any one of] the sprinklings [of blood] which are to be placed on the outer altar

[M. Zeb. 5:3-7] does not impair the validity of one another [M. Zeb. 4:1, M. Men. 3:6].

T. 6:13 The blue and white [of the show-fringes] do not impair the validity of one another [M. Men. 4:1A]. The proper conduct of the rite is to give precedence to the white over the blue. But if one gave precedence to the blue over the white, he has fulfilled his obligation.

M. 4:2 (5) The [absence of] bullocks and the rams and the he-lambs seven lambs, [absence of] one bullock, and two rams offered with the two loaves on Shabuot and two bullocks, [absence of] a ram, and seven lambs for the additional offering of Shabuot, Lev. 23:18, Num. 28:11ff.] do not impair the validity of one another. R. Simeon says, "If they had [funds for] many bullocks but did not have [funds for] drink offerings [sufficient for all of them], let them bring a single bullock and its drink offerings. But let them not offer up all of them without their [meal and] drink offerings."

T. 6:14 The drink-offerings of a beast and the flour impair the validity of one another [vs. M. Men. 4:2A]. Bullocks, rams, and lambs impair the validity of one another. R. Judah says, "Bullocks do not impair the validity of one another, because they are diminished [in number] on the festival [of Sukkot]. "But rams and lambs impair the validity of one another."

T. 6:15 They do not bring the bullocks, rams, and lambs, and then bring the drink-offerings. [But they bring] the bullocks with their drink-offerings, the rams with their drink-offerings, and the lambs with their drink-offerings. R. Judah says, "An individual who owed bullocks, rams, and lambs and has no drink-offerings [sufficient for all of them] should bring bullocks with their drink-offerings, but he should not bring bullocks, rams, and lambs without drink-offerings" [M. Men. 4:3B-C].

T. 6:16 The community which was liable for bullocks, rams, and lambs and had not [sufficient funds for] drink-offerings should bring bullocks with their drink-offerings. But let it not bring bullocks, rams, and lambs without drink offerings.

T. 6:17 An individual who brought drink-offerings and had no need for them should give them to the community. The community which brought drink-offerings and had no need for them should give them to an individual.

T. 6:18 [If] one brought his drink-offerings for a burnt-offering and the animal-sacrifice was made unclean or invalidated, he should give them for peace-offerings. [If] he brought his drink-offerings for peace-offerings and the animal-sacrifice was made unclean or invalidated, he should give them for use with a burnt-offering. And drink-offerings which were not offered one day may be offered on the next day. Under what circumstances? When they have not been sanctified in a utensil. But when they have been sanctified in a utensil, let them be offered on that day, and let them not be offered on the next day, for they are invalidated by being left overnight.

M. 4:3 The [absences of] the bullock and the rams and the he-lambs and the he-goat [of Pentecost/Shabuot] do not impair the validity of the bread. Nor does [the absence of] the bread impair their validity. "The [absence of] bread impairs the validity of the lambs, but the [absence of] lambs does not impair the validity of the bread," the words of R. Aqiba. Said Simeon b. Nannos, "That is not so. But the [absence of] lambs impairs the validity of the bread, and [absence of] the bread does not impair the validity of the lambs [= M. 2:3]. For so do we find that, when the Israelites were in the wilderness, for forty years they offered up lambs without bread [since they had only manna]. Likewise here, let them offer up lambs without bread." Said R. Simeon, "The law is in accord with the opinion of Ben Nannos. But the operative consideration [therefore] is not in accord with his opinion. For every [offering, Num. 28:27ff.] stated in the Book of Numbers was offered in the wilderness. But every [offering] stated in the Book of Leviticus was not offered in the wilderness [inclusive of that under discussion, Lev. 23:18-19]. When they came to the Land, both these and those were offered. And on what account do I rule, 'Let the lambs be offered without bread'? For the lambs [once the blood is sprinkled on the altar] render their own offering permissible without bread [so that the priests may then eat their share]. [But as to] bread without lambs, it has nothing which renders it permissible [for priestly use (M. 2:5)]."

M. 4:4 (1) The [absence of] continual offerings [daily whole offerings] does not impair the validity of the additional offerings, and (2) [the absence of] the additional offerings does not impair the validity of the continual offerings, and (3) the additional offerings do not impair the validity of one another. [If] they did not offer a lamb in the morning, let them offer it at twilight. Said R. Simeon, "Under what circumstances? When they were subject to constraint or in error. But if they deliberately did not offer a lamb in the morning, they should not offer it at twilight." [If] they did not burn the incense in the morning, they should burn it at twilight. Said R. Simeon, "But all of it [the incense offering] is offered at twilight. For they dedicate[d] (1) the golden altar only with incense of sweet spices that are offered in the afternoon, and (2) the altar of the burnt offering only by the continual offering in the morning, and (3) the table only by the showbread that was laid on the table on the Sabbath."

T. 5:4 The two lambs [offered at] "Asseret [Pentecost] sanctify the bread only when they are slaughtered [M. Men. 4:3]. The thank-offering and ram of the Nazirite sanctify the bread only when they are slaughtered. [If] one slaughtered them for their own name and tossed their blood for their own name, the bread is sanctified [thereby]. [If] one slaughtered them not for their own name and tossed their blood not for their own name, the bread is not sanctified. [If] one slaughtered them for their own name and tossed their blood not for their own name, the bread is sanctified and not sanctified," the words of Rabbi. R. Eleazar b. R. Simeon says, "Under no circumstances is the bread sanctified unless one will slaughter them for their own name and toss their blood for their own name."

T. 5:5 There are times that (1) they are deemed refuse and the bread is deemed refuse, (2) they are deemed refuse and the bread is valid, (3) they are valid and the bread is deemed refuse, (4) they are valid and the bread is valid. (1) [If] one slaughtered them for their own name [but with the improper intention] to eat them on the next day, they are deemed refuse, and the bread is deemed refuse. (2) [If] one slaughtered them not for their own name [with the improper intention] to eat of them on the next day, they are deemed refuse, but the bread is valid. (3)[If] one slaughtered them for their own name [but with the intention] to eat of the bread on the next day, they are valid, and the bread is valid [Better: deemed refuse]. (4)[If] one slaughtered one of them for its own name [with the improper intention] to eat its fellow on the next day, they are valid, and the bread is valid.

T. 6:19 The 'omer does not impair the validity of the lamb, and the lamb does not impair the validity of the 'omer. "The bread impairs the validity of the lambs [M. Men. 4:3C]. What should they do? Let it be waved and its appearance become disfigured, and then go out to the place of burning," the words of R. Aqiba. Said R. Simeon ben Nannos, "Not so. But lambs impair the validity of the bread. The bread does not impair the validity [of the lambs]" [M. Men. 4:3]. Said to him R. Aqiba, "The matter is still suspended. Who will settle it?" Said Ben Nannos, "I shall settle it. And so do we find that when the Israelites were in the wilderness for forty years, they offered lambs without bread. So here, let the lambs be offered without bread." Said R. Simeon, "The law is in accord with the opinion of Ben Nannos, but the reason is not in accord with his view "[M. Men. 4:31.-H].

T. 6:20 "You turn out to maintain that once the Israelites crossed the Jordan, they became liable to the laws of the dough-offering and to the prohibitions of 'orlah fruit and to that concerning the new crops. When the sixteenth of Nisan came, they became liable for the 'omer and to that which is offered with it. Fifty days later they became liable to the two loaves of bread and to that which is offered with them. At the end of fourteen years, they became liable to observe the prohibition against using the fruit of a vineyard in its fourth year." R. Yosé b. R. Judah and R. Eleazar b. R. Simeon say, "They became liable to the prohibition against using the fruit of a vineyard in its fourth year only after fourteen years. When they conquered and divided [the land], they became liable to tithes. They began counting the first year and the second year and the third year. Afterward, they became liable to the prohibition against using the fruit of a vineyard in its fourth year. In the twenty-first year, they observed the year of release. In the sixty-fourth year, they observed the jubilee. On what account do I rule, let the lambs be offered without bread? Because the lambs [when properly offered] permit themselves [to be eaten], but not the bread. [Bread] without lambs has nothing to render it permitted [for eating]" [M. Men. 4:3M].

T. 7:1 Cinnamon [may be offered in] halves, as it is said, "[Take the finest spices: of liquid myrrh five hundred shekels, and] of sweet-smelling cinnamon half as much, that is two hundred and fifty, and aromatic cane two hundred and fifty, and of cassia five hundred, according to the shekel of the sanctuary, and of olive oil a hin" (Ex. 30:23-24). Twelve logs of incense, half of which was not offered in the morning — let the whole of it be offered in the evening in fulfillment of the obligation of twilight [M. Men. 4:4E].

T. 7:2 The meal-offering of the high priest, half of which was not offered in the morning — let the whole of it be offered in the evening, in fulfillment of the obligation of twilight.

T. 7:3 [If] the he-goats of the festival were not offered on the festival, let them be offered on the New Moon. [If] they were not offered on the New Moon, let them be offered on the Day of Atonement. [If] they were not offered on the Day of Atonement, let them be offered on the next festival. For to begin with the offerings of the congregation were sanctified only on condition that they be offered on the outer altar.

T. 7:4 The additional offerings of the Sabbath which were not offered on this Sabbath may be offered on another Sabbath in fulfillment of the obligation of the next Sabbath to follow. The additional offerings of the New Moon which were not offered on this New Moon may be offered on the next New Moon in fulfillment of the obligation of the next New Moon to follow. [If] the lamb was not offered in the morning, let it be offered at twilight [M. Men. 4:4B]. [If] they did not offer incense in the morning, let them offer the incense at twilight.

T. 7:5 Said R. Simeon, "Under what circumstances? When the court was under constraint or did so inadvertently. But if they did so deliberately...For [if] it was the dedication of the altar, and they [deliberately] did not offer a lamb in the morning, let them not offer it at twilight." [If] one did not offer the incense in the morning, let them not offer it at twilight [M. Men. 4:4E]. Said R. Simeon, "All of it was offered at twilight. For they dedicate the golden altar only with incense of sweet spices, and the altar of the burnt-offering only with the continual offering of the morning, and the table only with show bread on the Sabbath, and the candelabrum only with lights at twilight" [M. Men. 4:4F-J].

T. 7:6 R. Yosé says, "All the seven days of dedication the table was left vacant, without bread. For the work of making it was not completed at the end of the Sabbath. They arranged the bread on it only on the Sabbath, in its proper time."

T. 7:7 Lo, it says, "And Moses saw all the work, and behold, they had done it as the Lord had commanded, so had they done it" (Ex. 39:43). And where did he thus command him? "And let them make for me a sanctuary" (Ex. 25:8). "And he put the table in the tent of meeting" (Ex. 40:22). And set the bread in order on it before the Lord as the Lord had commanded" (Ex. 40:23). Where did he command him to do so? "Every Sabbath day Aaron shall set it in order before the Lord continually" (Lev. 24:8). And he put the lampstand in the tent of meeting opposite the table...and set up the lamps before the Lord, as the Lord had commanded Moses" (Ex. 40:24-25). Where did he command him to do so? "He shall keep the lamps in order upon the lampstand of pure gold before the Lord continually" (Lev. 24:4). "And he put the golden altar in the tent of meeting before the veil, and burnt fragrant incense upon it, as the Lord had commanded Moses" (Ex. 40:26-27). Where did he command him to do so? "And Aaron shall burn fragrant incense on it. Every morning when he dresses the lamps, he shall burn it "(Ex. 30:7). "And he put in place the screen for the door of the tabernacle. And he set the altar of burnt offering at the door of the tabernacle of the tent of meeting, and offered upon it the burnt-offering and the meal-offering, as the Lord had commanded Moses" (Ex. 40:28-29). Where did he command him to do so? "The one lamb you shall offer in the morning" (Num. 28:4).

T. 7:8 Another matter: "And Moses saw all the work, and behold, they had done it, as the Lord had commanded, so had they done it. And Moses blessed them" (Ex. 39:43). With what blessing did he bless them? He said to them, "May the Presence of God dwell with the work of your hands." R. Meir says, "Thus did he bless them: May the Lord, the God of your fathers, make you a thousand times as many as you are, and bless you as he has promised you" (Deut. 1:11). He said to them, 'Just as you have been engaged in the work of making the tabernacle and the Presence of God has dwelled with the work of your hands, so may you have the merit of building before me the chosen house, and may the Presence of God dwell with the work of your hands.' And they say, 'Let the favor of the Lord, our God, be upon us, and establish thou, the work of our hands upon us, yes, the work of our hands, establish thou it' (Ps. 90:17).

T. 7:9 When Israel is in favor before the Omnipresent, what is said concerning them? "My offering, my food [for my offerings by fire, my pleasing odor, you shall take heed to offer to me in its due season" (Num. 28:2) — like children who derive sustenance from their father. And in a time of rebuke, what does it say? For my offerings by fire, my pleasing odor — All the offerings which you bring are destined only for the fire. And so it says, "I do not reprove you for your sacrifices; your burnt offerings are continually before me. I will accept no bull from your house, nor he-goat from your folds. For every beast of the forest is mine, the cattle on a thousand hills. I know all the birds of the air. And all that moves in the field is mine. If I were hungry, I would not tell you, for the world and all that is in it is mine. Do I eat the flesh of bulls or drink the blood of goats?" (Ps. 50:8-13). Now is hunger a problem to him? And he said, "[If] hunger were a problem to me, the lamb which you offer in the morning and the lamb which you offer at twilight — would they be sufficient? If you have enough in your power, I shall give the food concerning which you spoke: Offer to God a sacrifice of thanksgiving, and pay your vows to the Most High" (Ps. 50:14)."

M. 4:5 The griddle cakes of the high priest were not offered in half [tenths of an ephah at a time]. But one brings a whole tenth and divides it, and offers half in the morning and half at twilight. And a priest who offered half in the morning and died, and in whose place [on that same day] they appointed another priest — [the latter, at twilight] should not bring a half-tenth [of an ephah] from his own property, nor half of the tenth of the first priest. But he brings a whole tenth and divides it and offers half. And the other half is left to perish. It turns out that two halves are offered, and two halves are left to perish. [If] they did not appoint another priest [in place of the one who died], of whose [property] was it offered? R. Simeon says, "Of the community." R. Judah says, "Of the heirs [of the deceased]." And the whole [tenth] was offered.

T. 7:10 A priest who offered half in the morning and died, and in whose place they appointed another priest — [the latter] should not bring half a tenth [ephah] from his own property nor a half tenth [ephah] of the first. But he brings a whole tenth and divides it [M. Men. 4:5D-G]. This half [of his, which he does not offer] and the first half — their appearance is left to become disfigured, and the whole is sent out to the place of burning.

T. 7:11 A priest who offered half in the morning, and the second half, thereof, became unclean — Lo, this one brings a whole tenth and divides it up. This half [which he does not offer up, of the second lot] and the first [unclean] half — their appearance is left to become disfigured, and the whole is sent out to the place of burning.

T. 7:12 [If] they did not appoint another priest, of whose property was it offered? R. Simeon says, "Of the property of the community, as it is said, 'And one shall take from it a handful of the fine flour...and burn this as its memorial portion of the altar' (Lev. 6:15) — he with whom the covenant is made." R. Judah says, "Of the property of his heirs, as it is said, 'And one [of the sons of Aaron] shall take' (Lev. 6:15)." And the whole was offered, whether in the morning or in the evening, as it is said, "It shall be wholly burned" (Lev. 6:15) [M. Men. 4:5I-L].

T. 7:14 These are the differences between the meal-offering of the high priest and the meal-offering of an ordinary priest: The meal-offering of a high priest is brought daily [even on the Sabbath]; it is brought regularly [even if the high priest died, M. Men. 4:5]; it is brought soaked; it is offered in halves; it requires two acts of taking a handful [of frankincense], one in the morning and one at twilight; and it requires three logs of oil, one and a half in the morning, and one and a half at twilight. Under what circumstances? In the case of a meal-offering which is brought in fulfillment of the obligation of a high priest. But in the case of a meal-offering brought as a thank-offering of a high priest, Lo, it is like the meal-offering brought as a thank-offering of an ordinary priest.

T. 7:15 "The meal-offering which is [offered on] a high place — a non priest takes the handful and offers it up on the fires," the words of R. Meir. And sages say, "There is no meal-offering on a high place" [M. Zeb. 14:10].

We move from the particular hermeneutics of Menahot (Zebahim) to the generic hermeneutics. The key-issue, given the subject-matter, presents no surprise: it is the matter of mixtures, from M. 3:2 onward. A further generic issue distinguishes what is primary from what is subordinate in a mixture. That yields a huge and successful exercise of differentiation of the principal from the secondary, M. 3:5ff., with further attention to mixtures. In the first group all components of a mixture are equally critical, at M. 3:6. In these cases, every component of a composite is equally required, and the loss of any invalidates the entire composite. In the second sequence, M. 4:1, all components are not equally required, and omitting a peripheral item does not invalidate the central one(s). The appropriateness of the entire generic issue is demonstrated (rather deftly, as a matter of fact) at M. 4:3-4, which pertain, in particular to meal-offerings (e.g., bread). As much as does the particular hermeneutics in I/A, the generic hermeneutics of I/B homogenizes the diverse meal-offerings by imposing upon them all a uniform set of rules. This exercise, "all meal-offerings...," "there are meal-offerings that..., and there are meal-offerings that...," and similar constructions, continues at unit II.

II. THE PROPER PREPARATION OF MEAL-OFFERINGS

A. GENERAL RULES

M. 5:1 All meal-offerings are brought unleavened [Lev. 2:4-5, 6:7-9], except for the leavened cakes of thank-offerings [M. 7:1] and the two loaves of bread [of Pentecost], which are brought as leavened bread [Lev. 7:13, 23:17]. R. Meir says, "The leaven is set aside for them from their own [contents], and it leavens them." R. Judah says, "Also: that is not of the best way [for the yeast is too fresh and not sufficiently potent to leaven the rest of the meal-offering properly]. But one brings the leaven and puts it into the measure and [then] fills the measure [with meal]." They said to him, "Also: it would be either too little or too much."

M. 5:2 All those meal-offerings [that must be unleavened] are kneaded in lukewarm water. And one watches them, that they not leaven. And if the residue became leavened, one transgresses a negative commandment. As it is said [in proof], "No meal-offering which you shall offer to the Lord shall be made with leaven" (Lev. 2:11). And they are liable [on account of leavening] in connection with (1) kneading it, (2) rolling it, and (3) baking it.

T. 7:13 As to all meal-offerings: They do not knead them in boiling water, because they form [too thick] a paste, nor in cold water because they dilute [it so that the meal does not cohere]. But they knead them in lukewarm water and watch them, that they not become leavened. And if one leavened the residue, he transgresses [M. Men. 5:2A — C] [a negative commandment] on four counts [of leavening]: On the counts of not kneading, not stirring, not smoothing the surface [of the dough], and not baking. Baking was subsumed in the general principle [of Lev. 2:11]. And why was it differentiated [at Lev. 6:17]? To serve by way of analogy: Just as baking is a specific act, in that it is a distinct action, so that they are liable for doing it alone, so I treat as equivalent kneading it, rolling it out, baking it [M. Men. 5:2E], and each and every action concerning it, on account of each one of which separately one is liable. As to the soaked cake: They knead it in boiling water. You have only three kinds of [meal-offering] which require soaking [in oil]: the cakes of the anointed priest and the soaked cake which goes with the thank-offering and [one offered with] the ram of ordination [Lev. 8:22].

M. 5:3 There are [meal-offerings which] require oil and frankincense, oil but not frankincense, frankincense but not oil, neither oil nor frankincense. And these are they that require oil and frankincense: (1) the meal-offering of fine flour [Lev. 2:1,

6:8], and (2) the meal-offering prepared in the baking pan [Lev. 2:5], and (3) the meal-offering prepared in the frying pan [Lev. 2:7], and (4) the meal-offering of the cakes, and (5) of the wafers [Lev. 2:4], (6) the meal-offering of the priests, and (7) the meal-offering of the anointed priest [Lev. 6:20ff.], (8) the meal-offering of gentiles, and (9) the meal-offering of women, and (10) the meal-offering of the 'omer (Lev. 2:14-15, 23:9-14). The meal-offering which is brought with drink offerings requires oil but does not require frankincense [Num. 15:4ff.]. The showbread requires frankincense but does not require oil [Lev. 24:7]. The two loaves, the meal-offering of a sinner, and the meal-offering of the woman accused of adultery [require] neither oil nor frankincense [Lev. 5:11, Num. 5:15].

M. 5:4 And one is liable [for putting on a meal-offering which does not require oil and frankincense] on account of the oil by itself and on account of the frankincense by itself. [If] one put oil on it, he has invalidated it. [If he put] frankincense on it, he should gather it up [and remove it]. [If] he put oil on its residue, he does not violate a negative commandment. [If] he put a utensil above a utensil [one containing oil or frankincense, the other containing the meal-offering], he has not rendered it invalid.

M. 5:5 There are those [offerings] which require bringing near but do not require waving, waving but not bringing near, waving and bringing near, neither waving nor bringing near. These [are offerings] which require waving but do not require bringing near: (1) the meal-offering of fine flour, and (2) the meal-offering prepared in the baking pan, and (3) the meal-offering prepared in the frying pan [Lev. 2:8], and (4) the meal-offering of cakes, and (5) the meal-offering of wafers, and (6) the meal-offering of priests, and (7) the meal-offering of an anointed priest, and (8) the meal-offering of gentiles, and (9) the meal-offering of women, and (10) the meal-offering of a sinner. R. Simeon says, "To the meal-offering of priests, the meal-offering of an anointed priest, bringing near does not apply, because the taking of a handful does not apply to them. And whatever is not subject to the taking of a handful is not subject to the act of bringing near."

M. 5:6 These [are offerings which] require waving and do not require bringing near: (1) the log of oil of the person healed of the skin ailment; (2) his guilt offering [Lev. 14:12] and (3) first fruits — this is in accord with the opinion of R. Eliezer b. Jacob [M. Bik. 2:4, 3:6]; and (4) the sacrificial parts of the peace offerings of an individual; and (5) their breast and thigh [Lev. 10:15] — both those of Israelite men and women but not those of others — and the (6) two loaves of bread, and the two lambs of Pentecost [Aseret/Shabuot]; How does one carry out the rite? One puts the two loaves of bread on top of the two lambs and places his two hands below and swings them forward and backward and upward and downward, as it is written, "Which is waved and which is raised up" [Ex. 29:27]. The waving was at the east [of the altar], and the bringing near of the west [at the southwestern corner]. And the wavings come before the bringings near. The meal-offering of the omer [on the sixteenth of Nisan, Lev. 23:11], and the meal-offering of the woman accused of adultery [Num. 5:25] require [both] waving and bringing near. The showbread and the meal-offering brought with drink offerings [require] neither waving nor bringing near.

T. 7:19 How does one wave the two loaves of bread? One places one loaf on this lamb and one on the other. A priest places his hand under the hoof of one lamb, and another priest places his hand under the hand of the priest. And he swings them forward and backward and upward and downward. And thus was the manner of waving them [M. Men. 5:6J-K].

T. 7:20 R. Yosé ben Hammeshulam says, "The lambs were located on top of the bread", as it is said, "And the priest shall wave them with the bread of the first fruits as a wave-offering [before the Lord on the two lambs] (Lev. 23:20)." They said to him, "But is it not also said, As a wave-offering before the Lord on the two lambs?" He said to them, "We find that the matter is still in the balance. Who will settle the question?" They said to him, "Just as in the case of the ram of initiation, the bread is located on top [Lev. 8:26], so here too the bread should be on the top." All meal-offerings are valid only if prepared in an oven. [If] one made them in a stove or on hot tiles, they are invalid. R. Judah says, "A stove is equivalent to an oven" [M. Men. 5:51A-B].

M. 5:7 R. Simeon says, "Three kinds [of offering] require three rites, two [apply] to each of them, but [all] three apply to none of them. And these are they: The sacrifices of peace offerings of an individual, and the sacrifices of peace offerings of the community, and the guilt offering of the person healed of the skin ailment. The sacrifices of peace offerings of an individual [M. 5:6G4-5] require (1) laying on of hands while the animal is yet alive [Lev. 3:2], and (2) waving of the slaughtered animals, but (3) waving does not apply to them while they are alive [Lev. 10:15]. The sacrifices of peace offerings of the community [the lambs of Pentecost/Shabuot], M. 5:6I1 require (1) waving while they are alive and (2) when they are slaughtered, but (3) the laying on of hands does not apply to them [Lev. 23:20]. The guilt offering of the person healed of the skin ailment requires (1) laying on of hands and (2) waving while it is alive [Lev. 14:12-13], but (3) waving does not apply to it when it has been slaughtered."

T. 7:17 How does one wave the peace-offerings of an individual? One separated from [the carcasses] the two kidneys and the large lobe of the liver and the fat-tail of the lamb, the breast and the thigh, and adds to them the shoulder and the heave-offering of bread. And he puts them into the hand of the owner. And the priest puts his hand under the hand of the owner and swings them forward and backward and upward and downward. And thus, was the manner of waving them.

T. 7:18 The breast, thigh, shoulder, and heave-offering of bread were eaten by the priests. The large lobe of the liver, the fat-tail, the breast and thigh does he give to another priest. And he puts his hand under the hand of the priest, and swings them forward and backward and upward and downward. And thus, was the manner of waving it. The breast and thigh were eaten by the priests. And the remaining items are offered on the fires.

T. 8:12 R. Simeon says, "Three kinds [of offering] require three rites. Two apply to each of them, but all three apply to none of them. And these are they: the sacrifices of peace-offerings of an individual, and the sacrifices of peace-offerings of the community, and the guilt-offering of the *mesora'*."

T. 8:13 "The sacrifices of peace-offerings of an individual require laying on of hands while the animal is yet alive and waving of the slaughtered animals, but waving does not apply to them while they are alive" [M. Men. 5:7A-D]. What is the rule of waving in the case of sacrifices of peace-offerings of the community? The sacrifices of peace-offerings of the community require waving while they are alive and when they are slaughtered, but the laying on of hands does not apply to them [M. Men. 5:7E]. And what is the rule of waving in the case of the guilt-offering of the *mesora'*? The guilt-offering of the *mesora'* requires laying on of hands and waving while it is alive, but waving does not apply to it when it has been slaughtered [M. Men. 5:7F].

M. 5:8 He who says, "Lo, I pledge myself to a meal-offering baked in a baking pan," should not bring one prepared in a frying pan. [If he says, "Lo, I pledge myself to] a meal-offering prepared in a frying pan," he should not bring one prepared in a baking pan. And what is the difference between a baking pan and a frying pan? But: "The frying pan has a cover, and the baking pan has no cover," the words of R. Yosé the Galilean. R. Hananiah b. Gamaliel says, "A frying pan is deep, and what is cooked in it is spongy, and a baking pan is flat, and what is cooked in it is hard."

M. 5:9 He who says, "Lo, I pledge myself [to bring] a meal-offering baked in the oven" should not bring one baked in a stove, or one baked on hot tiles, or one baked in the cauldrons of

Arabs [M. Kel. 5:10]. R. Judah says, "If he wanted, he may bring one baked in a stove [which is a kind of oven]". [He who says,] "Lo, I pledge myself [to bring] a meal-offering which is baked," should not bring one which is half in cakes and half in wafers [i.e., he should bring ten of one kind or the other, not five of each]. R. Simeon permits, because it is one kind of offering.

T. 8:11 And so did R. Simeon state, "He who says, ['Lo, I pledge myself to bring a meal-offering] baked in an oven' brings half in the form of loaves and half in the form of wafers" [M. Men. 5:9C — D]. One stirs in the oil and takes [the handful of cake] from the middle. And if he gave from one sort for its fellow, he has fulfilled his obligation [M. Men. 5:9C-D].

M. 7:1 [so the Bavli = Mishnah 6:1] And these are meal-offerings [from which] the handful is taken, and the residue of which belongs to the priests [Lev. 7:7-9]: (1) the meal-offering of fine flour [Lev. 2:21], and (2) [the meal-offering prepared in] a baking pan [Lev. 2:9, 7:8], and (3) [the meal-offering prepared in] a frying pan, and (4) the loaves, and (5) the wafers [Lev. 2:9-10], and (6) the meal-offering of gentiles, and (7) the meal-offering of women, and (8) the meal-offering of the first sheaf of barley [Lev. 2:16], and (9) the meal-offering of a sinner [Lev. 5:12], and (10) the meal-offering of a woman accused of adultery [Num. 5:26]. R. Simeon says, "[From] the meal-offering of a priest who was a sinner [Lev. 7:16], the handful is taken [even though the whole of it in any case is offered on the altar], and the handful is offered by itself, and the residue [thereof] is offered by itself."

T. 8:3 The two loaves of bread and the show bread are eaten [M. Men. 6:2L]. But a handful is not taken from them. The meal-offering of a high priest [and] the meal-offering of an anointed priest and the meal-offering which comes with drink-offerings are not eaten [M. Men. 6:2A]. And a handful is not taken from them. R. Simeon says, "From the meal-offering of a sinner who was a priest a handful is taken" [M. Men. 6:1C].

T. 8:4 The handful is offered by itself, and the residue is offered by itself [M. Men. 6:1C]. R. Eleazar b. R. Simeon says, "The handful is offered by itself. But the residue is scattered on the ashes."

M. 7:2 The meal-offering of priests [Lev. 7:15-16] and the meal-offering of an anointed priest and the meal-offering brought with drink offerings [Num. 23:20, 24:91] [belong] to the altar [without the removal of the handful]. And the priests have no [portion] in them. In this regard, the right of the altar is greater than the right of the priests. The two loaves of bread [Lev. 23:20, 24:9] and the showbread belong to the priests. And the altar has no [portion] in them. And in this regard the right of the priests is greater than the right of the altar.

M. 7:3 All meal-offerings that are prepared in a utensil [a baking pan or a frying pan] require three applications of oil: (1) pouring [oil into the utensil], (2) stirring [the meal into the oil], and [then again], (3) putting oil into the utensil prior to their preparation. "And as to the loaves [baked in an oven], one stirs them [with oil]," the words of Rabbi. And sages say, "The fine flour [alone was mixed with oil]." The loaves require stirring. The wafers are anointed. How does one anoint them? In the form of a chi [an X] [that is, in the form of a cross]. And the remainder of the oil is eaten by the priests.

T. 8:5 All meal-offerings [which are] prepared in a utensil and require three acts of applying the oil. Pouring [oil into the utensil], stirring [the meal into the oil], and putting oil into the utensil prior to their preparation [M. Men. 6:3A-B]. How does one do this? He puts oil into the utensil and fries it. [Then he puts] oil into the flour and stirs it and breaks it up. And he [then] pours oil on it as one pours oil on pounded beans.

T. 8:6 Loaves require mixing [with oil], but a wafer [requires anointing with oil] [M. Men. 6:3E-F]. You turn out to rule: What is valid for loaves is invalid for wafers. What is valid for wafers is invalid for loaves.

T. 8:7 How do they stir them? In the case of loaves, they stir [oil into them]. The words of Rabbi, as it is said, "Loaves mixed with oil" [Lev. 7:12]. And sages say, "[With] fine four" [M. Men. 6:3C-D], as it is said, "Flour mixed with oil" [Lev. 7:23]. He said to them, "Still is the matter subject to debate. Who shall settle the matter?" They said to him, "Here loaves is stated, and in connection with the thank-offering loaves is stated. Just as loaves stated in connection with the thank-offering [means] that it is not possible to stir them without fine flour, so loaves stated in this case [means] that it is not possible to stir them without fine flour." Said Rabbi, "I prefer their opinion to my opinion."

T. 8:8 How does one anoint them [with oil] [M. Men. 6:3G]? One anoints the entire surface of the wafer. R. Simeon says, "One anoints the wafers in the form of a chi (X)." And the rest of the oil is eaten by the priests [M. Men. 6:3H-I].

T. 8:10 A half-log of water is used in connection with the woman accused of adultery. And a half-log of oil is used for the thank-offering. One puts half into the loaves and half into the wafers. R. Simeon says, "One anoints the wafers in the form of a chi, and the remainder of the oil is eaten by the priests" [M. Men. 6:3H-I].

M. 7:4 All meal-offerings that are prepared in a utensil require breaking up [for the taking of the handful]. [As to] the meal-offering of an Israelite: one folds it one into two, then two into four [parts], and divides it [at each fold]. [As to] the meal-offering of priests: one folds it one into two, then two into four [parts] but does not divide it. [As to] the meal-offering of the anointed priest: one did not fold it up. R. Simeon says, "The meal-offering of priests and the meal-offering of an anointed priest are not subject to [the requirement of] breaking up. For they are not subject to the taking of a handful. And anything which is not subject to the taking of a handful is not subject to breaking up. And all of them are to be broken up into pieces at least the size of olive's bulks."

T. 8:9 [As to] a meal-offering which was brought half as loaves and half as wafers, one puts in half for the loaves and half for the wafers [M. Men. 6:3A-B]. R. Simeon says, "One anoints the wafers in the form of a chi. And the rest of the oil one puts into the loaves" [vs. M. Men. 6:3]. And so did R. Simeon say, "The excess of the wafers of the meal-offering of an Israelite — their broken parts are the size of an olive's bulk, so that one can grasp them for taking the handful" [M. Men. 6:4H].

M. 7:5 As to all meal-offerings [the flour used therefor] require three hundred [acts of] rubbing [to remove dirt] and five hundred [acts of] beating [to remove husks]. And rubbing and beating [apply to grains of] wheat. R. Yosé says, "Also: [to the] dough." "All meal-offerings [of loaves or wafers] are brought ten at a time, except for showbread [Lev. 24:5: twelve] and the baked cakes of a high priest [Lev. 7:13-15], which are brought twelve at a time," the words of R. Judah. R. Meir says, "All of them are brought twelve at a time, except for the loaves of the thank-offering [M. 7:1] and of the Nazirite [M. 7:2], which are brought ten at a time."

T. 8:1 All meal-offerings, the number of the loaves of which was too many, or the number of the loaves of which was too few, or the measure of one of which was less than that of its fellow or greater than that of its fellow — Lo, these are invalid.

T. 8:2 The two loaves of bread and the show-bread, the loaves of the thank-offerings and the wafers of the Nazir, the number of loaves of which was too great, or the number of loaves of which was too small, or the measure of one of which was greater than that of its fellow or less than that of its fellow — Lo, these are invalid. But all other meal-offerings, whether they come from an individual or from the community, have no fixed measure. But this is on condition that they shall bring them from the best.

T. 8:14 All meal-offerings require three hundred [acts of] rubbing and five hundred [acts of] beating [for the grain used therein]. Others say, "Rubbing and beating [apply to grains of] wheat" [M. Men. 6:5A — B]. R. Yosé says, "In the case of dough" [M. Men. 6:5C]. As to the 'omer. There was in it a tenth [of an ephah] from three seahs [M. Men. 6:6A]. How much is its tenth? Three seahs. It turns out that its tenth is a qab and a half. The 'omer did one sift in thirteen sieves, the two loaves in twelve, the show-bread in eleven [M. Men. 6:7A-C]. [One made use] of a thin and a thick [sieve], a thin one so that it will hold the fine flour, and a thick one so that it will hold the refuse. R. Simeon b. Eleazar says, "The thirteen sieves were located one on top of the other. The lowest of all of them was so made as to hold the fine flour. "

M. 7:6 The [meal-offering of] the offering of the first sheaf of barley was offered of a tenth [of an ephah of flour] taken from three seahs. The two loaves of bread [come from] two tenths taken from three seahs [Lev. 23:17]. The showbread comes from twenty-four tenths taken from twenty-four seahs [Lev. 24:5 twenty-four loaves, each of two tenths].

M. 7:7 The [meal-offering of the] offering of the first sheaf of barley was sifted through thirteen sieves [each finer than the former]. And the two loaves [Lev. 23:17] [were sifted through] twelve sieves. And the showbread [was sifted through] eleven sieves, R. Simeon says, "There is no prescribed limit to the matter [of C]. But flour that was sifted as much as necessary did one bring, as it is said, And [in the case of showbread] you will take fine flour and bake it [Lev. 24:5] — that it should be sifted as much as necessary."

T. 8:15 The 'omer and the two loaves and the show-bread, the tenth of which was too large or too small, the measure of which was greater than that of its fellow or smaller than that of its fellow, Lo, these are invalid. [If] the measure of the seah was too large or too small, Lo, these are valid.

From the particular and the generic hermeneutics and the results thereof, we proceed to the corpus of established facts — whether from Scripture or tradition — that pertain, but that do not precipitate or sustain a penetrating analytical exercise. The focus throughout is "all meal-offerings," and the differentiation among the several types will follow, from M. 5:3-6+7 forward, in a systematic way, the whole worked out through a process of systematization through comparison and contrast. M. 5:8-9 then translate the difference among offerings into effective language of vowing, showing that the distinctions make a difference throughout. It is hard to imagine a more systematic presentation of complex and diverse data. That is how homogenization works. We now proceed to particular meal-offerings, beginning with the one made special by the meat-offering that it accompanies.

B. THE MEAL-OFFERING THAT ACCOMPANIES THE THANK-OFFERING

M. 8:1 [Mishnah: 7:1, Bavli: 8:1] [The flour for the loaves of the] thank-offering was brought [from] five seahs by the Jerusalem measure, which are six by the wilderness measure [equivalent to], two ephahs — the ephah is three seahs [by the wilderness measure] — twenty tenths [of an ephah]: (1) ten [tenths of an ephah] for what was to be leavened, and (2) ten for what was to be unleavened. Ten for what was to be leavened — a tenth [of an ephah] for a loaf. And ten for what was to be unleavened. And in the unleavened part are three kinds: (1) loaves, (2) wafers, and (3) [oil] — soaked cake[s] [Lev. 8:12]. There turn out to be three and a third tenths [of an ephah] for each kind, three loaves for each tenth [of an ephah]. [And] in the Jerusalem measure were thirty qabs [six qabs = one seah], (1) fifteen [qabs] for that which was unleavened, and (2) fifteen for that which was leavened. Fifteen for that which was unleavened: a qab and a half per loaf. And fifteen for that which was leavened: and in that which was unleavened were three kinds: loaves and wafers and soaked cake[s]. They turn out to be five qabs for each kind, two loaves per qab.

M. 8:2 For the [bread brought with] consecration [offering, Lev. 8:22-28] they brought [the offerings] like the unleavened [bread of the meal-offering] which goes with the thank-offering: (1) loaves and (2) wafers and (3) [oil-] soaked cakes. The [wafers of the] Nazirite's [meal-offering] consisted of two — thirds of the unleavened [cakes] of the thank-offering: [ten unleavened] loaves and [ten unleavened] wafers. But soaked cakes are not [brought along] with it. They [the Nazirite's offering] turn out to be ten Jerusalem qabs [five for unleavened loaves, five for unleavened wafers] which are six tenths [of an ephah]; and something left over [six and two-thirds tenths]. And from all of them did one take one [loaf of each kind] out of ten as heave offering, as it is said, "And he shall offer one out of each offering as a heave offering to the Lord" [Lev. 8:14] — "one" — that he should not take a broken one; "out of each offering" — (l) that all the offerings should be equivalent [ten loaves for each kind of animal], and (2) that he should not take [two loaves] from one offering [and none at all] for its fellow [that is, he should take one loaf of each kind], "to the priest who tosses the blood of the peace offerings it shall belong" [Lev. 8:14] — and the remainder [of the bread] is eaten by the owner.

T. 8:16 The flour for the loaves of the thank-offering was brought from five seahs by the Jerusalem measure, which are six by the wilderness measure [M. Men. 7:1A]. The Jerusalem measure turns out to be larger than that of the wilderness by a sixth.

T. 8:17 The [bread brought with the] ram of the consecration-offering was brought like the unleavened [bread of the meal-offering] which goes with the thank-offering: loaves, wafers, and soaked cakes [M. Men. 7:2A]. Their oil was in like measure as the oil of the thank-offering, and the waving is done as is the waving of the bread of the thank-offering. The [wafers brought with the] ram of a Nazir consisted of two-thirds of the unleavened cakes of the thank-offering: loaves and wafers. But soaked cakes are not brought along with it. Its oil was in like measure as the oil of the thank-offering, and its waving is done as is the waving of the thank-offering.

M. 8:3 He who slaughters the thank-offering inside [the Temple court], [while] its bread-offering is located outside the wall — the bread is not sanctified. [If] he slaughtered the thank-offering before its bread-offering had formed a crust in the oven — even if all of them [the loaves] formed a crust except for one of them — the bread is not sanctified. [If] he slaughtered it [intending to eat its flesh or to toss the blood or to offer up the sacrificial parts] outside of its proper time or outside of its proper place, the bread is sanctified [and is deemed refuse, M. 2:3]. [If] he slaughtered it [the thank-offering], and it turned out to be terefah, the bread is not sanctified [M. Zeb. 9:2-3]. [If] he slaughtered it and it turned out to be blemished — R. Eliezer says, "It [the bread] is sanctified." And sages say, "It is not sanctified." [The blemished animal which goes up on the altar is not removed, so Aqiba, M. Zeb. 9:2-3. Eliezer is of the same view.] [If] he slaughtered it not for its own name [=not under the classification of offering for which the animal originally was designated], and so with the ram of consecration, and so the two lambs of Aseret which one slaughtered not for their own name [=not under the classification of offering for which the animal originally was designated] — the bread is not sanctified.

T. 8:17 The bread brought with the ram of the consecration-offering was brought like the unleavened [bread of the meal-offering] which goes with the thank-offering: loaves, wafers, and soaked cakes [M. Men. 7:2A]. Their oil was in like measure as the oil of the thank-offering, and the waving is done as is the waving of the bread of the thank-offering. The wafers brought with the ram of a Nazir consisted of two-thirds of the unleavened cakes of the thank-offering, loaves and wafers. But soaked cakes are not brought along with it. Its oil was in like measure as the oil of the thank-offering, and its waving is done as is the waving of the thank-offering.

T. 8:18 He who slaughters the thank-offering inside the wall of Beth Page — the bread is not sanctified [M. Men. 7:3A]. Even if all of them are inside and one of them is outside, the bread is not sanctified [M. Men. 7:3B-D]. [If] one slaughtered it [a thank-offering], and it turned out to have been a beast which had had sexual relations with a human being, or one with which a human being had had sexual relations, a beast set aside for the purposes of idolatry or one which actually had been worshipped, a beast used in the hire or a harlot or in payment for a dog.

T. 8:19 [If] one slaughtered it and it turned out to be terefah, the bread has not been sanctified. If one slaughtered it and it turned out to be blemished — R. Eliezer says, "It [the bread] has been sanctified." R. Joshua says, "It has not been sanctified," [M. Men. 7:3G], the words of R. Meir. R. Judah said, "R. Eliezer and R. Joshua did not dispute the case in which one has slaughtered it [with improper intention to eat what is eaten] outside of the proper time, that the bread indeed has been sanctified. Nor did they dispute a case in which one slaughtered it and it turned out to be blemished, that the bread has not been sanctified." Concerning what case did they dispute? Concerning a case in which one slaughtered it [with the improper intention to eat what is to be eaten, etc.] outside of the proper place. For R. Eliezer says, "It has been sanctified." And R. Joshua says, "It has been sanctified." Said R. Eliezer to him [Joshua]. "Do you not agree that [if] one slaughtered it [with improper intention to eat what is to be eaten, etc.] out side of its proper time, that the bread has been sanctified? Also in the case of one who slaughtered it [with improper intention to eat what is to be eaten, etc.] outside of its proper place, the bread should be deemed sanctified." Said to him R. Joshua, "Do you not agree that if one slaughtered it and it turned out to be blemished, that the bread has not been sanctified? So too in the case of one who has slaughtered it [with improper intention to eat what is to be eaten, etc.] outside of its proper place, the bread should not be deemed sanctified." Said to him R. Eliezer, "You compare it to the case of a blemished animal, and I compare it to the case of [improper intention to eat what is to be eaten] outside of its proper time." Let us see to which sort of case it is comparable. If it is comparable to the case of a blemished animal, let us derive the law from that of a blemished animal. And if the case is comparable to [one in which improper intention has focused upon carrying out the specified actions] outside of its proper time, let us derive the law from a case of improper intention concerning the proper time. R. Eliezer says, "[A case of improper intention about eating] outside of the proper time produces invalidation through improper intention and one in which improper intention [about eating] outside of the proper place produces invalidation through improper intention. But let not the case of the blemished animal prove the point, for in such a case, invalidation is not on account of intention but on account of the facts of the matter." R. Joshua says, "A blemished animal is invalid, and extirpation does not apply to it, and a case of [invalidating the animal through improper intention to eat] outside of the proper place produces invalidation, and extirpation does not apply to it. But let not the case of improper intention [to eat] outside of the proper time prove the matter, because in such a case the status of refuse applies, and they are liable on its account to extirpation."

T. 8:26 [If] before he slaughtered it [the thank-offering] its bread went forth beyond the wall, one may bring it back and then slaughter [the animal] to which it belongs, and it is valid. [If] after he slaughtered [the thank-offering] its bread went outside of the wall, the blood is to be tossed. But the man has not fulfilled the conditions of his vow. The thank-offering is permitted to be eaten, but the bread is forbidden. [If this happened] after the blood was tossed, they take a tenth [loaf M. Men. 7:2D-F] from the loaves which are inside the wall for those which are outside the wall.

T. 8:27 [If] before the animal was slaughtered, the bread was broken [M. Men. 7:2E], let him bring other bread and slaughter the animal to which it belongs, and it is valid. [If] after he slaughtered [the animal], its bread was broken, the blood [nonetheless] is tossed. And the man has fulfilled the conditions of his vow. The thank-offering is permitted to be eaten, but the bread is prohibited. [If this happened] after the blood was tossed, they take the heave offering [owing to the priest, one in ten loaves] from the whole loaves for the broken ones. [If] after the animal was slaughtered, its bread was made unclean, the blood is tossed. But the owner has not fulfilled the conditions of his vow. The thank-offering is permitted for eating, but the bread is prohibited. [If this happened] after the blood was tossed, they take the heave offering [owing to the priest] from what is clean for what is unclean.

M. 8:4 Drink offerings which were sanctified in a utensil, and the animal sacrifice [with which they were brought] turned out to be invalid — if there is another animal sacrifice [requiring drink offerings], let them be offered with it. And if not, let them be invalidated by being kept overnight. (1) The offspring of a thank-offering and (2) a beast designated as its substitute [in line with Lev. 27:10] — and (3) he who sets aside his thank-offering, and it was lost, and he separated another in its place [and thereafter the lost one was found] — [when they are offered, as they must be,] they do not require bread, as it is said, "And he shall offer up with the sacrifice of the thank-offering" [Lev. 8:12] — the [one which is offered as a] thank-offering requires bread, but (1) its offspring, and (2) its substitute do not require bread, and (3) that which is brought in its place.

T. 8:20 A thank-offering requires bread, but [a thank-offering brought by] the one who errs does not require bread. What is the case of one who errs? He who separates a thank-offering and it got lost, and he set aside another in its stead, and did not have time to offer it before the first was located [M. Men. 7:4E] — Lo, both of them are available — the first is offered and requires bread and requires drink-offerings. And the second is offered, but it does not require bread, although it requires drink-offerings.

T. 8:21 He who separates coins for his thank-offering and they were lost, and who then separated coins in their stead, and who did not have time to purchase a thank-offering with them before the first coins were found — let him bring with each of them a thank-offering and offer them up. And it requires bread and it requires drink-offerings. And with the remainder of the coins, let him bring a thank-offering, and it is offered up. But it does not require a bread-offering, although it requires drink-offerings.

T. 8:22 He who separates coins for his thank-offering and they were lost, and he set aside a thank-offering in their place, and did not have time to offer it up before the coins were found — let him bring with them a thank-offering, and let it be offered up. And it requires a bread-offering, and it requires drink-offerings. And the thank-offering [which he also set aside] is to be offered up. But it does not require a bread-offering, although it requires drink-offerings.

T. 8:23 He who sets aside his thank-offering and it was lost, and who then set aside coins in its stead, and who did not have time to purchase with them [another] thank-offering before the [first] thank-offering was found — the thank-offering is to be offered up. And it requires bread and requires drink-offerings. With the coins, he purchases a thank-offering, and this [too] is offered up. But it does not require a bread-offering, although it requires drink offerings.

T. 8:24 He who sets aside his thank-offering and it was lost, and who sets aside another in its place, and he offered it up, and afterward the first is found — [the first] is to be offered up. And it requires a bread-offering and it requires drink-offerings.

T. 8:25 He who sets aside coins for his thank-offering, and they were lost, and who set aside coins in their stead and who purchased with them a thank-offering and offered it up, and afterward the first coins were found — let him bring from both [groups of coins] a thank-offering. Let it be offered up. And it requires a bread-offering, and it requires drink-offerings. If he purchased with them [the coins] a thank-offering and had money left over, let him bring with the excess funds a thank-offering. And let it be offered up. But it does not require a bread-offering, although it does require drink-offerings.

M. 8:5 He who says, "Lo, I pledge myself [to bring] a thank-offering" brings it and its bread from that which is unconsecrated [not purchased with second-tithe coins]. [He who says], "A thank-offering from that which is unconsecrated, and its bread from tithe," brings its bread from that which is unconsecrated. [He who says], "A thank-offering from tithe and its bread from

that which is unconsecrated," brings [the things just as he has specified]. [He who says], "A thank-offering — it and its bread from tithe," brings [the things just as he has specified].

M. 8:6 How on the basis of Scripture do we know that he who says, "Lo, I pledge myself [to bring] a thank-offering," should bring it only from unconsecrated beasts? As it is said, "And you will slaughter a Passover to the Lord, your God, of the flock or of the herd" [Dt. 16:2] — And does not the Passover derive only from lambs or goats? If so, why is flock or herd said? But: it is to compare whatever derives from the flock or from the herd to the Passover. Just as the Passover, which is brought in fulfillment of an obligation, is brought only from unconsecrated beasts, so everything which is brought in fulfillment of an obligation is brought only from unconsecrated beasts. Therefore: He who says, "Lo, I pledge myself [to bring] a thank-offering," "Lo, I pledge myself [to bring] peace offerings" — since they are brought in fulfillment of an obligation, should bring them only from unconsecrated [funds]. And drink offerings under all circumstances [even at M. 8:5D-E] should derive only from unconsecrated [funds].

T. 8:28 [He who says, "Lo, I pledge myself to bring] a thank-offering deriving half from unconsecrated funds and half from second tithe," brings its bread from coins which derive in the same way, half from unconsecrated funds and half from second tithe money. [He who vows to bring] a thank-offering, it and its bread from consecrated coins [may do so] [M. Men. 7:5D]. But one in fulfillment of his obligation he brings only from unconsecrated funds, as it is said, "And you will keep this service in this month" [Ex. 13:5] — Just as this service derives only from unconsecrated funds, so all matters which are done in fulfillment of an obligation derive only from unconsecrated funds [M. Men. 7:6].

T. 8:29 One should bring second tithe only from funds which derive from second tithe. [He who says,] "Lo, I pledge myself to bring a thank-offering," "Lo, I pledge myself to bring peace-offerings" — since they are brought in fulfillment of an obligation, should bring them only with unconsecrated funds [M. Men. 7:6G-H].

T. 8:30 Drink-offerings under all circumstances should derive only from unconsecrated funds [M. Men. 7:6I]. They do not bring meal-offerings and drink-offerings, the meal-offering which goes with a beast, and the bread-offering which goes with a thank-offering, from produce, from which tithes have not been taken, or from produce from which only first tithe has been taken, first-tithe from which the heave offering has not been taken, and from second tithe, and produce which was sanctified and then not redeemed, from produce which has been mixed up with heave-offering, from new crops [before the 'omer has been offered on the sixteenth of Nisan] and from produce which has grown in the seventh year. And if one brought [meal-offerings and drink-offerings, etc.] from such sources, Lo, these are invalid. And one need hardly add, [One does not bring meal-offerings and drink-offerings, etc.] from produce which is subject to the restrictions of 'orlah or from produce which is prohibited by reason of sanctification as mixed seeds in a vineyard.

We turn to a special case, a meal-offering presented with the thank-offering and its particular requirements. The rules seem to me to respond to no more encompassing program, e.g., the generic hermeneutics, although the issues of such pericopes as M. 8:3 transcend the case. Now we revert to the "all-meal offerings..." mode, which makes me wonder why the bread-offering that accompanies the thank-offering has found its place where it has. The same mode goes forward to the end of the unit. Only then do we meet the other singular meal-offering, the 'omer. The upshot is, the topical organization contains an anomaly, rare indeed in the Halakhah.

C. SOURCES OF FLOUR, OIL, AND WINE USED FOR THE MEAL-OFFERING

M. 9:1 [Mishnah: 8:1, Bavli: 9:1] All [meal] offerings of the community and of the individual derive (1) from [wheat grown] in the Land [of Israel] or from [wheat grown] abroad, (2) from fresh produce [wheat, grown in the present year] or from old [wheat, grown in the preceding year], except for the offering of a sheaf of the first crop of barley [Lev. 23:10] and two loaves of bread [Lev. 23:1617], which derive only from new [wheat, grown in the present year] and from [wheat grown in the] Land. But all of them derive only from the choicest [produce] [Dt. 12:11]. And what is deemed to be the choicest [produce]? Mikhmas [Ezra 2:27] and Zanuhah [Josh. 15:35, 56] are alpha as to fine flour. Second to them is Hapharayim [2 Chron. 13:19, Josh. 19:19] in the valley. All lands were valid [as sources for the grain], but from here did they bring [the flour for the meal-offering].

M. 9:2 They do not bring [wheat for flour for the meal-offering] either from a manured field or from an irrigated field or from a tree-planted field. But if they brought [wheat from these areas], it is valid. How does one do it? One broke up fresh ground in the first year of the sabbatical cycle, and in the second of the sabbatical cycle sows it seventy days before Passover, and it produces abundant flour. How does one examine it [the flour]? The [Temple] treasurer sticks his hand into it [the flour]. [If] dust came up on it [his hand], it is invalid, until one will sift it [afresh]. And if it had become maggoty, it is invalid.

T. 9:1 All offerings of the community and of the individual derive from the Land [of Israel] and from abroad [M. Men. 8:1A] — even from gentiles, except for the firstling and tithe, which derive only from the Land and derive only from Israelites.

T. 9:2 All meal-offerings derive from the Land and from abroad, from new and from old [produce], except for the 'omer and the two loaves of bread, which derive only from new produce and from the Land [M. Men. 8:1A — D]. And all of them derive only from the choicest [produce] [M. Men. 8:1 E], as it is said, "And all the choice-offerings which you shall vow [RSV: And all your votive offerings]" [Deut. 12:11]. And what is deemed to be the choicest [produce]? Mikmas [— this is Lahah —] is alpha as to fine pour. Second to it is Aphrayam in the valley [M. Men. 8:1F-H]. R. Yosé says, "Also Hiti Berehayim and Kefar Ahus." These were near Jerusalem, and from them did they bring [the wheat ground for flour for the meal-offerings].

T. 9:3 They bring [the wheat] only from fields which have been repeatedly ploughed over for that purpose. How does one do it? In the first year he broke fresh ground, and in the second he ploughs and sows it seventy days before Passover [M. Men. 8:2C — D], so that it will [sprout up] near the [season of] sunshine, and it produces abundant flour [M. Men. 8:2E]. And it would produce stalks one span long and ears two spans long. Then they winnowed it and threshed it and ground it and sifted it and brought it to the treasurer. The treasurer sticks his hand into it. If dust came up from it, they go and winnow it a second time [M. Men. 8:2H]. In the name of R. Nathan they said, "His hand did he anoint with oil, and he pushed it into it [the wheat] so that [all] the dust should go up out of it."

T. 9:4 Flour which had become maggoty, Lo, this is deemed blemished for the altar [M. Men. 8:21]. Grains of wheat which became maggoty or which rotted, Lo, these are deemed blemished for the altar.

M. 9:3 Teqo'ah [2 Sam. 14:2] is alpha for olive oil. Abba Saul says, "Second to it is Reqeb in Transjordan." All lands were valid, but from here did they bring [oil]. They do not bring [olives for olive oil] from a manured field or from an irrigated field or from a field among [the trees of which] seed was sown. And if one did bring [olives for the oil from such fields, the oil produced therefrom] is valid. They do not bring it from unripe olives. And if one did bring it [from such a source], it is invalid. They do not bring [oil produced] from dried olives which had been soaked in water, nor from pickled olives, nor from seethed olives. And if one did bring [it from such a source], it is invalid.

T. 9:5 A. Teqo'ah is alpha for olive-oil. Abba Saul says, "Second to it is Reqeb in TransJordan" [M. Men. 8:3A-B]. R. Eliezer

b. Jacob says, "Third to it is Gush Halab in Galilee."

M. 9:4 There are three [ways of preparing] olives, and each one of them [produces] three [kinds of] oil. The first [way of preparing the] olive [is as follows]: (1) One gathers it from the top of the olive tree, and (2) crushes it, and (3) puts it into a basket — R. Judah says, "Around the sides of the basket [oozing down to the bottom]" — this is the first [kind of oil produced in the first of the three ways]. One pressed them under the beam. R. Judah says, "Under stones" — this is the second [kind of oil produced by the first of the three ways]. One went and ground and pressed [them]. This is the third [kind of oil]. The first [kind of oil] is used for the candelabrum, and the rest for meal-offerings. The second [way of preparing] olives [is as follows]: (1) one gathers [the olives when they are] at the [level of the] top of the roof, and (2) presses [them], and (3) puts them into the basket — R. Judah says, "Around the sides of the basket" — this is the first [kind of oil produced in the second way]. One pressed them under the beam — R. Judah says, "Under stones" — This is the second. One ground and pressed [them] — this is the third. The first [kind of oil] is used for the candelabrum, and the rest for meal-offerings. The third [way of preparing] olives [is as follows]: (1) [Since the olives are on the lowest branches, in the shade, and will not ripen on the tree], one packs them in the house, until they are fully ripe, and (2) brings them up and dries them on the top of the roof, and (3) crushes and puts them into a basket — R. Judah says, "Around the sides of the basket" — this is the first. One pressed it under the beam — R. Judah says, "Under stones" — this is the second. One went and ground and pressed [it] — this is the third. The first is for the candelabrum, and the rest for meal-offerings.

M. 9:5 The first [kind of oil, deriving from] the first process — there is nothing better than it. The second [kind of oil deriving from the] first [process] and the first [kind of oil deriving from the] second [process] are equivalent. The third [kind of oil produced by] the first [process] and the second [produced by the] second [process] and the first [produced by the] third process are equivalent. The third [kind of oil produced by the] second [process] and the second [kind of oil produced by the] third [process] are equivalent. The third kind of oil produced by the third process — there is nothing beneath it. Also: meal-offerings might logically be deemed to require the purest kind of oil: Now if the oil used for the candelabrum, which is not destined to be eaten, requires the purest kind of olive oil, meal-offerings, which are destined to be eaten, logically should require the purest kind of olive oil. Scripture therefore states, "Pure olive oil beaten for the light" [Ex. 20:27] — And not pure olive oil beaten for meal-offerings.

T. 9:6 They bring [olive-oil] only from olives which are set aside for that purpose. R. Judah says, "They did not grind it in a mill, but they crushed it in an olive crusher. They did not grind it under a beam but under stones" [M. Men. 8:4F].

T. 9:7 "They do not place the 'bread' [the olive-pulp] into the basket, but the basket into the 'bread' [M. Men. 8:4C], and it exudes from the basket." The first [oil] is for the candelabrum, the second and the third for meal-offerings [M. Men. 8:4J].

T. 9:8 Oil of unripe olives is invalid, for it is only sap [M. Men. 8:3F]. Oil [produced from olives which had been] soaked in water or seethed or boiled, that of the lees, and that which has a bad smell — Lo, this is deemed blemished for the altar [M. Men. 8:3F-I].

M. 9:6 And from whence did they bring wine? Qarutim and Hattulim are alpha as to wine. Second to them are Bet Rimmah and Bet Laban in the hills, and Kefar Signah in the valley. All lands were valid, but from here did they bring it. They do not bring [the wine from grapes grown] either in a manured field, or in an irrigated field, or from vineyards sown with seed between the vines. And if they brought [it from such areas], it is valid. They do not bring [wine which derives from] sun-dried grapes. And if they brought [it from such a source], it is valid. "They do not bring last year's [wine]," the words of Rabbi. And sages declare valid. They do not bring sweet, or smoked, or boiled wine. And if one did bring [such kinds of wine], it is invalid. They do not bring [wine made from grapes grown on] trellised vines, but only from vines growing from the ground and from vineyards which are tended.

M. 9:7 They did not collect it in large store utensils but in little jars. And one does not fill the jars up to their rims, so that its fragrance spreads. One does not draw [the wine] from its mouth, because of the scum, or from its bottom, because of the lees. But one draws it from the middle of the middle-third [of the jar]. How does one test it? The [Temple] treasurer sits, with a reed in his hand. [When] it tossed off the froth, then he struck it with the reed [as a sign that it is to be sealed]. R. Yosé bar Judah says, "Wine on which scum came up is invalid, as it is said, 'And they shall be to you without blemish, and their meal-offering' [Num. 29:23], and 'They shall be unto you without blemish, also their drink offering' [Num. 29:31]."

T. 9:9 Sour wine, mixed wine, wine which had been left uncovered, wine lees, and wine with a bad smell — Lo, this is deemed blemished for the altar. Wine deriving from sun-dried grapes [M. Men. 8:6G], and dark wine, and effervescent wine, and wine made of raisins, and wine kept in a store room one should not bring [M. Men. 8:6K-L]. And if one brought [such wine], it is valid. Rabbi says,

"Also: wine two years old or three years old, the color of which has changed and grown dim, one should not bring. But if he brought [such wine], it is valid."

T. 9:10 They do not bring [wine produced from grapes of] vines trained over the wall or from those trained on espaliers but only from vines growing from the ground [M. Men. 8:6M], which are set aside for that purpose. They did not cut the grapes and let them shrink [before putting them into the press], but cut and forthwith pressed them. And they did not collect it [the wine] in large store-utensils or in little jars [vs. M. Men. 8:7A], but in medium-sized jugs. They did not leave them either in the cellar or on the roof. But they left them as they were. And one did not fill the jar up to the brim, but only two-thirds of the jar [did he fill], so that its fragrance spreads [M. Men. 8:7B]. One does not draw [wine] from the mouth, because of the scum, or from the bottom, because of the lees, but one pierces it and draws it from the middle of the middle-third [of the jug] [M. Men. 8:7C-D].

T. 9:11 How does one test it? The [Temple] treasurer sits, with a reed in his hand. Once it tosses off the froth [M. Men. 8:7E–F], he gives orders, and they take it away from him and bring another instead. And they say, "Come and take for yourselves that which is invalid for the altar."

T. 9:12 They do not bring wine which is less than forty days old. But if one brought the wine directly from its vat, it is valid.

T. 9:13 Rams [were brought] from Moab, calves from Sharon, lambs from the wilderness, pigeons from the Royal hill-country. R. Judah says, "Lambs whose height is equal to their breadth."

T. 9:14 All sorts of wood are valid for the altar, except for the wood of an olive-tree and of a grapevine. R. Eleazar adds, "Five kinds of wood are invalid: also the wood of a sycamore and that of a carob and that of a palm and that of a mayish [a tall tree with fruits like myrtle-berries] and that of an oak." And [pieces of] wood of any kind taken from a building which had been torn down — Lo, these are invalid. But these were they accustomed [to bring to the altar]: wild fig-trees and wood of an oil-tree, and wood of a nut-tree.

T. 9:15 Salt — this is salt from Sodom, as it is said, "Thou shalt not leave off salt" [Lev. 2:13]. Bring salt which is not lacking [which has no Sabbath], and this is salt of Sodom. And how do we know that if one did not find salt of Sodom, he should bring salt of Istria? Scripture states, Salt, Salt, by way of inclusion.

T. 9:16 Blue is valid only if it comes from the purple-shell [used for that purpose]. [If] one brought blue which did not come from the purple-shell, it is invalid, as it is said, "Blue" [Ex. 28:31]. It is to derive from blue of the hill-country. [If] one brought it not of the blue of the hill country, it is invalid.

T. 9:17 Linen — this is [linen made from] flax. If one made it from canvas, it is invalid.

T. 9:18 The candelabrum and the consecrated utensils — their requirement is to derive from the [funds] left over [from those used to purchase] drink-offerings. If there is insufficient [money] for that purpose, let one bring them from funds of the heave-offering of the chamber. The candelabrum is valid only if it is made from a gold bar. [If] one made it from filings, it is invalid. [If one made it] from other sorts of metal, it is valid.

T. 9:19 The trumpet is valid only if it is made from silver. [If] one made it from ore, it is valid. [If one made it] from other sorts of metal, it is invalid.

T. 9:20 You turn out to rule: What is invalid in the case of the candelabrum is valid in the case of the trumpet. What is invalid in the case of the trumpet is valid in the case of the candelabrum. [One made] of tin, lead, *assiterum*, or of metal — Rabbi declares invalid. And R. Yosé bar Judah declares valid. One of wood and of bone and of glass — all agree that it is invalid.

T. 9:21 Utensils of service, before they have been used — an ordinary person may make use of them once they have been used for the sanctuary, an ordinary person may not make use of it. Utensils which to begin with were made for an ordinary person — they do not use them [for the sanctuary].

T. 9:22 Utensils of service which were perforated — they do not melt them, and they do not put lead into them, and they do not grind away its blemish.

T. 9:23 A knife which broke off — they do not restore. And they do not grind away its blemish. Abba Saul says, "A knife was causing terefot [invalidating damage to the beast], and they gave orders concerning it, to hide it away."

Seeing the composite in the aggregate, I discern here only data particular to the topic, inert facts, no generative issues of any kind. In detail some of the compositions work over issues that transcend the case at hand, but no systematic program, such as we have discerned elsewhere, operates throughout. Now we revert, to the end of the unit, to rules governing all meal-offerings.

D. *MEASURING THE MATERIALS USED FOR THE OFFERING*

M. 10:1 Two dry measures were in the sanctuary: (1) a tenth [ephah measure], and (2) a half-tenth [ephah measure]. R. Meir says, "A tenth measure, [another] tenth measure, and a half-tenth measure" [M. 10:5]. A tenth measure: how did it serve? In it did one measure [flour for] all meal-offerings. One did not measure either with a three-tenths measure for [the meal-offering of] a bullock, or with a two-tenths measure for [the meal-offering of] a ram [Num. 15:6, 9, 28:12], but they measured them with tenth measures. A half-tenth measure: how did it serve? In it did one measure the baked cakes of a high priest [M. 4:5], half [a tenth-ephah measure] for the morning, half [a tenth-ephah measure] for twilight [M. 10:5].

T. 10:1 R. Meir says, "What is the meaning of the Scripture's saying, 'A tenth [a tenth for every lamb' (Num. 28:29)]? One which is heaped up, and one which is not heaped up. With this one which was heaped up did one measure for all meal-offerings. With this one which was not heaped up did one measure for the cakes of an anointed priest" [M. Men. 9:3B]. And so there was not a measure of three [tenths] for a bullock or a measure of two [tenths] for a ram. But even if there were sixty bullocks and sixty rams, with one tenth ephah did one measure out [flour and oil] for all of them [M. Men. 9:3E], as "For a meal-offering and a log of oil" [Lev. 14:21] — oil for every meal-offering, [and] a log of oil.

M. 10:2 Seven liquid measures were in the sanctuary: (1) a hin [= twelve logs], and (2) a half-hin, and (3) a third-hin, and (4) a fourth-hin, (5) a log, and (6) half-log, and (7) a quarter-log. R. Eleazar b. Sadoq says, "Notches were in the hin: 'Up to here for a bullock [a half-hin of oil and wine],' 'up to here for a ram [a third-hin],' 'up to here for a lamb [a fourth hin, Num. 28:14].'" R. Simeon says, "There was no hin there, and for what purpose would a hin serve? [There was no need for a hin-measure. It was used only for Moses' anointing oil, Ex. 30:24.] But there was a further measure of a log and a half [= an eighth-hin], in which one did measure out [oil for] the high priest's meal-offering. A log and a half in the morning, and a log and a half at twilight."

M. 10:3 A quarter-log: how did it serve? It served to measure out the quarter-log of water for the person afflicted with the skin ailment [Lev. 14:5], and a quarter-log of oil for the Nazirite [M. 7:2]. A half-log: how did it serve? It served to measure out the half-log of water for the woman accused of adultery [Num. 5:17], and a half-log of oil for the thank-offering [M. 7:1]. And with a log did one measure out [oil] for all meal-offerings. Even [for] the meal-offering containing sixty tenths did one measure out sixty [individual] logs. R. Eliezer b. Jacob says, "Even a meal-offering of sixty tenths gets only its [one] log, as it is said, 'For a meal-offering, and a log of oil' [Lev. 14:21]." Six [logs = a half-hin] [the drink offerings of] a bullock, four [logs = a third-hin] for a ram, three [logs = a quarter-hin] for a lamb, and three and a half for the lamp, a half-log for each light.

T. 7:16 How does one measure out the oil? As to a meal-offering of one tenth of an ephah: they put in it one log [of oil]. As to one of sixty tenths: they put in it sixty logs. But as to the handful of frankincense and the handful for remembrance, one takes one handful for all of them. R. Nehemiah and R. Eleazar say, "Just as for the handful of the frankincense and the handful of remembrance, one takes one handful for all of them, so in the case of the meal-offering made of one tenth of an ephah and one of sixty tenths of an ephah, one log of oil serves all of them, 'as it is said, [And a tenth of an ephah of fine flour mixed with oil] for a cereal offering, and a log of oil [Lev. 14:21] — for every meal-offering, one log of oil'" [M. Men. 9:3].

T. 10:2 Seven liquid measures were in the sanctuary [M. Men. 9:2A]: A quarter-log, a half-log, a log, a quarter-hin, a third-hin, a half-hin, R. Judah says, "A hin, a half-hin, a third-hin, a quarter-hin, a log, a half-log, and a quarter-log" [M. Men. 9:2A].

T. 10:3 A quarter-log. How did it serve [M. Men. 9:3A]? With it did one take the measure for the cakes of an anointed priest a half-log. How did it serve? With it did one take the measure for the three logs and a half for the lamp, and a half-log for each light. A log? With it did one take the measure for all meal-offerings. A quarter-hin — how did it serve? [For the meal-offering accompanying] every sort of animal of the flock, large and small, male and female, because all of them are equivalent as to the [meal-offerings which accompany their] drink-offerings. They are stirred together with one another.

T. 10:4 The third-hin. It was the poorest of all of them. It served only for measuring out the [flour for the meal-offerings which accompanied] the drink-offerings of rams, whether for two or more than that. The half-hin. How did it serve? [It served for measuring out the flour for the meal-offerings which accompanied the drink-offerings for] every kind of cattle, large and small, male and female, because all of them are equivalent as to the [meal-offerings which accompany their] drink-offerings. And they are stirred together with one another. R. Simeon says, "There were not seven measures in the sanctuary, [for there was no need of a] hin [M. Men. 9:2C]. For they do not give a single measure for two bullocks, or a single measure for two rams." "What did one bring in their stead? A log-and-a-half-measure." Said R. Judah, "But was there not a half-log and a log?" Said to him R. Simeon, "If so, one can take care of all of them with a quarter-log-measure. But no measure in the sanctuary served in place of its fellow."

T. 10:5 R. Eleazar bar Sadoq says, "There were four liquid-measures in the sanctuary: A quarter-log, a half-log, a log, and a hin were there. And there were notches in the hin: Up to here for a bullock ...up to here for a lamb [M. Men. 9:2B], a half-log for a thank-offering, and a quarter-log for the Nazirite" [M. Men. 9:3B-C].

M. 10:4 They stir together (1) [the meal-offering which accompanies] drink offerings of rams along with [that for] drink offerings of bullocks, (2) [the meal-offering which accompanies] drink offerings of lambs along with [that for] drink offerings of lambs, (3) those of an individual along with those of the community, (4) those of one day along with those of the preceding day [for drink offerings may be offered up to ten days after the sacrifice which they accompany]. But they do not stir the drink offerings of lambs along with the drink offerings of bullocks or rams. And if one stirred them, these by themselves and those by themselves, and they [then] become confused, they are valid. If before one stirred them [they became confused], it is invalid. The lamb which is brought with the sheaf of first barley that is waved — even though its meal-offering was doubled [two tenths instead of one, Lev. 23:13], its drink offerings were not doubled [but each lamb gets three logs of wine and oil].

T. 10:6 They do not sanctify inside but outside [M. Men. 9:3A — C]. They do not stir the drink-offerings of lambs with the drink-offerings bullocks and rams [M. Men. 9:4B]. Under what circumstances? In the case of meal-offerings made with fine flour and oil. But in the case of drink-offerings, they do stir the drink-offerings of an individual with the drink-offerings of another individual, and the drink offerings of the community with the drink-offerings of the community, those of an individual with those of the community, those of today with those of the day before, and those of today with those of tomorrow [M. Men. 9:4A]. Under what circumstances? When they have not been sanctified [poured] in a utensil. But when they have been sanctified in a utensil, they do not mix those of today with those of tomorrow, because they [those of today] are rendered invalid by being kept overnight.

M. 10:5 All measures which were in the sanctuary were heaped up, except for that of the high priest, which he did heap up into its own midst. Liquid measures: their overflow was consecrated. And dry measures: their overflow was unconsecrated. R. Aqiba says, "The liquid measures are consecrated, therefore, their overflow is consecrated. And dry measures are unconsecrated, therefore, their overflow is unconsecrated." R. Yosé says, "Not on this account, but [the reason is] that [by adding a surplus, what is in] the liquid measure is stirred up, but [by adding a surplus] what is in the dry measure is not stirred up."

T. 10:7 All the overflow of [liquid-] measures: in the case of liquid-measures, it is consecrated, and in the case of dry measures, it is unconsecrated [M. Men. 9:5C — D]. On what account in the case of liquid is it holy? Because they are anointed inside. On what account in the case of dry is it unconsecrated? Because they are not anointed [M. Men. 9:5E].

T. 10:8 All the overflow of these measures: if there is another animal-sacrifice, let them be offered with it. And if not, let them be invalidated through being kept overnight. [And if not, let their appearance be spoiled and let them go out to the place of burning.] And if not, let them be sold to those who are liable to offer another animal sacrifice. Let him bring with the proceeds what is needed for the time that the altar is unused for private offerings. [To provide] what is needed for the time that the altar is unused for private offerings do they purchase with the funds burnt-offerings and with them they keep the altar occupied.

M. 10:6 All offerings of the community and the individual require drink offerings, except for (1) the firstling, (2) tithe of cattle, (3) the Passover, (4) the sin offering, and (5) the guilt offering. But (4) the sin offering of the person afflicted with the skin ailment and (5) his guilt offering require drink offerings.

M. 10:7 All offerings of the community do not receive laying on of hands, except for the bullock which is brought on account of [the community's transgression of] any of the commandments [Lev. 4:15] and the goat which is sent forth [Lev. 16:21]. R. Simeon says, "Also: the goats which are brought on account of idolatry [Num. 15:2]." All offerings of the individual require laying on of hands, except for (1) the firstling, (2) tithe of cattle, and (3) the Passover. And the heir [of a man who died before bringing a vowed sacrifice] "lays on hands and brings drink offerings and has the power to effect substitution [Lev. 27:10]."

M. 10:8 All lay on hands, except for (1) the deaf-mute, (2) the idiot, and (3) the minor, (4) the blind person, and (5) the gentile, and (6) the slave, and (7) the agent, and (8) the woman. And laying on of hands constitutes the residue of the requirement [which may, in fact, be omitted without affecting the efficacy of atonement]. [It is done] on the head [of the animal] with both hands. And in the place in which they lay on hands [there do] they slaughter [the animal]. And forthwith after laying on of hands is the act of slaughter, which is not the rule for laying on of hands.

M. 10:9 A more strict rule applies to laying on of hands than to waving, and to waving than to laying on of hands. For: one person waves for all associated [with the sacrifice], but one person does not lay on hands for all associated [with the sacrifice]. A more strict rule applies to waving. For: Waving applies to offerings of an individual and to offerings of the community, to living animals and to slaughtered animals, to something animate and to something inanimate, which is not the rule for laying on of hands.

T. 10:9 "All offerings of the community do not receive laying on of hands, except for the bullock which is brought on account of the community's transgression of any of the commandments [M. Men. 9:7A-B]. And the goats brought on account of idolatry, which do require laying on of hands," the words of R. Simeon. R. Judah says, "The goats which are brought on account of idolatry do not require laying on of hands. What does one bring in their stead? The goat which is sent forth." Said to him R. Simeon, "And does not the laying on of hands apply only to the owners? The goat which is sent forth — Aaron and his sons lay their hands on it simultaneously." Said to him R. Judah, "They also find atonement through it."

T. 10:10 A general rule did R. Simeon lay down: "Whatever is brought on account of violations of a specific commandment and the blood of which is brought inside [to the inner altar] requires laying on of hands. Whatever is not brought on account of transgressions of a specific commandment and the blood of which is not brought inside does not require laying on of hands."

T. 10:11 "The heir [M. Men. 9:7F] and the eleventh of the tithe [M. Bekh 9:8] — Lo, these effect substitution. They require laying on of hands, and drink-offerings," the words of R. Meir. R. Judah says, "The heir does not effect substitution, and the eleventh of the tithe does not effect substitution, because it itself is a substitute, and that which is a substitute cannot effect substitution." He said to R. Judah, "If this were [merely] a substitute, it would be offered. But it was a sacrifice [unto itself] and it had drink-offerings [to be offered] unto themselves."

T. 10:12 "How does one lay on hands? The animal to be sacrificed stands at the north with its face to the west. The one who lays on hands is in the west, with his face to the west. He puts his two hands onto the horns of the animal. But he did not put his hands on the shoulder, and he did not put his hands on top of one another, and nothing intervened between his hands and the horns. He made confession of sin or transgression over it: over a sin offering, [he confessed] the particular sin he had committed, over the guilt offering, the particular transgression of which he was guilty. Over a burnt-offering, [he confessed] the particular sin concerning transgression of the rules of gleaning, the forgotten sheaf, and the corner of the field [of which he was guilty], to which confession does not apply," the words of R. Yosé the Galilean. Said to him R. Aqiba, "For what sins does the burnt-offering effect atonement? For those things which incur a specific punishment. Lo, a punishment is stated [and the punishment atones for the deed]. For a negative precept, their own modes of punishment are stated. For what does the burnt-offering effect atonement? For transgression of a positive commandment and for transgression of a negative commandment which involves positive action."

T. 10:13 The laying on of hands applies in the case of priests, Levites, Israelites, proselytes, freed slaves, Hallalin, Netinin, Mamzerin, a male rendered a eunuch by human action or naturally, a man with crushed testicles and one with a damaged penis. It does not apply to gentiles, women, slaves, or minors.

T. 10:14 Five men who brought a single animal-sacrifice all lay hands on. But all of them do not simultaneously lay hands on it, but each one does so separately and stands aside.

T. 10:15 Laying on of hands [for ordination] is by three: The laying on of hands of elders [Lev. 4:15] is by three. R. Judah says, "By five." All of them do not simultaneously lay hands on it, but each individual lays on hands and stands aside. As to the ram of consecration: Aaron and his sons simultaneously [lay hands on it].

T. 10:16 Just as the laying on of hands is done by those who are clean, so slaughter is done by those who are clean. Forthwith after laying on of hands is the act of slaughter [M. Men.] In the place in which they lay on hands, there do they slaughter [the animal] [M. Men. 9:8E].

T. 10:17 Waving [the offering] applies to priests, Levites, and Israelites, proselytes, freed slaves, Hallalin, Netinin, Mamzerin, a male rendered a eunuch by human action or naturally, a man with crushed testicles and one with a damaged penis. It does not apply to gentiles, women, slaves, or minors.

T. 10:18 Five who brought a single animal-sacrifice: One [of them] waves it in behalf of all of them. He who sends his sacrifice through another — a priest waves [the sacrifice] in his behalf. As to a woman: A priest waves [her sacrifice] in her behalf.

The only point of interest among these merely-informative rulings is at M. 10:4, where various types of meal-offerings are classified, some to be mixed together, some not. The comparisons and contrasts at M. 10:7-9 successfully systematize a fair amount of data as well. The Toseftan statements manage to broaden the interest of the entire repertoire.

III. SPECIAL MEAL-OFFERINGS

A. *THE 'OMER*

M. 6:1 [Mishnah: 10:1, Bavli: 6:1] R. Ishmael says, "The offering of the first sheaf of barley was brought (1) on the Sabbath from three seahs [of barley], (2) and on a weekday, from five." And sages say, "All the same are the Sabbath and the weekday: from three [seahs] was it brought." R. Hananiah, Prefect of the Priests, says, "On the Sabbath it [the barley] was reaped (1) by one man, and with one sickle, and into one basket, (2) and on a

weekday by three men, into three baskets, with three sickles."
And sages say, "All the same are the Sabbath and the weekday: [it is done] by three men, into three baskets, with three sickles."

T. 10:19 R. Ishmael says, "The 'omer was brought on the Sabbath from three seahs, and on a weekday from five." And sages say, "All the same are the Sabbath and the weekday: from three seahs was it brought" [M. Men. 10:1A-B].

T. 10:20 Abba Saul says, "On the Sabbath it [the grain] was reaped by one man, with one sickle, into one basket. On a weekday, [it was reaped] by three men into three baskets with three sickles." And sages say, "All the same are the Sabbath and the weekday: By three [men] into three baskets and with three sickles" [M. Men. 10:1C-D].

M. 6:2 The requirement of the offering of the first sheaf of barley is to bring it from [barley growing] nearby to Jerusalem. [If] it [the crop] did not ripen near Jerusalem [in time for use on Nisan 16] [however,] they bring it from any place.

T. 10:21 The 'omer was brought from the valley of Bet Miqlah in Qidron valley. It [produced a crop] early, and it contained three seahs, and the sun rises [shining] into it, and sets [shining] into it. It was [left] half unploughed and half sown.

T. 10:22 [There] they watch the aftergrowth in years of release and jubilee-years, to bring from them the 'omer and the two loaves. They receive their salary from the heave-offering of the chamber [compare M. Sheq. 4:1]. And from there did they bring [the necessary funds] whether from ample or sparse [funds], they were the [fixed] funds [used for that purpose]. He who wants to volunteer [the necessary funds] — they do not listen to him. R. Yosé says, "He who wants to volunteer may volunteer [the necessary funds], on condition that he give them over to the community" [compare M. Sheq. 4:1].

M. 6:3 How did they do it? Agents of the court go forth on the eve of [the afternoon before] the festival [of Passover]. And they make it into sheaves while it is still attached to the ground, so that it will be easy to reap. And all the villagers nearby gather together there [on the night after the first day of Passover], so that it will be reaped with great pomp. Once it gets dark [on the night of the sixteenth of Nisan], he says to them, "Has the sun set?" They say, "Yes." "Has the sun set?" They say, "Yes." "[With] this sickle?" They say, "Yes." "[With] this sickle?" They say, "Yes." "[With] this basket?" They say, "Yes." "[With] this basket?" They say, "Yes." On the Sabbath, he says to them, "[Shall l reap on] this Sabbath?" They say, "Yes." "[Shall I reap on] this Sabbath?" They say, "Yes." "Shall I reap?" They say, "Reap." "Shall I reap?" They say, "Reap"- three times for each and every matter. And they say to him, "Yes, yes, yes." All of this [pomp]

for what purpose? Because of the Boethusians, for they maintain, "The reaping of the [barley for] the offering of the first sheaf of barley is not [done] at the conclusion of the festival."

M. 6:4 They reaped it, and they put it into baskets, They brought it to the court [of the Temple]. "They did parch it in fire, so as to carry out the requirement that it be parched with fire [Lev.2:14]," the words of R. Meir. And sages say, "With reeds and with stems of plants do they [first] beat it [to thresh it], so that it not be crushed. And they put it into a tube. And the tube was perforated, so that the fire affect all of it." They spread it out in the court, and the breeze blows over it. They put it into a grist mill and took out therefrom a tenth ephah, which is sifted through thirteen sieves [M. 6:7]. And the residue is redeemed and eaten by anyone. And it is liable for the dough offering, but exempt from tithes. R. Aqiba declares it liable for both dough offering and tithes. He came [on the sixteenth of Nisan] to the tenth [ephah of flour], and put in its oil and frankincense [M. 6:3]]. He poured in [oil] and mingled it and waved it. And he brought it near [M. 5:6] and took out the handful and offered it up. And the residue is eaten by the priests.

M. 6:5 After the offering of the first sheaf of barley was offered, they go out and find the market of Jerusalem full of meal and parched grain [of new produce] — not with the approval of sages. The words of R. Meir. R. Judah says, "With the approval of sages did they do so." After the offering of the first sheaf of barley was offered, new produce was permitted forthwith. And [for] people who are distant [from Jerusalem] it is permitted from noontime and thereafter [on the sixteenth of Nisan]. After the Temple was destroyed, Rabban Yohanan b. Zakkai ordained that the day of waving [of the offering of the first sheaf of barley, the second day of Passover] should be wholly prohibited [in respect to new produce]. Said R. Judah, "And is it not so that it is prohibited by the Torah, as it is said, 'To this selfsame day' (Lev. 23:14)?" On what account are those who are distant [from Jerusalem] permitted [to make use of new produce] from noontime and thereafter? Because they are certain that the court is not slovenly in dealing with it.

T. 10:23 The day of waving [the 'omer] which coincides with the Sabbath overrides [the prohibitions of] the Sabbath in respect to the reaping of [barley for] the 'omer [M. Men. 10:9K]. How did they do it? Agents of the court go forth on the eve of [the afternoon before] the festival [of Passover] [M. Men. 10:3B-C]. They take baskets and sickles, and they plait there [baskets] for three seahs, and they leave the baskets and the sickles and come home. On the festival near dark they would go forth, and a great mob would go forth with them. Once it got dark, he said to them, "On this Sabbath [shall I reap grain for the 'omer]? On this Sabbath? On this Sabbath?" "With this basket? With this basket? With this basket?" R. Eliezer bar Sadoq adds, "Also: 'With this sickle? With this sickle? With this sickle?'" Three times for each detail. And they say, "Yes, yes, yes." "Shall I reap?" They say to him, "Reap." All of this [pomp] for what purpose? Because of the Boethusians, who say, "The reaping of the [barley for the] 'omer does not [take place] at the conclusion of the festival" [M. Men. 10:2AA-BB].

T. 10:24 They reaped it, and they put it into baskets, and they brought it to the court [of the Temple] [M. Men. 10:4A]. "They did parch it in fire, so as to carry out the requirement that it be parched with fire [Lev. 2:14]," the words of R. Meir [M. Men. 10:4D]. And sages say, "This is not the meaning of the language. But there was a copper tube which was perforated with holes, so that the fire would affect the whole of it" [M. Men. 10:4E]. And they spread it out in the court, and a breeze blows over it. And they put it into a grist-mill to take out of it a tenth-ephah, which [then] is sifted in thirteen sieves. And the residue is redeemed and eaten by any one [M. Men. 10:4F-H]. And it is liable for dough-offering and exempt from tithes. R. Aqiba declares it liable to dough-offering and to tithes [M. 10:4].

T. 10:25 He came to the tenth. He put in its oil and its frankincense. He mingled it and waved it. And he brought it near, took out the handful, and offered it up. And the residue is eaten by the priests [M. Men. 10:4K-N]. After the 'omer is offered, they go forth and find the market of Jerusalem full of meal and popcorn, "not with the approval of sages," the words of R. Meir. And sages say, " With the approval of sages did they do so" [M. Men. 10:5A-B].

T. 10:26 After the 'omer was offered, new produce was permitted forthwith. People who are [distant from Jerusalem] are permitted to make use of new produce from noon and thereafter. After the Temple was destroyed, Rabban Yohanan ben Zakkai ordained that the whole day of waving [the 'omer] should be prohibited [in respect to new produce. Said R. Judah, "And is it not so that it is prohibited by the Torah, as it is said, 'To this selfsame day' (Lev. 23:14)? On what account are those who are distant [from Jerusalem] permitted [to make use of new produce] from noon time and thereafter? Because they are certain that the court is not slovenly therewith" [M. Men. 10:5C-I].

M. 6:6 The offering of the first sheaf of barley rendered [the produce of the new crop] permitted in the country, and the Two Loaves [of Pentecost/Shabuot, Lev. 23:16,] rendered new produce [permitted for the meal-offering] in the sanctuary. Before the offering of the first sheaf of barley, they do not bring [from

new produce, grain that is to be used for] meal-offerings, first fruits, and the meal-offering which accompanies [drink] offerings along with beasts. And if one brought [grain for any of these before the offering of the first sheaf of barley], it is invalid. [As to bringing grain for any of these items of B] before the two loaves — one should not do so [Lev. 23:16]. And if one brought grain from the new crop for use in preparing them, it is valid.

M. 6:7 [Loaves of bread made from] wheat, barley, spelt, oats, and rye are liable to dough offering. And they join together with one another [to form the volume of dough liable to the dough offering]. And they are prohibited as to [the prohibition of] new produce before the offering of the first sheaf of barley, and [are prohibited] to be reaped before the offering of the first sheaf of barley. And if they took root before the offering of the first sheaf of barley, the offering of the first sheaf of barley renders them permitted [for reaping]. And if not, they are prohibited until the coming offering of the first sheaf of barley will have been brought.

T. 10:27 The 'omer did render [new produce] permitted in the country, and the two loaves [did the same] in the sanctuary [M. Men. 10:6A]. Once the two loaves were offered [at Pentecost], they began bringing meal-offerings and drink-offerings from all sources. They [at that time] do not hold back [produce from anywhere]. But they do not bring meal-offerings from produce from which tithes and heave-offering have not been taken at all.

T. 10:28 He who sanctifies standing grain for meal-offerings — it is free of the liability to tithes. R. Simeon b. Eleazar says, "They pluck [grain] before the 'omer and sell it after the 'omer and bring [grain for] meal-offerings from produce from which tithes and heave-offering have not been taken at all."

T. 10:29 He who sanctifies standing grain for meal-offerings — it is free of liability to tithes. And even though they have ruled, it is prohibited under the prohibition of new produce before Passover [M. Men. 10:7C], it is permitted for use in healing and for food for gentiles and dogs' food. They prohibited its use only for Israelites alone.

M. 6:8 [Before the presentation of the first sheaf of barley,] they may reap [the crop] in irrigated fields in valleys, but they may not heap it up. The people of Jericho reap, with sages' approval, and they heap up [the grain], not with sages' approval. But sages did not stop them. [Before the presentation of the first sheaf of barley,] one reaps unripe grain and feeds it to cattle. Said R. Judah, "Under what circumstances? When one begins [to reap] before the crop reaches a third of its full growth." R. Simeon says, "Also: [before the presentation of the first sheaf of barley,] one may reap and feed [it to cattle] even after it has reached a third of its full growth."

M. 6:9 [Before the presentation of the first sheaf of barley,] they reap [if the ground is needed] for seedlings, or as a station for mourning, [or] to prevent the interruption [of the activity] of the house of study. One should not [however] make them into bundles, but he leaves them in small heaps. The correct execution of the requirement of the offering of the first sheaf of barley is that it be brought from standing grain. [If] one did not find [standing grain], he may bring it from sheaves. The correct execution of the requirement is that it come from fresh grain. [If] one did not find [fresh grain], he may bring it from dried [grain]. The correct execution of the requirement is that one reap it by night. [If] it is reaped by day, it is valid. And it overrides [the rules of] the Sabbath.

T. 10:30 An Israelite who ate new produce before Passover, Lo, such a one receives forty stripes.

T. 10:31 [If] one was weeding on the thirteenth [of Nisan], and [an ear of grain] is uprooted in his hand, he plants it in swampy [soil] but not in a dry [place], for part of the day is deemed equivalent to the entire day. Even though they have stated, "It is prohibited to reap an irrigated field [M. Men. 10:8A] in the mountains," a naturally watered field in the valleys do they reap, on account of saplings, and on account of [making a station] for mourning, and because of the interruption [of the activity of] the bet hammidrash [M. Men. 10:9A-C]. One should not reap and make it into bundles [M. Men. 10:9D], but he reaps it and leaves it as he goes along.

T. 10:32 It is permitted to make a path in it. One reaps for the purpose of fodder before it has reached a third of its growth [M. Men. 10:8E]. Once it has reached a third of its growth, he should not begin to do so, but if he began to do so, he may complete it [M. Men. 10:8F-G]. Before [the grain] has reached a third of its growth, it is free of liability to the laws of gathering, the forgotten sheaf, and the corner of the field. After it has reached a third of its growth, it is liable to the laws of gathering, the forgotten sheaf, and the corner of the field. R. Simeon says, "Even after it has reached a third of its growth, it is free of liability to the laws of gathering, the forgotten sheaf, and the corner of the field, but it is liable for tithes."

T. 10:33 The requirement of the 'omer is that it be brought from standing grain. [If] one did not have [standing grain], he may bring it from sheaves [M. Men. 10:9E-F]. [If] he did not have [sheaves], he may bring it from the granary. [And its requirement is that it be brought] from that which was freshly-reaped. [If] he did not have [that kind], he may bring it from what is fresh. [If] he did not have [that kind], he may bring it from what is dried. [M. Men. 10:9G-H]. The two loaves of bread: the requirement is that they be brought from new [produce]. [If] he did not have [new produce], he may bring them from the upper chamber [in which last year's crop was stored].

The presentation of the first of the special meal-offerings, the *'omer,* which marks the advent of the new barley-crop in mid-Nisan, involves a narrative that conveys the rules of the procedure. The purpose, as specified at M. 6:6, is to render the produce of the new crop permitted at large, with a corresponding occasion for the sanctuary.

B. THE TWO LOAVES OF PENTECOST AND THE SHOW-BREAD

M. 11:1 The two loaves [of Pentecost/Shabuot] are kneaded one by one and baked [in the oven] one by one [one, then the next]. The [twelve loaves of] show bread are kneaded one by one and baked two by two. And in a mold did one make them. And when he takes them from the oven, he puts them into [another] mold, so that they [their shapes] will not be spoiled.

M. 11:2 All the same are the two loaves and the show bread: their kneading and their rolling out are [done] outside [the Temple courtyard], and their baking, inside. And they [= baking them] do not override [the prohibitions of] the Sabbath [= M. 11:9J]. R. Judah says, "All acts of preparing them are inside." R. Simeon says, "One should always be accustomed to state [the rule as follows]: 'The two loaves and the show bread are valid [if made] in the courtyard and are valid [if made] in Bethpage.'"

M. 11:3 The baked cakes of a high priest: their kneading and their rolling out are [done] inside. And they override [the prohibitions of] the Sabbath. Grinding their [grain] and sifting it do not override the Sabbath. A general principle did R. Aqiba state, "Any sort of work which it is possible to do on the eve of the Sabbath does not override the Sabbath, and [any sort of work] which it is not possible to do on the eve of the Sabbath does override the Sabbath [M. Shab. 19:1]."

M. 11:4 All meal-offerings are subject to preparation in a [consecrated] utensil [if they are prepared] inside, and are not subject to preparation in a [consecrated] utensil [if they are prepared] outside. How so? The two loaves: (1) their length is seven [handbreadths], (2) and their breadth, four, and (3) their horns [small pieces of dough placed on the four upper corners, like the horns of the altar], four fingerbreadths [high]. The show bread: (1) its length is ten [handbreadths], and (2) its breadth, five, and (3) its horns, seven fingerbreadths. R. Judah says, "So that you not err [make use of the mnemonic]: ZDDYHZ [= 7, 4, 4, 10, 5, 7]." Ben Zoma says, "'And you shall place on the table show bread in my sight [before my face] continually' (Ex. 25:30) — that it should have a face."

T. 11:1 "All the same are the two loaves and the show-bread: their kneading and their rolling are [done] outside, and their baking, inside. And they do not override the Sabbath" [M. Men. 11:2A-C], the words of R. Meir. R. Judah says, "All acts of preparing them are done inside" [M. Men. 11:2D]. R. Simeon says, "All acts of preparing them are done outside." For R. Simeon did rule, "One should never hesitate to state: All the same are the two loaves and the show-bread. Just as they are valid [when prepared] in the courtyard, so they are valid [when prepared] in Bethpage [M. Men. 11:2E]. Just as they are invalidated in the courtyard, so they are invalidated in Bethpage." And it had an upper chamber set aside and one made it therein.

T. 11:2 It had an oven shaped like a square hive. It held one of the two loaves, and two [loaves] of show bread [M. Men. 11:1A-B].

T. 11:3 Three moulds were there [M. Men. 11:1C-D]. One was for the [bread in] the oven, and one was for the dough, and one was for when one took the bread out of the oven. And one puts the dough into the mould so that they will not spoil the bread [M. Men. 11:1D].

T. 11:4 Meal-offerings are subject to preparation in a utensil inside [the court]. Grinding their grain and sifting it are done outside. Kneading it and rolling it and baking it are done inside [M. Men. 11:3B]. And [if it is done] by a non-priest, they are valid — until they are brought to the house [Temple] [for] the taking of a handful.

T. 11:5 All meal-offerings do not override either the Sabbath or [the consideration of] uncleanness, except for the baked cakes of an anointed priest, because it is subject to [be offered at] a fixed time. This is the general principle: Whatever is subject to a fixed time decreed by the Torah and cannot be done on the eve of the Sabbath overrides the Sabbath, and whatever is not subject to a fixed time decreed by the Torah and can be done on the eve of the Sabbath does not override the Sabbath [M. Men. 11:3E].

M. 11:5 "The table: Its length is ten [handbreadths] and its breadth, five [Ex. 25:33, two amahs by one, and the amah is five handbreadths, M. Kel. 17:10]. The show bread: its length is ten [handbreadths] and its breadth, five. One sets it lengthwise against the breadth of the table, and two and a half handbreadths does he double over [as a wall upward] on this side and on that [of the bread]. It turns out that its length fills the whole breadth of the table," the words of R. Judah. R. Meir says, "The table: its length is twelve [handbreadths, and its breadth, six]. [The amah is six handbreadths.] The show bread: its length is ten [handbreadths] and its breadth, five]: One sets it lengthwise against the breadth of the table, and two handbreadths on either side [of the bread] does he double [turn up as a wall], with two handbreadths

space in the middle [between the two sets of six loaves], so that the wind blows between them [preventing mould]." Abba Saul says, "There [in the open area] did they set the two dishes of frankincense of the show bread." They said to him, "Has it not already been stated, And you shall put pure frankincense upon each row (Lev. 24:7)?" He said to them, "And has it not already been said, 'And next to him shall be the tribe of Manasseh' (Num. 2:20)?"

T. 11:14 How do they lay out the show bread? One puts six loaves in this row and six rows in the other row. And if one put eight loaves in one row and four in the other, or made three rows of four loaves, he has done nothing. [If] one made two rows of fourteen [loaves] — Rabbi says, "They regard the ones on top as if they are not present, and the ones on the bottom are valid."

T. 11:15 How do they lay out the dishes [of frankincense]? One puts one dish on this row [of bread] and one dish on the other row. If one put the [two] dishes of [one handful of] frankincense [instead of two handfuls], or the [two handfuls of] frankincense of [two] dishes [into a single dish], or if there was something which intervened between the dishes and the bread or between the bread and the table, Lo, these are invalid. Abba Saul says, "Into the two handbreadths of empty space which are between one row and another did one put the dishes. And how do I explain, 'And you shall put on the row pure frankincense' (Lev. 24:7)? That all of it should be near the row" [M. Men. 11:5G].

M. 11:6 Four golden props were there [at the corners of the table], with their heads shaped into branches [like a Y], with which they would support them [the loaves of bread], two [props] for this row [of bread], and two for that row. And [there were, inserted into the props] twenty-eight [golden] rods [reeds], [each shaped] like half of a hollow reed, fourteen for this row, and fourteen for that row. Neither the work of ordering of the reeds nor the work of their removal overrides the Sabbath. But one enters on the eve of the Sabbath, draws them out, and places them parallel to the length of the table. All the utensils which were in the sanctuary [are laid out] lengthwise parallel to the length of the Temple [= east to west].

T. 11:6 Four golden props similar to pronged poles were there, on which they [the loaves of bread] would hang [M. Men. 11:6A-B]. For they [the loaves] are shaped like a boat, [and so are supported by the props] so that they should not shake. R. Yosé says, "There were no props there, but the height of the table was a handbreadth [high, and it supported the bread], as it is said, 'And you shall make around it a frame a handbreadth wide' (Ex. 25:25)." They said to him, "And is it not so that the rim of the table was only at the feet [of the table, not at its surface]."

T. 11:7 Twenty-eight rods of gold, shaped like half of a hollow reed, susceptible to receive uncleanness were there, inserted into the props [M. Men. 11:6C].

T. 11:8 All the utensils which were in the sanctuary [are laid] out lengthwise, parallel to the length of the Temple [M. Men. 11:6G], except for the ark, the lengthwise side of which was placed parallel to the breadth of the Temple. So were its staves set parallel to its width, and so was it taken up.

T. 11:9 Ten tables did Solomon make, as it is said, "And he also made ten tables" (11 Chron. 4:8). And even so, they laid out the showbread only on the table made by Moses, as it is said, "The golden table for the showbread" (I Kings 8:48).

T. 11:10 Ten golden lamp-stands did Solomon make, as it is said, "And he made ten golden lamp-stands" (11 Chron. 4:7). Nonetheless they only lit those of Moses, as it is said, ". . . and care for the golden lampstand that its lamps may burn every evening" (2 Chron. 13:1 I). The lampstand which Moses made did not require anointing oil, because when it was consecrated for the first time, it was consecrated for that time and consecrated for the future. R. Yosé b. R. Judah says, "All the tables did they use for the show bread, as it is said. So Solomon made all the things that were in the house of God: the golden [altar] the tables for the bread show-bread" (11 Chron. 4:19). And all the lamps did they kindle, as it is said — "the lampstands and their lamps of pure golden to burn before the inner sanctuary as prescribed" (2 Chron. 4:20). In the name of R. Eleazar b. Shammua did they state, "Why does Scripture say the golden [altar], the tables, and on them the show bread? This refers to the large golden table which was inside the sanctuary [hekhal], and the table which was in the porch at the door of the House, on which they placed the used show-bread" [M. Men. 11:7A].

T. 11:16 How do they arrange the rods? After the Sabbath did one enter. He raised up the head of a loaf, placing a rod under it. He raised up the head of the second, placing a rod under it, and one in the middle, and three under each and every loaf, and two under the topmost loaf, for there is no weight on top of it. The one loaf on the bottom was placed on the clean surface of the table. [If] before one broke [the mould], the bread was broken in half, the bread is invalid, and the dishes of frankincense were not burned. [If] after the mould was broken, the bread was broken in half, the bread is invalid, but the dishes of frankincense were burned [M. Men. 8A]. [If] the dishes of frankincense were offered up, and afterward the bread was broken in half, it is valid. [If] its bread was made unclean, whether after it was taken from the mould or before it was taken from the mould, the bread is invalid, and the dishes of frankincense were not offered up.

M. 11:7 Two tables were inside the porch, at the inside of the door of the house, one of marble, and one of gold. On the one of marble do they set the show bread when it is brought in, and on the one of gold when it is taken out. For in matters of holiness, they place something on a higher level of sanctification, but they do not lower something to a lower level of sanctification. And one of gold is inside, on which [is arrayed] the show bread continually. Four priests enter in, two in [whose] hands are two rows [of show bread], and two in [whose] hands are two dishes [of frankincense]. And four go in before them, two to take out the two rows [of bread], and two to take out the two dishes [of frankincense]. Those who bring them in stand at the north [side of the table], with their faces to the south. Those that bring them out stand at the south with their faces to the north. These draw out [the old loaves] and these lay down [the new ones]. And a handbreadth of one [new row] [lies] up against a handbreadth of another, as it is said, "Before me perpetually" (Ex. 25:30). R. Yosé says, "Even though these take away [the old loaves] and [then] the others put down [the new loaves], this too was [deemed to carry out the requirement that the bread be set forth] perpetually." They went forth and put them down on the golden table which was on the porch. And they burned the dishes [of frankincense that had been removed]. And the loaves are divided among the priests. [If] the Day of Atonement coincides with the Sabbath, the loaves are divided in the evening. [If] it coincided with the eve of the Sabbath, the goat of the Day of Atonement is eaten in the evening. The Babylonians would eat it raw, because they are not squeamish.

T. 11:11 How do they bring in the show-bread? On the eve of the Sabbath did one break [the bread] from the mould and put it on the table which was on the porch at the door of the House, on which they set the old show-bread [M. Men. 11:7C].

T. 11:12 How do they bring in the show-bread? On the eve of the Sabbath did one break them from the mould, and put it on the table which was on the porch at the door of the house? At dawn, once the blood of the daily whole-offering had been tossed, two priests took two dishes and put into them two handfuls of frankincense. All the dishes in the sanctuary did not have sides, except for these, which had sides. These draw out [the breadth by a handbreadth, and these insert [the bread] by a handbreadth. The handbreadth of one was within the handbreadth of the other, so that the table should not remain overnight without bread, as it is said, "Before me perpetually" (Ex. 25:30) [M. Men. 11:7K-M]. R. Yosé says, "Even if one removed the old bread in the morning and put in the new bread at twilight, even on the other days of the year they remove it from the court yard, and it is no matter. What is the meaning of Scripture's saying before me perpetually?

So that the table should not remain overnight without bread" [M. Men. 11:7N].

T. 11:13 These two priests, in whose hands are the two dishes of frankincense which has been with the old showbread, would put it on the altar with the limbs of the daily whole-offering. Once the two dishes of incense had burned up, they then give half of a loaf to each watch and divide it among themselves. R. Judah says, "This one who divided the show bread stands on the mosaic pavement of the porch. He divides and leaves [the bread], and each one then comes and takes his share. And the share for the blemished [men] of the priesthood did they take outside, for they cannot enter the area between the porch and the altar."

M. 11:8 [If] one set out the bread on the Sabbath but [set out] the dishes [of frankincense] after the Sabbath and burned the dishes [of frankincense] on the [next] Sabbath, it is invalid. [It was only on the table six days.] And they are not liable on their account [the loaves of bread] because of violation of the rules of refuse, remnant, and uncleanness. [The bread is not sanctified.] [If] one set out the bread and the dishes [of frankincense] on the Sabbath and burned the dishes [of frankincense] after the Sabbath, it is invalid. And they are not liable on their account because of violation of the laws of refuse, remnant, and uncleanness. [If] one set out the bread and the dishes [of frankincense] after the Sabbath and burned the dishes on [the next] Sabbath, it is invalid. [They have not been left from Sabbath to Sabbath.] How should one do it? Let him leave it for the coming Sabbath [thirteen days in all], for even if it is on the table for many days, that is of no account.

T. 11:17 [If] one set out the bread on the Sabbath and the dishes after the Sabbath and offered up the dishes on the Sabbath, it is invalid. And they are not liable on its account because of violation of the laws of refuse, remnant, and uncleanness [M. Men. 11:8A-B].

T. 11:18 [If] one set out the bread and the dishes on the Sabbath and offered up the dishes after the Sabbath, it is invalid. And they are liable on its account because of violation of the laws of refuse, remnant, and uncleanness. [If] one set out the bread and the dishes of frankincense after the Sabbath and offered up the dishes on the [next] Sabbath, it is invalid [M. Men. 11:8E]. If its bread, of the choicest quality, is there, they may bring it. And if not, let him wait for the next Sabbath [M. Men. 11:8G]. The bread is permitted to be eaten. And they are liable on its account because of violation of the laws of refuse, remnant, and uncleanness.

M. 11:9 The two loaves are eaten, neither earlier than two [days] nor later than three [days after being baked]. How so? [If] they are baked on the eve of the festival and eaten on the festival, [that would be an example of eating them] two days [after being

baked]. [If] the festival fell after the Sabbath, they are eaten three days [after being baked]. The show bread is eaten neither less than nine nor more than eleven days [after being baked]. How so? [If] it is baked on the eve of the Sabbath and eaten on the Sabbath [in the following week], [that would be an example of eating them] nine days [after they are baked]. [If] the festival coincided with the eve of the Sabbath, it is eaten ten [days after being baked]. [In the case of] two festival days of the New Year [that is, if the New Year began on Thursday and the Day of Atonement fell on the following Sabbath], it is eaten eleven [days after being baked]. And [baking it] does not override either the Sabbath or the festival [M. 11:2C]. Rabban Simeon b. Gamaliel says in the name of R. Simeon, son of the Prefect, "It overrides the festival, but it does not override the fast day."

The second class of special meal-offerings involve those displayed on the altar, the two loaves for Pentecost and the twelve loaves of show-bread. Once more, I discern nothing more than inert information.

IV. VOWS IN CONNECTION WITH MEAL-OFFERINGS

M. 12:1 Meal-offerings and drink offerings which were made unclean before one has sanctified them in a [consecrated] utensil are subject to redemption [for money, which is deemed consecrated in their stead]. [If they are made unclean] after one has sanctified them in a [consecrated] utensil, they are not subject to redemption. Fowl and wood and frankincense and a utensil of service are not subject to redemption [at all], for [the rule (Lev. 27:11-13) that permits redemption of a blemished offering] is stated only [in connection with offerings of] cattle.

T. 12:1 He who sanctifies fowl, and a blemish appears in it — it is subject to redemption. [If] he sanctified it as a blemished [bird], it is not subject to redemption. You have only a beast which requires redemption alone [M. Men. 12:1D]. In the case of a firstling, it is said, "You will not redeem it" [Num. 18:17], and in the case of tithe [of cattle], it is said, "It will not be redeemed" [Lev. 27:33].

M. 12:2 He who says, "Lo, I pledge myself [to bring a meal-offering prepared] in a baking pan," but brought one prepared in a frying pan, [or he who says, "Lo, I pledge myself to bring a meal-offering prepared] in a frying pan," but brought one prepared in a baking pan [M. 5:8] — what he has brought, he has brought [as a separate freewill offering]. But his obligation [for the original pledge] he has not carried out. [He who says, "Lo, I pledge myself to offer] this [fine flour as a meal-offering prepared] in a baking pan," but brought one prepared in a frying pan, [or he who says, "Lo, 1 pledge myself to bring this fine flour as a meal-offering prepared] in a frying pan," [but brought one prepared] in a baking pan, Lo, this is invalid. [He who says,] "Lo, I pledge myself to bring two tenths [of an ephah of fine flour prepared] in a single utensil," but brought [it] in two utensils, [or, "Lo, 1 pledge myself to bring two tenths of an ephah of fine flour prepared] in two utensils," but he brought [it] in one utensil — what he has brought, he has brought. But his obligation he has not carried out. [He who says, "Lo, I pledge myself to offer] these in one utensil," but brought [them] in two utensils, [or he who says, "Lo, I pledge myself to offer these] in two utensils," but he brought [them] in one utensil — Lo, these are invalid. [He who says,] "Lo, I pledge myself to bring two tenths [of an ephah of fine flour] in a single utensil," but brought them in two utensils, [if] they said to him, "In a single utensil did you vow [to bring the offering]," but he [then] offered them in a single utensil, they are valid. But [if he offered them] in two utensils, they are invalid [for they cannot now be deemed a separate freewill offering]. [He who says,] "Lo, I pledge myself to bring two tenths [ephahs of fine flour] in two utensils," but brought them in one utensil, [if] they said to him, "In two utensils did you vow [to bring them]," [but] he [then] offered them in two utensils, they are valid. [If] he gave them in a single utensil, they are deemed to be equivalent to two meal-offerings which were confused [M. 3:3].

T. 12:2 [He who says,] "Lo, I pledge myself to bring loaves," but who brought wafers...wafers," but who brought loaves — what he has brought, he has brought. But his obligation he has not carried out [M. Men. 12:2A-D]. [He who says, "Lo, I pledge myself] to bring these two tenths [of an ephah of fine flour] in one utensil," but who brought them in two utensils — the two utensils have not sanctified them. [If he said, "Lo, I pledge myself to bring these two tenths of an ephah of fine flour] in two utensils," but brought them in one utensil, he has not sanctified them in one utensil [M. Men. 12:2I]. [If he said, "Lo, I pledge myself to bring a meal-offering] in one utensil" [and] brought them in two utensils [M. Men. 12:2H], [and] they said to him, "You have vowed to bring it in one utensil" [M. Men. 12:20X], Lo, this one should not put it back. And if he put it back, Lo, it is equivalent to two meal-offerings which were confused [M. Men. 12:2Y]. [If he said, "Lo, I pledge myself to bring a meal-offering] in two utensils," and brought them in one utensil and they said to him, "In two utensils did you vow [to bring it]," Lo, this one should not put it back. And if he put it back, Lo, these are invalid.

M. 12:3 [He who says,] "Lo, I pledge myself [to bring] a meal-offering made of barley," [in any case] must bring one made of wheat. [Free will meal-offerings have to be made of wheat.] [He who says, "Lo, I pledge myself to bring a meal-offering made] of meal," must bring one made of fine flour. [He who says, "Lo, I pledge myself to bring a meal-offering] without wine and frankincense," must bring one with oil and frankincense. [He who says, "Lo, I pledge myself to bring a meal-offering made of] a half-tenth," must bring one made of a whole tenth. [He who says, "Lo, I pledge myself to bring a meal-offering made of a tenth and a half-tenth," brings one made of two [whole] tenths [of an ephah of fine flour]. R. Simeon declares free [of the obligation to bring a meal-offering in any of the foregoing cases], for [in so specifying,] he has not volunteered [a freewill meal-offering] in the way in which people volunteer [to make a freewill meal-offering].

T. 12:3 [He who says], "Lo, I pledge myself [to bring] a thank-offering without bread," or "a burnt-offering without drink-offerings" — they require him to bring a thank-offering with its bread, a burnt offering with its drink-offerings.

T. 12:4 A priest who said, "Lo, I pledge myself [to bring] a meal-offering, the handful of which will be taken, and [the residue of] which will be eaten, by an Israelite," — [If] he said, "Lo, I pledge myself [to bring] a meal-offering, the whole of which will be offered up on the fires" — "they force him to bring a meal-offering in accord with its requirement," the words of R. Judah. And R. Simeon declares [him] exempt [from bringing anything], for he has not volunteered in the way in which people volunteer [M. Men. 12:3G].

T. 12:5 [He who says,] "Lo, I pledge myself [to bring] a meal-offering of barley," — "they force him to bring one of wheat," the words of R. Judah. And R. Simeon declares [him] exempt, for he has not volunteered in the way in which people volunteer. [If he says,] "Lo, I pledge myself to bring one of wheat," — "they force him to bring one of flour," the words of R. Judah. And R. Simeon declares [him] exempt, for he has not volunteered in the way in which people volunteer. [He who says,] "Lo, I pledge myself [to bring a meal-offering made of] a half tenth" [M. Men. 12:3D], "they force him to bring one of a whole tenth," the words of R. Judah. And R. Simeon declares [him] exempt, for he has not volunteered in the way in which people volunteer. [He who says,] "Lo, I pledge myself [to bring a meal-offering of] one tenth in two utensils," — "they force him to bring two tenths in two utensils," the words of R. Judah. And R. Simeon declares [him] exempt, for he has not volunteered in the way in which people volunteer.

T. 12:6 [He who says,] "Lo, I pledge myself to bring a tenth and a half" [M. Men. 12:3E] — they force him to bring two whole tenths, for they do not volunteer [as a free will offering] half-tenths.

T. 12:7 [He who says,] "Lo, I pledge myself [to bring] a hundred tenths in one utensil," they force him to bring sixty in one utensil and forty in another utensil. And if he brought half in one utensil and half in another utensil, he has not fulfilled his obligation. [If he said, "Lo, I pledge myself to bring a hundred tenths] in two utensils," he brings half in one utensil and half in another utensil. And if he brought sixty in one utensil and forty in another utensil, he has fulfilled his obligation.

M. 12:4 A man volunteers to make a freewill offering of a meal-offering consisting of sixty tenths and brings it in a single utensil. If he said, "Lo, I pledge myself [to bring a meal-offering] of sixty-one [tenths of an ephah]," he brings sixty in a single utensil, and one in a single utensil. For so does the community bring on the first festival day of the Festival [Sukkot] which coincides with the Sabbath sixty-one [tenths]. It is enough for the individual to fall short of the community by one [tenth]. Said R. Simeon, "And are not these for bullocks, and these for rams, and they are not mixed up with one another [for the quantity of oil for the tenths is not uniform]? But [the reason is that] up to sixty tenths [of an ephah] can be mixed together [= Eliezer b. Jacob, M. 9:3]." They said to him, "Are sixty mixed together, and sixty-one not mixed together?" He said to them, "So it is in all measures [prescribed by] sages: In forty seahs [of water] one immerses. In forty seahs of water less a single qartob, one cannot immerse." They do not volunteer as a freewill offering a single log [of wine], two, or five. But they volunteer as a freewill offering three, four, or six, and any number more than six.

T. 12:8 Said R. Simeon, "My colleagues said to me, On what account [is it so that] he who says, 'Lo, I pledge myself sixty tenths' brings them in one utensil, [while he who says, 'Lo, I pledge myself to bring] sixty-one tenths' brings sixty in one utensil and one in another utensil [M. Men. 12:4A-B]? And I said to them, 'You state the reason.' They said, 'For so the community brings on the first day of the Festival [Sukkot] which coincides with the Sabbath sixty [tenths], but no more [M. Men. 12:4C].' I said to them, 'But do they not offer sixty-one?' They said to me, 'The individual falls short of the community by one' [M. Men. 12:4D]. I said to them, 'But are not these offered in the morning, and these are offered at twilight?' Another matter: And are there not there a meal-offering of bullocks, one of rams, and one of lambs, and they do not mix the meal-offering of bullocks, rams, and lambs together [M. Men. 12:4E]?' They said to me, 'If not, then you state the reason.'"

T. 12:9 I said to them, "Scripture says, Fine flour mixed with oil" (Lev. 2:5) — A meal-offering with which oil mixes for stirring. They said to me, "In sixty [tenths] it mixes, and in sixty-one it does not mix [M . Men. 1 2:4G].' I said to them, 'All the measurements which are in the Torah are fixed [and absolute].' In forty seahs [of water] does one immerse. In forty seahs less a single drop qartob one cannot immerse [M. Men. 12:4I]. 'Food of the volume of an egg imparts uncleanness as food. [If] it lacks even the volume of a sesame seed, it does not impart uncleanness as food.' [A piece of cloth] three by three handbreadths is susceptible to midras-uncleanness. [If] it lacks even a single thread, it is not susceptible to midras-uncleanness. 'It follows that all the measures which are in the Torah are fixed.'"

M. 12:5 "They volunteer wine [alone, unaccompanied by any animal offering] as a freewill offering, but they do not volunteer oil as a freewill offering," the words of R. Aqiba. R. Tarfon says, "They volunteer [also] oil as a freewill offering." Said R. Tarfon, "Just as we find in the case of wine that it is brought in fulfillment of an obligation, and it [also] is brought as a freewill offering, so in the case of oil, it is brought in fulfillment of an obligation, and it [also] is brought as a freewill offering." Said to him R. Aqiba, "No. If you have so stated the rule in connection with wine, it is because it is offered in fulfillment of one's obligation entirely by itself. But will you say so in connection with oil, which is not offered in fulfillment of one's obligation entirely by itself?" Two people do not volunteer as a freewill offering a single tenth. But they volunteer as a single freewill offering a burnt offering and peace offerings, and in the case of fowl, even a single bird.

T. 12:10 He who volunteers an offering of wine, in accord with the opinion of R. Aqiba and R. Tarfon, puts it into bowls. [He who volunteers] oil, in accord with the opinion of R. Tarfon — it is offered on the altar-fires [M. Men. 12:5A-B]. He who volunteers an offering of wine brings not one nor two nor five [logs] but brings three, so that they may be offered with a lamb four, so that they may be offered with the rams six, so that they may be offered with the bullock, or seven, so that they may be offered with the ram and with the lamb. From that point onward, you can divide it up.

M. 13:1 [He who says,] "Lo, I pledge myself [to bring] a tenth," brings one [tenth]. [He who says, "Lo, I pledge myself to bring] tenths" brings two [tenths]. [He who says,] "I expressly said [a certain number of tenths] but I do not know what I expressly said" brings sixty tenths [the maximum offered by an individual (M. 12:4)]. [He who says,] "Lo, I pledge myself [to bring] a meal-offering" brings any one [of the five kinds] he wants to. R. Judah says, "He brings a meal-offering of fine flour, for it is the distinctive one among [all types of] meal-offerings."

M. 13:2 [He who says, "Lo, I pledge myself to bring] a meal-offering" [or] "some kind of meal-offering" brings one [of the five kinds]. [He who says, "Lo, I pledge myself to bring] meal-offerings" [or] "some kind of meal-offerings" brings two [of the five kinds]. [He who says,] "I expressly said [which kind] but I do not know what I expressly said" brings all five kinds. [He who says,] "I expressly said a meal-offering of tenths, but I do not know what I expressly said" brings a meal-offering of sixty tenths. Rabbi says, "Let him bring meal-offerings of [every number] of tenths from one to sixty."

T. 12:11 [He who says,] "I expressly said a meal-offering, but I do not know what I expressly said, Lo, this one brings five meal-offerings, [one of each of] the five kinds [M. Men. 13:2C]." [He who says], "Lo, I pledge myself [to bring] some kind of meal-offerings" brings two meal-offerings of a single kind.... two kinds of meal-offerings" brings two meal-offerings of two kinds [M. Men. 13:2A-B]. [He who says,] "Lo, I pledge myself [to bring] some kind of tenths [of an ephah]" brings two tenths of one kind. ". . . kinds of tenths" brings two tenths of two kinds.

T. 12:12 [He who says,] "I expressly said a meal-offering of tenths, but I do not know which of them I expressly stated," Lo, this one brings five meal-offerings of five kinds [of meal-offering] of sixty tenths, which are three hundred tenths [M. Men. 13:2D].

T. 12:13 "[He who says], 'I expressly said a meal-offering of tenths, but I do not know of how many tenths I expressly stated,' Lo, this one brings meal-offerings of tenths, from one up to sixty, which are one thousand and eight [hundred] and thirty tenths," the words of Rabbi. And sages say, "One of sixty tenths" [M. Men. 13:2E].

T. 12:14 "[He who says,] 'I expressly said a meal-offering of tenths but I do not know which one of them I expressly said, and how many tenths I expressly said,' Lo, this one brings five meal-offerings of five kinds, of sixty tenths each, from one to sixty, which are nine thousand one hundred and fifty tenths," the words of Rabbi. And sages say, "Five meal-offerings of five kinds, sixty tenths which are three hundred tenths."

M. 13:3 [He who says,] "Lo, I pledge myself [to bring] wood" should not [bring] less than two bundles of wood. [He who says, "Lo, I pledge myself to bring] frankincense" should not [bring] less than a handful. They are five sorts of [rules pertinent to] handfuls: (1) He who says, "Lo, I pledge myself [to bring] rankincense" should not [bring] less than a handful. (2) He who volunteers a freewill offering of a meal-offering brings with it a handful of frankincense. (3) He who offers up a handful outside is liable. (4-5) And two dishes require two handfuls [of frankincense].

T. 12:15 [He who says,] "Lo, I pledge myself [to bring] frankincense" should not [bring] less than a handful [M. Men. 13:3B]. R. Judah says, "[He may bring frankincense] of the weight of ten denars." R. Yohanan b. Beroqah says, "A priest sanctifies it in a utensil of service and offers it up." Others say, "He who says, 'Lo, I pledge myself [to bring] iron' should not [bring] less than the scarecrow [an iron sheet studded with spikes" (M. Mid. 4:6)] which is in the sanctuary."

M. 13:4 [He who says,] "Lo, I pledge myself [to bring] gold" [for the upkeep of the Temple] should not [bring] less than a golden denar. [He who says, "Lo, pledge myself to bring] silver" should not [bring] less than a denar of silver. [He who says, "Lo, I pledge myself to bring] copper" should not bring] less than [the value of] a silver ma'ah. [He who says,] "I expressly said [how much I should give] but I do not know what I expressly said" must bring until he will state, "I did not intend that much."

M. 13:5 [He who says], "Lo, I pledge myself [to bring] wine" must not [bring] less than three logs [those for the drink offerings of a lamb, the smallest volume]. [He who says, "Lo, l pledge myself to bring] oil" must not bring less than a log [the smallest volume, that for a tenth of flour]. Rabbi says, "Three logs [as at A]." [He who says,] "I expressly said [how much I should give] but I do not know what I expressly said" brings in accord with [what is brought on] the day of the most abundant [offering of wine or oil which is the first day of Tabernacles when it coincides with the Sabbath].

M. 13:6 [He who says], "Lo, I pledge myself [to bring] a burnt offering" brings a lamb [the smallest acceptable burnt offering]. R. Eleazar b. Azariah says, "Or a turtledove, or a pigeon [a fowl also is acceptable as a burnt offering]." [He who says,] "I expressly said [that I should offer a beast] of the herd but I do not know what I expressly said" brings a bullock and a calf. [He who says, "I expressly said that I should offer a beast] of the cattle but I do not know what I expressly said" must bring a bullock, a calf, a ram, a goat, and a lamb. [He who says,] "I expressly said [what I should offer] but I do not know what I expressly said" adds to them a turtledove and a pigeon.

M. 13:7 [He who says,] "Lo, I pledge myself [to bring] a thank-offering and peace offerings" brings a lamb. [He who says,] "I expressly said [that I should bring a beast] of the herd but I do not know what I expressly said" brings a bullock, a heifer, a young bullock, and a young heifer. [He who says], "I expressly said [that I should bring a beast] of cattle, but I do not know what I expressly said" brings a bullock, a heifer, a young bullock, a young heifer, a ram, a ewe, a lamb, a she-lamb, a goat, a she-goat, a young ram, and a ewe-lamb.

T. 13:1 [He who says,] "Lo, I pledge myself [to bring] a burnt-offering [M. Men. 13:6A] from the herd" brings a heifer. ". . . from the flock" brings a lamb. [He who says], "Lo, I pledge myself [to bring a thank-offering and peace-offering [M. Men. 13:7A] from the herd" brings a heifer. And ". . . from the flock" ...brings a lamb.

T. 13:2 R. Simeon said, "If a man will say to you, 'In accord with the opinion of R. Aqiba, [One who vows a burnt-offering brings] a heifer' — accept [the tradition] from him: 'A ram' — accept the tradition from him, a lamb — accept the tradition from him. For in the case of all of them did R. Aqiba give the reason [that said animal fulfills the vow]: A heifer — for the claim of the All Highest is overriding. A ram — neither a large nor a small one but a middle sized one. A lamb — he who makes a claim against his fellow must bring proof [of the validity of his claim for something more than this]."

M. 13:8 [He who says,] "Lo, I pledge myself [to bring] an ox" brings it and its drink offerings to the value of a maneh. [He who says, "Lo, I pledge myself to bring] a young bullock" brings it and its drink offerings, to the value of five selas. [He who says, "Lo, I pledge myself to bring] a ram" brings it and its drink offerings to the value of two selas. ". . . a lamb" brings it and its drink offerings to the value of a sela. ". . . an ox to the value of a maneh" brings one at the value of a maneh, exclusive of the value of its drink offerings. ". . . a young bullock to the value of five selas" brings one of the value of five selas, exclusive of the value of its drink offerings. ". . . a ram at the value of two selas" brings one for two selas exclusive of the value of its drink offerings. ". . . a lamb at the value of a sela" brings one at the value of a sela, exclusive of the value of its drink offerings. ". . . an ox at the value of a maneh," and he brought two for a maneh has not carried out his obligation, even if this one is worth a maneh less a denar, and the other one is worth a maneh less a denar ". . . a black one" and he brought a white one, "a white one" and he brought a black one, he has not carried out his obligation. ". . . a small one" and he brought a large one — he has carried out his obligation. Rabbi says, "He has not carried out his obligation."

M. 13:9 [He who says,] "This ox is a burnt offering," and it became blemished, if he wants, he may bring with the proceeds [for the sale of the ox] two [oxen]. [He who says], "These two oxen are a burnt offering," and they got blemished, if he wants, brings with their proceeds one [ox]. Rabbi prohibits [doing so]. [He who says,] "This ram is a burnt offering," and it became blemished, if he wants, brings with its proceeds a lamb. [He who says,] "This lamb is a burnt offering," and it became blemished, if he wants, brings with its proceeds a ram. Rabbi prohibits [doing so]. He who says, "One of my lambs is dedicated, and one of my oxen is dedicated" — [if] he had two, the larger of them is dedicated. [If he had] three, the middle-sized one is dedicated. [If he said,] "I expressly said [which one I should give] but I do not know what I expressly said," [if] he said, "Father said to me [which one to give] but I do not know what [he said]" — the largest among them is dedicated.

T. 13:3 Just as he who dedicates without explanation, Lo, this one brings the largest among them, so he who says, "Lo, I pledge myself" without explanation, Lo, this one brings the largest one of them [the animals in a herd or a flock]. [He who says,] "Lo, I pledge myself [to bring] to the altar" brings frankincense, for dedication without explanation to the altar [refers to] frankincense. [He who says,] "I set aside [something] for the altar and I do not know what I set aside" — Lo, this one continues setting aside until he sets aside [animals in such wise] that one will come from each and every kind of animal which is offered on the altar.

T. 13:4 [He who says,] "This sela is for the altar" brings with it a heifer. [He who says,] "I set aside [something] for the altar and I do not know for what purpose I set it aside," Lo, this one continues to set aside until he will have brought something from every sort of thing which is offered on the altar.

T. 13:5 [He who says,] "This heifer is for the altar, this heifer is for the altar" must bring it. "...I set aside a burnt-offering for the altar, and I do not know which one I set aside" — it must pasture until it is blemished, and then be sold. And let the man continue setting aside [things for the altar] until he will have brought one of every sort of thing which is offered on the altar.

T. 13:6 [He who says,] "Lo, I pledge myself [to bring] a horned animal" and brought one whose horns are leveled, ...an animal whose horns are leveled" and brought a horned one — what he has brought, he has brought. But he has not fulfilled his obligation [M. Men. 12:2].

T. 13:7 [He who says,] "Lo, I pledge myself [to bring] an ox worth two hundred [zuz]" and went and brought two oxen worth a maneh each has not fulfilled his obligation [vs. M. Men. 13:9A]. [He who says,] "Lo, I pledge myself [to bring] an ox worth a maneh" and went and brought an ox worth two hundred, [for two hundred, or one worth two hundred for a] maneh — he has carried out his obligation, for included in two hundred [zuz] is a maneh. Rabbi says, "He has not fulfilled his obligation."

T. 13:8 [He who says,] "An ox, this ox is a burnt-offering," and it was blemished, should not bring two rams with its proceeds. But he may bring a ram with its proceeds. And Rabbi prohibits. For it is not a proper mixture [the meal-offerings are not the same].

T. 13:9 [He who says,] "This ram is a burnt-offering," and it was blemished, should not bring with its proceeds a lamb. But he brings with its proceeds two lambs. And Rabbi prohibits. For it is not a proper mixture. [He who says,] "This lamb is a burnt-offering" and it was blemished, [if] he wants, may bring with its proceeds a lamb.

But he brings with its proceeds two lambs. Rabbi prohibits. For it is not a proper mixture.

T. 13:10 [He who says,] "This ram is a burnt-offering," and it was blemished, if he wants, brings with its proceeds a ram. [He who says,] "This ram is a burnt-offering," and it was blemished, [if] he wants, brings with its proceeds a heifer. [He who says,] "This heifer is a burnt-offering" and it was blemished, [If] he wants, brings with its proceeds an ox. [He who says, "Lo, I pledge myself to bring an ox] of one of my oxen," it is a burnt-offering.

T. 13:11 And so: An ox set aside as a burnt-offering which was confused with his [other] oxen — Lo, this one brings the largest among them as a burnt offering. And the rest are to be sold to those who owe burnt-offerings. And the proceeds thereof are unconsecrated.

M. 13:10 [He who says,] "Lo, I pledge myself [to bring] a burnt offering" offers it in the sanctuary. And if he offered it in the House of Onias, he has not carried out his obligation. [He who says, "Lo, I pledge myself to bring a burnt offering] which I shall offer in the House of Onias" offers it in the sanctuary. But if he offered it in the House of Onias, he has carried out his obligation. R. Simeon says, "This is no burnt offering." [He who says,] "Lo, I am a Nazirite" shaves [Num. 6:13-18] in the sanctuary. And if he shaved in the House of Onias, he has not carried out his obligation. [If he said, "Lo, I am a Nazirite, and] I shall shave [that is, bring the offerings on the occasion of my shaving] in the House of Onias" shaves in the sanctuary. But if he shaved in the House of Onias, he has carried out his obligation. R. Simeon says, "This is no Nazirite." The priests who served in the House of Onias are not to serve in the sanctuary in Jerusalem. And one need not say [that this applies to those who have served] for another matter [idolatry], as it is said, "Nevertheless the priests of the high places came not up to the altar of the Lord in Jerusalem, but they ate unleavened bread among their brethren" [Kings 23:9]— Lo, they are like blemished priests, taking a share and eating [it] but not offering up [sacrifices].

T. 13:12 [He who says,] "Lo, I pledge myself [to bring] a burnt-offering" offers it in the sanctuary. And if he offered it in the House of Onias, he has not carried out his obligation [M. Men. 13:10A-B]. And they are liable on account of its animal sacrifices to extirpation.

T. 13:13 [He who says,] "Lo, I am a Nazirite" shaves in the sanctuary and thereby fulfills his obligation. And if he shaved in the House of Onias, he has not carried out his obligation [M. Men. 13:10F — G]. And they are liable for his sacrifices [offered therein] to extirpation.

T. 13:14 The priest (5) who served in the House of Onias or in other places at the time of the prohibition of the high place[s] — is prohibited [from serving in Jerusalem]. [If he did so] at the time of the permission of the high place[s], he is permitted [M. Men. 13:10K-L]. As it is said, "Nevertheless the priests of the high places came not up to the altar of the Lord in Jerusalem, but they ate unleavened bread among their brethren" [2 Kings 23:9].

T. 13:15 May one therefore conclude, if they ate unleavened bread in the midst of their brethren, they should be prohibited, and if not, they should be permitted [even if they have officiated? Obviously not!] Conclude, therefore, [that] they are valid to take their share but prohibited to offer [sacrifices], like [other] blemished [priests].

T. 13:16 Lo, if [a priest] was clean at the time of slaughter and at the time of the tossing of the blood, but at the time of the burning of the fat was made unclean, Lo, this one takes a share of the flesh. R. Nehora'i says, "Even if he was clean at the time of the tossing of the blood, but at the time of the burning of the fat he was made unclean, he does not take a portion in the flesh. Under no circumstances does he take a portion of the flesh unless he is clean at the time of the slaughter and at the time of the tossing of the blood and at the time of the burning of the fat."

T. 13:17 [If] a priest comes and offers his Holy Things in a watch which is not his, the hide and their [fee for] service belong to him. And if he was aged or ill, they give [the work] to any priest whom he wants. Its hide and its flesh are his. But if he was blemished, they give to the men of that watch its hide, and [the fee for] its service belongs to them. And that which is taken from a gentile belongs to any priest whom he chooses. And a field of possession is given to the men of the watch on the New Year which marks the beginning of the Jubilee year.

T. 13:18 At first did they bring the hides of Holy Things to the room of bet happarvah and divided them in the evening to each household which served on that day. But the powerful men of the priesthood would come and take them by force. They ordained that they should divide it on Fridays to each and every watch.

T. 13:19 But still did violent men of the priesthood come and take it away by force. The owners went and dedicated them to Heaven [T. Zeb. 11:16]. They said, The days were not few before the priests covered the face of the entire porch [of the Temple] with golden trays, a hundred by a hundred [handbreadths], with the thickness of a golden denar. Thus did they lay them together until the festival. And on the festival they remove them. And they leave them on the stairs of the Temple Mount, so that the people should see their work, that it is beautiful [and] that there was no imperfection in them. After the festival they go and put them up in their place.

T. 13:20 Abba Saul says, "Beams of sycamore were in Jericho. And strong-fisted men would come and take them by force. The owners went and dedicated them to Heaven." They said, "The owners dedicated to Heaven only beams of sycamore alone" [T. Zeb. 11:16-17].

T. 13:21 Concerning these and people like them and people similar to them and people who do deeds like their deeds did Abba Saul b. Bitnit and Abba Yosé b. Yohanan of Jerusalem say, Woe is me because of the House of Boethus. Woe is me because of their staves. Woe is me because of the house of Qadros. Woe is me because of their pen. Woe is me because of the house of Elhanan. Woe is me because of their whispering. Woe is me because of the house of Ishmael ben Phiabi. "For they are high priests, and their sons, treasurers, and their sons in law, supervisors, and their servants come and beat us with staves."

M. 13:11 It is said of the burnt offering of a beast, "An offering by fire, a smell of sweet savor" [Lev. 1:9] and of the bird offering, "An offering by fire, a smell of sweet savor" [Lev. 1:17] and [even] of the meal-offering, "An offering by fire, a smell of sweet savor" [Lev. 2:9] — to teach that all the same are the one who offers much and the one who offers little, on condition that a man will direct his intention to Heaven.

T. 13:22 Said R. Yohanan b. Torta, "On what account was Shiloh destroyed? Because of the disgraceful disposition of the Holy Things which were there? As to Jerusalem's first building, on what account was it destroyed? Because of idolatry and licentiousness and bloodshed which was in it? But [as to] the latter [building] we know that they devoted themselves to Torah and were meticulous about tithes. On what account did they go into exile? Because they love money and hate one another? This teaches you that hatred of one for another is evil before the Omnipresent, and Scripture deems it equivalent to idolatry, licentiousness and bloodshed."

T. 13:23 But as to the final building which is destined to be built — may it be in our lifetime and in our days! — what is stated? "And it shall come to pass in the latter days that the mountain of the house of the Lord shall be established as the highest of the mountains, and shall be raised above the hills, and all the nations shall flow to it, and many people shall come and say, 'Come, let us go up to the mountain of the Lord, to the house of the God of Jacob'" [Is. 2:2-3]. "For there shall be a day when watchmen will call in the hill country of Ephraim: 'Arise, and let us go up to Zion our God'" [Jer. 31:6].

Because of the homogeneous character of meal-offerings, the language that one uses in referring to them ("a meal-offering" without further qualification) encompasses them all, even though one has specified details particular to one type rather than another. The exercise before us underscores the homogeneity of the category-formation. This it does by highlighting the encompassing character of the category-formation, "meal-offerings," so that if one vows one prepared in a baking pan but brings one prepared in a frying pan, the result is the same: it is a meal-offering in accord with the rule, even though the one who has made the pledge has still to carry out its details. But if he made specific reference to the flour in hand and did not prepare it in line with the language he used, that is another matter. So the rule, M. 12:2, works out important points of differentiation. One must, moreover, conform to accepted usage, and if one pledges a meal-offering not in accord with the correct mode of preparing it, he must nonetheless conform to the rule, M. 12:3. The main point, then, transcends the cases, and it is that the commonly accepted meaning of language governs, and the appropriate rule pertains, whatever one has specified as his distinctive intentionality. We do not take account of idiosyncratic intentionality, the outer limits are set by those that conform to an effective norm.

IV. DOCUMENTARY TRAITS

A. THE MISHNAH AND THE TOSEFTA

The usual pattern reproduces itself: the Tosefta vastly enriches and amplifies the Halakhah but does not recast the category-formation in any significant way. The Tosefta time and again shows itself a critical component of the Halakhic exegetics, not of the Halakhic hermeneutics. Since the Mishnah in order comes before the Tosefta, which cites the Mishnah constantly and depends on the Mishnah for its program and for the order of inquiry, we must regard the corpus of category-formations as the contribution of the Mishnah in particular.

B. THE BAVLI

The Bavli conducts a systematic exegesis of the Halakhah of the Mishnah and some of that of the Tosefta but does not extend the category-formation.

V. THE HERMENEUTICS OF MENAHOT

A. WHAT FUSES THE HALAKHIC DATA INTO A CATEGORY-FORMATION?

The preoccupations of the Halakhah of Menahot accord with the ones that engaged those in charge of Zebahim. The order and the logic of presentation are identical: [1] intentionality, [2] general rules covering all cases, [3] particular rules for special cases and, finally, [4] extrinsic problems, principles of law for another range of transactions as these principles pertain to the topic at hand (vows yielding vows in connection with meal-offerings). That fixed order tells us the generic logic of exposition that the framers found self-evident: [1] from the general to the particular, [2] from the abstract to the concrete, [3] from the material to the intangible, and so on. But within that framework, in conformity with those rules of natural history, the specificities of Menahot dictate the entire Halakhic program. No one took the step from principle to case and back to principle, viewed in still greater abstraction; no one in the Halakhic framework set forth the principles of natural history and analysis thereof. Much of the Halakhah before us proves intensely particular to its topic. But that made possible the accomplishment of the goal of the category-formation, one of homogenization of the specificities of the details. That is in two aspects.

If first of all, someone is deeply persuaded of the autonomy of the genus of animal from that of vegetable, then he is going to find deeply puzzling the utilization of both animals and vegetables for one and the same purpose in the offerings on the altar. For such a person, it will not suffice to say, the adventitious character of the social order, some rich, some poor, some able to present entire oxen, others a mere handful of flour — the accidents of this world cannot sufficiently account for the facts. So the Halakhah will take as its starting point some deeper explanation of the congruence of what is deemed categorically incompatible.

Exactly how are meal-offerings equivalent to animal offerings, as Scripture dictates them to be? The answer to that question fuses the category-formation before us. As with animal offerings, so with meal-offerings, intentionality plays a critical role. This is expressed in the following language: All meal-offerings from which the handful was taken not for the purpose for which the meal-offering was originally designated ("not for their own name") are valid for offering up, and, in the case of the residue, for the priests' eating. But they have not gone to their owner's credit in fulfillment of an obligation, except for the meal-offering of a sinner and the meal-offering of jealousy of a suspected adulteress which, if improperly designated for a purpose other than that for which originally designated, are invalid. The same points made at Zebahim are recapitulated at Menahot. But that bears considerable weight, because it means meal-offerings indeed are equivalent to animal offerings. The contrary view is that meal-offerings, from which the handful was taken not for their own name are valid. And they do go to their owner's credit in fulfillment of an obligation (M. Men. 1:1A-B).

Second, if someone focuses upon the diversity of meal-offerings, he is likely to wonder at the possibility of stating rules that cover them all equally. So to validate the category-formation, built as it is on the model of the homogeneity of animal-offerings, the rules for each must be shown to conform to patterns governing them all. That is why the category-formation accomplishes its goal of homogenization through the tedious work of specification of which encompassing rule applies to which group of otherwise differentiated meal-offerings. True to its generative hermeneutics, the Halakhah engages in an exercise of comparison and contrast. One powerful demonstration emerges by showing the comparability of offerings of different genera for exactly the same cultic purpose. And that, it is made manifest, is not only in matters of attitude but also in action. Just as the same attitude governs, so too the pattern of actions are shown identical. The four principal actions of the rite of the meal-offering form counterparts to the four pertaining to the blood rite: taking the handful, putting it into a utensil, bringing it to the altar, and offering it up on the fire. This is expressed in the following language:

> What is the order of meal-offerings? One would bring it from home in a silver or a golden utensil. He put it into a utensil of service and sanctified it in a utensil of service and put its oil and its frankincense on it. He went in to the courtyard and offered it up at the southeastern corner of the altar, at the southern side of the corner. He puts it on the altar and that suffices. Then he removes its frankincense from one side and takes up a handful of meal-offering from the place at which the oil is located and puts it into a utensil of service and sanctifies it in a utensil of service. Then he gathers the frankincense and puts it on top of it. And he raises it onto the altar and salts it and puts it onto the altar fires. And the residue do they give to the priests.
>
> T. 1:16

The priest then forms an intention in connection with these critical procedures, and if it is improper, then, as with the blood rite, the action is null and the rite spoiled. All meal-offerings equally are subject to the rule. Like the blood rite of the animal offering, the taking of the handful of the meal-offering for placement on the altar must be done by a properly qualified and vested priest. The contrary view holds that if things are done wrong, the meal-offering is not invalidated; a properly qualified priest simply repeats the action. Here the difference is, once the blood is collected, the effective part of the rite is underway and is irreversible; the beast is dead. But the meal-offering is not comparable here; it is still available. That view is expressed by Ben Beterah when he says in the case of the priest's using his left hand, "Let him put it back, and go and take up a handful in his right hand."

The work of homogenization generates its own problems. Once we admit that intentionality makes a difference at the specified stages of all meal offerings, we have to address the differentiated components of the meal-offering and ask whether the improper intentionality must affect the entirety — all components — or even only one of them, so as to invalidate the meal-offering. We see three positions. One distinguishes the handful of meal-offering from the frankincense, so that if the improper intention regarding the time of offering up the frankincense applies, the sacrifice is invalid, but not made refuse. Others hold that the sacrifice is made refuse. Still others maintain that only when the whole of that which renders the offering permissible has been subjected to improper intentionality do we dispose of the offering by treating it as refuse. The normative position is, improper intention concerning what is primary to the offering affects what is secondary, but improper intention concerning what is secondary does not affect what is primary. Thus, an improper intentionality concerning the thank-offering makes the bread brought along with the thank-offering (Lev. 7:13, M. 7:1) refuse, but an improper intentionality concerning the bread does not make the thank-offering refuse. How so? He who slaughters the thank-offering with the improper intention to eat of it on the next day — it and the bread are made refuse. If he does so with the improper intention to eat of the bread on the next day, the bread is made refuse, but the thank-offering is not made refuse. Improper intentionality concerning the lambs make the bread (Lev. 23:19, 20, M. 2:2) refuse, but improper intentionality concerning the bread does not make the lambs refuse. How so? He who slaughters the lambs with the improper intention to eat of them on the next day — they and the bread are made refuse. If he does so with the improper intention to eat of the bread on the next day, the bread is made refuse, but the lambs are not made refuse.

    Meal-offerings not only are compared with animal offerings, they also are shown to differ from them. And this too underscores their homogeneity. The second component of the category-formation — the differentiation of the meal-offerings — contrasts with its counterpart in Zebahim. All animal offerings, we saw at Zebahim, conform to a single set of regulations as to their preparation. But Scripture has already indicated that that is not the case for meal-offerings, for which there are five different modes of preparation, and which are further differentiated in various classifications. The activity of the category-formation focuses upon the differentiated regulations, for reasons just now specified. At issue is whether the diverse rites that differentiate types of meal-offerings make a difference in sorting out the Halakhah that governs, or whether the principles for animal offerings pertain equally to meal-offerings. The blood-rite, the taking of the handful of meal-offering, and the drink-offering are treated as equivalent. If they are made unclean, the priestly frontlet effects atonement for that fact in all three cases. If the meat, grain, or oil should contract uncleanness and nonetheless be offered, no one knowing in advance of what has happened, the priestly frontlet effects atonement equally in all three cases. That fact once again captures what is the single most important point of the Halakhah is that meal-offerings and animal sacrifices are analogous and subject to the same rule. Just as the tossing of the blood renders the sacrificial meat available to the priests and, where pertinent, to the sacrifier, so the offering up of the handful of meal-offering renders the residue permissible to the priests.

Why should anyone have thought otherwise? First, because the blood, meat, and sacrificial parts of the animal sacrifice are of a single genre, but the meal-offering is made up of components that are not of the same genre, e.g., the frankincense is not of the same sub-classification as the flour. The second reason is, while animal offerings of whatever classification involve one and the same four rites — killing the animal, collecting the blood, conveying the blood, tossing the blood — meal-offerings are differentiated by diverse procedures and modes of preparation. Thus, it is argued, meal-offerings are not comparable to animal-sacrifices. For if the priest takes a handful from meal-offering prepared on a griddle and refers to it as one prepared in a pan, the rites pertaining to it in any case indicate that he is dealing with one prepared on a griddle. If he is dealing with a dry meal-offering and refers to it as one mixed with oil, this is of no consequence because the rites pertaining to it indicate that he is dealing with a dry one. But in the case of animal sacrifices, there is only one rite for all of them, and one mode of slaughter for all of them. The Halakhah takes the position that the meal-offering serving as a thank-offering could never be designated as the meal-offering of a sinner, and the meal-offering of a sinner and of a woman accused of adultery must be designated in particular for those purposes. Not only so, but in more general terms, animal offerings involve a particular place, at the north of the altar, and a particular place for the cut, at the neck of the animal. But meal-offerings can be offered anywhere on the altar, and, as a matter of obvious fact, no particular spot in the offering is reserved for the taking of the handful. Meal-offerings involve a more strict side, the priest having to wear vestments, and only a priest may take up the handful; an ordinary person may kill the animal, though a priest is required to collect the blood and carry out the blood-rite. What is implicit is, the very costly animal offering and the inexpensive meal-offering bear exactly the same weight in the cult. What is implicit in the Halakhah is articulated in the same context, as we shall note presently.

The Halakhah cannot impose uniformities that do not exist in the facts dictated by Scripture and tradition. It can and does organize and systematize what Scripture leaves disparate by reason of its quite different way of organizing data, the distinctive perspectives implicit in its category-formations. This work of reorganization, the Halakhah does by comparing and contrasting the like and the unlike. Or it accomplishes the same end by listing a rule and then exceptions thereto. The systematization (not homogenization) of Scripture's diverse offerings comes to expression in formulations of the rule with the exception, as the following show: All offerings of the community and the individual require drink offerings, except for (1) the firstling, (2) tithe of cattle, (3) the Passover, (4) the sin offering, and (5) the guilt offering. Individuals lay hands on their offering, but no communal counterpart exists: All offerings of the community do not receive laying on of hands, except for the bullock which is brought on account of the community's transgression of any of the commandments (Lev. 4:15) and the goat which is sent forth (Lev. 16:21). In rules such as these the Halakhah collects and organizes data but does not force those data to serve its principal purpose. So, in all, the category-formation fuses the data in a massive exercise of homogenization, which serves the larger hermeneutics of the category-formation: the demonstration of the fundamental genus that encompasses the media of expiation and atonement, however these are themselves speciated.

B. THE ACTIVITY OF THE CATEGORY-FORMATION

The category-formation extends its range to a number of concrete issues: laying on of hands, proper preparation of meal-offerings in general, special meal-offerings, the 'omer and the show-bread, and vows in connection with meal-offerings. Only the last-named component contains rulings that transcend the cases at hand. But the presentation of all of the issues that are actively considered responds to that same hermeneutics that fuses the data into a highly coherent and purposive category-formation.

PROPER PREPARATION OF MEAL-OFFERINGS IN GENERAL: The grain for meal-offerings in all cases may derive from abroad, from current or prior crops, and from a field that is validly devoted to grain. It is not intrinsically holy, e.g., by reason of its having grown in the Holy Land. It becomes holy in the transaction at hand, that is, in relationship to the Israelite's intentionality to atone for his sins through this meal-offering. Thus: All meal-offerings of the community and of the individual derive (1) from wheat grown in the Land of Israel or from wheat grown abroad, (2) from fresh produce wheat, grown in the present year or from old wheat, grown in the preceding year. But there are two meal-offerings that derive from grain deemed holy by reason of its having been grown in the Land of Israel. The offering of a sheaf of the first crop of barley Lev. 23:10 and two loaves of bread Lev. 23:1617, derive only from new wheat, grown in the present year and from wheat grown in the Land. But the grain used for all of them derives only from the choicest produce. It may derive even from gentiles, except for the firstling and tithe, which derive only from the Land and derive only from Israelites. They do not bring wheat for flour for the meal-offering either from a manured field or from an irrigated field or from a tree-planted field. But if they brought wheat from these areas, it is valid. How does one do it? One broke up fresh ground in the first year of the sabbatical cycle, and in the second of the sabbatical cycle sows it seventy days before Passover, and it produces abundant flour.

The Halakhah formulates general rules out of the facts supplied by the Written Torah. Here the particular gift of the framers of the Halakhah, their power to compare and contrast and so generalize out of diverse data, facilitates the main work, thus: There are meal-offerings which require oil and frankincense, oil but not frankincense, frankincense but not oil, neither oil nor frankincense. And these are they that require oil and frankincense. And again, there are those offerings which require bringing near but do not require waving, waving but not bringing near, waving and bringing near, neither waving nor bringing near. So, for another example of the generalizing power, the recasting of Scripture's law now states: All meal-offerings are brought unleavened except for the leavened cakes of thank-offerings (M. 7:1) and the two loaves of bread of Pentecost, which are brought as leavened bread. All those meal-offerings that must be unleavened are kneaded in lukewarm water. And one watches them that they not leaven. And if the residue became leavened, one transgresses a negative commandment. They do not knead them in boiling water, because they form too thick a paste, nor in cold water because they dilute it so that the meal does not cohere. But they knead them in lukewarm water and watch them, that they not become leavened. And if one leavened the residue, he transgresses a negative commandment.

The operative actions in preparing meal-offerings involve taking the handful, putting it into a utensil (comparable to the bowl for collecting the blood), conveying it to the altar, and pouring the handful of the meal-offering onto the fires. Failing to carry out the other required actions — e.g., (1) did not pour oil over the fine flour, (2) did not mingle the oil with unleavened cakes, (3) did not break up the meal-offering prepared in a baking pan, (4) did not salt it, (5) did not wave it — the offering remains valid. Then what happens if the handfuls of meal-offerings presented for diverse purposes are mixed together? The offering remains valid: If its handful of meal-offering was mixed with the handful of its fellow meal-offering — (1) with the meal-offering of priests, (2) with the meal-offering of the anointed priest, (3) with the meal-offerings brought with drink offerings (M. 6:2) — it is valid. So some components of the rite are essential, and improper performance of any one of those will invalidate the entire rite. Others have no affect upon one another.

Since Scripture classifies meal-offerings by the taxonomic indicators of mode of preparation, the Halakhah insists on the differentiation by those indicators, e.g., when one is vowing to present a meal-offering. Then if he specifies preparation in one mode, he cannot carry out the vow by presenting a meal-offering prepared in another: He who says, "Lo, I pledge myself to a meal-offering baked in a baking pan," should not bring one prepared in a frying pan. If he says, "Lo, I pledge myself to a meal-offering prepared in a frying pan," he should not bring one prepared in a baking pan. Meal-offerings prepared in a utensil have to be broken up for the handful to be taken; breaking them up facilitates taking the handful, and hence offerings that yield no residue and no handful do not have to be broken up in the same way that applies to those that do.

Some meal-offerings were thick in consistency, some thin. That variable complicates the consideration of mixtures and the disposition thereof. If several types of meal-offerings were of an equivalent consistency, there is no reason not to mix them together. But when one is thicker than another, they should not be mixed together. Thus: In the case of mixture with the meal-offering of the anointed priest or with the meal-offering brought with drink offerings, it is invalid. For in the case of one, its mixture is thick, and in the case of the others, its mixture is thin, and each absorbs from the other. That explains the following general distinctions among diverse offerings: They stir together (1) the meal-offering which accompanies drink offerings of rams along with that for drink offerings of bullocks, (2) the meal-offering which accompanies drink offerings of lambs along with that for drink offerings of lambs, (3) those of an individual along with those of the community, (4) those of one day along with those of the preceding day for drink offerings may be offered up to ten days after the sacrifice which they accompany. But they do not stir the drink offerings of lambs along with the drink offerings of bullocks or rams. And if one stirred them, these by themselves and those by themselves, and they then become confused, they are valid.

Just as the priests eat certain parts of the animal-offerings in most though not all cases, so they eat the residue of the meal-offerings in most though not all cases. If a handful is removed and offered up, the residue is ordinarily eaten by them. But ordinarily if no handful is removed but the whole meal-offering is burned up, then the priests have no claim on residue. So far as the facts permit, then, that provision for the meal-offering runs parallel to the burnt-offering, which yields no meat for the priests to eat. But there are meal-offerings that are not burnt up and from which no handful is removed, yet that are eaten by the priest. These are the special meal-offering constituted by the two loaves of bread and the show bread placed on the altar a week at a time. And there are meal-offerings that are not eaten and from which no handful is removed, specifically, the meal-offering of the high priest, of the anointed priest, and the one that comes with drink-offerings. What the priests present as their own meal-offerings yields no residue for them (Lev. 6:16). Here again, we find the articulation of ad hoc rules of Scripture.

SPECIAL MEAL-OFFERINGS: Having stated rules that govern all meal-offerings, the Halakhah also differentiates one from the next. Even here, so far as the facts permit, principles with broad implications for a variety of meal-offerings come to bear. For example, what is the relationship between an animal-offering and the meal-offering that accompanies it? If the animal-sacrifice is invalid, is the bread that is presented still valid, and vice versa? The answer is given as follows: He who slaughters the thank-offering inside the Temple court, while its bread-offering is located outside the wall — the bread is not sanctified. If he slaughtered the thank-offering before its bread-offering had formed a crust in the oven — even if all of them the loaves formed a crust except for one of them — the bread is not sanctified. If he slaughtered it intending to eat its flesh or to toss the blood or to offer up the sacrificial parts outside of its proper time or outside of its proper place, the bread is sanctified and is deemed refuse. If he slaughtered it the thank-offering, and it turned out to be terefah, the bread is not sanctified. The point then is, the principal governs the ancillary component of a composite offering. And that principle transcends the particular problem in which it is set forth.

Secondary points include these: the bread-offering must be appropriately situated where it may be eaten; it must be wholly baked, otherwise it is dough; the invalidation of the animal-sacrifice does not prevent the sanctification of the bread; the animal-sacrifice must be valid; the animal must be offered under the proper designation so that the bread is to begin with required. The same exercise concerns drink offerings. Drink offerings which were sanctified in a utensil, and the animal sacrifice with which they were brought turned out to be invalid — if there is there another animal sacrifice requiring drink offerings, let them be offered with it. And if not, let them be invalidated by being kept overnight.

LAYING ON OF HANDS: When the Halakhah expounds a given rite, it commonly broadens the discussion to articulate the purpose of the rite, making explicit what is at stake. That is shown in the presentation of the laying on of hands: How does one lay on hands? The animal to be sacrificed stands at the north with its face to the west. The one who lays on hands is in the west, with his face to the west. So the animal is situated to the north of the altar, facing the west. That leaves the one who lays on hands east of the animal and facing the animal. He puts his two hands onto the horns of the animal. But he did not put his hands on the shoulder, and he did not put his hands on top of one another, and nothing intervened between his hands and the horns. All of this sets the stage for the act of contrition. The sacrifier made confession of sin or transgression over it: over a sin offering, he confessed the particular sin he had committed, over the guilt offering, the particular transgression of which he was guilty. Then, as we noted in our survey of the main points of the law, all who bear complete responsibility for their actions lay on hands. The laying on of hands applies in the case of priests, Levites, Israelites, proselytes, freed slaves, Hallalin, Netinin, Mamzerin, a male rendered a eunuch by human action or naturally, a man with crushed testicles and one with a damaged penis. Excluded from the explicit confession of sins are gentiles, women, slaves, or minors. The difference is, priests, Levites, Israelites, and the like all are deemed to act entirely in accord with their own free will and are not subject to the will of others. Gentiles, women, slaves, and minors either are excluded from the system altogether or, for women, slaves, and minors, these classes of persons do not bear complete responsibility for their actions because they are subject to the will of others. That the cult embodies a transaction of wills once more accounts for the details of the Halakhah.

But then, since in one way or another, all of these classes of persons are represented by one offering or another — even the gentile may present an offering — exactly what difference does the distinction make between laying on of hands and not laying on of hands? In fact, the Halakhah logically declares, while desirable, the laying on of hands constitutes the residue of the requirement. That means the procedure may, in fact, be omitted without affecting the efficacy of atonement. It is done on the head of the animal with both hands. And in the place in which they lay on hands there do they slaughter the animal. And forthwith after laying on of hands is the act of slaughter, which is not the rule for laying on of hands. Simeon would carry the logic of the laying on of hands to its ultimate realization: Whatever is brought on account of violations of a specific commandment and the blood of which is brought inside to the inner altar requires laying on of hands. Whatever is not brought on account of transgressions of a specific commandment and the blood of which is not brought inside does not require laying on of hands. Simeon then recognizes that those offerings that are linked to specific sins carried out by particular persons deemed wholly responsible for what they do — hence adult Israelite males of sound senses — are the ones where a physical link between the man and the offering must be established to complete the circle: inadvertent sin, discovery, atonement for that particular sin, forgiveness and reconciliation.

THE 'OMER, THE SHOW BREAD: The offering of the first sheaf of barley rendered the produce of the new crop permitted in the country, and the Two Loaves of Pentecost/Shabuot, Lev. 23:16, rendered new produce permitted for the meal-offering in the sanctuary. Before the offering of the first sheaf of barley, they do not bring from new produce, grain that is to be used for meal-offerings, first fruits, and the meal-offering which accompanies drink offerings along with beasts. And if one brought grain for any of these before the offering of the [first sheaf of barley], it is invalid. Once the two loaves were offered at Pentecost, they began bringing meal-offerings and drink-offerings from all sources. They at that time do not hold back produce from anywhere. What distinguishes the 'omer, a public offering consisting of the first crop of barley presented from the sixteenth of Nisan until Pentecost, is its effect. Once presented for the first time, the offering marks the beginning of the season in which new crops, those harvested from Nisan forward, may be utilized. The grain was ground, sifted, mixed with oil and frankincense, and "brought near," and then a handful was taken out and offered up, the residue being eaten by the priests. That signaled the point at which the new crops could be traded in the market: After the offering of the first sheaf of barley was offered, new produce was permitted forthwith.

VOWS IN CONNECTION WITH MEAL-OFFERINGS: Because of the diversity of meal-offerings, one must be careful to provide exactly the type of meal-offering that he has vowed to give. If he vows one sort but presents another, the former remains a valid offering, but the vow has yet to be carried out: He who says, "Lo, I pledge myself to bring a meal-offering prepared in a baking pan," but brought one prepared in a frying pan, or he who says, "Lo, I pledge myself to bring a meal-offering prepared in a frying pan," but brought one prepared in a baking pan (M. 5:8) — what he has brought, he has brought as a separate freewill offering. But his obligation for the original pledge he has not carried out. Whatever one promises, he still must abide by the prevailing rule. Meal-offerings are made of wheat; if one pledges one of barley, he still must provide one of wheat, so too, fine flour and meal and the like. The ordinary usage governs in the interpretation of what one has pledged. A further qualification concerning vows involves the precise pledge, no less but also no more. The basic principle is, one must do exactly what he has said, and if one does more than what he has promised to do, that is not accepted in fulfillment of his pledge.

C. THE CONSISTENCY OF THE CATEGORY-FORMATION

I see no point at which the category-formation accommodates kinds of Halakhah out of phase with its principal concerns. The inquiry loses all interest. Since homogenization is at issue, the category-formation would find itself reshaped were an effort at differentiation to take priority; that we do not find in the Tosefta or in the Bavli, except as the program already defined by the Mishnah requires it for some special consideration (e.g., systemization of anomalous facts).

D. THE GENERATIVITY OF THE CATEGORY-FORMATION

The Halakhic category-formation thus insists upon the systematic character of the cult, underscoring the ways in which the various, diverse offerings conform to a single pattern, and so it is with animal- and meal-offerings. That point of stress differs from Scripture's. Indeed, in its taxonomic inquiry, the Halakhah homogenizes what Scripture has differentiated. Not only so, but, as we realize in the comparison and contrast of Zebahim and Menahot, the Halakhah further homogenizes its own speciated category-formations. Indeed, the demonstration of the comparability of the two forms a critical point of interest, and a mark of the generativity of the encompassing category-formation for Zebahim and Menahot, identified in Chapter One. When it comes to offerings of vegetable and of animal classifications, respectively, the taking of the handful is equivalent to the slaughtering of the beast by cutting its throat, the placing of the handful of meal into the bowl forms the counterpart to collecting the blood in a bowl, the conveying of the meal to the altar runs parallel to the conveying of the blood, and the tossing of the meal on the fires corresponds to the tossing of the blood on the altar. To underscore the fundamental comparability of the offerings, the Halakhah then dismisses as appropriate but not essential all other variables that would differentiate one rite from the other!

What further defines the generativity of the present category-formation, as already noted for Zebahim, also is what is omitted. Everything else is secondary. That is why these are the four actions that, in each case, must be carried out for the purpose of the offering to be achieved. The comparability of the types of offerings moreover makes possible the recapitulation of the principles pertaining to animal-offerings in connection with the regulation of meal-offerings. For example, if we have a case in which the blood of an animal offering was sprinkled, and then the meat became unclean, the offering remains valid, in Eliezer's view, while in Joshua's, both elements must remain valid: "If there is no blood, there is no meat, and vice versa." Exactly the same dispute is played out here, now in the language (for Joshua's position): "If there is no handful, there is no residue, and if there is no residue, there is no handful." It would be difficult to state more forcefully the basic principle of the Halakhah that no difference separates offerings of discrete classifications of matter. So much for the extension of the limits of the category-formation in its Halakhic framework. And all of this is for a single purpose: it is to insist upon the comparability, the interchangeability, of the media of expiation and atonement, animal-offerings and meal-offerings. If I had to identify the single point of these two massive bodies of Halakhah, pervading the details and shaping the way they are presented is that single point of insistence.

What about the Aggadic reading of the matter? It is explicit in its insistence upon the unity of the species of the genus comprised by Zebahim and Menahot. Here is how the Aggadah states the equivalency of the meal-offering to the animal-offering:

> It is said of the burnt offering of a beast, "An offering by

fire, a smell of sweet savor" (Lev. 1:9) and of the bird offering, "An offering by fire, a smell of sweet savor" (Lev. 1:17) and even of the meal-offering, "An offering by fire, a smell of sweet savor" (Lev. 2:9) — to teach that all the same are the one who offers much and the one who offers little, on condition that a man will direct his intention to Heaven.

M. 13:11

That proposition is illustrated in rich detail by the Halakhah, which embodies the equivalency of the two offerings. And the same proposition explains what is at stake in their point of verbatim coincidence: the centrality of intentionality in all details of both species of the genus, "Media for atoning sin or crime to which intentionality of the empowered actor, the priest, is critical, the animal- and meal-offerings, Zebahim and Menahot."

Reading the statement of M. 13:11 within the framework of hermeneutical analysis imposes a very specific meaning: "Directing intention to Heaven" means, "to Heaven," and not to the inappropriate directions specified in the Halakhah. It is not a statement of mere sentimentality, praising good intention and minimizing the importance of the *materia sacra* under discussion. It is itself a statement that draws upon the specificities of the Halakhah to state the generalization: the meal- and animal-offerings represent a transaction of intentionality, a way of demonstrating the sacrifier's and the sacrificer's acceptance of God's will expressed in the Torah. Having found he has inadvertently sinned, the sacrifier hastens to the altar to atone for his lapse of acceptance of God's will in the Torah and to atone intentionally for what he has unwittingly done. That, I contend, is not an exercise in the leveling power of intentionality to even out differences between rich and poor (though that is the effect). The rite, whatever its medium, animate or inanimate, bears the same statement, and to make that statement, the animate, so rich in symbolic meaning, had to be homogenized with the inanimate. On its own, the animate leaves space for reflection on the interplay of blood and blood, the substantive transfer of guilt, and other obvious considerations of the cult as a transaction of a material character. But the animate joined with and treated as equivalent to the inanimate removes from the transaction at the altar that same enchanted character that, in its way, the Halakhah of Zebahim denies as well. All things are made relative to the absolute of intentionality. Just as with reference to the animal offerings, the altar sanctifies only what is appropriate to it, so here too the tangibility, the materiality of "the holy" gives way to the transitive power of will.

The hermeneutics of Menahot and Zebahim, therefore, begins with a prior corpus of data altogether, selecting those data and interpreting them in such a way that, at a later stage of logical thought, the hermeneutics of the

Halakhah that we have identified would emerge. Specifically, the setting for the institution of the offerings, both animate and inanimate, is the sin at the base of Sinai and on the occasion of the very giving of the Torah itself. It is embodied in the calf made by Aaron the priest — with Moses yet on the mountain. No wonder the sacrificer, the priest, exercises the same taxonomic power as the sacrifier; he too bears a burden of sin and guilt that the very rite embodies. Israel outside of the Land forms the counterpart of man beyond Eden. Adam and Eve rebelled and lost Eden; Israel rebelled even before entering Eden. But it is with the difference that the Torah intervenes, complete with its provision for a medium of atonement that Adam and Eve did not possess. And for inadvertent sin, that medium of atonement worked through its demonstration of a change of heart, an assurance to God that the sin was not deliberate. That explains why all the same are the one who offers much and the one who offers little, on condition that a man will direct his intention to Heaven. So much for the components of the transaction. But whence the dynamism?

So far as the Halakhah of Menahot makes a statement on how Israel relates to God at the altar, it consists of a single proposition: those who bear full responsibility for their actions by reason of enjoying full command of their own will stand before God as equals. They are equal because all, rich and poor, unintentionally sin. To all equally is accorded responsibility for their actions. And to everyone, rich and poor alike, possessed of the right attitude, God affords the possibility of atonement and reconciliation. That striking fact then underscores that it is not the blood rite that makes the difference, for the meal-offering — at drastically diminished cost — accomplishes exactly the same thing.

To state the matter simply, concrete actions take on consequence only by reference to the intention with which they are carried out. What matters in the offerings is intentionality; the size of the offering makes no difference, only the intent of the person who presents it, so b. Men. 13:11 I.2/110a:

> 2. A. It has been taught on Tannaite authority:
> B. Said R. Simeon b. Azzai, "Come and take note of what is written in the passage that deals with sacrifices: neither the name of God that is *el* nor the name of God that is *elohim* but only the Lord. This is so as not to give contentious folk an occasion to rebel.
>
> C. "Furthermore it is said: It is said of the burnt offering of a beast, 'An offering by fire, a smell of sweet savor' (Lev. 1:9) and of the bird offering, 'An offering by fire, a smell of sweet savor' (Lev. 1:17) and [even] of the meal offering, 'An offering by fire, a smell of sweet savor' (Lev. 2:9) — to teach that all the same are the

one who offers much and the one who offers little, on condition that a man will direct his intention to Heaven.

D. "Now might you say, 'Then it is because God needs the food,' Scripture states, 'If I were hungry, I would not tell you, for the world is mine and the fullness thereof' (Ps. 50:12); 'For every beast of the forest is mine and the cattle upon a thousand hills; I know all the fowl of the mountains and wild beasts of the field are mine; do I eat the meat of bulls or drink the blood of goats' (Ps. 50:10, 11, 13). I did not order you to make sacrifices so you might say, 'I will do what he wants so he will do what I wants.' You do not make sacrifices for my sake but for your sake: 'you shall sacrifice at your own volition' (Lev. 19:5)."

So to conclude: just as sanctification constitutes a taxonomic status, not a substantive quality, so the altar carries out its task only when man's attitude and activity warrant: what is appropriate for the altar, not what is not appropriate for it, is what ascends. The Halakhah in its norms for actualities then characterizes man's relationship with God: man is responsible for his own will, and God responds to man's will. But knowing who and what man is, God gives man ample occasion to manifest the character of his conscience, the quality of his conviction. It is when man discerns the inadvertent sin that he has committed and atones therefor that man makes his will conform with God's will: freely to love, freely to obey. That is why the Halakhah in such an elaborate manner requires a massive set of category-formations in order in detail to equate the hugely costly ox with the paltry handful of flour. In the hermeneutics of the category-formation, media of atonement at the altar (animal, vegetable), the Halakhah makes a statement to which even the critical issues of intentionality must be deemed subordinate to the specificities of rules shown in detail to work together in a homogeneous construction.

3.
TRACTATE HULLIN

I. THE DEFINITION OF THE CATEGORY-FORMATION

Hullin takes as its problem the concrete preparation of meat, whether for the table at home or for the altar in the Temple. The Written Torah repeatedly asserts that "the blood is the life," making provision for the disposition of blood produced in slaughtering an animal. If killed for God, that is to say, in the Temple courtyard, the animal yields blood for the altar, to be sprinkled at the corners in an act of expiation; it further produces the sacrificial parts to be burned up in smoke on the altar-fires and thence to ascend to God's nostrils; and the beast may also yield meat for the priests and their families to eat. If killed for man's needs, the animal produces blood to be covered with dust, returned to the earth. Scripture's laws on this subject reach their logical conclusion in the Halakhah of Hullin. For once Scripture treats as analogous the killing of a beast for the altar and for the domestic table, then analogical-contrastive thinking will take over. The consequent analysis defines the hermeneutics of the category-formation through a process, to be reconstructed here, of comparison and contrast.

In the stated genus the Halakhah knows two species, [1] shedding blood for food preparation for God's altar, [2] doing the same for food preparation for Israel's table. The category-formation, then, is so constructed as to underscore the comparability of the two foci of nourishment, God's in Zebahim and holy Israel's in Hullin. The contrasts flow, the Halakhah sorting out the results. What are the variables indicated by analogical-contrastive analysis that will distinguish the genus's two species, Hullin and Zebahim? Once we have established that the two belong to the same genus, then the obvious opposites must be food preparation [1] in the Temple or outside the veils, that is, in the Land of Israel, [2] by priests or by householders, and therefore, by extension of both points, food preparation done [3] anywhere Israelites live, by any qualified person. The first two represent counterpoised opposites. The third carries forward what is implicit. This I take to mean, if not in the Temple, then anywhere, not even in the Land of Israel; if not by the priests, then by anyone, not even a householder, within the hierarchy of castes culminating in the priesthood. The analogical-contrastive analysis, then, will find its data in rules of food preparation, and its hermeneutics will take shape in the likeness and unlikeness of the rules covering God's and Israel's food, respectively.

So much for the theory of matters. How do the facts of the category-formation measure up? As we shall see, in concrete terms what is at issue is sorting out the contrasts from the analogies. When it comes to the domestic preparation of meat, the Halakhah in fact deals with three settings: [1] the Temple, [2] the Land of Israel, and [3] foreign land. These represent the three classifications indicated by considerations of sanctification of locality. The Halakhah further contrasts [1] the time that the Temple is standing from [2] the time that the Temple is destroyed. But the contrasts having been established, what is the analogical side to things — for therein lies the operative hermeneutics? For all three, the Halakhah insists, *the same rules pertain*. That is the case even despite the considerable differences as to sanctification, from the most holy space of the Temple to the utterly unclean that lies beyond the Land of Israel. And the very presence of the Temple does not determine. Even when the Temple rites no longer are practiced, the acts analogous to them persist. "Why does sanctification endure beyond locative and even temporal boundaries, and what preserves the generative analogy, sanctification of the shedding of blood for food, God's and Israel's?" It is the indelible and hierarchically paramount sanctification of Israel, God's people, that registers. And that takes priority now, without consideration of localization or even enlandisement, and also without consideration of the age, whether then, whether now.

At what cost? The sanctification of the Land is subordinated to the sanctification of Israel. Since all territory outside of the Land of Israel is by definition unclean, the premise of the Halakhah is that, despite that fact, Israel is to consume its secular meat in accord with those rules of sanctification that pertain to food and its preparation. The laws of cultic cleanness may apply to the household in the Land of Israel but cannot pertain abroad; nonetheless, the other principal admonitions apply overseas when blood is shed for food. So much for space, what about time? The age graced by the presence of the Temple, placed by M. Zeb. 14:4-8 at the apex of time differentiated by the location and activity of the cult, is marked as less holy Israel's time, with or without the cult. As we know, time is marked by the condition of the Temple, fully in service or utterly in ruins. That too in the present context is a distinction that makes no difference. The existence of the Temple or its destruction, the location of Israel, in the Land or in the lands of the gentiles — so far as taking animal life for man's purpose, these change nothing. That represents a profound judgment that under all circumstances, temporal and locative, Israel sustains its life in conditions of sanctification. Israel's condition of sanctification persists even without the atonement of the working Temple and its priesthood. To state the obvious: Israel's sanctification is what survives the calamities of destruction and exile, incarnate whenever and wherever Israel endures.

This carries us a step forward. Implicit in the hermeneutics particular to the category-formation, then, is the analogy of Israel and God, both sanctified, neither being truly enlandised in its sanctification or restricted by considerations of time and its speciation or periodization. Blood is shed to yield meat for God's table, and blood is shed to provide meat for Israel's household. Here is where the remarkable analogy, that of Israel to God, enters in. Both are holy, in a single hierarchization of sanctity. What, therefore, happens when the fires have gone out on the Temple altar, when Israel locates itself outside of the Land of Israel, and when animals no longer are consecrated for divine service at all? Then the initial balance, the perfect match of slaughter for the altar and slaughter for everyday food, is lost — but the generative analogy, blood to blood, persists. If we read as a set of interdependent categorical actions, the requirements of the Written Torah in connection with taking the life of an animal for God's and for man's use, then what law persists in this time? That is the question answered in the depths of the law of Hullin, certainly the high point of the entire Halakhic system.

But whatever my theory of the workings of the analogical-contrastive analytical process as key to the hermeneutics of the Halakhah throughout, the topical program does not sustain formal comparison with the counterpart in Zebahim, as a glance at the outline of the category-formation will indicate:

I. RULES OF SLAUGHTERING UNCONSECRATED ANIMALS FOR USE AT HOME OR IN THE TEMPLE

    A. General Rules of Slaughter
    B. Specific Regulations. *Terefah*-Rules
    C. Slaughter and Illicit Sacrifice
    D. *Terefah*- and Valid Carcasses
    E. The Affect of Valid Slaughter on the Parts of a Beast's Body, e.g., on the Foetus

II. OTHER RULES GOVERNING THE PREPARATION OF MEAT FOR USE AT HOME

    A. Not Slaughtering "It and Its Young" (Lev. 22:28)
    B. The Requirement to Cover Up the Blood (Lev. 17:13-14)
    C. The Prohibition of the Sciatic Nerve (Gen. 32:32)
    D. The Separation of Milk and Meat (Ex. 23:19, 34:26, Dt. 12:21) Connection for the Purposes of Contracting Uncleanness
    E. The Gifts to the Priest Taken from a Beast Slaughtered for Secular Purposes: The Shoulder, Two Cheeks, and Maw (Dt.

18:3)
F. The Gift to the Priest of the First Fleece of a Sheep (Dt. 18:4)
G. Letting the Dam Go from the Nest When Taking the Young (Dt. 22:6-7)

The second unit systematically works through Scripture's special rules, all the while working through the hermeneutical program just now outlined [1] whether the law applies both in the Temple and outside; [2] whether it applies when the Temple is standing or even after its destruction; [3] whether it applies only to Holy Things or also to unconsecrated beasts. I cannot point to a more systematic or cogent composition, among the many remarkably coherent constructions of the Halakhah.

Since Menahot and Zebahim match, we should have anticipated an equally well-articulated and systematic contrastive comparison of Hullin and Zebahim. But there is none. Why no formal comparison with Zebahim? Because here the issue is the disposition of the blood and, along the way, other Scriptural concerns. Those concerns flow directly from the Scripture: once the comparison of the species is drawn in the aspect of disposition of the blood (Chapters One through Four) other comparisons are drawn in the further aspects of meat-preparation that Scripture defines for Israel (Chapters Five through Twelve). To that undertaking — blood to blood — Zebahim makes no necessary contribution, other than in its opening unit on intentionality. Beyond that point, Zebahim, Menahot, and Hullin go their separate ways, each engaged by Halakhah particular to itself. Then for its part, while touching on the matter of intentionality in appropriately modest proportions, Hullin can state the entire message within its governing structure. Where there is secondary exposition, the generic hermeneutics takes over. The articulation of the Halakhah goes over quite familiar, uniform problems of an interstitial character; or grids of intersecting rules will generate a variety of tertiary rulings. This we see again in unit II, that is, in Chapters Five through Twelve, where a sequence of particular rules or problems is worked out systematically; a single pattern provided by the generic hermeneutics applies throughout.

If the generative issue throughout the articulation of the Halakhic category-formation is, how is the table like the altar? Then the complementary issue follows, how is it different? Then the way in which the circumstance of the one imposes a different rule from that of the other will demand detailed attention. Since the table compares with the altar, how and where and why is it subject to a different rule from that pertaining to the altar? The hermeneutics of the category-formation then interprets the appropriate data by an exercise in hierarchical classification — the point of the analogical part of the analogical-contrastive analysis to which I made reference a moment ago. To understand what follows, readers will need to know that, for unit II, a persistent formal pattern, embodying a hermeneutics I, shall now identify, dictates the course of exegesis. The following provides a preview of that recurrent formal pattern:

M. 5:1 [The prohibition against slaughtering on the same day] "it and its young" (Lev. 22:28) applies (1) in the Land and outside the Land, (2) in the time of the Temple and not in the time of the Temple, (3) in the case of unconsecrated beasts and in the case of consecrated beasts. How so? He who slaughters it and its offspring, (1) which are unconsecrated, (2) outside [the Temple courtyard] —both of them are valid. And [for slaughtering] the second he incurs forty stripes. [He who slaughters] (1) Holy Things (2) outside — [for] the first is he liable to extirpation, and both of them are invalid, and [for] both of them he incurs forty stripes. [He who slaughters] (1) unconsecrated beasts (2) inside [the Temple courtyard] — both of them are invalid, and [for] the second he incurs forty stripes. [He who slaughters] (1) Holy Things (2) inside — the first is valid, and he is exempt [from any punishment], and [for] the second he incurs forty stripes, and it is invalid.

M. 6:1 [The requirement to] cover up the blood applies in the Land and abroad, (2) in the time of the Temple and not in the time of the Temple, (3) in the case of unconsecrated beasts, but not in the case of Holy Things. And it applies (4) to a wild beast and a bird, (5) to that which is captive and to that which is not captive. And it applies (6) to a *koy*, because it is a matter of doubt [whether it is wild or domesticated]. And they do not slaughter it [a *koy*] on the festival. But if one has slaughtered it, they do not cover up its blood.

The same pattern recurs. What requires explanation, then, is why the triplet of concerns: in the Land and abroad, at the time of the Temple and not, in the case of the Israelite household's meat and in the case of God's? What is at stake here is the hermeneutics of the category-formation, which governs throughout.

The main lines of the category-formation in hand, we return to the basic question of the Halakhic hermeneutics of comparison and contrast of species of a common genus: what accounts for the Halakhic judgment that the nourishment of Israel is analogous to the nourishment of God? My answer is, it is the inherent sanctification of Israel, rendering Israel consubstantial with God ("in our image, after our likeness"). This is stated by Scripture itself, in such language as that of Ex. 22:30: "You shall be holy men to me, and [it must follow from your status as to sanctification, like me] meat in the field that is torn you shall not eat, you shall toss it to the dogs [just as you would not place such meat on the altar]." What follows from the analogy that compares (and hierarchizes) Israel's and God's status as to sanctification in one consequent requirement is self-evident. Israel sustain itself in accord with the rules of sanctification of food that is offered to God himself. Stated simply, Israel is holy and God is holy, thus "You shall be holy, for I, the Lord, your God, am holy" (Lev. 19:3). Scripture explicitly says so and equally blatantly links Israel's sanctification to the rules governing Israel's nourishment. So, within the established hierarchy of the classification of sanctified persons, where pertinent, the same rules dictate the appropriate source and correct preparation of food for both. And that further explains why the Halakhah of meat-preparation explicitly insists that Israel at home, outside of the Temple, even outside of the Land, retains that same status of sanctification that imposes the food-taboos involving blood. The sanctification of Israel, the people, survives [1] in the absence of the cult and the — not unemployment but — dis-employment of the priesthood, and [2] in alien, unclean territory, and [3] whatever the source of the food that Israel eats. Israel's sanctity is eternal, uncontingent, absolute. The sanctification that inheres in Israel, the people, transcends the Land and outlives the Temple and its cult. Since the sanctity of Israel, the people, persists beyond the Temple and outside of the Land, that sanctity stands at a higher point in the hierarchy of domains of the holy that ascend from earth to heaven and from (Israelite) Man to God.

The Halakhah to make its statement about the eternal sanctification of the people, Israel, explicitly responds to three facts: [1] enlandisement does not register, for Israelites live not only in the holy land but abroad, in unclean land; [2] the character of the age does not pertain (such as M. Zebahim 14:4-8 classified and hierarchized so precisely), for the Temple has been destroyed, a situation not contemplated in the pertinent hierarchization of Zebahim, but the rules of sanctification persist; [3] and, consequently, animals are slaughtered not only in the Temple in the Land but in unconsecrated space and abroad, and the meat is eaten not only in a cultic but in a profane circumstance. Although the sanctity of the Temple stands in abeyance, the sanctity of the Israelite table persists; although Israel is in exile from the Holy Land, Israel remains holy; although in the Temple rules of uncleanness are not now kept, they continue in force where they can be. Birds and animals that flourish outside of the Land when prepared for the Israelite table are regulated by the same rules that apply in the Land and even (where relevant) at the altar. So Israel, the people, not only retains sanctity but preserves it outside of the Land, and the sanctity of Israel transcends that of the Temple and its altar. No category-formation can have supplied a setting for such a statement so effective as the one at hand, and no hermeneutics can have been devised more effectively to translate the statement into the selection and interpretation of facts than the one embodied in the tripartite construction that predominates. But, as usual, once we reach the definition of the category-formation and identify its particular hermeneutics, we find that the generic hermeneutics of the Halakhah take over. And that is as it should be, for the power of the Halakhah is generated by its specificity and particularity.

II. THE FOUNDATIONS OF THE HALAKHIC CATEGORY-FORMATION

As at the Babas, so here too, Scripture provides a considerable corpus of facts, but the Halakhah recasts and reshapes these facts and makes of them a statement that is quite independent of Scripture's presentation of the same topic, as I have just now indicated. What the hermeneutics of the Halakhah does, essentially, is to form diverse facts into a single coherent construction and through them to make a striking point, which I have already laid out. The verses of Scripture that pertain are these:

> "When the Lord your God enlarges your territory...and you say, 'I will eat meat,' because you crave meat, you may eat as much meat as you desire. If the place that the Lord your God chooses to put his name there is too far from you, then you may kill any of your herd or your flock that the Lord has given you as I have commanded you, and you may eat within your towns, as much s you desire. Just as the gazelle or the hart is eaten, so you may eat of it; the unclean and the clean alike may eat of it. Only be sure that you do not eat the blood, for the blood is the life, and you shall not eat the life with the meat. You shall not eat it, you shall pour it out upon the earth like water."
>
> Dt. 12:20-24

> "You shall be holy men to me, and meat in the field that is torn you shall not eat, you shall toss it to the dogs."
>
> Ex. 22:30

> "You shall not eat any carrion. You will give it to the stranger that is within your gates and he may eat it, or you may sell it to a gentile, for you are a people holy to the Lord your God. You shall not boil a lamb in its mother's milk."
>
> Dt. 14:21

> "An ox or a sheep — it and its offspring you shall not slaughter on the same day."
>
> Lev. 22:28

> "Any man also of the people of Israel or of the strangers that sojourn among you who takes in hunting any beast or bird that may be eaten shall pour out its blood and cover it with dust, for the life of

every creature is the blood of it. Therefore, I have said to the people
of Israel, you shall not eat the blood of any creature, for the life of
every creature is its blood; whoever eats of it shall be cut off."

Lev. 17:13-14

"Therefore, to this day the Israelites do not eat the sinew of
the hip that is upon the hollow of the thigh, because he touched the
hollow of Jacob's thigh on the sinew of the hip."

Gen. 32:33

"This shall be the priests' due from the people, from those
offering a sacrifice, whether it be ox or sheep: they shall give to the
priest the shoulder and the two cheeks and the stomach."

Dt. 18:3

"If you chance to come upon a bird's nest in any tree or on
the ground with young ones or eggs and the mother sitting upon the
young or upon the eggs, you shall not take the mother with the young;
you shall let the mother go, but the young you may take to yourself,
that it may go well with you and that you may live long."

Dt. 22:6-7

What is it that the Halakhah makes of these several rules about meat-preparation in the household? We now examine in detail the answer to that question. Here, the paramount source of energy is the generic hermeneutics of the Halakhah, joined with the corpus of Scripture's facts.

III. THE EXPOSITION OF THE COMPONENTS OF THE GIVEN CATEGORY-FORMATION BY THE MISHNAH-TOSEFTA-YERUSHALMI-BAVLI

I. RULES OF SLAUGHTERING UNCONSECRATED ANIMALS FOR USE AT HOME OR IN THE TEMPLE

A. *GENERAL RULES OF SLAUGHTER*

M. 1:1 (1) All slaughter, (2) and their act of slaughter is valid, except for a deaf-mute, an imbecile, and a minor lest they impair [the fitness of the carcass] through their act of slaughter. But all of them who performed an act of slaughter, with others watching them — their act of slaughter is valid. The act of slaughter of a gentile [produces] carrion. And it [the meat] imparts uncleanness through being carried. He who slaughters at night — and so too a blind person who slaughtered — his act of slaughter is valid. He who slaughters on the Sabbath or on the Day of Atonement, even though he [thereby] becomes liable for his life — his act of slaughter is valid.

T. 1:1 All are valid to [carry out an act of] slaughter [M. Hul. 1:1A], even a Samaritan, even an uncircumcised man, and even an Israelite apostate. The act of slaughter done by a min[4] is [deemed to be for the purpose of] idolatry. And the act of slaughter done by a gentile, Lo, this is invalid. And the act of slaughter done by an ape, Lo, this is invalid, as it is said, "And you shall slaughter . . . and you shall eat" [Deut. 12:2 1] — not that which the gentile slaughters, nor that which an ape slaughters, nor that which is slaughtered on its own [accidentally].

T. 1:2 An Israelite who slaughtered, and [the act of] slaughter [of whom] a gentile finished [by cutting further than is required] — his act of slaughtering is invalid. [If] he slaughtered in it [the animal] two or the greater part of two [organs of the throat], his act of slaughtering is valid. A gentile who slaughtered, and [the act of] slaughtering [of whom] an Israelite finished [by cutting further than is required] — his act of slaughtering is invalid. [If] he [the gentile] slaughtered in it something which does not render it *terefah*, and an Israelite came and completed it [the act of slaughter], it is permitted for eating.

T. 1:3 A. An Israelite and a gentile who were holding a knife and slaughtering, even [if] the hand of one was above and that of the other was below — their act of slaughtering is valid [M. Hul. 1:1D]. And so a blind person who knows how to slaughter — his act of slaughter is valid [M. Hul. 1:1H]. A minor who knows how to slaughter — his act of slaughter is valid [M. Hul. 1:1B, D].

B. 1:1 I.5/3B [MEAT FROM AN ANIMAL] SLAUGHTERED BY A SAMARITAN IS PERMITTED. IN WHAT CIRCUMSTANCE? IF AN ISRAELITE WAS STANDING OVER HIM [TO SUPERVISE]. BUT IF ONE CAME AND FOUND THAT HE DID SLAUGHTER, THEY CUT OFF AN OLIVE'S BULK OF MEAT AND OFFER IT TO HIM. IF HE EATS IT, THEN OTHERS ARE PERMITTED TO EAT FROM [ANIMALS] HE SLAUGHTERED. AND IF HE DOES NOT [EAT IT], THEN OTHERS ARE FORBIDDEN TO EAT FROM [ANIMALS] HE SLAUGHTERED. SIMILARLY, IF ONE FOUND IN HIS POSSESSION A BASKET OF BIRDS [THAT WERE SLAUGHTERED] HE CUTS OFF THE HEAD OF ONE OF THEM AND GIVES IT TO HIM. IF HE EATS IT, THEN OTHERS ARE PERMITTED TO EAT FROM [ANIMALS] HE SLAUGHTERED. AND IF HE DOES NOT [EAT IT], THEN OTHERS ARE FORBIDDEN TO EAT FROM [ANIMALS] HE SLAUGHTERED.

B. 1:1 I.14 THE KNIFE OF AN IDOLATER — IT IS PERMITTED TO SLAUGHTER WITH IT BUT IT IS FORBIDDEN TO CUT MEAT WITH IT. IT IS PERMITTED TO SLAUGHTER WITH IT BECAUSE [TECHNICALLY SPEAKING] HE DIMINISHES [THE

---

[4] I leave "min" untranslated for the most part. In some contexts it clearly stands for an idolater, in others for an Israelite sectarian or heretic.

VALUE OF THE ANIMAL THROUGH ITS SLAUGHTER. IT CAN NO LONGER BE USED FOR BREEDING OR WORK]. IT IS FORBIDDEN TO CUT MEAT WITH IT BECAUSE [THEREBY] HE ENHANCES [THE VALUE OF THE ANIMAL BY PREPARING IT FOR CONSUMPTION AND THIS IS DEEMED TO BE A FORBIDDEN BENEFIT DERIVED FROM A UTENSIL BELONGING TO IDOLATRY].

M. 1:2 He who slaughters with [the smooth edge of] a hand sickle, with a flint, or with a reed — his act of slaughtering is valid. All slaughter. And at any time do they slaughter. And with anything do they slaughter, except for (1) a scythe, and (2) a saw, and (3) teeth, and (4) a fingernail, because they [do not cut but tear the windpipe and] choke [the animal]. He who slaughters with a scythe, [drawing the scythe] forward — it is valid. And if they filed down its teeth, Lo, it is equivalent to a knife.

T. 1:4 At any time do they slaughter [M. Hul. 1:2D] — whether by day or by night. [And in any place do they slaughter —] whether on a ship or whether on a roof.

T. 1:5 With anything do they slaughter [M. Hul. 1:2B] — even with a flint, even with glass, even with the point of a reed. With anything do they slaughter — whether it is something joined to the ground or detached from the ground, whether one passed the knife over the throat or passed the throat over the knife, and one thereby slaughtered, [the beast] his act of slaughter is valid.

T. 1:6 He who holds [the animal for] the gentile, so that he [the gentile] slaughtered — his act of slaughter is valid [M. Hul. 1:1E]. A tooth which is detached and a fingernail which is detached — they slaughter therewith [M. Hul. 1:2E3, 4].

T. 1:7 [If] one stuck the knife into the waterwheel and slaughtered with it his act of slaughter is invalid. A knife which has many notches is deemed to be equivalent to a saw. If there is between one notch and another a space equivalent to the space between two organs of the throat, his act of slaughtering is valid. [If] there is only a single notch, if it catches and slaughters, it is valid. If it chokes, it is invalid [M. Hul. 1:2E, G].

M. 1:3 He who slaughters [by cutting] through the [top cartilage] ring [of the windpipe] and left in it a thread's breadth of its whole circumference [towards the head], his act of slaughter is valid.

T. 1:8 [If] one tossed the knife or the dagger and slaughtered [thereby] his act of slaughtering is valid

M. 1:4 He who slaughters [an animal by cutting] at the sides [of the throat] — his act of slaughter is valid. He who wrings off [the neck of a bird with his fingernail for sacrificial purposes, M. Zeb. 6:4] at the sides [of the throat] — his act of wringing the neck is invalid. He who slaughters [by cutting] at the back [of the neck] — his act of slaughter is invalid. He who wrings the neck [of a bird] at the back [of the neck] — his act of wringing the neck is valid [Lev. 5:8]. He who slaughters [by cutting] at [the front of] the throat — his act of slaughter is valid. He who wrings the neck at [the front of] the throat — his act of wringing the neck is invalid. For the whole back of the neck is valid for wringing the neck, and the whole [region about] the throat is valid for slaughtering. It turns out that what is valid for slaughtering is invalid for wringing the neck, what is valid for wringing the neck is invalid for slaughtering.

T. 1:9 The requirement of [the act of] slaughter [is to] draw the knife forward and backward. [If] one drew it forward but not backward, or [if] one drew it backward but not forward, it is valid. [And this is] on condition that the knife be sufficiently long to allow for drawing forward and backward. If one drew the knife forward and backward, even though the knife is not sufficiently long to cover two organs in the throat, his act of slaughter is valid [M. Hul. 2:3A].

T. 1:10 The requirement of slaughtering [is to cut] from the ring to the lungs. [If] it slants downwards [that is], if one let the knife slide beyond the space prescribed for cutting, so that the windpipe was cut at or below the point where the thyroid cartilage narrows, it is invalid. [If] one left in it so much as a thread the size of a hair near the top — [if it extends] around the whole circumference, it is valid.

T. 1:11 The whole [region of the] throat is valid for slaughtering [M. Hul. 1:4L]. [If] one slaughtered it below, the slaughtering of the animal is valid. [If one did so] at the top, at the sides, his act of slaughtering is invalid. And the whole [area] at the back is valid for wringing the neck. [If] one wrung the neck above [at the back], his act of wringing the neck is valid. [If one did so] at the sides or at the bottom, his act of wringing the neck is invalid.

T. 1:12 Slaughtering is [done] with a utensil, wringing the neck by hand. You turn out to rule: That which is valid in wringing the neck is invalid in slaughtering. That which is valid in slaughtering is invalid in wringing the neck [M. Hul. 1:4M].

T. 1:13 The slaughtering of fowl inside [the court] is invalid. The wringing of the neck [of fowl] inside is valid. The wringing of the neck of fowl outside is invalid, and slaughtering [of fowl] outside is valid. You turn out to rule: The place which is valid for slaughtering is invalid for wringing the neck. The place which is valid for wringing the neck is invalid for slaughtering.

M. 1:5 That which is valid in the case of turtledoves is invalid in the case of pigeons. What is valid in the case of pigeons is invalid in the case of turtledoves. The beginning of the brightening [of the neck feathers like gold] in both this one and that one is invalid.

T. 1:14 The blood of a sin-offering of cattle is sprinkled above the red line of the altar, and the blood of all [other] sacrifices is sprinkled below the red line. You turn out to rule: That which is valid [as to the sprinkling of blood] in the case of a sin-offering is invalid in the case of all [other] animal sacrifices. That which is valid in the case of all [other] animal sacrifices is invalid in the case of a sin-offering. What is valid for the outer altar is invalid for the inner altar. What is valid for the inner altar is invalid for the outer altar. What is valid in the case of rams is invalid in the case of lambs. What is valid in the case of lambs is invalid in the case of rams. The *palgas* in both cases is invalid [M. Par. 1:3]. What is valid in the case of the red cow is invalid in the case of the heifer [whose neck is to be broken]. What is valid in the case of the heifer whose neck is to be broken] is invalid in the case of the red cow. An [extraneous act of] labor invalidates in the case of both.

T. 1:15 Pigeons, once they have grown old enough to sip, or until the beginning of the brightening [of the neck feathers], [are valid]. [M. Hul. 1:5C] Turtle-doves, once they have flown, even if they are old, [are valid]. You turn out to rule: That which is valid in the case of turtle-doves is invalid in the case of pigeons. What is valid in the case of pigeons is invalid in the case of turtle-doves [M. Hul. 1:5A-B].

M. 1:6 What is valid [as a mode of killing] in the case of the [red] cow is invalid in the case of the calf [whose neck is to be broken]. What is valid in the case of the calf is invalid in the case of the cow. What is valid in the case of priests is invalid in the case of Levites. What is valid in the case of Levites is invalid in the case of priests. What is clean [insusceptible to uncleanness] in the case of clay utensils is unclean [susceptible] in the case of all [other] utensils. What is clean in the case of all [other utensils] is unclean in the case of the clay utensils. What is clean in the case of wooden utensils is unclean in the case of metal utensils. What is clean in the case of metal utensils is unclean in the case of wooden utensils. What is liable [for tithes] in the case of bitter almonds is exempt [from tithes] in the case of sweet [almonds]. What is liable in the case of sweet ones is exempt in the case of bitter ones.

T. 1:16 Priests, when they will produce two pubic hairs, and even if they are old, are valid. But a blemish invalidates them. Levites from the age of thirty to the age of fifty are valid. But the blemish does not invalidate them. You turn out to rule: What is valid for priests is invalid for Levites. What is valid for Levites is invalid for priests [M. Hul. 1:6C-D]. Under what circumstances? In the case of the Tent Meeting in the wilderness. But in the case of the Eternal House, Levites are invalidated only by reason of [having a poor] voice.

T. 1:17 What is valid for a high priest is invalid for an ordinary priest. What is valid for an ordinary priest is invalid for a high priest. What is valid for golden garments is invalid for white garments. What is valid for white garments is invalid for golden garments.

T. 1:18 A lampstand is suitable only when made from a gold bar. If one made it from filings, it is invalid. [If one made it] from other kinds of metal, it is valid.

T. 1:19 A trumpet is valid only when made from silver [bar]. [If] one made it from filings, it is valid. [If one made it] from other kinds of metal, it is invalid. You turn out to rule: What is valid in the case of a lampstand is invalid in the case of a trumpet. What is valid in the case of a trumpet is invalid in the case of a lampstand.

T. 1:20 The contained airspace of a clay utensil is susceptible to uncleanness, but its outer side is insusceptible to uncleanness. The contained airspace of all [other] utensils is insusceptible. But its outer side is susceptible. You turn out to rule: What is insusceptible in the case of clay utensil is susceptible in the case of all utensils. What is insusceptible in the case of all utensils is susceptible in the case of a clay utensil [M. Hul. 1:6E-F].

T. 1:21 Flat wooden utensils are insusceptible, and when in incomplete form, they are susceptible. Flat metal utensils are susceptible, but when in incomplete form, they are insusceptible. You turn out to rule: What is insusceptible in the case of wooden utensils is susceptible in the case of metal utensils. What is insusceptible in the case of metal utensils is susceptible in the case of wooden utensils [M. Hul. 1:6G].

T. 1:22 He who brings chests and ovens, bowls and clay utensils from abroad to the Land, [if this is] before they have been fired — they are susceptible because of deriving from the land of the gentiles, but are insusceptible as clay utensils. [If this is] after they have been fired, they are susceptible as clay utensils, but insusceptible by reason of deriving from the land of the gentiles. You turn out to rule: When they are susceptible by reason of deriving from the land of the gentiles, they are insusceptible as a clay utensil. And when they are susceptible as a clay utensil, they are insusceptible by reason of deriving from the land of the gentiles.

T. 1:23 What is susceptible when it is dry is insusceptible when it is moist. Seeds are susceptible when in moist state and insusceptible when they are dry. You turn out to rule: What is insusceptible in dry state is susceptible in moist state. What is insusceptible in moist state is susceptible in dry state.

T. 1:24 Small bitter almonds are liable [to tithes], but large ones are exempt. And large sweet [almonds] are liable [to tithes], but small ones are exempt. You turn out to rule: What is liable in the case of bitter almonds is exempt in the case of sweet ones. What is liable in the case of sweet ones is exempt in the case of bitter ones [M. Hul. 1:61-J].

T. 1:25 What is valid in the case of a writ of divorce is invalid in the case of a prosbul. What is valid in the case of a prosbol is invalid in the case of a write of divorce. What is valid in the case of an [ordinary] woman is invalid in the case of a Levirate wife. What is valid in the case of a Levirate wife is invalid in the case of an [ordinary] woman. What is valid in the case of a divorcée is invalid in the case of a halusah. What is valid in the case of a halusah is invalid in the case of a divorcee.

B. 1:6A-B I.1/23B OUR RABBIS TAUGHT ON TANNAITE AUTHORITY: A [RED] COW KILLED BY SLAUGHTERING IS VALID; KILLED BY BREAKING THE NECK IS INVALID. A CALF KILLED BY BREAKING THE NECK IS VALID; KILLED BY SLAUGHTERING IS INVALID. WE FIND THAT, WHAT IS VALID [AS A MODE OF KILLING] IN THE CASE OF THE [RED] COW IS INVALID IN THE CASE OF THE CALF [WHOSE NECK IS TO BE BROKEN]. WHAT IS VALID IN THE CASE OF THE CALF IS INVALID IN THE CASE OF THE COW.

M. 1:7 Grape skin wine: before it has fermented, it is not purchased with funds deriving from [second] tithe and invalidates the immersion pool. After it has fermented, it is purchased with funds deriving from tithe and does not invalidate the immersion pool. Brothers who are partners: when they are liable to surcharge, they are exempt from tithe of cattle. When they are liable to tithe of cattle, they are exempt from surcharge. In any situation in which there is a right of sale, there is no fine. And in any situation in which there is a fine, there is no right of sale. In any situation in which there is a right of refusal, there is no *halisah*. And in any situation in which there is *halisah*, there is no right of refusal. In any situation in which there is a sounding [of the *Shofar*], there is no *habdalah* (i.e., prayer of separation). And in any situation in which there is *habdalah*, there is no sounding [of the *Shofar*]. A festival which coincided with Friday [the eve of the Sabbath] — they sound the *Shofar,* and they do not say *habdalah.* And [a festival which coincided with] Sunday [the day after Sabbath] they say *habdalah* and they do not sound [the *Shofar*]. How do they say *habdalah*? "Who distinguishes between one holy [season] and [another] holy [season]."

T. 1:26 In any situation in which there is a sounding [of the Shofar] there is no habdalah. And in any situation in which there is habdalah, there is no sounding of the Shofar. On a festival which coincides with Friday, they sound the Shofar and they do not say habdalah. On one which coincides with Sunday, they say habdalah and they do not sound the Shofar [M. Hul. 1:71-1]. How does one sound [the Shofar]? One plain [unbroken] one, and one does not sound the teru'ah-[notes].

No more striking contrast between the Halakhic category-formation, slaughter of animals for the altar, and the one at hand can be drawn than the one before us. Only priests can validly slaughter at the altar, here, nearly anyone. The rite is done by day, here, by night as well. The Toseftan refinements, e.g., an Israelite starts, a gentile finishes, remain well within the defined limits of the category-formation. The mode of slaughtering, a bird for the altar is contrasted with that for the domestic table, M. 1:4. Here, the Tosefta's formulation, T. 1:9-10 to M. 1:4, states matters in more general terms. The contrasts drawn from M. 1:5-7 represent a different mode of framing category-formations than the topical one that predominates in the Halakhah. But as we examine the Toseftan complement, we see how totally the second document of the Halakhah depends upon the first for its category-formation. It rarely recasts matters within a theory of its own of how data should be chosen and interpreted.

B. SPECIFIC REGULATIONS. TEREFAH-RULES

M. 2:1 He who slaughters [cuts] one [organ, either the windpipe or the gullet] in the case of fowl, or two [both the windpipe and the gullet] in the case of a beast — his act of slaughter is valid. And the greater part of one [of the organs] is equivalent to [the whole of] it. [He who cuts through] half of one [organ] in the case of fowl and one and a half [organs] in the case of a beast — his act of slaughter is invalid. [He who cuts through] the greater part of one [organ] in the case of fowl or the greater part of two [organs] in the case of a beast — his act of slaughter is valid.

T. 2:1 He who slaughters [cuts through] two halves [of the principal organs of the throat] in the case of fowl — his act of slaughter is invalid [M. Hul. 2:1B]. [And] it is not necessary to state, two halves in the case of a beast. [If one cut through] one [organ] or the greater part of one [organ] in the case of fowl, even though he delayed [completing the act of slaughter] for a very long time, his act of slaughter is valid [M. Hul. 2:1E].

M. 2:2 He who slaughters [cuts through] two heads [of cattle] simultaneously — his act of slaughter is valid. [If] two people hold the knife and effect an act of slaughter [of a single beast], even if [one holds the knife at] the upper [end], and one at the lower, their act of slaughter is valid.

T. 2.4 [If] one slaughtered [cut through] the gullet and afterward the windpipe was detached, his act of slaughter is valid. [If] the windpipe was detached and afterward one slaughtered [cut through] the gullet, his act of slaughter is invalid. [If] one slaughtered [cut through] the gullet and the windpipe turned out to be detached, [if further,] it is a matter of doubt [whether this took place] before the act of slaughter or after the act of slaughter — this was a case, and they came and asked sages, who ruled: Any matter of doubt in connection with an act of slaughter leads to a decision of invalidation.

M. 2:3 [If] one chopped off the head with a single stroke, it is invalid. [If] one was engaged in the act of slaughter and chopped off the head with a single stroke, if the knife is [as long again as] the width of the neck, it is valid. [If] one was engaged in the act of slaughter and chopped off two heads simultaneously, if the knife was [as long again as] the width of the neck of one [of them], it is valid. Under what circumstances? When [the slaughterer moved the knife] forward but not backward, or backward but not forward. But if he moved it forward and backward, however short [the knife], even with a scalpel, it is valid. [If] the knife fell and effected the act of slaughter, even if it effected the act of slaughter properly, it is invalid. As it is said, "And you will slaughter...and you will eat..." [Deut. 12:21] — just as *you* effect the act of slaughter, so do *you* eat. [If] the knife fell and one raised it up, [or] if his clothing fell and he picked them up, [or if] he was whetting the knife, [or if] he became weary, [and he ,therefore, interrupted the act of slaughter], and his fellow came and [completed the act of] slaughter — if the delay was sufficient for an act of slaughter [cutting of two organs], it is invalid.

T. 2:3 [If] one was slaughtering and chopped off the head in a single stroke [M. Hul. 2:3B] — if he intended to do so, his act of slaughter is invalid. And if not, his act of slaughter is valid.

T. 2:6 He who finds a slaughtered chicken in the market place, and so too: he who gave his chicken to someone in the market place for slaughter and does not know the character of the person [to whom he gave it] — they follow the status of the majority [of slaughterers in the market place].

T. 2:7 [If] a knife fell and slaughtered it [an animal] [M. Hul. 2:3L], or pressed down on it and slaughtered it, or [if] it was butchered on its own — it is carrion [M. Hul. 2:4A-E]. And it imparts uncleanness through carriage [to the one who carries it].

T. 2:8 [If] one was engaged in an act of slaughter and trembled, or grew tired, or [if] his fellow pushed him, or [if] the wind pushed him, or [if] the knife fell from his hand and he picked it up [M. Hul. 2: 3Q], or [if] the corner of his garment fell and he picked it up [M . Hul. 2:3R], and [in doing any of these things] he interrupted [the act of slaughter] for a time sufficient to perform another act of slaughter, it [the act of slaughter] is invalid [M. Hul. 2:3U-V].

M. 2:4 [If] one slaughtered [cut through] the gullet and tore open the windpipe, or slaughtered [cut through] the windpipe and [afterward] tore open the gullet, or slaughtered [cut through] one of them and waited until [the animal] died, or [after properly cutting one organ], thrust the knife into the second [of the organs] and tore it [from below to above], it is carrion. Whatever is invalidated while it is being slaughtered is deemed carrion. Whatever is subject to an act of slaughter which is proper, but which some other matter caused to be invalidated, is *terefah*.

T. 2:10 [If] one slaughtered [cut through] the smaller part of the gullet and interrupted [the act of slaughter] for sufficient time for an [other] act of slaughter [M. Hul. 2:3T-V], and afterward slaughtered [cut through] both of them, or [if] the gullet was perforated and afterward one slaughtered [cut through] both of them [the principal organs], it is *terefah* [M. Hul. 2:4E]. And the act of slaughtering it renders it insusceptible to uncleanness [M. Hul. 2:5E].

M. 2:5 He who slaughters a beast, a wild animal, or fowl, from which blood did not exude — they are valid. And they are eaten with [hygienically] dirty hands, because they have not been made susceptible to uncleanness by blood.

T. 2:12 [If] it put forth its foreleg and did not withdraw it, it is invalid, for [this is] only la token of 1, its expiring alone [M. Hul. 2:6J-K]. And in the case of the hind-leg: [if] it put it forth but did not withdraw it, [or] withdrew it but did not put it forth, it is valid. Under what circumstances? In the case of a small beast [M. Hul. 2:6], but in the case of a large beast, whether in the case of the fore-leg or the hind-leg, [if] it put it forth and did not bring it back, or brought it back but did not put it forth, it is valid. Under what circumstances? In the case of a beast. But in the case of fowl, even if it jerked only the tip of the wing or the tip of the tail, it is valid.

As before, I see little of generative interest in the Halakhah of the act of slaughter. But the generic hermeneutics transforms the facts into problems, e.g., at M. 2:2-3.

C. *SLAUGHTER AND ILLICIT SACRIFICE*

M. 2:7 He who slaughters [a gentile's beast] on behalf of a gentile — his act of slaughter is valid.

T. 2:13 He who slaughters a beast [intending] to toss its blood for the purposes of idolatry and to burn its fat for the purposes of idolatry, Lo, this is meat of the sacrifices of corpses [M. Hul. 2:7C]. If after one slaughtered it, he tossed its blood for the purposes of idolatry or burned its fat for the purposes of idolatry, Lo, this was an actual case in Caesarea. So they came and asked sages, who did not rule either to prohibit or to permit [the meat].

T. 2.14 He who slaughters in the [Temple-] courtyard an unclean beast, wild beast, or bird — they are prohibited for any sort of gain, and, it is not necessary to say, for eating. [He who slaughters in the Temple-courtyard] a clean beast, wild beast, or bird — they are permitted for gain [but not for eating].

T. 2:15 He who slaughters [an animal for the purposes of] healing, for consumption by gentiles, or for consumption by dogs — it is prohibited for [use for any sort of] gain [M. Hul. 2:7A, C]. He who slaughters [an animal] and it turns out to be carrion on account of his act — and he who kills by stabbing, and he who tears loose the organs to be cut — [in the case of] an act of slaughter for a gentile — it is permitted for [use for some sort of] gain.

T. 2:20 Meat which is found in the possession of a gentile is permitted for gain. [If it is found] in the possession of a sectarian [min], it is prohibited for gain. That which goes forth from a pagan temple, Lo, it is deemed to be meat from the sacrifices of corpses. For they have stated, "The act of slaughter of a min [is routinely deemed to be for the purposes of] idolatry [M. Hul. 2:7E]." Their bread [is deemed] the bread of a Samaritan, and their wine is deemed wine used for idolatrous purposes, and their produce is deemed wholly untithed, and their books are deemed magical books, and their children are mamzerim.

M. 2:8 He who slaughters (1) for the sake of mountains, (2) for the sake of valleys, (3) for the sake of seas, (4) for the sake of rivers, (5) for the sake of deserts — his act of slaughter is invalid. [If] two take hold of a knife and perform an act of slaughter, one for the sake of any of the forenamed, and one for the sake of a valid purpose, their act of slaughter is invalid.

T. 2:18 He who slaughters for the sake of the sun, for the sake of the moon, for the sake of the stars, for the sake of the planets, for the sake of Michael, prince of the great host, and for the sake of the small *Shilshul* [sic!] — Lo, this is deemed to be flesh deriving from the sacrifices of corpses [M. Hul. 2:8A-B].

M. 2:9 They do not perform an act of slaughter [in such a way that the blood falls] either into seas, or into rivers, or into utensils. But one slaughters [so that the blood falls] into a dish filled with water, or, [when on board] a boat, on to the backs of utensils. They do not slaughter [in such a way that the blood falls] into a hole. But one makes a hole in his house, so that the blood will flow down into it. And in the market, one may not do so, so that one will not imitate the minim [in their ways].

T. 2:19 They do not perform an act of slaughter in such a way that the blood falls either into seas or into rivers [M. Hul. 2:9A]. But into turbid water [one may do so]. But one performs an act of slaughter in such a way that the blood falls into a dish of water, or, on a ship, on the sides of utensils [M. Hul. 2:9B-C]. And if one has no place on a ship [in which to perform the act of slaughter in the way just now prescribed], one performs the act of slaughter [so that the blood flows over the sides of the ship and then] into the sea. And if one does not want to make his house dirty, he performs an act of slaughter [so that the blood flows] into a utensil or into a hole [M. Hul. 2:9C, D]. But in the market one may not do so, because he [thereby] carries out [the act in accord with] the rules of minim [M. Hul. 2:9E]. And if he has done so, it requires examination.

M. 2:10 He who slaughters [an unconsecrated beast outside of the Temple] (1) for the sake of a burnt-offering, (2) for the sake of animal offerings, (3) for the sake of a suspended guilt-offering, (4) for the sake of a Passover-offering, (5) for the sake of a thank-offering — his act of slaughtering is invalid. Two hold onto a knife and perform an act of slaughter, one for the sake of one of all the forenamed items, and one for the sake of a valid purpose — their act of slaughter is invalid. He who slaughters [an unconsecrated beast outside of the Temple] (1) for the sake of a sin-offering, (2) for the sake of an unconditional guilt-offering, (3) for the sake of a firstling, (4) for the sake of tithe [of cattle], (5) for the sake of a substitute offering — his act of slaughter is valid. This is the general principle: As to anything which is [offered as fulfillment of] a vow or as a freewill offering, he who slaughters it for the sake of its own name — it is prohibited. But as to anything which is not [offered as fulfillment of] a vow or as a freewill offering — he who slaughters it for its name — it is valid.

T. 2:16 A. He who slaughters in the courtyard of women an unclean beast, wild beast, or bird [M. Hul. 2:10A] — they are permitted for eating, and it is not necessary to say, for any other sort of gain.

T. 2:25 He who slaughters [an unconsecrated beast outside of the Temple] for the sake of a burnt-offering, for the sake of peace-offerings, for the sake of a suspended guilt-offering, for the sake of a Passover, for the sake of a thankoffering — his act of slaughter is invalid.

T. 2:27 He who slaughters [an unconsecrated beast outside of the Temple for the sake of a sin-offering, for the sake of a guilt-offering, for the sake of a firstling, for the sake of tithe [of cattle, for the sake of a substitute-offering — his act of slaughter is valid [M. Hul. 2:10F-G]. This is the general principle: As to anything which is [offered as fulfillment of] a vow or as a freewill-offering — he who slaughters it for its own name — it is invalid. And as to anything which is not [offered as fulfillment of I, a vow or as a freewill-offering — he who slaughters it for its name — it is valid [M. Hul. 2:10H-J].

Israelites may slaughter beasts for gentiles, but intentionality enters in when gentiles' beasts are involved, so T. 2:13 to M. 2:7. The intention to kill the beast as an act of sacrifice to idolatry invalidates the meat, just as the counterpart intentionalities in the Temple invalidate the offering. M. 2:8 is explicit on that point. Slaughtering an unconsecrated beast outside of the Temple with the intentionality of designating it for an offering invalidates the beast as well. So among common Israelites, beyond the limits of the Temple, or when the Temple is no longer standing, intentionality still bears tangible, transformative consequences.

D. *TEREFAH- AND VALID CARCASSES*

M. 3:1 These are the *terefah* [carcasses] among cattle: (1) one in which the gullet is pierced, (2) and one in which the windpipe is torn. (3) [If] the membrane of the brain is pierced, (4) [if] the heart is pierced up to the cavity thereof; (5) [if] the backbone is broken so that the spinal cord is severed; (6) [if] the liver is removed [missing], so that nothing whatsoever remains of it. (7) The lung that is pierced or lacking [any part thereof]. (8) [If] the belly [abomasum] is pierced, (9) [if] the gallbladder is pierced, (10) [if] the intestines are pierced; (11) [if] the innermost belly [rumen] is pierced. (12) The greater part of the outer [exterior coating] which is pierced. (13) The omasum or the second stomach [reticulum] which are pierced on the outer side [exterior]. (14) [If] it fell from the roof, (15) [if] the greater number of its ribs are broken. And one which has been mauled by a wolf. This is the general principle: Any the like of which does not live is *terefah*.

T. 3:1 And these are the *terefah* [carcasses] among cattle: one in which the gullet is pierced, and the windpipe torn [M. Hul. 3:1A-B] — horizontally — Lo, this is invalid. [If] its backbone is broken and the greater part of the spinal cord is severed, it is invalid [M. Hul. 3:1C]. [If] the lung was crushed [and its membrane is not left] it is invalid. If the spinal cord was snapped, it is invalid.

T. 3:2 [If] the liver is missing, so that an insufficient amount remained of it to produce healing, it is invalid [M. Hul. 3:1C].

T. 3:3 One mauled by a wolf [M. Hul. 3: I-J] so far as the cavity is invalid. One mauled by a falcon so far as the cavity is invalid.

T. 3:4 [If] it fell from the roof [M. Hul. 3:1] and its limbs were crushed, if it remained alive for twenty-four hours and one slaughtered it, it is valid [M. Hul. 3:3E]. If it got up forthwith, one way or the other, it is valid.

M. 3:2 And these are the valid [carcasses] among cattle: [if] the windpipe is pierced or is slit [lengthwise] (2) [if] the skull is damaged, but the membrane of the brain is not pierced, [if] the heart is pierced, but not up to the empty space [cavity] thereof, [if] the backbone is broken, but the spinal cord is not severed, [if] the liver is removed, but an olive's bulk of it remains, the omasum or the second stomach [reticulum] that are pierced [so that the holes lead] one into the other, [if] the spleen is removed, [if] the kidneys are removed, [if] the lower jaw is removed, [if] the womb is removed. (11) And one [the lung] of it is dried naturally. (12) One that has lost its hide [having been flayed] — it is invalid.

T. 3:9 There are those sorts of fetuses which are invalid: one born at four months in the case of a small animal, and at eight in the case of a large one. [If] it was born with two backs and two backbones, since such as this cannot live, it is invalid.

T. 3:10 And these are the valid [carcasses] among cattle: one the windpipe of which is pierced of which is slit [M. Hul. 3:2A] lengthwise — Lo, this is valid. [If] the backbone is broken, but the greater part of the spinal cord is not severed [M. Hul. 3:2C4] — it is valid. [If] the liver is removed [M. Hul. 3:2CS] but a sufficient amount remains to bring about healing, it is valid. [If] the lung softened, but the membrane thereof remained, it is valid. If its womb was removed, it is valid [M. Hul. 3.2C10]. [If] its liver decayed, it is valid.

T. 3:11 A needle which is found in the thick wall of the reticulum [M. Hul. 3:2C6], when it protrudes from one side — it [the animal] is valid. [When it protrudes] on both sides, it is invalid. If there is in its place a coagulated drop of blood, one may be certain that [the needle was in place] before slaughter. [If] there is not in its place a coagulated drop of blood, one may be certain that [the needle was in place] after slaughter. [If] the surface of a wound formed a scab, one may be certain that [it was there] three days before slaughter. [If] the surface of a wound did not form a scab, [then] he who makes a claim against his fellow must bring proof [that the animal is invalid].

T. 3:12 And one [the lung of which] is dried naturally [M. Hul. 3:2D] is valid. What is [a lung which] has dried? Any [animal] whose lung is shrunk.

M. 3:3 And these are the *terefah* [carcasses] among fowl: (1) one the gullet of which is pierced, (2) one the windpipe of which is torn. (3) [If] the weasel pierced its head at a point which renders it *terefah*; (4) [if] the gizzard is pierced; (5) [if] the small intestines are pierced. (6) [If] it fell into the fire and the intestines were scorched — if they are green, they are invalid. If they are red, they are valid. (7) [If] one trampled it or knocked it against the wall, or [if] a beast trampled on it, and it flutters — if it remains alive for twenty-four hours, and one [then] slaughtered it, it is valid.

T. 3:13 There are among limbs those which are valid: A dangling limb in the case of a beast — [if] it is sufficient[ly connected so that] it can bring about healing [it is valid.] Dangling flesh on a beast — [if] it is sufficient[ly connected so that] it can bring about healing — [it is valid]. [If] the bone broke and protruded, but the greater part of the hide and flesh cover it, it is valid.

T. 3:14 There are those among fetuses which are valid: one born at the age of five months in the case of a small animal, and one born at nine months in the case of a large one. [If] they were born with three eyes or five legs, since such as these are capable of surviving, it is valid.

T. 3(4):15 And these are the *terefah*-[carcasses] among fowl. one the gullet of which is pierced and one the windpipe of which is torn [M. Hul. 3:3A] horizontally, Lo, this is invalid. [If] the weasel pierced its head at a point which renders it *terefah* [M. Hul. 3:3B], it is invalid. That is, a piercing of the brain in which the membrane thereof is pierced — it is invalid. [If it is] a piercing of the heart to the cavity thereof — it is invalid.

M. 3:4 And these are valid [carcasses] among fowl: (1) [if] the windpipe is pierced or severed [lengthwise], (2) [if] the weasel pierced its head at a point which does not render it *terefah*, (3) [if] the crop was pierced, (4) [if] the intestines protrude but are not pierced, (5) [if] its wings are broken, (6) [if] its legs are broken, (7) [if] its wing feathers are plucked.

T. 3(4):16 [If] it fell into the fire and the intestines were scorched [M . Hul. 3:3C], it is invalid. Which intestines did they mean? The stomachs, the liver, and the heart.

T. 3(4):17 These are valid [carcasses] among fowl, one the gullet of which is pierced, one the windpipe of which is torn [M. Hul. 3:4A] vertically — Lo, this is valid. [If] the weasel pierced its head at a point which does not render it *terefah* [M. Hul. 3:4B] — it is valid. [If] the heart is perforated, but not to the cavity, it is valid. [If] it fell from the roof and its limbs were crushed, or [ill its fellow ran] and crushed its limbs, and one slaughtered it forthwith, it is valid. [If] it survived for twenty-four hours, one way or the other, it is valid [M. Hul. 3:3E].

M. 3:5 (1) [A beast which suffers from] congestion of blood, (2) and one [which has suffered from] smoke, (3) and one [which has suffered from] cold, (4) and one which has eaten oleander, (5) and one which has eaten chicken shit, (6) or which has drunk dirty water is valid. [If] it ate deadly poison, or if a snake bit it, it is permitted [to eat it] in respect to [the laws of] *terefah*,

but it is prohibited as a danger to life.

T. 3(4):19 A beast which suffers from congestion of blood, and one [which has suffered from] smoke, and one [which has suffered from] cold. [If] one force-fed it asafoetida, root of crowfoot, oleander, deadly poison, [or] chicken-shit — it is valid. One bitten by a snake, or bitten by a rabid dog in respect to *terefah* is permitted, but is prohibited as a danger to life [M. Hul. 3:5C]. A token that an animal is *terefah* is any which does not produce offspring.

M. 3:6 The tokens [by which we know whether or not animals are deemed clean or fit] of cattle and wild beasts have been stated by the Torah [cf. Lev. 11:3]. "Any fowl that seizes is unclean. Any [fowl] that has an extra talon [the hallux] and a craw, and the skin of the stomach of which [can] be stripped off is clean."

T. 3:6 [If] its femur slipped from the socket, below — it is valid. [If its femur slipped] from the socket, above — it is invalid. [If] the bone broke and the juncture of the thigh-sinews is removed, it is invalid [M. Hul. 4:6]. One, [the lung of which] is dried by man [M. Hul. 3:2D] is invalid.

T. 3:8 There are among the limbs those which are invalid, a dangling limb on a beast [which] is not [so connected] as to bring about healing; dangling flesh on a beast [which] is not [so connected] as to bring about healing. [If] the bone broke and protruded outside, so that the larger part of the hide and flesh do not cover it — how does one proceed? He removes it and tosses it out, and the rest, Lo, this is permitted.

T. 3(4):20 These are the tokens of cattle [by which] we know whether or not animals are deemed blemished [M. Hul. 3:6A]: Whatever parts the hoof and is cloven footed and chews the cud among animals you may eat [Lev. 11:3]. Whatever chews the cud has no upper teeth. What is the sort of ox, the horns of which are similar to its cloven hooves? This is the heifer of the first man, as it is said. This will please the Lord more than an ox or a bull with horns and hooves [Ps. 69:31]. 3(4):21 A. What are the tokens [by which] we know whether an animal is a wild beast? Any which has horns and hooves.

T. 3(4):24 They purchase eggs from any source and do not scruple lest they are of carrion- or *terefah*-birds. They do not sell eggs of carrion-birds [or] of *terefah*-birds to a gentile unless they were cracked open into a dish. Therefore, they said, "They do not purchase from a gentile eggs which are cracked open into a dish."

B. 3:6 II.12/64A THESE ARE THE TOKENS [OF CLEANNESS] FOR EGGS: ANY [EGG] THAT IS ARCHED AND ROUNDED, [THAT IS] WITH ONE END BROAD AND ONE END NARROW, IS CLEAN. [ANY EGGS THAT HAVE] BOTH ENDS BROAD OR BOTH ENDS NARROW ARE UNCLEAN. [ANY EGG]

WITH THE WHITE ON THE OUTSIDE AND THE YOLK ON THE INSIDE, IS CLEAN. [ANY EGG] WITH THE YOLK ON THE OUTSIDE AND THE WHITE ON THE INSIDE, IS UNCLEAN. [T. HAS THIS VERSION: ANY [EGG] THAT IS ARCHED (ON TOP, NOT POINTED) AND ROUNDED, ONE MAY BE CERTAIN, DERIVES FROM AN UNCLEAN BIRD, AND ANY THAT IS NOT ARCHED AND ROUNDED, ONE MAY BE CERTAIN, DERIVES FROM A CLEAN BIRD [T. 3:23 C].

M. 3:7 And among locusts: Any that has (1) four legs, (2) four wings, and (3) jointed legs [Lev. 11:21], and (4) the wings of which cover the greater part of its body. And among fish: Any that has fins and scales. And what are scales? Those that are immovable. And fins? Those with which it swims [but not propelling itself on dry land with them].

The exposition of the category, terefah-carcasses, that is, "any the like of which does not live," is taken up with inert facts. If there is an initiative provoked by the generic hermeneutics, I do not discern it.

E. *THE AFFECT OF VALID SLAUGHTER ON THE PARTS OF A BEAST'S BODY, E.G., ON THE FOETUS*

M. 4:1 A beast that was in hard labor, and its offspring put its hoof out and withdrew it — [when the dam is properly slaughtered], it [the offspring] is permitted to be eaten. [Not being deemed born, it is not a living beast that itself must be slaughtered before being eaten.] [If] it put forth its head, even though it withdrew it, Lo, this is [deemed] as fully born. [If] one cuts off part of the offspring that is in its womb — it [what is cut off] is permitted to be eaten. [If he cut off] part of the spleen or kidneys [of the beast itself], it is prohibited to be eaten. This is the general principle: Something that is part of its [the dam's] body is prohibited [as a limb cut from a living beast]. Something that is not part of its body is permitted.

T. 4(5):1 A beast which was in hard labor, land the offspring [of which] put its head out and withdrew it [M. Hul. 4:1A, C], and which he afterward slaughtered — [if] he slaughtered it [the dam] and afterward it [the offspring] withdrew it [the head] — it is forbidden. [If] he chopped it [the head] off and afterward slaughtered it [the dam], it [the dam] is permitted to be eaten, but the offspring is prohibited. [If] it put forth its head and the greater part of the body, Lo, this is as if it were fully born [M. Hul. 4:1C]. [If] it put forth its hand and he chopped it off, and afterward he slaughtered it, that which has gone forth is prohibited [delete: unclean]. But that which is inside, is permitted.

T. 4(5):2 A strict rule applies to limbs which does not apply to offspring, and [a strict rule applies] to offspring which does not apply to limbs. For [if] the offspring put forth its head and withdrew it, it is prohibited. [If] it put forth its hoof and withdrew it, it is permitted. A strict rule applies to limbs, for he who cuts off the offspring in the belly of its dam — it is permitted to be eaten. [If he cut off] part of the spleen and kidneys, it is prohibited to be eaten [M. Hul. 4:1F].

T. 4(5):3 A beast which was in hard labor and the offspring [of which put forth its hoof and withdrew it, and which one afterward slaughtered — the hoof is permitted [M. Hul. 4:1A-B]. [If] he slaughtered it and afterward it withdrew [the hoof], it is prohibited. [If] he cut it off and afterward slaughtered it, that which it put forth is prohibited. But that which is inside is permitted. [If] he slaughtered it and afterward cut it off, that which it put forth is prohibited and unclean. And that which is inside is permitted.

M. 4:2 A beast producing its firstborn that is in hard labor — one cuts off the limbs [of the offspring] one by one and throws them to the dogs. [If] the greater part of it came forth, Lo, this is to be buried. And it [beast] is free of [the law of] the firstling.

M. 4:3 A beast, the foetus of which died in its womb, and [that foetus] the shepherd put in his hand and touched — whether in the case of an unclean beast or a clean beast — he is clean. The woman whose foetus died in her womb, whose [foetus] the midwife put in her [the midwife's] hand and touched — the midwife is unclean with a seven-day uncleanness, and the woman is clean until the foetus will emerge.

M. 4:4 A beast that is in hard labor, and the young put forth its hoof [and] that one cut off, and afterward one slaughtered its dam — [the hoof is unclean as carrion but] the meat [of the offspring in the womb] is clean. [If] he slaughtered its mother and afterward cut it off, it is in the status of that which [has touched] *terefah* that has been slaughtered.

M. 4:5 He who slaughters a beast and found in it an eight-months' birth, living or dead, or a dead nine-months' birth, tears it out and removes its blood. [If] he found a live nine-months' birth, the slaughtering of its mother renders it clean. [If] one cut [into a beast] and found in it a living nine-months' birth, it requires slaughtering, because its mother has not been slaughtered.

M. 4:6 A beast, the [hind] legs of which are cut off below the knee, is valid. [If they are cut off] above the knee, it is invalid. And so [if] the juncture of the thigh sinews was removed [it is invalid]. [If] the bone broke [but was not cut off], if most of the meat remains, slaughtering it renders it [the broken leg] clean. And if not, slaughtering it does not render it clean [and the broken leg cannot be eaten, but the rest of the beast is valid].

M. 4:7 He who slaughters the beast and found in it an afterbirth — [slaughtering the mother renders it clean, so] a robust person will eat it. But it is subject to neither the uncleanness of foods nor [if the beast dies] the uncleanness of carrion. [If] he gave thought to it [for use as food], it imparts the uncleanness of foods [M. Uqsin 3:1], but not the uncleanness of carrion. An afterbirth, part of which emerged, is prohibited to be eaten. It is a token of [the birth of] an offspring in a woman, and the token of [the birth of] an offspring in a beast. A beast which, producing its first born, dropped an afterbirth — one should throw it to the dogs. And in the case of Holy Things, it is to be buried. They do not bury it at the crossroads. And they do not hang it on a tree, because of [the prohibition against imitating] the ways of the Amorites.

T. 4(5):7 A beast which died, and which one tore open, and in which one found a live offspring nine months old — it requires slaughtering. And it is liable to [the priestly] gifts. But it is invalid for use on the altar, because it is an animal taken out [of the dead mother's womb].

T. 4(5):8 He who slaughters a *terefah*-animal and found in it a live nine-month-old birth — it requires slaughtering and is liable for [priestly] gifts. And if it died, it is clean of imparting uncleanness through carriage, because the slaughter of its dam renders it clean. He who slaughters the sin-offering and found in it a live offspring four months old — even after three days, and even if it went forth beyond the veils — it is permitted to be eaten.

T. 4(5):9 A beast producing its first-born which dropped an afterbirth — one should throw it to the dogs. And in the case of Holy Things, it should be buried [M. Hul. 4:7G-I], because it grew in a state of sanctity. An afterbirth [subjected to improper intention] does not render the sacrifice, refuse either with respect to [intention to] eat it outside of the proper time or with respect to offer it up outside of the proper place. Improper intention does not invalidate it because of refuse. And he who offers it up outside is free of liability to punishment.

Now the matter of interstitiality produces a variety of problems of special interest by reason of the complex of classifications that pertain here. At what point has the offspring become a fully-autonomous entity, subject to a proper act of slaughter, M. 4:1, 3. So to T. 4(5):2 compares and contrasts the offspring to the limb of the beast, each with its own indicative traits awaiting hierarchization.

II. OTHER RULES GOVERNING THE PREPARATION OF FOOD, PRINCIPALLY FOR USE AT HOME

A. *NOT SLAUGHTERING "IT AND ITS YOUNG" (LEV. 22:28)*

M. 5:1 [The prohibition against slaughtering on the same day] "it and its young" [Lev. 22:28] applies (1) in the Land and outside the Land, (2) in the time of the Temple and not in the time of the Temple, (3) in the case of unconsecrated beasts and in the case of consecrated beasts. How so? He who slaughters it and its offspring, (1) which are unconsecrated, (2) outside [the Temple courtyard] —both of them are valid. And [for slaughtering] the second he incurs forty stripes. [He who slaughters] (1) Holy Things (2) outside — [for] the first is he liable to extirpation, and both of them are invalid, and [for] both of them he incurs forty stripes. [He who slaughters] (1) unconsecrated beasts (2) inside [the Temple courtyard] — both of them are invalid, and [for] the second he incurs forty stripes. [He who slaughters] (1) Holy Things (2) inside — the first is valid, and he is exempt [from any punishment], and [for] the second he incurs forty stripes, and it is invalid.

T. 5(6):1 [The prohibition against slaughtering on the same day] it and its offspring applies to hybrid animals and to the koy.

M. 5:2 [He who slaughters] (1) unconsecrated beasts and (2) Holy Things *outside* [the Temple courtyard], the first is valid, and he is free [on its account of the penalty of extirpation], and [for] the second he incurs forty stripes, and it is invalid. [He who slaughters] (1) Holy Things and (2) unconsecrated beasts *outside*, [for] the first he is liable to extirpation, and it is invalid. And the second is valid. And [for] both of them he incurs forty stripes. [He who slaughters] (1) unconsecrated beasts and (2) Holy Things *inside* [the Temple], both of them are invalid. And [for] the second he incurs forty stripes. [He who slaughters] (1) Holy Things and (2) unconsecrated beasts *inside*, the first is valid. And he is free [on its account of the penalty of extirpation]. And [for] the second he incurs forty stripes, and it is invalid. [He who slaughters] unconsecrated beasts (1) outside and (2) inside, the first is valid, and he is free [of the penalty of extirpation]. And [for the second] he incurs forty stripes, and it is invalid. [He who slaughters] Holy Things (1) outside and (2) inside, [for] the first he is liable to extirpation, and both of them are invalid. And [for] both of them he incurs forty stripes. [He who slaughters] unconsecrated beasts (1) inside and (2) outside, the first is invalid. And he is free [of the penalty of extirpation]. And [for] the second he incurs forty stripes. And it is valid. [He who slaughters] Holy Things (1) inside and (2) outside, the first is valid. And he is free [of the penalty of extirpation]. And [for] the second he incurs forty stripes, and it is invalid.

M. 5:3 (1) He who slaughters [a beast], and it turns out to be *terefah*, (2) he who slaughters a beast for idolatrous purpose, (3) and he who slaughters a cow [to be burned] for purification [water], and an ox which is to be stoned, and a heifer whose neck is to be broken [none of these is eaten] is liable. (1) He who slaughters [a beast], and it is made carrion by his own deed, (2) he who pierces [the windpipe], (3) and he who tears out [the windpipe] is exempt on account of violating the prohibition against slaughtering it and its offspring on one day. Two who purchased, [one] a cow, and [the other] its offspring — that one who purchased the first slaughters first. But if the second did it first, he has acquired the right [to do so]. [If] he slaughtered a cow and afterward its two offspring, he incurs eighty stripes. [If] he slaughtered its two offspring and afterward slaughtered it, he incurs forty stripes. [If] he slaughtered it, its daughter, its granddaughter, he incurs eighty stripes. [If] he slaughtered it and its granddaughter and afterward slaughtered its daughter, he incurs forty stripes.

T. 5(6):3 He who slaughters [a beast] and it is made carrion by his own deed, he who pierces the windpipe, and he who tears out the windpipe [M. Hul. 5:3F-H], and the act of slaughter of a gentile — it is permitted because of violating the prohibition against slaughtering it and its offspring.

T. 5(6):4 He who purchases an animal from a householder takes precedence over the householder [in the right to slaughter the animal], for to begin with, he purchased it only for that purpose.

T. 5(6):5 Two who purchased a cow and its offspring — the one who purchased first has the right to slaughter first. But if the second went ahead and slaughtered [his animal], Lo, this one is rewarded for his promptness [M. Hul. 5:3J-L].

T. 5(6):6 [If] one [on the same day] slaughtered it and its mother, even up to five generations [of the same family], he is liable only for one [violation of the prohibition]. [If] he slaughtered it and the daughter of its son and the daughter of its daughter, even for five generations, he is liable only for the last. [If] he slaughtered it and someone else came and slaughtered its mother, and someone else came and slaughtered its daughter, the latter two are liable. But the one in the middle is exempt. [If] he slaughtered it and afterward he slaughtered its five sons, he is liable because of violating the negative commandment five times.

T. 5(6):8 [If] he slaughtered it and afterward slaughtered its mother, he who slaughters the mother is liable, but [he who slaughters] the daughter is free. [If] he slaughtered it before it got dark, it is permitted to slaughter its [If he slaughtered it] after it got dark, it is prohibited to slaughter its daughter that entire day and night.

M. 5:4 At four seasons in the year does he who sells a beast to his fellow have to inform him, "Its mother did I sell for slaughter, its daughter did I sell for slaughter," and these are they: (1) On the eve of the last festival day of the Festival [of Sukkot;] (2) on the eve of the first festival day of Passover; (3) on the eve of Aseret [Shabuot], (4) and on the eve of the New Year. At these four seasons do they force the butcher to slaughter [an animal] against his will. Even if it was an ox worth a thousand denars, and the purchaser has only one denar, they force him to slaughter it. Therefore, if it dies, the loss is that of the customer. But on the rest of the days of the year, it is not so. Therefore, if it dies, the loss is that of the seller.

M. 5:5 [Concerning the phrase], "One day" which is stated in connection with "it and its young" [with regard to the law this means] the day [accords] with the preceding night.

Now, with reference to Scripture's repertoire of rules on meat-preparation, begins the patterned sequence — Land/outside, in time of Temple/not, in case of unconsecrated beasts +/- not — to which I made reference earlier. The amplification of the law not to slaughter the offspring on the same day as the mother now fully responds to the generic hermeneutics, e.g., M. 5:2's interest in polythetic classification. The usual clarifications of fact, M. 5:4, 5, follow at the end. The distinction between the particular and the generic hermeneutics alongside the designation of inert facts is handsomely illustrated.

B. *THE REQUIREMENT TO COVER UP THE BLOOD (LEV. 17:13-14)*

M. 6:1 [The requirement to] cover up the blood applies in the Land and abroad, (2) in the time of the Temple and not in the time of the Temple, (3) in the case of unconsecrated beasts, but not in the case of Holy Things. And it applies (4) to a wild beast and a bird, (5) to that which is captive and to that which is not captive. And it applies (6) to a *koy*, because it is a matter of doubt [whether it is wild or domesticated]. And they do not slaughter it [a *koy*] on the festival. But if one has slaughtered it, they do not cover up its blood.

T. 6:1 [The requirement to] cover up the blood applies to hybrids and to the koy [M. Hul. 6:1C].

M. 6:2 (1) He who slaughters [a wild beast or a bird] and it turns out to be *terefah*, (2) he who slaughters for the purpose of idolatry, (3) he who slaughters an unconsecrated [wild animal or bird] inside [the Temple] or consecrated ones outside [M. 5:1], (4) a wild beast and a bird which are to be stoned is free [of the liability]. (1) He who slaughters [a wild beast or a bird] and it is made carrion by his own deed, (2) he who pierces [the windpipe], (3) he who tears out [the windpipe], is free [of the obligation] to cover up [the blood].

T. 6:4 He who slaughters for healing, and for food for a gentile, and for food for dogs, is liable to cover up the blood. He who slaughters and it is made carrion by his own deed, he who pierces and he who tears out [M. Hul. 6:2G — H], and the act of slaughter of a gentile — one is free of liability to cover up the blood.

T. 6:5 He who slaughters on the Sabbath or on the Day of Atonement even though he thereby assumes liability for his life, once it gets dark, if the blood was still available, is liable to cover it up.

T. 6:6 He who slaughters on a boat, once he reaches dry land, if the blood is still available, is liable to cover it up. Even though they have said, "A man should not slaughter on a boat unless he had dirt ready," he who slaughters and needs the blood should not slaughter in the usual way. But how should he do it? He should pierce it or wring its neck.

M. 6:3 A deaf-mute, an imbecile, and a minor who slaughtered, and others oversee them [M. 1:1] are liable to cover up [the blood]. [If they did so] all by themselves, they are free of liability to cover up [the blood]. And so with regard to the matter of, "It and its offspring:" [If] they have slaughtered and others oversee them, it is prohibited to slaughter [the offspring] after them [If they did so] all by themselves, it is prohibited. But if one has slaughtered [the offspring after the deaf-mute, imbecile, or minor has slaughtered the dam], he does not incur forty stripes.

M. 6:4 (1) [If] one has slaughtered a hundred wild beasts in one place, a single covering up of the blood [serves] for all of them. (2) [If one has slaughtered] a hundred birds in one place, a single covering up of the blood [serves] for all of them. (3) [If one has slaughtered] a wild beast and a bird in one place, a single covering up of the blood [serves] for all of them. [If] he slaughtered [a wild beast or a bird] and he did not cover up [its blood] and another person saw him, he [the other person] is liable to cover up [the blood]. [If] he covered up [the blood] and it became uncovered, he is free of liability to cover it up [again]. [If] the wind [blew dirt and] covered it up [and it became uncovered], he is liable to cover it up.

T. 6:7 He who slaughters and sanctified the blood [to Heaven] is liable to cover it up, because the requirement of covering the blood takes precedence over the requirement of sanctification. He who slaughters and the earth absorbed it [the blood] is free of the obligation to cover it up. [If] the wind covered it up, he is liable to cover it up [once again] [M. Hul. 6:4G].

T. 6:9 He who slaughters has to say a blessing for that action by itself. He who covers up the blood has to say a blessing for that action by itself. [If] one slaughtered and did not cover up the blood and someone else saw him, he [the witness] is liable to cover it up [M. Hul. 6:4E], even on a festival.

T. 6:10 He who covers up the blood should cover it up by hand and should not cover it up by his foot, for they do not carry out the commandments in a slovenly way.

M. 6:5 Blood that was mixed with water, if it has the appearance of blood, one is liable to cover it up. [If] it was mixed with wine, they regard it as if it were water. [If] it was mixed up with blood of a [domesticated] beast or with blood of a wild beast, they regard it as if it were water.

M. 6:6 Blood that splashes and that is on the knife, one is liable to cover it up.

M. 6:7 With what do they cover up [the blood], and with what do they not cover up the blood? They cover up the blood (1) with fine dung and (2) with fine sand and (3) with lime and (4) with [pieces of] potsherd and (5) with brick and (6) with the plug of a jar [both (5,6)] of which one has crushed. But they do not cover up the blood either (1) with coarse dung or (2) with coarse sand or (3) with a brick or (4) with the plug of a jar neither [(3,4)] of which one has crushed. And one should not turn a utensil over on it. With something in which one grows plants, they cover it up, and with something in which one does not grow plants, they do not cover it up.

T. 6:11 With what do they cover up the blood and with what do they not cover up the blood [M. Hul. 6:7A]? They do not cover up the blood (1) with straw, (2) with stubble, (3) with chips, (4) with peastalks, (5) with down, (6) with wings of a dove, with (7) scrapings of earthenware, (8) with hatchelled flax, (9) with metal shavings, (10) with broken utensils, (11) with metal strips, (12) with flour, or (13) with fine flour. Nor should one put a stone on the blood and cover it up. But one covers it up with lime, with gypsum, and with shards which one has crushed and made into dust. This is the general principle: With anything which is a kind of dirt [which] absorbs and [in which plants] sprout do they cover up the blood [M. Hul. 6:7F].

Once the particular hermeneutics shapes the topic, the generic hermeneutics, M. 6:2ff., does the rest. The issue of responsibility, M. 6:3, deals with one set of interstitial problems, the division of single action and multiple effect or vice versa, M. 6:4, another, and of mixtures, M. 6:5, a third. The inert facts, as the pattern requires, then are tacked on, M. 6:7.

C. *THE PROHIBITION OF THE SCIATIC NERVE (GEN. 32:32)*

M. 7:1 [The prohibition of] the sinew of the hip [sciatic nerve, Gen. 32:32] applies (1) in the Land [of Israel] and outside of the Land, (2) in the time of the Temple and not in the time of the Temple, (3) to unconsecrated animals and to Holy Things. It applies (1) to domesticated cattle and to wild beasts, (2) to the right hip and to the left hip. But it does not apply (3) to a bird, because it has no hollow [of the thigh or spoon-shaped hip and its fat is permitted. Butchers are believed (1) concerning it and (2) concerning the [forbidden] fat [Lev. 3:17, 7:23].

T. 7:1 A. The [prohibition against eating] the sinew of the hip applies to hybrids and to a *koy*. It applies to both hips: to the right hip and to the left hip. This is the general principle: Any beast which has a right thigh, the prohibition of the sinew of the hip applies thereunto. Any beast which does not have a right thigh, the prohibition of the sinew of the hip does not apply thereunto.

T. 7:3 He who sends a cut-up hip to his fellow must separate from it the sinew of the hip. [If he sends] a whole [one to his fellow], he does not have to separate from it the sinew of the hip. He who purchases a cut-up hip from the butcher does not have to separate from it the sinew of the hip. [If he purchases] a whole one, he has to separate from it the sinew of the hip. He who sells a cut-up hip to a gentile does not have to separate from it the sinew of the hip. On condition that he does not sell it to him before an Israelite, because he [the Israelite] goes and purchases it from him. And on account of two considerations did they say, They do not sell carrion-meat and *terefah*-meat to a gentile: because he goes and sells [feeds] it to an Israelite; another consideration: because they do not feed a person something by which he may err. And for two considerations did they state: An Israelite person should not say to a gentile, "Buy me meat": (1) because of carrion, and (2) because of *terefah*-meat. Another consideration: because of the possibility of thugs [who may not pay the butcher and may just steal the meat].

M. 7:2 A man sends to a gentile a thigh in which the sinew of the hip [is located], because its place [presence] is known. He who removes the sinew of the hip must remove the whole of it.

T. 7:4 As to the sinew of the hip: One digs after it in every place in which it is located and removes it. Its fat — Lo, this is permitted [M. Hul. 7:2B].

B. 7:2A I:2/94A A PERSON SHOULD NOT SELL TO HIS FELLOW A SANDAL [MADE FROM THE HIDE] OF AN ANIMAL THAT DIED OF NATURAL CAUSES AS IF IT CAME FROM A LIVE ANIMAL THAT HAD BEEN SLAUGHTERED FOR TWO REASONS. ONE, BECAUSE HE MISLEADS HIM. AND THE OTHER, BECAUSE

OF THE DANGER [THAT THE HIDE IS TAINTED IN SOME WAY]. A PERSON SHOULD NOT SEND TO HIS FELLOW A CASK OF WINE WITH OIL FLOATING AT THE OPENING. AND ONCE A PERSON SENT HIS FELLOW A CASK OF WINE WITH OIL FLOATING AT ITS OPENING. AND HE WENT AND INVITED GUESTS [THINKING IT WAS A BARREL OF OIL]. AND THEY CAME. WHEN HE FOUND OUT THAT IT WAS WINE HE HANGED HIMSELF. AND GUESTS ARE NOT PERMITTED TO GIVE FROM WHAT IS BROUGHT BEFORE THEM TO THE SON OR THE DAUGHTER OF THE HOUSEHOLDER UNLESS THEY ASKED FOR PERMISSION FROM THE HOUSEHOLDER. AND ONCE A PERSON INVITED THREE GUESTS DURING A YEAR OF FAMINE AND HE HAD ONLY THREE EGGS TO SERVE THEM. THE SON OF THE HOUSEHOLD CAME IN. ONE OF THE GUESTS TOOK HIS PORTION AND GAVE IT TO HIM [I.E., THE SON]. AND SO DID THE SECOND [GUEST] AND SO DID THE THIRD. THE FATHER OF THE CHILD CAME AND FOUND HIM WITH ONE EGG GORGED IN HIS MOUTH AND ONE IN EACH HAND. [ENRAGED] HE THREW HIM TO THE GROUND AND HE DIED. WHEN HIS MOTHER SAW WHAT HAPPENED SHE WENT UP TO THE ROOF AND JUMPED OFF AND DIED. THEN EVEN HE WENT UP TO THE ROOF AND JUMPED OFF AND DIED.

M. 7:3 He who eats an olive's bulk of the sinew of the hip incurs forty stripes. [If] he ate it and it does not contain an olive's bulk, he is [nonetheless] liable. [If] he ate an olive's bulk of [the sinew of] this [hip] and an olive's bulk of that one, he incurs eighty stripes.

M. 7:4 A thigh with which the sinew of the hip [which was not removed] was cooked, if it [the sinew] is sufficient to impart a flavor [to the thigh], Lo, this is prohibited. How do they estimate the matter? Like meat [cooked] with turnips.

M. 7:5 The sinew of the hip which was cooked with [other] sinews, and one recognizes it — [it must be removed, and the remainder is prohibited if there is enough] to impart a flavor. And if [one does] not [recognize the presence of the sinew of the hip], all of them are prohibited [for any one might be the sciatic nerve]. As to the broth, [it is prohibited if] it imparts a flavor. And so with a piece of carrion, and so with a piece of unclean fish which were cooked with [other] pieces: When one recognizes their [presence], [they must be removed and the rest are forbidden if there is enough] to impart flavor. And if [one does] not [recognize their presence] they are all forbidden. As to the broth, [it is forbidden only if the carrion or unclean fish] imparts a flavor.

T. 7:6 A thigh with which the sinew of the thigh was cooked, if it was cooked so much that it imparts a flavor, Lo, this is prohibited. How do they estimate it? Like meat [cooked] in turnips [M. Hul.

7:4A-C]. [If] it was cooked with sinews, Lo, this is [prohibited if it] imparts a flavor [M. Hul. 7:5A].

T. 7:7 A forbidden piece [of meat] which was mixed with [other] pieces, even if they are a thousand — all of them are prohibited [M. Hul. 7:5B]. In the case of a broth, [it is prohibited if] it imparts a flavor [M. Hul. 7:5C]. [If] it was dissolved, Lo, this is [prohibited if] it imparts a flavor.

M. 7:6 [The prohibition of the sinew of the hip] applies to a clean [beast], but it does not apply to an unclean [beast].

T. 7:10 He who eats a limb cut from a living animal transgresses a negative commandment. [He who eats] fat from a living animal transgresses on that account because of two negative commandments, because of the fat, and because of [its originating in a] living [beast]. [He who eats] blood from a living beast is liable on account of violating two negative commandments, because of the prohibition of blood, and because of the prohibition of eating that which is cut from a living beast. [He who eats] a limb cut from a living beast is liable because of the prohibition of carrion. [He who eats] fat of carrion is liable because of violating two negative commandments, because of fat, and because of carrion.

T. 7:12 [He who eats] the fat tail of Holy Things is liable for violating two negative commandments, because of the fat tail, and because of Holy Things. [He who eats] fat from Holy Things is liable for violating two negative commandments, because of fat, and because of Holy Things.

The established pattern governs.

D.   *THE SEPARATION OF MILK AND MEAT (EX. 23:19, 34:26, DT. 12:21)*

M. 8:1 Every [kind of] flesh [i.e., meat, of cattle, wild beast, and fowl] is it prohibited to cook in milk, except for the flesh of fish and locusts. And it is prohibited to serve it up onto the table with cheese, except for the flesh of fish and locusts. He who vows [to abstain] from flesh is permitted [to make use of] the flesh of fish and locusts.

T. 8:1 [The prohibition against cooking] meat and milk applies in the Land and outside of the Land, in the time of the Temple and not in the time of the Temple, to [meat of] unconsecrated beasts and to consecrated ones.

T. 8:2 He who vows to abstain from flesh is prohibited from every kind of flesh, and permitted [to make use of], the flesh of fish and locusts [M. Hul. 8:1E]. The fowl does not go up, [onto the table on which cheese is located] and is not eaten.

M. 8:2 A man ties up meat and cheese in a single cloth, provided that they do not touch one another.

T. 8:4 They put [meat and cheese] into a basket or into a strike and throw them over their shoulder [M. Hul. 8:2A]. One must [conclude] they prohibited it only in the case of a table used for eating.

T. 8:5 Two who came into an inn, this one coming from the north, and that one coming from the south — this one eats his piece of meat, and that one eats his cheese and they do not scruple [M. Hul. 8:2C]. One must [conclude]: They prohibited [meat and cheese on one table] only when they [the people eating the food] all were a single group.

M. 8:3 A drop of milk which fell on a piece [of meat], if it is sufficient to impart flavor to that piece [of meat] — it is prohibited. [If] one stirred the pot, if there is in it sufficient [milk] to impart flavor to that [entire] pot]'s [contents], it [the contents of the pot] is prohibited. The udder: one cuts it open and takes out its milk. [If] he did not cut it open, he does not transgress on that account. The heart: One cuts it open and takes out its blood. [If] he did not cut it open, he does not transgress on that account. He who serves up fowl with cheese on the table does not transgress a prohibition.

T. 8:7 [If] hot [milk fell] into hot [meat], or cold into hot, it is prohibited. [If] hot [fell] into cold, one dries it off and eats it [the meat].

T. 8:8 The udder of a nursing cow: one cuts it open and takes out its milk. [If] he did not cut it open, he does not transgress on that account. The heart. One cuts it open and takes out its blood. If he cooked it, he cuts it open after it is cooked [M. Hul. 8:3C-H].

M. 8:4 (1) The meat of clean cattle with the milk of a clean cattle — it is prohibited to cook [one with the other] or to derive benefit [therefrom]. (2) The meat of clean cattle with the milk of an unclean cattle, (3) the meat of unclean cattle with the milk of clean cattle — it is permitted to cook and permitted to derive benefit [therefrom].

T. 8:10 He who cooks [meat] in the juice of milk is free [of liability to punishment]. [He who does so] in the milk of a male is free. Blood which one cooked in milk — he is free. The bones and sinews and horns and hooves which one cooked in milk — he is free. That which is refuse, remnant, or unclean [of consecrated meat] which one cooked in milk — he is liable on their account because of refuse, remnant, and uncleanness.

T. 8:11 The meat of clean cattle [cooked] in the milk of clean cattle is prohibited for use for purposes of healing and for benefit [M. Hul. 8:4A-B].

M. 8:5 [The milk in] the stomach of [a beast slaughtered by] a gentile [which is carrion, M. 1:1], and that [in the stomach of] carrion — Lo, this is prohibited. He who curdles [milk] in the skin of the stomach of a valid[ly slaughtered beast], if it is sufficient to impart a flavor — Lo, this [cheese] is prohibited. A valid beast which sucked from a *terefah* beast — [the milk in] its stomach is prohibited. A *terefah* beast which sucked from a valid beast — [the milk in] its stomach is permitted, [in both cases] because [the milk remains] collected together in its intestines.

T. 8:9 An udder which one cooked in its milk is permitted. A maw which one cooked [in its milk] — one is liable [M. Hul. 8:5B]. One who cooks milk and meat, Lo, this one is liable. How much does one cook so as to be liable? A half olive's bulk of meat and a half olive's bulk of milk, so that it [the result of cooking the two together] should be an olive's bulk. Just as one is liable for cooking it, so he is liable for eating it. How much does one eat so as to be liable? Sufficient so that it is eaten as something which is cooked.

T. 8:12 The milk in the stomach of a beast slaughtered by a gentile, and that in the stomach of a beast which is carrion — Lo, this is prohibited [M. Hul. 8:5A]. They reverted to rule: They curdle milk in the stomach of a beast slaughtered by a gentile and in the stomach of a beast which is carrion, and do not scruple on that account.

M. 8:6 A more strict rule applies to fat than to blood, and a more strict rule applies to blood than to fat. A more strict rule applies to fat: For as to fat: (1) the laws of sacrilege apply to it. And (2) they are liable on its account to the laws of refuse, remnant, and uncleanness, which is not the case with blood, for [the law forbidding] blood applies to cattle, a wild beast, and a bird, whether unclean or clean. But [the prohibition of] fat applies only to a clean cattle alone.

T. 8:14 A more strict rule applies to fat than to blood, and to blood than to fat: For the prohibition of fat applies to raw and cooked fat. And it is offered on the altar-fires And the laws of sacrilege apply to it, and they are liable on its account because of violation of laws of refuse, remnant, and uncleanness which is not the case of blood [M. Hul. 8:6-D]. A more strict rule applies to blood. For blood renders [the offering] permitted [to be eaten by the priests], it renders the offering valid [when it itself is properly tossed], and it renders the offering refuse [when tossed with improper intention], which is not the case with fat.

The Tosefta, not the Mishnah, invokes the established hermeneutics in presenting the prohibition of mixing milk and meat, T. 8:1 to M. 8:1. The rest of the exposition, M. 8:1ff., concerns the problem of mixtures, and here is a case in which the subject-matter and the generic hermeneutics intersect and coincide. But the key-ruling, M. 8:3, concerns how we know which portion of a mixture determines the status of the whole, and that is a question fundamental to the generic hermeneutics. The answer, invoking the principle that what imparts the flavor to the whole determines the status of the whole, is standard for the Halakhic repertoire on liquid-mixtures. M. 8:6 results from another component of the generic hermeneutics, the hierarchization of comparable classifications.

> E. *CONNECTION FOR THE PURPOSES OF CONTRACTING UNCLEANNESS*
>
> M. 9:1 The (1) hide, and (2) grease, and (3) sediment, and (4) flayed-off meat, and (5) bones, and (6) sinews, and (7) horns and (8) hooves join together [with the meat to which they are attached to form the requisite volume] to impart food uncleanness, but [they do] not [join together to impart] uncleanness of carrion. Similarly: He who slaughters unclean cattle for a gentile — while it yet is writhing, it imparts food uncleanness, but [it does] not [impart] uncleanness of carrion — (1) until it dies, or (2) until one cuts off its head. [Scripture thus] has [prescribed] more [conditions] to impart food uncleanness than uncleanness of carrion.
>
> M. 9:2 [In the case of] these, their skin [hide] is deemed equivalent to their meat: (1) the skin of man, and (2) skin of a domesticated pig — and (3) skin of the hump of a young camel, and (4) the skin of the head of a young calf, and (5) the skin of the hooves, and (6) the skin of the genitals, and (7) the skin of the foetus, and (8) the skin which is under the fat tail, and (9) the skin of the hedgehog, and the chameleon, and the lizard, and the snail. And all of them which one tanned, or on which one trampled so [that they are fit for] use are clean [and do not impart food uncleanness], except for the skin of man.
>
> M. 9:3 He who flays a beast or a wild animal, whether clean or unclean, whether large or small for the purpose [of making] a covering — [the skin is deemed connected to the carcass so that it contracts from, and conveys uncleanness to, the carcass, as long as there is not yet flayed] enough for a hold [on the carcass]; for the purpose of a water-skin — [the skin is deemed connected to the carcass] until he will flay the breast. [He who flays] from the feet upwards — it is wholly connected for uncleanness, for contracting uncleanness and for imparting uncleanness. [If he did not yet flay the] hide which is on the neck — it is connected, until he will flay off the whole of it.
>
> M. 9:5 The marrow bone of the corpse and the marrow bone of [invalidated] consecrated animals — he who touches them, whether [they are] stopped up or hollowed out, is unclean. The marrow bone of carrion and the marrow bone of a creeping thing

— he who touches them, [if they are] stopped up, is clean. [If they are] hollowed out in any amount at all — they impart uncleanness to the one who touches them. How do we know that also to the one who carries them [the marrow bones of carrion that they do impart uncleanness]? Scripture states, "He who touches" and "he who carries" [Lev. 11:39, 40]. That which enters the category of touching enters the category of carrying. That which does not enter the category of touching does not enter the category of carrying.

M. 9:6 The egg of a creeping thing [in which the foetus is] formed is clean. [If] it was pierced in any measure at all, it is unclean. A mouse, half of which is flesh and half dirt — he who touches the flesh is unclean. [He who touches] the dirt is clean.

T. 8:20 The egg of a creeping thing [in which the foetus is] formed is clean [M. Hul. 9:6A]. And how much is it formed [to fall under this rule]? So that one may discern the creeping thing inside of it. If the shell is perforated in any amount at all, it is unclean [M. Hul. 9:6B]. And how large is the perforation to be? The breadth of a hair.

M. 9:7 The dangling limb and flesh in the case of cattle impart food uncleanness [when they are] in their place [attached]. And they require preparation [i.e., wetting down, to receive uncleanness].

M. 9:8 The dangling limb and flesh in the case of man are clean. [If] the man died, the flesh is clean.

To invoke the considerations of uncleanness or prohibition on some other grounds, a minimum volume of a given substance is required. That is because if the volume is trifling and not noteworthy, no one is assumed to pay attention to it, and, absent the possibility of intentionality, the volume is null. We need to know, therefore, how to classify the distinct parts of a beast for the purpose of forming the requisite volume for food uncleanness. M. 9:1 both answers that question and then differentiates food-uncleanness from carrion-uncleanness, a neat exercise in taxonomy. Considerations of issues of connection, therefore, carries forward the matter of mixtures of the prior unit in this composite, which disrupts the flow of the Halakhic exposition. The final units resume it.

F. *THE GIFTS TO THE PRIEST TAKEN FROM A BEAST SLAUGHTERED FOR SECULAR PURPOSES: THE SHOULDER, TWO CHEEKS, AND MAW (DT. 18;3)*

M. 10:1 [The requirement to give to the priests] the shoulder, the two cheeks, and the maw [Deut. 18:3] applies (1) in the Land and outside of the Land, (2) in the time of the Temple and not in the time of the Temple, (3) to unconsecrated beasts, but not to consecrated beasts. For it [the contrary to 3] might have appeared logical: Now, if unconsecrated animals, which are not liable for the breast and thigh [which are taken from peace offerings for the priests, (Lev. 7:31)], are liable for the [priestly] gifts [of the shoulder, cheeks, and maw], Holy Things, which *are* liable for the breast and thigh, logically should be liable to the priestly gifts. Scripture therefore states, "And I have given them to Aaron the priest and to his sons as a due for ever" [Lev. 7:34] — he has a right [in consecrated beasts] only to that which is explicitly stated [namely, the breast and thigh].

T. 9:1 [The requirement to give to the priest] the shoulder, the two cheeks, and the maw [M. Hul. 10:1 A] applies to hybrid beasts and to the koy. T. Hallah 2:1ff. Twenty-four gifts for the priesthood were given to Aaron and his sons, and all of them were granted through a generalization [Num. 18:8] followed by a particularization [Num. 18:9-18] followed by a generalization [Num. 18:19], and 'a covenant of salt' [Num. 18:8-19], so that if one carries them out, it is as though he has carried out the entirety of the generalization, particularization, and generalization, covering all sacrifices that comprise the covenant of salt; and to violate them is to violate the entirety of the generalization, particularization, and generalization, covering all sacrifices that comprise the covenant of salt. These are they: ten to be eaten inside the Temple, four in Jerusalem, ten within the borders of the Land of Israel. Ten to be eaten in the precincts of the Temple: a sin offering of an animal, sin offering of a bird, guilt offering for a known sin, guilt offering for a sin that is subject to doubt, peace offering of the community, log of oil in the case of a person afflicted with the skin ailment, residue of the wave offering, two loaves, show bread, and residue of meal offerings. The four to be eaten in Jerusalem: the firstling, first of the first fruits, portions separated from the thank offering for the priesthood and the ram of the Nazirite, and the hides of most Holy Things. The ten to be eaten within the borders of the Land of Israel: food designated as priestly rations [heave-offering], the priestly rations taken up from the tithe, dough offering, first fleece, portions of the unconsecrated animals assigned to the priesthood, the beast that serves for the redemption of the first born son, the beast that serves for the redemption of the firstling of an ass, a field of possession, a field that has been devoted, and what has been handed over in restitution for a robbery committed against a proselyte.

M. 10:2 All Holy Things in which a permanent blemish occurred before they were sanctified, and which were redeemed, (1) are liable to the law of the firstling and for priestly gifts, (2) and they go forth for unconsecrated purposes, to be sheared and to be used for labor, (3) and their offspring and their milk are permitted after they are redeemed, (4) and he who slaughters

them outside of the sanctuary is free [of liability to punishment], (5) and they are not subject to the law of the substitute, (6) and if they died, they [the carcasses] are redeemed, except for the firstling and tithe. All [Holy Things] in which a permanent blemish occurred after they were sanctified or in which a transient blemish occurred before they were sanctified, and afterward a permanent blemish appeared in them, and which were redeemed (1) are free of the law of the firstling and of the priestly gifts, (2) and they do not go forth for unconsecrated purposes, to be sheared and to be used for labor, (3) and their offspring and their milk are prohibited after they are redeemed, (4) and he who slaughters them outside is liable [Aqiba, M. Zeb. 9:3], (5) and they are subject to the law of the substitute, (6) and if they died, they are to be buried.

M. 10:3 A [blemished] firstling which was mixed up among a hundred [other unconsecrated beasts] — When a hundred [people, in addition to the owner of the firstling] slaughter all [one hundred and one] of them, they render all of them free [of priestly dues]. [If] one slaughters all of them, they free one for him. He who slaughters for a priest or for a gentile — it is free [of requirement to give the priestly dues]. And one who is a partner with them has to give some indication [that the animal is exempt from the priestly dues]. And if [the priest or gentile who sold the beast to an Israelite] said, "[The beast is sold] except for the priestly gifts," he [the one who slaughters (D)] is free of the priestly gifts. [If] he said, "Sell me the intestines of the cow [= the maw]," and the priests' dues were in them, he gives them to the priest, and does not deduct their value from [what he pays] him. [If] he purchased it from him by weight, he gives them to the priest, and he does deduct their value [from what he pays] him.

T. 9:2 He who slaughters for purposes of healing, [and he who slaughters] for food for a gentile or for dog-food — it [the slaughtered beast] is liable to the priestly gifts.

T. 9:3 He who slaughters [a beast] [and he] by whose hand it is made carrion, he who tears, and he who pierces, and the act of slaughter of a gentile — [a beast killed in any of these invalid ways] is free of the priestly gifts. C. A priest or a gentile who sold their beast to an Israelite to slaughter — it is liable to the priestly gifts. If they were killed while in their [the priest's or the gentile's] possession, and afterward they sold it to him — it is free of the liability for the priestly gifts [M. Hul. 10:3E].

T. 9:4 An Israelite who sold his beast to a priest to slaughter — it is exempt from the priestly gifts. [If] it was slaughtered while yet in his possession and afterward he sold it to him, it is liable for the priestly gifts.

T. 9:5 A priest is exempt, and one who is a partner with a priest is exempt. A gentile is exempt, and one who is partner with a gentile is exempt. A partner with a priest must make a mark [M. Hul. 10:3F]. One who is a partner with a gentile does not have to give evidence. And [a partner of priests] who are invalid for consecrated purposes F. does not have to make a mark.

T. 9:6 [If] a priest said to him, "It is entirely yours, but the fore-leg is mine," even if one among a hundred are in the fore-leg, it is exempt from the gifts of the shoulder. [If] he said, "The whole shoulder is yours, and the head is mine," even one among a hundred, it is exempt from the gift of the cheek. [If he said], "The whole cheek is yours, and the intestines are mine," even if one in a hundred are among the intestines, it is exempt from the requirement to give the maw.

T. 9:7 In a place in which they are accustomed to flay the head, one is not permitted to flay the cheek. [In a place in which they are accustomed] to strip [off the hair by scalding] the heifers, one is not permitted to strip [off the hair by scalding] the shoulder. And if there is a priest, one gives them to the priest. And if not, one exchanges them for money.

T. 9:8 [If] one sold him the hand as it is and the head as it is and the intestines as they are, he gives them to a priest. And he does not deduct from [what he pays] the butcher the cost thereof [M. Hul. 10:3H].

T. 9:9 [If] he purchased from him by weight, he gives them to the priest. But he deducts from [what he pays] the butcher their value [M. Hul. 10:3]. The priestly gifts are in no way subject to sanctity. Even if one sold them to a gentile, and even if one put them before his dog, they are subject only to the requirement of [being given to] the priesthood alone.

T. 9:10 He who sends meat to his fellow, and there were in it [the meat] the gifts [the parts usually given to the priests] — they do not scruple lest they be the priestly gifts.

M. 10:4 A convert who converted and had a cow — [if] it was slaughtered before he converted, it is free of priestly dues. [If it was slaughtered] after he converted, it is liable. [If it is a matter of] doubt, it is free of liability, for he who makes a claim against his fellow bears the burden of proof. What is the shoulder? From the joint to the shoulder socket of the foreleg. And that pertains also to the Nazirite [Num. 6:19]. And the corresponding part in the hind leg is the thigh. What is the cheek? From the joint of the jaw to the knob of the windpipe [the tip of the thyroid cartilage, the whole lower jaw and the tongue].

T. 9:11 What is the shoulder [M. Hul. 10:4D-E]? One removes it from the socket, and all the socket with it. As is the shoulder [defined] in the case of Holy Things, so is the shoulder [defined] in the case of [offerings of the shoulder in] the provinces [M. Hul. 10:4F]. What is the cheek? One removes it from the place at which the animal is slaughtered, and the whole place where the animal is slaughtered with it. The maw is as its name implies. The fat which is on the maw does one give to the priest.

M. 10:1 not only invokes the particular hermeneutics but introduces an uncommon, but not unknown, initiative of an exegetical character, showing how the Halakhah defies the natural reason of the argument a fortiori and depends upon the exegetically-dictated taxonomy. M. 10:2, 4 introduce an interstitial problem, M. 10:3, one of mixtures, and the composite produces no surprises.

G. *THE GIFT TO THE PRIEST OF THE FIRST FLEECE OF A SHEEP (DT. 18:4)*

M. 11:1-2 [The laws concerning the obligation to donate to the priest] the first shearings [of wool from the sheep of one's flock (Deut. 18:4)] apply both inside the Land of Israel and outside the Land of Israel, in the time the Temple [in Jerusalem stands] and in the time the Temple does not [stand]. [And the laws apply] to [the fleece of] unconsecrated [animals] but not to [the fleece of animals that were] consecrated [to the Temple]. A stricter rule applies to [the obligation to give to the priest] the shoulder, the two cheeks and the maw [of one's animals] than to [the obligation to give to the priest] the first shearings [of wool from the sheep of one's flock]. For [the obligation to give to the priest] the shoulder, the two cheeks and the maw [of one's animals] applies both to the [large] animals of one's herd and to the [small] animals of one's flock. And [the law applies] to [a case where one slaughtered] a large number [of animals] or a small number [of animals — even one animal]. But the [law regarding the] first shearings [of wool from the sheep of one's flock] applies only to sheep, and only in [a case where one slaughtered] a large number [of animals]. And how much must one give to him [i.e., to the priest from the first shearings of the flock]? [An amount equivalent to] the value of five *sela* in Judea. And this is equivalent to [the value of] ten *sela* in the Galilee. [And he must give] white [bleached] wool and not soiled [unbleached] wool [i.e., the higher quality of wool]. [And he must give] enough to make a small garment [from the wool]. As it says in scripture, "You shall give to him [Deut. 18:4]." [This implies that you must give him enough] so that [legitimately] it can be considered a gift. If he did not have a chance to give to [the priest a share from the first shearings] before they dyed [the wool], he is free of his obligation [to give the shearings to the priest after dying it]. If they bleached [the wool before giving a share to the priest] but as yet did not dye it, he is liable [to give a share of the wool to the priest]. One who buys shearings of wool from a gentile is exempt from the obligation to give from it a gift of the first shearings [to the priest]. One who buys shearings of wool from his fellow [is subject to the following rules]: If [the buyer did not buy the entire lot of the wool but] left over [some of the wool of the lot in the possession of the seller], the seller is liable [to give from that a gift of wool to the priest]. [But if the buyer] did not leave over [any wool in the possession of the seller, but purchased the entire lot], the buyer is liable [to give the priest a gift from the wool]. If [the seller] had two kinds [of wool], gray and white [the rule is as follows]: If he sold him the gray wool, but not the white wool, [or if he had separate lots of wool from males and from females and] he sold him [the wool from] the males, but not from the females, this one [the buyer] gives of his own [a gift of wool to the priest] and this one [the seller] gives of his own.

T. 9:12 The shoulder — this is the right shoulder. You say it is the right shoulder. But perhaps it is only the left one? Lo, you argue: Since the thigh is a gift to the priest, and the shoulder is a gift to the priest, just as the thigh applies only to the right one, so the shoulder should apply only to the right one.

T. 9:13 What is the breast? Whatever is visible from the ground and upward, through to the neck, and downward through to the belly. One cuts it off and removes it from between the two walls on either side. And what is the fat-tail? One cuts off in a downward direction until one touches the backbone. Once it enters beyond the backbone up to one reaches the joint — one cuts it off and removes the whole of it.

T. 10:1 [The requirement to give to the priest] the first of the fleece applies to a *terefah*-sheep. And it does not apply to a dead sheep. And it applies to a hybrid-sheep and to a koy.

T. 10:2 A priest and a gentile who gave their beast to an Israelite — it is free of the first of the fleece. This rule is more strict for the [shoulder and] two cheeks and maw than for the first of the fleece.

T. 10:3 All Holy Things, the permanent blemish of which came before they were sanctified, and which were redeemed, are liable to the first of the fleece. But if they were sanctified before they were blemished, or there was a transient blemish before they were sanctified, or afterward a permanent blemish appears in them, and they were redeemed, they are free of the first of the fleece.

T. 10:4 He who shears his goats is free [of the requirement to give to the priest] the first of the fleece. The partner — his ewes are liable for the first of the fleece. He who purchases from the householder is liable.

T. 10:5 How much does he give him? The weight equivalent to five selas in Judah, which are ten selas in Galilee, bleached and not dirty [M. Hul. 11:2F-H]. And it is not that he should bleach it and give it to him. But he gives him dirty wool sufficient so that, when he bleaches it, there will remain in his possession a weight equivalent to five selas in Judah, which are ten selas in Galilee, as it is said, "You shall give him" [Deut. 18:4] — that it be sufficient to be a gift [M. Hul. 11:2J].

T. 10:6 [If] one had two flocks, he shears one and leaves it, shears the other and leaves it, even though he is going to add to them, they do not join together [to form the volume liable to the gift of the first fleece]. [If] he had five, he shears and leaves, shears and leaves, even for two or three years. Lo, these join together. [If] he dyed them and spun them and sold them, they do not join together.

T. 10:7 He who separates the fleece of his flock and it was lost — he is responsible for it. The first of the fleece — its requirement [applies] at the outset [of shearing]. If [however] he gave it, whether at the beginning or at the middle of or at the end [of the shearing], he has fulfilled his obligation. And what is its measure [which one must give of his first shearing]? One-sixtieth part of the whole, as in the case of heave-offering.

T. 10:8 He who purchases the fleece of the flock of his fellow and did not separate from it the first of the fleece — the purchaser is free of the obligation to do so. A more strict rule applies to the shoulder, the cheeks, and the maw than to the first of the fleece in this regard.

This unit conforms in every way to the established pattern, and the Tosefta's complement typifies the Tosefta's framers at their most systematic and original — and talmudic.

H. *LETTING THE DAM GO FROM THE NEST WHEN TAKING THE YOUNG (DT. 22:6-7)*

M. 12:1 [The requirement to] let [the dam] go from the nest [Deut. 22:6-7] applies (1) in the Land and outside of the Land, (2) in the time of the Temple and not in the time of the Temple, (3) to unconsecrated [birds] but not to consecrated ones. A more strict rule applies to covering up the blood than to letting [the dam] go from the nest: For the requirement of covering up the blood applies (1) to a wild beast and to fowl, (2) to that which is captive and to that which is not captive. But letting [the dam] go from the nest applies only (1) to fowl and applies only (2) to that which is not captive. What is that which is not captive? For example, geese and fowl which make their nest in an orchard. But if they make their nest in the house [and so Herodian doves], one is free of the requirement of letting the dam go.

T. 10:9 Geese and fowl and Herodian pigeons who escaped or who made their nest in an orchard — they are liable for sending forth [M. Hul. 12:1D-F]. A male is exempt from the requirement of sending forth.

M. 12:2 An unclean bird is exempt from the requirement of letting the dam go. [If] an unclean bird sits on the eggs of a clean bird, or a clean bird sits on the eggs of an unclean bird, one is free of the requirement of letting the dam go.

M. 12:3 [If the dam] was hovering [over the nest], when its wings touched the nest, one is liable to send forth the dam. [If] its wings are not touching the nest, he is exempt from the requirement to send forth the dam. [If] there was there only one nestling or one egg, one is liable to send forth the dam, as it is said, "A bird's nest" [Deut. 22:6] — a bird's nest of any kind. [If] there were nestlings able to fly or spoiled eggs, one is exempt from the requirement of sending forth the dam, as it is said, "And the dam sitting upon the young or upon the eggs" — Just as the nestlings are those likely to live, so the eggs must be those likely to live, excluding those which are spoiled. And just as the eggs require their dam, so the nestlings require their dam, excluding those that can fly. [If] one sent it forth and it returned, even four or five times, he is liable [to send it forth again], as it is said, "You shall surely send it forth." [If] one said, "Lo, I shall take the dam and send forth the young," he is liable to send forth [the dam], as it is said, "You shall surely send forth the dam." [If] one took the young and then returned them to the nest and afterward the dam returned to them, he is free of the obligation to send forth [the dam from the nest].

T. 10:10 An unclean bird is exempt from the requirement of sending forth. A clean bird setting on the eggs of a clean bird which is not of its kind is exempt from the requirement of sending forth. [If] it was standing [not sitting] among them, it is exempt from the requirement of sending forth. [If] it was sitting on them, it is liable to the requirement of sending forth. [If] it was hovering lover [the nest], when its wings are touching it, one is liable to the requirement of sending forth. [If] its wings are not touching it, one is exempt from the requirement of sending forth [M. Hul. 12:3A-D]. [If] the mother of the nestlings is *terefah*, one is exempt from sending forth. [If] the eggs [are *terefah*], one is exempt from the requirement of sending forth [M. Hul. 12:3K].

M. 12:4 He who takes the dam with the young sends forth [the dam], but does not incur the penalty of stripes. This is the general principle: for any [negative] prohibition that is overridden by affirmative [commandment] to rise up and do something, one does not incur the penalty of stripes.

M. 12:5 One would not take the dam with the young even for the purpose of purifying a *mesora'*. Now if concerning an unimportant commandment, [the loss incurred in the performance of] which is worth only an *issar*, scripture has said, "That it may be well with you and that you may prolong your days" [Deut. 22:7], how much the more so for the weightier commandments that are in the Torah [will reward be given].

T. 10:11 [In the case of] nestlings which have flown and do not require their dam, one is free of the requirement of sending forth. [If] one took the dam and did not have time to take the young before she died or before they were made *terefah*, one is free of the requirement of sending forth.

T. 10:12 [If] one took the dam and afterward took the young, he is liable to the requirement of sending forth. [If] he took the young and afterward took the dam, he is exempt from the requirement of sending forth. [If] one person took the dam and another took the young, the one who takes the dam is liable to the requirement of sending forth.

T. 10:13 He who finds a nest in pits, ditches, or caverns — they are permitted as to the prohibition of robbery and liable as to the requirement of sending forth. And if they were tied up, they are prohibited as to robbery and free of liability for sending forth. The pigeons of a dovecote and the pigeons of an attic are liable to the requirement of sending forth and prohibited because of robbery, in order to keep peace.

T. 10:14 He who finds a nest should not purify, therewith, a *mesora'*, as it is said, "And he will purchase" [Lev. 14:4].

I see nothing that diverges from the established pattern.

IV. DOCUMENTARY TRAITS

A. THE MISHNAH AND THE TOSEFTA

No significant revision in the particular hermeneutics of the category-formation characterizes the Tosefta's treatment.

B. THE BAVLI

I do not see a single point at which the Bavli contributes a fresh exegetical issue, let alone an original interpretative initiative.

V. THE HERMENEUTICS OF HULLIN

A. WHAT FUSES THE HALAKHIC DATA INTO A CATEGORY-FORMATION?

The Halakhic data are fused by the particular hermeneutics of analogy and contrast into the category-formation at hand to make the statement that Israel is holier than the Land and than the Temple and, therefore, subjects to considerations of sanctity, the animals slaughtered for its nourishment. The selection of the data and the interpretation, thereof, realize the result of analogical-contrastive analysis, which is that Israel is holy like God, in consequence of which what sustains Israel's life, the shedding of blood, must accord with the rules of sanctification that govern the shedding of blood in the Temple. Then the whole holds tightly together.

How does the hermeneutics dictate the choice of data? The answer is illustrated by its selection of a particular Scriptural law for a principal focus. The Written Torah supplies a law that realizes the entire analogical-contrastive hermeneutics, when it imposes the same requirements that pertain to slaughter of an animal sacrifice for the altar in Jerusalem, to killing an animal for the use of Israel at home. That means meat Israel eats, is subject to the same regulations that apply to meat God receives on the altar-fires, and meat for those who are not holy, that is, gentile-idolaters, is not subject to the same rules (Ex. 22:30, Dt. 14:21). So the point cannot be missed: Food for God and for Israel must be prepared in comparable manner, which does not apply to food for gentiles.

The Halakhic category-formation indeed has done little more than explore the consequences of that rule when it states that the requirements of slaughter in the cult pertain also outside of the cult. But then the outer limits are set not by the Land but by the locus: wherever Israelites are located. And, concomitantly, when the physicalization of sanctification in Israel is fully appreciated, considerations of time give way. Then, the rule persists, both whenever the act takes place — even outside of the Land altogether, even during the time that the Temple is no longer standing. If within the logic set forth by the Written Torah at Dt. 12:20-24 and fully probed at M. Zebahim 14:4-8's ordering of Scripture's other (contradictory) data is contained an Israel outside of Jerusalem, then the next step, and it is not a giant step, is to contemplate an Israel outside of the Land altogether, not to say a Temple in ruins. The integral connection of slaughter of animals and sacrifice at the altar having been broken when all cultic activity was focused by Deuteronomy within Jerusalem, all that the Oral Torah has done is to address in so many words the extreme consequences of that situation: If the rules apply even to unconsecrated beasts, and even to the Land beyond Jerusalem, and even outside of the Temple, then by the same token, logic dictates a utopian consequence. The same laws apply even when no animals are being consecrated at all, and they apply even when no Temple stood, and they pertain even abroad.

What about the contrastive side of the hermeneutics? How are God and Israel differentiated when it comes to killing animals for nourishment? The category-formation in the context of analogical-contrastive analysis will lay stress on the contrast of altar to table — the contrast's implicitly highlighting the main point, which is their commonality. The requirements for the two settings to be sure exhibit striking differences. In the Temple priests ordinarily slaughter the beast and are the only ones who can sprinkle the blood on the altar. In the household, any Israelite performs the act of slaughter, and, as to the disposing of the blood, anyone may cover it up. Temple rites take place in daylight, the counterpart act of slaughter in the household may be done at night, and so on. The main point, however, is not to be missed: Any Israelite (here including a Samaritan or an apostate) may perform the act of slaughter, and it may be carried out at any time, day or night. Then how are the two settings comparable? They compare in all the ways that count: that have to do with life and death, blood and earth. That is to say, the actual act is the same: with a knife, applied to the throat, drawn across the two organs of the throat, windpipe and gullet (M. 2:1). The upshot is, it is in exactly the same way that a beast is slaughtered for the altar and for the household. Since that is not the case for killing fowl, the point should not be missed. The rule joining household to altar goes a step further. The act of slaughter for domestic use must be intentional and carried out by man, just as in the case of the altar: [If] the knife fell and effected the act of slaughter, even if it effected the act of slaughter properly, it is invalid. As it is said, "And you will slaughter...and you will eat..." (Deut. 12:21) — just as *you* effect the act of slaughter, so do *you* eat. The introduction of the issue of correct intentionality underscores that the altar and the table form a single genus, the operative traits being dictated by the altar.

So, the Written Torah in any event, set the stage when it took up the situation of slaughter not in behalf of the transaction at the altar and not in the setting of the holy place at all. And consequently, the Halakhah worked out in the critical detail of the sustenance of life, the conviction that Israel the people forms the locus of sanctification. Then all else follows. That allegation about the ubiquitous and eternal sanctification inherent in Israel, the people pervades the exposition of the laws in detail. It is an amazing statement in its insistence upon the priority and permanence of that act of sanctification — the sanctity of Israel — whatever may become of the holiness of the altar and of the Land.

From the particular hermeneutics, let us turn briefly to take note of the familiar generic hermeneutics. A single example of the working of the hermeneutics of interstitiality suffices. Since the main point of the act of slaughter is deliberately to take the life of the living beast, rather than allowing the animal to die of natural causes and only then to use its meat, a category between suitable and unsuitable has to take account of an interstitial case. A suitable act of slaughter kills the beast and attends to its blood. An unsuitable act of slaughter does not. But what about a beast that has not died on its own, but that also has not been slaughtered in the ordinary manner, out of the fullness of life? Such an interstitial case is taken up under the word *terefah*. That word, at Ex. 22:31, refers to a beast clawed by a wild animal: "You shall be men consecrated to me; therefore, you shall not eat any flesh that is born by beasts in the field; you shall cast it to the dogs." *Terefah* then pertains to carrion, a beast that dies without a proper act of slaughter. Ex. 22:31 then refers to a beast that has not yet died but that cannot survive. This yields the notion that beasts that bear some imperfection capable of causing death cannot be eaten by Israelites. Thus, both beasts that die on their own, carrion, and those that are going to die by reason of wounds or imperfections, *terefah*-beasts, are prohibited. The hermeneutics that yields the choice and interpretation of these data is absolutely standard for the Halakhah across its entire surface.

B. THE ACTIVITY OF THE CATEGORY-FORMATION

Now comes the speciation always commencing with the particular hermeneutics, then working its way through the generic hermeneutics. Let me give some concrete cases that show the activity of the category-formation.

Just as, in the Temple, offerings may be presented in behalf of gentiles, so an Israelite may slaughter a gentile's beast in behalf of the gentile. But if the intent is improper, the act is null, just as it would be if the officiating priest declared an improper intentionality in connection with a critical component of the rite, e.g., tossing the blood with the wrong purpose in mind. So the law is explicit: He who slaughters a beast [intending] to toss its blood for the purposes of idolatry and to burn its fat for the purposes of idolatry, Lo, this is meat of the sacrifices of corpses. And again, for intentionality in more general terms: He who slaughters (1) for the sake of mountains, (2) for the sake of valleys, (3) for the sake of seas, (4) for the sake of rivers, (5) for the sake of deserts — his act of slaughter is invalid. As in the Temple, so at home, the blood must be collected, not allowed to run out into a stream, and it is then covered with dirt, that is, given burial. On the other hand, slaughtering an unconsecrated beast outside of the Temple with the intent of offering up a sacrifice produces carrion. So a clear distinction differentiates slaughtering in the household and for its purposes from slaughtering in the Temple for its appropriate considerations. But what links the two venues proves equally striking: what renders an animal unfit for the altar invalidates it for the table as well.

And conversely, what the altar will not accept the household table cannot receive either. So, to state matters simply, when Israel eats meat, it eats the meat of the same classification and character that God consumes at the altar.

Accordingly, beasts (but not fowl) are slaughtered for the altar and the domestic table in accord with one and the same protocol, and the critical consideration that pertains to the altar — the attitude of the officiating priest — pertains to the table. That is, the attitude of the person who carries out or supervises the act of slaughter (as the case requires). But there is a striking difference between the household and the Temple. The Halakhah encompasses the Israelite household both in the Holy Land and abroad, and systematically states that prohibitions set forth in the Written Torah concerning preparation of meat and poultry apply in both settings, and pertain whether or not the Temple is standing, as well as to both unconsecrated and consecrated beasts. The recurrent formula, "(1) in the Land and outside the Land, (2) in the time of the Temple and not in the time of the Temple, (3) in the case of unconsecrated beasts and in the case of consecrated beasts," insists that these rules transcend boundaries of space, time, and circumstance — the principal result of the contrastive side of the hermeneutics. Thus for example, M. 5:2 sets up a grid: [1] unconsecrated versus consecrated beasts, [2] inside and outside the Temple courtyard, and that yields a variety of results as the possible cases are systematically considered. Then, at M. 6:1, another distinction is introduced. Blood of a consecrated beast is to be tossed on the altar; that of a secular one is to be buried. So that difference enters the complex.

What then is excluded? Rules pertaining to vegetables and fruits grown in the Land apply only to what is produced in the Land (in those parts of the Land possessed by Israel); tithes and heave-offerings are required only there. So the Halakhah of Hullin establishes a fundamental distinction between meat and grain (and other produce). Preparation of meat whether for the altar or for the table is subject to the same rules, which is why those rules extend the sanctity of the altar to the home. Preparation of fruits and vegetables, in which God has a different interest — these are for the priesthood and the poor, not consumed by God at the altar — does not.

What about cultic cleanness in the household? The Halakhah does not state that meat even consumed at home is to be eaten in the state of cultic cleanness as it is in the Temple (whether by the altar, whether by the priests) but the exposition at Chapter Nine rests on that premise (just as the whole of tractate/category-formation Tohorot assumes the same). The rule we should have would state, "The rules of cultic cleanness even for meat eaten at home apply (1) in the Land of Israel but not outside of the Land [where by definition everything suffers from corpse-uncleanness], (2) in the time of the Temple and not in the time of the Temple; (3) to unconsecrated animals and to Holy

Things. It applies (1) to domesticated cattle and to wild beasts, (2) to all parts of the beast, and it does apply (3) to a bird." These principles form the foundations of the rules that we do have.[5]

But the pertinent Halakhah addresses a different matter, which is the comparison and contrast of two categories of uncleanness that affect meat: food-uncleanness and carrion. Food contracts uncleanness from various specified sources, e.g., a corpse or a dead creeping thing. What we have, therefore, is a tertiary exercise in sorting out two sources of uncleanness affecting food, each with its own consequences for the status and handling of said food. Meat untouched by a corpse or dead creeping thing falls into one category, meat classified as unclean as carrion into another. The consequences of the one kind of uncleanness differ from those of the other. The Halakhah, generated as it is by the labor of hierarchical classification that defines the work of the Mishnah, exhibits a systematic concern for asking how different species of the same genus (two different sources of uncleanness affecting meat) join together or function together to produce the same result — if they do.

The issue is drawn: since a minimum volume of food is required for contracting uncleanness — a negligible volume is deemed null and outside of the system altogether — in estimating whether that requisite volume of food has been formed, do we differentiate food that has become unclean by reason of a corpse from food that has become unclean by reason of being declared carrion? That is to say, do we regard the semi-attached or distinct components of the carcass to form part of the carcass for purposes of assessing whether or not the requisite volume for receiving uncleanness has been reached. Thus, the issue is framed in terms of "connection," meaning, treating as a single entity distinct parts of the beast, e.g., the hide, which separates from the flesh, the grease or sediment or bones or sinews or horns or hooves. If we do treat these as part of the beast, they contribute to the formation of the requisite volume to contract uncleanness. If not, we do not. The distinction governing is stated at the outset: the specified, distinct components of the carcass do join together, when attached, to form the requisite volume to impart food uncleanness; for that purpose they are deemed integral to the carcass. But they do not joint together to impart uncleanness by reason of carrion, meaning, in a beast that has died of natural causes, the specified components of the carcass are not assigned an integral part in the carcass. Clearly, the entire discussion presupposes a domes-

---

[5]Those who argue that the laws of cultic purity in the theory of the Halakhah pertained to the Temple and only there seem to me not to have opened the Mishnah or paid any attention to the context presupposed by the Halakhah in general. Hullin Chapter Nine could not be more explicit, but an examination of the cases and premises of tractate Tohorot yields the same result.

tic venue and not a setting in the Temple, where, for example, no one is going to slaughter unclean cattle for a gentile!

The upshot is, the Halakhah everywhere takes for granted that considerations of uncleanness, not only those of suitability (proper slaughter and the like) pertain. So the picture is clear and one-sided: the Halakhah makes sense only if its fundamental premise, comparing the altar to the table, extends even to imposing cleanness-taboos of the former upon the latter. That general uncleanness should enter the picture presents no surprise; the Halakhah takes for granted that Israelites will eat their meat not only in accord with the requirements of the Written Torah, such as are specified, but also in accord with the rules of cultic cleanness that govern, to begin with, in the Temple itself. And that carries us deep into the religious conception of the Halakhah at hand, one that is hardly unfamiliar: the sanctity that encompasses Israel, which is distinct from the sanctity that permeates the Land of Israel, which itself forms a category-formation separate from the sanctity that is embodied in the Temple and on upward to its altar. Granted, the one is holier than the other. But how do the realms of the holy relate — and interpenetrate? That is what the Halakhah at hand addresses.

C. THE CONSISTENCY OF THE CATEGORY-FORMATION

"In the Land and outside, in the time of the Temple and afterward, in connection with consecrated and secular beasts" — the consistent program of the category-formation pertains throughout. The topical program of the Halakhah is in two parts, first what pertains to preparation of meat, covering up the blood, the prohibition of the sciatic nerve, separation of meat from dairy products ("cooking meat in milk"), and the cultic uncleanness of food, second, what involves gifts of meat or animal by-products to the priests. Letting the dam go from the nest when taking the young is placed at the end, because it has no bearing on the altar at all ("to unconsecrated birds but not to consecrated ones"). The ordering of the topics, the entire topical program, and the analytical inquiry cohere and admit no inconsistencies of either message or method.

D. THE GENERATIVITY OF THE CATEGORY-FORMATION

The Halakhic hermeneutics establishes that the sanctity of Israel is higher in the taxonomic hierarchy of types (embodiments, dimensions, locations) of sanctity than the sanctity of the Land and of the Temple and its altar. But, for all that, I cannot point to marks of generativity in the category-formation. It accommodates those facts of Scripture that pertain. But I see no extensions of the established particular hermeneutics, no amplification of the received components of the category-formation. The generativity of the category-formation comes to expression in its selection of the data that make its point — there alone. We have seen, and shall again encounter, category-formations far more powerful in their capacity to generate Halakhic extensions and amplifications than this one, with its dependence upon Scripture for so large a portion of its exegetical program.

4.
TRACTATE BEKHOROT

I. THE DEFINITION OF THE CATEGORY-FORMATION

The hermeneutics of Bekhorot, complex in its architectonics, yields a coherent construction, in which the whole exceeds in its outreach and implications the sum of the parts. Here to begin with is the program of the category-formation:

> I. THE FIRSTBORN OF ANIMALS. GENERAL RULES
>   A. The Firstborn of an Ass
>   B. The Firstborn of a Cow
>   C. The Resolution of Matters of Doubt
>   D. Not Shearing the Firstling
>   E. The Requirement to Tend the Firstling before Handing It over to the Priest
>
> II. SLAUGHTERING A FIRSTLING BY REASON OF BLEMISHES
>   A. Examining a Firstling to See Whether or Not It Is Blemished
>   B. Further Rules of Slaughtering the Firstling
>   C. Blemishes in Animals
>   D. Blemishes in Priests
>
> III. THE FIRSTBORN OF MAN
>
> IV. TITHE OF CATTLE

The topical program is clear: the firstborn of animals and the conditions that will permit the householder to slaughter it for meat (I, II). But two other subdivisions alert us to a deeper consideration, the firstborn of man and how he is redeemed (III), and tithe of cattle (IV), tacked on, it would appear, but integral to the particular hermeneutics that animates the category-formation. As this brief outline indicates, the program of the category-formation on the face of matters does not define the parameters of analogical-contrastive analysis. But as I shall show, the selection of data and the principles of interpreting them clearly respond to the result of systematic comparison and contrast of identifiable category-formations, the species of an identifiable genus.

Determining the genus of which the Halakhic category-formation, Bekhorot, firstborn, defines a species depends upon our choice of candidates for analogical-contrastive analysis. What possibilities present themselves? For a genus encompassing firstlings as a species alongside some other(s) that for at least formal reasons are deemed congruent, I see four candidates, and, while distinct, they interrelate and cohere, accounting for the particular hermeneutics of the category-formation before us.

First, we may posit a genus, food sanctified for divine purposes, with the species, (A) food that *man* designates as holy, e.g., priestly rations, tithes, and firstfruits, (B) food that *God* selects, firstlings.

Second comes the comparison and contrast of firstborn and others, Israel and the nations, the priesthood and Israel. Thus, we deal with processes of God's hierarchization of humanity and of Israel, Israel being the select, the firstborn of humanity, the priesthood, of Israel.

The third is comprised by the initial produce of field and man: (A) firstfruits, (B) firstlings, respectively.

The fourth dictates that we compare the tithe of cattle (unit IV above) with tithe of produce.

All four sets of species, respectively, comprise genera, and each set of species, when compared and contrasted, yields up its principles of selection of data and interpretation thereof. On that basis, I account for the particular hermeneutics of this category-formation, so far as that hermeneutics makes its impact; the rest of the exegetical work on the chosen topics derives from the generic hermeneutics of the Halakhah.

THE GENUS, GOD'S FOOD: We begin with the most obvious and promising hermeneutics of the category-formation: God's food (meat, fruit, vegetables and grains) and the comparison and contrast of its species. Then come the species, distinguished by the taxic indicator, *who does the choosing?* First comes food designated as holy by man, second, food selected by God for sanctification. The former congeries of isomorphic species for produce would then encompass sub-species in such category-formations as Terumot, Heave-Offering, Maaserot, tithes, and Bikkurim, firstfruits. Meat for the altar is chosen by man through an act of designation of a particular beast for a specified sacred purpose. The pertinent category-formation would then be Zebahim. These subspecies form the species: Man's choice for God's nourishment. Man by his act of intentionality sanctifies most offerings for the altar and for God's designated purposes. Whether beast or bird, the offering is the Israelite's choice. But, identifying his selection among animals and man, God too effects acts of particularized consecration as well: this specific beast or person is holy to God, by indicators defined by God.

In God's view, what he wants, the best, is what comes first. Specifically, he selects the firstfruits of the life-processes of Israel itself — counterpart to the firstfruits of the Land taken by the householder to the priest. These God designates: the firstborn males among animals, the firstborn only of Israel among the nations, and the priesthood among Israel. Then, logic dictates, we further should compare firstlings and firstfruits. The classifications having been established, the hierarchization will compare the level of sanctification inherent in the Land's produce with that inherent in Israel's produce (encompassing also Israel's herds and flocks, made holy by forming Israel's possession, wherever Israel is located). The result can only be as follows: utopian sanctification effected through carnate Israel exceeds in sanctity locative sanctification effected through the Land of Israel. In concrete terms, the outcome is, Israel's crops overseas are not subject to God's domain, but Israel's firstborn sons and the tithe of its herd and flock are.

THE GENUS, ISRAEL AND THE NATIONS: Having hierarchized the People of Israel above the Land of Israel, the logical next step carries us to Israel and the nations, that is, from a locative taxon to a utopian one in the work of hierarchization. The second genus, the Israelite species of the genus of humanity, fits integrally into the Halakhic category-formation, Bekhorot. That is because, as the Halakhah explicitly states, the class of animals that ends up on the altar, that God chooses, corresponds to a class of mankind linked to the altar and a class of Israel also chosen by God. The first is comprised by firstborn animals, the second, by firstborn male Israelites, redeemed from the altar, and the third, by the priesthood, fed from the altar and accorded special rights over the firstborn of animals and of Israel. What these three classes bear in common, then, is that all are sanctified by God's, not man's, selection. The analogical initiative then produces a contrast. While the Halakhah of firstlings encompasses the firstborn of man, the firstborn of a clean beast, and the firstborn of an unclean beast, the exposition of the Halakhah explicitly treats the priesthood, within Israel, as equivalent to the firstborn among clean beasts, meaning, blemishes that disqualify beasts from the altar disqualify priests from serving at the altar. So the equivalency of the firstborn of any Israelite couple (here the woman's condition is essential to the transaction) and the priests is established. That rather subtle exercise of serial comparison and contrast then forms the logical next step beyond the opening one.

THE GENUS, FIRSTLINGS AND FIRSTFRUITS, COMPARED AND CONTRASTED: The third of the three theoretical genera — the logical continuation and complement of the first and the second — involves the obvious comparison and contrast: firstfruits and firstlings, that is, the inanimate and the animate selections of God. The classifications — firstborn of man and wife, firstborn of beasts, firstfruits of the Land — are readily situated in relationship to one another. The self-evident, descending order, man, beast, crops underscores God's role in the selection of the first and the second, giving way to man's exercise of choice (through random selection to be sure) in the third. Firstlings and the tithe of the herd and flock compare to firstfruits and the tithe of the field and orchard and express the same conception. God claims his share out of the best of the produce. But here in Bekhorot (and, *mutatis mutandis,* in Bikkurim) God's claim takes effect not when man determines to make use of the produce of the Land, as in the case of tithes and heave-offerings of crops of the Land of Israel. Rather, God's claim on the fruit of the womb comes into view as soon as the offspring, human or animal, or the crop, emerges. Upon birth or ripening, then, the firstling or first fruit is holy, belonging to God, hence the priesthood, and has to be redeemed in the case of man or otherwise disposed of in the case of animals or presented to the priesthood in the case of firstfruits. Man's will bears no consequence in the selection of the firstling, man or beast or the first-ripening fruit.

The analogy having been established, what of the contrast of firstlings and firstfruits? Here again, the firstfuits represent a locative species, firstlings and firstborn, a utopian (and therefore, hierarchically holier) one. What is required is firstfruits of those species in which the Land specializes; who is obligated is, the Israelite who not only possesses a share in the Land but also derives from the Israel to whom the Land was initially handed over. Birth to an Israelite father and mother (within the qualifications the Halakhah sets forth) imposes the liability of redemption upon the father, and birth to an Israelite owner imposes liability to tithing the herd or flock. A more striking contrast would be difficult to locate than the one that differentiates firstfruits from the firstborn of man and beast and the obligation to tithe the herd and flock. By contrast to firstfruits, obligatory only for Israelite landholders, firstlings must be presented by all Israelites. So in this aspect, possession of the Land ceases to differentiate one group of Israelites from another. Tithes of cattle are owing, furthermore, not only in the Land of Israel but wherever Israelites are located who own herds and flocks. And, along these same lines, all Israelites' firstborn male children, wherever they are born, must be redeemed. So the source of sanctification is personal, utopian, and not enlandised and locative, and here we find ourselves within a hermeneutics of sanctification that derives from genealogy, not geography.

THE GENUS, TITHE OF CROPS, TITHE OF CATTLE, COMPARED AND CONTRASTED: The final genus, dealing with the tithe of cattle/tithe of crops, stands on its own but finds an integral position within the larger construction of the category-formation. What we have is a continuation of the comparison and contrast of the genus, agricultural offerings to God (e.g., firstfruits, firstlings). All natural-born cattle are subject to the tithe. The designation of the tenth beast is done by the householder in a random manner, just as the designation of tithe and heave offering must be done by chance, not by deliberate choice. So in that important detail, the agricultural offerings form a single genus. But then the contrast is striking. The tithe of cattle is required even from herds and flocks located outside of the Land of Israel, and it is required even when the Temple is not standing. It is an on-going obligation, inherent in animate property of Israel, meaning, the tithe is collected from one's entire herd and flock. But in the present context the fact that the tithe is required outside of the Land means that it is the possession by the Israelite, not location in the Land, that imposes the obligation to tithe. So operative is a personal, not a locative, criterion. Then the analogy begins with the obligation to redeem the firstborn Israelite male and extends to the parallel obligation to redeem the tithe of Israel's flocks and herds, wherever situated. Genealogy shades over into possession, not location.

So much for identifying the genus and the species, an exercise in four parts, which identifies the logical context for details of the Halakhah. We can now account for the components of the category-formation and can identify the particular hermeneutics that, analogical-contrastive analysis shows, will guide selection and interpretation of data. Within the theory of the present project, we may account for the expositions of the category-formations by appeal to three sources of data, their selection and interpretation: the particular hermeneutics, now reviewed, the generic hermeneutics, and a corpus of inert facts, often deriving from Scripture. Now to Scripture's data, which form the raw materials for the category-formation.

II. THE FOUNDATIONS OF THE HALAKHIC CATEGORY-FORMATION

The pertinent verses of the Written Torah began with the most general, covering firstborn whether of man or beast:

> "Sanctify to me all the firstborn, whatever opens the womb among the children of Israel, both of man and of beast"
>
> Ex. 13:2

The firstborn of man and of unclean beasts are redeemed, the proceeds assigned to the priests; the firstborn of clean beasts is slaughtered in the Temple court, the meat then going to the priest:

> "Howbeit the firstborn of man shall you surely redeem...but the firstling of an ox you shall not redeem; they are holy...and the flesh of them shall be yours"
>
> Num. 18:15-18

If the firstborn of a clean beast was blemished, it is given to the priest; he may eat it anywhere or sell it or give it away, as his own property:

> "And if there be any blemish therein, lameness of blindness...the unclean and the clean may eat it alike, as the gazelle and as the hart"
>
> Dt. 15:21-22

One must sanctify the firstling of an ox and declare it holy:

> "You shall sanctify it to the Lord your God"
>
> Dt. 15:10

Firstlings may not be brought to the Land from outside:

> "And you shall eat before the Lord your God...the tithe of your grain of your wine and of your oil and the firstling of your herd and of your flock"
>
> Dt. 14:23

A firstling must be eaten during its first year, whether blemished or otherwise:

> "You shall eat it before the Lord your God year by year...and if there be any blemish therein...you shall eat it within your gates"
>
> Dt. 15:20-22

What renders a firstborn animal unfit for the altar renders a priest unfit for service, a signal of the comparability of the firstborn and the priesthood. As to blemishes that disqualify priests for service at the altar, Scripture states the following:

> "For no one who has a blemish shall draw near: a man blind or lame, or one who has a mutilated face or a limb too long or a man who has an injured foot or an injured hand or a hunchback or a dwarf or a man with a defect in his sight or an itching disease or scabs or crushed testicles"
>
> Lev. 21:18-20

So much for the Halakhah of firstlings. But these are not the only portion of the herds and the flocks that God requires. There is a counterpart, among the animal possessions of Israel, to the crops of the Land and its fields and orchards, and a tithe for the priests is required of these as well. Accordingly, the Halakhah encompasses, also, the tithe of the herds and the flocks:

> "And all the tithe of herds and flocks, every tenth animal of all that pas under the herdsman's staff, shall be holy to the Lord. A man shall not inquire whether it is good or bad, neither shall he exchange it; and if he exchanges it, then both it and that for which it is exchanged shall be holy; it shall be redeemed."
>
> Lev. 27:32-33

Like other gifts to the priesthood, the law of the firstborn applies both when the Temple is standing and when the Temple is not standing. But the priest himself owes firstborn animals born to him to the altar; sacrificial portions are burned up, and the priest gets the rest of the meat, Scripture being explicit, at Dt. 15:19, "All the firstling males that are born of your herd and of your flock," encompassing those born to the priesthood. But priests and Levites do not have to redeem their firstborn sons, as ordinary Israelites do.

III. THE EXPOSITION OF THE COMPONENTS OF THE GIVEN CATEGORY-FORMATION BY THE MISHNAH-TOSEFTA-YERUSHALMI-BAVLI

I. THE FIRSTBORN OF ANIMALS. GENERAL RULES

A. *THE FIRSTBORN OF AN ASS*
M. 1:1 (1) He who purchases the unborn offspring of the ass of a gentile, (2) and he who sells it to him (even though one is not permitted to do so), (3) and he who is a partner with him; (4) and [either] he who receives [asses] from him [under contract to rear them and share in the profit], and [or] he who delivers [asses] to him under contract [to rear them and share in the profit] — it [the foetus, when born] is exempt from the law of the firstling, since it is said, "[All the firstborn] in Israel" (Num. 3:13) — but not [the firstborn produced] among others. Priests and Levites are exempt [from the law of giving a lamb in redemption of the firstborn of an ass], by an argument *a fortiori:* If those of Israelites were exempted in the wilderness [by reason of the Levites, Num. 3:45], how much the more so should they exempt their own?

T. 1:1 He who purchases the unborn offspring of the ass of a gentile, and he who sells it to him (even though he is not permitted to do so), and he who is a partner with him, and he who receives [one] from him under contract [to rear and share in the profit], and he who hands over to him under contract, is exempt from the law of the firstling, since it is said, "All the firstborn in Israel" (Num. 3:13) — and not among others [M. Bekh. 1:1A-E].

T. 1:2 And so do you rule in the case of priests and Levites [M. Bekh. 1:1F]. Since priests and Levites are liable to the law of the firstling in the case of a clean beast, one might have supposed that they should be liable to the law of the firstling in the case of an unclean beast. Accordingly, Scripture states, "Both of man and of beast [they shall be mine]" (Num. 3:13). That to which you are subject in the case of man, you are subject in the case of beast. That to which you are not subject in the case of man, you are not subject in the case of beast. Levites are exempt in the case of the firstling of an unclean beast. But they give redemption [-money] for the firstborn son, or a redemption [lamb] for the firstborn of an ass only to priests alone.

T. 1:3 Among all unclean beasts, you have liable to the law of the firstling only for the ass alone. Among all wild animals you have only the dog which is prohibited because of the price [received therefor] alone.

T. 1:4 R. Meir did say, "Anyone who carries out the commandment concerning the firstborn of an ass — they accredit it for him as if he carried out the commandment of every unclean beast. Anyone who does not carry out the commandment concerning the firstborn of an ass — they credit it to him as if he annulled the commandment for every unclean beast."

M. 1:2 A cow which bore [an offspring] like an ass, or an ass which bore [an offspring] like a horse — it [the offspring] is exempt from the law of the firstling, since it is said, "The firstling of an ass" (Ex. 13:13), "The firstling of an ass" (Ex. 34:20) — two times, [meaning that the rule applies] only when that which gives birth is an ass and that which is born is an ass. What is the rule as to eating them? A clean beast which bore [an offspring] like an unclean beast — it [the offspring] is permitted as to eating. And an unclean beast which bore [an offspring] like a clean beast — it [the offspring] is prohibited as to eating. For that which comes forth from the unclean is unclean, and that which comes forth from the clean is clean. An unclean fish which swallowed a clean fish — it [the clean fish] is permitted as to eating. A clean fish which swallowed an unclean fish — it [the unclean fish] is prohibited as to eating, for it is not its product.

T. 1:5 R. Yosé the Galilean says, "But the firstborn of an ox or the firstborn of a sheep or the firstborn of a goat you shall not redeem. They are holy (Num. 18:17). The firstborn of an ox [means that the rule applies] only when that which gives birth and that which is born is an ox. The firstborn of a sheep [means that the rule applies] only when that which gives birth and that which is born are sheep. The firstborn of a goat [means that the rule applies] only when that which gives birth and that which is born are goats" [M. Bekh. 1:2A-D]. And if it [the offspring] exhibits some of the traits of the dam, it is liable to the law of the firstborn.

T. 1:6 A clean beast which bore an offspring like an unclean beast — it [the offspring] is permitted for eating [M. Bekh. 1:2F]. And if it exhibits some of the traits [of the dam], it is liable to the law of the firstborn. And an unclean [beast] which bore an offspring like a clean beast — it is prohibited for eating [M. Bekh. 1:2G]. For that which comes forth from the unclean is unclean, and that which comes forth from the clean is clean [M. Bekh. 1:2H].

T. 1:7 An unclean fish which swallowed a clean fish — it [the clean fish] is permitted as to eating. And a clean fish which swallowed an unclean fish — it [the unclean fish] is prohibited as to eating, for it is not its [the clean fish's] product [M. Bekh. 1:2I-K].

T. 1:8 On what account [then] did they rule that the honey of bees is permitted? For they do not bring it forth [from their own bodies] but store it up. The honey of gazin-bees is prohibited, for it is only saliva.

T. 1:9 R. Simeon says, "Why does Scripture say, 'Camel, Camel' (Lev. 11:4, Deut. 14:7) — two times? To encompass the camel which is born of a cow as equivalent to one born of a camel. And if its head and the greater part of its body are similar to those of its dam, it is permitted for eating." And sages say, "That which goes forth from the unclean is unclean and that which goes forth from the clean is clean [M. Bekh. 1:2H]. For an unclean beast does not give birth to a clean one, nor does a clean one give birth to an unclean one, nor does a large one come out of a small one, nor does a small one come out of a large one, nor does a human being come out of any of them, nor does any of them come out of a human being."

T. 1:10 A small clean beast gives birth at five months. A large clean beast gives birth at nine months. A large unclean beast gives birth at twelve months, the dog at fifty days, the cat at fifty-two, the pig at sixty days, the fox and all creeping things at six months; the wolf, the lion, the bear, the panther, the leopard, the elephant, the baboon, and the ape at three years, and the snake at seven years.

T. 1:11 The dolphins give birth and raise [their young] as does man. An unclean fish casts forth young. A clean fish lays eggs.

T. 1:12 The innards of fish and the foetus [thereof] are eaten only on the advice of an expert. Fowl are eaten in accord with tradition [as to which are clean]. A hunter is believed to state, "This fowl is clean."

M. 1:3 An ass which had not given birth and which bore two males [and it is not known which of them came forth first] — the farmer gives a single lamb to the priest. [If it bore] male and female [and it is not known which of them came forth first] — one separates a single lamb [but keeps it] for himself. Two asses which had not given birth and which bore two males — one gives two lambs to the priest. [If they bore] (1) a male and a female or (2) two males and a female, one gives a single lamb to the priest. [If they bore] (1) two females and one male, (2) or two males and two females, there is nothing whatsoever here for the priest.

M. 1:4 [Two asses], one [of which] had given birth and one which had not given birth, and which bore two males — one gives a single lamb to the priest. [If they produced] a male and a female, the farmer separates a single lamb for himself. For it is said, "And every firstling of an ass you shall redeem with a lamb" (Ex. 34:20) — (1) [A lamb deriving] from sheep or from goats, (2) male or female, (3) large or small, (4) blemished or unblemished. (1) And one redeems with [a single lamb] many firstlings. (2) And it enters the fold to be tithed. (3) And if it dies, they derive benefit from it.

T. 1:19 An ass which had not given birth and which gave birth to two males [and it is not known which is the firstborn] — one gives [for redemption] a single lamb to the priest. [If it gives birth to] a male and a female, one separates a lamb. But it is for himself. [M. Bekh. 1:3A-D]. Two asses which had [not] given birth and which gave birth to two males — one gives two lambs to the priest. [If they gave birth to] a male and a female or to two males and a female one gives one lamb to the priest. [If they gave birth to] two females and a male or to two males and two females, and one does not know [which is which], there is nothing whatsoever here for the priest [M. Bekh. I-J]. But one separates one lamb and redeems with it each one by itself [M. Bekh. 1:4I].

T. 1:13 A cow which gave birth to a kind of lamb — they do not redeem therewith [the kind of lamb] the firstborn of an ass. For every place in which lamb is stated encompasses sheep and goats, large and small, males and females, unblemished and blemished [M. Bekh. 1:4E-H]. One redeems [the firstborn of an ass] with [a redemption-lamb], does it a second and a third time [with the same lamb] [M. Bekh. 1:4I]. And he brings it in fulfillment of a vow and as a thank-offering, for his sin-offering and for his guilt-offering. And it is liable to the law of the firstborn and to the priestly gifts [the two cheeks, shoulder, and maw]. R. Eleazar says, "The hybrid of a ewe and a goat — they redeem therewith [the firstborn of an ass]. That of a koy — they do not deem therewith [the firstborn of an ass]" [M. Bekh.

1:5B].

T. 1:15 What is the least one gives? R. Yosé bar Judah says, "One should give no [redemption-lamb] of less than the value of a sheqel." What is [the sort of lamb used for] the redemption of the firstborn of an ass which enters the fold for tithing [M. Bekh. 1:4J]? (1) An Israelite who had [firstborn asses] the status of which was in doubt and who redeemed them [M. Bekh. 1:3D, 1:4C]; (2) and so too a priest who inherited from his mother's father, an Israelite; (3) or if one gave him [a priest] the firstborn of an ass as a gift to redeem it [and the priest redeemed it] — this [lamb (D, E, F)] is the redemption-lamb of a firstborn of an ass which enters the fold for tithing. Lo, [if] one has a firstling and does not have [a lamb] with which to redeem it.

T. 1:16 [and] a priest said to him, "Give it to me, and I shall redeem it," Lo, this one should give it to him only if he knows that he will [most certainly] redeem it.

M. 1:5 They do not redeem [a firstling of an ass] with (1) a calf, or (2) with a wild beast, or (3) with an animal which has been properly slaughtered, or (4) with an animal which is terefah, or (5) with a hybrid [of a he-goat and a ewe], or (6) with a koy [the offspring of a he-goat and a hind]. R. Eliezer permits in the case of a hybrid, because it is deemed a lamb, and prohibits in the case of the koy, because it is a matter of doubt [whether it is deemed a lamb]. [If] one gave it [the offspring of an ass directly] to the priest, the priest is not permitted to keep it unless he sets aside and designates a lamb in its place [which he also, of course, keeps].

T. 1:14 Just as they do not redeem [the firstborn of an ass] with a slain [lamb], so they do not redeem the firstborn of an ass who died [M. Bekh. 1:6F, H]. The firstborn of an ass — its requirement is that one keep it for thirty days. Thereafter, one must either redeem it or break its neck [M. Bekh. 1:7A B].

M. 1:6 He who separates a redemption-lamb for a firstborn of an ass and who died — R. Eliezer says, (1) "They [the heirs] are responsible for it [to give the redemption-lamb to the priest], (2) as [the heirs are liable for replacing, should the money be lost] the five selas [paid in the redemption of the firstborn] son." And sages say, (1) "They are not liable for it [to give the redemption-lamb to the priest], (2) as [the are not liable in the case of] the redemption of second tithe." Testified R. Joshua and R. Sadoq concerning the redemption-lamb which was set aside for the firstling of an ass [and] which had died, that there is nothing whatsoever for the priest here [=C]. [If] the firstling [of an ass] died, R. Eliezer says, "It is to be buried. And [the owner] is permitted to derive benefit from the lamb [which had been set aside to redeem it]." And sages say, "It need not be buried. And the

lamb belongs to the priest."

M. 1:7 [If] one did not want to redeem it [the firstling of an ass], he breaks its neck from behind with a hatchet, and buries it. The requirement of redemption takes precedence over the requirement of breaking the neck, since it is said, "And if you will not redeem it, then you will break its neck" (Ex. 34:20). The requirement of espousing [a Hebrew bondwoman] takes precedence over the requirement of redemption, since it is said, "So that he has not espoused her, then he shall let her be redeemed" (Ex. 21:8). The requirement of Levirate marriage takes precedence over the ceremony of halisah — at first, when they would consummate the Levirate marriage for the sake of fulfilling a commandment. But now, that they do not consummate the Levirate marriage for the sake of fulfilling a commandment, they have ruled: The requirement of halisah takes precedence over the requirement of Levirate marriage. The requirement of redeeming [an unclean beast dedicated to the Temple] is incumbent upon the master. He takes precedence over every other person [M. Ar. 8:2], since it is said, "[Then he shall ransom it...] or if it is not redeemed, then it shall be sold according to thy estimation" (Lev. 27:27).

T. 1:17 One breaks its neck from behind with a hatchet and buries it [M. Bekh. 1:7A]. And it is prohibited for benefit. One should not kill it with a staff or a reed or lock the door in its face so that it will die. And if one has done so, Lo, he has not carried out his obligation.

T. 1:18 While it is alive [and unredeemed] it is prohibited for shearing or for any sort of labor. And R. Simeon declares permitted. And the firstling of man is permitted in all instances.

In line with the hermeneutics outlined at the outset, we should not find surprising that the Halakhic repertoire commences with the main point: the firstborn produced in Israel are subject to the law of the firstling, not those produced among outsiders, M. 1:1. This is framed in terms of the offspring of the ass of a gentile, but the rule transcends the case. The further rules, M. 1:2ff., go over issues of the generic hermeneutics, e.g., precision in categorization, problems of mixtures, confusion, interstitial cases, and the like. What is not covered by the particular or the generic hermeneutics forms the detritus of inert facts that the Halakhah has, also, to deliver.

B. *THE FIRSTBORN OF A COW*

M. 2:1 (1) He who purchases the unborn offspring of the cow of a gentile, (2) and he who sells it to him (even though one is not permitted to do so), (3) and he who is a partner with him, (4) and he who receives [cows] from him (5) and he who delivers [cows] to him under contract [to rear them and share in the profit] is exempt from the law of the firstling, since it is said, "[All the firstborn] in Israel" (Num. 3:13) — but not [the firstborn produced] among others. Priests and Levites are liable. They are not exempted from the law of the firstborn of a clean beast. But they are exempt only from the redemption of the firstborn son and from [the law of the firstling in regard to] the firstborn of an ass.

T. 2:1 He who purchases the unborn offspring of the cow of a gentile and he who sells it to him (even though one is not permitted to do so), and he who is a partner with him, and he who gives one to him as a partner, and he who receives one from him or gives one to him under contract [to raise it and share in the profits], is exempt from the law of the firstling [M. Bekh. 2:1A-C]. R. Judah says, "Also he who receives one from a gentile [under contract to raise it and share in the profits] (even though one is not permitted to do so), Lo, this one estimates its value and gives half of its price to the priest. And one who gives one over to him [a gentile] under contract (even though one is not permitted to do so), Lo, this one estimates it, and even ten times its price, and gives all of its price to the priest." And sages say, "Since the finger of a gentile is mixed up in the matter, it is free of the law of the firstling."

T. 2:2 A beast in the time of the Wilderness, a beast of the sanctuary, and a beast of a gentile who died without heirs is exempt from the law of the firstling. A beast set aside for payment of the arnonah-tax is liable to the law of the firstling.

M. 2:2 All Holy Things, the permanent blemish of which came before their consecration, and which were redeemed are liable to the law of the firstling, and to the priestly gifts, and go forth for secular purposes, for sheering and for labor. And their offspring and their milk are permitted after their redemption. And he who slaughters them outside [the Temple court] is free of punishment. And they are not subject to the law of the substitute. And if they died, they are redeemed, except for the firstling and for tithe [of cattle].

M. 2:3 [All Holy Things], the consecration of which came before their blemish, or [in which was] a transient blemish before their consecration, and in which afterward a permanent blemish appeared, and which were redeemed, are free of the law of the firstling, and from the priestly gifts, and do not go forth for secular purposes, for sheering and for labor. And their offspring and their milk are prohibited [even] after their redemption. And he who slaughters them outside is liable. And they are subject to the law of the substitute. And if they die, they are buried.

T. 2:3 All Holy Things, the permanent blemish of which came before their consecration and which were redeemed, are liable to the law of the firstling, and to the priestly gifts [M. Bekh. 2:2A-B]. And their offspring are unconsecrated. And they are redeemed when unblemished. And one brings them for any sort of animal-sacrifice which he likes before they are redeemed. And the laws of sacrilege apply to them after they are redeemed. But whether before they are redeemed or after they are redeemed, they do not impart the status of substitute [to an animal designated in their stead]. Whether before they are redeemed or after they are redeemed, he who shears them and he who does work with them is not smitten with forty stripes [M. Bekh. 2:2B]. The general principle of the matter is this: Lo, they are deemed unconsecrated beasts for every purpose, and they are subject only to the requirement of evaluation alone.

T. 2:4 But if their consecration came before their blemish, or a transient blemish [appeared] before their consecration and afterward a permanent blemish appeared in them, and they were redeemed, they are free of the law of the firstling and of the priestly gifts [M. Bekh. 2:3A-B]. And their offspring are holy. And they are not redeemed when unblemished. And one does not bring them for any sort of animal sacrifice which he likes. And before they are redeemed the laws of sacrilege apply to them. And after they are redeemed the laws of sacrilege do not apply to them. And whether before they are redeemed or after they are redeemed, they do impart the status of substitute. And whether before they are redeemed or after they are redeemed, he who shears them or performs work with them, Lo, this one is smitten with forty stripes [M. Bekh. 2:3B]. The general principle of the matter is this: Lo, they are deemed equivalent to consecrated beasts for every purpose, and there applies to them [the right of secular use] only if they are permitted through a proper act of [sacrificial] slaughter alone.

M. 2:4 He who receives [under contract to raise and share in the profits] a flock from a gentile on "iron-flock terms"— the offspring are exempt [from the law of the firstling]. But the offspring of the offspring are liable. [If the Israelite] had stipulated [that they] should stand in place of their mothers, the offspring of the offspring are exempt. And the offspring of the offspring of the offspring are liable. Rabban Simeon b. Gamaliel says, "Even up to ten generations are they exempt, for the right [to lay claim to] them belongs to the gentile."

T. 2:5 [He who receives under contract to raise and share in the profits] a flock from a gentile on 'iron terms' — the offspring are exempt [from the law or the firstling]. The offspring of the offspring are liable. [If] the mothers died and one set up the offspring instead of their mothers, the offspring are exempt. And the offspring of the offspring are liable [M. Bekh. 2:4A-F]. Rabban Simeon b. Gamaliel says, "They, their offspring, and the offspring of their offspring are exempt from the law of the firstling and from the priestly gifts, even to the end of time" [M. Bekh. 2:4G-H].

M. 2:5 A sheep which gave birth [to an offspring] something like a goat, or a goat which gave birth [to an offspring] something like a sheep — it [the offspring] is exempt from the law of the firstling. But if it bears some of the traits [of the mother], it is liable.

T. 2:6 A sheep which gave birth [to an offspring] something like a goat, or a goat which gave birth [to an offspring] something like a sheep — it [the offspring] is exempt from the law of the firstling. But if it bears some of the traits [of the mother], it is liable to the law of the offspring [M. Bekh. 2:5].

M. 2:6 A sheep which had not given birth and which bore two males, and both of their heads emerged simultaneously — R. Yosé the Galilean says, "Both of them belong to the priest, since it is said, 'The males [even more than one, e.g., when the two were born simultaneously] belong to the Lord' (Ex. 13:12)." And sages say, "It is not possible to determine exactly [for there to be simultaneous birth]." But: "One belongs to him and one to the priest." R. Tarfon says, "The priest selects for himself the better." R. Aqiba says, "They compromise between them" [with the one who takes the fatter giving the other half the excess value]. And as to the second, it pastures until it becomes blemished. "And it is liable to the priestly gifts. R. Yosé declares it exempt [from the priestly gifts]." [If] one of them died, R. Tarfon says, "Let them divide [the value of the living one]." R. Aqiba says, "He who lays claim against his fellow bears the burden of proof." [If it bore simultaneously] a male and a female, there is nothing whatsoever for the priest here.

M. 2:7 Two sheep which had not given birth and which bore two males — one gives both of them to the priest. [If they bore] a male and a female, the male goes to the priest. [If they bore] two males and a female, one of them goes to him [the owner] and one to the priest. R. Tarfon says, "The priest selects the better of them for himself." R. Aqiba says, "They compromise between them." And as to the second: it pastures until it is blemished. And it is liable for priestly gifts. R. Yosé declares it exempt [from priestly gifts]. [If] one of them died, R. Tarfon says, "They divide it." R. Aqiba says, "He who lays claim against his fellow bears the burden of proof." [If they bore] two females and a male or two males and two females, there is nothing whatsoever for the priest here.

M. 2:8 [Two, of which] one had given birth and one had not given birth, which bore two males — one is for him and one for the priest. R. Tarfon says, "The priest selects for himself the better of the two." R. Aqiba says, "They compromise between them." And as to the second: it pastures until it is blemished. And it is liable for the priestly gifts. R. Yosé declares exempt. R. Yosé did rule: "Any [animal] the exchange of which is in the hand of a priest is free of the obligation to priestly gifts." R. Meir declares liable. [If] one of them died, R. Tarfon says, "They divide it." R. Aqiba says, "He who lays claim against his fellow bears the burden of proof." [If they bore] male and female, there is nothing whatsoever for the priest here.

T. 2:7 A sheep which had not given birth and which gave birth to two males and their heads came forth simultaneously — R. Yosé the Galilean says, "Both of them belong to the priest, since it is said, 'The males belong to the Lord' (Ex. 13:12)." And sages say, "It is not possible. But one belongs to him and one to the priest." R. Tarfon says, "The better of them." R. Aqiba says, "The worse of them." The second is set out to pasture until it is blemished. And it is liable to the priestly gifts [when it is slaughtered]. And R. Yosé declares it exempt [M. Bekh. 2:6A-K].

T. 2:8 [If] one of them died, R. Tarfon says, "Let them divide it." R. Aqiba says, "He who lays claim against his fellow bears the burden of proof. [If] it bore male and female, and it is not known [which came first], there is nothing whatsoever for the priest here [M. Bekh. 2:6L-O]. But the male is set out to pasture until it is blemished, and then it is sold, and the owner eats it when it is blemished. Two sheep which had not given birth and which bore two males — One gives both of them to the priest. [If it bore] male and female, the male goes to the priest. [If it bore] two males and a female, one of them belongs to him and one to the priest [M. Bekh. 2:7A-D]. R. Tarfon says, "The better of them." R. Aqiba says, "The worse of them."

T. 2:9 ([If the firstborn is] a koy, it is set to pasture until it is blemished.) And it is liable to the priestly gifts. And R. Yosé declares one of them exempt. R. Tarfon says, "Let them divide it." And R. Aqiba says, "He who lays claim against his fellow bears the burden of proof."

T. 2:10 [If there were two sheep, which had not given birth and they bore] two females and a male, or two males and two females, and it is not known [which is which], there is nothing whatsoever for the priest here [M. Bekh. 2:7M-N]. But the males are set to pasture until they are blemished and are eaten on account of their blemish by the owner. [If] one had given birth and one had not given birth, and they gave birth to two males, one belongs to him and one to a priest [M. Bekh. 2:8A-B]. R. Tarfon says, "The better of them." R. Aqiba says, "The worse of them." The second is set to pasture until it is blemished, and it is liable for the priestly gifts. R. Yosé declares it exempt, for R. Yosé did rule, "Any animal, the exchange of which is in the hand of a priest, is free of the obligation to priestly gifts. R. Meir declares liable [M. Bekh. 2:8E-J]. For he did rule, "[The priest may claim], 'If it is a firstling, give it to me. And if not, give me its [priestly] gifts." [If] one of them died, R. Tarfon says, "They divide it." R. Aqiba says, "He who lays claim against his fellow bears the burden of proof." [If] they bore a male and a female, and it is not known [which is which], there is nothing whatsoever here for the priest [M. Bekh. 2.8N-O]. But let the male be set to pasture until it is blemished, and then the owner eats it on account of its blemish.

The pattern repeats itself, making the same principal point for a new case, so M. 2:1. Now we deal with species that yield animals for the altar, so M. 2:2-3 raise an interstitial problem, what to do with the firstling of a consecrated beast that has been redeemed and is therefore liable to the law of the firstling. If the permanent blemish is prior to consecration, then the firstling has been conceived not in a condition of sanctification, but if after, it has. So too, if the ownership is ultimately vested in a gentile, even though the beast is under an Israelite's care, the beast is not liable to the law of the firstling. Once more, generic hermeneutics take over, with problems of confusion, mixture, and other aspects of interstitiality.

C. *THE RESOLUTION OF MATTERS OF DOUBT*

M. 2:9 A beast born from the side and that which comes after it — R. Tarfon says, "Both of them pasture until they are blemished. And they are eaten by the owner when blemished." R. Aqiba says, "Both of them are not subject to the law of the firstling: The first, because it is not that which opens the womb, and the second, because the other came before it."

M. 3:1 He who purchases a beast from a gentile, and it is not known whether it has given birth or whether it has not given birth — R. Ishmael says, "A goat a year old [which produced an offspring] — it [the offspring] certainly belongs to the priest. From that age and onward it is a matter of doubt [whether or not the offspring is a firstborn]. A sheep two years old [which produced an offspring] — it certainly belongs to the priest. From that age and onward it is a matter of doubt. A cow and an ass three years old [which produced offspring] — they certainly belong to the priest. From that age and onward it is a matter of doubt." Said to him R. Aqiba, "If by the offspring alone [and not by a discharge] the beast were exempted [from the law of the firstling], it would be in accord with your words. But they have said: The token of [having given birth to] an offspring, in a small beast is womb-discharge, in a large beast is afterbirth. And in a woman are the foetus-sack and afterbirth." This is the general principle: [In the case of] any [beast] of which it is known that it has given birth, the priest has nothing whatsoever here. And [in the case of] any beast [of which it is known] that it has not given birth, Lo, this goes to the priest. If it is a matter of doubt, let it [the new-born beast] be eaten by the owner when it is blemished. R. Eliezer b. Jacob says, "A large beast which discharged a clot of blood — Lo, this [the clot] is to be buried. And the mother, thereby, is exempted from the law of the firstling."

T. 2:11 He who purchases a beast from a gentile, and it is not known whether it has given birth or whether it had not given birth — [The offspring of] a goat a year old certainly belongs to the priest. From that age and onward it is a matter of doubt. The offspring of a sheep two years old certainly belongs to the priest. From that age and onward it is a matter of doubt. [The offspring of] a cow three years old certainly belongs to the priest. From that age and onward, it is a matter of doubt. And [the offspring of] an ass is deemed equivalent to a cow. R. Yosé bar Judah says, "[The offspring of] an ass four years old [certainly belongs to the priest]." To this point are the words of R. Ishmael [M. Bekh. 3:1A-H].

T. 2:12 And when these words were stated before R. Joshua, he said, "Go and say to Ishmael, 'You have erred. If by the offspring alone [and not by a discharge] the beast were exempted from the law of the firstling, well should you have ruled.'" But they have said: The token [of having given birth to] an offspring: in a small beast is womb-discharge. In a large beast, afterbirth. And in a woman, the foetus-sack and afterbirth. But I rule: A goat which has produced a womb-discharge at the age of six gives birth when one year old. A sheep which has produced a womb discharge in her first year gives birth at the age of two." R. Aqiba says, "It does not derive from this reasoning, but: In the case of any [beast] of which it is known that it has given birth, the priest has nothing whatsoever here. And [in the case] of any beast [of which it is known] that it has not given birth, Lo, this goes to the priest. And if it is a matter of doubt, let it be eaten by the owner when it is blemished" [M. Bekh. 3:1P-R].

T. 2:13 R. Eliezer b. Jacob says, "A large beast which discharged a clot of blood — It [the clot] requires burial [M. Bekh. 3:1]. 'But it does not impart uncleanness to the one who carries it.' And that which is born after it is exempt from the law of the firstling."

M. 3:2 Rabban Simeon b. Gamaliel says, "He who purchases from a gentile a beast that was nursing does not scruple lest it [the sucking animal] be the offspring of another [beast]. [If] he went into his fold and saw beasts which had not previously given

birth nursing, and those which had previously given birth nursing, he does not scruple lest the offspring of one has come to another or that the offspring of the other has come to this one."

T. 2:14 He who purchases from a gentile a beast that was nursing that which is born after it is exempt from the law of the firstling on account of doubt, because it cares for that to which it has not given birth. Rabban Simeon b. Gamaliel says, "Lo, it remains in its presumed condition [of having given birth to the beast which it nurses, and for that reason, is exempt from the law of the firstling]."

T. 2:15 And so did Rabban Simeon b. Gamaliel state, "He who enters his fold at night and saw that ten or fifteen animals which had not given birth produce offspring, and at dawn he came and found lambs sucking from old beasts and females from those which had not given birth, "does not scruple lest the offspring of this one has come to another, or that the offspring of the other has come to this one" [M. Bekh. 3:2B].

T. 2:16 And so did Rabban Simeon b. Gamaliel state, "He who hands over his beast to a gentile to pasture (even though one is not permitted to do so), and at dawn he came and found males nursing from old beasts and females nursing from those which had not given birth, "does not scruple lest the gentile have brought the offspring of one to another and the offspring of the other to this one."

This set of rulings carries forward the generic hermeneutics.

D.   NOT SHEARING THE FIRSTLING

M. 3:3 [With reference to Deut. 15:19: You shall do no work with the firstling of your herd, nor shear the firstling of your flock,"] R. Yosé ben Hammeshullam says, "He who slaughters the firstling makes a place with the hatchet on either side and pulls out the hair. And [this is so] on condition that he does not remove it [the wool] from its place." And so he who pulls up the hair to examine the place of a blemish.

M. 3:4 "The hair of a blemished firstling which fell out, and which one put in a wall-niche, and which [firstling] one afterward slaughtered — "Aqabya b. Mahalalel permits [the priest to use the wool, for as killing the beast makes the meat and skin and wool attached to the animal available for priestly use, so the part that was detached can also be used], and sages prohibit. [If you permit the use of wool plucked when the animal is alive, people may hold the firstling to benefit from the wool, and this may ultimately break the law against working and shearing the beast]," the words of R. Judah. Said R. Yosé, "Not in this case did Aqabya declare permitted, but in the case of: The hair of a blemished firstling which fell out, and which one put in a wall-niche, and which [firstling] afterward died — in this case Aqabya b. Mahalalel permits and sages prohibit." The wool which dangles from a firstling['s hide after the firstling is slaughtered] — that which appears [distinct] from the [rest of the] wool is permitted. And that which does not appear [distinct] from the [rest of the] wool is prohibited.

T. 2:17 He who uproots wool from an unblemished firstling and leaves it in a wall-niche, even though a blemish appeared in it [the firstling] afterward and one slaughtered it, Lo, this [wool which he plucked] is to be buried.

T. 2:18 A blemished firstling from which one plucked hair and which afterward died — Aqabya b. Mahalalel permits and sages prohibit. Said R. Judah, "Aqabya concedes in this case that it is prohibited." Concerning what case did they differ? "Concerning one which was made unclean [=blemished] from which hair was plucked and which afterward was slaughtered, for — Aqabya b. Mahalalel permits and sages prohibit."

T. 2:19 Said R. Yosé, "R. Halafta concedes in this case that it is permitted." But most specifically did sages say, 'Let him leave it in a wall-niche, as there may be some sort of way of righting matters.' "For if it should die, it is prohibited; if one slaughters it, it is permitted." Concerning what did they dispute? Concerning one which was made unclean [blemished], from which hair was plucked, and which afterward died, for "Aqabya b. Mahalalel permits, and sages prohibit" [M. Bekh. 3:4].

Now we turn to components of the law of the firstling. How these laws are carried out yields secondary problems. Not shearing the hide raises the question of how to slaughter the beast without doing so. The disposition of the hair of a slaughtered beast raises problems of connection and disposition of the hair.

E. *THE REQUIREMENT TO TEND THE FIRSTLING BEFORE HANDING IT OVER TO THE PRIEST*

M. 4:1 How long are Israelites liable to tend to the firstling [before handing it over to the priest]? In the case of a small beast, for thirty days. And in the case of a large beast, for fifty days. R. Yosé says, "In the case of a small one, three months." [If] the priest said to him during this period, "Give it to me," Lo, this one does not give it to him. If it was blemished, [if] he said to him, "Give it to me that I might eat it," it is permitted. And in the time of the Temple, if it was perfect, [if] he said to him, "Give it to me that I may offer it up," it is permitted. The firstling is eaten within a year, whether it is unblemished or blemished, since it is said, "Before the Lord your God will you eat it year by year" (Deut. 15:20).

M. 4:2 [If] a blemish appeared in it during its first year, it is permitted to keep it for the whole twelve months. [If a blemish appeared in it] after its first year, it is permitted to keep it only for thirty days.

T. 3:1 How long are Israelites liable to tend to the firstling [before handing it over to the priest]? In the case of a small beast, for thirty days. And in the case of a large beast, for fifty days. R. Yosé says, "In the case of a small one, three months [M. Bekh. 4: 1A-D], because the care it requires is considerable."

T. 3:2 An unblemished animal at this time — one is permitted to keep it alive two or three years before showing it to an expert. Once one has shown it to an expert, [if] a blemish appears in it, one is permitted to keep it all twelve months. After twelve months one is not permitted to keep it thirty days [M. Bekh. 4:2].

T. 3:3 All Holy Things which are sanctified in the womb and delivered through the side — sanctity applies to them. The firstling and the tithe [of cattle born by caesarian section] — sanctity does not apply to them [M. Bekh. 2:10].

T. 3:4 All Holy Things concerning which "a year" is written, once their year has passed, Lo, they are invalid. The firstling and tithe of cattle, even for two or three years, Lo, they are valid.

T. 3:5 All the same are the firstling and tithe of cattle and all Holy Things which have been kept back for a year without [three] festivals, or for [three] festivals [without] a year — one transgresses on their account because of the requirement not to delay.

The rules are inert and do not lead to problems beyond the cases at hand.

II. SLAUGHTERING A FIRSTLING BY REASON OF BLEMISHES

A. *EXAMINING A FIRSTLING TO SEE WHETHER OR NOT IT IS BLEMISHED*

M. 4:3 He who slaughters a firstling and [then] shows its blemish [to an expert] — R. Judah permits. R. Meir says, "Since it was slaughtered not at the authority of an expert, it is prohibited."

T. 3:6 He who slaughters a firstling assuming that it is blemished and it turns to be unblemished — "As to blemishes in the eye, they do not examine them, because they [the eyes] change after death. But as to those in the body, they do examine them," the words of R. Meir. R. Judah says, "Also those in the body they do not examine. But Lo, this is to be buried."

M. 4:4 He who was not an expert and examined the firstling, (and) which was slaughtered on his instructions — Lo, this [firstling] is to be buried. And he [the amateur] pays [compensation] from his own funds. [If] one [who was not an expert] judged a case, declaring the liable person to be free of liability, declaring the person free of liability to be liable, declaring what is clean to be unclean, declaring what is unclean to be clean — what he has done is done. And he pays from his own funds. But if he was an expert recognized by a court, he is free from the liability of paying. There was the following case: the womb of a cow was removed. And R. Tarfon had it [the cow] fed to the dogs. The case came before sages, and they declared it permitted. Said Todos, the physician, "Neither a cow nor a pig leaves Alexandria without their ripping out its womb, so that it will not bear offspring." Said R. Tarfon, "There goes your ass, Tarfon." Said to him R. Aqiba, "Rabbi Tarfon, You are exempt, for you are an expert recognized by a court. And any expert recognized by a court is free from the liability of paying."

T. 3:7 He who is not an expert and examined a firstling which was slaughtered on his instructions [M. Bekh. 4:4A] — this was a case. And Eleazar ben Tadda'i came and asked sages, and they ruled, "He pays half the value in the case of a small beast, and a quarter in the case of a large one."

B. 4:4A-C III.1/28B AND HE [THE AMATEUR] PAYS FROM HIS OWN FUNDS: IT WAS TAUGHT BY A TANNAITE AUTHORITY: WHEN HE PAYS THE PRIEST, HE PAYS A QUARTER OF THE LOSS, FOR A FIRSTLING OF SMALL CATTLE, AND HALF OF THE LOSS, FOR A FIRSTLING OF LARGE CATTLE [HALF BECAUSE THE MONEY MAY OR MAY NOT BE COMING TO THE PRIEST, AS ONE MAY SAY THE ISRAELITE CAUSED A COMPLETE LOSS, FOR AN EXPERT MIGHT HAVE ASSIGNED THE BEAST TO A PRIEST, BUT NOW IT HAS TO BE BURIED; BUT PERHAPS THERE WAS NO PERMANENT BLEMISH, AND THE EXPERT WOULD NOT HAVE PERMITTED IT, BUT THE FIRSTLING CAN HAVE DIED WITHOUT A BLEMISH AT ALL].

M. 4:5 He who takes payments for examining firstlings — they do not slaughter upon his advice [a blemished firstling], unless he was an expert like Ila in Yabneh, whom sages permitted to receive four *issars* for [examining] a small beast, and six for a large one, whether [he ruled it to be] unblemished or blemished.

M. 4:6 He who takes payment for judging — his judgments are null. [He who takes payment] for testifying — his testimony is null. [He who takes payment] to sprinkle [purification-water on one made unclean by a corpse] and to mix [ash of a red cow with water for the purpose of making purification-water] —

his water is cave-water, and his ash is hearth-ash. If he was a priest, and [by examining the beast] he was made unclean for [eating] his heave-offering, one feeds him [ordinary food] and gives him to drink and anoints him. And if he was an elder, one puts him up on an ass and gives him a wage in accord with that paid to a day-laborer.

T. 3:8 He who is suspected of taking a salary and judging, or of taking a salary and giving testimony — all the judgments which he has made and all the testimony which he has given, Lo, they are null [M. Bekh. 4:6A-D]. But one pays a fee to a judge for his time and a fee to the witness for his testimony, even though they have ruled. It is valid for a judge to take a salary and for a witness to take a salary for his testimony.

T. 3:9 He who is suspected of taking a fee for sprinkling purification-water and for mixing [the ashes of a red cow with water for purification-water] — his water is cave-water and his ash is hearth-ash. And if he was a priest [and by judging the condition of the firstling] he is made unclean for eating his heave-offering, one feeds him and gives him something to drink and anoints him. And if he was an elder, one puts him up on his ass and pays him a wage in accord with that paid to a day-laborer [M. Bekh. 4:6E-H] — even though they have said, Like a blind man is a judge who takes a salary.

M. 4:7 He who is suspected [of breaking] the law of firstlings — they do not purchase from him meat of gazelles or untanned hides. R. Eliezer says, "They purchase from him the hide of a female." And they do not purchase from him bleached wool or dirty [wool]. But they purchase from him spun wool and [wool made into] garments.

M. 4:8 He who is suspected [of transgressing] the Seventh Year — they do not purchase from him flax, and even if it is combed. But they purchase from him spun flat and woven [flax].

M. 4:9 "He who is suspected of selling heave-offering as unconsecrated food — they do not purchase from him even water or salt," the words of R. Judah. R. Simeon says, "Whatever is subject to the rules of heave-offerings and tithes they do not purchase from him."

M. 4:10 He who is suspected of [violating] the Seventh Year is not suspected on account of tithes. He who is suspected on account of tithes is not suspected on account of [violating] the Seventh Year. He who is suspected both in this regard and in that regard is suspected in regard to [observance of the law of] purities. And there is he who is suspected on account of [violating] the laws of purities but is not suspected either on this account or on that account. This is the general principle: Whoever is suspected on account of any matter does not make judgments nor testify concerning that matter.

T. 3:10 He who is suspected [of breaking] the law of firstlings — they do not purchase from him the hides of gazelles or hides which are not tanned. R. Eleazar says, "They purchase from him the hides of a female, for it has never entered into the category of sanctity" [M. Bekh. 4:6A-C].

T. 3:11 R. Simeon says, "He who is suspected of selling heave-offering as unconsecrated food — they do not purchase from him anything which is subject to the rules of heave-offering or tithes [M. Bekh. 4:9A, C]. And he is suspect in respect to the rules governing cleanness of foods and concerning the sources of uncleanness which are in the Torah."

T. 3:12 He who is suspected of making himself unclean with corpses is [nonetheless] believed concerning the marking out of graves. He who is suspected concerning the Seventh Year is [not] suspected concerning tithes. There is one who is suspected concerning tithes and not suspected concerning [observance] of the Seventh Year. One suspected for this and for that is suspected in regard to the laws of clean foods. There is he who is suspected concerning the laws of purities and not suspected either concerning the laws of the Seventh Year or concerning tithes [M. Bekh. 4:10A-D]. One who is suspected concerning idolatry is suspect concerning all the commandments in the Torah. This is so not retroactively, but only henceforward, since it is said, "From the day on which the Lord commanded and thenceforward for your generations" (Num. 15:23).

A firstling that is blemished may be slaughtered, so the issue is, who examines it for permanent blemishes, and under what conditions? The examination may or may not be post facto. An expert, uncompensated veterinarian that a court has declared qualified need not pay compensation should he err. Here, the Bavli makes a contribution to the Halakhah by defining the range of compensation. A generic issue arises in the matter of dealing with a person of poor repute. If he is suspect of not keeping the law, people may not rely on him, even though they do not know for sure that he has violated the law in a particular case.

B. FURTHER RULES OF SLAUGHTERING THE FIRSTLING

M. 5:1 All invalidated Holy Things [after they have been redeemed] — their advantage falls to the sanctuary, and they are sold in the marketplace, and are slaughtered in the marketplace, and are weighed by the *litra,* except for the [blemished] firstling and tithe of cattle. For the advantage [of selling them in the market, where demand is higher, would fall] to the owner. Invalidated Holy Things — their advantage [falls] to the sanctuary. But: they weigh a *maneh* against a *maneh* in the case of the meat of the firstling.

T. 3:13 All invalidated Holy Things [after they have been redeemed] are sold in the marketplace, and are slaughtered in the marketplace, and weighed by measure, except for the firstling and tithe of cattle, for the advantage [of selling them in the market, where demand is higher, would fall] to the owner.

T. 3:14 Rabban Simeon b. Gamaliel says, "A man persuades himself by weighing by the pound in the case of a firstling to find out what has come to him" R. Judah says, "[If] a man found his fellow in Jerusalem [and] said to him, 'What did you eat today,' [if] he said to him, 'Manna,' he knows for sure that he ate tithe. Just as manna is beyond price, so tithe is beyond price. [If] he said to him, 'Summer-fruit,' he knows for sure that he ate a firstling. Just as summer-fruit is sold cheaply, so the firstling is sold cheaply."

M. 5:2 The House of Shammai say, "An Israelite is not numbered with a priest [for eating] a firstling." And the House of Hillel permit, And even in the case of a gentile. "A firstling which suffered from a congestion of blood, even though [if one does not let blood] it [may] die — they do not draw blood from it," the words of R. Judah. And sages say, "one draws blood from it, on condition that one not make a blemish in it. And if he made a blemish in it, Lo, this one should not be slaughtered on that account." R. Simeon says, "One draws blood from it, even though one make a blemish in it thereby."

T. 3:15 The House of Shammai say, "Only priests are numbered with [those who eat] firstlings." And the House of Hillel say, "Even Israelites" [M. Bekh. 5:2A-B]. R. Aqiba permits even a gentile, as it is said, 'As of the gazelle and as of the hart' (Deut. 12:15)."

T. 3:16 The meat of a firstling — The House of Shammai say, "They do not feed it to menstruating women." And the House of Hillel say, "They feed it to menstruating women."

T. 3:17 A firstling which suffered from congestion of blood [M. Bekh. 5:2D] — "They do not draw blood from it in a place on which one makes a blemish. But they draw blood from it in a place on which one does not make a blemish," the words of R. Meir. And sages say, "Also they draw blood from it in a place on which one makes a blemish. It is not slaughtered on account of that blemish, but on account of some other blemish." R. Judah says, "Also: It is slaughtered on account of that blemish." R. Simeon says, "Even if it is on the point of death, they do not draw blood from it."

M. 5:3 He who slit the ear of the firstling — "Lo, this should never be slaughtered [by reason of a blemish]," the words of R. Eliezer. And sages say, "When another blemish will appear in it, it is slaughtered on its account." There was the case of an old

ram, with its hair dangling. A Roman detective saw it. He said, "What sort of thing is this?" They said to him, "It is a firstling. And it is slaughtered only if there is a blemish on it." He took a dagger and slit its ear. And the case came before sages, and they declared it permitted. He saw that they permitted [it] and went and tore the ears of other firstlings. And they declared [them] prohibited. Another time children were playing in the field, and they tied the tails of lambs to one another. And the tail of one of them split off. And Lo, it was a firstling. And the case came before sages, and they declared it permitted. They saw that they declared it permitted, and they went and tied together the tails of other firstlings. And they declared [them] prohibited. This is the general principle: Anything [done] deliberately — it is prohibited. And anything [done] unintentionally — it is permitted.

T. 3:24 He who makes a blemish on a blemished animal, Lo, this one is smitten with forty stripes. He who causes that which is leavened to leaven, Lo, this one receives forty stripes. He who castrates a castrate, Lo, this one receives forty stripes.

M. 5:4 [If] a firstling was running after him, and he kicked it and made a blemish in it — Lo, this is slaughtered on that account. Any blemishes which are likely to happen at the hands of man — Israelite-cast shepherds are believed [to testify that the blemishes came about unintentionally]. But priestly-cast shepherds are not believed. Rabban Simeon b. Gamaliel says, "He [a priest] is believed concerning another's [firstling] but is not believed concerning his own." R. Meir says, "He who is suspect in a given matter neither judges nor bears witness in that matter."

T. 3:18 [If a firstling was running after him and he kicked it and made a blemish on it [M. Bekh. 5:4A] — if he intended to do so, it is prohibited, and if not, it is permitted.

T. 3:19 All blemishes which are likely to happen at the hands of man — Israelite shepherds are believed. Priestly-shepherds are not believed [M. Bekh. 5:4C-E]. They reverted to rule: He is believed concerning that of his fellow, but he is not believed concerning his own [M. Bekh. 5:4F]. R. Joshua b. Qepusai says. "They slaughter the firstling only on the instructions of two [witnesses]." R. Simeon b. Gamaliel says, "Even his son and even his daughter." Rabbi says, "Even ten in the household are not believed. For one who is suspect in a given matter neither judges nor bears witness in that matter" [M. Bekh. 5:4G].

T. 3:20 They do not have unblemished firstlings estimated for an Israelite. But they have blemished firstlings estimated for them. They have unblemished firstlings estimated for priests. And it is not necessary to say, blemished ones.

T. 3:21 They do not examine firstlings for Israelites. And if one said, "A priest sent me to you," or one who inherited the estate of the father of his mother who is a priest, they do examine them.

T. 3:22 A priest who was the shepherd of the flock of an Israelite should not say to him, "Give me these firstlings." But he says to him, "The four unclean ones which are in your flock — give them to me."

T. 3:23 All firstlings does a man declare permitted except for his own firstling. He oversees his own Holy Things and his own tithes. And he accepts inquiry concerning [the legal status of] his own unclean and clean matters.

M. 5:5 A priest is believed to state, "I showed this firstling [to an expert] and [he ruled that] it is blemished." All are believed [to testify] concerning blemishes of tithe of cattle [that they were not deliberately caused]. A firstling, the eye of which is blinded, the hoof of which is cut off, the hind-leg of which is broken — Lo, this is slaughtered on the advice of three members of the assembly [M. Zeb. 3:2]. R. Yosé says, "Even if there are twenty-three there, he is to be slaughtered only on the advice of an expert."

T. 3:25 A blemish which is visible — "Lo, this [firstling] is slaughtered at the decision of three members of the congregation," the words of R. Meir. R. Yosé says, "Even if his leg was cut off or his eye was blinded, it should be slaughtered only at the instruction of an expert."

M. 5:6 He who slaughters the firstling and sold it, and it becomes known that he did not show it [to an expert] — that which they [the purchasers] have eaten, they have eaten. And he returns to them the cost [of the meat]. And [as to] what they have not eaten — the meat is to be buried. And he returns to them the cost [what they paid for it]. And so: He who slaughters a cow and sold it and it becomes known that it is *terefah* — What they have eaten, they have eaten. And [as a penalty] he returns to them the cost. And [as to] what they have not eaten — they return the meat. And he returns their money. [If] they sold it to gentiles or tossed it to the dogs, they return to him the value of the *terefah* [meat, which is cheap, and he repays the difference between what they paid and what they received].

The firstling is both like and not like Holy Things, depending on its condition, and that leads to comparison and contrast of the firstling and Holy Things. M. 5:1 compares the sale in the market of invalidated Holy Things and invalidated firstlings, with the result that is made explicit. The upshot is, the status of the invalidated firstling is different from that of the invalidated Holy Thing, the former losing all sanctity and becoming private property, upon which God lays no further claim. Then what about the special rights of the priesthood to Holy Things, when it comes to a firstling that was unblemished and that was offered and given over to the priests for consumption? The Hillelites reaffirm its essential secularity, the Shammaites, its basic sanctification. Issues of reliability and rules of evidence recur.

C. BLEMISHES IN ANIMALS

M. 6:1 On account of these blemishes do they slaughter the firstling: (1) [If] its ear is damaged in the gristle but not in the skin [ear lobe]; (2) [if] it is slit, even though there is no loss of substance; (3) [if] it has a hole as big as a vetch, or (4) [if] it is dried up. What is the meaning of 'dried up'? Any which, if pierced, does not produce a drop of blood. R. Yosé b. Meshullam says, "So dried up that it crumbles."

M. 6:2 (1) The eyelid which is perforated, which is damaged, (3) which is slit. Lo, [if] in its lid is (1) a cataract, (2) a commingling, (3) a snail-shaped [growth], (4) a snake-shaped [growth], and (5) a berry-shaped [growth.] What is the meaning of "commingling?" The white breaks through the ring and enters the black. In the case of the black's entering the white, it is not a blemish, for blemishes do not affect the white [of the eye].

M. 6:3 (1) A white cataract and (2) rheum which are lasting [constantly drip]. What is a white cataract that is lasting? Any which remained eighty days. R. Hanina b. Antigonos says, "They examine it three times in eighty days." What is rheum that is lasting? [If] it ate fresh or dry [fodder] from rain-watered fields, [and the water in the eye remained — this is rheum which is lasting]. [If it ate] fresh or dry [fodder] from irrigated fields, [or if] it ate dry [fodder] and afterward ate fresh [and the water remained in the eyes], it is not a blemish — unless it ate dry [fodder] after fresh [fodder].

M. 6:4 (1) Its nose which is perforated, (2) which is damaged, (3) which is slit. Its lip (1) which is perforated, (2) which is damaged, (3) which is slit. (1) Its front teeth [incisors] which are damaged, (2) or worn down; (3) and the back ones [molars] which are uprooted. R. Hanina ben Antigonos says, "They do not examine the double teeth backward, or even the double-teeth [themselves]."

M. 6:5 [If] the sheath [of the male organ] is damaged or the female organ in female beasts in the case of Holy Things. (1) [If] the tail is damaged at the bone, but not at the joint; or (2) [if] the root-[end] of the tail has a divided bone, or (3) [if] there is a finger's breadth of flesh between one link [of the tail] and the next link.

M. 6:6 [If] it has no testicles, or has only one testicle. R. Ishmael says, "If it has two pouches, it has two testicles. [If] it has only one pouch, it has only one testicle." R. Aqiba says, "One sets it on its buttocks and squeezes: if there is a testicle there, it ultimately will descend." There was the case in which someone squeezed and it did not descend. And it was slaughtered. And it [the testicle] was found cleaving to the groin. And R. Aqiba declared the beast permitted, and R. Yohanan b. Nuri prohibited it.

M. 6:7 A beast with five legs, or which has only three; one the legs of which are closed [not cloven], like those of the ass; and one with a dislocated hip; and one with a deformed hip. What is one wit a dislocated hip? That the thigh-bone has slipped [from its socket]. And deformed? That one of its hips is higher [than the other].

M. 6:8 [If] a bone in the foreleg is broken, or a bone in the hind-leg, even if it is not visible. These blemishes did Ila list in Yabneh. And sages concurred with him. And three more did he add. They said to him, "We have not heard these." (1) That [beast] the eye of which is round like that of a man; (2) and the mouth of which is like that of a pig; (3) and that, the greater part of fore-tongue of which is removed. And the court which succeeded them said, "Lo, these are deemed blemishes."

T. 4:1 All blemishes [which] invalidate in the case of Holy Things (and) invalidate in the case of the firstling. The split [of the ear, M. Bekh. 6:1B2] in any amount damages [the ear]. And as to the ear [if it is damaged, M. Bekh. 6:1 B2] whether by man or naturally — what is the sort of damage [to which reference is made]? Any one in which one puts his finger and it catches. To what extent is it perforated [so that a hole in the ear constitutes a blemish, M. Bekh. 6:1B3]? A hole the size of a vetch [M. Bekh. 6:1B2]. R. Yosé bar Judah says, "As large as a lentil." How much should it dry [and be deemed a blemish, M. Bekh. 6:1 B4]? R. Yosé Hammeshullam says, "So that it crumbles." And their opinions are so close as to be identical.

T. 4:2 What is a cataract? That which floats on the surface of the eye, and is not sunk into the base of the eye [M. Bekh. 6:2BI]. A snail-shaped growth [M. Bekh. 6:2B3]? As its name implies. A snake-shaped growth [M. Bekh. 6:2B4]? As its name implies. A berry-shaped growth [M. Bekh. 6:2B5]? As its name implies. [If] there was a wart and one cut it off, if there is a bone in it, it [the firstling] may be slaughtered. And if not, it may not be slaughtered. A cataract which is lasting [M. Bekh. 6:3A1] — forty days [vs. M. Bekh. 6:3C].

T. 4:3 "Rheum which is lasting — eighty days" [M. Bekh. 6:3B,C], and the sages say, "A cataract which is lasting — eighty days [M Bekh. 6:3B-C], and rheum which is lasting — eighty."

T. 4:4 [If] it ate fresh and dry fodder from a rain-watered field, and not fresh and dry fodder from an irrigated field — [If] it ate fresh and afterward dry fodder — it counts for it [to signify that this is rheum which is lasting (M. Bekh. 6:3F)]. [If it ate] dry fodder and afterward ate fresh, it does not count [to signify that this is rheum which is lasting (M. Bekh. 6:3H)]. Under no circumstances does it matter unless it ate dry fodder after fresh. R. Hananiah b. Antigonos says, "And as to a cataract: they examine it three times in thirty days, lest it disappear and return." R. Simeon b. Eleazar says, "If its eye was tearing, one may be certain that the rheum will pass. [If] it ceased to tear, one may be certain that the rheum is lasting" [M. Bekh. 6:3]. [If] its nose is perforated from one side to the other on the inside, it should not be slaughtered [on account of such a blemish]. [If the perforation is] on the outside [wall of the nose], it may be slaughtered [M. Bekh. 6:4A].

T. 4:5 What are the double-teeth [M. Bekh. 6:4D3]? Inside from the double teeth, or from the double teeth and inside. R. Joshua b. Qepusai says, "They slaughter the firstling only on account of the incisors." R. Hananiah b. Antigonos says, "They do not examine the molars at all" [M. Bekh. 6:4E-F].

T. 4:6 [If] the container of the fat-tail is broken in the case of Holy Things, Lo, this is a blemish. [If] the sheath [of the male organ] is damaged [M. Bekh. 6: A] in any amount at all, Lo, this may be slaughtered. What is the sheath? The container, and not the penis. Said R. Yosé b. Hammeshullam, "A wolf ripped off that of one [beast], and it grew back."

T. 4:7 [If] the tail is cut off at the bone but not at the joint, or [if] the root [end] of the tail is divided into two bones — or [if] there is flesh between one link [of the tail] and the next link to the breadth of a link [vs. M. Bekh. 6:5C], Lo, this should not be slaughtered. If it has only one testicle, Lo, this may be slaughtered [M. Bekh. 6:6B]. [If] it had two, even though the two are doubled [in one sack], Lo, this should not be slaughtered.

T. 4:8 Said R. Yosé, "A heifer of the house of Menahem did they set up on its buttocks, and they squeezed it at the testicles, and only one came forth. So it was slaughtered. But it was found cleaving to the groin. And the case came before R. Aqiba, and he declared it valid. But when the matter was reported before R. Yohanan b. Nuri he said, 'Aqiba has fed them carrion'" [M. Bekh. 6:6E-G]. [If] the horns and hooves were removed, and marrow with them, Lo, this may be slaughtered.

T. 4:9 What is an animal with too many? Any which has three eyes or five legs [M. Bekh. 6:7A]. And that which is lacking? One which has three legs or one eye.

T. 4:10 What sort of beast is invalid? Any the loins of which protrude. [If] the larger number of its ribs were broken, or if it had an internal blemish, this is not deemed a blemish, since it is said, "For no one who [has a blemish shall draw near], a man blind or lame or one who has a mutilated face or a limb too long" (Lev. 21:18) — just as the blind or lame is distinctive in that it is a blemish which is in the open and which does not go away [so any blemish which is in the open invalidates, but not an internal one].

T. 4:11 Said R Yosé b. Hammeshullam, "Imla did list blemishes in Yabneh, and stated them before sages, and they concurred with him" [M. Bekh. 6:8D-E]. Three more did he add. They said to him." We have not heard [these]" [M. Bekh. 6:8F-G]. That [beast] the eye of which is round like that of man, and that the mouth of which is like that of a pig, and that, the greater part of the tongue of which is removed [M. Bekh. 6:8H]. R. Hanina b. Antigonos said, "The greater part of the fore-tongue." The court which succeeded them said, "Lo, these are deemed blemishes" [M. Bekh. 6:8I].

M. 6:9 There was a case in which the lower jaw stretched beyond the upper one. And Rabban Simeon b. Gamaliel consulted sages. And they said, "Lo, this is a blemish." The ear of a kid which was doubled up — Sages said, "When it is all a single bone, it is a blemish. And if it not all a single bone, it is not a blemish." R. Hanania b. Gamaliel says, "The tail of a kid which is like that of a pig, and that which does not have three links [vertebrae] — Lo, this is a blemish."

T. 4:12 [If] the lower lip stretched beyond the upper one, Lo, this is a blemish. B Rabban Simeon b. Gamaliel says, "If the upper stretched beyond the lower like that of a pig, Lo, this is a blemish" [M. Bekh. 6:9A-C].

T. 4:13 [If] its mouth is closed or its feet joined together — [if] it is on account of itself, it may be slaughtered. [If] it is on account of the wind, it may not be slaughtered. [If] its ears are closed with one system of cartilages, it may not be slaughtered. [If they are closed] with two systems of cartilages, it may be slaughtered. R. Hananiah b. Rabban Gamaliel says, "The tail of a sheep on which are three links — it may not be slaughtered. [If] there are two, it may be slaughtered."

M. 6:10 R. Hanina b. Antigonos says, "[If] it has a wart in its eye; and [if] the bone of its fore-leg was damaged; and the bone of its hind-leg; and [if] the bone of the mouth of which is severed; and [if] one eye is large and one small, and [if] one ear is large and one small — in appearance [upon visual examination], but not by [actual] measure." R. Judah says, "[If] one of its testicles is twice as large as its fellow." And sages did not concur with him.

M. 6:11 The calf's tail which does not reach the knee-joint — [it is a blemish]. Sages said, "Through the whole period of growth of calves it is so. All the time that they are growing, they grow longer [so the tail always reaches the knee-joint]." To what joint did they refer? R. Hanina b. Antigonos says, "To the joint in the middle of the thigh." On account of these blemishes do they slaughter the firstling. And invalidated Holy Things are redeemed on their account.

T. 4:14 The calf's tail which does not reach the knee joint [M. Bekh. 6:1 IA] — Lo, this may be slaughtered. To what joint did they refer? R. Hananiah b. Antigonos says, "To the joint in the middle of the thigh, up to the upper joint, and not up to the lower joint" [M. Bekh. 6:11E].

M. 6:12 These are the ones on account of which they do not slaughter [firstlings] either in the sanctuary or in the provinces: (1) a white cataract or rheum [in the eye] which are not lasting [by contrast to M. 6:3A]; (2) and back teeth that are damaged but are not uprooted [by contrast to M. 6:4D]; (3) and [a beast] with scurvy; (4) and [a beast] with warts; (5) and [a beast] with lichen [Lev. 22:22]; (6) and an old [beast] [M. Par. 1:2]; (7) and a sick [beast]; (8) and a smelly [beast]; (9) and a beast on which a bestial transgression was committed [M. Zeb. 8:1]; (10) and one which killed a man, according to the testimony of a single witness or according to the testimony of the owner; (11) and a beast of doubtful sex; (12) and a beast of double sex — neither in the sanctuary nor in the provinces. R. Ishmael says, "There is no greater blemish than that." And sages say, "It [a beast of double sex] is not deemed a firstling [at all], but it may be sheared and used for labor."

T. 4:15 There are things which are like blemishes, but on which account they [nonetheless] slaughter [the animal, deeming it valid] in the sanctuary. And they [also] do not slaughter [for secular purposes] on their account in the provinces [since these are not blemishes so severe as to invalidate the animal in the sanctuary, therefore, they are not so serious as to allow it to be slaughtered in the provinces (M. Bekh. 6:12A)]. And these are they: *A gamun, a someah,* and *a Somin*, and a female which has horns.

T. 4:16 What is a *gamun*? That which lacks horns. What is a *someah*? That which lacks ears. What is *a somin*? That one, the ears of which are closed up. R. Ilai says in the name of R. Ishmael, "A beast of double sex is a firstling, but on account of that blemish, it may be slaughtered" [M. Bekh. 6:12E]. And sages say, "Sanctity does not pertain to it at all. But it is sent forth to pasture in the fold" [M. Bekh. 6:12F]. R. Simeon says, "Lo, it says, 'Every firstling which will be born in your herd and your flock — the male you shall sanctify to the Lord your God.' Any passage in which male is stated means to exclude from the rule the one of doubtful sex and the one of double sex."

The catalogue of disqualifying blemishes, which permit the householder to slaughter the firstling for his own use in the theory that this is not the kind of firstling that God values for his altar and for the priesthood, is comprised by inert facts, which yield the distinction between enduring or disfiguring and transient and trivial blemishes. The latter mark the firstling as unsuitable to its purpose.

D. BLEMISHES IN PRIESTS
M. 7:1 [With reference to the verse, "For no one who has a blemish shall draw near: a man blind or lame, or one who has a mutilated face or a limb too long or a man who has an injured foot or an injured hand or a hunchback or a dwarf or a man with a defect in his sight or an itching disease or scabs or crushed testicles" (Lev. 21:18-20): These blemishes [that have been listed in the preceding chapter], whether permanent or transient, disqualify man [from serving in the Temple]. In addition to them in the case of man: (1) the one whose head is wedge-shaped, (2) or turnip-shaped, (3) or hammer-shaped. (4) And the on Hump-backs — R. Judah declares valid. And sages declare invalid.

M. 7:2 A bald-headed man is invalid. What is a bald-headed man? Any who does not have a row of hair going around from ear to ear. But if he has, Lo, this one is valid. [If] he does not have eyebrows, [or] if he has only one eyebrow, he is that *gibben* [Lev. 14:9] of which the Torah speaks. R. Dosa says, "Any whose eyebrows hang down." R. Hananiah b. Antigonos says, "He who has two backs and two backbones."

M. 7:3 The man who is flat-nosed is invalid. What is the man who is flat-nosed? He who paints both eyes in one movement. [If] (1) both eyes are above, or (2) both eyes are below, or (3) one eye is above and one eye is below [so that] he sees the room and the attic simultaneously, (1) those who cover [their eyes from] the sun, (2) [if he has] unmatched [eyes], (3) [if he has] bleary [eyes], — [he is disqualified]. And he whose eyelashes have fallen out is invalid, for appearance's sake.

M. 7:4 (1) [If] his eyes are as large as those of a calf, (2) or as small as those of a goose, (3) [if] his body is too big for his limbs, (4) or too small for his limbs, (5) [if] his nose is too big for his limbs, (6) or too small for his limbs — [he is disqualified]. [If he is] *simmem* or *simmea* — [he is disqualified]. What is the meaning of *simmea?* That his ears are too small. And of *simmen?*

That his ears look like sponges.

M. 7:5 (1) [If] his upper lip stuck out over the lower, (2) or the lower stuck out over the upper, Lo, this is a blemish. And [if] his teeth are taken out, he is invalid, for appearance's sake. (1) If his breasts like those of a woman, (2) [if] his belly is swollen, (3) [if] his bellybutton protrudes, (4) [if] he is smitten with epilepsy, even once in a while, (5) [if] lockjaw affects him, (6) the one whose testicles are too large, (7) and the one whose penis is too large, (8) [if] he has no testicles, (9) or has only one testicle. this is "he that has his stones broken" (Lev. 21:20) of which the Torah speaks. R. Ishmael says, '[Scripture refers to] any who has testicles crushed.' R. Aqiba says, "It refers to any who has wind in his testicles." R. Hananiah b. Antigonos says, "It refers to any whose complexion is very dark."

M. 7:6 (1) He who knocks together his ankles or his knees, (2) and one who has swellings [in the feet], (3) and one who is bow-legged. Who is bow-legged? Any who puts together his soles and whose knees do not touch one another. (1) [If] he has a swelling on the big toe, (2) [if] his heel juts out backward, (3) [if] his sole is as wide as that of a goose, (4) [if] his toes lie one above the other, (5) or are webbed to the middle-joint, he is valid. [If they are webbed] below the middle joint [at the toes] and one cut it [the tissue], he is valid. [If] there was an extra finger on him and he cut it off, if there is a bone in it, he is invalid. And if not, he is valid. [If] he has excess on his hands and feet — six in each limb, twenty-four in all — R. Judah declares valid. And sages declare invalid. He who is ambidextrous — Rabbi declares invalid. And sages declare valid. The (1) Ethiopian [swarthy], and (2) the red-skinned, and (3) the albino, and (4) the giant, and (5) the dwarf, and (6) the deaf-mute, and (7) the imbecile, and (8) the drunkard, and (9) the one who has clean *nega'im* are invalid among men, and valid among beasts. Rabban Simeon b. Gamaliel says, "An imbecile among beasts is not the choicest." R. Eliezer says, "Also: those who have dangling warts are invalid among men, and valid among beasts."

T. 5:1 These blemishes, whether permanent or transient, invalidate in the case of a man [M. Bekh. 7:1A]. In addition to them in the case of man: One whose neck is long or compacted.

T. 5:2 The bleary-eyed [M. Bekh. 7:3G], the bald-headed [M. Bekh. 7:2A], the ones who have no teeth [M. Bekh. 7:5D], and hump-backed [M. Bekh. 7:1C-D] are valid. But they are invalid for appearance's sake. One castrated by man or castrated by nature, one whose testicles are crushed, and one whose penis is missing, and the one with abnormally long eye-brows [M. Bekh. 7:2H], and the one with an unequal pair of eyes [M. Bekh. 7:3F] [are disqualified].

T. 5:3 What is the one with long eye-brows? One whose eyebrows lie flat. And what is the one with an unequal pair of eyes? That one of his eye-brows is black, and one white. What is the one who covers his eyes from the sun [M. Bekh. 7:3E]? One who sees the room and the attic simultaneously [M. Bekh. 7:3D] looking at one, seeing two. How so? [If] he looks [directly] at his fellow and he says that he does not see him. [If] his nose is stopped up or turned up or hangs over, [if] his ears are stopped up [if] his ears are strips, [if] his eyes are bleary, [if] his eyes are dripping, [if] his eyes are large or small — large as those of a calf, small as those of a goose [M. Bekh. 7:4A-B]. [If] he has worts, if lockjaw affects him, if he has falling disease, even once in a great while [M. Bekh. 7:5 1, M] [he is disqualified].

T. 5:4 What is "He that hath his stones broken" (Lev. 21:20)? "One that is suffering from a scrotal hernia, into the testicles of whom the wind enters," the words of R. Aqiba. R. Ishmael says, "This is one whose genitals are wasted." [If] his instep is hollow, turned inward like a scythe, [if] his leg is set in the middle of his foot, knocking in the middle and spread out below, one afflicted with lumps, or [if] his fingers are split apart, [if] his fingers are stumped, [if] his fingers lie above one another [M. Bekh. 7:61], or [if] his large finger was turned inward, he is invalid.

T. 5:5 [If] there was a mole on him, if it has hair in it, he is invalid. [If] there is no hair in it, he is valid. [If it is] large, he is invalid. [If it is] small, he is valid And what is the size of a large one? Rabban Simeon b. Gamaliel says, "The size of an Italian issar."

T. 5:6 As to an extra finger [M. Bekh. 7:6M] — if there is a bone in it, he is invalid. If not, he is valid. Extra — as it said: "[If] the fingers on his hands and feet are six [each]" — R. Judah declares valid. And R. Yosé declares invalid [M. Bekh. 7.6N-P].

T. 5:7 Said R. Judah, "A case came before R. Tarfon [of a priest with twenty-four]." And he said, "Such as he increases high priests in Israel." Said to him R. Yosé, "Thus did he say, 'May such as he diminish [as] Netinin and mamzerim in Israel.'"

T. 5:8 A left-handed person, whether in hand or in foot, is invalid. One who is ambidextrous — Rabbi declares invalid. And sages declare valid [M. Bekh. 7:6P-R]

T. 5:9 One whose eyes are unsteady, one with bushy eyebrows, one who has no eyebrows, the albino [M. Bekh. 7:613], and the bandy-legged, and the one who is bow-legged, and the knock-kneed, are unfit in the case of man and fit in the case of beasts [M. Bekh. 7:7U].

M. 7:7 These are valid among men and invalid among beasts: (1) progenitor and his offspring [M. Hul. 5:1], (2) and a *terefah*, (3) and one born from the side, (4) and that upon whom a

sin was committed, (5) and one who killed a man. He who marries women that are forbidden is invalid until he will vow not to derive benefit. And he who contracts corpse-uncleanness is invalid until he will undertake not to contract corpse-uncleanness.

The comparability of the priesthood to the firstborn forms the basis for the present catalogue, which treats as equivalently blemishing those faults that exclude the beast from the altar and the priest from service at the altar. Once that point registers, no further issues transcend the cases. The predictable contrast — valid among men and invalid among beasts — contains nothing of special consequence.

III. THE FIRSTBORN OF MAN

M. 8:1 There is a firstborn in respect to inheritance, who is not a firstborn in respect to the priest, a firstborn in respect to the priest who is not a firstborn in respect to inheritance, a firstborn in respect to inheritance and in respect to the priest, and there is one who is not a firstborn either in respect to inheritance or in respect to the priest. Who is he who is a firstborn in respect to inheritance and not a firstborn in respect to the priest? (1) He who comes after an untimely birth whose head emerged alive, (2) or [after] a nine-month-old birth the head of which emerged [but which was] dead, and [he who comes after] an abortion which was like a beast, a wild animal, or a bird," the words of R. Meir. And sages say, "Only if [the abortion] bears the appearance of man." (3) She who aborts a sandal, an afterbirth, or a fully-formed foetus, and that which goes forth in pieces — that which is born after them is a firstling in respect to inheritance but not a firstling in respect to the priest. (1) He who had no children and who married a woman who already had given birth — (2) [or] if she was a bondwoman and then made free, (3) a gentile and converted, after she came to the Israelite, she gave birth, he is a firstborn in respect to inheritance but not a firstborn in respect to the priest. R. Yosé the Galilean says, "He is a firstling for inheritance and for the priest, since it is said, 'Whatsoever opens the womb among the children of Israel' (Ex. 13:2) — [this is applicable] once they [the offspring] will open the womb of Israelite[s]." He who had children, and who married a woman who had not given birth, (2) she converted when pregnant, (3) [or if] she was freed when pregnant, (1) [if] there gave birth she and a priest's wife [and the babies were mixed up], (2) she and a Levite's wife [and the babies were mixed up], (3) she and a woman who had already given birth [and the babies were mixed up], and so she who did not wait after her husband['s death] for three months but got married and gave birth — [so] it is not known whether it is an offspring at nine months attributed to the first husband or at seven months attributed to the second — it is a firstborn in respect to the priest but not a firstborn in respect to inheritance. Who is he who is a firstborn in respect to inheritance and in respect to the priest? (1) She who aborts a foetus filled with blood, filled with water, filled with variegated matter, (2) she who aborts something like fish, locusts, insects, or creeping things, (3) she who aborts on [up to] the fortieth day [after conception] — he who comes after them is a firstling in respect to inheritance and in respect to the priest.

M. 8:2 That which goes forth from the side and that which comes after it — both of them are neither a firstborn in respect to inheritance nor in respect to the priest [M. 2:9]. R. Simeon says, "The first is [a firstborn] in respect to inheritance. And the second is [a firstborn] in respect to the five *selas* [to be paid to the priest]."

T. 6:1 He who was born after an untimely birth [M. Bekh. 8:1 F], in the eighth month, or one born in the ninth month of pregnancy, whose head emerged [but who was dead [M. Bekh. 8:1F2] is a firstborn in respect to inheritance but not a firstborn in respect to the priest [M. Bekh. 8:1E], since it is said, "He may not treat the son of the loved as the firstborn in preference to the son of the disliked, who is the firstborn" (Deut. 21:16). This is the general principle: Any [offspring], the head and greater part of the body of whom went forth alive exempts the one who is born afterward from the [right of the] firstborn. But not from the five selas of the son [owing to the priest] [M. Bekh. 8:1R].

T. 6:2 Two wives of two men who had not given birth and who gave birth to two males [M. Bekh. 8:5A] in hiding [so that we do not know which is which] — one of them died, the second is a firstborn in respect to inheritance but not a firstborn in respect to the priest. [If] she and a woman who was [married to] a priest, she and a woman who was [married to] a Levite, she and a woman who had already given birth gave birth to two males, it is a firstling born in respect to the priest but not a firstborn in respect to inheritance [M. Bekh. 8:1U-W, Z]. [If] one of them died, or it was a male and a female [to which they gave birth], it is not a firstborn either in respect to inheritance or in respect to the priest.

M. 8:3 He whose wife had not given birth and [whose wife] gave birth to two males gives five *selas* to the priest. [If] one of them died during the first thirty days [after birth], the father is exempt [from the obligation to give five *selas* to the priest]. [If] the father died and the sons live, R. Meir says, "If they had given [the five *selas*] before they divided [the inheritance], they have given it.

[The priest keeps it, since one of the two is surely liable as firstborn]. And if not, they are exempt. [We do not know which one is liable to pay the money]." R. Judah says, "The estate is liable. [The father is in any case liable for the five *selas*]." [If she bore] male and female, there is nothing whatsoever here for the priest.

M. 8:4 Two women [married to the same man] who had not given birth and who bore two males — he [the father] gives ten *selas* to the priest. [If] one of them died during the first thirty days [after birth], if [the father] had given [the ten *selas*] to one priest, he [the priest] returns five *selas* to him [the father]. If he had given [the ten *selas*] to two priests, he cannot recover [the funds] from their hand. [If they bore] a male and a female, or two males and a female, he gives five *selas* to the priest. [If they bore] two females and a male, or two males and two females, there is nothing whatsoever here for the priest. [If] one had given birth and one had not given birth, and they bore two males, he [the father] gives five *selas* to the priest. [If] one of them died during the first thirty days after birth, the father is exempt. [If] the father died, and the sons live, R. Meir says, "If they had given [the five *selas*] before they divided [the inheritance], they have given [them]. And if not, they are exempt." R. Judah says, "The estate is liable." [If they bore] male and female, there is nothing whatsoever here for the priest.

M. 8:5 Two wives of two men, who had not given birth, and who gave birth to two males — this one gives five *selas* to the priest, and that one gives five *selas* to the priest. [If] one of them died during the first thirty days [after birth], if they had given [the five *selas*] to one priest, he returns the five *selas* to them. If they had given [the five *selas*] to two priests, they cannot recover [the funds] from their hand. [If they gave birth to] a male and a female, the fathers are exempt. But the son is liable to redeem himself. [If they gave birth] to two females and a male or to two males and two females, there is nothing whatsoever here for the priest.

M. 8:6 [If] one had given birth and one had not given birth, to two men, and they gave birth to two males, this one whose wife had not given birth gives five *selas* to the priest. [If they gave birth to [a male and a female [and the children were mixed up], there is nothing whatsoever here for the priest. [If] the son died during the first thirty days [after birth], even though he [the father] had given to the priest [five *selas* to the priest], he must return the money. If it was after thirty days, even though he has not yet given the money, he must give it. [If the male] died on the thirtieth day, it is deemed equivalent to the day before it [the twenty-ninth, and the father owes nothing]. R. Aqiba says, "If he gave [the five *selas*, but the son died on the thirtieth day], he [the father] should not take [the money back]. And if he did not give [over the five *selas*], he [the father] should not give [over the five *selas*]." [If] the father died during the thirty days [and it is not known whether or not he had redeemed the firstborn male], it is assumed that he [the firstborn] has not been redeemed until one will bring proof that he has been redeemed. [If the father died] after thirty days, it is assumed that he has been redeemed, until they will tell him that he has not been redeemed. [If a man who was firstborn son had a firstborn son and was told that he had not been redeemed so that he is] to redeem himself and [he is] to redeem his son, he comes before his son. R. Judah says, "His son comes before him. For the requirement of redeeming him [the father] falls upon *his* father, while the requirement of redeeming his son falls on him."

T. 6:3 There is he who pays [the five selas to the priest] in his own behalf, and there is he whose father pays [the five selas to the priest] in his behalf, and there is he who with his father pays [the five selas to the priest] in his behalf, and there is he who does not pay and whose father does not pay [the five selas to the priest]. Who is he who pays [the five selas] in his own behalf? [If] his conception was not in conditions of sanctity and his birth is not in conditions of sanctity, he pays in his own behalf [M. Bekh. 8:1S]. [If] it is a matter of doubt whether he is born at nine months to the priest husband] or at seven months to the second, he pays in his own behalf [M. Bekh. 8:1X-Y]. Two wives of two men who had not given birth and who gave birth to two males in secret and one of them [the sons] died, the second pays [five selas to the priest] in his own behalf.

T. 6:4 Who is he whose father pays [the five selas to the priest] in his behalf? Two wives of two men who had not given birth and who gave birth to two males in secret — this one gives five selas, and this one gives five selas to the priest [M. Bekh. 8:5A-B]. [If] the father gave five selas [to the priest] and the father died, the second one is liable, but the sons are exempt.

T. 6:5 [If] she and a priestess, she and a Levitess, she and a woman who had already given birth gave birth to two males [M. Bekh. 8:1U-W], the father gives [five selas to the priest] in his behalf. [If] one of them died, or [if] it was a male and a female, neither he nor his father give [five selas to the priest] [M. Bekh. 8:6D].

T. 6:6 Who is he who pays with his father [the five selas to the priest]? Two wives of two men who had not given birth and who gave birth to two males in secret — this one gives five selas to the priest, and that one gives five selas to the priest [M. Bekh. 8:5A-B]. [If] the father gave five selas [to the priest], and the father died, the second [of the two husbands] is liable. And the sons are exempt. [If] one of the sons died, the second son is liable [to pay in his own behalf], and the fathers are exempt. [If] the father gave five selas, and one of the sons died, Lo, all of them are exempt.

T. 6:7 [If] one had given birth and one had not given birth [who were wives of] two men, and they gave birth to two males [M. Bekh. 8:6A-B] [if] one of them died during the first thirty days [after birth], Lo, all of them are exempt.

T. 6:8 Two wives of two men had not given birth and who gave birth to two males in secret, this one gives five selas to the priest, and that one gives five selas to the priest [M. Bekh. 8:5A-B]. [If] the father gave five selas to the priest and died, the sons, before they have divided the estate of their father, are liable. [If this is] after they have divided the estate of their father, they are exempt [M. Bekh. 8:3F-G]. R. Judah says, "Even after they have divided the estate of their father, if one of them has ten denars of their father, they are liable. And if not, they are exempt" [M. Bekh. 8:3H].

T. 6:9 Two women had not given birth and who gave birth to two males in secret give ten selas to the priest. [If] one of them [the sons] died during the first thirty days after birth they retrieve [the money] from their [the priests'] possession [M. Bekh. 8:6E]. R. Judah says, "If they gave to one priest, they retrieve the funds from his possession. "If they gave to two priests, they cannot retrieve the funds from his possession, for he who lays claim against his fellow bears the burden of proof."

T. 6:10 [If a man is obligated] to redeem himself and to make a pilgrimage for a festival, he redeems himself and afterward he makes the pilgrimage for the festival [M. Bekh. 8:6M — P]. R. Judah says, "He makes the pilgrimage for the festival and afterward he redeems himself." For this [the pilgrimage] is a requirement which is transient [and the opportunity will not recur]." [If a man is obligated] to learn Torah and to marry a wife, he learns Torah and afterward marries a wife. R. Judah said, "If he cannot sit [and study] without a wife, he marries a wife and afterward he learns Torah." [If one is obligated] to study Torah and his son [is obligated] to study Torah, [if] he is obligated to marry a wife and his son to marry a wife, he comes before his son. R. Judah says, "If his son was eager, while his [own] Torah would be preserved in his possession, then his son comes first."

T. 6:11 There was one who encouraged his son to learn Torah, imposing upon him a vow not to do any other labor. And R. Yosé permitted him [the son] to fill a bucket of water for him and to light a lamp for him [the father].

M. 8:7 The five *selas* for redeeming the firstborn son are in Tyrian coinage. (1) The thirty for the slave [Ex. 21:32], and (2) the fifty to be paid by the rapist and seducer [Ex. 22:15-16, Deut. 22:28-29], and (3) the hundred to be paid by the gossip [Deut.

22:19] — all are to be paid in the value of *sheqels* of the sanctuary, in Tyrian coinage. And everything which is to be redeemed [is redeemed] in silver or its equivalent, except for *sheqel*-dues.

T. 6:12 The five selas for the redemption of the son, the thirty for the slave, the fifty to be paid by the rapist and the seducer, the hundred to be paid by the gossip — all are to be paid in the value of sheqels of the sanctuary, in Tyrian coinage. And everything which is to be redeemed may be redeemed with silver or its equivalent [M. Bekh. 8:7B-D], except for the excess of the sheqels of the pilgrims' burnt-offering, and of the redemption of second tithe, which derive only from minted coins.

M. 8:8 They do not [pay the price of five shekels for the] redemption [of the firstborn] either with slaves or with deeds or with land, nor [is] anything which has been sanctified [redeemed with slaves, deeds, or land]. [If] one wrote a document for the priest that he owes him five *selas*, he is liable to pay him [the five *selas*], but his son is not yet redeemed [until the father pays five *selas*]. Therefore, if the priest [did not choose to collect the five *selas*, but decided] to give [the five *selas* of the bond] to him as a gift, he has the right. He who sets aside the redemption [money] for his son, and it was lost, is liable for it, since it is said, "It shall be yours, and you shall surely redeem it" (Num. 18:15).

T. 6:13 [If one said], "This heifer is for the redemption of my son," his son is not redeemed. But if he said, "This heifer which is worth five selas is for the redemption of my son," or, "This cloak, which is worth five selas, is for the redemption of my son," his son is redeemed. But they do not [pay the price of redemption] either with slaves or with deeds or with land [M. Bekh. 8:8A]. And even if one said, "This slave is worth five selas for the redemption of my son." "This land is worth five selas for the redemption of my son," his son is not redeemed.

T. 6:14 [If] the father gave five selas to five priests, his son is redeemed. 13. [If] he gave them to him [one priest] one after another, his son is redeemed. [If] he [the father] gave them to him [the priest] and went and took them back, his son is redeemed. Thus did R. Tarfon perform the act: He took them from him [the father] and went and gave them back to him.

M. 8:9 The firstborn takes a double portion in the estate of the father. But he does not take a double portion in the estate of the mother. And he does not take a double portion of the increased value or [a double share] of what is going to accrue to the estate [of the father] as [he receives a double share] of what already is in hand. [And the same applies to] (1) the wife in respect to her marriage-settlement, and (2) to the daughters in respect to their maintenance, and (3) to the Levir. None of them takes [what

is owing] the increased value or of what is expected to accrue to the estate as [they receive a double share] of what already is in hand.

T. 6:15 The firstborn does not take a double portion of the increase which the estate of the father enjoyed after the death of the father. 13. Rabbi says, "I rule that the firstborn takes a double portion of the increase of the estate after the death of the father." For his share increased in value with theirs.

T. 6:16 [Continuing the foregoing:] "How so? [If] he had a beast which was let out to a sharecropper or hired out to others or a cow which was feeding in the dirt, the firstborn takes a double share. And the firstborn takes a double portion of the shoulder, cheeks, and maw." And sages say, "Only of that which the heirs did not take over after the death of their father does the firstling take a double portion." But he takes a double portion only of that which is accessible to him. But if the father built houses and the firstborn planted a vineyard, all agree that he takes a double portion thereof.

T. 6:17 How does he take a double portion? [If] they inherited deeds of debt, he takes a double portion. [If] deeds of debt are laid against him [the estate], he pays out a double portion. If he said, "I want neither to take nor to pay out [the double portion]," the right is his.

T. 6:18 How does he not take a double portion of what is expected to accrue to the estate as they take a double portion of what already is in hand [M. Bekh. 8:9G]? [If] his father died during the life of his [own] father, he [the firstborn son] takes a double portion of the estate of his father, but he does not take a double portion of the estate of his grandfather. But if his father was a firstborn, he takes a double portion even of the estate of his grandfather.

M. 8:10 These are the things which do not revert [to the original owners] in the Jubilee [Lev. 25:10]: (1) the portion of the firstborn; (2) and [the inheritance of] one who inherits his wife['s estate]; (3) and [the inheritance of] the one who performs Levirate marriage. "And what is given as a gift," the words of R. Meir. And sages say, "That which is given as a gift is equivalent to that which is sold." R. Eleazar says, "All of them revert in the Jubilee." R. Yohanan b. Beroqah says, "He who inherits his wife['s estate] restores [the property] to the members of [her] family and allows them a deduction from the purchase-money."

T. 6:19 The portion of the firstborn, and the inheritance of one who inherits his [wife's estate] and [the inheritance] of one who takes in Levirate marriage the wife of his brother, and that which is given as a gift [M. Bekh. 8:10A 1-3, B], and that which is paid for damages, and half-damages, and double payment, and payment in fourfold or fivefold — none of them take what is expected to accrue as they take what already is in hand [M. Bekh. 8:9G]. But one gives to them out of a field which returns in the Jubilee [vs. M. Bekh. 8:10A — B]. R. Yohanan b. Beroqah says, "He who inherits his wife's estate — the members of the family give him coins and retrieve the field from his hand, since it is said, 'No inheritance shall be transferred from one tribe to another' (Num. 36:9)" [M. Bekh. 8:10E].

Once the firstborn of man contributes a component of the category-formation and so responds to the governing hermeneutics thereof, the Halakhah does little more than fill out the spaces opened by the generic hermeneutics, e.g., interstitial cases of being firstborn for one purpose but not for another, M. 8:1; exceptions as to status by reason of formal considerations, M. 8;2; cases of confusion and of mixtures, M. 8:3-6. Then we conclude with inert facts, M. 8:7-8. In a rough way, therefore, the program that guides the presentation is [1] exegesis of cases generated by the particular hermeneutics of the category-formation; [2] exegesis of cases provoked by the generic hermeneutics; [3] exposition of facts that are necessary but not sufficient to exemplify rules beyond the cases they embody. I do not know why M. 8:9 is separated from its obvious position, in the sequence commencing at M. 8:1.

IV. TITHE OF CATTLE

M. 9:1 [With reference] to the verse, "And all the tithe of herds and flocks, every tenth animal of all that pass under the herdsman's staff, shall be holy to the Lord. A man shall not inquire whether it is good or bad, neither shall he exchange it; and if he exchanges it, then both it and that for which it is exchanged shall be holy; it shall be redeemed" (Lev. 27:32-33),] [The law concerning] tithe of cattle applies (1) in the Land and outside of the Land, (2) in the time of the Temple and not in the time of the Temple, (3) in the case of unconsecrated beasts but not in the case of consecrated beasts. (1) And it applies to the herd and to the flock, but they are not tithed one for another; (2) to sheep and to goats, and they are tithed one for another; (3) to what is new [born after new year] and to what is old [born before new year (M. 9:5-6)], but they are not tithed one for another. For it might have been logical [to conclude as follows]: Now if that which is new and that which is old, which are not prohibited as mixed kinds with one another, are not tithed one for another, sheep and goats, which are prohibited as mixed kinds with one another, logically should not be tithed one for another. Scripture [accordingly is required] to state, "And of the flock," (Lev. 27:32) — implying that all flock is one [and tithed together].

M. Ma'aser Sheni 1:2 [As to] the tithe of cattle: (1) the [farmers] do not sell it [when the animal is] unblemished [and] alive; (2) and not [when the animal is] blemished, [whether it is] alive or slaughtered. (3) And they do not give it as a token of betrothal to women. [As to] the firstling [the first calves of the year's herd]: (1) they [the priests] sell it [when the animal is] unblemished [and] alive; (2) and [when the animal is] blemished, [whether it is] alive or slaughtered. (3) And they give it as a token of betrothal to women. They do not deconsecrate [produce in the status of] second tithe with (1) a poorly minted coin nor with (2) coin that is not [currently] circulating, nor with (3) money that is not in one's possession.

T. 7:1 [The law concerning] tithe of cattle applies to large ones and to small ones, to males and to females, to unblemished ones and to blemished ones [M. Bekh. 9:1A-C]. "And they tithe them from one year to the next, since it says, 'Tithing, you shall tithe' (Deut. 14:22). It speaks, therefore, of two acts of tithing." One tithes grain and afterward one tithes cattle," the words of R. Aqiba. And sages say, "Year by year (Deut. 14:22) — [Cattle] of one year do you tithe, but you do not tithe that of one year for that of the next" [M Bekh. 9:1 H].

T. 7:2 A she-kid which produced three females, and the females produced three [at the end of their first year] — [all] three enter the corral to be tithed. Said R. Simeon, "I saw a she-kid, [the offspring of] which was tithed in its first year." If one had beasts two or three years old, if one recognizes those of one year as distinct from those of another, it enters the corral to be tithed. And if not, it does not enter the corral to be tithed.

M. 9:2 [For purposes of] tithe of cattle [those cattle which are found] within the radius of pasturing cattle are included together. And how much is the radius of pasturing cattle? Sixteen miles. [If] there was between these and those [cattle] thirty-two miles, they do not join together [for the purposes of tithing]. [If] he had [cattle] in the middle, he brings and tithes them [with those which are] in the middle. R. Meir says, "The Jordan is a boundary [to a herd for purposes of] tithe of cattle."

T. 7:3 [For purposes of tithe of cattle] are included together [those cattle which are found] within the radius of pasturing cattle [M. Bekh. 9:2A] — and not within the day's radius of a wandering beast. How much is the radius of a beast? Thirty-two miles. How so? If one had five in Kefar Hananiah and five in Kefar 'Otenai and five in Sepphoris, Lo, these join together. [If he had] five in Kefar Hananiah and five in Kefar 'Otenai, these do not join together, unless he had at least one in Sepphoris. [If] he had [cattle] across the Jordan on either side, for example, in Hashshulmi and Nemuri, or in two autonomous cities, they do not join together with one another. And one need not say [the same rule applies to those] in the Land and outside of the Land [M. Bekh. 9:2F].

T. 7:4 The stream which emerges from the cave of Pamias and crosses the lake of Sopni and the lake of Tiberias, even though it is called Jordan, is not reckoned with the Jordan. What is the Jordan? From the area of Jericho and downward [M. Bekh. 9:2F].

M. 9:3 That which is purchased or that which is given to one as a gift is exempt from [the law to] tithe cattle. Brothers in partnership who are liable to a surcharge are exempt from tithe of cattle. And those who are liable to tithe of cattle are exempt from surcharge [M. Sheq. 1:7]. [If] they acquired [cattle] from the property of the estate [of their father], they are liable. And if not, they are exempt. [If] they divided [the estate] and then went and formed a partnership, they are liable to surcharge and exempt from tithe of cattle.

T. 7:5 What is deemed that which is purchased [M. Bekh. 9:3A]? And which one has sold to someone and gone and purchased from him, or which one has given to someone as a gift and gone and purchased from him. But one who purchases the unborn foetus of the cow of his fellow, even though it was born in the domain of the owner, enters the corral to be tithed.

M. 9:4 Every [sort of beast] enters the corral to be tithed, except for (1) hybrid-beasts, and (2) terefah-beasts. and (3) beasts born from the side, and (4) that which is not yet old enough, and (5) the orphan. What is the orphan? Any, the dam of which has died or been slaughtered. R. Joshua says, "Even if its dam is slaughtered, but the hide is whole, this is not deemed an orphan."

T. 7:6 "Every [sort of beast] enters the corral to be tithed, except for the hybrid-beast and the terefah-beast," the words of R. Eliezer b. Judah of Bartuta, which he cited in the name of R. Joshua. Said R. Aqiba, "I heard in his name: Also: That which is born from the side, and that which is not yet old enough, and the orphan" [M. Bekh. 9:4A-F]. True. What is the hybrid beast? A sheep which gave birth to a kind of a young animal, even a kind of a lamb, and a goat which gave birth to a kind of lamb, even something like a young sheep. Terefah — in accord with its normal meaning. That which is born from the side — in accord with its normal meaning. That which is not yet old enough — none [is tithed which is] less than eight days. R. Simeon says, "That which is too young enters the corral to be tithed."

T. 7:7 A beast with which a human has had sexual relations, one set aside for idolatrous worship, one which has been worshipped, the hire of a harlot the price of a dog, a beast of doubtful sex, and one of double sex do not enter the corral to be tithed [vs. M. Bekh. 9:4A].

R. Simeon bar Judah says in the name of R. Simeon, "A beast of doubtful sex and a beast of double sex do not enter the corral to be tithed. For wherever it is said, 'male', Scripture means to exclude from consideration a beast of doubtful sex and one of double sex."

T. 7:8 What is the harlot's hire? Any [case in which] one has given her the unborn foetus of his cow and gone and repurchased it from her. What is the price of a dog? A dog which one has exchanged with him for the unborn foetus of his cow and gone and repurchased from him.

M. 9:5 There are three seasons ["threshing-floors"] for the tithe of cattle [in which one takes the tenth of animals born in the stated period, at which point one may not use the animal until the tithing process is complete]: "Peras [that is, half a month] before Passover, Peras [half a month] before Pentecost [Hebrew: Aseret], and Peras [half a month] before the Festival [Sukkot]," the words of R. Aqiba. Ben Azzai says, "On the twenty-ninth of Adar, on the first of Sivan, and on the twenty-ninth of Ab." R. Eleazar and R. Simeon say, "On the first of Nisan, on the first of Sivan, and on the twenty-ninth of Elul." And why did they say on the twenty-ninth of Elul and they did not say on the first of Tishré? Because it is a festival, and it is not possible to tithe on the festival. Therefore, they pushed it up to the twenty-ninth of Elul. R. Meir says, "On the first of Elul is the New Year for the tithe of cattle." Ben Azzai says, "[Cattle born in] Elul are tithed by themselves."

M. 9:6 "All beasts born from the first of Tishré to the twenty-ninth of [the following] Elul, Lo, they join together [for purposes of tithe]. "Five [born] before New Year and five [born] after New Year do not join together [to form the requisite herd of ten beasts for tithing]. Those born five days before the tithing season and those born five days after the tithing season do join together." If so, then why have they said, "There are three seasons for tithe of cattle"? For: until the season has come, it is permitted to sell and to slaughter. Once the season has come, one should not slaughter. But if he has slaughtered, he is exempt [from penalty].

T. 7:9 There are three seasons for the tithe of cattle. Half a month before Passover, and half a month before Aseret, and half a month before the Festival [M. Bekh. 9:5B]. "They are without limit," The words of R. Aqiba. R. Yosé bar Judah says, "They are not less than fifteen days before the festival." Said R. Simeon b. Azzai, "Since these rule, 'On the first of Elul,' and these rule, 'On the first of Tishré,' those born in Elul are tithed by themselves [M. Bekh. 9:5I]. "How so?" [If] there were born to a person five in Ab and five in Elul and five in Tishré, then those five born in Ab and those five born in Tishré do not join together. The five born in Tishré and the five born in Ab, Lo, these do join together [to form ten for the purposes of tithing]."

M. 9:7 How does one tithe them? He brings them into a corral and makes a small chute, so that two cannot exit simultaneously. And he counts [using] a staff: One, two, three, four, five, six, seven, eight, nine. And the one which exits tenth does he mark with a red mark, saying, "Lo this is tithe." [If] (1) one did not mark it with a red mark, or (2) did not count them with a staff, or (3) if one counted them while they were crouching or standing, Lo, these are deemed tithed. [If] he had a hundred and took [any] ten [of them], or had ten and took [any] one of them, this is not deemed tithe. R. Yosé bar Judah says, "Lo, this is tithe." [If] one of those which had already been numbered jumped among them [which had not been numbered], Lo, these are exempt. [If one of those which was marked as] tithe [jumped] into their midst, all of them must pasture until they are blemished. And by reason of their blemish they may be eaten by their owners.

M. 9:8 [If the first] two exited simultaneously, he counts them two by two. [If] he counted them as one, then the ninth and the tenth are spoiled. [If] the ninth and the tenth exited simultaneously, the ninth and the tenth are spoiled. [If] he called the ninth, tenth, and the tenth, ninth, and the eleventh, tenth, all three are sanctified: (1) the ninth is eaten by reason of its blemish; (2) the tenth is tithe; (3) and the eleventh is offered as peace-offerings. "And it [the eleventh] is subject to the law of the substitute," the words of R. Meir. Said R. Judah, "And is there a substitute which imparts the status of a substitute to another?" They said in the name of R. Meir, "If it had been a substitute, it could not have been offered." [If] he called the ninth, tenth, and the tenth, tenth, and the eleventh, tenth — the eleventh is not sanctified. This is the general principle: In any case in which the tenth was not deprived of its proper designation, the eleventh is not sanctified.

T. 7:10 How do they tithe? One sets up the mothers outside and they low, and the offspring go forth toward them [M. Bekh. 9:7A]. [If] the eighth and the ninth go out simultaneously, Lo, one combines them [with others]. [If] the ninth and the tenth [go forth simultaneously], they are set out to pasture until they are blemished. [If] the tenth and eleventh [went forth simultaneously], all of them are left to die. [If] one was numbering one by one, [if] the first died [or if] the first was slaughtered, Lo, one combines them [with others].

T. 7:11 [If] one was counting, and one of them put forth its head and the greater part of its body outside the corral and then came back, it is deemed to have been counted in every respect. [If] one counted them while they were crouching or while they were standing, Lo, this one combines them [with others] [M. Bekh. 9:7F]. [If] one was counting and one's fellow called him to talk with him, Lo this one combines them [with others]. [If] one was counting and the darkness of the Sabbath night came upon him, Lo, this one combines them [with others].

T. 7:12 [If] one was counting and one of those already counted jumped among those which were not counted, if he can discern it, he is free of further obligation, and the remainder are liable [to be tithed]. And if not, Lo, all of them are exempt [M. Bekh. 9:7I]. [If] an orphan became mixed up with them, or one which had been purchased, Lo, all of them are exempt [from tithe]. [If] he had ten and had counted five and one of those which had been counted died, Lo, this one combines them [with others] from those which had not been counted. Those which had been counted are free [from tithe]. And the remainder join together [for counting] at the next season of tithes.

T. 7:13 [If] one had fifteen, he should not say, "Lo, I shall bring ten of them into the corral." But he brings all of them and counts ten of them, and the rest are tithed in the coming year. [If] he counted them in reverse, the tenth of all of them is sanctified. [If] he called the ninth, ninth, the tenth, tenth, and the eleventh, eleventh, the ninth is unconsecrated, the tenth is tithe, and the eleventh is unconsecrated.

T. 7:14 [If] he called the ninth, tenth, and the tenth, ninth, and the eleventh, eleventh, the ninth is eaten when it is blemished; the tenth is tithe; and the eleventh is unconsecrated. [If] he called the ninth, ninth, and the tenth, eleventh, and the eleventh, tenth, the ninth is unconsecrated, the tenth is tithe, and the eleventh is offered as peace-offerings. [If] he called the ninth, tenth and the tenth, ninth and the eleventh, tenth, all three are sanctified. The ninth is eaten when it is blemished. The tenth is tithe. And the eleventh is offered as peace-offerings, and it is subject to the law of the substitute [M. Bekh. 9:8D-E]. [If] he called the ninth, ninth, and the tenth, tenth, and the eleventh, tenth, the eleventh is not deemed sanctified. This is the general principle. In any case in which the eleventh was not deprived of its proper name, the eleventh is not sanctified until one will pass by the ninth silently and call the tenth, ninth, and the eleventh, tenth.

T. 7:15 A herd in which was confused a beast which is subject to doubt as to being the tenth at this time — they [the whole herd] are set out to pasture until they will be blemished. [If] the doubt concerns one which is in doubt as the eleventh, lo, all of them are left to die. The tithe of cattle of an estate — they sell it, on account of the consideration of returning that which is lost to its owner. A tithe of cattle which one slaughtered — the hooves, horns, bones, fat, hide, and hair, Lo, these are permitted.

B. 9:8 II.2 IF TWO ANIMALS CAME OUT OF THE CORRAL AT THE NINTH, AND HE CALLED THEM THE NINTH, THE TENTH

AND UNCONSECRATED BEASTS ARE TREATED AS A SINGLE GROUP ['MIXED TOGETHER'] [AND MAY NOT BE EATEN UNTIL BLEMISHED, BUT ARE OTHERWISE CLASSIFIED AS UNCONSECRATED]. THE TENTH IS SANCTIFIED EO IPSE [EVEN THOUGH NOT CALLED TENTH], AND THE NINTH IS UNCONSECRATED, HAVING BEEN DESIGNATED, CORRECTLY, AS NINTH. IF HE CALLED THEM THE TENTH, THE TENTH AND THE NINTH ARE TREATED AS A GROUP. HOW COME? HE HAS CALLED BOTH OF THEM TENTH. IF TWO OF THEM CAME OUT SIMULTANEOUSLY AS TENTH, AND HE CALLED THEM TENTH, THE TENTH AND THE ELEVENTH ARE TREATED AS A GROUP TOGETHER [THE TENTH IS ACTUALLY TITHE, THE ELEVENTH IS A PEACE OFFERING]. IF HE CALLED [THE TWO LAMBS THAT CAME OUT WHEN THE TENTH WAS TO MAKE ITS APPEARANCE] THE ELEVENTH, THE TENTH AND UNCONSECRATED BEASTS ARE DEEMED TO HAVE FORMED A SINGLE GROUP [AND BOTH ARE EATEN BY THE OWNER WHEN BLEMISHED]. IF TWO ANIMALS CAME OUT OF THE CORRAL AT THE NINTH, [AND HE CALLED THEM THE NINTH], THE TENTH AND UNCONSECRATED BEASTS ARE TREATED AS A SINGLE GROUP ['MIXED TOGETHER'] [AND MAY NOT BE EATEN UNTIL BLEMISHED], BUT ARE OTHERWISE CLASSIFIED AS UNCONSECRATED. THE TENTH IS SANCTIFIED EO IPSE EVEN THOUGH NOT CALLED 'TENTH, AND THE NINTH IS UNCONSECRATED, HAVING BEEN DESIGNATED, CORRECTLY, AS NINTH. IF HE CALLED THEM THE TENTH, THE TENTH AND THE NINTH ARE TREATED AS A GROUP"] — ONE TANNAITE VERSION STATES, "LET THEM BE PUT OUT TO PASTURE." ANOTHER TANNAITE VERSION STATES, "THEY ARE TO BE LEFT TO DIE."

It would be difficult to find a more explicit statement of the particular hermeneutics of the category-formation, tithe of cattle, than is given at M. 9:1. For the sake of a full presentation of the Halakhah I, include M. M.S. 1:2. The rest of the components of the composite, M. 9:2ff., respond to the generic hermeneutics, e.g., M. 9:3, complex ownership or acquisition; M. 9:4, designation of the classes of beasts that are exempt from the requirement. Then come necessary facts of the law, M. 9:5ff., and confusion that may result from the designated procedures.

IV. DOCUMENTARY TRAITS

A. THE MISHNAH AND THE TOSEFTA

A review of the Tosefta's contribution once again shows an imaginative and wide-ranging reflection on what is implicit in, or required by, the Mishnah's Halakhah. But though the Tosefta encompasses compositions of an independent-minded character, it does not recast the category-formation in any way.

B. THE BAVLI

The massive character of the Bavli's contribution to the exegesis of the received Halakhah is hardly adumbrated by the rather paltry cases in which the Bavli contributes hard data to the Halakhic category-formation.

V. THE HERMENEUTICS OF BEKHOROT

A. WHAT FUSES THE HALAKHIC DATA INTO A CATEGORY-FORMATION?

Among the four genera with their respective choices of species that I proposed at the outset, the third genus, firstlings/firstfruits, provides the integrating hermeneutics. Firstlings and firstfruits celebrate the procreation of life, the one brought about by animate Israel (encompassing its herds and flocks), the other by the Land of Israel. Then the two classifications are readily hierarchized, as we have seen throughout. Firstfruits focus upon the Land as the particular medium for the celebration of life, the Land as the womb for the seed planted by the householder and nurtured by God and taken over by the priesthood. The laws of the firstborn and of tithing the flock and the herd celebrate life in a different way, now, life formed in the womb of the seed planted by animate Israel (including, once more, Israel's flocks and herds). So the Halakhah compares Israel in the Land and Israel detached from the Land. Like Hullin, the category-formation works out the hermeneutics of utopian Israel in contrast to locative Israel. The choice of data and interpretation thereof then present no surprises.

But what about the hierarchization of the produce of the Land itself? What signifies the priority of firstfruits over other produce is, God has indicated his selection, and has specified the mode of delivery and the agency to receive delivery of his choice fruit: transportation to Jerusalem, presentation to the priesthood, with the remarkable declaration linking the householder to the entire sanctified existence of Israel in that one action. In this context we recall the contrast between ordinary offerings and firstfruits. Anyone may buy a beast or bird or cereal and designate it for a personal purpose. Only the householder presents firstfruits. Anyone may declare the classification of a beast or bird or cereal, e.g., a sin-offering, a guilt-offering, a freewill-offering, a peace-offering. Only the householder may classify the produce as firstfruits by an explicit designation. When it comes to the firstling and the tithe of the herd and flock, any Israelite participates through ownership, but only God by his action designates what or who qualifies — which beast, which son. That the firstborn son must be redeemed from God contains the entire statement. The rite of firstfruits defines the relationship of Israel and God in acutely personal terms, invoking the "I" and the "my", in giving back to God the first testimonies to God's on-going benevolence. Firstfruits makes the relationship between God and Israel personal and immediate, personal, familial and genealogical — wholly through the nexus of the Holy Land.

Firstlings, by contrast, represent God's giving back to Israel the fruit of the womb of herd or flock or of woman. Whoever owns animals, wherever he lives, like any husband and wife in the appropriate circumstance, is a candidate for entry into that relationship, for receiving that gift of a future and a hope, and for giving back to God the first of what God has given to him. So the Halakhah wishes to state that Israel in its fleshly embodiment of families through genealogical ties relates to God at the Temple through the gifts of grace presented by the Land. Then the Halakhah can make no more particular and concrete statement than it does through the laws of the firstfruits. So too, the Halakhah wishes to state that God shows grace to Israel in the fleshly embodiment of families by giving firstborn sons to their mothers and fathers, and by giving firstborn offspring to herds and flocks. And it finds in the Written Torah's laws of firstlings the ideal medium for that statement. I cannot imagine a more just and exact match between the medium and the message. That is why I maintain, the category-formation fuses with remarkable solidity.

B. THE ACTIVITY OF THE CATEGORY-FORMATION

The Halakhah has chosen, out of the topic of firstlings, a diverse program of inquiry, not so well focussed as elsewhere. But out of the details, a few striking generalizations do emerge, and these pertain to the critical tensions and generative concerns of the Halakhah overall: Land of Israel, people (genealogy) of Israel, and how the sanctification of each dictates their respective obligations to God.

WHO IS OBLIGED TO DISTINGUISH THE FIRSTBORN: The obligation to assign to God the beasts, wholly owned by Israelites, that he has chosen for himself by bringing them out of the womb first of all pertains only to Israel. Gentiles are not subject to the requirement, and gentile ownership of beasts subject to Israelite control exempts the firstborn of that flock or herd. Priests and Levites also are exempt from having to redeem the firstborn of an unclean beast. God only wants Israelite firstborn, as he only wants his share of the Israelite crops of the Land of Israel. But it is Israel unbounded by the limits of the Land, bearer of sanctity wherever located.

REDEEMING THE FIRSTLING: Like all Holy Things, the firstlings under certain conditions may be "redeemed", that is, may be transferred to a secular status in exchange for a substitute, specifically, a replacement of the value of what has been consecrated. The firstborn of man is redeemed for five sheqels (Num. 18:16). In this way Israel's sanctity, inherent in the firstborn, differs from the declared, imposed sanctity of a beast, for, in line with Lev. 27:10, a beast that an Israelite has declared holy remains holy; a beast consecrated in substitution for the originally-sanctified beast does not take its place and release its sanctity. But when it comes to God's choice, the firstborn, five silver coins suffice to substitute for the firstborn son. It is a transaction that, in the most secular and banal sense, is symbolic, not actual. God asks only the heart: the intention to acknowledge his dominion, but not the physical actuality.

Animals conform to their own species' rule, as one would expect, in line with Lev. 27:10. The firstborn of a clean beast, of the flock or herd, is deemed holy and is given to the priest whether or not it is blemished. If it is not blemished, it is offered up on the altar, and the priests eat the meat; it is Lesser Holy Things. If it is blemished, God relinquishes possession, and it is the property of the priest, not of the altar of God, and is slaughtered as an unconsecrated animal and eaten without restrictions.

THE PRIESTHOOD AS ISRAEL'S FIRSTFRUITS/FIRSTLINGS: The analogy is explicit and detailed: blemishes that disqualify the firstling from the altar disqualify the priest from the altar. As the blemish disqualifies the priest, despite his genealogy, so the blemish now secularizes the beast, despite his primogeniture. Other details complete the recapitulation of Scripture. The firstborn of the unclean beast, e.g., the ass, is redeemed in exchange for a lamb, or the neck of the unclean firstborn is broken. The lamb belongs to a priest and is not deemed consecrated. The ass is then unconsecrated as well. The program of the Halakhah, as set forth in the Oral Torah, proceeds from the firstborn of an ass to the firstborn of clean cattle and finally the firstborn of man.

THE FIRSTBORN OF AN ASS (=UNCLEAN BEAST): Among all unclean beasts, liable to the law of the firstling is only the ass alone. One has either to kill the beast by breaking its neck or to redeem the firstborn of an ass with the designation of a lamb in its place. If one did not want to redeem it the firstling of an ass, he breaks its neck from behind with a hatchet, and buries it. The requirement of redemption takes precedence over the requirement of breaking the neck The redemption-lamb belongs to the priest, and the firstling no longer falls into the priest's domain.

THE FIRSTBORN OF A COW (=CLEAN BEAST): If a clean beast's offspring is unblemished, the law of the firstling applies; but if the offspring is blemished permanently, then the animal is available for secular purposes; if the beast was consecrated before the blemish came, or if the blemish was transient, the beast is consecrated: All Holy Things, the permanent blemish of which came before their consecration, and which were redeemed are liable to the law of the firstling, and to the priestly gifts, and go forth for secular purposes, for sheering and for labor. And their offspring and their milk are permitted after their redemption, they are deemed unconsecrated beasts for every purpose. All Holy Things, the consecration of which came before their blemish, or in which was a transient blemish before their consecration, and in which afterward a permanent blemish appeared, and which were redeemed are free of the law of the firstling, and from the priestly gifts. They also do not go forth for secular purposes, for sheering and for labor.

NOT SHEARING THE FIRSTLING (DT. 15:19): One may not pluck the wool of the firstling or cut it in the process of breaking the neck. If hair falls out before slaughter, and then the beast is killed and so rendered permitted for appropriate purposes, the hair becomes available as well. The act of slaughter renders the firstling permitted.

BLEMISHES THAT PERMIT SLAUGHTERING A FIRSTLING, REMOVING IT FROM THE PRIESTHOOD AND THE ALTAR, AND BLEMISHES THAT PROHIBIT A PRIEST FROM SERVING AT THE ALTAR: Israelites must take the trouble to tend the firstling for a month or so before handing it over to the priest. The firstling must be eaten during the first year, whether it is unblemished and redeemed, or blemished and not. If the beast is blemished, the owner may eat it. If the owner slaughters it and then shows the blemish to an expert, who determines that it was permanent, he may or may not eat the animal. If someone who was not expert examined the firstling and said it was permanently blemished, the firstling is buried and may not be eaten. If the beast is slaughtered and the meat sold, it may not be sold in the market place, where demand is higher; that would be to the advantage of the owner. When the advantage falls to the sanctuary, it is permitted to sell the redeemed meat in the market, to yield a better price to the sanctuary; the private person does not enjoy the same advantage. When the firstling is eaten under priestly auspices, Israelites may join in, as may gentiles. If someone deliberately blemished a firstling, it may not be slaughtered by reason of that blemish, but it may be slaughtered by reason of some other. If an animal is blemished by a man, Israelite shepherds may testify that they came about unintentionally, but priest-shepherds may not testify, since it is to their advantage that the beast be deemed validly blemished; then it is given to them.

The blemishes that disqualify the beast for the altar and so permit slaughtering and eating a firstling at home (Dt. 15:21) and those that disqualify a priest run parallel, with additional points of disqualification affecting the priesthood.

FIRSTBORN OF MAN: The topic having been defined, the generic hermeneutics takes over — to the extent that the category-formation does more than collect and organize information. The firstborn male belongs to the priest and has to be redeemed, as Scripture says through the payment of five shekels. The payment must be in cash, not in something of equivalent value. The firstborn in regard to the priesthood may not be firstborn in respect to the rights of primogeniture. There is a firstborn in respect to inheritance, who is not a firstborn in respect to the priest, a firstborn in respect to the priest who is not a firstborn in respect to inheritance, a firstborn in respect to inheritance and in respect to the priest, and there is one who is not a firstborn either in respect to inheritance or in respect to the priest. Who is he who is a firstborn in respect to inheritance and not a firstborn in respect to the priest? (1) He who comes after an untimely birth whose head emerged alive, (2) or after a nine-month-old birth the head of which emerged but which was dead, and he who comes after an abortion. (1) He who had no children and who married a woman who already had given birth — (2) or if she was a bondwoman and then made free, (3) a gentile and converted, after she came to the Israelite, she gave birth, he is a firstborn in respect to inheritance but not a firstborn in respect to the priest. So the claim of God through the priest applies only in the most literal sense: the firstborn to emerge from the womb.

TITHE OF CATTLE: Since the tithe is not enlandised, it also is not connected with the agricultural calendar of the Land of Israel, commencing as it does with Passover. Instead, wherever one is located, one tithes the animals born in a stated period over a cycle, marked by Passover, Pentecost, and Tabernacles. The only point of differentiation — taking account of the agricultural calendar of the Land of Israel without imposing that cycle upon the tithe of the herds and the flocks — is that animals born after Passover ("new") are tithed as a group, those already in being prior ("old") likewise. Like the tithe of the crops of the Land, the tithe of the herds and flocks is paid over to the priest. The manner of identifying what is to be tithed must be random and casual, allowing chance to take over, as with the heave-offering and other agricultural offerings in the Land. The act of tithing must be detailed and explicit; it is not enough to separate ten out of a hundred, but a process of selection by chance must be effected. The animals must pass before the farmer to be explicitly counted out, with every tenth one taken for the tithe. That is the counterpart process to the taking up of grain from the harvested crop, that is, the "heave-offering."

C. THE CONSISTENCY OF THE CATEGORY-FORMATION

If the exposition of the category-formation contains evidence of a process of hermeneutics other than the analogical-contrastive ones I have proposed, I do not discern evidence of its working.

D. THE GENERATIVITY OF THE CATEGORY-FORMATION

The capacity of the category-formation to generate results that vastly transcend the array of laws emerges in the contrast of the message of the Halakhah of Bikkurim, firstfruits, with that of Bekhorot, firstlings. The presentation of the firstfruits defines the occasion for declaring who is, and who is not, that Israel of whom Scripture speaks, the one to whom reference is made in the statement,

> "A wandering Aramean was my father, and he went down into Egypt and sojourned there, few in number; and there he became a nation, great, mighty, and populous. And the Egyptians treated us harshly and afflicted us and laid upon us hard bondage...and the Lord brought us out of Egypt with a mighty hand and an outstretched arm, with great terror, ...and he brought us to this place and gave us this land, a land flowing with the milk and honey. And behold, now I bring the first of the fruit of the ground that thou, O Lord, have given me."
>
> DT. 26:6FF.

Presenting firstfruits and reciting the declaration characterize one who is wholly Israel, possessing both the Land by inheritance and the genealogy that mark one as such.

But firstlings, also presented to the priesthood, require no such declaration, a confession both public and personal, involving both Israel and the Israelite. God possesses the firstlings from the womb, and, if unblemished, they are offered up to him or redeemed from him, with reference to beast and man respectively. So firstfruits testify to enlandised Israel, firstlings to genealogical Israel. When it comes to utopian, hence genealogical, Israel, as distinct from enlandised Israel, everyone participates — from the womb. That is the critical point. Converts, on the one side, and non-householders (landowners) on the other, fall outside of the rite of firstfruits. Those who cannot state that the Land is theirs find themselves excluded from the Israel, possessed of the Land, who celebrate their relationship with God in the rite at hand. But all Israel, wherever they are located, tithe their herds and flocks, and all Israel men and women may potentially produce firstborn.

That message, the manifest outcome of the analogical-contrastive analysis of the category-formation in its particular-hermeneutical context, extends the boundaries of the category-formation, opening vast territories for exploration. But, within the Halakhic framework, I can provide no evidence of an effort to map the new lands.

5.
TRACTATE ARAKHIN

I. THE DEFINITION OF THE CATEGORY-FORMATION

The generic topic of the category-formation, Arakhin, is readily defined: individual acts of consecration of abstract, intangible "value" to God's service in the Temple. Principally as a matter of personal initiative individuals consecrate the value of persons, real estate or movables. That is, specifically, the value of persons or real estate is estimated, and the cash paid to redeem from the sanctuary the pledged value, whether personal or landed, goes to the Temple for its upkeep. Scripture explicitly makes provision for such votive offerings of personal worth, specifying the requisite number of sheqels that measure the worth of a person of a given classification. But those who sanctify their own value and cannot pay the fixed sum may be subjected to an individual evaluation. When it comes to real estate, the category-formation focuses upon the disposition of real estate received by inheritance, that is, real estate assigned in the original, perfect division of the Land to one or another specific party to the entry into the Land. Both personal valuations and dedications of real property — fields and houses under specified circumstances — represent donations to God through the Temple and the priesthood.

All of this, as we shall see, derives from Scripture, none emerges from that (theoretical) thought process of comparison and contrast between two or more species of a common genus that I have proposed. Then we must wonder, what of the components of the category-formation and the processes of thought that identified and fused those parts into a transcendent whole? The category-formation, Arakhin, joins together four scriptural expositions, internally cogent and free-standing in their Pentateuchal presentation. The particular hermeneutics of comparison — the theory, framed through a process of comparison and contrast of species of a common genus, of how data are selected and interpreted — has no decisive contribution to make to the exposition of that complex but one. That is to address the one obvious question left open by Scripture: why join these four items? But, in context, that very question of fusion of topics has time and again defined the hermeneutical question for us. Here, once more, even where Scripture has designed the category-formation, we are well served by the theory of the thought-process I have put forth in this systematic account.

To reconstruct the process that has yielded the present category-formation, we begin with the topical outline, introducing the pertinent verses of Scripture that supply the corpus of facts. The underlined phrases take on consequence in due course.

I. VALUATIONS AND VOWS FOR THE BENEFIT OF THE TEMPLE

>The Lord said to Moses, "Say to the people of Israel, When a man makes a special vow of persons to the Lord *at your valuation*, then your valuation of a male from twenty years old up to sixty years old shall be fifty sheqels of silver according to the sheqel of the sanctuary. If the person is a female, your valuation shall be thirty sheqels. If the person is from five years old up to twenty years old, your valuation shall be for a male twenty sheqels and for a female ten sheqels. If the person is from a month old up to five years old, your valuation shall be for a male five sheqels of silver and for a female your valuation shall be three sheqels of silver. And if the person is sixty years old and upward, then your valuation for a male shall be fifteen sheqels, and for a female ten sheqels. And if a man is too poor to pay your valuation, then he shall bring the person before the priest and the priest shall value him; according to the ability of him who vowed the priest shall value him.
>
>Lev. 27:1-8

    A. Basic Rules
    B. Special Rules
    C. Ability to Pay in Assessing Vows
    D. The Difference between Pledging a Valuation and Vowing the Worth, or Price, of Someone or Something
    E. Collecting Valuations

II. THE DEDICATION AND REDEMPTION OF A FIELD THAT HAS BEEN RECEIVED AS AN INHERITANCE

>"If a man dedicates to the Lord part of the land *that is his by inheritance*, then your valuation shall be according to the seed for it; a sowing of a homer of barley shall be valued at fifty sheqels of silver. If he dedicates his field from the year of jubilee, it shall stand at your full valuation, but if he dedicates his field after the jubilee, then the priest shall compute the money-value for it according to the years that remain until the year of jubilee, and a deduction shall be made from your valuation. And if he who dedicates the field wishes to redeem it, then he shall add a fifth of the valuation in money to it, and it shall remain his. But if he does not wish to redeem the field, or if he has sold the field to another man, it shall not be redeemed any more; but

the field, when it is released in the jubilee, shall be holy to the Lord as a field that has been devoted; the priest shall be in possession of it. If he dedicates to the Lord a field that he has bought, which is not part of his possession by inheritance, then the priest shall compute the valuation for it up to the year of jubilee, and the man shall give the amount of the valuation on that day as a holy thing to the Lord. In the year of jubilee, the field shall return to him from whom it was bought, to whom the land belongs as a possession by inheritance. Every valuation shall be according to the sheqel of the sanctuary: twenty gerahs shall make a sheqel.

Lev. 27:16-25

III.   THE DEVOTED THING [HEREM]

"But no devoted thing that a man devotes to the Lord of *anything that he has*, whether of man or beast or of his inherited field, shall be sold or redeemed; every devoted thing is most holy to the Lord. No one devoted, who is to be utterly destroyed from among men, shall be ransomed; he shall be put to death."

Lev. 27:28-29

IV.   THE SALE AND REDEMPTION OF A FIELD THAT HAS BEEN RECEIVED AS AN INHERITANCE AND OF A DWELLING PLACE IN A WALLED CITY

"In this year of jubilee each of you shall return *to his property*. And if you sell to your neighbor or buy from your neighbor, you shall not wrong one another. According to the number of years after the jubilee you shall buy from your neighbor, and according to the number of years for crops he shall sell to you. If the years are many you shall increase the price, and if the years are few you shall diminish the price, for it is the number of the crops that he is selling to you."

Lev. 25:13-17

"If your brother becomes poor and *sells part of his property*, then his next of kin shall come and redeem what his brother has sold. If a man has no one to redeem it, and then himself becomes prosperous and finds sufficient means to redeem it, let him reckon the years since he sold it and pay back the overpayment to the man to whom he sold it; and he shall then return to his property. But if he has not sufficient means to get it back for himself, then what he sold shall remain in the hand of him who bought it until the year of jubilee; in the jubilee it shall be released and he shall return to his property."

"If a man sells a dwelling house in a walled city, he may redeem it within a whole year after its sale; for a full year he shall have the right of redemption. If it is not redeemed within a full year, then the house that is in the walled city shall be made sure in perpetuity to him who bought it, throughout his generations; it shall not be released in the jubilee. But the houses of the villages that have no wall around them shall be reckoned with the fields of the country; they may be redeemed and they shall be released in the jubilee. Nevertheless, the cities of the Levites, the houses in the cities of their possession, the Levites may redeem at any time. And if one of the Levites does not exercise his right of redemption, then the house that was sold in a city of their possession shall be released in the jubilee; for the houses in the cities of the Levites are their possession among the people of Israel. But the fields of common land belonging to their cities may not be sold; for that is their perpetual possession."

Lev. 25:25-34

Pledges to the Temple of the worth of a person, his formal valuation, and dedicating to the Temple an inherited field and the devoted thing (herem) bear an obvious trait in common. They represent the sanctification of abstract value, the devotion of something fungible that is of personal worth and ownership. That covers the first three items. The fourth item, then, expands upon the second matter, the inherited field. That component concerns the restoration of land in the Land of Israel to its original, genealogical possessors, as of the moment of the division of the country by Joshua. That conception of the periodic recovery of the conditions of stasis and perfection that prevailed in the beginning forms part of the larger Pentateuchal account of the restoration of Eden; it is a theological key to the system as a whole, but it does not belong and need not detain us here, except as an appendix of useful information. Then why tack it on as the fourth item, rather then place it in sequence after the second? True to its established preferences, the Halakhah organizes its category-formation topically, only then tacking on an appendix important to complete the exposition of one of the integral topics. So the three integral components of the category-formation cohere: gifts to the Temple of the value of persons or property, other than animals for use on the altar.

Now comes the definition of the category-formation through the now-familiar process of analogical-contrastive analysis. To identify the genus of which the stated complex of topics constitute a species, we ask, what would constitute for a common genus a like-yet-unlike species, for comparison with, and contrast to, the one at hand? The obvious answer must encompass the traits that characterize the components supplied by Scripture. The gift of personal valuations ("the special vow of persons to the Lord") or Land or objects involves

[1] What is votive, not obligatory;
[2] What concretely embodies abstract value (fungible in the case of valuations of persons, no less fungible in the case of land), and, above all,
[3] What is individual in ownership. At each point Scripture stresses the individual ownership of what is dedicated, as the underlined phrases indicate. What then presents itself as the opposite? What is

[1] Not votive but obligatory,
[2] Not of fungible value but itself serviceable in the divine liturgy,
[3] What is public and corporate, not private and personal.

Now the analytical process is complete, with its specification of the indicative traits of species, the analogical-contrastive traits of a genus. For we know (at least in theory) what a contrastive category-formation will have looked like. The consequent genus is donations in support of the Temple, both votive and obligatory, both generic and particular, both corporate and individual. In the setting of that genus and its matched species, what requires comparison are the laws of Zebahim-Menahot, on the one side, Yoma+Sheqalim-Tamid, and on the other, the laws of Arakhin.

That is to say, we turn to what is implicit, and then the contrast is Sheqalim-Tamid (+Yoma) to Arakhin. Sheqalim-Tamid for the year and Yoma for the Sabbath of Sabbaths are corporate, obligatory, of fixed value, and the very opposite of fungible. They also involve the expiation of sin. As noted, the principal gifts covered by Arakhin by contrast are individual, votive, and of variable value; and at no point is the expiation of sin raised as an issue. Having gained perspective on the category-formation through this brief exercise of analogy and contrast, how may we characterize the species, Arakhin (with reference to its three principal components, omitting the fourth)?

Here then is what I take to be the meaning that analogical-contrastive analysis suggests, the hermeneutics of the category-formation, dictating the selection of data and its particular interpretation (so far as a particular interpretation is required). Israel not only constitutes a corporate moral entity but also encompasses private persons, all of them capable of independent volition and action. How to hold together the public and the personal dimensions of the relationship of Israel with God? For Israel, both a singular and a collective-plural noun, looks to God not only in its entirety but also turn to God in *their* individuality.[6]

Let us dwell on that defining aspect of the matter, the individuality of the donor, the context in which his individuality comes to embodiment. All Israelites bear equally the obligation to support the public offerings of atonement. No Israelite is assigned a counterpart, obligatory offering, except in cases of uncleanness and purification or of inadvertent sin, in which case he or she may present a sin-offering to atone for the unintended act. Other individual offerings are votive and supererogatory, not obligatory. So while embodied, corporate Israel is required to present the half-sheqel, forming the parts into the whole for purposes of cultic atonement, no counterpart obligation is imposed on individuals. But when it comes to the votive side, variations of personal taste and judgment enter in. Then, what Israelites may do to express their devotion to God, their supererogatory acceptance of his will even where that will is unarticulated, involves the actions outlined here: give what God has not required. In the setting of the *Shema*, loving God with all one's heart, soul, and might, Arakhin takes up the third of the three components of love: the devotion of one's power, meaning, one's possessions, as an act of love — the very opposite of the (inadvertent) sin that has to be expiated through obligatory gifts to the altar.

We therefore have to consider what it means for an individual to donate to God through the Temple on his own something subject to his will and possession, whether his own worth, whether the worth of a material good. For we now take up the way in which the Halakhah makes provision for individual's to single themselves out in devotion to God through the Temple: what may they do, and what meaning does the deed possess?

Reinforcing the lesson of Sheqalim, the main point of Arakhin is negative, which helps us understand why the active hermeneutics of the principal parts of Arakhin is generic and not particular. The Halakhah by its silence stresses that *only* corporate Israel carries out God's commandments concerning public atonement offerings; individuals may not on their own initiative provide them. One person may not atone for another person's sin, but all Israel may atone for the sin for which all equally bear corporate responsibility.[7] The

---

[6] In British English, which treats collective nouns as plural, e.g., "the Government say," that distinction works better than in American English. Since we treat the collective noun as singular, e.g., the Government says, this sentence jars. But I cannot think of a more precise way of formulating matters.

[7] In the cult, the priest acts in behalf of the sinful sacrifier (the person in whose behalf an offering is made). When the high priest atones for Israel, it is for all Israel, encompassing the high priest and his family as well, for sins for which all bear responsibility.

community alone acts in behalf of entire Israel. Not only so, but corporate Israel acts not on its own volition but only when instructed to by God's explicit commandment. And God does not respect persons or provide for individuals an occasion for self-aggrandizement through acts of obligatory piety. That is why — a triumph for the Halakhah! — by the law of Sheqalim no one may contribute more than the half-sheqel for the public atonement offerings. Recognizing neither wealth nor poverty, neither utter purity nor total corruption of a given person, God permits no distinctions when it comes to atonement. All Israel equally bear[8] guilt, having sinned collectively, not merely individually, for example with the Golden Calf, which set the stage for the provision of the cult. At God's word Israel formed itself into a collectivity, a moral entity at Sinai; the Torah, once accepted voluntarily by the entirety of Israel, explicitly dictated commandments pertaining to the whole community, not only to persons one by one (or, more to the point, by families, as at Exodus 12).

Then what place do individuals find for themselves, for the natural and concrete expression of their personal devotion to, love of God, in line with the *Shema*? Whatever derives from individuals, by reason of personal initiative and idiosyncratic motivation to contribute to the public interest goes to the upkeep of the Temple, not to the altar except in special circumstances to which the Halakhah just now surveyed has made reference.[9] True, individuals may present offerings as well. This they may do in three contexts, all of a single class. The first is the offering presented when private persons are commanded to, for instance, in connection with purification-rites. The second comes when an existing obligation is augmented, for example, in the added offerings on the occasion of pilgrimage rites.[10] The third is when the individual is permitted to present an optional votive offering, e.g., a peace-offering or a thank-offering. In all three cases, God has provided for occasions to accommodate private circumstances, encompassing even individually-motivated offerings. But these do not respond to the act of commandment of all Israel, as the public offerings do. And even individual gentiles may present offerings of a specified character.

With the stated exception of the augmentative offerings, provision to present these offerings represents an accommodation of the individual's exceptional situation. That may prove negative in the case of uncleanness or positive in the case of devotion. Personal offerings do not represent occasions for obe-

---

[8] Once again, the collective and therefore, in the British usage, the plural verb.

[9] That would be, for instance, a donation including beasts that may serve as offerings, but these then are processed into the system of obligations, as we saw in our survey of the Halakhah.

[10] We considered these at category-formation Hagigah.

dience to commandments, with the exceptions of the Passover and the festal offering (*Hagigah*). These, we note are incidental to the encompassing commandment concerning the festival pilgrimage. In this context then, the stress in Arakhin upon the consecration of "value" or scarce resources for the upkeep of the Temple house bears both a positive and a negative point. The positive is, when people wish to act for God in the public interest, they do so through helping to maintain the public place. The negative is, when people propose to distinguish themselves in divine service, they only contribute to the location, not to the activity that takes place in behalf of entire Israel (or classes of Israel involved in expiation, as noted).

The sharp distinction between obligatory participation in the Temple cult, involving all male Israelites in the presentation of the public sacrifices of atonement, the whole-offerings, and the voluntary participation emerges as the most striking provision of the Halakhah — unarticulated but everywhere implicit. When it comes to the public, obligatory offerings of corporate Israel, — I cannot overstress — all males must participate in exactly the same measure, and females may participate as well. When it comes to supererogatory and votive participation in the cult, no one may undertake the obligatory corporate offerings. For the sin that requires atonement by entire Israel, each individual is equally guilty, none less, no more. The upshot is, unless subject to a commandment to do so, for instance, in connection with the Passover, individuals may present offerings only in their own behalf, e.g., when required by reason of inadvertent and unintentional sinful actions and their counterparts, or when motivated by reason of celebration, e.g., offerings to augment the obligatory ones for the pilgrimage or for Passover. So when it comes to presenting offerings to God on the altar, corporate Israel acts by reason of God's instructions and commandments, and individual Israelites cannot act in behalf of the entirety of Israel.

Individuals, accordingly, contribute their own scarce resources, whether property, personalty, or realty, to the public space that is consecrated to God. That they have the right to do, because they possess and may dispose of goods and land and — in a world that countenanced slavery (the buying and selling of persons) — also themselves, their own market-value. Of this they may dispose in accord with their own will; then, in so doing, they make his will their will, their property his. So they give what they command, in proportion to what they hold. And that to which they give then corresponds to what is given: individual worth to the worth of the Temple building, individually-possessed land to the sacred space that sustains the Temple. In that they really are distinguished from one another; in that they willfully distinguish themselves in Godly dedication.

So much for the particular hermeneutics of the category-formation.

What we shall now see is that, once the exegetical work begins, the generic hermeneutics predominates. Only here and there do we see the particular hermeneutics at work. That, I think, is because all components of the category-formation are amply expounded in Scripture, and the Halakhah takes as its problem the secondary exposition and refinement of Scripture's explicit rules. As a matter of hypothesis, I should suggest that, where Scripture is less than ample in the provision of detailed rules, there the particular hermeneutics will generate exegetical problems for Halakhic exposition; where Scripture provides a corpus of detailed rules, these will define the course of exegesis. Hullin is a fine instance of what I take to be a common phenomenon. Where Scripture sets forth a topic and its embodiment in rules, there the Halakhah merely refines and amplifies matters. Then the particular hermeneutics of the category-formation dictates mainly the overall presentation of the matter, the opening proposition in particular, but not the course of Halakhic exegesis, which in the nature of things, responds routinely, that is, to the generic hermeneutics that everywhere serves.

II. THE FOUNDATIONS OF THE HALAKHIC CATEGORY-FORMATION

Principally as a matter of personal initiative individuals consecrate something of value. Such supererogatory acts of sanctification may pertain either to persons or to real estate, and both are covered within the Halakhic category of Arakhin, Valuations. A person may sanctify himself or his property, or he may sanctify the worth of another party, and in either case is obligated to pay to the Temple the value of what he has declared sacred. That represents the process of "redemption," that is, redeeming with a payment of money what has been sanctified for the purposes of the Temple. The process of redemption regularizes the matter. The pertinent statement of Scripture is Lev. 27:1-8, already cited. The value of persons or real estate is estimated, and the cash paid to redeem from the sanctuary the pledged value, whether personal or landed, goes to the Temple for its upkeep. Scripture explicitly makes provision for such votive offerings of personal worth, specifying the requisite number of sheqels that measure the worth of a person of a given classification. For an adult male, it is one hundred times the half-sheqel paid annually, for an adult female, sixty, and so on down. But those who sanctify their own value and cannot pay the fixed sum may be subjected to an individual evaluation.

The Halakhah treats as part of the same category the dedication of real estate, not only one's personal Valuation, to the Temple. Scripture treats the subject at Lev. 27:16-25. When it comes to real estate, the Halakhah of the

Oral Torah focuses upon the disposition of real estate received by inheritance, that is, real estate assigned in the original, perfect division of the Land to one or another specific party to the entry into the Land. Finally, the Halakhah takes up the disposition of things that are declared herem, at Lev. 27:28-29.

The final topic is the sale and redemption of a field that has been received as an inheritance and of a dwelling place in a walled city, Lev. 25:13-17, 25-34.

III. THE EXPOSITION OF THE COMPONENTS OF THE GIVEN CATEGORY-FORMATION BY THE MISHNAH-TOSEFTA-YERUSHALMI-BAVLI

I. VALUATIONS AND VOWS FOR THE BENEFIT OF THE TEMPLE

> The Lord said to Moses, "Say to the people of Israel, When a man makes a special vow of persons to the Lord at your valuation, then your valuation of a male from twenty years old up to sixty years old shall be fifty sheqels of silver according to the sheqel of the sanctuary. If the person is a female, your valuation shall be thirty sheqels. If the person is from five years old up to twenty years old, your valuation shall be for a male twenty sheqels and for a female ten sheqels. If the person is from a month old up to five years old, your valuation shall be for a male five sheqels of silver and for a female your valuation shall be three sheqels of silver. And if the person is sixty years old and upward, then your valuation for a male shall be fifteen sheqels, and for a female ten sheqels. And if a man is too poor to pay your valuation, then he shall bring the person before the priest and the priest shall value him; according to the ability of him who vowed the priest shall value him.
>
> Lev. 27:1-8

A. *BASIC RULES*

M. 1:1 All pledge the Valuation [of others] and are subject to the pledge of Valuation [by others], vow [the worth of another] and are subject to the vow [of payment of their worth by another]: priests and Levites and Israelites, women and slaves. A person of doubtful sexual traits and hermaphrodites vow [the worth of another] and are subject to the vow [of payment of their worth by another], pledge the Valuation [of others], but are not subject to the pledge of Valuation by others, for only [a person of] clear masculine or clear feminine [traits] is subject to the pledge of Valuation [by others]. A deaf-mute, an imbecile, and a minor are subject to the vow [of payment of their worth by another], and are subject to the pledge of Valuation by others, but do not vow the worth, and do not pledge the Valuation, of others, for they do not possess understanding.] One who is less than a month old is subject to the vow [of payment of worth by another], but is not subject to the pledge of Valuation.

T. 1:1 R. Meir says, "Greater is the applicability of the rule of being subject to the pledge of Valuation than the applicability of the rule of pledging the Valuation of others. For: A deaf-mute, an imbecile, and a minor are subject to the pledge of Valuation by others but do not pledge the Valuation of others [M. Ar. 1:1F]." R. Judah says, "Greater is the applicability of the rule of pledging the Valuation of others than the applicability of being subject to the pledge of Valuation [by others]. For: A person of doubtful sexual traits and a person who exhibits traits of both sexes pledge the Valuation [of others] but are not subjected to the pledge of Valuation [to be paid by others] [M. Ar. 1:1D]. Also: The Samaritan should be subject to the rule of pledging the Valuation of others but should not be under the rule of being subject to the pledge of Valuation [by others]" [M. Ar. 1:2A, C].

T. 1:2 Women and slaves vow [the value of others] and are subject to vow [of payment of their worth by others], are subject to the pledge of Valuation [by others] and pledge the Valuation [of others] [M. Ar. 1:1A-C]. If at this time they have [sufficient property], they collect from them. If not, they write a writ of indebtedness and collect it from them after some time. Gentiles vow [to give the value of others] and are subject to vow [that others will give their value] [M. Ar. 1:2D]. Those missing limbs and afflicted by sores, even though they are not of worth, are subject to the pledge of Valuation.

B. 1:1 I.1/2A [WHEN THE FRAMER EXPLICITLY REFERS TO THE FORMULATION] ALL PLEDGE THE VALUATION, [IN FRAMING THE MISHNAH-PARAGRAPH AT HAND, SAYING ALL PLEDGE...,] WHAT [CLASSIFICATION OF PERSONS DOES HE INTEND] TO INCLUDE, [SEEING THAT IN WHAT FOLLOWS, HE LISTS THE AVAILABLE CLASSIFICATIONS OF PERSONS IN ANY EVENT, AND, FURTHER, HE SPECIFIES CATEGORIES OF PERSONS THAT ARE EXCLUDED. ACCORDINGLY, TO WHAT PURPOSE DOES HE ADD THE ENCOMPASSING LANGUAGE, ALL, AT THE OUTSET?] IT SERVES TO ENCOMPASS A MALE NEARING PUBERTY [WHO HAS NOT YET PASSED PUBERTY. SUCH A ONE IS SUBJECT TO EXAMINATION TO DETERMINE WHETHER HE GRASPS THE MEANING OF A VOW, SUCH AS IS UNDER DISCUSSION. A CHILD YOUNGER THAN THE SPECIFIED AGE, TWELVE YEARS TO THIRTEEN, IS ASSUMED NOT TO HAVE SUCH UNDERSTANDING, AND ONE OLDER IS TAKEN FOR GRANTED TO HAVE IT.] [WHEN THE FRAMER EXPLICITLY FRAMES MATTERS AS ALL] ARE SUBJECT TO THE PLEDGE OF VALUATION, WHAT [CLASSI-

FICATION OF PERSONS DOES HE INTEND] TO INCLUDE? IT IS TO INCLUDE A PERSON WHO IS DISFIGURED OR AFFLICTED WITH A SKIN AILMENT. [AT I.31 WE ARE GIVEN A SCRIPTURAL BASIS FOR THAT STATEMENT.]

M. 1:2 The gentile - R. Meir says, "He is subject to the pledge of Valuation [by others], but he does not pledge the Valuation [of others]." R. Judah says, "He pledges the Valuation [of others] but is not subject to the pledge of Valuation [by others]." And this one and that one agree that they vow and are subject to the vow [of payment of worth].

M. 1:3 He who is on the point of death or he who goes forth to be put to death is not subject to the vow [of payment of his worth by others] nor subject to the pledge of Valuation [by others]. R. Hananiah b. 'Aqabya says, "He is subject to the pledge of Valuation, because its [a Valuation's] price is fixed. But he is not subject to the vow [of payment of his worth by others], because its [a vow's] price is not fixed." R. Yosé says, "He may vow [the value of another] and may pledge a Valuation [of another] and may declare something sanctified. And if he caused damage, he is liable to make restitution."

M. 1:4 The [pregnant] woman who goes forth to be put to death — they do not postpone [the execution] for her until she will give birth. [If] she sat on the travailing stool, they postpone [the execution] for her until she will give birth. The woman who is executed — they derive benefit from her hair. A beast which is executed — it [the hair] is prohibited from benefit.

T. 1:3 "He who is on the point of death or one who is eight days old is not subject to the vow [of payment of his worth by others] nor subject to the pledge of Valuation [by others]. And he who goes to be put to death is not subject to the vow [of payment of his worth by others] nor subject to the pledge of Valuation [by others]," the words of R. Meir [M. Ar. 1:3A-B]. R. Hanina b. Aqiba says, "He is subject to the pledge of Valuation, because its price is fixed. But he is not subject to the vow [of payment of his worth by others], because its price is not fixed" [M. Ar. 1:3C-F]. R. Yosé says, "He vows [the value of another] and pledges a Valuation [of another] and declares something sanctified. And if he caused damage, he is liable to make restitution" [M. Ar. 1:3G-H].

T. 1:4 A woman who goes forth to be put to death [M. Ar. 1:4A] — [If] the offspring put forth its hand, they postpone [the execution] for her until she will give birth. For if she had given birth, her offspring would have been stoned. The woman who goes forth to be put to death — [if] she said, "Give my hair to my daughter," they give it to her. [If] she died without specifying [to whom the hair should be given], they do not give it to her [the daughter]. For those that are dead are prohibited from the benefit [of any possessions, hence cannot after death be supposed to have disposed of property in this wise].

In the hermeneutical context established in section i, the opening rule contains a weighty message with its "all pledge the Valuation." That is the centerpiece, provision for persons of all classifications. Then the generic hermeneutics takes over, with its interstitial question: what of persons of an unclear classification? And the Tosefta, for its part, mimics the analogical-contrastive analytical approach with its sub-speciation, that is, the comparison of one thing to another within the same species, now the comparison of the rule governing pledging the Valuation of others with that of having one's own Valuation pledged. The Tosefta further highlights the particular hermeneutics at T. 1:2, encompassing women and slaves in the system. The rest of the exposition pursues the interstitialities, as we should expect. The opening, seen whole, typifies the Halakhic discourse: first the particular hermeneutics, then the generic, first the main rules, then the secondary cases.

B. SPECIAL RULES
M. 2:1 In paying a Valuation one may not pay less than a sela, or more than fifty selas. How so? [If] one [pledged a Valuation as a poor man and paid the minimum due, a sela,] but [then] got rich, he gives nothing [more]. [If he gave] less than a sela but [then before paying what was owing of the remainder of the sela] got rich, he gives fifty selas. [Since he did not pay the minimum to begin with he has not discharged his obligation.] [If] he had five selas — R. Meir says, "He gives only one [of them]." And sages say, "He gives all of them." In paying a Valuation, one may not pay less than a sela, or more than fifty selas.

T. 1:5 The Valuation of a poor man is a sela. The Valuation of a rich one is written in the Torah. [If] one had a sela in hand and had given of it three denars but did not finish handing over the fourth denar before he became rich, they assign to him the whole [required amount, fifty selas]. But if in the first place he had given it over, he should have been exempt [from paying the whole fifty selas] [M. Ar. 2:1D]. [If] he had in hand thirty selas and had given twenty-nine of them but did not finish handing over the last before he became rich, they assign to him the whole [required amount, fifty selas].

M. 3:1 There is in respect to Valuations [the possibility] to rule leniently and to rule stringently; in respect to the law of the field of possession (Lev. 27:16ff) [the possibility] to rule leniently and to rule stringently, in respect to an ox which is an attested danger which killed a slave [the possibility] to rule leniently and to rule stringently; in the case of the rapist (Deut. 22:28f.) and seducer (Ex. 22:15f.), and the one who brings forth an evil name (Deut. 22:17f.) [the possibility] to rule leniently and to rule stringently. There is in respect to Valuations [the possibility] to rule leniently and to rule stringently: How so? The same rule applies to one who pledged the Valuation of the most beautiful among Israelites and [one who pledged that] of the ugliest among Israelites — he gives fifty selas [in either case]. [If, however,] he said, "Lo, his [actual] value is incumbent on me," he gives his actual value.

M. 3:2 In respect to the law of the field of possession [the possibility] to rule leniently and to rule stringently: How so? The same rule applies to one who sanctifies a field in the desert of Mahoz and he who sanctifies a field among the orchards of Sebaste: [if he wants to redeem it] he pays fifty sheqels of silver [for every part of a field that suffices for] the sowing of a homer of barley (Lev. 27:16) [M. 7:10]. And in the case of a field which he has bought (Lev. 27:22), he gives its actual value. R. Eliezer says, "The same rule applies to a field of possession and a field which he has bought. What is the difference between a field of possession and a field which he has bought? Rather in the case of a field of possession he pays an added fifth, and in the case of a field which he has bought he does not pay an added fifth" [M. 7:2].

T. 2:8 In respect to the law of the field of possession [the possibility exists] to rule leniently and to rule stringently. How so? He who sanctifies a field among the orchards of Saposta and in the desert of Mahoz gives fifty selas for a bet kor. R. Judah says, "Also: He who sanctifies a field in the orchards of Jericho and in the desert of Yabneh gives fifty selas for a bet kor" [M. Ar. 3:2A-B].

T. 2:9 "In the case of a field which he has bought (Lev. 27:22), he gives its actual value [M. Ar. 3:2D], as it is said, then the priest shall compute the valuation for it up to the year of jubilee, and the man shall give the amount of the valuation on that day as a holy thing to the Lord (Lev. 27:23). The amount of the valuation is only its value," the words of R. Judah. Said to him R. Eleazar, "If he does not give its whole value, why does Scripture say, And the priest shall compute? But here it is stated, He shall compute, and below it is stated, He shall compute. Just as compute stated below refers to a sela for a bet kor, so compute which is stated here refers to paying fifty selas to redeem a bet kor [of ground]."

The fixed and variable Valuations define the framework for this secondary exposition of matters. The fixed value extends to real estate, not only to persons, M. 3:2. We note a different theory of category-formation, one resting on a common principle covering varied topics, at M. 3:1ff.

C.   *ABILITY TO PAY IN ASSESSING VOWS*

M. 4:1 [The estimate of] ability to pay [is made in accord with the status of] the one who vows [Lev. 27:8]. And [the estimate of] the years [of age is made in accord with the status of] the one [whose Valuation] is vowed. And [when this is according to] the Valuations [spelled out in the Torah], it is in accord with the status [age, sex] of the one whose Valuation is pledged. And the Valuation [is paid in accordance with the rate prescribed] at the time of the pledge of Valuation. [The estimate of] ability to pay [is made in accord with the status of] the one who vows: How so? A poor man who pledged the Valuation of a rich man gives the Valuation required of a poor man. And a rich man who pledged the Valuation of a poor man gives the Valuation required of a rich man.

M. 4:2 But in the case of offerings, [the rule] is not so. Lo, [if] one said, "The [obligation to bring] the offering of this person with skin disease (*mesora'*) is incumbent on me," if the person with the skin ailment (*mesora'*) was poor, he brings the offering of a poor man. [If the *mesora'* was] rich, he brings the offering of a rich one. Rabbi says, "I say, 'Also in the case of Valuations the rule is so. And on what account does the poor man who pledged the Valuation of the rich man give the Valuation of a poor man? Because the rich man [under such circumstances, in any case] owes nothing. But a rich man who said, 'My Valuation is incumbent on me,' and a poor man heard and said, 'What this one has said is incumbent on me [too],' he [the poor man] gives the Valuation of the rich one." [If] he was poor and got rich, or rich and grew poor, he gives the Valuation of a rich man. R. Judah says, "Even if he was poor and got rich and then became poor again, he gives the Valuation of a rich man."

M. 4:3 But in the case of offerings, the rule is not so. Even if his father [is about to] die and leave him ten thousand, [even if] his ship was at sea and [about to] arrive with ten thousand, the sanctuary has no claim whatsoever on them.

T. 2:12 A poor man and a rich man who pledged the Valuation of a poor man and a rich man — this one gives in accord with his status, and that one gives in accord with his status [M. Ar. 4:1F-G].

T. 2:13 [He who says] without further specification, "Lo, I pledge myself to give a Valuation" brings the least of Valuations. And how much is the least of Valuations? Five selas.

T. 2:14 He who says, "The Valuation of ten people is incumbent on me, if he was a poor man, gives for all of them the Valuation of a poor man. If he was a rich man, he gives for all of them the Valuation of a rich man. [If] he was a poor man and got rich, he gives for all of them the Valuation of a rich man. [If] he was a rich man and grew poor, he gives for all of them the valuation of a poor man. R. Judah says, "[He gives] the valuation of a rich man, since for one moment he has entered the category of wealth" [M. Ar. 4:2G].

T. 2:15 "He who says, 'The Valuation of such-and-so is incumbent on me, Lo, this one gives a sela," the words of R. Meir. For it is said, "Every valuation shall be according to the sheqel of the sanctuary" (Lev. 27:25). And sages say, "He gives only in accord with his capacity, as it is said, "According to the ability of him who vowed the priest shall value him' (Lev. 27:8)."

T. 2:16 A poor man who pledged his own Valuation — they do not say to him, "Go, borrow money for yourself. Do work. Then bring the Valuation of a rich man." But it is better that he bring the Valuation of a poor man now. And let him not bring the Valuation of a rich man only after a while.

T. 2:17 R. Judah says, "[If] his father was sick or dying, or his ship was out at sea, so that he may [shortly] bring the Valuation of a rich man, it is better that he bring the Valuation of a poor man now. And let him not bring the Valuation of a rich man after a while."

T. 2:18 R. Eleazar says, "[If] he owed a rising-and-falling offering, they do not say to him, 'Go, borrow money for yourself. Do work, and bring the offering of a rich man.' But it is better that he bring the offering of a poor man now. And let him not bring the offering of a rich man after a while."

T. 2:19 R. Simeon says, "The burning of the fats is valid at the end of the Sabbath. The Torah [however] has said, 'Let them override the Sabbath in the proper time. But let them not be offered up at the end of the Sabbath, not in the proper time.' And so it says, A wise-hearted man heed the commandments (Prov. 10:8) — he who makes his commandment a commandment [to be done right away]."

M. 4:4 [The estimate of] the years [of his age is made in accord with the status of] the one [whose Valuation] is vowed: How so? A child who pledged the Valuation of an elder gives the Valuation of an elder. And an elder who pledged the Valuation of a child gives the Valuation of a child. And [when this is reckoned according to] the Valuation [spelled out in the Torah], it is in accord with the status of the one whose Valuation is pledged: How so? A man who pledged the Valuation of a woman gives the Valuation of a woman. And a woman who pledged the Valuation of a man gives the Valuation of a man. And the Valuation [is paid in accordance with the rate prescribed] at the time of the pledge of

Valuation: How so? [If] one pledged the Valuation of another when the latter was less than five years old, and [that one] passed five, less than twenty years old and he passed twenty, he pays in accord with what is required at the time of the pledge of Valuation. [If a man pledged the Valuation of a child who on that day had reached his] thirtieth day [he is considered] less than that. [And if the person whose Valuation was pledged reached his] fifth year or twentieth year [he is considered] less than that. [That is, in order to fall into the category of a five year old or twenty year old he must be five years and a day or twenty years and a day.] As it says, "And if it be from sixty years old and upward, if it be a male" (Lev. 27:7). Lo, we derive the rule for all cases from that applicable to the sixtieth year. Just as the sixtieth year is deemed equivalent to less than that age, so the fifth year or the twentieth year is deemed equivalent to less than that age. Is this so? If Scripture has treated the sixtieth year as less than it, it is to impose a more stringent rule. Shall we then treat the fifth year and the twentieth year as less than they, to impose a more lenient rule? Scripture says, "Year ... year ...," for the purposes of establishing an analogy. Just as year stated in connection with the sixtieth year is deemed equivalent to less than it, so year stated in connection with the fifth year and the twentieth year are deemed equivalent to less than they, whether this imposes a lenient or a stringent ruling. R. Eleazar says, "The foregoing applies so long as they are a month and a day more than the years [which are prescribed]."

B. 4:4A-J I.1/18A OUR RABBIS HAVE TAUGHT ON TANNAITE AUTHORITY: YOU HAVE PLACED IN THE SAME CLASSIFICATION VOWS OF WORTH AND VALUATIONS, WITH REGARD TO [THE VALUATION OF] A PEARL FOR THE POOR, AND WITH REGARD TO THE RULE THAT THE VALUE OF A LIMB BE JUDGED IN ACCORD WITH ITS IMPORTANCE. [IF A POOR MAN OWNED A PEARL WHICH IS IN HIS PLACE OF RESIDENCE, FOR LACK OF DEMAND, IS WORTH BUT THIRTY SELAS, WHEREAS IN A LARGE TOWN WHERE THERE ARE MANY BUYERS, IT WOULD BE WORTH FIFTY, ONE MUST ASSUME THAT IT IS WORTH ONLY WHAT THE POOR MAN CAN GET FOR IT NOW, IN HIS PLACE OF RESIDENCE. THE POOR MAN WHO VOWED HIS OWN VALUATION WOULD HENCE NOT HAVE TO PAY FIFTY SELAS (IF HE WERE BETWEEN TWENTY AND FIFTY YEARS OF AGE , ALTHOUGH THE PEARL MIGHT FETCH THAT PRICE ELSEWHERE. NOW THE SAME RULE APPLIES TO THE CASE OF ONE WHO SAID, 'I TAKE IT UPON MYSELF TO PAY TO THE SANCTUARY THE VALUE OF THIS PEARL." HERE TOO, SINCE WE COMPARED VALUATION TO VOW OF MARKET-VALUE, THE VOWER WOULD HAVE TO PAY THE LOWER PRICE....] IS IT POSSIBLE THAT WE SHOULD ALSO PLACE

IN A SINGLE CLASSIFICATION PLEDGES OF VALUATION AND VOWS OF THE ACTUAL VALUE [OF AN OBJECT, PAYABLE TO THE SANCTUARY], SO THAT THE DONOR MUST PAY IN ACCORD WITH THE PRICE PREVAILING AT THE TIME HE *ACTUALLY* PAYS THE FUNDS? [TO FORESTALL THAT CONCLUSION], SCRIPTURE STATES, "ACCORDING TO YOUR VALUATION IT SHALL STAND" (LEV. 27:17). ONE PAYS ONLY WHAT THE OBJECT WAS WORTH AT THE TIME OF VALUATION, [AND NOT AT THE TIME OF PAYING OVER WHAT HE OWES, AT WHICH POINT A DIFFERENT VALUE MIGHT ATTACH TO THE OBJECT].

The clarification on the criterion by which ability to pay is established depends on the distinction between the one who vows a Valuation and the one whose Valuation is vowed. Here, again, the generic hermeneutics comes to bear. The Tosefta's amplification is particularly rich.

D. *THE DIFFERENCE BETWEEN PLEDGING A VALUATION AND VOWING THE WORTH, OR PRICE, OF SOMEONE OR SOMETHING*

M. 5:1 He who says, "My weight is incumbent on me [as a pledge to the sanctuary]" pays his weight — if [he said], "Silver," [then he pays] in silver; if [he said], "Gold," [then he pays] in gold. It once happened that the mother of Yirmatyah said, "The weight of my daughter is incumbent on me." And she went up to Jerusalem, and weighed her [Yirmatyah], and paid her weight in gold. [He who says], "The weight of my hand is incumbent on me [as a pledge to the sanctuary]" — R. Judah says, "He fills up a jar and pokes it [his hand] in up to the elbow. And he weighs out the meat of an ass, with the sinews and bones. And he puts it [the ass-meat] into it [the jar] until it [the jar] is filled [to the brim as the water rises]." Said R. Yosé, "And how is it possible to treat as equivalent one kind of flesh and another, and one kind of bones and another? But: They estimate how much the hand is likely to weigh."

T. 3:1 He who says, "Lo, incumbent on me is a staff the full measure of my height" brings the full measure of his height with a staff which is not bent. M'SH B: The mother of Yirmatyah, whose daughter was sick, said, "If my daughter will recover from her illness, I shall give her weight in gold." She [the daughter] recovered from her illness. She [the mother] went to Jerusalem and weighed her in gold [M. Ar. 5:1D].

T. 3:2 [He who says], "The weight of my hand is incumbent on me" gives [the equivalent of the weight] up to the elbow. [He who says], "The weight of my foot is incumbent on me" gives [the equivalent of the weight] up to the ankle. How does he carry out [the measure]? He brings a jar full of water and puts his hand in it up to the elbow. He puts in his foot up to the ankle. And he brings ass-meat, sinews and bones. He weighs it out and puts into it meat equivalent in volume to his meat and bones equivalent in volume to his bones [M. Ar. 5:1F]. Even though there is no proof for such a procedure, there is an allusion to it: Whose flesh is the flesh of asses (Ez. 23:20)," the words of R. Judah. Said to him R. Yosé, "How is it possible to treat as equivalent one kind of flesh and another, and one kind of bones and another [M. Ar. 5:1G]?" Said to him R. Judah, "They make a rough estimate of it." Said to him R. Yosé, "While they are making a rough estimate of it, let them make a rough estimate of the hand — how much it weighs, and of the foot — how much it weighs [M. Ar. 5:1G-H]."

M. 5:2 [He who says], "The price of my hand is incumbent on me" — they make an estimate of him: how much is he worth with a hand, and how much is he worth without a hand? This rule is more strict in connection with vows than in connection with Valuations. More strict is the rule in connection with Valuations than in connection with vows. How so? He who says, "My Valuation is incumbent on me" and then dies — the heirs must pay [the Valuation]. [He who says], "My worth is incumbent on me" and then dies — the heirs do not pay [the vow]. For corpses have no price [worth]. [He who says], "The Valuation of my hand, or the Valuation of my foot is incumbent on me" has not said a thing. [He who says], "The Valuation of my head," or "the Valuation of my liver is incumbent on me" pays the Valuation of his whole person. This is the general principle: [If he refers to] something on which life depends, he pays the Valuation of his whole person.

T. 3:3 A. [He who says], "Half of my Valuation is incumbent on me" pays half his Valuation [M. Ar. 5:3A]. R. Judah says, "They impose a fine on him and he pays his entire Valuation." [He who says], "Half of my price is incumbent on me" pays half his price [M. Ar. 5:3D]. R. Yosé bar Judah says, "They impose a fine upon him and he pays his entire price."

M. 5:3 [He who says], "Half of my Valuation is incumbent on me" pays half his Valuation. [He who says], "The Valuation of half of me is incumbent on me" pays the whole of his Valuation. [He who says], "Half of my price is incumbent on me" pays half of his price. [He who says], "The price of half of me is incumbent on me" pays the whole of his price. This is the general principle: [If he refers to] something on which life depends, he pays the Valuation of his whole person.

M. 5:4 He who says, "The Valuation of so-and-so is incumbent on me" — [If] the one who makes the vow and the one concerning whom the vow is made die — the heirs [of the former] pay the pledge. [If he said], "The price of so-and-so is incumbent on me" [and] the one who makes the vow dies, the heirs must pay the vow. [If] the one concerning whom the vow is made dies, the heirs do not have to pay. For corpses have no price [value].

T. 3:4 A He who says, "The Valuation of so-and-so is incumbent on me" — [if] the one whose Valuation has been pledged dies, the one who has pledged the Valuation is [nonetheless] liable [M. Ar. 5:4A-C].

T. 3:5 A strict rule applies to [vows to pay] the price which does not apply to Valuations, and to Valuations which does not apply to [vows to pay] the price. [For vows to pay] the price apply to man and beast, to live and slaughtered [beasts], to whole ones and to limbs. And they apply without regard to ability to pay, which is not the case for Valuations.

T. 3:6 A more strict rule applies to Valuations For Valuations are subject to a fixed sum deriving from the Torah which is not the case of [vows to pay] the price. He who says, "The Valuation of so-and-so is incumbent on me," and who dies, is liable [through his estate to pay the pledged Valuation]. [He who says], "The price of this beast is incumbent on me" and who dies is liable. [He who says], "The price of this beast is incumbent on me," and the beast dies — the one who vows [nonetheless] is liable.

T. 3:7 A strict rule applies to man which does not apply to beast, and [a strict rule applies to] a beast which does not apply to man. For he who says, "The price of this beast is incumbent on me," if it died, is still liable. [He who says], "The price of so-and-so is incumbent on me," if he dies, is exempt [M. Ar. 5:2F]. A more strict rule applies to Valuations, for Valuations apply to man and do not apply to beast.

M. 5:5 [He who says], "This ox is a burnt-offering," "This house is qorban," [if] the ox died or the house fell down, is not liable to pay. [If he said], "[The price of] this ox is incumbent on me for a burnt-offering," or "[the price of] this house is incumbent on me as qorban," [if] the ox died or the house fell down, he is liable to pay.

T. 3:8 He who sanctifies the produce of his wife's hands, lo, this one provides for her maintenance therefrom. And only the remainder is deemed sanctified. He who sanctifies the produce of his servant's hands, lo, this one provides him with maintenance therefrom. And [only] the remainder is deemed sanctified. He who sanctifies himself, lo, this one labors and benefits from the fruit of his labor. He has sanctified only his value.

T. 3:9 [He who says], "The head of this servant is sanctified" — he and the sanctuary are partners in him. [He who says], "The head of this ass is sanctified," he and the sanctuary are partners in it. [He who says], "The head of this servant is sold to you" — they work the matter out between them. [He who says], "The head of this ass is sold to you" — they work the matter out between them.

T. 3:10 [He who says], "The head of this cow is sold to you" has sold only its head. And not only so, but even if he had said, "The head of this cow is sanctified," he has sanctified only its head.

T. 3:11 [He who says], "This ox is a burnt-offering" — the ox is deemed a burnt-offering. And it is subject to the laws of sacrilege. And they are not responsible for [replacing] it [if it should be lost]. [He who says], "This ox is incumbent on me as a burnt-offering" — the ox is deemed a burnt-offering. And it is subject to the laws of sacrilege. And they are responsible for [replacing] it [if it should be lost].

T. 3:12 [He who says], "The price of his ox is a burnt-offering" — the ox is deemed unconsecrated. And the laws of sacrilege do not apply to it. And they are not responsible [to replace] it [if it is lost]. [He who says], "The price of this ox is incumbent on me as a burnt-offering," the ox is unconsecrated. And the laws of sacrilege do not apply to it. But they are responsible [to replace] it [if it should be lost].

T. 3:13 [He who says], "This house is sanctified" — the house is sanctified. And the laws of sacrilege apply to it. But he is not responsible for it. "This house is incumbent on me as sanctified" — the house is sanctified. And the laws of sacrilege apply to it. And they are responsible for it. The price of this house is sanctified" — the house is unconsecrated. The laws of sacrilege do not apply to it. And they are not responsible for it. The price of this house is incumbent on me as sanctified" — the house is unconsecrated. And the laws of sacrilege do not apply to it. But they are liable to be responsible [for the funds].

The same issue continues, now with attention to assessing the appropriate Valuation. The governing distinctions present no surprises.

E. *COLLECTING VALUATIONS*

M. 5:6 Those who owe Valuations [to the Temple] — they exact pledges from them. Those who owe sin-sufferings or guilt-offerings — they do not exact pledges from them. Those who owe burnt-offerings or peace-offerings — they exact pledges from them. Even though he does not make atonement [that is, atonement is not effected for him] unless he acts of his own will, as it is said, "At his good will" (Lev. 1:3), [nonetheless], they compel him until he says, "I will it." And so do you rule in the case of writs of divorce for women: They compel him until he says, "I will it."

T. 3:14 Those who are liable for vows, freewill-offerings,

Valuations, things which have been declared *herem* things which have been declared sanctified — the court exacts a surety from them [M. Ar. 5:6A]. And if they die, the heirs are liable to provide [what has been lost].

T. 3:15 A Those who owe sin-offerings and guilt-offerings or the price [thereof] — the court does not exact a surety from them [M. Ar. 5:6C]. And if they die, the heirs are not liable to provide [what is owed]. And as to the price which has been laid on them, Lo, it is deemed the equivalent of Valuations.

T. 3:16 Burnt-offerings which are brought with sin-offerings — the court exacts a surety for them. And if they died, the heirs are liable to provide [what is owed]. [If] one brought his sin-offering and did not bring his burnt-offering the court exacts a surety on its account. And if they died, the heirs are liable to provide [what is owed] [If] he brought his burnt-offering and did not bring his sin-offering the court does not exact a surety on its account. And if they died, the heirs are not liable to provide [a sin-offering].

T. 3:17 Those who owe burnt-offerings and the price [thereof], peace-offerings, Valuations, things which have been declared *herem* things which have been declared sanctified, vows, free-will-offerings, sin-offerings, guilt-offerings, gifts of charity, tithes, gleanings, the forgotten sheaf, the corner of the field, firstlings, tithe of cattle, and the Passover — once three festivals have gone by, transgress on their account the rule against postponing [and not doing the matter in proper time].

T. 3:18 R. Simeon says, "Three festivals in proper order, and the festival of unleavened bread comes first." R. Eleazar bar Simeon says, "Once the festival of Sukkot passes by, one transgresses on their account the rule against postponing." And all the same are the firstling and the tithe, and all the same are all Holy Things which one has sanctified — a year of festivals and the festivals of a year [having gone by] one transgresses on their account the rule against postponing [= T. Bekh. 3:5].

M. 6:1 [The proclamation of the sale of goods of] orphans evaluated [by the court to meet the father's debt] is for thirty days. And [the proclamation of the sale of goods of] the sanctuary evaluated [by the court] is for sixty days. And they make an announcement morning and night. He who sanctifies his property, and there was incumbent upon it the payment of his wife's *ketubah* — R. Eliezer says, "When he divorces her, he takes a vow not to enjoy any benefit [from her]." [This indicates he has no intention of committing fraud. For had he not taken the vow, he might have divorced the woman, so that her ketubah would be paid from the sanctified property, whereupon he would remarry her. But by vowing that she have no benefit from him, he indicates this is not the case.] R. Joshua says, "He need not do so." Along these same lines did Rabban Simeon b. Gamaliel say, "Also: He who was a guarantor for a woman in respect to her ketubah, and her husband divorced her — let him [the husband] impose on her a vow not to enjoy any benefit from him. lest he [the husband] conspire against the property of this one [the guarantor], and then take his wife back [after she had collected her ketubah from the guarantor]."

T. 4:1 [The proclamation of the sale of goods of [orphans evaluated] by the court to meet the father's debt is for thirty days. And [the proclamation of the sale of goods of 1 the sanctuary evaluated [by the court] is for sixty days. And they make an announcement morning and night [M. Ar. 6:1 A-C] — when the workers come in and when the workers go out. They state the traits [of the property]: how much it was worth, and how much one demands for its redemption for the purpose of paying a woman her ketubah and a creditor his debt. Just as an ordinary person who took precedence before another ordinary person — Lo, this is deemed precedence for all purposes, so an ordinary person who took precedence over the Most High, Lo, this is deemed precedence for all purposes.

T. 4:2 Movables which belong to the sanctuary, the produce of the fourth year, and second tithe, the price of which are not known, are redeemed at the decision of three purchasers, and not at the decision of three who are not purchasers. [If] there is a blemish on its leg, Lo, this may be slaughtered at the instruction of members of the Congregation," the words of R. Meir. R. Yosé says, "Even if his leg was cut off or his eye was blinded, it should be slaughtered only at the instruction of an expert" [T. Bekh. 3:25].

T. 4:3 He who sanctifies a beast and it dies — it is subject to redemption. He who sanctifies a dead beast — it is not subject to redemption. He who redeems [something] from the possession of the sanctuary without a [specified] price — it is deemed to have been redeemed, for the claim of the sanctuary is paramount. This cow worth five selas is in place of a cow of the sanctuary," "This cloak worth five selas is in place of a cloak of the sanctuary" — it is deemed to have been redeemed, for the claim of the sanctuary is paramount. This cow worth five selas in place of a cow of the sanctuary," "This cloak worth five selas is in place of a cloak of the sanctuary" — the first requires an added fifth, and the second does not require an added fifth.

T. 4:4 [If] one effected possession for a maneh, but did not have time to complete the act of redemption before the price went up to two hundred [zuz, two manehs] — Lo, this one pays two hundred zuz, as it is said, "And he will pay the money and depart." If he has given the money, Lo, these belong to him. But if not, it is not his. [If] one acquired possession for two hundred but did not have time to complete the act of redemption before the price went to a maneh, Lo, this one pays two hundred. For an act of acquisition by word in the case of the Most High is equivalent to an act of acquisition through actual handing over in the case of an ordinary person. [If] one redeemed it for a maneh but did not have time to effect possession before the price went to two hundred, that which he has redeemed is deemed to have been redeemed. [If] he redeemed it for two hundred and did not have time to effect possession before the price went to a maneh, that which he has redeemed is deemed redeemed. For in the case of the sanctuary, an act of redemption is deemed to constitute an act of acquisition [to effect possession]. Rabban Simeon b. Gamaliel and R. Yohanan b. Beroqah say, "Even in the case of second tithe, its redemption is deemed equivalent to an act of effecting possession."

T. 4:5 He who sanctifies his property and gave thought to divorcing his wife — R. Eliezer says, "Let him take a vow not to enjoy any benefit from it, and she collects her ketubah from the sanctuary. And if he wants to remarry her, he may do so." R. Joshua says, "If he wants to remarry her, he may not remarry her." And the House of Hillel say, "If he wants to remarry her, he may not remarry her." R. Eliezer rules in accord with the House of Shammai, and R. Joshua rules in accord with the House of Hillel.

M. 6:2 He who sanctifies his property, and there were incumbent upon him payment of his wife's ketubah and a debt — the wife cannot collect her ketubah from the sanctified property, nor the creditor his debt. But he who redeems [the property] redeems it on condition of paying the woman her ketubah and the creditor his debt. He who sanctified [property worth] ninety manehs, and his debt was a hundred manehs — he [the debtor] adds another denar and redeems these possessions, on condition of paying the woman her ketubah and the creditor his debt.

M. 6:3 Even though they have said [M. 5:6]: Those who owe Valuations — they exact a surety from them, they [nonetheless] supply him with food for thirty days, and clothing for twelve months, and bedding, shoes, and *tefillin* — for him, but not for his wife or his children. If he was a craftsman, they give him two of every kind of the tools of his craft. [To a] carpenter they give two axes and two saws. R. Eliezer says, "If he was a farmer, they give him his yoke [of oxen]. [If he was] an ass-driver, they give him his ass."

T. 4:6 [If] one sanctified [property worth] ninety manehs, and his debt was a hundred — he [the creditor] adds a denar and redeems it [M. Ar. 6:2E-F] from the sanctuary even for a denar. For that which is sanctified does not go forth without redemption. Rabban Simeon b. Gamaliel says, "If his debt was larger than that which he has sanctified, he has sanctified nothing." Even though they have said,

"Those who owe things which have been sanctified — the court exacts a surety from them," they [nonetheless] supply him with food for thirty days and a garment for a year [M. Ar. 6:3A-B]. Under what circumstances? In respect to things which concern the court. But as to things which do not concern the court — they provide him with bedding, his shoes, and his tefillin [M. Ar. 6:3B]. R. Eliezer says, "If he was a farmer, they provide him with his yoke [of oxen]" [M. Ar. 6:3F]. R. Eliezer says, "As to an ass-driver, they give him his asses" [M. Ar. 6:3G].

M. 6:4 [If] one sort [of tools] was abundant and one was few, they do not tell him to sell some of the abundant kind and to buy for himself some of the few. But: They give him two from every kind which is abundant, and all of those of which he has only few. He who sanctifies his property — they take away his tefillin.

M. 6:5 The same rule applies to one who sanctifies his property and the one who pledges his own Valuation: he has no claim either on his wife's garment, or on his children's garment, or on dyed clothes which he dyed for them, or on new shoes which he bought for them. Even though they have said: Slaves are sold with their clothing to improve their value, so that if for him [the slave] a garment should be purchased for thirty denars, it improves his value by a maneh, and so in the case of a cow: if they keep it for sale in a market place, it fetches a better price, and so in the case of a pearl: if they bring it up to a city, it fetches a better price — the sanctuary [nonetheless] has a claim only in its own place and in its own time.

T. 4:7 He who sanctifies his property and included were slaves — they do not instruct him to feed the slaves and to provide them with clothing, so that they will bring a good price. And not only so, but: Even pearls in a little village [a man is not required to bring to a city for sale in a larger market]. The sanctuary has a claim only in its own place and in its own time [M. Ar. 6:5C-G].

That alternative theory of category-formation — abstract principle over concrete topic — leads to the combination of topically-distinct units in a single composition, cohering around the contrast of exacting/not exacting pledges. The governing principle is that, where one's own volition is the key, the court may compel volition; the whole then ignores the particular hermeneutics of Arakhin. Had this other approach prevailed, the hermeneutics of the Halakhah would have predominated even on the surface of matters, the generic hermeneutics playing a subordinate role.

II.   THE DEDICATION AND REDEMPTION OF A FIELD THAT

HAS BEEN RECEIVED AS AN INHERITANCE

"If a man dedicates to the Lord part of the land that is his by inheritance, then your valuation shall be according to the seed for it; a sowing of a homer of barley shall be valued at fifty sheqels of silver. If he dedicates his field from the year of jubilee, it shall stand at your full valuation, but if he dedicates his field after the jubilee, then the priest shall compute the money-value for it according to the years that remain until the year of jubilee, and a deduction shall be made from your valuation. And if he who dedicates the field wishes to redeem it, then he shall add a fifth of the valuation in money to it, and it shall remain his. But if he does not wish to redeem the field, or if he has sold the field to another man, it shall not be redeemed any more; but the field, when it is released in the jubilee, shall be holy to the Lord as a field that has been devoted; the priest shall be in possession of it. If he dedicates to the Lord a field that he has bought, which is not part of his possession by inheritance, then the priest shall compute the valuation for it up to the year of jubilee, and the man shall give the amount of the valuation on that day as a holy thing to the Lord. In the year of jubilee, the field shall return to him from whom it was bought, to whom the land belongs as a possession by inheritance. Every valuation shall be according to the sheqel of the sanctuary: twenty gerahs shall make a sheqel.

Lev. 27:16-25

M. 7:1 They do not sanctify [a field of possession] less than two years before the year of Jubilee. And they do not redeem it less than a year after the year of Jubilee. [In redeeming the field] they do not reckon the months against the sanctuary. But the sanctuary reckons the months [to its own advantage]. He who sanctifies his field at the time of the Jubilee's [being in effect] [compare M. 8:1] pays the fifty sheqels of silver [for every part of a field that suffices for] the sowing of a homer of barley. [If] there were there crevices ten handbreadths deep or rocks ten handbreadths high, they are not measured with it. [If they were in height] less than this, they are measured with it. [If] one sanctified it two or three years before the Jubilee, he gives a sela and a pondion for each year. If he said, "Lo, I shall pay for each year as it comes," they do not pay attention to him. But he pays the whole at once.

T. 4:8 They do not declare [the field of possession sanctified less than two years before the year of Jubilee [M. Ar. 7:1 A] — [two years] of crops [M. Ar. 9: 1 A], as it is said, Then the priest shall compute the money-value for it according to the years [that remain until the year of Jubilee] (Lev. 27:18). Behold, if one sanctified it in the Jubilee-year itself, Lo, this is deemed sanctified.

T. 4:9 "Years" (Lev. 27:1 8) — There are no fewer than two. Or [may one hold:] Just as they do not sanctify [a field of possession] less than two years [before the Jubilee], so they do not redeem [a field of possession which has been sanctified] less then two years [thereafter]? Scripture states, And a deduction shall be made from your valuation (Lev. 27:18) — even a single year [Vs. M. Ar. 7:1B].

T. 4:10 You turn out to rule: A jubilee of forty-nine years requires forty-nine selas and forty-nine pondions. [If] the sanctuary had the usufruct for ten or fifteen years, the owner deducts from it[s redemption price] a sela and a pondion per year. [If] it enjoyed the usufruct for ten or fifteen years, he pays a sela and a pondion per year.

T. 4:11 He who sanctified his field in the time of the Jubilee pays fifty sheqels of silver [for every part of a field that suffices for] the sowing of a homer of barley [M. Ar. 7:1F]. [For every part of a field that suffices for] the sowing of a homer of barley — and not by measure. All the same are a field in which one may sow a kor [of seed], a field of trees, and a field of reeds — all are subject to this measure. [If] they are less than this or more than this, one pays by reckoning.

T. 4:12 [If] there were there crevices ten handbreadths deep or rocks ten handbreadths high [M. Ar. 7:1G], Lo, they are not deemed sanctified and measured with it. [If they were] less than this, they are measured with it and are deemed sanctified [M. Ar. 7:1H].

T. 4:13 The house, the hut, the tower, and the dovecote which are in it, Lo, they are measured with it. When they are redeemed, they are redeemed in the status of houses which are in courtyards. [If] one sanctified the field and then went and sanctified the tree, when he redeems, he redeems the tree by itself and the field by itself. [As to a field of possession], if one sanctified it and redeemed it, it does not pass out of his possession at the Jubilee year [M. Ar. 7:3A].

M. 7:2 The same rule applies to the owner [of the field] and every [other] man [in regard to what is paid (M. 7-1/1-K) for the redemption of the field]. What is the difference between the owner and every other man? But: the owner pays the added fifth, and no other person pays the added fifth [M. 8:1].

M. 7:3 [If] he sanctified it and redeemed it, it does not go forth from his domain on the Jubilee. [If] his son redeemed it, it goes forth to his father on the Jubilee. [If] someone else redeemed it, or one of the relatives, and he redeemed it from his domain, it does go forth from his domain in the Jubilee. [If] one of the priests redeemed it, and Lo, it is in his [the priest's] domain, he may not say, "Since it goes forth to the priests in the Jubilee, and since,

Lo, it is in my domain, it is mine." But it goes forth and is divided among all his brethren, the priests.

T. 4:14 [If] his son redeemed it, it goes forth to his father on the Jubilee. [If] another person or one of his relatives redeemed it, [and] he redeemed it from his possession, it does not go forth from his possession on the Jubilee [M. Ar. 7:3B-C]. You have nothing which leaves one's possession for that of the father in the case of provision [for the female slave] and of that for the Hebrew slave and of field of possession except in the case of the son alone.

M. 7:4 [If] the Jubilee arrived and [the field] was not redeemed, "The priests enter into [the possession of] it but pay its price," the words of R. Judah. R. Simeon says, "They enter, and they do not pay." R. Eliezer says, "They neither enter nor pay. But: It is called an abandoned field until the second Jubilee. [If] the second year of the Jubilee came and it was not redeemed, it is called a twice-abandoned field, up to the third Jubilee. The priests under no circumstances do not [directly] enter into possession until another [party] has redeemed it."

T. 4:15 [If] the Jubilee arrived and it was not redeemed, "The priests enter into possession of it and pay its price," the words R. Judah. R. Simeon says, "They enter but do not pay." R. Eleazar says, "They do not enter and do not pay. But: It is called an abandoned field, until the second Jubilee. If the second Jubilee came and it was not redeemed, it is called a twice-abandoned field, up to the third Jubilee." The priests under no circumstances enter into possession until another will redeem it [M. Ar. 7:4A-H]. Under what circumstances? In the case of a field of possession of an Israelite But in the case of a field which is purchased of an Israelite, they sanctify it any time that they want, and they redeem it any time that they want. [If] another person redeemed it, it goes forth to the [original] owner at the Jubilee.

M. 7:5 He who purchases a field from his father, [if] his father died, and afterward he sanctified it, lo, it is deemed a field of possession (Lev. 27:16). [If] he sanctified it and afterward his father died, "Lo, it is deemed in the status of a field which has been bought," the words of R. Meir. R. Judah and R. Simeon say, "It is deemed in the status of a field of possession." Since it is said, "And if a field which he has bought which is not a field of his possession (Lev. 27:22) — a field which is not destined to be a field of possession, which excludes this, which is destined to be a field of possession [i.e., when his father dies]." A field which has been bought does not go forth to the priests in the Jubilee, for a man does not declare sanctified something which is not his own. Priests and Levites sanctify [their fields] at any time and redeem them at any time, whether before the Jubilee or after the Jubilee.

T. 4:16 A field which has gone forth from the power of the sanctuary to the priests in the Jubilee year, Lo, it is in the status of a field of possession of an Israelite. The priests and Levites in a field in a city of their dwelling sanctify [property] any time they like. And they redeem property at any time [that they like]. [If] another person redeemed it, it returns to the owner at the Jubilee.

T. 4:17 A field which has gone forth from the possession of the sanctuary to the priests, Lo, it is deemed equivalent to the field of possession of an Israelite. The priests and Levites in the field of their possession in the cities of their dwelling sanctify [property] at any time they like and redeem it at any time they like. [If] another person redeemed it, it goes forth to the [original] owner at the Jubilee.

T. 4:18 A priest who inherited the estate of the father of his mother who was a Levite and so the son of a Levite, a Netin, a Mamzer who inherited a field of his fathers — Lo, it is deemed to be equivalent to a field of possession of an Israelite.

M. 8:1 He who sanctifies his field when the Jubilee is not [observed, i.e. after the destruction of the Temple] — they say to him, "You declare first" [how much you wish to pay for the redemption of the field, since, when the Jubilee is not in force, the field is redeemed at market value, not at the fifty sheqels for each homer's area]. For the owner pays an added fifth. But no other man pays an added fifth [M. 7:2]. It once happened that a man sanctified his field because of its poor quality. They said to him, "You declare first." He said, "Lo, it is mine for an issar." Said R. Yosé, "This one said not for an issar but only, 'For [the value of] an egg.'" For what is sanctified is redeemed by money or by something worth money.) He [i.e. the Temple treasurer] said to him, "It's yours!" He turned out to lose an issar, and his field was still his.

T. 4:19 A. He who sanctifies his field when the Jubilee is not [in force] — they say to him, "You declare a price of redemption first. For the owner pays an added fifth. But no other man pays an added fifth" [M. Ar. 8:1A-D].

T. 4:20 M'SH B: One sanctified his field because of its poor quality They said to him, "You state a price of redemption first." He said, "Lo, it is mine for an issar." R. Yosé said, "Even if he had not said this, but rather, 'For an egg,' he [would have] said to him, 'It's yours!' For what is sanctified is redeemed by money or by something worth money" [M. Ar. 8:1E-J].

M. 8:2 [Concerning the case of a field that will be redeemed by the highest bidder, if] one [bidder] said, "Lo, it is mine for ten selas," and one said, "For twenty," and another says, "For thirty," and one says, "For forty," and one says, "For fifty" — [if] the one who said fifty retracted, they exact a surety from his property for ten [selas] [and sell it to the next highest bidder. In this way the Temple loses no money]. [If] the one who said forty retracted, they exact a surety from his property for ten. [If] the one who said thirty retracted, they exact a surety from his property for ten. [If] the one who said twenty retracted, they exact a surety from his property for ten. [If] the one who said ten retracted, they sell it [the sanctified field] for its market value. And they collect the remainder from the one who bid ten. [If] the owner says, "Twenty," and any other person says, "Twenty," the owner takes precedence [M. Bekh. 1:7]. For [in any event] he adds the fifth.

M. 8:3 [If] one said, "Lo, it is mine for twenty-one," the owner pays twenty-six. [That is, they do not sell it to the first man but allow the owner to up his bid as well]. "Twenty-two" — the owner pays twenty-seven. "Twenty-three" — the owner pays twenty-eight. "Twenty-four" — the owner pays twenty-nine. "Twenty-five" — the owner pays thirty. For they do not add the fifth to what the other bids more [than the owner's bid]. [If] one said, "Lo, it is mine for twenty-six" — if the owner wants to pay thirty-one and a denar, the owner takes precedence. And if not, they say, "It's yours!"

T. 4:21 [If] one said, "Lo, it is mine for ten selas," and one says, "For twenty," and one says, "For thirty," and one says, "For forty," and one says, "For fifty" [M. Ar. 8:2A] — [If] the one who said fifty retracted, they take from him ten selas and bring the [right of] purchase back to the one before him. [If] the one who said forty retracted, they take from him ten selas, and bring the [right of] purchase back to the one before him. [If] the one who said thirty retracted, they take from him ten selas, and bring the [right of] purchase back to the one before him. [If] the one who said twenty retracted, they take ten selas from him, and bring the [right of] purchase back to the one before him. [If] they all retracted, if he [the Temple agent] took from all of them ten selas each the [right of] purchase is left in the hands of the first.

T. 4:22 He who sanctifies a field of possession not in the time of the Jubilee — [or sanctifies] his houses and his movables whether in the time of the Jubilee or not in the time of the Jubilee — they force the owner to open [the bidding for redemption] first. [If] one said, "Lo, it is mine for twenty-one," they force the owner to give twenty-six. "Twenty-two" — they force the owner to give twenty-seven. "Twenty-three" — they force the owner to give twenty-eight. "Twenty-four" — they force the owner to give twenty-nine. "Twenty-five" — they force the owner to give thirty. Less than this — they do not force the owner, for they force the owner to pay only as much as [the base price plus] the added fifth [M. Ar. 8:3]. [If] the owner wanted to redeem [the property], he has the right. He pays thirty selas and one denar. The House of Shammai say, "The added fifth applies to the additional sum." And the House of Hillel say, "The added fifth does not apply to the additional sum."

The exposition of the theme focuses upon the evaluation of the field of possession that has been dedicated. The variable is, with the Jubilee the field reverts to the inheritors who have dedicated it. So the value is for the possession, not ownership, and that is for the specified span of time. The exposition at no point comes under the influence of the particular hermeneutics I have posited for the category-formation viewed whole; the entire amplification responds to issues defined by the generic hermeneutics.

III. THE DEVOTED THING [HEREM]

> But no devoted thing that a man devotes to the Lord of anything that he has, whether of man or beast or of his inherited field, shall be sold or redeemed; every devoted thing is most holy to the Lord. No one devoted, who is to be utterly destroyed from among men, shall be ransomed; he shall be put to death.
>
> Lev. 27:28-29

M. 8:4 "A man may declare herem part of his flock, part of his herd, some of his Canaanite man-servants and maid-servants, and part of his field of possession. But if he declared herem the whole of them, they are not deemed herem," the words of R. Eleazar. Said R. Eleazar b. Azariah, "Now if to the Most High a man is not permitted to declare all of his property herem, all the more so that a man must take care of his property."

T. 4:23 A man is not permitted to sanctify all his possessions. If he sanctified all of them, Lo they are deemed sanctified. A man is not permitted to declare all his possessions herem. And if he declared all of them herem, Lo, they are deemed herem [vs. M. Ar. 8:5A].

T. 4:24 R. Eliezer says, "Part of a man (Lev. 27:28), and not the whole of one's man-servants. Part of a herd, and not the whole of the herd. Part of the field of his possession, and not the whole of the field of his possession. Therefore if he sanctified [better: declared herem] all of them, they are not deemed herem" [M. Ar. 8:5A].

T. 4:25 Said R. Eleazar b. Azariah, "If to the Most High a man is not permitted to declare all of his property herem, for the Omnipresent has a care for It, "all the more so that a man must have a care for his own property" [M. Ar. 8:4B].

T. 4:26 R. Eleazar b. Azariah says, "Lo, it says, 'When the Lord your God enlarges your territory, as he has promised you, and you say, "I will eat flesh," because you crave flesh, you may eat as much flesh as you desire' (Deut. 12:20). 'If the place which the Lord your God will choose to put his name there is too far from you, then you may kill any of your herd or your flock, which the Lord has given you..., and you may eat within your towns, as much as you desire' (Deut. 12:21)]. Is it possible that the meat should stink in the pot and this one should want it? Lo, it says, And you say, 'I will eat flesh'"— only when you have an appetite for it. Might one say that he should buy it in the market and eat it? Scripture says, 'And you will kill any of your herd or your flock and eat.' Might one say that he should slaughter all of them? Scripture says, 'Of your herd' — and not your whole herd. 'Of your flock' — and not your whole flock."

T. 4:27 And so did R. Eleazar b. Azariah say, "He who has ten manehs gets himself vegetables in a pot every day. Twenty manehs — gets himself vegetables in a pot and a pan. Fifty manehs — a litra of meat from Friday to Friday. A hundred manehs — a litra of meat every day. Even though there is no proof for the proposition, there surely is an allusion to it, as it is said, In that day a man will keep alive a young cow and two sheep, and because of the abundance of milk which they give, he will eat curds; for every one that is left in the land will eat curds and honey (Is. 7:21-22)."

T. 4:28 Rabbi says, "Lo it says, 'Any man.... who takes in hunting any beast or bird that may be eaten shall pour out its blood and cover it with dust' (Lev. 17:13). Now are we not going to include what he has inherited, purchased, or received as a gift [under the state rule, not merely things taken in hunting]? Lo, Scripture says, 'And you say, "I will eat flesh"' only in the present connection."

M. 8:5 He who declares herem his son, his daughter, his Hebrew man-servant or maid-servant, a field which he has purchased — they are not deemed herem. For a man does not declare herem that which is not his own. "Priests and Levites do not declare [anything] herem," the words of R. Judah. R. Simeon says, "Priests do not declare [anything] herem. For things declared herem belong to them. But Levite declare [something] herem, for things declared herem do not belong to them." Rabbi says, "The opinion of R. Judah appears to me correct in the case of real estate. Since it is said, For it is their personal possession (Lev. 25:34). And the opinion of R. Simeon [appears to me correct] in the case of movables, for things declared herem do not belong to them."

T. 4:33 "Priests and Levites do not declare anything herem," the words of R. Judah. R. Simeon says, "Priests do not declare anything herem, for things declared herem belong to them. Levites declare things herem, for things declared herem do not belong to them." Said Rabbi, "The opinion of R. Judah appears to me correct in the case of real estate, For it is their perpetual possession (Lev. 25:34). The opinion of R. Simeon [appears to me to be correct] in the case of movables, for things declared herem do not belong to them" [M. Ar. 8:5D-H].

T. 4:34 There are three sorts of things which are herem. "But no devoted thing that a man devotes to the Lord, of anything that he has, whether of man or beast or of his inherited field, shall be sold or redeemed" (Lev. 27:28) — this refers to things declared herem for the priests." Every devoted thing is most holy to the Lord" (Lev. 27:28) — this refers to things declared herem for the Most High. "No one devoted who is to be utterly destroyed from among men shall be ransomed, he shall be put to death" (Lev. 27:29). This refers to those who are declared by a court to be subject to the death-penalty.

M. 8:6 Things which are declared herem for priests are not subject to redemption but are given to the priests. R. Judah b. Betera says, "What is declared herem without further explanation is for the repair of the Temple house, since it is said, 'Every devoted thing is most holy to the Lord' (Lev. 27:28)." And sages say, "What is declared herem without further explanation is for the priests, since it is said, ;As a field devoted to the possession thereof shall be the priest's; (Lev. 27:21). If so, why is it said, 'And every devoted thing is most holy to the Lord'? That it applies to Most Holy Things and to Lesser Holy Things."

T. 4:31 Things which are declared herem for priests are not subject to redemption [M. Ar. 8:6A]. And they do not go forth at the Jubilee. Things declared herem by Israelites — [if] the owners want to redeem them, the right is in the power of the priest [to allow him to do so]. Things declared herem by an Israelite, once they have come into the domain of a priest, Lo, they are deemed equivalent to unconsecrated things in every respect.

T. 4:32 What is declared herem without further specification is for ordinary purposes, and what is made explicit is for the Most High. As it is said, Every devoted thing is most holy to the Lord (Lev. 27:28). R. Judah b. Betera says, "What is declared herem without further specification is for the Most High. And that which is made explicit is for an ordinary purpose, as it is said, As a field devoted (Lev. 27:21)" [M. Ar. 8:6B-E].

M. 8:7 A man declares herem things he has declared holy, whether they are in the status of Most Holy Things or of Lesser Holy Things [M. 8:6G]. If it is a vow, he gives it value. If it is a freewill-offering, he gives what it is worth to him. [If he says,] "This ox is a burnt-offering," they estimate how much a man is willing to pay for this ox to offer it up as a burnt-offering for which he is not liable [that is, as a freewill-offering]. The firstling, whether unblemished or blemished, do they declare herem. How do they redeem it? They estimate how much a man is willing to pay for this firstling to give it to his daughter's son or his sister's son [who are priests and have a right to it]. R. Ishmael says, "One Scripture says, 'You will sanctify [all the firstling males]' (Deut. 15:19). And one Scripture says, 'You will not sanctify [the firstling among beasts]' (Lev. 27:26). It is not possible to rule, 'You will sanctify,' for it already has been said not to sanctify. And it is not possible to rule, 'You will not sanctify,' for it already has been said to sanctify. Rule on this basis: You sanctify it as something whose additional value is sanctified. But you do not sanctify it as an offering which falls to the altar."

T. 4:29 He who declares half of his man-servant or half of his maidservant to be herem — he and the priest are partners in him.

T. 4:30 Things declared herem for priests which one sanctified for the sacred purposes of the altar or for the sacred purposes of the upkeep of the Temple-House — one has done nothing whatsoever. Truly: that which is sanctified to the altar which one sanctified as herem for priests or for the sacred purposes of the altar — he has done nothing whatsoever. But that which is sanctified for the upkeep of the Temple-House which one sanctified as herem for the priests or for the sacred purposes of the altar — what he has done is indeed done [and valid].

B. 8:6-7 I.1/29A OUR RABBIS HAVE TAUGHT ON TANNAITE AUTHORITY: THINGS WHICH ARE DECLARED HEREM FOR PRIESTS ARE NOT SUBJECT TO REDEMPTION BUT ARE GIVEN TO THE PRIESTS [M. 8:6A]. AS TO THINGS THAT HAVE BEEN DECLARED HEREM, SO LONG AS THEY ARE IN THE HOUSEHOLD OF THE OWNER [WHO HAS CONSECRATED THEM], LO, THEY ARE IN THE STATUS OF HOLY THINGS IN ALL MATTERS PERTAINING TO THEM, AS IT IS SAID, "EVERYTHING DECLARED HEREM IN ISRAEL IS MOST HOLY TO THE LORD" (LEV. 27:28). ONCE ONE HAS HANDED OVER THOSE SAME OBJECTS TO THE PRIESTS, LO, IN ALL MATTERS RESPECTING THEM THEY ARE IN THE CATEGORY OF ORDINARY THINGS [NOT HOLY], AS IT IS SAID, "EVERY DEVOTED THING IN ISRAEL SHALL BE YOURS" (NUM. 18:14).

Once more, the topic having registered, the exposition proceeds wholly in accord with the program of the generic hermeneutics. Standard rules, e.g., one does not declare sanctified what is not his own property, are recast to fit the topic. The particular point, that priests possess herem so do not declare anything herem, is hardly surprising. M. 8:7 sets forth the only subtlety, declaring herem what he has declared holy, and the disposition of the object subject to the double declaration.

IV. THE SALE AND REDEMPTION OF A FIELD THAT HAS BEEN RECEIVED AS AN INHERITANCE AND OF A DWELLING PLACE IN A WALLED CITY

"In this year of jubilee each of you shall return to his property. And if you sell to your neighbor or buy from your neighbor, you shall not wrong one another. According to the number of years after the jubilee you shall buy from your neighbor, and according to the number of years for crops he shall sell to you. If the years are many you shall increase the price, and if the years are few you shall diminish the price, for it is the number of the crops that he is selling to you."

Lev. 25:13-17

"If your brother becomes poor and sells part of his property, then his next of kin shall come and redeem what his brother has sold. If a man has no one to redeem it, and then himself becomes prosperous and finds sufficient means to redeem it, let him reckon the years since he sold it and pay back the overpayment to the man to whom he sold it; and he shall then return to his property. But if he has not sufficient means to get it back for himself, then what he sold shall remain in the hand of him who bought it until the year of jubilee; in the jubilee it shall be released and he shall return to his property."

"If a man sells a dwelling house in a walled city, he may redeem it within a whole year after its sale; for a full year he shall have the right of redemption. If it is not redeemed within a full year, then the house that is in the walled city shall be made sure in perpetuity to him who bought it, throughout his generations; it shall not be released in the jubilee. But the houses of the villages that have no wall around them shall be reckoned with the fields of the country; they may be redeemed and they shall be released in the jubilee. Nevertheless, the cities of the Levites, the houses in the cities of their possession, the Levites may redeem at any time. And if one of the Levites does not exercise his right of redemption, then the house that was sold in a city of their possession shall be released in the jubilee; for the houses in the cities of the Levites are their possession among the people of Israel. But the fields of common land belonging to their cities may not be sold; for that is their perpetual possession."

Lev. 25:25-34

M. 9:1 He who sells his field [of possession, that is, one received by inheritance] at the time of the Jubilee['s being in effect] is not permitted to redeem it in less than two years [M. 7:1A], since it is said, "According to the number of years [plural, hence at least 2 years] of the crops he shall sell to you" (Lev. 25:15). [If it was a year of blight or mildew or a Seventh Year, it does not count in the reckoning [of the crop-years]. [If] he only broke the ground or left it fallow, it does count in the reckoning [of the crop-years]. R. Eliezer says, "[If] he sold it to him before the New Year and it was full of produce, Lo, this one enjoys the usufruct from it of three crops in a period of two years."

T. 5:1 He who sells his field [of possession] at the time of the Jubilee['s being in effect] is not permitted to redeem it for less than two years of crops, since it is said, "According to the number of years of the crops he shall sell to you" (Lev. 25:15) [M. Ar. 9:1A-B]. [If] it was a Seventh Year or [if the] years were like the years of Elijah [drought-ridden], it does not count in the reckoning [of the crop-years] [M. Ar. 9:1 C]. [If] he only broke the ground for a year, or made use of the crop for a year and left it fallow for a year, it does count in the reckoning [of the crop-years] [M. Ar. 9:1D]. R. Eleazar says, "There are times that one can enjoy the usufruct of it for three crops in a period of two years. How so? [If] one left it and went forth, [and] there were in it [the field] grain to cut or olives to pick or grapes to harvest, he may not say to him, 'Leave it before me full [of fruit], just as I left it before you full [of fruit].' But he makes use of the usufruct one year and takes his leave" [M. Ar. 9:1E]. Reeds, prunings, and sycamore-fruit in it, lo, they are deemed equivalent to fruit.

M. 9:2 [If] one sold it to the first party for a maneh [a hundred zuz], and the first party sold it to the second for two hundred, one [who repurchases the field] reckons only with the first [buyer], since it is said, "[Let him restore the surplus] to the man to whom he sold it" (Lev. 25:27). [If] one sold it to the first for two hundred, and the first sold it to the second for a maneh, one reckons only with the second, since it is said, "Let him restore the surplus to the man" — to the man who is now in full possession of it. (1) One should not sell [a field] at a distance and redeem [with the proceeds] one which is near by, or a poor one and redeem [with the proceeds] a good one. (2) One should not borrow and redeem [a field]. (3) One should not redeem [a field] in halves. But in the case of that which has been sanctified, one is permitted in all of these respects. This rule is more strict in the case of common property than in that of what has been sanctified.

T. 5:2 A tree which was cut down or which had dried out — both of them are prohibited in it. How should one act? Let it be sold and let him purchase with proceeds land, and let him enjoy the usufruct. If he sold it to the first for a maneh, and the first sold it to the second for two hundred, he reckons only with the first, since it is said, "[Let him restore the overplus to the man] to whom he sold it" (Lev. 25:27) [M. Ar. 9:2A-C].

T. 5:3 [If he sold it] to the first for two hundred, and the first sold it to the second for a maneh, he reckons only with the last, since it is said, to the man — to the man who is now in full possession of it [M. Ar. 9:2D-F]. [If] his father or brother or one of the relatives of the first wanted to redeem it, the right to do so is his. [But if one of the relatives] of the second [wanted to do so], they do not listen to him.

T. 5:4 One should not sell a field at a distance and redeem [with the proceeds] one which is near by, or a poor one and redeem a good one. One should not borrow and redeem [a field] — or redeem a field in halves. But in the case of that which has been sanctified, one is permitted in all aspects. This rule is more strict in the case of common property than in that of what has been sanctified [M. Ar. 9:2H-L].

T. 5:5 Said R. Simeon, "On what account did Scripture not press [the process of redemption] in the case of common property? For if the Jubilee comes and it is not redeemed, it goes forth to the original owner at the time of the Jubilee. On what account did Scripture press [the process of redemption] in the case of what has been sanctified? For if the Jubilee comes and it is not redeemed, the field is permanently assigned to the sanctuary."

T. 5:6 A man is not permitted to sell a field of possession and [merely] to leave them [the proceeds] in his money-bag, or [merely] to purchase with them a beast, to purchase with them garments, or to purchase with them slaves, or to raise with them a small beast, even to [invest them in commerce and] trade unless he was in dire need. But if he has sold it, Lo, it is sold.

T. 5:7 A man is not permitted to sell his daughter and [merely] to leave them [the proceeds] in his money-bag, or to purchase with them a beast, or to purchase with them garments, or to purchase with them slaves, or to raise with them a small beast, and even to [invest them in commerce and] trade, unless he was in dire need. But if he has sold her, Lo, she is sold.

T. 5:8 A man is not permitted to sell himself and to leave them [the proceeds] in his money-bag, or to purchase with them a beast, or to purchase with them garments, or to purchase with them slaves, or to raise with them a small beast, and even to [invest them in commerce and] trade, unless he is in dire need. But if he has sold himself, Lo, he is sold.

T. 5:9 Said R. Yosé bar Hanina, "Come and see how difficult are agricultural occupations indirectly related to those forbidden in the Seventh Year. How so? [If] a man does work on produce of the Seventh year, he begins to sell his movables, as it is said, [In this year of Jubilee each of you shall return to his property]. And if you sell to your neighbor... (Lev. 25:13-14). [If] he pays no attention [to this bad omen], he begins to sell off his field of possession, as it is said, If your brother becomes poor and sells part of his property (Lev. 25:25). It [the proceeds] scarcely reaches his domain before he has sold his house, as it is said, If a man sells a dwelling house in a walled city (Lev. 25:29). It scarcely reaches his domain, before he has sold his daughter, as it is said, When a man sells his daughter as a slave (Ex. 21:7). It scarcely reaches his domain, before he has borrowed on interest as it is said, If your brother becomes poor and cannot maintain himself...take no interest from him or increase (Lev. 25:35 — 36). It scarcely reaches his domain, before he has sold himself, as it is said, And your brother... becomes poor and sells himself to the stranger or sojourner with you (Lev. 25:47). And not to you, but to a stranger, as it is said, And sell himself (Lev. 25:47). And not to a righteous stranger, but a resident alien, as it is said, And sell himself to a sojourner (Lev. 25:47). Even to an idolater, as it is said, To a member of the stranger's family (Lev. 25:47) — he becomes an apostate to idolatry."

M. 9:3 He who sells a house among the houses in walled cities, lo, this one may redeem [the house] forthwith. And he redeems it at any time within twelve months. Lo, this is a kind of usury which is not usury. [If] the seller died, his son may redeem [it]. [If] the purchaser died, he may redeem it from the domain of his son. He reckons the year only from the time that he sold it to him, since it is said, "Within the space of a full year" (Lev. 25:30). And when it says, "Full", it means to encompass the month added in an intercalated year. Rabbi says, "One allows him a year and its intercalated days."

T. 5:10 He who sanctifies a house among the houses in walled cities, lo, this one redeems it forthwith. And he redeems it at any time. [If] he did not redeem it, it is permanently assigned to the sanctuary. He who sells a house among the houses in walled cities, Lo, this one redeems the house forthwith. And he goes along and redeems it at any time in the next twelve months [M. Ar. 9:3A-B]. [If] he did not redeem it during the twelve months, it falls permanently into the possession of the purchaser. [If] he sold it to the first party, and the first party went and sold it to the second, Lo, this one redeems it forthwith. [And] he goes along and redeems it at any time in the next twelve months. [If] he did not redeem it in the next twelve months, it falls permanently into the possession of the second party.

T. 5:11 He who sanctifies a house among houses in courtyards, Lo, this one redeems it forthwith and redeems it at any time. [If] someone else redeemed it, it goes forth to the [original] owner at the Jubilee [M. Ar. 9:7A].

T. 5:12 He who sells a house among houses in courtyards, Lo, this one redeems it forthwith [and] redeems it at any time. For if the Jubilee comes and one has not redeemed it, it goes forth to the [original] owner at the Jubilee. Houses of courtyards even though they have a wall formed by their roofs, are not equivalent to houses in cities surrounded by a wall [M. Ar 9:6A].

M. 9:4 [If] the [last] day of the twelve months has come and it has not been redeemed, it becomes his permanently. All the same are the one who purchases and the one to whom it is given as a gift, since it says, "In perpetuity" (Lev. 25:30). At first someone would hide on the day on which the twelve months were completed, so that it [the house] should become his permanently. Hillel the Elder ordained that one should deposit his money in the [Temple] office, break down the door [of the house], and take possession. Whenever the other wants, he may come and take his money.

M. 9:5 Whatever is inside the wall, lo, it is deemed in the status of a dwelling house in a walled city (Lev. 25:29) except for the fields. R. Meir says, "Also the fields." A house which is built into the wall — R. Judah says, "It is not a dwelling house in a walled city." And R. Simeon says, "The outer partition, Lo, it is its [the city's] wall."

T. 5:13 A city, the wall of which has fallen down — the whole of this commandment applies to it. [If] one built a house outside of it [the fallen wall], it is deemed equivalent to houses in courtyards.

T. 5:14 As to houses in cities surrounded by a wall but outside of the Land, all follows the root [of the tree]. As to Jerusalem and cities of refuge and second tithe — all follows the bough. The hut, tower, and dovecote which are in it, lo, they are in the status of houses in cities surrounded by a wall. And the storehouses and the gardens and orchards which are in it — R. Meir says, "Lo, they are deemed equivalent to houses in cities surrounded by a wall." And sages say, "Lo, they are like fields." A house built into the wall — R. Judah says, "It is as if it were outside." And R. Simeon says, "It is as if it were inside" [M. Ar. 9:5D-F].

T. 5:15 Olive-presses, the doors of which face inward, and the open space of which faces outwards, or the doors of which face outwards and the open space of which faces inwards — The House of Shammai say, "They do not redeem therein second tithe [as one does in Jerusalem], as if they are inside [the wall of Jerusalem]. But they do not eat therein Lesser Holy Things, as if they were outside [the walls of Jerusalem]." The House of Hillel say, "From the space directly beneath the wall and inward, it is as if it were inside. From the space directly beneath the wall and outward, it is as if it were outside." Said R. Yosé, "This [version] is the Mishnah of R. Aqiba. The first Mishnah [states matters as follows]: The House of Shammai say, 'They do not redeem therein second tithe, as if they [the spaces] are outside. And they do not eat therein Lesser Holy Things, as if they are inside.' The House of Hillel say, 'Lo, they are deemed equivalent to the chambers [of the Temple]. That, the entry of which is inside, is deemed equivalent to space inside [the wall], and that, the entry of which is facing outside, is deemed equivalent to space outside the wall.'"

M. 9:6 [A house in] a city the roofs of which form its wall, or one in a city which was not surrounded by a wall from the time of Joshua ben Nun, is not deemed a dwelling house in a walled city. And what is a dwelling house in a walled city? [A city in which are not less than] three courtyards, each with two houses, surrounded by a wall from the time of Joshua ben Nun, such as: the old castle of Sepphoris; the fortress of Gush-Halab, old Yodpat, Gamala, Gadwad, Hadid, Ono, Jerusalem, and the like.

M. 9:7 As to houses in courtyards [without a surrounding wall] — they assign to them the privilege of a dwelling house in a walled city and the privilege of fields: They may be redeemed forthwith [M. 9:3], and they may be redeemed for a full year — like houses. And they go forth at the Jubilee, and [at an earlier time] by [payment of] a reduced price [M. 9:1] — like fields. And what are houses in courtyards? [A city in which are] two courtyards, having each two houses, even though surrounded by a wall from the time of Joshua ben Nun — Lo, these are deemed houses in courtyards.

T. 5:16 Said R. Ishmael bar Yosé, "And do we have only these alone as cities surrounded by a wall? Lo, it says, [And we took all his cities at that time — there was not a city which we did not take from them] sixty cities, the whole region of Argob, the kingdom of Og in Bashan (Deut. 3:4). All these were cities fortified with high walls, gates, and bars, besides very many unwalled villages (Deut. 3:5) But when the Israelites were exiled to Babylonia, the commandment concerning cities with a wall was annulled. And when they came up from the Exile, they found these which were surrounded with a wall from the time of Joshua ben Nun. And they declared them sacred. And not these only, but all which you will prove in tradition were surrounded by a wall from the time of Joshua ben Nun — the whole of this commandment applies to it. And to those which they consecrated henceforward the whole of this commandment applies."

T. 5:17 A strict rule applies to houses in cities surrounded by a wall which does not apply to a field of possession, and [a strict rule applies] to a field of possession which does not apply to houses in cities surrounded by a wall. For houses in cities surrounded by a wall do not go forth in the Jubilee. If not redeemed in the preceding twelve months, they are permanently assigned to the purchaser, which is not the case in the field of possession [M. Ar. 9:7A1-2]. A strict rule applies to the field of possession: For one who sanctifies his field of possession not in the time of the Jubilee — it is not permitted to be redeemed in less than two years. They go forth in the Jubilee, and [at any earlier time] by payment of] reduced [price] [M. Ar. 9:7], which is not the case for houses in cities surrounded by a wall.

M. 9:8 "An Israelite who inherited [a house in the city of the Levites] from his mother's father, a Levite, may not redeem the house in accord with this procedure. And so too a Levite who inherited [a house in a city of Israelites] from his mother's father, an Israelite, may not redeem the house in accord with this procedure." Since it is said, 'For the houses in the cities of the Levites are their possession' (Lev. 25:33) — unless it is a Levite and [the house is in one of] the cities of the Levites,' the words of Rabbi. But sages say, "These rules have been stated only with respect to cities of Levites." They may not turn (1) a field into a city's outskirts, or (2) a city's outskirts into a field, or (3) a city's outskirts into a city, or (4) a city into a city's outskirts. Said R. Eleazar, "With respect to what were these rules stated? With respect to cities of Levites. But as for cities of Israelites, they may (1) turn a field into a city's outskirts, and (2) a city's outskirts into a field, (3) a city's outskirts into a city, but (4) not a city into a city's outskirts, so as not to wipe out the cities of Israel." Priests and Levites may sell at any time and redeem at any time [even in less than two years, (M. 9:1A), and even after one year, (M. 9:5, 7)], since it is said, "[The houses of the cities of their possession] may the Levites redeem at any time" (Lev. 25:32).

T. 5:18 They do not turn a field into a city's outskirts, nor a city's outskirts into a field, nor a city's outskirts into a city, nor a city into a city's outskirts. R. Eleazar says, "Under what circumstances? In the case of cities of Levites. But in the case of cities of Israelites, they do turn a field into a city's outskirts and a city's outskirts into a field, a city's outskirts into a city, but not a city into a city's outskirts, so as not to wipe out the cities of Israel" [M. Ar. 9:8H].

T. 5:19 A man should not tear down his house to make the area into a garden. A man should not plant a garden in an area of his ruin[ed house], because it is as if he is destroying the land of Israel. Rabban Simeon b. Gamaliel says, "A man may plant a garden in the area of his ruined house, for such is a means of settling it." R. Eleazar son of R. Yosé the Galilean says, "Two thousand amahs are the border of the cities of the Levites. Deduct from them a thousand amahs as outskirts. You have a quarter of that area as outskirts, and the rest is used for fields and vineyards."

The rules governing sale and redemption of inherited property and of dwelling places in walled cities form an appendix to the the me of unit II.

IV. DOCUMENTARY TRAITS

A. THE MISHNAH AND THE TOSEFTA

The Tosefta performs its anticipated tasks, amplifying, extending, clarifying, complicating — but rarely originating ideas, let alone classes of ideas, not adumbrated by the Mishnah's initial statement of the Halakhah.

B. THE BAVLI

The Bavli's contribution to the Halakhah is, as usual, exegetical, not fundamental, and never categorical. But the Aggadic component proves innovative.

C. THE AGGADAH AND THE HALAKHAH IN THE BAVLI

The system of the Talmud, as distinct from its structure, emerges in the inclusion of subjects not dealt with by the Mishnah. Here the Talmud speaks for its framers — those who made connections not made in the Mishnah, yielding, therefore and consequently, conclusions not set forth by the Mishnah. One important composite calls attention to itself, outlined as follows:

> XVII.   MISHNAH-TRACTATE ARAKHIN 3:5
>
> A.   IN THE CASE OF THE ONE WHO IS A TALE BEARER [I.E., ONE WHO FALSELY ACCUSES A WOMAN OF PREMARITAL RELATIONS, DT. 22:29] [THE POSSIBILITY] TO RULE LENIENTLY AND TO RULE STRINGENTLY: HOW SO? THE SAME RULE APPLIES TO ONE WHO IS A TALE BEARER CONCERNING THE GREATEST WOMAN IN THE PRIESTHOOD AND THE LEAST AMONG ISRAELITES: HE PAYS A HUNDRED SELAS [DEUT. 22:19].
> IT TURNS OUT THAT THE ONE WHO SAYS SOMETHING WITH HIS MOUTH [SUFFERS] MORE THAN THE ONE WHO ACTUALLY DOES A DEED. [THAT IS, FOR ACTUALLY SEDUCING A VIRGIN ONE PAYS ONLY FIFTY SELAS (M. 3:4B) BUT FOR GOSSIPING ONE PAYS 100.]
> 1. I:1: How we know that gossip was the real cause.
>
> B.   FOR SO WE FIND THAT THE DECREE AGAINST OUR FOREFATHERS IN THE WILDERNESS WAS SEALED ONLY ON ACCOUNT OF EVIL SPEECH [NUM. 13:32], AS IT IS SAID, AND THEY TEMPTED ME THESE TEN TIMES AND HAVE NOT HEARKENED TO MY VOICE (NUM. 14:22).
> 1. II:1: On what account [do we reach the conclusion just now stated]? Perhaps it was because the measure [of their guilt] was not yet full?
> 2. II:2: Come and see how great is the power of slander [evil speech]. From whence do we learn that lesson? From the case of the spies.

A. II.3: The ten trials by which God was tried by the Israelites.

C. THE POWER OF THE POWER OF GOSSIP AND SLANDER
1. II:4: Whoever repeats slander is as if he denied the very principle of God's rule.
2. II:5: Slander is the cause of leprosy, as in the case of Miriam.
3. II:6: Whoever speaks slander is worthy of being stoned.
4. II:7: What remedy is there for those who speak slander? If it is a disciple of a sage, let him keep busy in Torah.
5. II:8: Whoever speaks slander inflates his sins [so that they are as great] as the three cardinal sins of idolatry, fornication, and bloodshed.
6. II:9: What is the meaning of the verse of Scripture, 'Death and life are in the hands of the tongue' (Prov. 18:21)? "Now does the tongue have a hand? Rather it is to indicate to you that just as the hand can commit murder, so the tongue can commit murder.
7. II:10: How shall we define slander?
8. II:11: "What is the meaning of the verse of Scripture, 'He who blesses his friend with a loud voice, rising early in the morning, it shall be regarded as a curse to him' (Prov. 27:14)?
9. II:12: On account of seven causes plagues come [upon someone]: slander, bloodshed, a vain oath, incest, arrogance, theft, and envy.
10. II:13: The tunic of the priesthood achieves atonement for the sin of bloodshed. Elaboration on a secondary entry in the foregoing. Included because of N: "Bloodshed [is atoned through] the calf whose neck is broken, and slander is atoned for through the incense offering."
11. II:14: Why is the one afflicted with the skin ailment (*mesora'*) treated separately?

D. CRITICIZING OTHERS IN A LEGITIMATE MANNER AS NOTED, THERE IS SLANDER, WHICH IS TO BE AVOIDED, AND THERE IS PROPER REBUKE, WHICH IS TO BE ENCOURAGED.
1. II:15: "You shall not hate your brother in your heart" (Lev. 19:17). Is it possible to suppose that all one should not do is not smite, slap, or curse him, and that is what is at issue only? Scripture says, "...in your heart," thus speaking of the sort of hatred that is in the heart as much as hatred expressed through physical means.

2. II:16: Eloration on foregoing. The importance of rebuke.
3. II:17: As above. Sincere reproof as against hypocritical restraint.
4. II:18: To what extent does one administer reproof?
A. II:19: Formal match to foregoing: To what extent [should a person accept discomfort] before changing his lodging place?
B. II:20: How do we know [on the basis of Scripture] that a person should not change his calling and that of his ancestors?

E. TRIVIAL PENALTIES FOR SINNING.
1. II:21: To what trivial degree do penitential troubles extend? That is, there are chastisements for sin which one suffers in this world, so that, in the world to come, there is no unpenalized sin, and one will enjoy the world to come. The question then is what are the most trivial sorts of inconvenience that constitute adequate chastisement in this world for some sort of sin, so that, on their account, one may be confident of enjoying the world to come? There follows a catalogue of the most trivial sorts of inconvenience.
2. II:22: If the Holy One, blessed be he, came to judgment with Abraham, Isaac, and Jacob, they could not stand before his rebuke.
3. II:23: A generation is judged in accord with its principal leader. Or a principal leader is judged in accord with the character of his generation.

Identify the important initiatives that transcend Halakhic exegesis, extension, and refinement, as follows:

IV.C: This entry simply adds a rule within the thematic structure defined by the Mishnah, that is, laws governing those who are to be put to death. It forms no important statement outside of the framework of the Mishnah's topical program or principles.

XVII.C: The Mishnah's own topic of tale-bearing, gossip, and other forms of sinning through speech, is expanded here and at the next two items. First comes the power of gossip and slander, with an explanation of why slander is a sin and how Heaven penalizes the sinner. The character of slander as a social, not a personal, infraction is underscored.

XVII.D: There is a difference between slander and legitimate criticism. Rebuke is worthy, slander is despicable. There is a difference between sincere reproof, moreover, and hypocritical restraint.

XVII.E: This item is tacked on. The general theme, how Heaven penalizes sin, accounts for the introduction of XVII.E.1, that is, trivial sufferings that exact a penalty for small-scale sins. II.22-23 then are equally occasional. Without this item, the systematic exposition of XVII.C and D would have yielded precisely the same point. My guess is that something in II.20 explains the addition of II.21, and I suspect that the reference-point of II.22 and 23 is the Mishnah, not the foregoing entries; that is to say, XVII.B has Israel punished by reason of the actions of the spies and leaders in the wilderness, e.g., Miriam and Aaron (through speaking ill of the land and through gossip against Moses, respectively). If that is so, then the final items are meant to draw to a close by a final reference to the theme of the Mishnah this massive composite on the principle, but not the thematic materials, of the Mishnah.

XXVII.B: This is simple a further discussion of the established topic, selling estates.

The one genuinely important systemic composite introduces a theme on which the Talmud-compilers find much to say: gossip and slander, as well as other forms of anti-social behavior that they deem common among Israelites. Had the Talmud's writers not introduced that topic, the presentation of the Mishnah-tractate in its own terms would have suffered in no way that I can perceive. But by forcing consideration of sins of speech, the Talmudic compositors have made a striking and interesting comment on the Mishnah-tractate's theme, which is, acts of religious consequence that are carried out through speech. For a statement of pledge of one's own, or another party's, Valuation to the purposes of the Temple and the service of God therein does not demand that we also discuss the very opposite of the use of speech for God's purpose. But once we do consider how an act of speech may destroy, as much as build, the sacred community, our appreciation for the matter of Valuations deepens, and its moral meaning comes to the surface. What our sages of blessed memory in the Talmud add to the Mishnah-tractate, therefore, is the profound statement indeed: through an act of speech, one may sanctify, but through an act of speech one may also destroy, the holy community of Israel. The one — the act of sanctification through an act of speech — devotes to God through the Temple the results of good will. The other — the act of slander through an act of speech — diminishes God's people through the expression of ill will.

What the Talmud's compilers do, therefore, is make a connection of opposites: sanctification through speech as against sin through speech. In this context we call to mind other connections formed through the juxtaposition of opposites that our sages of blessed memory bring about in Talmud-making. In connection with tractate Moed Qatan, we wondered what the Talmud's principal topical innovation had to do with the Mishnah-tractate's interest: the rules of burial and mourning with the intermediate days of the festival? Precisely what has death to do with the intermediate days of the festival? The principal mode of thought of the Mishnah is that of comparison and contrast. Something is like something else, therefore, follows its rule; or unlike, therefore, follows the opposite of the rule governing the something else. So as a matter of hypothesis, let us assume that the framers of Talmud-tractate Moed Qatan found self-evidently valid the modes of thought that they learned from the Mishnah and so made connections between things that were alike, on the one side, or things that were opposite, on the other. How do death and mourning compare to the intermediate days of the festival? The point of opposition — the contrastive part of the equation — then proves blatant. Death is the opposite of the celebration of the festival. The one brings mourning, the other, joy. But death and the festival also form moments of a single continuum, one of uncleanness yielding to its polar opposite, sanctification, sanctification yielding to uncleanness. Death, we must not forget, also serves as a principal source of uncleanness, the festival, the occasion for sanctification beginning with the removal of cultic uncleanness and the entry into a state of cultic cleanness. These opposites also take their place on a single continuum of being.

So in establishing the connection, through treating the categories as equivalent and counterpart to one another, between death and the festival's intermediate days, sages make the connection between the one and the other — death and the festival's intermediate days — so as to yield a conclusion concerning the everyday and the here and now. These are neither permanently sanctified nor definitively unclean. Now we find the same mode of thought — finding the opposite of the topic at hand, drawing conclusions from the comparison and contrast of the connection that is made between opposites. And, we also observe, we may point to a systemic conclusion that coheres. Just as death and the Festival form opposites yet stand on the single continuum of life, so speech that consecrates and speech that demolishes stand on the single plane of social being: the community of Israel is sanctified through holy speech or it is diminished through evil speech (the exact equivalent in English to the Hebrew words translated as gossip or slander, *lashon hara*). Tractate Arakhin sets forth how through an act of speech one carries out a deed of sanctification; the Talmud's important and fresh composites explain how through an act of speech one does a deed that is the opposite of sanctification, which is, a deed that is unclean in that it contaminates the holy community.

Temple and holy Israel: these form the comparable components; an act of speech then is the variable, yielding the sanctification of goods and persons to the Temple, or the act of contamination of persons in the holy community. The framers of the Talmud contribute the making of connections in the Mishnah's manner but for a purpose of their own devising, and they, therefore, set forth an important element of a large-scale system, one that, it becomes clear, the Talmud is meant — in a remarkably subtle manner to be sure — to set forth. As the Bavli's tractates pass in review, the outlines of the Bavli's compilers' system begin to emerge. The method continues the familiar mode of thought that through comparison and contrast identifies like and unlike, something and its opposite. The message emerges from the connection that is made between opposites, the conclusion that is to be drawn from the making of that connection. So the modes of thought that produce the Halakhic category-formations work, also, to revise them in the dialogue with the Aggadah.

V. THE HERMENEUTICS OF ARAKHIN

A. WHAT FUSES THE HALAKHIC DATA INTO A CATEGORY-FORMATION?

In line with the Written Torah, the Halakhah deems it entirely rational to devote scarce resources to the upkeep of the Temple, entirely proper for individuals to do so on their own. And, — a point we should not miss — also in line with the provisions of Leviticus, supererogatory donations to the priesthood, either immediately, through the herem, or in the course of nature at the end of the Jubilee-cycle, certainly had their place. It is God's, not man's, perspective that fuses the Halakhah into a category-formation — votive gifts of worth to the Temple by individuals. If the genus is, votive gifts of worth, then the species are, [1] classifications of things all of the same value, [2] classifications of things of variable value. When it comes to God's Valuation of persons, all are equal; when it comes to man's, by contrast, the beautiful people are worth and give more, the ugly less. God's perspective comes to expression in Sheqalim-Tamid+Yoma, that is, everyone's equal share in the sin of Israel and its expiation through the daily whole offering. Man's perspective, recognizing differences in the value of persons, predominates in Arakhin, with its fascinating distinctions between fixed and market value or between the thing valued and the person obligated to pay the value.

The genus yielding comparison and contrast then encompasses two species.

[1] When the Halakhah takes the measure of individuals within entire Israel, all weigh equally and give appropriately, yielding Sheqalim-Tamid-Yoma.

[2] When the Halakhah accords to individuals the right to distinguish themselves, it carefully defines that by which they take their own measure and restricts to appropriately-corresponding loci and foci that to which they then may donate. That produces Arakhin. That is why, when moved to volunteer to God something of per-

sonal value, individual Israel have[11] every right to pledge the value of their persons or property.

This brings us to a second aspect of the fusion of the category-formation. It comes in the answer to the question, Why is it that individuals have the right voluntarily to contribute to enhance public space in the holy place, on the one side, and to sustain the priesthood, on the other? To answer that initial question out of the Halakhah but now another, if kindred, sector of the Halakhah, we ask necessary, second question: Under ordinary circumstances, who must support the priesthood and its activities? The answer is, the householder, and that comes out of the produce of his land. The upshot is simple. The category-formation fuses its data into a coherent statement concerning the power of individuals, not householders in the Land of Israel, not householders (landowners) at all, not resident in the Land of Israel, to volunteer "value" to the Temple, just as householders in the Land of Israel may donate supererogatory gifts, animate or inanimate, deriving from the Land that the possess in partnership with God.

Here I find the hermeneutical heart of the category-formation, the particular hermeneutics that dictate the selection and interpretation of the data of said category-formation: Israel, whatever its circumstance, wherever located, possesses "value" that God values and that may appropriately serve within the transaction embodied in the Temple and its rites. Like Bekhorot, like Hullin, the category-formation at hand underscores the sanctity of Israel and hierarchizes it, by necessity, above the sanctity of Land and even Temple.[12] In permitting individuals to pledge personal Valuations of themselves for the support of the Temple, the Halakhah treats the population without land, including the population outside of the Land, as equal in all ways to the enlandised householder. The entire population of Israel, at home in the Land and in the Exile, finds itself in a position of equality vis à vis the holy place and its staff.

That is not merely an abstraction, an inchoate theme. The stress on the equalization of all Israel in the matter of personal Valuations is explicit and tangible when wealth and poverty, beauty and its opposite play no role in assessing the worth of a person who pledges his, or another's, Valuation to the

---

[11] A usage explained in footnote 1.

[12] The Division of Holy Things, then, takes shape around two poles: the enlandised and locative as against the utopian and ubiquitous, embodiments and activities of sanctity and sanctification (respectively), thus on the one side, Zebahim-Menahot, and on the other, Hullin-Bekhorot-Arakhin. No wonder the sages of Babylonia found powerful motivation to carry forward the Halakhic program of Mishnah-Tosefta Qodoshim and produce the Bavli's continuation, and those of the Land of Israel did not. Then the key to Qodoshim lies in the contrast between Zebahim-Menahot and the rest.

upkeep of the Temple and its priesthood. But it also is implicit in opening the way to dedications from overseas and from others besides householders. To take the concrete case of Bikkurim, just as the householder, alone able to present firstfruits, may contribute more than the prescribed minimum, may decorate his firstfruits and contribute the supplementary decorations, for example, so every individual enjoys the same option here. He or she has every right to pledge not the fixed Valuation — the *price fixe* — but the actual worth, and the Halakhah takes pains to differentiate the fixed Valuation from the actual worth and dictate how the latter is assessed. That point of stress represents the workings of the particular hermeneutics of the category-formation.

But the system does distinguish the enlandised from the non-enlandised Israelite, those who are not householders or do not live in the Land to begin with. So we must wonder, when it comes to optional acts of devotion, how does the Halakhah realize its established recognition of the special position of the enlandised class? If the Halakhah makes provision for those without land and without the Land to participate in the support of the sacred space and its servants, it accords to a particular class of householders a very special opportunity. That class consists of Israelites who hold shares in the Land by reason of inheritance, that is, Israelites who are enlandised by genealogy. They represent the incarnate union of Israel and the Land — the family bound to the Land from the very beginning. Theirs is something very particular to give, if they wish. It is land within the Land that is received by inheritance. What makes that property precious is that it was received in the initial division of the Land. It embodies that perfect moment at which Israel came to rest, before sin renewed the wanderings within and out of Israelite Eden. Sages in the Aggadah maintain that, had Israel not sinned, Scripture would have concluded with the book of Joshua; there would be no further story to tell. That accounts for the conception of the original division, in stasis, as the point at which sinless Israel attained perfection — if only for a brief spell. And that conception explains the Halakhah before us, that is, the reversion to the perfect beginning of Israel in the Land. Specifically, when that part of Israel that hold Land from the originally-perfect division in stasis are moved to sanctify their portion of the Land to God, that land in the natural course of events finds its way into the possession of the priesthood. If the original family attached to the Land — to a particular plot of land — no longer holds it, then how better to regain perfection than assign the plot to the priesthood, to hold in perpetuity in behalf of all Israel, beneficiaries of the priesthood and its labor in the divine service.

Here the circle closes; now we identify the ultimate medium for the incarnation of Israel in the Land, that class of Israel that is sustained by God's portion of the produce and that is required to eat God's portion of the produce in conditions of cultic purity. The priesthood, denied a portion by family-inheritance in the Land and nourished instead by God's share, now collectively, as a genealogical entity, enters upon possession of the Land, which, in consequence, returns to God's dominion in an exact sense. Of that which the priesthood can never own, as private persons own, they enter into possession. The full implications of the Halakhah of God's and the householder's partnership, realized in Ma'aserot, Terumot, and the other category-formations that distinguish ownership from possession and establish the rules of the divine-Israelite partnership in the Land, here are realized in a remarkably subtle way. Here, then, a particular class of Israel, the genealogically-enlandised, as I said, representative of the perfection of old, has in its power to take a step toward the restoration: the repossession of the Land in behalf of entire Israel.

How does the process realize itself? We recall that if someone dedicates a field received by inheritance, he redeems it from the Temple (that is, contributes the cash in place of the land) by a fixed valuation set in relationship to the Jubilee: an annual payment collected for the years that the purchaser of the land may utilize the field before restoring ownership to the original donor at the advent of the Jubilee. If someone dedicates a field he has (merely) purchased, it is sold for whatever it is worth; the one who bought and then dedicated it never gets it back. If the field is not redeemed by the person who received it in the lineage of the original division of the Land, the priests get it. The upshot is simple: over time, through the working of the Jubilee through the priesthood Israel restores to God the possession, not merely the ownership, of the Land. That is in two distinct processes. First of all, a part of the Land returns to God's dominion through the priesthood, which receives title as noted to those fields received as an inheritance that are not redeemed at the Jubilee. Second, at the Jubilee, the climax of seven Sabbatical years, the entire Land not only reverts to the condition of public, ownerless property — all now belonging to God — but also regains its original condition. That is to say, the Land is restored to that condition of stasis that it attained when Israel first entered into, and divided the Land and before Israel's sin, leading to the loss of the Land, commenced. The Jubilee reclaims for the Land the condition it enjoyed before Israel sinned and the Land passed into other hands.

B. THE ACTIVITY OF THE CATEGORY-FORMATION

The category-formation accomplishes its exegesis principally within the generic hermeneutics of the Halakhah, as we have noted in detail. A brief review suffices.

SANCTIFYING ABSTRACT WORTH, NOT ONLY TANGIBLE AND ALTAR-APPROPRIATE, OBJECTS TO THE TEMPLE: At this point, the particular hermeneutics governs. In all cases we deal with statements of sanctification of something of intangible, fungible worth to the Temple. A person may sanctify himself or his property, or he may sanctify the worth of another party, and in either case is obligated to pay to the Temple the value of what he has declared sacred. That represents the process of "redemption," that is, redeeming with a payment of money what has been sanctified for the purposes of the Temple. Such statements apply even to a portion of the value or the person: He who says, "The head of this servant is sanctified" — he and the sanctuary are partners in him. He who says, "The head of this ass is sanctified," he and the sanctuary are partners in it. And the process of redemption regularizes the matter.

WHO MAY OR MAY NOT PLEDGE A PERSONAL VALUATION OF ONESELF OR OF ANOTHER PARTY: All normal Israelites, capable of an informed statement of intentionality, including women and slaves, may pledge the valuation of third parties and may be subjected to such a pledge of their worth by third parties. That means, within the range of sanctification of Israel fall women and slaves, not only men, as bearers of sanctity and of value suitable for merger with the Temple and its rites.

What about gentiles? Since the pledge is one of volition, and since gentiles may sanctify offerings for thanksgiving or free-will donations to the cult, they may also pledge the value of others and are subject to such a vow. Those in a special class of persons may do so as well, but only within their own class. That class is formed of those whose volition is unclear, or whose traits are not certain. That is to say, a person of doubtful sexual traits may participate in his own class, but may not cross the lines to be valued on the pledge of third parties, for only a person of clear masculine or clear feminine traits is subject to the pledge of Valuation by others. Persons of imperfect senses, minors, and imbeciles may be the object of a Valuation but may not undertake a valuation, being assumed not to possess understanding.

VARIABLE PAYMENT AND THE ABILITY TO PAY: The minimum payment of a vow of Valuation is a sela, so Lev. 27:8, and the maximum, fifty. One's status at the moment of valuation dictates what is owing. But within the stated limits — age, condition — all persons are worth the same fifty selas, and that is without regard to looks or other gifts. The same rule applies to one who pledged the Valuation of the most beautiful among Israelites and one who pledged that of the ugliest among Israelites — he gives fifty selas in either case. If, however, he said, "Lo, his actual value is incumbent on me," he gives his actual value. The important point then concerns a vow of Valuation. Pledges of personal worth involve actual, individual assessment.

The actual payment is assessed in terms of the governing variable: the person concerning whom the vow of Valuation is made, the person who takes the vow of Valuation. The former governs what is to be paid, e.g., the matter of age, sex; the latter, the matter of ability to pay, which is relative to the ability of the one who takes the vow. A poor man who pledged the Valuation of a rich man gives the Valuation required of a poor man. And a rich man who pledged the Valuation of a poor man gives the Valuation required of a rich man.

PLEDGES OF PERSONAL WORTH: In addition to the vow of Valuation, fixed by the Written Torah, the vow of personal worth further individuates. Vows to pay the value apply to anything, man or beast, live or slaughtered beasts, whole persons and limbs, and ability to pay is not an issue. Now the individual is singled out as to his or her actual traits — another point marking the activity of the particular hermeneutics.

But the amplification and extension of the Halakhah, once the sub-category is established, work out of the generic hermeneutics. The cases and distinctions then are predictable. One may vow to give his weight to the sanctuary, even in silver or in gold. He may pledge to give the worth of his hand, in which case he pays the difference between his value with, and without, a hand. If one pledges his own Valuation and dies, his estate pays; the obligation takes effect forthwith. If he pledges his worth and dies, the estate pays nothing. At the moment of payment, when the obligation takes effect, he is worth nothing. But if someone pledges the Valuation of a third party and dies, or the person concerning whom the pledge is made dies, the estate of the one who took the vow pays. If it is not the Valuation but the worth, the situation changes. If he said, "The price of so-and-so is incumbent on me" and the one who makes the vow dies, the heirs must pay the vow. If the one concerning whom the vow is made dies, the heirs do not have to pay. For corpses have no price value. The same conception emerges in the following: He who says, "This ox is a burnt-offering," "This house is qorban," if the ox died or the house fell down, is not liable to pay. If he said, "The price of this ox is incumbent on me for a burnt-offering," or "the price of this house is incumbent on me as qorban," if the ox died or the house fell down, he is liable to pay. All of this embodies the common sense of the Halakhic process of analysis.

COLLECTING VALUATIONS: This sub-set of the Halakhah presents inert information, vivified only in modest measure by the generic hermeneutics. The obligation to present obligatory offerings, sin- and guilt-offerings, expires with the death of the donor. Votive offerings must be paid even if the donor dies: Those who are liable for vows, freewill-offerings, Valuations, things which have been declared herem things which have been declared sanctified — the court exacts a surety from them. And if they die, the heirs are liable to provide what has been lost. Those who owe sin-offerings and guilt-offerings or the price thereof — the court does not exact a surety from them. And if they die, the heirs are not liable to provide what is owed. And as to the price which has been laid on them, lo, it is deemed the equivalent of Valuations. The obligation in the latter case concerns the expiation of sin incurred inadvertently; death accomplishes the same purpose. The obligation in the former case is a freely-undertaken one, and that devolves upon the man's estate. One must not postpone paying other such obligations, e.g., pledges of offerings or the value thereof, Valuations, and the like. One has three festivals in which to pay them. Once these have gone by, one transgresses the rule against postponing obligations and not carrying them out.

What is owing to the Temple must be sold at public auction, with the widest possible circulation of the prospectus and call for bids. By contrast, the sale of the property of an estate, requiring an auction, does not entail such a broad circulation of the call for bids. When the Temple is concerned, its interests always take priority. But the obligation to the Temple will not be met by depriving the donor of the necessities of life. They supply him with food for thirty days, and clothing for twelve months, and bedding, shoes, and tefillin. If he was a craftsman, they give him two of every kind of the tools of his craft. To a carpenter they give two axes and two saws. And it goes without saying that one who sanctifies his property has no claim on what belongs to his wife or children.

DEDICATING AND REDEEMING REAL ESTATE POSSESSED BY INHERITANCE: The Halakhah differentiates between a field received by inheritance and one that has been purchased. A field acquired by inheritance is subject to a fixed valuation, the later is evaluated in accord with its actual worth. The former, when dedicated, corresponds to a pledge of personal Valuation, the latter to a pledge of one's worth. If one dedicates a field that one has purchased, he loses all claim to it. At the Jubilee year it reverts to the person who sold it, assumed to be one who has received the field as an inheritance. But if it is a field that he has inherited ("a field of possession"), then the field is redeemed at a fixed valuation in relationship to the Jubilee year; if it is not redeemed, when the Jubilee year releases it from the hands of the titleholder, the field is taken over by the priests.

To redeem a field that has been dedicated to the sanctuary, one pays the sanctuary a sela (sheqel) and a pondion for each year remaining in the Jubilee, e.g., four years, four selas and four pondions. If the owner redeems the field, he pays an additional fifth. A jubilee of forty-nine years requires forty-nine selas and forty-nine pondions. If the sanctuary had the usufruct for ten or fifteen years, the owner deducts from its redemption price a sela and a pondion per year. If it enjoyed the usufruct for ten or fifteen years, he pays a sela and a pondion per year. The priest has no special rights in connection with redeeming a property. If one of the priests redeemed it, and lo, it is in his the priest's domain, he may not say, "Since it goes forth to the priests in the Jubilee, and since, Lo, it is in my domain, it is mine." But it goes forth and is divided among all his brethren, the priests.

DECLARATIONS OF HEREM: The counterpart to sanctifying a person's worth or Valuation, on the one side, and to sanctifying a field, on the other, is the declaration that one's possessions are herem, meaning, dedicated to God. I find little of particular interest here. Social policy intervenes in the rule that a man is not permitted to sanctify all his possessions. A man is not permitted to declare all his possessions herem. In a law analogous to that of Valuations, one may declare herem not only goods but persons, e.g., one's own children or slaves. These then are redeemed, and the value goes to the Temple, for the upkeep of the buildings. He may also declare herem what he has already sanctified: whether in the status of Most Holy Things or of Lesser Holy Things. If it is a vow, he gives its value. If it is a freewill-offering, he gives what it is worth to him. If he says, "This ox is a burnt-offering," they estimate how much a man is willing to pay for this ox to offer it up as a burnt-offering for which he is not liable that is, as a freewill-offering. The firstling, whether unblemished or blemished, do they declare herem. How do they redeem it? They estimate how much a man is willing to pay for this firstling to give it to his daughter's son or his sister's son who are priests and have a right to it. None of these rules seems to me to derive from the workings of the particular hermeneutics of Arakhin.

C. THE CONSISTENCY OF THE CATEGORY-FORMATION

It is difficult to invoke the criterion of consistency, when the category-formation itself encompasses three distinct sub-divisions plus an appendix. It suffices to say that within the limits set by the result of analogical-contrastive analysis, the category-formation holds together three quite coherent components and makes room for nothing that violates its basic definition. But I do not regard that judgment as consequential.

D. THE GENERATIVITY OF THE CATEGORY-FORMATION

On the surface, the Halakhah of the category-formation, Arakhin, addresses some rather superficial questions about the definition of a particular kind of verbal undertaking, a vow of one's (fixed) Valuation or of one's (market) value, with special reference to technical questions of the effect of language and the like. But on the other hand, as a category-formation viewed whole, Arakhin writes a complex account of Israel's relationship with God without the Land and within, through the medium of value represented (conventionally) by the Land and (idiosyncratically) through other media of value altogether. Provision for landless individuals to sanctify their worth, either a fixed Valuation or their actual value, accommodates Israel wherever located. And that provision finds its match in the occasion for enlandised individuals to sanctify their land in the Land, which, we see, transcends the mere transfer of value and restores the condition of perfect stasis disrupted by Israel's own sin. However complex the details, though, the statement proves simple: Israel has the power to effect the sanctification of what is subject to Israel's own will. Individually, not only jointly, Israel engages with God as God wishes to be engaged with. And that engagement brings about transactions both enlandised and transcendent.

6.
TRACTATE TEMURAH

I. THE DEFINITION OF THE CATEGORY-FORMATION

Reconstructing the thought processes that define the hermeneutics — the theory of selection and interpretation of pertinent data — for the category-formation, Temurah, follows a simple course. [1] Scripture here defines the category-formation and leaves no doubt as to the genus of which it forms a species for purposes of comparison and contrast. Nonetheless, [2] the Halakhah sets forth its particular hermeneutics in presenting the category-formation. And [3] the generic hermeneutics of the Halakhah takes its share in the work, the three components yielding a remarkably lucid statement of the main point, which is not Scripture's nor the generic hermeneutics' contribution but that of the particular hermeneutics.

Specifically, Scripture defines the category-formation, "substitution," meaning, the declaration that one beast substitutes for another that has been sanctified, the result being, the proposed substitute indeed is sanctified but the originally-designated beast remains sanctified. The particular hermeneutics of the Halakhah then selects and interprets pertinent data to make a negative judgment on any such procedure, which the Halakhah deems disreputable. The individual Israelite has the will-power to violate with effect the will of the Torah and its rules. He is penalized, but his action — one of sanctification no less — is effective. And the exegetical program of the completed category-formation not defined by the particular hermeneutics derives from the standard, generic kind. But in so stating, we have moved ahead of our story.

To begin at the beginning, as usual we identify the particular hermeneutics of a category-formation through a theoretical analysis of analogical-contrastive relationships of species of a common genus. To do so here, we define the genus of which the category-formation, Temurah, forms a species, then posit the contrastive traits of another species of the same genus. And, as I said, it is Scripture that presents the species, from which we easily reconstruct a hypothetical genus and a theoretical counterpart-species for comparison, then contrast. As I said, the species, this category-formation, encompasses the effect of the act of substituting a beast for an already-consecrated one and the effect of doing so. Leviticus 27:9-10 states the substance of the category-formation in so many words:

> "If it is an animal such as men offer as an offering to the Lord, all of such that any man gives to the Lord is holy. He shall not substitute anything for it or exchange it, a good for a bad or a bad for a good; and if he makes any exchange of beast for beast, then both it and that for which it is exchanged shall be holy."

The traits of the species are clear. The beast designated as a substitute for an already-sanctified beast becomes holy, but the beast that was already consecrated remains holy. Once the Israelite has made a statement that a beast is sanctified, he cannot nullify it. Nor can he change his mind, declaring profane a beast designated as holy and replacing that beast with some other. Scripture does not make a judgment upon the action of substitution, only defines the consequences. The intent of the Israelite, to substitute one beast for another, without regard to the case, is null. Here is a case in which the power of the Israelite intentionality is limited. Once expressed to God, that intentionality, sanctifying the original beast, stands, and the Israelite cannot change his mind. So much for Scripture's contribution to the category-formation.

Now to the specific application of our procedure: the hypothetical definition of a companion-species for comparison and then contrast. If the species is, the effect of sanctifying a beast as a substitute for an already-sanctified one, then [1] what of the genus, and [2] what counterpart species is required to form the other component of the common genus? The simplest common genus clearly is, verbal acts of sanctification of beasts for the altar. Then the counterpart species, rendering the genus complex, must be, the act of sanctification of a secular beast to the altar. Then what we first compare and then contrast are [1] an act of sanctifying a beast *ab initio* and [2] an act of sanctifying a beast in place of an already-sanctified beast.

The question is not how the two actions compare, for Scripture answers that question in so many words. They yield identical taxonomic results. The latter of the two actions produces exactly the same effect as the former. So if the two species of acts of sanctification produce exactly the same result — a holy cow — the species surely are comparable, as in classical physics like actions produce equivalent reactions. But what contrasts present themselves? That sets what is for us the generative question. Before we pursue it and identify the particular hermeneutics of the category-formation, we must ask whether the outline of the category-formation of the Halakhah points to the activity of a particular hermeneutics. Here is the outline.

I. THE RULES OF SUBSTITUTION: WHO MAY DO SO, AND IN WHAT CONTEXT

    A. Liability to the Law of Substitution
    B. Exemptions from the Law of Substitution
    C. The Individual's Offerings are Subject to the Law of Subtitution, Those of the Community are Not

II. THE STATUS OF THE OFFSPRING OF SUBSTITUTES

    A. Diverse Sacrifices, their Substitutes and Offspring
    B. The Supererogatory Sin-Offering

III. THE LANGUAGE USED IN EFFECTING AN ACT OF SUBSTITUTION

IV. FORMAL APPENDIX

Even the most superficial encounter with the category-formation, fully exposed, yields results. Clearly, I/A may contain, and I/C certainly does present, signals of the presence of considerations that Scripture's simple rule does not on the surface introduce. I/A will tell us who bears the power or the standing to "effect an act of substitution," which is to say, to make a declaration that produces the stated effect. On the surface, I/C makes distinctions hardly suggested by Scripture but clearly generative for the Halakhah.

Now let us turn to a systematic comparison of our two species. We start with the Halakhah, which, predictably, itself conducts the contrast,[13] as usual in this language of hierarchical classification:

> M. 2:3 A more strict rule applies to consecrated animals than to a substitute, and [a more strict rule] applies to a substitute than to

---

[13] That simple fact validates the hypothetical procedure that I have followed so many times. All I have done is define in general terms the rules for analysis that are instantiated and apply those rules myself, where the Tosefta (often) and the Mishnah (sometimes) would be expected to do so. One might even propose the argument that the framers of the Tosefta carry to their logical conclusion the occasionally-articulated but always-present modes of hierarchical-classificatory thought that pervade the Mishnah. These are what account for that huge proportion of the Mishnah that transcends inert facts and transforms cases into examples, inviting the hearers of the Mishnah to recast examples into general rules.

consecrated animals. A more strict rule applies to consecrated animals than to a substitute: for consecrated animals impart the status of a substitute [to that animal declared by its owner to be a substitute in their stead]. But a substitute does not impart [to another animal, designated in its stead] the status of a substitute [M. 1:5]. A community or partners declare [animals] to be sanctified, but do not effect a declaration of substitution [so that should a group of people or partners declare an animal substitute for one already consecrated, the former is not deemed consecrated] [M. 1:6]. And they sanctify limbs and fetuses, but do not effect substitution [for limbs or fetuses] [M. 1:3].

A more strict rule applies to the substitute. For sanctity applies to [a substitute] which is afflicted with a permanent blemish [M. 1:2], so that it does not go forth for unconsecrated purposes, for shearing and for labor. R. Eleazar says, "A beast that is crossbred and a terefah and one born from the side, a beast lacking in clear-cut sexual characteristics and one which bears both male and female characteristics are not made holy and do not impart [to a substitute] the status of holiness."

The Mishnah's comparison of the two species yields these consequential points:
1. Corporate Israel may declare a beast sanctified but not effect an act of substitution;
2. Only an unblemished, whole beast may be sanctified for the altar, but even a blemished beast and limbs or fetuses may be sanctified through a statement of substitution;
3. If someone declares a beast to be a substitute for a beast substituted for a consecrated animal, that beast is not sanctified; the outer limits of the power of metaphor are reached.

These three results of hierarchical classification (within the routine framework, more strict/less strict) underscore difference among like things. In this case, it is difference among statements that produce a common result, the status of sanctification.

The first difference is the most striking: corporate Israel cannot commit an act of substitution. That corporate Israel cannot collectively commit the action at hand, e.g., the community as a whole through its agents or all together cannot declare a beast substitute for an already consecrated one with the result that the substitute is deemed consecrated too, bears a clear implication. It is that, whatever the actions of individuals, the community cannot carry out a deed that is at one and the same time not permitted but effective: "even though it is not permitted to do it, the act of substitution takes effect," a slight paraphrase of the Mishnah will say. Idiosyncratic, but not collective actions register in this context.

Let me expand on this matter. The community's effective acts of intentionality must conform with the Torah. Individual Israelites may effect an improper intentionality; corporate Israel cannot effectively will what is contrary to the repertoire of accepted acts of intentionality defined by the Torah. The analogy of the oath comes to mind. All Israel took an oath to God at Sinai, which takes priority, so no Israelite oath contrary to the Torah takes effect. But when it comes to acts of sanctification, while the public offerings subject to corporate intentionality (the Tamid for instance) are unaffected by an act of improper intentionality, individual offerings, sanctified by private persons for idiosyncratic purposes, are indeed effected by individual's improper, but effective, acts of intentionality such as substitution. That distinction accounts for a formidable component of the Halakhic category-formation, the entire range of anomalies that gain admission.

But the second is no less consequential: blemished beasts become sanctified through an act of substitution. What a permitted and valid act cannot accomplish, the sanctification of a blemished beast as an offering, the not-permitted but-nonetheless-effective act can. That fact underscores what we have already noted: we deal with a deed that is illicit but nonetheless effective. Once the intentionality of the private person registers even in the commission of a not-permitted action, the normative law opens the way toward other anomalies.

And the third difference, ending the chain of substitution, leads to the same conclusion as the first two. We deal with a marginal situation, where intention to do what is irregular produces irregular effects. Even though the beast one has substituted for a sanctified beast is sanctified too, it is not sanctified in the same way. For yet another beast declared a substitute for the substitute is not affected. The taxonomic power of improper language does not carry beyond its initial effect.

But the first point is the most interesting: Israel seen whole cannot sin in the way in which an individual can. The distinction between corporate and idiosyncratic Israel — the same Hebrew word, Yisra'el, standing for the community and the individual Israelite — this registers in the heart of the Halakhah.

A systematic survey of the Halakhah of Temurah yields a comparable result, that the act of substitution is a sin.

THE INITIAL ACT OF SANCTIFICATION	AN ACT OF SUBSTITUTION
1. Anyone who owns a beast may consecrate it.	1. M. 1:1 All effect a valid [consequential] substitution [that is, through a statement of consecration of a secular beast propose to substitute that beast for one they have first designated as a sacrifice, so that, by making a statement of substitution, that second beast enters the status of the originally-consecrated one] — all the same are men and women.
2. It is permitted to sanctify a beast for the altar, and one incurs no penalty for doing so.	2. M. 1:1 Not that a person in any event is permitted to effect a substitution. [For it is forbidden to make such a statement of substitution of a now-secular beast for one already consecrated.] But if one has effected a substitution, it [that which is designated instead of the beast already consecrated] is deemed a substitute [and also consecrated]. And the person [who does so moreover] incurs the penalty of forty stripes.
3. A person may not consecrate an animal he does not own.	3. T. 1:1 He who effects a substitution, even on the Sabbath — lo, this [animal] indeed is substituted [for that originally consecrated, and it too is holy]. And he incurs forty stripes. Priests do not effect an act of substitution in the case of Holy Things of Israelites, and Israelites do not effect an act of substitution in the case of Holy Things of priests [M. Tem. T. 1:IF-G]. For a man does not effect an act of substitution in the case of an animal-offering which does not belong to him.
4. One may not consecrate a blemished animal for use on the altar, though one may consecrate it value for the upkeep of the Temple house.	4. M. 1:2 They substitute [= impose the law of substitution upon] [an animal] (1) from the herd for one from the flock, and one from the flock for one from the herd, (2) from sheep for goats, and from goats for sheep, (3) from males for females, and from females for males, (4) from unblemished for blemished animals, and from blemished for unblemished animals, since it is said, "He shall not substitute anything for it or exchange it, a good for a bad, or a bad for a good" (Lev. 27:10).

5. Parts of beasts may not be consecrated for use on the altar, though they may be consecrated for their value.	5. M. 1:3 They do not substitute (1) limbs for fetuses, or fetuses for limbs, or (2) limbs and fetuses for whole beasts, or whole beasts for them.
6. Not only an individual, but group of people or partners may share in the consecration of a beast, e.g., lay hands on its head.	6. M. 1:6 Birds and meal offerings do not produce a substitute [impose the status of a substitute upon birds or meal designated as their replacement] . For only in the case of cattle is [substitute] mentioned [Lev. 27:10]. A congregation and partners do not produce a substitute, since it is said, "He shall not change it" (Lev. 27:10) — The individual produces a substitute, and neither a congregation nor partners produce a substitute. Offerings for the upkeep of the Temple do not produce a substitute
7. As above.	7. M. 2:1 There are [rules] applying to offerings of an individual, which do not apply to offerings of the community. And there are [rules] applying to offerings of the community which do not apply to offerings of an individual. (1) For offerings of an individual impose the status of substitute, but offerings of the community do not impose the status of substitute

The more systematic comparison confirms our initial results. First comes the comparison, then the contrast.

No. 1 shows the comparability of the two species. Anyone who owns a beast may sanctify it to the altar. Any one may propose a substitution of a beast that he owns for an already-sanctified beast. No. 2 then captures the critical point of the particular hermeneutics of Temurah: here is an act of sanctification that is not permitted, that is penalized with a flogging, but that, nonetheless takes effect when an individual Israelite carries it out.

That produces two conclusions. First, corporate Israel cannot sin in this way.

Second, even though Israelites individually may sin in effecting an act of substitution, nonetheless, when an Israelite declares something holy, even doing so illicitly, his statement constitutes a valid act of taxonomy. In my judgment, the particular hermeneutics of Temurah comes to full exposure here, accounting for the selection of data and the interpretation thereof. The contrast between the licit, initial act of sanctification and the effective-but-illicit act of substitution is drawn at the point of flogging.

No. 3 goes over the same ground. But an unarticulated point should be noted. While one may not consecrate an animal that he does not own, and while one may also not effect a valid act of substitution for an animal he does not own (saying, "That cow over there, which belongs to Mr. Jones, is sanctified in place of that ox over here, which belongs to Mr. Smith"), one does have an anomalous power. It is to say, "This cow over here, which belongs to me, is substituted for that already-holy cow over there, which belongs to Mr. Jones." *So someone may adopt for himself the condition of sanctification brought about by a third party!*

Nos. 4, 5 go over the same issue, that of comparability. While one may not sanctify a blemished animal for the altar but only for the upkeep of the Temple house, if one uses of a blemished animal or one that actually cannot serve for other reasons language that signifies substitution of an animal for one designated for the altar, the language, though impossible of realization, still takes effect. That is yet another outcome of the principle that when an Israelite uses the language of sanctification, he exercises taxonomic power even where the situation is merely theoretical and utterly inaccessible of realization. In concrete terms, only male beasts serve for communal offerings. If one declares a female beast to be a substitute for a male beast sanctified for a communal offering, the act of substitution takes effect; the female beast is sanctified, even though it cannot actually have replaced the beast for which it was declared a substitute.

No. 6 goes over familiar ground, repeated at No. 7. Sanctification may represent a corporate intentionality, but substitution can result from an utterly idiosyncratic one.

If I had to select the critical hermeneutics, I should choose a simple formulation: sanctification comes about both licitly and otherwise. What Israel does corporately as an act of will always is licit and, as I said above, by definition cannot take effect otherwise. Corporate Israel has accepted the Torah, corporate Israel cannot perish, and its will has thereby been defined; hence corporate Israel cannot contradict itself with consequence. Stated simply: when it comes to the intentionality to effect an act of sanctification eternal Israel's effective public will invariably conforms with God's will. But individual Israelites differ from corporate Israel, because they die, and so, for individuals matters are otherwise. The private person with effect may form an improper, idiosyncratic intentionality. He is flogged in expiation of the sin, but the sin yields results. That intentionality may violate the objective conditions that pertain, e.g., to substitute a blemished for an unblemished beast, yet produce the consequence, *ex opere operato,* of sanctification. The outer limit of the matter is reached with other-than-animate offerings; substitution does not take effect for meal-offerings and the like. So much for the particular hermeneutics of Temurah. But as usual, the generic hermeneutics accounts for the bulk of the Halakhah — everything but what is distinctive to the category-formation.

II. THE FOUNDATIONS OF THE HALAKHIC CATEGORY-FORMATION

We have already taken note of Scripture's definition of the present category-formation.

III. THE EXPOSITION OF THE COMPONENTS OF THE GIVEN CATEGORY-FORMATION BY THE MISHNAH-TOSEFTA-YERUSHALMI-BAVLI

I. THE RULES OF SUBSTITUTION: WHO MAY DO SO, AND TO WHAT

A. *LIABILITY TO THE LAW OF SUBSTITUTION*
M. 1:1 All effect a valid [consequential] substitution [that is, through a statement of consecration of a secular beast propose to substitute that beast for one they have first designated as a sacrifice, so that, by making a statement of substitution, that second beast enters the status of the originally-consecrated one] — all the same are men and women. Not that a person in any event is permitted to effect a substitution. [For it is forbidden to make such a statement of substitution of a now-secular beast for one already consecrated.] But if one has effected a substitution, it [that which is designated instead of the beast already consecrated] is deemed a substitute [and also consecrated]. And the person [who does so moreover] incurs the penalty of forty stripes. Priests effect a substitution in the case of what belongs to them. And Israelites effect a substitution in the case of what belongs to them. Priests do not effect a substitution in the case either of a sin offering or of a guilt offering or of a firstling. [They own no share in sin- or guilt-offering prior to their being killed and their blood's being tossed on the altar.] Said R. Yohanan ben Nuri, "And on what account do they [the priests, who own firstlings] not effect a substitution in the case of a firstling?" Said R. Aqiba, "A sin offering and a guilt offering are a gift to the priest, and a firstling is a gift to the priest. Just as, in the case of a sin offering and a guilt offering, they do not effect a substitution, so in the case of a firstling, they should not effect a substitution." Said to him R. Yohanan b. Nuri,

"What difference does it make to me that one does not effect a substitution in the case of a sin offering and a guilt offering? For in case of these, they [the priests] have no claim while they [the beasts] are alive. Will you say the same in the case of the firstling, to which they [the priests] have a claim while [the firstling] is still alive?" Said to him R. Aqiba, "But has it not already been stated, 'Then both it and that for which it is changed shall be holy' (Lev. 27:10)? At what point does sanctity descend on to it? In the house of the owner. So the substitute [becomes holy] in the house of the owner."

T. 1:1 He who effects a substitution, even on the Sabbath — lo, this [animal] indeed is substituted [for that originally consecrated, and it too is holy]. And he incurs forty stripes. Priests do not effect an act of substitution in the case of Holy Things of Israelites, and Israelites do not effect an act of substitution in the case of Holy Things of priests [M. Tem. T. 1:1F-G]. For a man does not effect an act of substitution in the case of an animal-offering which does not belong to him.

T. 1:2 "A firstling born to an Israelite is subject to the law of substitution. One born to a priest is not subject to the law of substitution," the words of R. Aqiba [M. Tem. 1:1H]. R. Simeon b. Eleazar says, "Once they have come into the possession of a priest, neither one is subject to the law of substitution. What should one do with this substitute? It should be left to pasture until disfigured and then is eaten by the owner by reason of its blemish."

T. 1:3 All the same are Most Holy Things and Lesser Holy Things: one is not permitted to effect a substitution [M. Tem. 1:1C], whether on a weekday or on the Sabbath. They do not change them from their status as to sanctification, even from a lesser [lower] status of sanctification to a greater [higher] status of sanctification, and it is hardly necessary to say, from a greater status to a lesser status of sanctification.

T. 1:4 [If] one said concerning a firstling or concerning peace-offerings, "Lo, these are a burnt-offering," he has said nothing. And it is not necessary to say, [if he said] concerning a burnt-offering, "Lo, this is a firstling," "Lo, this is peace-offering." They do declare them to be herem. and they treat them as sanctified in value [for the upkeep of the House (M. Tem. 7:3)].

T. 1:5 What are objects which are deemed to be herem? He who says, "This herem is for a priest." What are objects which are deemed to be holy? He who says, "This holy thing is for the upkeep of the Temple House." From how much does one give [if he has declared herem] Holy Things for which he bears responsibility, for example, a sin-offering and a guilt-offering? He who says, "Lo, this [animal] is incumbent on me as a burnt-offering," "Lo, this is incumbent on me as a peace-offering," gives their whole value.

T. 1:6 Holy Things for which one does not bear responsibility, for example, a firstling and tithe [of cattle] — he who says, "Lo, this is incumbent on me as a burnt-offering," "Lo, these are peace-offerings" — he pays [only] the value of enjoying benefit from them [but not their total cost, if they should be lost]. And how much is the value of enjoying benefit from them? One says how much a man is willing to pay for this burnt-offering which in point of fact he does not need in fulfillment of an obligation [M. Ar. 8:7D] or to purchase this firstling to give it to the son of his daughter [who is married to a priest and whose son thus permitted to eat it] [M. Ar 8:7G].

B. 1:1A-E I.2 2A WHAT DOES THE LANGUAGE, "ALL," SERVE TO ENCOMPASS? IT SERVES TO ENCOMPASS THE HEIR [OF THE OWNER OF A BEAST, WHO EFFECTS A SUBSTITUTION WHILE THE OWNER OF THE BEAST, E.G., THE FATHER, IS STILL ALIVE. HE DOES NOT YET OWN THE BEAST, AND ONLY THE OWNER OF A BEAST CAN DESIGNATE IT AS HOLY. FOR A PERSON MAY NOT CONSECRATE PROPERTY THAT HE DOES NOT HIMSELF OWN. BUT HE IS PRESUMED TO BE HEIR AND THEREFORE FUTURE OWNER OF THE BEAST. THE LEGAL EFFECT OF HIS PRESUMPTIVE OWNERSHIP THEN IS AT ISSUE.]

M. 1:2 They substitute [=impose the law of substitution upon] [an animal] (1) from the herd for one from the flock, and one from the flock for one from the herd, (2) from sheep for goats, and from goats for sheep, (3) from males for females, and from females for males, (4) from unblemished for blemished animals, and from blemished for unblemished animals, since it is said, "He shall not substitute anything for it or exchange it, a good for a bad, or a bad for a good" (Lev. 27:10). What is a good for a bad? [Substituting unblemished animals for already consecrated] blemished ones, the sanctification of which took place before their blemish [M. Bekh. 2:2-3. Those sanctified when already blemished are unfit for the altar and exempt from the law of substitution]. They substitute [a valid act of substitution takes place in the case of a statement concerning] one for two and two for one, one for a hundred and a hundred for one. R. Simeon says, "They substitute only one for one, since it is said, 'Then both it and that for which it is substituted' (Lev. 27:10) — just as it is singular, so its substitute is singular."

T. 1:7 They substitute [one animal] for others [different from it, M. Tem. 1:2A-E]. They effect an act of substitution one for another. They substitute one for two and two for one, one for a hundred and a hundred for one. R. Simeon says, "They substitute only one for one" [M . Tem. 1:2H-I] since it says, Beast — I spoke of a beast for a beast, not beasts for a beast." They said to him, "Just as a single beast is called a beast, so many cattle are called beast, since it is said, 'Much cattle' (Jonah 4:11)."

T. 1:10 He who sanctifies [and sacrifices] a blemished animal for the altar transgresses five negative commandments: against the negative commandments of not sanctifying, not slaughtering, not tossing the blood, not burning the fat, and not burning part of it, since it says, "And when any one offers a sacrifice of peace offerings to the Lord, to fulfill a vow or as a freewill offering, from the herd or from the flock, to be accepted it must be perfect, there shall be no blemish in it." R. Yosé bar Judah says, "Also [one transgresses] because of not receiving its blood."

T. 1:11 [If] one sanctified it but did not slaughter it, he is liable only on account of violating one negative commandment. [If] one sanctified it and slaughtered it and tossed its blood, he is liable for each and every action.

T. 1:12 He who sanctifies a beast which has committed an act of bestiality and one upon which such an act has been committed, a beast set aside for idolatrous worship and one actually worshipped, the fee of a harlot and the purchase price of a dog, one with one hip larger than the other, or one with uncloven hooves, transgresses on account of these counts. For Lo, they are deemed equivalent to the blemished animals the sanctification of which has taken place before the appearance of their blemish. And they never revert to the status of unconsecrated animals except on account of a permanent blemish alone.

T. 1:13 "He who sanctifies unblemished animals for the upkeep of the house violates a positive commandment and a negative commandment," the words of R. Judah. And sages say, "He is liable only on account of a negative commandment alone." He who sanctifies unblemished animals for the upkeep of the Temple House — they redeem it only for the purpose of the altar alone.

As we have come to expect, the general tendency of the Halakhic program is to set forth cases that conduct exegesis in line with the particular hermeneutics, then those that respond to the generic hermeneutics, then inert data. The opening composition, M. 1:1, contains within itself the principal point, which is that it is forbidden to do such a deed, but if done, the deed bears actual results, in the sanctification of the substituted beast and the flogging of the one who has made the improper statement concerning his own property. Everything else flows from these two points. The particular hermeneutics furthermore takes up the effects of the metaphorical speech ("this is like that"): to what extent do the limits that pertain to that to which comparison is made impose themselves on that which is compared? And, in simpler language, "this is like that," to what extent does the "that" govern the limits of the "this"? T. 1:1 frees the "this" of the limitations of the "that," so that an act of substitution done on the Sabbath is effective. Not only so, but, the Tosefta amplifies, if one's language violates the rules of the rite, it is null, e.g., "if one said concerning a firstling," "Lo, these are a burnt-offering," that is null. The generic language of sanctification must apply. But then there are no limits; the act of substitution applies to an animal from the herd for one from the flock and so for the various other regnant classifications of offerings, M. 1:2. The exposition of the particular hermeneutics through the exegesis of the law and its cases now continues.

B. EXEMPTIONS FROM THE LAW OF SUBSTITUTION

M. 1:3 They do not substitute (1) limbs for fetuses, or fetuses for limbs, or (2) limbs and fetuses for whole beasts, or whole beasts for them. R. Yosé says, "They substitute limbs for whole beasts but not whole beasts for limbs." Said R. Yosé, "And is it not so that in the case of animals which have been consecrated, he who says, 'The foot of this is a burnt offering' — the whole beast is a burnt offering? So when one states, 'The foot of this is instead of that'— the whole of it should be a substitute in its stead."

T. 1:8 [If] one said, "The foot of this [ox] is a burnt-offering," the whole of it is not a burnt-offering, but only that foot alone. What should one do to it? Let it be sold to those who owe burnt-offerings except for its foot. And the proceeds [except for the value of the limb] are unconsecrated," the words of R. Meir and R. Judah. R. Yosé and R. Simeon say, "The whole of it is not a burnt-offering." Said Rabbi, "The opinion of R. Meir and R. Judah appears correct in the case of a part of the animal on which life does not depend, and the opinion of R. Yosé and R. Simeon in the case of a part of the animal on which life depends."

T. 1:9 R. Yosé says, "They effect an act of substitution in the case of whole animals or limbs" [M. Tem. 1:3C]. They effect an act of substitution in the case of an animal [in fact unfit for the altar, e.g.,] which has committed an act of bestiality and in the case of one upon which such an act has been committed, in the case of an animal set aside for idolatry and one which has been subjected to idolatrous worship, in the case of an animal used for the fee of a harlot and the purchase-price of a dog, in the case of a hybrid, one which is terefah, and one which is born from the side. R. Eliezer says, "As to a hybrid, a terefah, one which goes forth from the side, one without clearly defined sexual traits, and one with sexual traits of both male and female, they are not holy and are not made holy [and therefore are not subject to the law of substitution at all]."

M. 1:4 That which contains heave offering imparts the status of heave offering [to other produce] only by due measure [in the prescribed proportion] That which contains leaven imparts the

status of leaven [to something else] only by due measure. Drawn water spoils the immersion pool only in due measure.

M. 1:5 Purification water is made purification water only with the putting in of the ashes [of the red cow]. A grave area does not make [another field into] a grave area. And heave offering [does] not follow [the taking of] heave offering. [There is no valid heave offering after heave offering has been removed from a quantity of produce.] And a substitute [for a substitute] does not produce a substitute. [A substitute does not impart the status of a substitute to that animal put forward in its stead.] And an offspring [of a consecrated animal] does not impart the status of a substitute [to that animal put forward in its stead]. R. Judah says, "An offspring [of a consecrated animal] does produce a substitute." [An offspring does not impart the status of a substitute to that animal put forward in its stead.] They said to him, "That which has been sanctified produces a substitute, but the offspring and the substitute do not produce a substitute."

T. 1:14 He who sanctifies a blemished animal for sacrifice on the altar — [if] he wanted to redeem it for sanctification for the upkeep of the Temple-house, he has the right to do so. An offspring [of a consecrated animal] does not produce a substitute [M. Tem 1:5E]. And it is not necessary to say, the offspring of an offspring. R. Judah says, "The offspring does not produce a substitute." A congregation does not produce a substitute [M. Ar. 1:6C].

M. 1:6 Birds and meal offerings do not produce a substitute [impose the status of a substitute upon birds or meal designated as their replacement]. For only in the case of cattle is [substitute] mentioned [Lev. 27:10]. A congregation and partners do not produce a substitute, since it is said, "He shall not change it" (Lev. 27:10) — The individual produces a substitute, and neither a congregation nor partners produce a substitute. Offerings for the upkeep of the Temple do not produce a substitute. Said R. Simeon, "And was not tithe [of cattle] included [among the offerings for which a substitute may be brought] (Lev. 27:10)? And why was it excluded [And the tithe of herds and flocks . . . shall be holy unto the Lord. A man shall not inquire whether it is good or bad, neither shall he exchange it; and 'if he exchanges it, then both it and that for which it is exchanged shall be holy; it shall not be redeemed (Lev. 27:32-33)]? To allow for an analogy: Just as the tithe [of cattle] is a sacrifice of an individual [M. Bekh. 9:3], excluding sacrifices of the congregation, so tithe is an offering of the altar, excluding offerings to the Temple treasury [for the upkeep of the Temple]." [A dedication for Temple repairs also is called an offering, and therefore there is need for a text to exclude dedications for Temple repairs from the law of exchange.]

T. 1:15 A beast owned by a congregation does not produce a substitute [M. Tem. 1:6C]. Partners do not produce a substitute [M. Tem. 1:6C]. And a beast owned by partners does not produce a substitute [M. Tem. 1:6C].

T. 1:16 A beast half of which is consecrated and half of which is not consecrated does not produce [a substitute] and is not made into a substitute. Nor does an animal-sacrifice which is brought on account of a substitute produce a substitute.

The logical second question is, within the broad framework in which an illicit act of substitution does bear consequences for the sanctification of what is substituted, where are the limits? The answer comes in the exposition of the principle, not the topic, at M. 1:4-5: a substitute does not impart the status of a substitute to the animal put forward in its stead. Birds and meal offerings do not impose the status of a substitute upon birds or meal offerings designated as their substitutes. A congregation or partners cannot act to produce a substitute: only the individual has that power.

C. THE INDIVIDUAL'S OFFERINGS ARE SUBJECT TO THE LAW OF SUBSTITUTION, THOSE OF THE COMMUNITY ARE NOT

M. 2:1 There are [rules] applying to offerings of an individual, which do not apply to offerings of the community. And there are [rules] applying to offerings of the community which do not apply to offerings of an individual. (1) For offerings of an individual impose the status of substitute, but offerings of the community do not impose the status of substitute. (2) Offerings of an individual pertain to male and female [beasts], but offerings of the community pertain only to male ones. (3) For offerings of an individual are they liable to be answerable [replacing animals set aside for the individual if said animals are lost] and answerable for their drink offerings, but for offerings of the community they are liable to be answerable neither for them nor for their drink offerings, but they are liable to be answerable for their drink offerings once the animal sacrifice is offered. There are [rules] applying to offerings of the community which do not apply to offerings of the individual. For offerings of the community override the Sabbath and [the prohibitions of] uncleanness, and offerings of an individual override neither the Sabbath nor [the prohibitions of] uncleanness. Said R. Meir, "And are not the baked cakes [M. Men. 4:5] of the high priest and the bullock of the Day of Atonement the offering of an individual, and they override both the Sabbath and [the prohibitions of] uncleanness? But [the reason is that] their time is fixed." [The reason both offerings of the community and the aforementioned offerings of an individual override the Sabbath and the prohibitions of uncleanness is that their time is fixed.]

T. 1:17 "The offerings of the community override the Sabbath and the prohibitions of uncleanness. The offerings of the individual override neither the Sabbath nor the prohibitions of uncleanness" [M. Tem. 2:1H], the words of R. Judah. Said to him R. Meir, "We find in the case of the baked cakes of the high priest, the bullock of the Day of Atonement, and the Passover, which are offerings of an individual, that they override the Sabbath and [the prohibitions of] uncleanness" [M. Tem. 2:1I]. We find in the case of the bullock which is brought on account of having committed the sin of idolatry and the festal offering, which are offerings of the community, that they do not override the Sabbath and [the prohibitions of] uncleanness. A general rule did R. Jacob state, "Anything which is subject to performance at a fixed time by the authority of the Torah and cannot be done on the eve of the Sabbath overrides the Sabbath, and anything which is not subject to performance at a fixed time by the authority of the Torah and can be done on the eve of the Sabbath does not override the Sabbath."

T. 1:18 These are the points of difference between offerings of the community and offerings of an individual. For: In the case of offerings of the community, [from] the beginning of [the time of] their consecration the law of sacrilege applies to them. In the case of offerings of an individual, to some of them the law of sacrilege applies, and to some of them the law of sacrilege does not apply. There is among them a sin-offering which derives from the flock, namely, that which is brought in connection with an unwitting sin. And in the case of all of them [communal offerings]: Most Holy Things are eaten within the veils and eaten by the males of the priesthood and eaten for one day and one night, which is not the case of offerings of an individual. Offerings of an individual impose the status of substitute and are brought in partnership. And there are among them a sin-offering which is female, and a guilt-offering brought because of certainty and a suspensive guilt-offering, and they are acquired with [funds from] tithe, and they require a laying on of hands, which is not the case for communal offerings.

T. 1:19 These are the points of difference between [offerings of] a beast and those of fowl. For: A beast overrides the Sabbath and overrides [the prohibitions of] uncleanness and pertains to the community as to the individual, and five sorts of sin-offerings of a beast are left to die [M. Tem. 2:2D-E], and a female sin-offering is brought, and [so are] a guilt-offering brought because of certainty and a suspensive guilt-offering and a thank-offering and peace-offerings, and it is purchased with [money of] tithe, and it is offered on a high place, and it requires laying on of hands and drink-offerings and the waving of the shoulder and thigh, and in requires four acts of tossing [of the blood], and there are instances in which some of its blood is brought inside, (and) into the innermost area, [none of] which applies in the case of fowl.

T. 1:20 These are points of difference between [offerings of] fowl and those of a beast. For: In the case of fowl, from the beginning of [the time of] their consecration, the law of sacrilege applies to them. But in the case of offerings of beast, there are some of them to which the law of sacrilege applies, and there are some of them to which the law of sacrilege does not apply. And they are deemed fit to be brought as females [or] as males for burnt-offerings. And those which are blemished are equivalent to females in respect to the altar. And there is among them a sin-offering of fowl which is offered on account of doubt. And all of them are Most Holy Things and are eaten inside the veils and are eaten by the males of the priesthood and are eaten for a day and a night, which is not [invariably] the case for offerings of beasts.

T. 1:21 And these are the points of difference between meal-offerings and offerings of fowl. For: Meal-offerings apply to the community as to the individual. And they override the Sabbath and [the prohibitions of] uncleanness. And they require bringing near and waving. And they require [sanctification in a] utensil and other things which must be brought as a requirement along with them, which is not the case for offerings of fowl.

T. 1:22 And these are the points of difference between offerings of fowl and meal-offerings. For: Fowl are brought in partnership. And they render permitted those whose rites of atonement are not yet complete. And they are rendered freed of the category of prohibition in the case of Holy Things. And they [who sacrifice fowl] are liable on their account when they are offered outside [the Temple], which is not the case for meal-offerings.

M. 2:2 **The sin offering of an individual, the owner of which has effected atonement [through another animal] [is left to] die. And that of the community [which has effected atonement through another animal] is not [left to] die. R. Judah says, "Let it be left to die." Said R. Simeon, "Just as we find in the case of the offspring of a sin offering, and the substitute of a sin offering, and a sin offering the owner of which has died, [that] it is in the case of an individual that matters are stated, but not in the case of the community, so in the case of that [animal], the owner of which has effected atonement, or the year of which has passed [and which has become superannuated (M. Par. 1:3-4)], it is in the case of an individual that matters are stated, but not in the case of the community."**

T. 1:23 The offspring of a sin-offering and the substitute of a sin-offering the owner of which has died, are left to die. A sin-offering, the owner of which has died, does not impart the status of a substitute [to an animal designated in its stead]. And one which was lost and found before the owner has effected atonement imparts the status of substitute. [But that which is lost and found] after the owner has effected atonement [through another beast] does not impart the status of a substitute [but left to die, M. Tem. 2:2A]. R. Simeon says, "Also: that animal, the owner of which has effected atonement, or that which is superannuated, in the case of an individual['s offering] should be left to die. We find that the law for the offspring of a sin-offering and the substitute of a sin-offering and the sin-offering, the owner of which has died is stated in the case of an individual, not in the case of the community. So for these it is in the case of an individual that matters are stated and not in the case of the community" [M. Tem. 2:2D].

M. 2:3 A more strict rule applies to consecrated animals than to a substitute, and [a more strict rule] applies to a substitute than to consecrated animals. A more strict rule applies to consecrated animals than to a substitute: for consecrated animals impart the status of a substitute [to that animal declared by its owner to be a substitute in their stead]. But a substitute does not impart [to another animal, designated in its stead] the status of a substitute [M. 1:5]. A community or partners declare [animals] to be sanctified, but do not effect a declaration of substitution [so that should a group of people or partners declare an animal substitute for one already consecrated, the former is not deemed consecrated] [M. 1:6]. And they sanctify limbs and fetuses, but do not effect substitution [for limbs or fetuses] [M. 1:3]. A more strict rule applies to the substitute. For sanctity applies to [a substitute] which is afflicted with a permanent blemish [M. 1:2], so that it does not go forth for unconsecrated purposes, for shearing and for labor. R. Yosé b. Judah says, "[The law] has treated that which is done unintentionally as equivalent to that done intentionally in the case of the substitute. But it has not treated that which is done unintentionally as equivalent to that which is done intentionally in the case of consecrated beasts." R. Eleazar says, "A beast that is crossbred and a terefah and one born from the side, a beast lacking in clear-cut sexual characteristics and one which bears both male and female characteristics are not made holy and do not impart [to a substitute] the status of holiness."

T. 1:24 A strict rule applies to an animal-sacrifice which does not apply to a substitute, and [a strict rule applies] to a substitute which does not apply to an animal-sacrifice. For an animal-sacrifice overrides the Sabbath and [the prohibitions of] uncleanness and pertains to the community as to the individual and imparts the status of a substitute, which is not the case of a substitute. A more strict rule applies to the substitute: For sanctity applies to a substitute which is afflicted with a permanent blemish, which is not the case for an animal-sacrifice [M. Tem. 1:2, 2:3F]. R. Yosé bar Judah says, "[In the case of a substitute] that which is done unintentionally is equivalent to that which is done intentionally" [M. Tem. 2:3G].

The particular hermeneutics continues to govern. Offerings of an individual impose the status of substitute, but those of the community do not, and so throughout at M. 2:1, a fundamental statement. The main point is, the individual alone has the power to act in this context, and he can act only upon what he himself possesses. M. 2:3 then systematically compares the consecrated animal with the substitute put forth to replace such an animal, a fine composition. The Tosefta's amplification of the rule of the Mishnah is particularly wide-ranging and cogent; once more, such coherent composites as T. 1:17-22 show us a different theory of category-formation, therefore of presentation, around principles rather than particular topics, from the Mishnah's. Within the alternative theory another hermeneutics altogether is to be identified than the one I have tried to show pervades the Halakhah, that of analogical-contrastive analysis of the species of a common genus.

II. THE STATUS OF THE OFFSPRING OF SUBSTITUTES

A. *DIVERSE SACRIFICES, THEIR SUBSTITUTES AND OFFSPRING*

M. 3:1 These are the consecrated animals, the offspring, and the substitutes of which are deemed of equivalent status: (1) the offspring of peace offerings, (2) and their substitute, (3) and their [the offspring's and the substitute's] offspring, (4) and the offspring of their offspring, to infinity — Lo, these are deemed equivalent to peace offerings. And [like the animal for which they have been substituted or from which they derive], they require laying on of hands, drink offerings, and waving of the breast and thigh [M. Zeb. 10:2]. R. Eliezer says, "The offspring of peace offerings is not offered as peace offerings [but is left to die]." And sages say, "It is offered." Said R. Simeon, "They did not dispute concerning the offspring of an offspring of peace offerings and concerning the offspring of an offspring of a substitute, that it should not be offered. Concerning what did they dispute? Concerning the offspring [itself], for: R. Eliezer says, 'It is not offered.' And sages say, 'It is offered.'" Testified R. Joshua and R. Pappyas concerning the offspring of peace offerings, that it is offered as peace offerings [=Sages]. Said R. Pappyas, "I bear witness that we had a cow deriving from sacrifices of peace offerings and we ate it on Passover And we ate its offspring a peace offer-

ings on the [next] Festival [Sukkot]."

M. 3:2 (1) The offspring of a thank offering, and (2) its substitute, (3) their offspring, and (4) the offspring of their offspring, to infinity, Lo, these are deemed equivalent to a thank offering, But with the proviso that they do not require bread.(1) The substitute of a burnt offering, and (2) the offspring of the substitute, and (3) their offspring, and (4) the offspring of their offspring, to infinity, Lo, these are deemed equivalent to a burnt offering. And they require flaying and cutting up and are wholly burned upon the altar fires.

M. 3:3 He who sets aside a female beast as a burnt offering [and a burnt offering can be made only of a male beast], which bore a male — [the offspring] pastures until it is blemished, then it is to be sold, and [the owner] brings with its proceeds a burnt offering. R. Eleazar says, "It itself is offered as a burnt offering." He who sets aside a female beast as a guilt offering — [the beast] pastures until it is blemished, then it is to be sold, and [the owner] brings with its proceeds a guilt offering, If his guilt offering has been offered, then its proceeds fall [to the Temple treasury] as a freewill offering. R. Simeon says, "It is sold [even] without a blemish." The substitute of a guilt offering, the offspring of its substitute, and their offspring, and the offspring of their offspring, to infinity, are to pasture until they are blemished. Then they are to be sold. And their proceeds are to fall [to the Temple treasury] as a freewill offering. R. Eleazar says, "Let them be left to die." R. Eliezer says, "Let him purchase with their proceeds a burnt offering." A guilt offering, the owner of which died, or the owner of which effected atonement [with another animal], is set out to pasture until it suffers a blemish. Then it is sold. And the proceeds are to fall [to the Temple treasury] as a freewill offering. R. Eliezer says, "Let it be left to die." R. Eleazar says, "Let him purchase with its proceeds a burnt offering."

M. 3:4 And is not also [that which falls to the Temple treasury as] a freewill offering a burnt offering? So what is the difference between the opinion of R. Eleazar and the opinion of sages [M. 3:3I, K]? But when it [a burnt offering] is brought in fulfillment of an obligation, he lays his hands on it and brings drink offerings on its account and the drink offerings derive from his own funds. And if he was a priest, the service of offering it up and the hide belong to him. But when it [a burnt offering] is brought as a freewill offering, he does not lay his hands on it and he does not bring drink offerings on its account, and its drink offerings derive from public funds. Even though he is a priest, the service of offering it up and the hide belong to the men of that particular course.

T. 2:1 He who sets aside a female beast as a burnt-offering [M. Tem. 3:3A] — it [the beast] pastures until it is blemished, then is sold, and its proceeds fall [to the Temple-treasury] as a freewill-offering. R. Simeon says, "[If] one said concerning an unclean beast or concerning a blemished beast, 'Lo, these are a burnt-offering,' he has said nothing whatsoever.[If] he said, 'Lo, these are for a burnt-offering,' even [if he said so in regard to] manure or stones, let them be sold and let him bring a burnt-offering with their proceeds."

T. 2:2 He who sets aside a female beast for a guilt-offering — it [the beast] pastures until it is blemished, then is sold, and its proceeds fall [to the Temple-treasury] as a freewill-offering [M. Tem. 3:3D].

T. 2:3 He who separates a female as a Passover — it pastures until it is blemished, then is sold, and with its proceeds let him bring [another] Passover. R. Simeon b. Judah says in the name of R. Simeon, "It may be sold even if it is not blemished" [M. Tem. 3:3F]. [If] it bore a male, it pastures until it is blemished, then is sold, and with its proceeds let him bring [another] Passover. R. Eleazar says, "It itself is offered as a Passover" [M. Tem. 3:3C].

T. 2:4 The substitute of the Passover, the offspring of the substitute of the Passover, their offspring, and the offspring of their offspring — to infinity — let them pasture until they are blemished, then let them be sold, and let [the owner] bring peace-offerings with their proceeds. R. Eleazar says, "The offspring themselves may be offered as peace-offerings." The offspring of the substitute of peace-offerings, their offspring, and the offspring of their offspring — to infinity — let them pasture until they are blemished, then let them be sold, and let [the owner] bring peace-offerings with their proceeds. R. Eleazar says, "The offspring themselves may be offered as peace-offerings."

T. 2:5 He who separates a female for his burnt-offering, his Passover, and his guilt-offering, has effected an act of substitution [the female being deemed holy as the substitute for the specified- offerings]. R. Simeon says, "For his burnt-offering he has effected an act of substitution. For his Passover and his guilt-offering he has not effected an act of substitution." "You have nothing which imparts the status of substitute except something which may be put out to pasture until blemished." Said Rabbi, "I prefer the opinion of R. Simeon in the case of a Passover, for from that which is sanctified as a Passover peace-offerings are brought."

T. 2:6 He who sets aside his guilt-offering [which] is lost, and set aside another in its stead, and did not suffice to offer it up before the first turns up, and lo, both of them are available — let him bring whichever one he prefers. And the second is set to pasture until it is blemished, then sold, and its proceeds fall to [the Temple-treasury] as a freewill-offering [M. Tem. 3:3L]. R. Eleazar says, "Let it be left to die" [M. Tem. 3:3M].

T. 2:7 He who separates coins for his guilt-offering [which] are lost, and who separated coins in their stead, and who did not suffice to purchase a guilt-offering with them before the first coins turned up — let him bring a guilt-offering [purchased] with some of these and with some of those. And the remainder falls [to the Temple-treasury] as a freewill-offering.

T. 2:8 He who separates coins for his guilt-offering, [which were lost] and separated coins in their stead, and did not suffice to purchase a guilt-offering with them before the coins turned up, Let him bring with them a guilt-offering and let it be offered.

T. 2:9 He who separates his guilt-offering, which was lost, and separated coins in its stead, and did not suffice to purchase [another] with them before the guilt-offering was turned up — the guilt-offering is offered up, and the coins fall [to the Temple-treasury] as a freewill-offering.

T. 2:10 He who separates his guilt-offering, which was lost, and who separated another in its stead and offered it up, and afterward the first turned up — let it be put out to pasture until it is blemished, then let it be sold. and its proceeds fall [to the Temple-treasury] as a freewill-offering. R. Eleazar says, "Let him purchase a burnt-offering with its proceeds" [M. Tem. 3:3N].

T. 2:11 He who separates coins for his guilt-offering, which were lost, and who separated coins in their stead, and who purchased with them a guilt-offering (and) which he offered it up — and afterward the first coins turned up — let them fall [to the Temple-treasury] as a freewill-offering. Rabbi says, "Let them go to the Salt Sea." R. Eleazar says, "Let him bring with them a burnt-offering." And is it not so that also the freewill-offering was a burnt-offering. What is the difference between the opinion of R. Eliezer and the opinion of sages [M. Tem. 3:4B]? R. Eliezer says, "It imparts the status of a substitute [to the animal designated in its stead]." And sages say, "It does not impart the status of a substitute."

M. 3:5 The substitute of a firstling or of a beast designated as tithe, their offspring, and the offspring of their offspring, to infinity, Lo, they are deemed equivalent to a firstling or to a beast designated as tithe, And they are eaten by the owners after they are blemished. What is the difference between the [blemished] firstling and a beast designated as tithe and all [other blemished] Holy Things? For all other Holy Things [when blemished] are sold in the market and are slaughtered in the market and are weighed by the litra, except for the firstling and a beast designated as tithe [M. Bekh. 5:1]. And they are subject to redemption, and their substitutes are subject to redemption, except for the firstling and a beast designated as tithe. And they are brought from abroad, except for the firstling and a beast designated as the tithe [which derive only from cattle raised in the Land of Israel] [compare M. Bekh. 9:1]. If they are brought without blemish, they are offered up, and if they are blemished, they are eaten by their owners after they are blemished. Said R. Simeon, "What is the reason [for G]? For the firstling and a beast designated as tithe have a remedy in their original location. But all other Holy Things, even though a blemish affects them, lo, they remain in their sanctity."

T. 2:16 The substitute of a firstling and of tithe, their offspring, and the offspring of their offspring, to infinity — Lo, they are deemed equivalent to the firstling or to tithe. And they are eaten by the owner after they are blemished [M. Tem. 3:5A-D].

T. 2:17 What is the difference between the firstling and tithe and all other Holy Things [M. Tem. 3:5E]: For all other Holy Things — one is liable [to replace them if they are lost]. And one must take the trouble to bring them from abroad to the Land of Israel [M. Tem. 3:5H], which is not the case for the firstling or tithe.

The comparison of the offspring of a consecrated beast and the substitute put forth for such a consecrated beast now takes over. The main point is, where the substitute is deemed of equivalent, specific status, so the offspring will enjoy the same. In the cases listed at M. 3:1ff., the substitute and the offspring are equivalent to that to which they have been compared (for the former) or from which they have been produced (for the later). Since the substitution takes effect even when the animal put forth as a substitute is not of the same classification as the already-sanctified beast, the issue here is a logical question for the particular hermeneutics. Once more, what we need to find out is the outer limits of the analogical process: in what way is the substitute like the beast for which it is substituted? Here we see, it is not only like the already-consecrated beast in that it too is now holy. It also takes on the distinctive traits of consecration that define the already-consecrated beast, entering its status just as does its offspring. That is an important clarification. It furthermore yields the kind of problems in which the generic hermeneutics specializes, e.g., at M. 3:3. The Tosefta's complementary composite, T. 2:1ff., once more shows us a highly original exegetical intellect at work, applying the same principle to diverse cases to good effect.

B. *THE SUPEREROGATORY SIN-OFFERING*

M. 4:1 (1) The offspring of a sin offering, (2) the substitute of a sin offering, and (3) a sin offering, the owner of [any ox] which died are left to die. (4) One which was superannuated or (5) one which was lost and turned up blemished, if this is after the owner has effected atonement, is left to die. And it does not impart the status of substitute [to an animal designated in its stead]. People do not derive benefit from it, but it is not subject to the laws of sacrilege. If this is before the owner has effected atonement, it is set out to pasture until it is blemished, then is sold, and [the owner] brings another with its proceeds. And it imparts the status of substitute [to an animal] designated in its stead, and it is subject to the laws of sacrilege.

M. 4:2 He who sets aside his sin offering and [the animal] was lost, and [who] offered another in its stead, and afterward the first [animal, that had been originally set aside] turned up — [the first animal] is left to die. He who sets aside coins for a sin offering, which were lost, and [who] offered up a sin offering in their stead, and afterward the coins turned up — let them go to the Salt Sea.

M. 4:3 He who sets aside coins for his sin offering, which were lost, and [who] set aside other coins in their stead — he did not suffice to buy with them [the replacement coins] a sin offering before the first coins turned up [that is, the proceeds of the sale of the blemished sin offering]. Let him bring a sin offering with some of these and with some of those, and let the others fall [to the Temple treasury] as a freewill offering. He who separates coins for his sin offering, which were lost, and [who] set aside a sin offering in their stead — he did not suffice to offer it up before the coins turned up — and Lo, the sin offering is blemished — let it be sold and let him bring a sin offering with some of these and with some of those [coins, the original ones as well as the ones which were the And let the rest fall [to the Temple treasury] as a freewill offering. He who separates his sin offering, which was lost, and [who] separated coins in its stead- he did not suffice to purchase a sin offering with them before his sin offering turned up — and lo, it is blemished — let it be sold, and let him bring a sin offering with some of these and with some of those [coins]. And let the rest fall [to the Temple treasury] as a freewill offering. He who separates his sin offering, which was lost, and [who] separated another in its stead- — he did not suffice to offer it up before the first turned up — and lo, both of them are blemished — let them both be sold. And let him bring a sin offering with some of these and some of those [coins received for the two blemished animals]. And let the rest fall [to the Temple treasury] as a freewill offering. He who separates his sin offering, which was lost, and [who] separated another in its stead — he did not suffice to offer it up before the first turned up — and Lo, both of them are totally unblemished — "one of them is to be offered as a sin offering. And the other is to be left to die," the words of Rabbi. And sages say, "Only that sin offering is left to die in the case in which the owners have effected atonement. And coins do not go to the Salt Sea except in the case of those which are found after the owner has effected atonement."

T. 2:12 He who sets aside his sin-offering, which was lost, and who separated another in its stead, but did not suffice to offer it up before the first turned up, and Lo, both of them are unblemished — One of them is offered up, and the second is left to die, the words of Rabbi [M. Tem. 4:6]. [If] one of them is unblemished and one of them is blemished, the unblemished one is offered up, and the blemished one is slaughtered. [If] the blemished one is slaughtered before the blood of the unblemished one is tossed, it is permitted. [If this is] after the blood of the unblemished one is tossed, it is prohibited. R. Eleazar bar Simeon says, "Even flesh in the pot — Lo, this is to be buried" [under the circumstances of F] [M. Tem. 4:4].

T. 2:13 He who sets aside his sin-offering, which was lost, and who separated another in its stead, but did not suffice to offer it up before the first turned up, and Lo, both of them are in hand — let him bring whichever one he wants. The second is put out to pasture until it is blemished and then sold, and the proceeds fall [to the Temple-treasury] as a freewill-offering. Rabbi says, "It is left to die."

T. 2:14 He who separates coins for his sin-offering, which were lost, and who separated a sin-offering in their stead, but who did not suffice to offer it up before they were found — Rabbi says, "Let them go to the Salt Sea." And sages concur with Rabbi in the case of one who separates his sin-offering which was lost, and who separated another in its stead, and who offered it up, and afterward the first turned up, that it [the first] is left to die [M. Tem. 4:3EE].

T. 2:15 He who separates coins for his sin-offering, which were lost, and who separated a sin-offering, and afterward the coins turned up, (that) they should go to the Salt Sea. For Rabbi says, "The coins fall to the Temple-treasury as a freewill-offering only if one purchased with them a sin-offering and left over some money." And sages say, "A sin-offering is left to die, or coins go to the Salt Sea, only when they turn up after the owner has effected atonement."

M. 4:4 He who separates his sin offering, and Lo, it [turns out] to be blemished sells it and purchases another with its proceeds. R. Eleazar b. R. Simeon says, "If the second is offered before the first is slaughtered, it is left to die. For the owner already has effected atonement."

The entire composite is inserted here because of the reference at M. 4:1 to the substitute of a sin offering, but the focus is on the rules of the sin-offering, not those of the substitute in general. The point of insistence is that the animal designated as a sin-offering serve for the particular sin that a particular person has discovered he has inadvertently committed and wishes to expiate. Then a variety of possibilities and variations emerges, and the exegetical problems shade over into exercises in the generic hermeneutics.

III. THE LANGUAGE USED IN EFFECTING THE SANCTIFICATION OF BEASTS, INCLUDING THE LANGUAGE THAT BRINGS ABOUT AN ACT OF SUBSTITUTION

What follows is a formal composite, which covers a variety of topics and so violates the prevailing norm of Halakhic representation.

> M. 5:1 How do they [legitimately] practice deception in connection with the firstling [thereby evading the law and using the animal for another sacrifice which one owes]? [Concerning] a beast which had not given birth which was pregnant, one says, "What is in the womb of this, if it is male, is a burnt offering." [If] it gave birth to a male, it is to be offered as a burnt offering, "And if it is female, it is sacrifices of peace offerings." [If] it gave birth to a female, it is to be offered as peace offerings. If one says, "If it is male, it is a burnt offering. If it is female, it is sacrifices of peace offerings," [if] it gave birth to a male and a female, the male is to be offered as a burnt offering, and the female is to be offered as peace offerings.
>
> M. 5:2 [If] it gave birth to two males, one of them is to be offered as a burnt offering. And the second is to be sold to those who owe a burnt offering. But its proceeds are unconsecrated. [If] it gave birth to two females, one of them is to be offered as peace offerings, and the second is to be sold to those who owe peace offerings. But its proceeds are unconsecrated. [If] it gave birth to an offspring whose sexual traits cannot be discerned or to one bearing the traits of both sexes — Rabban Simeon b. Gamaliel says, "Sanctity does not apply to them [at all]."
>
> T. 3:1 He who says, "What is in the womb of this beast is consecrated" — it is permitted to be sheared, but prohibited to be used for ordinary labor, because one thereby weakens the consecrated [beast in the womb]. [If] one slaughtered it, the foetus is prohibited to be eaten. [If] it died, the foetus is prohibited for benefit.
>
> T. 3:2 [He who says], "This ox is consecrated after thirty days" — [if] he slaughtered it during the thirty-day period, it is permitted to be eaten. [If] it died, it is permitted for benefit. [If] he consecrated it for the sake of peace-offerings, Lo this is consecrated. [If he said], "From now and after thirty days" and slaughtered it during the thirty days, it is prohibited for eating. [If] it died, it is prohibited from benefit. [If] he sanctified it for the sake of peace-offerings, Lo, this is not sanctified.
>
> M. 5:3 "He who says, 'The offspring of this beast will be a

burnt offering, and it [itself] is peace offerings' — his words are confirmed. [He who says], 'It is peace offerings and its offspring is a burnt offering,' Lo, this is the offspring of peace offerings [and in the same status (M. 3:1A)]," the words of R. Meir. Said R. Yosé, "If to begin with he intended thus, since it is not possible to designate [them] by two names at once, his words are confirmed. But if after he said, 'Lo, this is peace offerings,' he changed his mind and said, 'his offspring is a burnt offering,' Lo, this is the offspring of peace offerings."

M. 5:4 "[He who with peace offerings and burnt offerings before him says], 'Lo, this [unconsecrated beast] is the substitute of a burnt offering and the substitute of peace offerings,' Lo, this is the substitute of a burnt offering," the words of R. Meir. Said R. Yosé, "If to begin with he intended thus, since it is not possible to designate [them] by two names at once, his words are confirmed. But if after he said, 'It is the substitute of a burnt offering,' he changed his mind and said, 'It is the substitute of peace offerings,' lo, this is the substitute of a burnt offering."

T. 3:3 "[He who says], 'This beast is a thank-offering, what it produces is a burnt-offering,' 'This beast is peace-offerings, what it will produce is a sin-offering,' Lo, this [offspring] is the offspring of a thank-offering, the offspring of peace-offerings, the words of R. Meir. And sages say, "His words are confirmed." R. Yosé says, "Let one investigate the matter. If he said, 'It was to this which I intended, but one cannot state two names at once,' his words are confirmed. If he said, 'I designated the first and then I went and designated the second,' his latter statement is null" [M. Tem. 5:3].

T. 3:4 R. Meir concedes to sages that [if he said], "That which this beast will produce is a burnt-offering, and it itself is a thank-offering," "That which this beast will produce is a sin-offering, and it is peace-offerings," that his words are confirmed. Sages concede to R. Meir in the case of one who says, "This beast is instead of these two animal-offerings," ". . . instead of two animal-offerings which I owe," that his latter statement is null.

T. 3:5 "[He who says], 'This beast is a substitute for a burnt-offering and the substitute of peace-offerings,' the whole is the substitute of a burnt-offering," the words of R. Meir. And sages say, "Let it be put out to pasture until it is blemished and be sold, and let [the owner] purchase a burnt-offering with the proceeds of half of it and peace-offerings with the proceeds of half of it." R. Yosé says, "Let one investigate the matter. If he said, 'It was this which I intended, but one cannot state two names at once,' his words are confirmed. If he said, 'I designated the first and then I went and designated the second,' his latter statement is null."

T. 3:6 "[He who says], 'This beast — half is a burnt-offering and half is peace-offerings' — the whole instead of a burnt-offering," the words of R. Meir. And sages say, "Let it be put out to pasture until it is blemished and be sold, and let [the owner] purchase a burnt-offering with the proceeds of half of it and peace-offerings with the proceeds of half of it." And R. Yosé says, "Let one investigate the matter. If he said, 'It was this which I intended, but one cannot state two names at once,' his words are confirmed. If he said, 'I designated the first and then I went and designated the second,' his latter statement is null."

T. 3:7 "[He who says], 'This beast is instead of a burnt-offering, instead of peace-offerings,' the whole is instead of a burnt-offering," the words of R. Meir. And sages say, "His words are confirmed." R. Yosé says, "Let one investigate the matter. If he said, 'It was this which I intended, but one cannot state two names at once,' his words are confirmed. If he said, 'I designated the first and then I went and designated the second,' his latter statement is null."

T. 3:8 "[He who says], 'This beast — half of it is a burnt-offering and half of it is peace-offerings,' and he effected an act of substitution in its regard — its substitute is in its status. Half of it is a burnt-offering and half of it is peace-offerings. [If he said], 'This beast — half of it is instead of a burnt-offering and half of it is instead of a sin-offering,' the whole is a burnt-offering," the words of R. Meir. And sages say, "Let it be left to die." [If he said], "Half of it is instead of a sin-offering and half of it is instead of a burnt-offering," all agree that it is left to die.

T. 3:9 Five who brought a single animal-sacrifice — one lays on hands for the sake of a burnt-offering, and all the rest laid on hands for the sake of peace-offerings — let it be put out to pasture until it is blemished and be sold with the proceeds of half of it a burnt-offering [is purchased], and with the proceeds of half of it, peace-offerings [are purchased]. [If] one slaughtered it, let its appearance become disfigured [through rotting], and let it go forth to the place of burning.

T. 3:10 [If] one found it as peace-offerings, let it go forth up onto the altar, because there was no court established for such a matter. Thus said R. Yosé, "Under what circumstances? When one intended thus to begin with. But if one laid hands for the sake of a burnt-offering and then changed his mind and said, 'For the sake of peace-offerings,' Lo, this remains in its original status as to sanctification. [If he said], 'Lo, this [as] at the outset,' but he laid on hands for the sake of a burnt-offering and changed his mind and said, 'For the sake of peace-offerings', Lo, this is in its original status as to sanctification."

M. 5:5 [He who says], "Lo, this is instead of that," ". . . the substitute of that" ". . . the exchange of that" — Lo, this is a substitute. [He who says, "Lo,] this is unconsecrated through that," — it is not a substitute. And if it was a blemished consecrated animal, it goes forth for unconsecrated purposes. But still one must make good its full value.

M. 5:6 [He who says,] "Lo, this is instead of a sin offering," ". . . instead of a burnt offering," — he has said nothing. [If he said], ". . . instead of this sin offering," ". . . instead of this burnt offering" ". . . instead of a sin offering," or "instead of a burnt offering, which I have in the house," [if] he had them, his words are confirmed. If he said concerning an unclean beast or concerning a blemished beast, "Lo, these are a burnt offering" he has said nothing. [If he said], "Lo, these are for a burnt offering," let them be sold, and let him bring a burnt offering with their proceeds.

T. 3:11 [He who says], "Lo, this is a substitute," "This is an exchange," "This, Lo, it is a substitute," "This is rendered unconsecrated by means of this," he has said nothing in the case of Holy Things. [If he so stated in regard to] the upkeep of the Temple, "This is rendered unconsecrated on its account," his words are confirmed. [If he said], "This is a substitute", "This is an exchange," he has said nothing [M. Tem. 5:6A].

T. 3:12 [He who says], "Lo, this is a sin-offering," and "Lo, this is a guilt-offering," even though he owes such sacrifices, has said nothing. [If] he said, "Lo, these are for my sin-offering" and "Lo, these are for my guilt-offering," if he owed [such sacrifices] his words are confirmed, and if not, he has said nothing [M. Tem. 5:6B]. [If] he said, "Lo, incumbent on me is the sin-offering or the burnt-offering [owed] by so-and-so," if he said so with [the other's] knowledge, he has fulfilled his obligation, and if he did not say so with [the other's] knowledge, he has not fulfilled his obligation. [If he said], "Lo, this is the sin-offering or the burnt-offering of so-and-so," if this other person went and brought the necessary sacrifices for himself, Lo, these are in the status of a sin-offering or a guilt-offering, the owners of which already have effected atonement.

T. 3:13 A burnt-offering which was mixed up with animal-sacrifices is to be put out to pasture until it is blemished, then be sold. And the owner brings with the proceeds of the best of them an animal-sacrifice, and with the proceeds of the best of them burnt-offerings. [If] he declared an animal substitute for one of them and does not know which of them he has subjected to the status of substitute, lo, this one brings coins or an animal-sacrifice from his own property. He then says, "If it is the substitute of the burnt-offering, Lo, this is peace-offerings. If it is the substitute of peace-offerings, this one, Lo, it is a burnt-offering." And Lo, they are like two animal-sacrifices which were mixed up with one another.

T. 3:14 [If] one went and effected an exchange with one of

them and does not know with which one of them he effected the exchange, Lo, this one brings coins from his own property and says, "If it is the substitute of a substitute, this one is unconsecrated, this one is a burnt-offering, this one is peace-offerings. If it is the substitute of peace-offerings, this one, Lo, this is a burnt-offering." And Lo, they are like an animal-sacrifice and a substitute which were mixed with one another.

T. 3:15 A thank-offering which was mixed up with its substitute — both of them are offered up, and he waves bread with them. [If] one of them died, the second should not be offered up. [If] he went and effected an exchange with one of them, Lo, this one should not be offered up. And so in the case of peace-offerings which were mixed up with a firstling: Both of them are to be put out to pasture until they suffer a blemish and are eaten in the status of a firstling. [If] one of them died, the second should not be offered up. [If] he went and effected an exchange in the case of one of them, Lo, this should not be offered up.

In the context of an exposition of the power of language to classify animals for purposes of sanctification, M. 5:1-4, we proceed to the language-rules for substitution. The generic hermeneutics takes over here.

IV. FORMAL APPENDIX

M. 6:1 All [animals] which are prohibited for the altar prohibit in any number at all [the utilization for sacred purposes of animals among which they are confused, and these are as follows]: (1) the one which has sexual relations with a human being; (2) and the one with whom a human being has sexual relations; (3) and the one which is set aside [for idolatrous worship]; (4) and the one which has actually been worshiped; (5) and the [harlot's] hire; (6) and the price of a dog [one given in payment for a dog]; (7) and the hybrid; (8) and the terefah; (9) and the one which is born from the side. What is the one which is set aside [A3]? The one which is set aside for idolatrous worship. It is prohibited, but what is on it is permitted. What is the one which is actually worshiped [A4]? Any which people serve. [Both] it and what is on it are prohibited. This and that [however] are permitted for eating.

M. 6:2 What is the hire [of a harlot]? He who says to a prostitute, "Here is this lamb for you as your fee." Even if [they were] a hundred [among which one such animal is confused], all of them are prohibited. He who says to his fellow, "Here is this lamb for you, and let your servant girl spend the night with my servant boy." Rabbi says, "It is not the hire of a harlot." And sages say, "It is the hire of a harlot."

M. 6:3 What is the price of a dog? He who says to his fellow, "Here is this lamb for you, in exchange for this dog." And so two partners who divided [property] — one took ten [lambs], and one took nine [lambs] and a dog. [All] hose which are set over against the dog are prohibited. [But] those which are with the dog are permitted. The hire [rental fee paid for use] of a dog and the price [paid for the purchase, e.g., as a slave] of a prostitute, lo, they are permitted, since it is said, "Even both these [two]" (Dt. 23:19) — but not four. Their offspring [that is, of animals paid for such] are permitted, since it is said, "They" — and not their offspring.

T. 4:1 An animal with which a human being has had sexual relations [M. Tem. 6:1A2], whether it belongs to him [who had sexual relations with it] or whether it belongs to someone else [other than the one who had sexual relations with it], whether it is [subjected to sexual relations] before it is sanctified or whether it is after it is sanctified, whether it is [done] unintentionally or intentionally, whether it is [done] inadvertently or willingly, is prohibited for use on the altar. In the case of that which has been set aside [for purposes of idolatry], if it belongs to him [who set it aside for idolatry], it is prohibited. [But if it belongs] to his fellow, it is permitted.

T. 4:2 From what point is it deemed to be set aside for idolatry [M. Tem. 6: 1 A3]? From the moment at which one actually does a deed [in that connection]. And that [beast] which is actually worshipped, whether it belongs to him [who worshipped it], or whether it belongs to his fellow, whether it is before it is sanctified or after it is sanctified, whether it is done unintentionally or intentionally, is prohibited for use on the altar. [If it is done] inadvertently, the beast remains valid. [If it is done] willingly [publicly], the beast is invalid.

T. 4:3 What is the definition of that which is actually worshipped [M. Tem. 6:1A4]? Any animal which people worship, whether inadvertently or willingly. What is an animal which is set aside [for idolatry, M. Tem. 6:1A2]? It is this which is set aside for idolatry. But if one said, "This ox is [consecrated] for idolatry," or "This house is [consecrated] for idolatry," he has said nothing. For an act of sanctification does not apply to the matter of idolatry.

T. 4:4 What is the price of a dog [M. Tem. 6:3A]? These are things given in exchange for a dog, as it is said, Thou has sold the people for a trifle (Ps. 44:13). Twigs with grapes and crowns of ears of corn, [bottles of] wine and oil and meal — anything the like of which is offered on the altar is prohibited.

T. 4:5 Brothers who had nine beasts and a dog — they divided four against four, and one against the dog — that which is over against the dog is prohibited. That which is with the dog is permitted

[M. Tem. 6:3D-E].

T. 4:6 What is the hire of a harlot? This is the fee paid to a harlot, as it is said, To all prostitutes will they be given (Ez. 16:33). The fee paid to a [male-] hustler, Lo, this [too] is prohibited. He who says, "Here is a lamb for you, so that your serving-girl will spend the night with my serving-boy" — Rabbi says, "It is the hire of a harlot." R. Yosé bar Judah says, "It is not the hire of a harlot" [M. Tem. 6:2D-F]. For the hire of a harlot pertains only in the case of prohibited sexual relations, intercourse with whom constitutes a transgression.

M. 6:4 [If] one gave her [pieces of] silver, Lo, they are permitted [e.g., for use in purchasing gifts for the altar]. [If he gave her bottles] of wine, [jars of] oil, meal, or anything the like of which is offered on the altar, it is prohibited. [If] he gave her [already] consecrated animals, Lo, they are permitted. [If he gave her] fowl, Lo, they are prohibited. For it might have been logical [to argue thus]: Now if to the case of consecrated animals, which a blemish invalidates, the consideration of the hire of a harlot and the price of a dog does not apply, to the case of fowl, which a blemish does not invalidate in any event, is it not logical that the consideration of the hire of a harlot and the price of a dog should not apply? Scripture states, "For any vow" (Dt. 23:19) — to encompass fowl.

T. 4:7 [If] one gave her wheat for the making of flour, grapes for the making of wine, olives for the making of oil, a cow which became pregnant [in his domain] and gave birth in his domain — Lo, these are prohibited [M. Tem. 6:4B]. But [if] one gave her coins with which to purchase wine, oil, flour, or a beast which became pregnant while in her domain and gave birth — Lo, these are permitted [M. Tem. 6:4A]. And just as they are prohibited for use in the tent of meeting which was in the wilderness, so they are prohibited for use in the tent of meeting which was in Gilgal. But they are permitted for use for consecration for the upkeep of the house.

T. 4:8 [If] one gave her gold — R. Yosé bar Judah says, "They do not make therewith beaten gold plates, even for the back of the Holy of Holies." [If] he gave her [such a thing] but did not have intercourse with her, Lo, these are permitted. [If] he had intercourse with her, even three years later, Lo, these [then] are prohibited. [If] he had intercourse with her and gave her nothing, [but] he then gave her something even three years later, Lo, these are prohibited. And what is a harlot's hire? Rabbi says, "It is only in the case of prohibited sexual relations, intercourse of a sort which constitutes a transgression." But he who gives his wife [something for having intercourse with him] during her menstrual period, or if she gave him something, or if he gave her a fee for her being taken away from her work, Lo, these are permitted. Even though there is no clear proof of that proposition, there is at least a hint pertaining to it: "If you were different from other women in your harlotries: none solicit you to play the harlot: and you gave hire, while no hire was given to you" (Ez. 16:34).

T. 4:9 [If] one gave her animals which had been consecrated, Lo, these are permitted. But logic suggests that they should be prohibited: Now if fowl, which a blemish does not invalidate, is subject to the prohibition by reason of being the hire of a harlot and the price of a dog, animals which have been consecrated, which a blemish does invalidate, is it not logical that they should be subject to prohibition by reason of being the hire of a harlot and the price of a dog? Scripture says, For any sort of vow — excluding that which [already] is subject to a vow [having been consecrated].

M. 6:5 All those animals which are prohibited for the altar — their offspring are permitted. The offspring of a terefah animal — R. Eliezer says, "It is not to be offered on the altar." And sages say, "It is to be offered." R. Hananiah b. Antigonos says, "A valid animal which sucked from a terefah animal is invalid on the altar." All Holy Things which became terefah — they do not redeem them. For they do not redeem Holy Things merely to feed them to the dogs.

T. 4:10 All those animals which are prohibited for the altar — their offspring are permitted [M. Tem. 6:5A]. R. Eleazar declares prohibited. The offspring of a terefah-animal — R. Eleazar says, 'It is not to be offered on the altar.' And sages say, 'It is to be offered on the altar' [M. Tem. 6:5B — D]. And R. Eleazar agrees in the case of a young bird which came out of the egg of a terefah-bird, that it is to be offered on the altar. R. Hanina b. Antigonos says in the name of R. Eleazar Hisma, "A valid animal which sucked from a terefah-animal is prohibited for the altar" [M. Tem. 6:5E].

T. 4:11 All Holy Things which were made terefah before they were consecrated and afterward died are subject to redemption. [If they were made terefah] after they were sanctified and then died, they are not subject to redemption, for they do not redeem Holy Things to feed them to the dogs [M. Tem. 6:5G]. The firstling and the tithe of cattle are subject to redemption.

M. 7:1 There are [rules applying] to [animals] sanctified for the altar which do not [apply] to things sanctified for the upkeep of the house [the Temple treasury]. And there are [rules applying] to things sanctified for the upkeep of the house which do not apply to [animals] sanctified for the altar. For (1) [all animals] sanctified for the altar impart the status of substitute [to animals designated in their stead]. And they are liable on their account [on account of things sanctified for the altar] because of

violation of the laws of refuse, remnant, and uncleanness. Their offspring and their milk are prohibited after they are redeemed [M. Hul. 10:2]. And he who slaughters them outside [of the Temple] is liable [M. Zeb. 14:1-2]. And they do not pay any part of them to craftsmen [who perform tasks for the Temple] as their salary [T to M. Meilah 3:6] [M. Sheq. 4:5-6] which is not the case of things sanctified for the upkeep of the house.

M. 7:2 There are [rules applying] to things sanctified for the upkeep of the house which do not apply to [animals] sanctified for the altar. For (1) Things which are sanctified without further specification go for the upkeep of the house [M. Sheq. 4:7]. (2) The sanctity pertaining to the upkeep of the house applies to anything [not merely to valid animals]. (3) And the laws of sacrilege apply to that which is produced by them [things which are sanctified for the upkeep of the house, e.g., to milk, wool, or eggs (M. Me. 3:5)]. (4) And the priests have no benefit from them.

M. 7:3 All the same are [animals] sanctified for the altar and things sanctified for the upkeep of the house. (1) They do not change them from one status of sanctification to another status of sanctification. (2) They sanctify [in the case of animals sanctified for the altar] their estimated value as a sanctified thing [=value dedication, M. Ar. 8:7]. (3) And they declare them devoted [=herem. assigned solely for the benefit of the priesthood]. And if they die, they are to be buried [M. Tem. 6:5G]. R. Simeon says, "Things sanctified for the upkeep of the house, if they die, are to be redeemed."

T. 4:12 A strict rule applies to that which is sanctified for the altar which does not apply to that which is sanctified for the upkeep of the house. And a strict rule applies to that which is sanctified for the upkeep of the house which does not apply to that which is sanctified for the altar. For: They hand over from it [that which is sanctified for the upkeep of the house] for the purposes of that which is sanctified for the altar that which is appropriate for it[s purposes] from this and not from this. But as to that which is consecrated for the upkeep of the house, it is only from this.

T. 4:13 A more strict rule applies to that which is sanctified for the upkeep of the house: At the outset of its sanctification, the laws of sacrilege apply to it. But as to that which is sanctified for the altar, there are things to which the laws of sacrilege apply, and these are things to which the laws of sacrilege do not apply [M. Tem. 7:3B3]. And it is permitted for eating only through redemption. If they died, whether unblemished or blemished, they are not to be redeemed [M. Tem. 7:3C]. R. Simeon says, "In the case of that which is sanctified for the altar: those animals which are unblemished are not to be redeemed. And those which are blemished are to be redeemed" [M. Tem. 7:3D].

T. 4:14 All the same are things sanctified for the altar and things sanctified for the upkeep of the house. For: if they died or miscarried or were made unclean, Lo, they are to be disposed of by burning [vs. M. Tem. 7:4A-B].

M. 7:4 And these are things which are to be buried: Sanctified animals which produced a miscarriage — they [the miscarriages] are to be buried. [If] it produced an afterbirth, it is to be buried. (1) An ox which is stoned to death, (2) and a heifer the neck of which is broken, (3) and the bird offerings of a *mesora'*, (4) and the hair of a Nazirite [which is cut off], (5) and the firstborn of an ass, (6) and meat mixed with milk. And unconsecrated beasts that have been slaughtered in the Temple courtyard. R. Simeon says, "Unconsecrated beasts slaughtered in the Temple courtyard are to be burned." And so: "A wild animal which is slaughtered in the Temple courtyard."

M. 7:5 And those are things which are to be burned: Leaven on Passover is to be burned. (1) And unclean heave offering, and (2) orlah fruit, and (3) mixed seeds in a vineyard — That which is usually burned is to be burned. That which is usually buried is to be buried. And they kindle [a flame] with [unclean] bread and oil of heave offering.

M. 7:6 All sanctified animals which were slaughtered [with improper intention to eat what is usually eaten or to burn what is usually burned] outside of their proper time or outside of their proper place, Lo, these are to be burned. A suspensive guilt offering is to be burned. R. Judah says, "It is to be buried." The sin offering of fowl which is brought in a case of doubt is to be burned. R. Judah says, "One tosses it into the gutter." All things which are to be burned are not to be buried, and all things which are to be buried are not to be burned. R. Judah says, "If one wanted to impose a more strict rule upon himself, to burn that which is to be buried, he is permitted [to do so]." They said to him, "One is not permitted to change [the established rule]."

T. 4:15 A sin-offering of fowl which is brought in a case of doubt [M. Tem. 7:6E], and a suspensive guilt-offering [M. Tem. 7:6C], And unconsecrated animals which are slaughtered in the courtyard [M. Tem. 7:4E] — R. Simeon says, "They are to be burned" [M. Tem. 7:4F]. R. Judah says, "They are to be buried" [M. Tem. 7:6D, F].

T. 4:16 How do they burn a sin-offering of fowl? They would put it into the water-gutter and it would roll down to the Qidron valley. R. Ishmael b. R. Yohanan b. Beroqah says, "There was a window outlet there on the western side of the ramp, a cubit by a cubit. It was called hollow (Rebukah). There did they put the sin-offering of fowl. It was left for its appearance to turn rotten and taken out to the place of burning" [T. Zeb. 7:6].

T. 4:17 Invalidated Most Holy Things and sacrificial parts of Lesser Holy Things and Most Holy Things which were made unclean inside the courtyard, and meal-offerings and flour and wine and oil — Lo, these are to be disposed of by burning. How do they burn wine and oil? They would put them on a bonfire as they are. Invalidated Lesser Holy Things and sacrificial parts of Most Holy Things which were made unclean outside the courtyard, and the Passover, the greater part of which went outside — they burn them before the Birah with wood of the altar.

We conclude with an appendix on mixtures. The reference to the power of animals sanctified for the altar to impart the status of substitute to animals designated in their stead, M. 7:1, which composition is integral to the larger composite, accounts for the inclusion of the entire construction in the account of substitution.

IV. DOCUMENTARY TRAITS

A. THE MISHNAH AND THE TOSEFTA

We have noted the Tosefta's occasional inclusion of compositions and composites formed within a different theory of category-formation from the one that governs in the Mishnah and is also paramount in the Tosefta.

B. THE BAVLI

I see no point at which the Bavli recasts the category-formation at hand.

V. THE HERMENEUTICS OF TEMURAH

A. WHAT FUSES THE HALAKHIC DATA INTO A CATEGORY-FORMATION?

What fuses the halakhic data into a category-formation is the pervasive principle that sanctification takes effect by reason of the individual Israelite's intentionality even in contradiction to what the Torah favors. The Torah forbids an act of substitution. If the will of the Torah were to prevail, then, logically, what has been subjected to an act of substitution — "this beast is holy in place of that" — should be unaffected by the Israelite's use of the formulaic language. But that is not the outcome specified by the (written) Torah itself. When the Israelite, on his own volition, uses the taxonomic language, sanctification results. So the Israelite's taxonomic power through use of correct language prevails, when activated by the Israelite's will, even over the logic of the rules of the Torah and even in violation of those rules. What the Halakhah contributes to the category-formation defined by Scripture is embodied in a simple rule. The Israelite power of intentionality even overrides the rules of what actually serves to realize the normative intentionality, which is to say, a blemished beast is consecrated, as it were, for the altar, in an act of substitution!

We find ourselves dealing with a familiar principle, the one encountered at M. Zeb. 10:1. There we are told that the altar sanctifies what is appropriate for it, but does not sanctify what is not appropriate for it. Then, it must follow, once an Israelite has sanctified to the altar what belongs there, the act is irrevocable, though its consequences may vary according to circumstance and procedure. There is, then, no possibility of changing one's mind, only the requirement of sorting out the results of one's initial decision and act of intentionality. And that same conception governs here: once one has sanctified a beast, he cannot deconsecrate it by replacing it with another. The initial act is valid, assuming that the beast is one that appropriately serves in the classification for which it has been designated. True, one may redeem from the status of sanctification an animal that he has consecrated, as Lev. 27:15 makes explicit: "And if he that sanctified it will redeem his house, then he shall add the fifth part of the money of thy valuation." But redeeming what has been sanctified is not the same thing as nullifying the original act, e.g., by an act of substitution of one thing for something else, specifically, the substitution of a secular beast for one already sanctified.

The basic issue of the Halakhah of Temurah is whether or not the status, as to sanctification, of that which is sanctified is subject to revision. And the position of the law is that once something has been sanctified, not only is the sanctification indelible (except through the Halakhah's own media of secularization) but it is permanent in its particular character. That is to say, one may not change the status of an already sanctified beast from consecrated to secular, and one also may not change the level of sanctification, e.g., declaring Most Holy Things to Lesser Holy Things or vice versa. This is stated in the following language: "All the same are Most Holy Things and Lesser Holy Things: one is not permitted to effect a substitution, whether on a weekday or on the Sabbath. They do not change them from their status as to sanctification, even from a lesser status of sanctification to a greater status of sanctification, and it is hardly necessary to say, from a greater status to a lesser status of sanctification. If one said concerning a firstling or concerning peace-offerings, 'Lo, these are a burnt-offering,' he has said nothing. And it is not necessary to say, if he said concerning a burnt-offering, 'Lo, this is a firstling,' 'Lo, this is peace-offering.'"

Because the act of substitution is both effective and null, the categories of offerings play no role in the working of the Halakhah. They substitute one animal for others different from it. And why not, since the originally-sanctified beast is unaffected by the declaration of substitution. The only trait of that beast that pertains is its generic classification of sanctification, not the particular sub-category as to sanctification that applies. That is how the Halakhah takes account of an act that is illegitimate but that produces effects: "One may not substitute a beast for an already-consecrated one, but if he does so, his act takes effect: Not that a person in any event is permitted to effect a substitution. For it is forbidden to make such a statement of substitution of a now-secular beast for one already consecrated. But if one has effected a substitution, it that which is designated instead of the beast already consecrated is deemed a substitute and also consecrated." And — as we have already noted — the person who does so moreover incurs the penalty of forty stripes. Not only so, but while on the Sabbath one may not effect an act of consecration, an act of substitution produces the anticipated result.

What defines the stakes of the Halakhah of Temurah? If I wished to make the statement that God not only hears and answers prayer and the other verbal formulations of their relationship with God that Israelites set forth, but that God also responds to Israelite language even when the language conveys an inappropriate or improper intention, I can imagine no more appropriate medium than the Halakhah of Temurah. And, predictably, as we have already noted, that is the opening theme of the Bavli's reading of the Halakhah: how one may violate the Torah's law and yet produce a practical result. I find two considerable points that follow.

First, language is not magical. The formula that transforms a secular beast into a sacred one accomplishes its act of transformation only when the prior condition is met that the one who uses the language has the right to use it. The language, on its own, bears no coercive quality and is not a formula that works without regard to circumstance. Scripture at Lev. 27:10 is mute on that point. The Halakhah makes explicit that the language of substitution works only when spoken by one who has the right to use it (just as the altar takes over what is appropriate to it but not what is not). Who carries out a valid act of substitution? One who owns the beast designated as a substitute. Then the language on its own does not suffice; the right person must use it, and he or she must have the power to effect it. Now, as we know, the Halakhah does not regard the act of sanctification as operative *ex opere operato* but only as conditional. Language constitutes an act of substance, not solely of status. It follows that, in connection with a beast belonging to someone else, one may use the language of substitution and produce no result at all.

The second pertains to the issue of language and actuality. The actualities of the originally-consecrated offering play no role whatsoever. The beast declared a substitute need not belong to the same category as the beast that has already been sanctified; the analogy — "this in place of that" — focuses upon the "this," not the "that." The trait of the initially-sanctified beast that registers is only its classification as holy, not the particularity of that for which it has been sanctified. And that violates the rule that one may not change the status, as to sanctification, of a designated beast. If it has been declared Most Holy Things, it cannot be reclassified as Lesser Holy Things, and so throughout. When it comes to the transformation of the substitute, by contrast, we ignore considerations of classification — specificities and particularities — and invoke only a single criterion: the classification of sanctification per se. God responds to the language and circumstance but need not take account of irrelevant details in the transaction at hand. So one may substitute an animal for others different from it — an amazing point that fits entirely within the present rationality.

The upshot is, the entire system of matching intentionality to actuality, the will of the sacrifier to the deed of the priest and the intentionality as to the offering expressed by the priest, here is suspended. Why should that be the case? Because at issue here is not the utilization of the substituted beast, only its status as to sanctification. The effective statement concerns only gross classification, not detailed disposition. The only limitation is that of comparability: limbs or fetuses do not compare with one another or with whole beasts; a statement of substitution then violates the rules of the governing metaphor: something must be like something else in the ways that count, but need not be like something else in the ways that do not count.

B. THE ACTIVITY OF THE CATEGORY-FORMATION THE MEANING OF "SUBSTITUTE:"

By the act of substitution, one beast is declared like another. "Substitute" bears several kindred meanings: (1) one beast takes the place of another; (2) one beast enters the status of a substitute, meaning, the same status as that enjoyed by the consecrated beast for which the substitution is proposed; (3) the status of substitute is invoked in connection with a given beast. All can invoke the status of substitute in connection with an originally-unconsecrated animal. One cannot exchange or substitute an animal for one that has been set aside as a sacrifice; the sanctity of the originally-consecrated beast applies in addition to the one that is set forth in its stead and both are now consecrated. Thus, "if one has effected a substitution," meaning, if one has proposed to offer as a holy sacrifice one beast in place of another, "it is deemed a substitute," meaning, it falls under the law of substitution and is holy just as the beast in the stead of which it was put forth is holy. But the substitute-beast does not necessarily enter into the exact status, as to sanctification, of the original beast; a female animal declared a substitute for a consecrated male animal does not serve the purpose of the male animal. Thus, the power of metaphorization — "this is like that," meaning, "this is instead of that" — finds itself restricted to the taxonomic generality: this is holy as that is holy. But when it comes to the specifics, the Halakhah draws back. It does not investigate the level of holiness imputed to the substitute nor insist that it is holy in exactly the same way as the originally-sanctified beast is holy, serving the same purpose for example.

WHAT CONSTITUTES AN ACT OF SUBSTITUTION. THE POWER OF LANGUAGE: The individual Israelite exercises power through the language that he uses, and that is the fundamental premise of the Halakhah here as elsewhere. And the power that he exercises is that of classification: "It is my intentionality that this thing enter into that taxon." That language having been spoken, the thing in reality responds and may well conform. The formulation and wording accordingly possess the power to classify and therefore to transform that to which reference is made.

In the case of the statement of substitution, the effective language is as follows: He who says, "Lo, this is instead of that," "...the substitute of that" "...the exchange of that" — Lo, this is a substitute. If the language that is used is that of deconsecration, it has no bearing on an act of substitution. That is explained in these terms: He who says, "Lo, this is unconsecrated through that," — it is not a substitute. That formulation does not constitute an act of substitution. And if under discussion was a blemished consecrated animal, it goes forth for unconsecrated purposes. But still one must make good its full value.

THE PARTICULARIZATION OF SPEECH: The formulation of a statement of substitution must be specific and refer to a particular animal. One cannot effect an act of classification through a language of generalities but must refer to concrete actualities. That is expressed in this way: He who says, "Lo, this is instead of a sin offering," "...instead of a burnt offering," — he has said nothing. If he said, "...instead of *this* sin offering," "...instead of *this* burnt offering" that language takes effect. If he said, "...instead of a sin offering," or "instead of a burnt offering that I have in the house [that is, that I have already designated for said purpose in my household]," if he had them, his words are confirmed. One must specify the particular consecrated animal for which an unconsecrated beast is to serve as a substitute; then alone does the act of substitution take effect. The requirement of specificity extends to the last detail, thus: He who says, "Lo, this is a sin-offering," and "Lo, this is a guilt-offering," even though he owes such sacrifices, has said nothing. If he said, "Lo, these are for my sin-offering" and "Lo, these are for my guilt-offering" if he owed such sacrifices his words are confirmed, and if not, he has said nothing.

WHO EFFECTS AN ACT OF SUBSTITUTION: Anyone who possesses an animal may carry out an act of substitution with effect. One does not effect an act of substitution in the case of an animal-offering which does not belong to him. That is because one also cannot sanctify something that does not belong to him. Anyone who may sanctify a beast may effect an act of substitution as well: All effect a valid substitution (that is, through a statement of consecration of a secular beast propose to substitute that beast for one they have first designated as a sacrifice, so that, by making a statement of substitution, that second beast enters the status of the originally-consecrated one) — all the same are men and women. Priests effect a substitution in the case of what belongs to them. And Israelites effect a substitution in the case of what belongs to them. That is why, also, an Israelite cannot dispose of what belongs to a priest, and vice versa. If a priest substituted an unconsecrated animal for one that he has set aside for himself, the substitute becomes sacred.

That principle yields an interesting refinement. If an Israelite gave a priest an animal to offer as a sin-offering and the priest substituted another animal for the one the Israelite gave him, the latter beast is not consecrated. That is because the priest has no share in the animal at that time, but only after it was sacrificed and burned. There is no possibility that before the sin-offering has been sacrificed, the priest can effect an act of substitution; the priest effects a substitution for what belongs to the priest but not for one that does not belong to him. So the governing criterion is the possession of title to the beast that is set forth as a substitute.

An act of consecration — "Lo, this beast is sanctified as the sin-offering that I must bring for such and such a sin done inadvertently and only now discovered" — must be deliberately articulated. But an act of substitution is not subject to the same limitation. The law has treated that which is done unintentionally as equivalent to that done intentionally in the case of the substitute. But it has not treated that which is done unintentionally as equivalent to that which is done intentionally in the case of consecrated beasts.

WHAT IS SUBJECT TO AN ACT OF SUBSTITUTION: Animals sanctified for the altar impart the status of substitute to animals designated in their stead, which is not the case of things sanctified for the upkeep of the house. The declaration of an act of substitution of one beast for another produces an effect — is valid — without regard to whether the beast set forth as a substitute actually falls into the same category as the beast that was initially sanctified. Here we see the broadening of the law: the metaphor ("this is like that") extends to the status as to sanctification, but not the original purpose for which the already-sanctified beast was consecrated. And that yields an important result. While it is the rule that people do not change them from one status of sanctification to another status of sanctification, in the case of an act of substitution, we ignore the matter of status. The reason is that all that matters about the already-sanctified beast is its status of consecration; whether the beast proposed as a substitute can actually serve makes no difference, the act being null. But the status of sanctification then overtakes the substitute; the prohibited action produces a result. The established classifications and categories of beasts — herd, flock, sheep, goats, males, females, unblemished, blemished — do not apply. The logic of the Halakhah rejects the notion that the act of substitution must bear within itself an appropriate and legal category of exchange.

A blemished beast cannot replace an unblemished, but that makes no difference; once the Israelite has declared the blemished beast a substitute, that fact takes over and produces its own consequences. All the same are Most Holy Things and Lesser Holy Things: one is not permitted to effect a substitution (M. Tem. 1:1C), whether on a weekday or on the Sabbath. They do not change them from their status as to sanctification, even from a lesser status of sanctification to a greater status of sanctification, and it is hardly necessary to say, from a greater status to a lesser status of sanctification. They substitute (=impose the law of substitution upon) an animal (1) from the herd for one from the flock, and one from the flock for one from the herd, (2) from sheep for goats, and from goats for sheep, (3) from males for females, and from females for males, (4) from unblemished for blemished animals, and from blemished for unblemished animals, since it is said, "He shall not substitute anything for it or exchange it, a good for a bad, or a bad for a good" (Lev. 27:10). What is a good for a bad? Substituting unblemished animals for already consecrated blemished ones, the sanctification of which took place before their blemish (M. Bekh. 2:2-3). Those sanctified when already blemished are unfit for the altar and exempt from the law of substitution. They substitute a valid act of substitution takes place in the case of a statement concerning one for two and two for one, one for a hundred and a hundred for one.

EXHAUSTING THE METAPHOR: Then what are the limits of the law of substitution? The metaphor breaks down when we deal with the parts of the consecrated beast, as distinct from the whole of it. They do not substitute (1) limbs for fetuses, or fetuses for limbs, or (2) limbs and fetuses for whole beasts, or whole beasts for them. "If one said, 'The foot of this ox is a burnt-offering,' the whole of it is not a burnt-offering, but only that foot alone; that is the case with a part of an animal on which life does not depend." Birds and meal offerings do not produce a substitute (impose the status of a substitute upon birds or meal designated as their replacement). For only in the case of cattle is substitute mentioned. The individual produces a substitute, and neither a congregation nor partners produce a substitute. Offerings for the upkeep of the Temple do not produce a substitute. For offerings of an individual impose the status of substitute, but offerings of the community do not impose the status of substitute.

A further limitation is to be noted. The beast consecrated by an act of substitution itself does not impart the same status to an animal designated in *its* stead: consecrated animals impart the status of a substitute to that animal declared by its owner to be a substitute in their stead. But a substitute does not impart to another animal, designated in its stead the status of a substitute. The process ends with the substitute-beast itself. A community or partners declare animals to be sanctified, but do not effect a declaration of substitution so that should a group of people or partners declare an animal substitute for one already consecrated, the former is not deemed consecrated (M. 1:6). And they sanctify limbs and fetuses, but do not effect substitution for limbs or fetuses.

THE EFFECTS OF AN ACT OF SUBSTITUTION. THE STATUS OF THE OFFSPRING OF SUBSTITUTES: The offspring of an animal sanctified by reason of being declared a substitute for a consecrated animal is in the status of the originally-substituted beast: These are the consecrated animals, the offspring, and the substitutes of which are deemed of equivalent status: (1) the offspring of peace offerings, (2) and their substitute, (3) and their the offspring's and the substitute's offspring, (4) and the offspring of their offspring, to infinity — lo, these are deemed equivalent to peace offerings. And like the animal for which they have been substituted or from which they derive, they require laying on of hands, drink offerings, and waving of the breast and thigh. The same is so of the offspring of an animal declared a substitute for thank-offering, burnt-offering, and the like. The logic clearly requires: just as the substitute shares in the status of the animal in the stead of which it is designated, so its offspring retains the same standing. The catalogue omits reference to the offspring of a burnt-offering. The owner has specified that a female substitute for the burnt-offering; the female can have given birth to a male. A burnt-offering must be male, so we cannot refer to the offspring of a burnt-offering. Then the rule is: He who sets aside a female beast as a burnt-offering — it the beast pastures until it is blemished, then is sold, and its proceeds fall to the Temple-treasury as a freewill-offering.

What about the substitute of a sin-offering, in a case in which the primary consecrated beast having turned out to be unneeded, for instance because the owner has died before the primary beast was offered? (1) The offspring of a sin offering, (2) the substitute of a sin offering, and (3) a sin offering, the owner of any ox which died are left to die. (4) One which was superannuated or (5) one which was lost and turned up blemished, if this is after the owner has effected atonement, is left to die. And it does not impart the status of substitute to an animal designated in its stead. If the owner has effected atonement, the animal is left to die. Then the animal left to die is not going to impart the status of a consecrated beast to one that is designated in its place.

C. THE CONSISTENCY OF THE CATEGORY-FORMATION

I see no component of the category-formation that violates the logic of the hermeneutics, e.g., that makes a point quite out of phase with the principal foci of the established program.

D. THE GENERATIVITY OF THE CATEGORY-FORMATION

The power of the hermeneutics that animates a category-formation to generate further Halakhic problems and solve them, even to extend the limits of the category-formation, should not be missed. The case, recast as a generalization, yields category-formations involving other cases altogether. The issue is, what is the law governing the consequence of performing an action that is illegal but may or may not be effective? Does a person bear the sanctions for an action that produces no valid effects? Or do we maintain that, since the action is null, there is no penalty for the consequences? That issue is active in but hardly limited to the Halakhah before us, and the achievement of the framer of this mighty passage is to show how broad and deep are the implications of the rather simple question, settled before us in an uncompromising way. Judah states the matter well (B. Tem. 2A): "All can be involved so as to effect a valid substitution — *not that a person is permitted to effect a substitution. But if one has effected a substitution, it [that which is designated instead of the beast already consecrated is deemed a substitute [and also consecrated. And the one who does so incurs the penalty of forty stripes.*" Then the opposed category to "forbidden but effective and therefore liable to penalty" must be "forbidden but not effective and therefore not liable to penalty," and a whole new range of Halakhic category-formations becomes theoretically possible. But we ought not be detained by theory, when the facts await analysis.

7.
TRACTATE KERITOT

I. THE DEFINITION OF THE CATEGORY-FORMATION

The category-formation, Keritot, works out a single, simple principle. If one has intentionally done a sin or a crime, for the sins or crimes dealt with here he pays the penalty of extirpation, death before age 60, and if he has done it inadvertently, he expiates the sin through a sin-offering, and if he does not know the facts of the matter, then he presents a suspensive guilt-offering. So the state of one's knowledge, critical to an assessment of intentionality, enters in. Predictably, the hermeneutical principle of taxonomic differentiation comes to expression with the Mishnah's usual lapidary clarity:

> "For those [thirty-six classes of transgressions listed at M. 1:1] are people liable, for deliberately doing them, to the punishment of extirpation, and for accidentally doing them, to the bringing of a sin offering, and for not being certain of whether or not one has done them, to a suspensive guilt offering."
>
> M. 1:2A

We, therefore, deal with penalties for sins or crimes that are differentiated by the attitude of the person who has done them, with special reference to the sin-offering and the suspensive guilt-offering or extirpation. At issue is whether a sin or crime is expiated through a sin-offering or through extirpation, early death or a suspensive guilt-offering. The category-formation then finds its hermeneutical problem in the differentiation of each of its components, and the hermeneutics once again, predictably, dictates the selection and interpretation of its data through the single variable, intentionality.

The subject-matter of the category-formation, Keritot, is only partially revealed in its title, "sins atoned for by extirpation," so we do best by beginning with an outline of the topical program.

    I.   THE SIN-OFFERING: THAT FOR WHICH IT EXPIATES

            A.   Classes of Transgressions that are subject to extirpation or the sin-offering, depending on intentionality

II. THE SIN-OFFERING: SPECIAL CASES

    A. The sin-offering in connection with childbirth
    B. The single sin-offering and multiple sins

III. THE OFFERING OF VARIABLE VALUE

IV. THE SUSPENSIVE GUILT-OFFERING

    A. Cases of doubt in which the suspensive guilt-offering is required
    B. When the animal designated for the suspensive guilt-offering may not be required

The topical program reveals little, but that offerings for various sins or crimes are subject to classification.

So much for the species, sins and their penalties, differentiated by intentionality and awareness. Now, to guide our inquiry into the hypothetical thought-processes that yield the species, what about the genus? Obviously, it is comprised by Sanhedrin-Makkot (with Shebuot), on the one side, and Keritot, on the other. What these category-formations bear in common is that they catalogue sins or crimes and the penalties therefor. The sins or crimes penalized by fines, capital punishment inflicted by man, or flogging are listed in the former, those penalized by offerings or extirpation, received by God or inflicted by God, in the latter. Thus man's power to inflict penalties is spelled out in Sanhedrin-Makkot, and those penalties inflicted by, or involving cultic engagement with, God (extirpation, the sin- or guilt-offering, respectively) are worked out in Keritot. The two species for a genus because of an effect in common: they produce the identical result, the reconciliation of the sinner or criminal with God. So much for the genus, now how does the comparison make possible illuminating contrasts?

To answer that question, we must address two others. First, how are we to contrast the comparable species? Instead of fines, capital punishment, or flogging, for the items of Sanhedrin-Makkot, what is required is either a sin-offering or a suspensive guilt offering or extirpation, for the items of Keritot. Second, what explains that contrast?

A negative experiment begins the inquiry. The point of differentiation between Sanhedrin-Makkot and Keritot does not emerge from a comparison of the sins or crimes the deliberate commission of which is penalized through the earthly court's inflicting the death penalty (and comparable penalties) or the Heavenly court's inflicting the death penalty through shortening of life. Here is a sample.

M. San. 7:4 These are [the felons] who are put to death by stoning: He who has sexual relations with his mother, with the wife of his father, with his daughter-in-law, with a male, and with a cow; and the women who brings an ox on top of herself; and he who blasphemes, he who performs an act of worship for an idol, he who gives of his seed to Molech, he who is a familiar spirit, and he who is a soothsayer; he who profanes the Sabbath, he who curses his father or his mother. he who has sexual relations with a betrothed maiden, he who beguiles [entices a whole town to idolatry], a sorcerer, and a stubborn and incorrigible son.

M. 9:1 And these are those who are put to death through burning: he who has sexual relations with both a woman and her daughter [Lev. 18:17, 20:14], and a priest's daughter who committed adultery [Lev. 21:9].

And these are those who are put to death through decapitation: the murderer, and the townsfolk of an apostate town. A murderer who hit his neighbor with a stone or a piece of iron [Ex. 21:18], or who pushed him under water or into fire, and [the other party] cannot get out of there and so perished, he is liable. [If] he pushed him into the water or into the fire, and he can get out of there but [nonetheless] he died, he is exempt.

M. 11:1 = Bavli 10:1 These are the ones who are to be strangled: he who hits his father and his mother [Ex. 21:15]; he who steals an Israelite [Ex. 21:16, Deut. 24:7]; an elder who defies the decision of a court, a false prophet, a prophet who prophesies in the name of an idol; He who has sexual relations with a married woman, those who bear false witness against a priest's daughter and against one who has sexual relations with her.

M. Keritot 1:1 Thirty-six [classes of] transgressions set forth in the Torah are subject to extirpation: he who has sexual relations with (1) his mother, and (2) with his father's wife, and (3) with his daughter-in-law; he who has sexual relations (4) with a male, and (5) with a beast; and (6) the woman who has sexual relations with a beast; he who has sexual relations (7) with a woman and with her daughter, and (8) with a married woman; he who has sexual relations (9) with his sister, and (10) with his father's sister, and (11) with his mother's sister, and (12) with his wife's sister, and (13) with his brother's wife, and (14) with his father's brother's wife, and (15) with a menstruating woman (Lev. 18:6ff.); (16) he who blasphemes (Num. 15:30), and (17) he who performs an act of blasphemous worship (Num. 15:31), and (18) he who gives his seed to Molekh (Lev. 18:21), and (19) one who has a familiar spirit (Lev. 20:6); (20) he who profanes the Sabbath day (Ex. 31:14); and (21) an unclean person who ate a Holy Thing (Lev. 22:3), and (22) he who comes to the sanctuary when unclean (Num. 19:20); he who eats (23) forbidden fat (Lev. 7:25), and (24) blood (Lev. 17:14), and (25) remnant (Lev. 19:6-8), and (26) refuse (Lev. 19:7-8); he who (27) slaughters and who (28) offers up [a sacrifice] outside [the Temple court] (Lev. 17:9); (29) he who eats leaven on Passover (Ex. 12:19); and he who (30) eats and he who (31) works on the Day of Atonement (Lev. 23:29-30); he who (32) compounds anointing oil [like that made in the Temple (Ex. 30:23-33)], and he who (33) compounds incense [like that made in the Temple], and he who (34) anoints himself with anointing oil (Ex. 30-32); [he who transgresses the laws of] (35) Passover (Num. 9:13) and (36) circumcision (Gen. 17:14), among the positive commandments.

The (abbreviated) lists overlap sufficiently to require a clear point of differentiation as to the same action between the death penalty imposed by man and extirpation imposed by God. The variable — so we now have seen — cannot be the severity or character of the sin or crime, and that is by definition. Nor can it be intentionality, for extirpation at the hands of Heaven, as much as the death penalty inflicted by man depends upon the attitude that motivates the action.

Even though the earthly court penalizes some sins or crimes that do not fall into the jurisdiction of the Heavenly court,[14] the point of differentiation between the Heavenly and earthly court can only be procedural. That is for two disparate reasons.

First, it is because some of the same crimes or sins for which the Heavenly court imposes the penalty of extirpation are those for which, under appropriate circumstances (e. g., sufficient evidence admissible in court) the earthly court imposes the death-penalty. That is, the Heavenly court and the earthly court impose precisely the same ultimate sanction — death — for the same crimes or sins. Where man cannot effect the sanction and consequent expiation, Heaven assures that justice will be done so that the sinner or criminal will pay in years of life but thereby retain his share of eternal life.

But, second, procedural considerations do not end there. The medium of expiation is the other, and obvious, point of differentiation between the Heavenly and the earthly court. The contrast sets God's engagement through the Temple sanctions against man's through the earthly penalties. The particular penalties outlined in the lists of Keritot then form the counterpart, in the specified cases of inadvertence, to the death penalty and that of flogging, in the specified counterpart cases in Sanhedrin-Makkot.

So the components of the genus are represented by these three institutions, [1] the altar or [2] the Heavenly court, represented by Keritot, and [3] the earthly court, represented by Sanhedrin-Makkot. All three exercise concrete and material power, utilizing legitimate violence to kill someone, exacting penalties against property, and inflicting pain. Power, therefore, flows through three distinct but intersecting dominions, each with its own concern, all sharing some interests in common. The Heavenly court attends to deliberate defiance

---

[14] The earthly court, for its part, penalizes social crimes against the community that the Heavenly court, on the one side, and the Temple rites, on the other, do not take into account at all. These are murder, apostasy, kidnapping, public defiance of the court, and false prophecy. The earthly court further imposes sanctions on matters of particular concern to the Heavenly court, with special reference to taboos of sanctification (e.g., negative commandments).

of Heaven, the Temple to inadvertent defiance of Heaven. The earthly court attends to matters subject to man's specific jurisdiction by reason of decisive evidence, proper witnesses, and the like. Then these same matters come under Heavenly jurisdiction when the earthly court finds itself unable to act. Accordingly, we have in our genus, Sanhedrin-Makkot Keritot, a tripartite system of sanctions — Heaven cooperating with the Temple in some matters, with the court in others, and, as noted, each bearing its own distinct media of enforcing the law as well — a complex system of criminal justice aimed at restoring the Israelite sinner or criminal to life in Eden.

Having established the common genus and differentiated principally upon procedural grounds between Sanhedrin-Makkot and Keritot, we turn to Keritot and ask about that category-formation's particular hermeneutics. And here the critical issue is, why does God supervise the process of expiation involving either the sin-offering (and its companions) or extirpation? The answer derives from God's unique knowledge: he knows what is deliberate and what is inadvertent, because he penetrates into the heart of man. That is why the distinction between an offering and extirpation makes a difference in the process of atonement. Offerings expiate those sins that do not are not committed as an act of rebellion against God. These God accepts, graciously, as an appropriate act of atonement for an act for which one bears responsibility but which was not meant as defiance of God. The ones that embody an attitude of rebellion, by contrast, can be expiated not through the surrogate, the blood of the beast, but through that of the sinner himself, who, if he is not put to death by the court here on earth or is not flogged by the court's agents, is cut off in the prime of life. Keritot, therefore, provides for God's intervention where man's justice fails and so forms a necessary link in the circle of reconciliation of Israel(ites) with God.

So the animating principle that pervades Keritot and rationalizes its formal distinctions into weighty differences is simple: God sees into man's heart. That is why the same act produces diverse consequences, based upon the intentionality with which the act is done. Indeed, in its own way that same conception animates the formal exercises on how many sin-offerings are owing for a single action or how many actions may be subsumed under, and expiated by, a single sin-offering. Beyond Keritot, the matter is expressed best in the Halakhah of Shabbat. There it is made explicit: A sin is atoned for by a sin-offering only when the act is inadvertent. A deliberate action is not covered:

> "This is the general principle: All those who may be liable to sin offerings in fact are not liable unless at the beginning and the end, their sin is done inadvertently. But if the beginning of their sin is inadvertent and the end is deliberate, or the beginning deliberate

and the end inadvertent, they are exempt — unless at the beginning and at the end their sin is inadvertent."

M. Shab. 11:6J-K

The distinction between deliberate sin and inadvertent law-violation permeates the Halakhah. But when it comes to the specification of the penalty for sin or crime, Keritot remains the principal point at which the Halakhah makes its statement of the prevailing distinction.

II. THE FOUNDATIONS OF THE HALAKHIC CATEGORY-FORMATION

The principal interest then is in animal-offerings that expiate sin committed inadvertently or unknowingly. The Written Torah contributes to the topic the following statement, at Lev. 5:17-19; I underline the key-language for the guilt-offering.

> "If any one sins, *doing any of the things that the Lord has commanded not to be done, though he does not know it, yet he is guilty and shall bear his iniquity.* He shall bring to the priest a ram without blemish out of the flock, valued by you at the price for a guilt offering, and the priest shall make atonement for him for the error that he committed unwittingly, and he shall be forgiven. It is a guilt offering; he is guilty before the Lord"

Since the generative premise of the Halakhah is the distinction between deliberate and inadvertent sin or crime, with extirpation the penalty for the former, the guilt offering expiating the latter, Scripture has defined the foundations for the articulation and exegesis of the Halakhah. The governing distinction set forth by the Halakhah simply builds upon Scripture's law.

As to expiation of sin through extirpation, the Torah at numerous points states, "that man will be cut off" (e.g., Lev. 17:4, 9; Ex. 30:33, 38, Gen. 17:14, Ex. 12:15, 19, 31:14, Num. 15:31), and the like, in many variations.[15]

---

[15] See H. Albeck, *Shishah Sidré Mishnah*. V. *Seder Qodoshim* (Tel Aviv, 1959), p. 243.

III. THE EXPOSITION OF THE COMPONENTS OF THE GIVEN CATEGORY-FORMATION BY THE MISHNAH-TOSEFTA-YERUSHALMI-BAVLI

I. THE SIN-OFFERING

A. *CLASSES OF TRANSGRESSIONS THAT ARE SUBJECT TO EXTIRPATION OR THE SIN-OFFERING*

M. 1:1 Thirty-six [classes of] transgressions set forth in the Torah are subject to extirpation: he who has sexual relations with (1) his mother, and (2) with his father's wife, and (3) with his daughter-in-law; he who has sexual relations (4) with a male, and (5) with a beast; and (6) the woman who has sexual relations with a beast; he who has sexual relations (7) with a woman and with her daughter, and (8) with a married woman; he who has sexual relations (9) with his sister, and (10) with his father's sister, and (11) with his mother's sister, and (12) with his wife's sister, and (13) with his brother's wife, and (14) with his father's brother's wife, and (15) with a menstruating woman (Lev. 18:6ff .); (16) he who blasphemes (Num. 15:30), and (17) he who performs an act of blasphemous worship (Num. 15:31), and (18) he who gives his seed to Molekh (Lev. 18:21), and (19) one who has a familiar spirit (Lev. 20:6); (20) he who profanes the Sabbath day (Ex. 31:14); and (21) an unclean person who ate a Holy Thing (Lev. 22:3), and (22) he who comes to the sanctuary when unclean (Num. 19:20); he who eats (23) forbidden fat (Lev. 7:25), and (24) blood (Lev. 17:14), and (25) remnant (Lev. 19:6-8), and (26) refuse (Lev. 19:7-8); he who (27) slaughters and who (28) offers up [a sacrifice] outside [the Temple court] (Lev. 17:9); (29) he who eats leaven on Passover (Ex. 12:19); and he who (30) eats and he who (31) works on the Day of Atonement (Lev. 23:29-30); he who (32) compounds anointing oil [like that made in the Temple (Ex. 30:23-33)], and he who (33) compounds incense [like that made in the Temple], and he who (34) anoints himself with anointing oil (Ex. 30-32); [he who transgresses the laws of] (35) Passover (Num. 9:13) and (36) circumcision (Gen. 17:14), among the positive commandments.

T. 1:1 He who anoints [himself] with the oil of anointing [like] that which Moses made in the wilderness, Lo, this one is liable to extirpation. Passover and circumcision, even though [people] are liable to extirpation for deliberate transgression thereof [M. Ker. 1:1P], are not subject to an offering, because they are [commandments] which require affirmative action ["they are subject to, 'Arise and do'"].

T. 1:2 An unclean person who ate Holy Things, and he who comes to the sanctuary while unclean [M. Ker. 1:1 K], even though they are liable for deliberately doing so to extirpation and for accidentally doing so to a sin-offering, are not subject to a suspensive guilt-offering, because they are subject to a sliding-scale-offering.

T. 1:3 He who curses his father and his mother, he who says to his fellow, "Go and carry out an act of liturgy to idolatry," he who incites and he who leads [Israel] astray, false prophets, and conspiring witnesses, even though they are liable to be put to death at the hands of a court, are not subject to bring an offering, because their [transgressions] do not contain a concrete action [M. Ker. 1:2F].

T. 1:6 This is the general principle: [For violation of] any negative commandment containing within itself a concrete deed do [violators] receive the penalty of forty stripes. And for the violation of any which does not contain within itself a concrete deed they do not receive the penalty of forty stripes. And as to all other negative commandments in the Torah, Lo, these are subject to warning. He who transgresses them violates the decree of the King.

T. 1:19 There are five guilt-offerings: a guilt-offering for theft, a guilt-offering for sacrilege, a guilt-offering brought for having sexual relations with a betrothed handmaiden, a guilt-offering of a Nazirite, and a guilt-offering of a *mesora'*.

B. 1:1 VI.1/6A HE WHO COMPOUNDS INCENSE IN ORDER TO LEARN ABOUT IT OR IN ORDER TO HAND IT OVER TO THE COMMUNITY IS EXEMPT. BUT IF HE DOES SO IN ORDER TO SNIFF IT, HE IS LIABLE. BUT HE WHO ACTUALLY SNIFFS IT IS EXEMPT FROM LIABILITY, EVEN THOUGH HE HAS COMMITTED AN ACT OF SACRILEGE.

B. 1:1 VII:1/6B HE WHO POURS ANOINTING OIL ON CATTLE OR UTENSILS IS EXEMPT FROM LIABILITY; IF HE DOES SO OVER GENTILES OR CORPSES, HE IS EXEMPT FROM LIABILITY.

M. 1:2 For those [thirty-six classes of transgressions] are people liable, for deliberately doing them, to the punishment of extirpation, and for accidentally doing them, to the bringing of a sin offering, and for not being certain of whether or not one has done them, to a suspensive guilt offering [Lev. 5:17] — [except for] the one who blasphemes, as it is said, "You shall have one law for him that does anything unwittingly" (Num. 15:29) — excluding the blasphemer, who does no concrete deed.

T. 1:4 He who hits his father and his mother, he who kidnaps an Israelite, an elder who rebels against a court ruling, a wicked and incorrigible son, and a murderer, even though [their transgressions] involve a deed and even though they are subject to be put to death by a court, are not subject to an offering, because they are punished by extirpation.

T. 1:5 These are those [transgressions] punishable by death: he who eats untithed food, a non-priest who ate clean heave-offering, an unclean priest who ate clean heave-offering, and a non-priest, one who had immersed that self-same day, one who lacked proper garments, one who lacked proper completion of rites of purification, one with unkempt hair, one who was drunk, [any of whom] served at the altar — all of them are subject to the death penalty. But the uncircumcised [priest], the priest in mourning, and the priest who [performed the rite while he] was sitting down, Lo, these are subject to warning.

T. 1:20 A drunkard is unfit for the sacred service, and [if he carries out an act of service in the cult] he is liable to the death penalty. What is a drunkard? Any one who has drunk a quarter-log of wine forty days old or older than that. [If] he drank [wine fresh] from his press in a volume of more than a quarter-log, he is exempt. [If] he drank less than a quarter-log of wine four or five years old, whether he mixed it and drank it, or drank it in little sips, he is liable.

M. 2:6 In all forbidden sexual relationships, [if] one is an adult and one is a minor, the minor is exempt. [If] one is awake and one is asleep, the one asleep is exempt. [If] one does the act inadvertently and one deliberately, the one who does it inadvertently is liable to bring a sin offering, and the one who does it deliberately is subject to extirpation [M. 1:2A].

T. 1:16 These are the points of difference between [intercourse with] the betrothed bondwoman and all other forbidden sexual relationships: All other forbidden sexual relationships which are stated in the Torah — Lo, these [others] are liable, in the case of deliberate transgression, to extirpation, and in the case of inadvertent transgression, to a sin-offering, and in a case of uncertain transgression, to a suspensive guilt-offering [M. Ker. 1:2], which is not the case for the one who has intercourse with a betrothed handmaiden [M. Ker. 2:4, M, 2:6D]. All [other] forbidden sexual relationships in the Torah treat the one who does the act under constraint as equivalent to the one who does it willingly, the one who does it unintentionally as equivalent to the one who does it intentionally, [M. Ker. 2:4M], the one who begins the act only as equivalent to the one who actually completes it [M. Ker. 2:4K], the one who is sleeping as equivalent to the one who is awake [M. Ker. 2:6C], the one who does it in the normal way as equivalent to the one who does it not in the normal way, [and the law] imposes a liability for each and every act of sexual intercourse [M. Ker. 2:3C/I], which is not the case with the betrothed handmaiden. In the case of all other forbidden sexual relationships, [the law] has treated a minor as equivalent to an adult, to impose the liability solely on the adult [M. Ker. 2:6B]. But in the case of a handmaiden, if he [the male who had sexual relations] was a minor, Lo, these are exempt from liability. In the case of all other forbidden sexual relationships, both of the participants receive stripes. But in the case of a handmaiden, she receives stripes but he does not receive stripes. In the case of all other forbidden sexual relationships, both parties bring an offering. But in the case of a handmaiden, he brings, but she does not bring [an offering]. In the case of all other forbidden sexual relationships, the penalty is a sin-offering. But in the case of a handmaiden, the penalty is a guilt-offering. In the case of all other forbidden sexual relationships, one brings a female [sin-offering]. But in the case of a handmaiden, one brings a male [guilt-offering] [M. Ker. 2:4G-H]. In the case of all other forbidden sexual relationships, one is liable for each and every act of sexual intercourse. But in the case of a handmaiden, one brings a single offering for many acts of sexual intercourse [M. Ker. 2:3C/I]. In the case of all other forbidden sexual relationships which are stated in the Torah, a court is liable to give instruction in their regard, which not the case for the betrothed handmaiden. In the case of all other forbidden sexual relationships, an anointed priest who gave instruction and did the deed is liable. In the case of the handmaiden, if he did the deed, even though he did not give instruction, he brings a guilt-offering on account of a confirmed case.

T. 1:18 He who has sexual relations with any one of all those who are prohibited by the Torah — he in a single spell of inadvertence, but she in five spells of inadvertence — he brings a single sin-offering. But she brings five sin-offerings. [If] she does so in a single spell of inadvertence, but he does so in five spells of inadvertence, she brings one sin-offering and he brings five sin-offerings. In respect to all prohibited relationships, [if] one is an adult and one is a minor, the minor is exempt. [If] one is awake and one asleep, the one asleep is exempt. [If] one does it inadvertently and the one does it intentionally: the one who does it inadvertently is liable to bring a sin-offering, and [he one who does it intentionally is subject to extirpation [M. Ker. 2:6].

Once the distinction is made between the sin- or guilt-offering and extirpation, all that remains is to form lists of the various crimes or sins. That is what M. 1:1 does for its stated data. The Tosefta then contributes a massive amplification of the entries. As already noted, M. 1:2 then introduces the operative variables. I move 2:6 to the present rubric because of its strong recapitulation of M. 1:2.

II. THE SIN-OFFERING: SPECIAL CASES

A. THE SIN-OFFERING IN CONNECTION WITH CHILDBIRTH

M. 1:3 (1) There are women who bring a [sin] offering [after childbirth], and it is eaten [by the priests], (2) and there are women who bring an offering, and it is not eaten, (3) and there are women who do not bring [an offering]. These [women after childbirth] bring an offering, and it is eaten: She who aborts (1) a sandal or (2) an afterbirth or (3) a fully fashioned foetus or (4) an offspring which is cut up [during delivery]. And so a slave-girl who gives birth brings an offering, and it is eaten.

M. 1:4 These bring [an offering], but it is not eaten: (1) She who aborts, and it is not known what it is that she has aborted; and so: two women who aborted, one [producing] something which is exempt [from the requirement of bringing an offering], and one [producing] something which is liable [to an offering].

T. 1:7 She who aborts after the completion of the days of purifying and she who aborts an eight-month-old foetus, alive or dead, or a child past term and a proselyte who converted while circumcised, and a deaf-mute, an imbecile, and a minor who lacked the completion of atonement rites bring an offering and it is eaten.

T. 1:8 [If] a woman is subject to doubt whether or not she gave birth to anything at all, or [if] she is subject to doubt that it is viable or not viable or [if] she is in doubt that the foetus does or does not bear human appearance, she brings an offering, but it is not eaten.

T. 1:10 A woman who is liable for the offering for giving birth and for yet another offering for giving birth, or an offering for flux and for yet another offering for flux brings a single offering. [If she is subject to an offering for] giving birth and an offering for suffering flux, she brings two offerings. [If she is subject to an offering] for possibly having given birth and [to an offering for] certainly having given birth, [to an offering for] possibly suffering a flux and [to an offering for] certainly having suffered a flux, she brings an offering for each obligation to which she is certainly subject among them [and] has fulfilled her obligation.

M. 1:5 These are those who do not bring [an offering at all]: She who aborts a foetus (1) filled with water, (2) filled with blood, (3) filled with variegated matter; she who aborts something shaped like (1) fish, (2) locusts, (3) abominable things, or (4) creeping things; she who aborts on the fortieth day. And [she who produces] that which comes forth from the side.

T. 1:12 All those who owe pairs of bird-sacrifices stated in the Torah — half of them [the sacrifices] are a sin-offering, and half of them are burnt-offerings, except for the bird-offering of a proselyte, for even though they are an obligation, both of them were burnt-offerings. [If] he wanted to offer beasts for those which are required, he may offer them [as he wishes]. [If] he offered beasts as burnt-offerings for atonement, he has fulfilled his obligation. [If he did so with] meal-offerings and drink-offerings, he has not fulfilled his obligation. They spoke of a pair of birds only to lighten the burden for him. [If] he brought one sort of offering for his purification from cereal, let him go and bring the same for his atonement-offering. [If he brought one sort of offering] for his Nazirite-offering, let him go and bring the same for his atonement-offering.

M. 2:1 [There are] four whose atonement is not complete [until they bring an offering]. And four bring [an offering] for [a transgression done] deliberately as they do for [one done] inadvertently. These are those whose atonement is not complete [until they bring an offering]: (1) The male-Zab [afflicted with flux in terms of Lev. 15], and (2) the female-Zabah, and (3) the woman who has given birth, and (4) the *mesora'* [afflicted with the skin disease discussed at Lev. 13-14].

B. 2:1 II.2/8B A PROSELYTE IS PREVENTED FROM EATING HOLY THINGS UNTIL HE HAS OFFERED HIS PAIR OF BIRDS. IF HE HAS PRESENTED ONE BIRD IN THE MORNING RITE, HE MAY EAT HOLY THINGS IN THE EVENING [THOUGH HE STILL OWES THE OTHER]. ALL OF THE PAIRS OF BIRDS THAT ARE LISTED IN THE TORAH ARE DESIGNATED, ONE FOR A SIN OFFERING AND ONE FOR A BURNT OFFERING, BUT HERE BOTH OF THEM ARE BURNT OFFERINGS. IF HE HAS BROUGHT HIS OBLIGATORY OFFERING IN THE FORM OF CATTLE [THIS COVERS TWO BIRDS], AND HE HAS CARRIED OUT HIS OBLIGATION. IF HE OFFERED A BURNT OFFERING AND A PEACE OFFERING, HE HAS CARRIED OUT HIS OBLIGATION. IF HE OFFERED A MEAL-OFFERING AND A PEACE-OFFERING, HE HAS NOT CARRIED OUT HIS OBLIGATION. THE PROVISION THAT HE MAY BRING A PAIR OF BIRDS HAS BEEN STATED ONLY AS A LENIENT RULING [TO MAKE THE PROCESS EASIER FOR THE PROSELYTE].

M. 2:2 These bring [an offering for a transgression done] deliberately as for [one done] inadvertently: (1) He who has sexual relations with a bondwoman; and (2) a Nazirite who was made unclean; and (3) for [him who utters a false] oath of testimony, and (4) for [him who utters a false] deposit oath.

The composite scarcely acknowledges the particular hermeneutics we have identified. The rules at M. 1:3-5 organize the data introduced at M. 1:3. These then establish a formal match with M. 2:1-2, which makes a point that does respond to the hermeneutical center of this category-formation, the distinction between deliberate and inadvertent action in the liability to an offering for atonement. The second group, joined for formal reasons to the first, then accounts for the inclusion of the entire complex here.

B. *THE SINGLE SIN-OFFERING AND MULTIPLE SINS*

M. 1:7 The woman who is subject to a doubt concerning [the appearance of] five fluxes, or the one who is subject to a doubt concerning five miscarriages brings a single offering. And she [then is deemed clean so that she] eats animal sacrifices. And the remainder [of the offerings] are not an obligation for her. [If she is subject to] five confirmed miscarriages, or five confirmed fluxes, she brings a single offering. And she eats animal sacrifices. But the rest [of the offerings, the other four] remain as an obligation for her [to bring at some later time]

M. 2:3 Five bring a single offering for many transgressions. And five bring a sliding scale offering. These bring a single offering for many transgressions: (1) He who has sexual relations with a bondwoman many times, and (2) a Nazirite who is made unclean many times. (3) he who suspects his wife of adultery with many men, and (4) a *mesora'* who was afflicted by nega'im many times. [If] he brought his birds and [then] was afflicted with a nega [the skin ailment discussed at Lev. 13-14], they [the birds] do not go to his credit until he brings his sin offering.

T. 1:13 Four sorts of transgressor bring [an offering] in [the case of deliberate transgression] as in the case of inadvertent [transgression]. In the case of all of them, if they are under constraint, they are exempt [from liability] except for the Nazir. Five bring a sliding-scale-offering [M. Ker. 2:3A]. There are among them poor and rich, there are among them the poorest of the poor. A *mesora'* and one who has given birth [M. Ker. 2:4E4-5] are poor and rich, bringing one for one. One who contaminates the sanctuary [M. Ker. 2:4E3] is the poorest of the poor, bringing two offerings for one infringement.

T. 1:21 He who has sexual relations with his mother is liable on two counts. He who has sexual relations with his father's sister is liable on two counts.

M. 2:4 A woman suffered many miscarriages — (1) she aborted a female during eighty days, and went and aborted another female during eighty days following, and (2) she who bore a multiple of abortions ["twins" — each in the period of purifying of the foregoing].

M. 3:2 [If] he ate [forbidden] fat and [again ate] fat in a single spell of inadvertence, he is liable only for a single sin offering, [If] he ate forbidden fat and blood and remnant and refuse [of an offering] in a single spell of inadvertence, he is liable for each and every one of them. This rule is more strict in the case of many kinds [of forbidden food] than of one kind. And more strict is the rule in [the case of] one kind than in many kinds: For if he ate a half-olive's bulk and went and ate a half-olive's bulk of a single kind, he is liable [since they are deemed to join together to form the requisite volume for incurring guilt]. [But if he ate two half-olive's bulks] of two [different] kinds, he is exempt.

T. 2:1 [If] one witness says, "He ate forbidden fat," and one witness says, "He ate permitted fat," [or if] one witness says, "He ate forbidden fat," and a woman says, "He ate permitted fat," [or if] one woman says, "He ate forbidden fat," and one woman says, "He ate permitted fat," he brings a suspensive guilt-offering. [If] one witness says to him, "You ate forbidden fat," and he says, "I ate permitted fat," he is exempt.

T. 2:2 All the same are he who eats and he who dissolves [produce into a liquid] and drinks it and one who anoints [with it] — if he ate and went and ate again and went and ate again — if there is from the beginning of the first act of eating to the end of the last act of eating sufficient time for the eating of a half-loaf of bread, the several acts of eating join together. And if not, they do not join together [M. Ker. 3:2E]. [If] he drank and went and drank again and went and drank again, if there i, from the beginning of the first act of drinking to the end of the last act of drinking sufficient time for the drinking of a quarter-*log*, the several acts of drinking join together [to form the requisite volume to render him unclean or culpable]. And if not, they do not join together.

M. 3:3 And how much should he who eats them tarry? [He is not liable] unless he tarries from beginning to end for sufficient time to eat a half-loaf [of bread]. [If] one ate unclean foods [or] drank unclean liquids, drank a quarter-*log* of wine, and entered the sanctuary and tarried there, [the measure of time between entering the Temple having eaten unclean food or drunk wine is] sufficient time to eat a half-loaf [of bread].

M. 3:4 There is he who carries out a single act of eating and is liable on its account for four sin offerings and one guilt offering: An unclean [lay] person who ate (1) forbidden fat, and it was (2) remnant, (3) of Holy Things, and (4) it was on the Day of Atonement.

M. 3:5 There is he who carries out a single act of sexual intercourse and becomes liable on its account for six sin offerings: He who has intercourse with his daughter is liable on her account because of violating the prohibition against having intercourse with (1) his daughter, and (2) his sister, and (3) his brother's wife, and (4) his brother's father's wife, and (5) a married woman, and (6) a menstruating woman. And who has intercourse with his daughter's daughter is liable on her account because of violating the prohibitions against having intercourse with (1) his daughter's daughter, and (2) his daughter-in-law, and (3) his wife's sister, and (4) his brother's wife, and (5) his brother's father's wife, and (6) a married woman, and (7) a menstruating woman.

M. 3:6 He who has sexual relations with his mother-in-law may turn out to be liable on her account because of the prohibitions against having sexual relations with (1) his mother-in-law, and (2) his daughter-in-law, and (3) his wife's sister, and (4) his brother's wife, and (5) his father's brother's wife, and (6) a married woman and (7) a menstruating woman. And so is the case for him who has sexual relations with the mother of his mother-in-law and with the mother of his father-in-law.

While a sin-offering must be presented to expiate a specifically-designated sin, there are circumstances in which a single offering serves, and these are listed at M. 1:7, 2:3-4, with a fine systematic study of mixtures at M. 3:2, 4-6. The generic hermeneutics does its work here.

III. THE OFFERING OF VARIABLE VALUE

M. 2:4 These bring an offering of variable value: (1) for [oaths such as are involved in] refusing to give evidence ["for hearing the voice" (Lev. 5:1)]; and (2) for an expression of the lips [a rash oath]; and (3) for contaminating the sanctuary and its Holy Things; and (4) the woman who has given birth, and (5) the *mesora'*. And what is the difference between the bondwoman and other forbidden sexual relationships (Lev. 18), that they are not alike (1) either in punishment or (2) in the offering [required for the transgression]? For all [other] forbidden sexual relations [are expiated] with a sin offering, but forbidden sexual relations with a bondwoman, with a guilt offering. All other sexual relations [are atoned] with a female animal, but the bondwoman, with a male animal. In respect to all other sexual relations, all the same are the man and the woman. They are equivalent as to flogging and as to an offering. But in respect to the bondwoman, the man is not treated as equivalent to the woman in regard to flogging, and the woman is not regarded as equivalent to the man in respect to an offering. In respect to all other forbidden sexual relations Scripture has treated him who begins the act as culpable as him who completes it, and he is liable for each and every act of sexual relations [which is not the case here, M. 2:3C1]. But this strict rule does the law stringently impose in the case of the bondwoman: that it treats in her regard the man who does the act intentionally as equivalent to the one who does it inadvertently.

B. 2:4D-E I.1/10B THERE ARE SOME WHO BRING THE OFFERING THAT IS REQUIRED BOTH IN POVERTY [BIRD] AND IN WEALTH [LAMB], SOME WHO BRING THE OFFERING REQUIRED ONLY IN POVERTY, SOME WHO BRING THE OFFERING REQUIRED OF THE POOREST OF THE POOR [A MEAL OFFERING]. A WOMAN WHO HAS GIVEN BIRTH PRESENTS THE OFFERING THAT IS REQUIRED OF THE POOR AND OF THE RICH [A DOVE, A LAMB]; A *MESORA'* BRINGS THE OFFERING REQUIRED OF THE POOR [THE PAIR OF BIRDS]; AND THOSE CULPABLE FOR REFUSING TO GIVE EVIDENCE ["FOR HEARING THE VOICE" (LEV. 5:1)]; AND (2) FOR AN EXPRESSION OF THE LIPS [A RASH OATH]; AND (3) FOR CONTAMINATING THE SANCTUARY AND ITS HOLY THINGS BRING THE OFFERING REQUIRED IN POVERTY OR OF THE POOREST OF THE POOR [A MEAL OFFERING]. SOMETIMES ONE BRINGS ONE OFFERING IN PLACE OF ONE [IN THE CASE OF POVERTY], TWO IN PLACE OF TWO, TWO IN PLACE OF ONE, AND ONE IN PLACE OF TWO — ON THIS BASIS YOU DERIVE THE LESSON THAT THE TENTH EPHAH MUST BE WORTH A PENNY. THE WOMAN WHO HAS GIVEN BIRTH ONE BRINGS ONE OFFERING IN PLACE OF ONE — THE PIGEON THAT SHE OWED ANYHOW AS A SIN OFFERING PLUS ONE BIRD IN PLACE OF A LAMB; A *MESORA'* BRINGS TWO IN PLACE OF TWO — TWO BIRDS IN PLACE OF TWO LAMBS; THOSE CULPABLE FOR REFUSING TO GIVE EVIDENCE ["FOR HEARING THE VOICE" (LEV. 5:1)]; AND (2) FOR AN EXPRESSION OF THE LIPS [A RASH OATH]; AND (3) FOR CONTAMINATING THE SANCTUARY AND ITS HOLY THINGS BRING TWO BIRDS IN PLACE OF ONE LAMB; AND THE POOREST OF THE POOR BRING ONE TENTH OF AN EPHAH IN PLACE OF TWO BIRDS.

Scripture has distinguished between a sin-offering of fixed value and one of variable value; I see little more here than the systematization of inert data.

IV. THE SUSPENSIVE GUILT-OFFERING

A. *Cases of Doubt in which the Suspensive Guilt Offering is Required*

M. 3:1 [If] they said to him, "You have eaten forbidden fat," he brings a sin offering. [If] one witness says, "He ate," and one witness says, "He did not eat" — [of if] a woman says, "He ate," and a woman says, "He did not eat," he brings a suspensive guilt offering. [If] a witness says, "He ate," and he says, "I did not eat" — he is exempt [from bringing an offering]. [If] two say, "He ate," and he says, "I did not eat" — he is exempt.

M. 4:1 It is a matter of doubt whether or not one has eaten forbidden fat, And even if he ate it, it is a matter of doubt whether or not it contains the requisite volume — Forbidden fat and permitted fat are before him, he ate one of them but is not certain which one of them he ate — His wife and his sister are with him in the house — he inadvertently transgressed with one of them and is not certain with which of them he transgressed — The Sabbath and an ordinary day — he did an act of labor on one of them and is not certain on which of them he did it — [in all the foregoing circumstances] he brings a suspensive guilt offering.

M. 4:2 Just as, if he ate forbidden fat and [again ate] forbidden fat in a single spell of inadvertence, he is liable for only a single sin offering [M. 3:2A], so in connection with a situation of uncertainty involving them, he is liable to bring only a single guilt offering. If there was clarification [of the facts of the matter] in the meantime, just as he brings a single sin offering for each and every transgression, so he brings a suspensive guilt offering for each and every [possible] transgression. Just as, if he ate forbidden fat, and blood, and remnant, and refuse, in a single spell of inadvertence, he is liable for each and every one [M. 3:2B], so in connection with a situation of uncertainty involving them, he brings a suspensive guilt offering for each and every one.

T. 2:4 [If] it is a matter of doubt whether or not one has sinned, he brings a suspensive guilt-offering [M. Ker. 4:1, 2A-B]. [If] he has sinned, but is not certain what particular sin he has committed, he brings a sin-offering. [If] he has sinned and is informed of the character of his sin but he has forgotten what sin he has committed, Lo, this one brings a sin-offering [M. Ker. 4:2C-D], and it is slaughtered for the sake of whichever [sin he has committed] and it is eaten. Then he goes and brings a sin-offering for that sin of which he is informed, and it is slaughtered for the sake of whatever [particular sin he has done] and it [too] is eaten.

T. 2:5 He who brings one sin-offering for two distinct sins — it is set out to pasture until it is disfigured, then sold. And [the man] brings with half of its proceeds one for this sin, and with half of its proceeds one for that sin. Two sin-offerings designated for a single sin — let the man offer whichever one of them he prefers. The second then is put out to pasture until it is blemished, and then it is sold, and its proceeds fall [to the Temple-treasury] as a freewill-offering. Two sin-offerings for two sins — this one is slaughtered for one of them, and that one is slaughtered for one of them.

T. 2:10 [If] one forgot the Torah and committed many transgressions, he is liable to bring a sin-offering for each and every one of them. How so? [If] he knew that there is such a thing as forbidden fat but said, "This is not the sort of forbidden fat for which we have been declared liable" — [if] he knew that there is such a thing as [the prohibition of] blood but said, "This is not the sort of blood for which we have been declared liable" — he is liable for each and every violation of the law.

T. 2:11 He who eats an olive's bulk of forbidden fat, an olive's bulk of refuse, an olive's bulk of remnant, and an olive's bulk of that which is unclean in one spell of inadvertence brings [one] sin-offering [M. Ker. 4:2E].

M. 5:1 If one ate the blood of slaughtering in the case of cattle, wild beast, and fowl, whether [said animals are] unclean or clean, the blood [shed in the case of] stabbing, and the blood [shed in the case] of tearing [the windpipe or gullet], and the blood let in bloodletting, by which the lifeblood flows out — they are liable on its account. Blood from the spleen, blood from the heart, the blood from the eggs [or testicles], the blood of fish, the blood of locusts, blood which is squeezed out [that is, blood which oozes out of the arteries after the lifeblood flows out] — they are not liable on their account.

T. 2:18 He who eats an olive's bulk of blood of a clean beast, wild animal or fowl brings a sin-offering. [If] it is a matter of doubt whether or not he ate [it], he brings a suspensive guilt-offering. But he is liable only for the blood of slaughtering alone.

T. 2:19 The blood shed in the case of stabbing, blood shed in the case of tearing the windpipe or the gullet, and blood let in bloodletting, by which the life-blood flows out — they are liable on its account [M. Ker. 5:1C]. Blood from the spleen, blood from the heart, blood from the kidneys, blood from the limbs — Lo, these are subject to a negative commandment. Blood of those who go on two feet, blood of eggs [testicles], blood of creeping things is prohibited. But they are not liable on their account. Blood of fish and blood of locusts, Lo, this is permitted.

T. 2:20 He who mashes forbidden fat and swallowed it, he who coagulates [forbidden] blood and ate it, if it is of the volume of an olive's bulk, is liable. [If] it was mixed up with others, if it is of the volume of an olive's bulk, Lo, this one is liable. [If] it was cooked with others, Lo, this is prohibited if it is of sufficient quantity to impart a flavor to the whole mixture. [If] one ate a half olive's bulk or drank a half olive's bulk of a single sort [of prohibited fat or blood], Lo, this one is liable.

M. 5:3 A woman [after giving birth] who brought a sin offering of fowl in a case of doubt [as to the character or viability of the foetus], if before the neck was severed, it became known to her that she had certainly brought forth [a viable foetus] — let her make it into an unconditional offering [for certainty]. For the kind of animal that she brings in the case of uncertainty she brings in

the case of certainty.

T. 2:22 The woman who brought a sin-offering of fowl in a case of doubt as to whether or not she has given birth to a viable offspring and learns that she has indeed not given birth [M. Ker. 5:3D-G], Lo, this [bird] is unconsecrated. She should give it to her girlfriend [who requires it]. And the one who discovers that she has certainly given birth — let her make it into an unconditional offering [M. Ker. 5:3F]. For the sort of animal which she brings in a case of uncertainty she brings in a case of certainty [M. Ker. 5:3G].

M. 5:4 A piece of meat of unconsecrated food and a piece of meat of Holy Things — [if] one ate one of them, and it is not known which of them he ate — he is exempt. [If] he ate the second, he brings an unconditional guilt offering.

T. 3:1 A piece of meat of forbidden fat of Holy Things and a piece of meat, of unconsecrated food — [if] one ate one of them and does not know which of them he ate he brings [delete: a sin-offering and] a suspensive guilt-offering. [If] he ate the second, he brings a sin-offering and an unconditional guilt-offering.

T. 3:2 A piece of meat of Holy Things and a piece of meat of unconsecrated food [M. Ker. 5:4A] — [if] one ate the first and then went and ate the second in a single spell of inadvertence he brings a sin-offering and an unconditional guilt-offering. [If] he ate them in two spells of inadvertence, he brings two sin-offerings and one unconditional guilt-offering

T. 3:3 A piece of meat [of forbidden fat] of refuse and a piece of meat of [if] one ate one of them and does not know which of them he ate, he brings a suspensive guilt-offering.

T. 3:4 A piece of meat of forbidden fat which is refuse and a piece of meat [of forbidden fat which is] of unconsecrated food — [if] one ate one of them and does not know which of them he ate he brings two suspensive guilt-offerings. [If] he ate the second, he brings two sin-offerings.

T. 3:5 A piece of meat of forbidden fat which is refuse and a piece of meat which is remnant — [if] one ate one of them and does not know which of them he ate he brings two suspensive guilt-offerings.

M. 5:5 A piece of meat of unconsecrated food and a piece of meat consisting of forbidden fat — [if] one ate one of them, and it is not known which of them he ate — he brings a suspensive guilt offering. [If] he ate the second, he brings a sin offering. [If] one person ate the first, and another came along and ate the second, this one brings a suspensive guilt offering and that one brings a suspensive guilt offering.

M. 5:6 A piece of meat consisting of forbidden fat and a piece of meat of Holy Things — [if] one ate one of them, and it is

not known which of them he ate — he brings a suspensive guilt offering. [If] he ate the second, he brings a sin offering and an unconditional guilt offering. [If] one person ate the first, and another came along and ate the second, this one brings a suspensive guilt offering, and that one brings a suspensive guilt offering.

M. 5:7 A piece of meat consisting of forbidden fat and a piece of meat consisting of forbidden fat of Holy Things — [if] one ate one of them, and it is not known which of them he ate — he brings a sin offering. [If] he ate the second, he brings two sin offerings and an unconditional guilt offering. If one person ate the first, and another came along and ate the second, this one brings a sin offering and that one brings a sin offering.

M. 5:8 A piece of meat consisting of forbidden fat and a piece of meat consisting of forbidden fat which is remnant — [if] one ate one of them, and it is not known which of them he ate, he brings a sin offering and a suspensive guilt offering. [If] he ate the second, he brings three sin offerings. [If] one person ate the first, and someone else came along and ate the second, this one brings a sin offering and a suspensive guilt offering, and that one brings a sin offering and a suspensive guilt offering.

T. 4:1 He who eats five pieces of meat from a single animal-sacrifice in five dishes in a single spell of inadvertence brings only a single sin-offering. And in a matter of doubt concerning them, he brings only a single suspensive guilt-offering. [But if he does so] in five spells of inadvertence, he brings five sin-offerings. And in a matter of doubt concerning them, he brings five suspensive guilt-offerings. This is the general principle: Whoever brings a sin-offering for a matter of certainty, brings a suspensive guilt-offering for a matter of uncertainty. And whoever does not bring a sin-offering for a matter of certainty does not bring a guilt-offering for a matter of uncertainty. But if he ate five pieces of meat from a single animal-sacrifice before the sprinkling of the blood, even in a single spell of inadvertence, he brings a sin-offering for each and every piece [which he ate].

The suspensive sin-offering covers a case in which a person is not certain whether or not he actually has committed a sin inadvertently. The cases that exemplify the interstitialities present no surprises and leave no ambiguities.

B. *WHEN THE ANIMAL DESIGNATED FOR THE SUSPENSIVE GUILT OFFERING MAY NOT BE REQUIRED*

M. 6:1 He who brings a suspensive guilt offering, and is informed that he did not commit a sin — if this was before it was slaughtered, it [the animal] is set out to pasture until it is blemished, then it is sold, and its proceeds fall [to the Temple treasury] as a freewill offering. If after it was slaughtered he is [so] informed, the blood is to be poured out. And the meat goes forth to the place of burning. [If the man is informed after] the blood is [properly] tossed, the meat is to be eaten.

M. 6:2 An unconditional guilt offering is not subject to the foregoing rule. If [the man is so informed] before it is slaughtered, it goes forth and pastures in the flock. [If the man is so informed] after it has been slaughtered, Lo, this is to be buried. [If the man is so informed after] the blood has been tossed, the meat goes out to the place of the burning. The ox which is stoned is not subject to the foregoing rule. If [it turns out that the ox has not killed a man] before it is stoned, it goes forth and pastures in the flock. [If it turns out that the ox has not killed a man] after it is stoned, it is available for benefit. The heifer whose neck is broken is not subject to the foregoing rule. If [the murderer is found] before its neck is broken, it goes forth and pastures in the flock. [If the murderer is found] after its neck is broken, it is buried in its place. For on account of a matter of doubt did it come in the first place. It has made atonement for its matter of doubt and goes its way [having served its purpose].

T. 2:6 Two people whose sin-offerings were mixed up in respect to two sins — it is set out to pasture until it is blemished and then sold. And let him bring with the proceeds of half of it a sin-offering for this one, and with the proceeds of half of it a sin-offering for that one. Two sin-offerings for a single sin — let the man offer whichever one of them he prefers. The second is put out to pasture until it is blemished, then it is sold, and its proceeds fall [to the Temple-treasury] as a freewill-offering. Two sin-offerings for two sins — this one is slaughtered for the sake of one of them, and that one is slaughtered for the sake of one of them.

T. 2:7 Two whose sin-offerings were confused — the sin-offering of an individual and the sin-offering of an individual, [or] the sin-offering of the community and the sin-offering of the community, [or] the sin-offering of an individual and the sin-offering of the community — even if they are two distinct sorts — this one is slaughtered for the sake of one of them, and that one is slaughtered for the sake of one of them.

T. 2:8 He who brings his sin-offering and slaughtered it — it is a matter of doubt whether or not its blood was [properly] tossed — he has carried out his obligation. If he was lacking the completion of his atonement, it is a matter of doubt whether or not it has gotten dark [so that the blood was tossed by night] — Lo, this one brings the sin-offering of fowl as a matter of doubt.

T. 2:17 The Day of Atonement which coincides with the Sabbath and he did an act of labor, whether before it or afterward, he is exempt from the requirement of bringing a suspensive guilt for the entire day effects atonement.

T. 2:23 In the case of her the neck of whose bird is broken, and who [then] is informed [that she certainly has given birth] — let its [the bird's] blood be drained out. [Its blood] has effected atonement. It is prohibited as to eating. [If this takes place] after its blood has been drained out [its blood] has effected atonement is prohibited for enjoyment. For to begin with it is brought on account of doubt. It has effected atonement for its matter of doubt and gone its way [M. Ker. 6:2K].

T. 4:2 He who brings a sin-offering or a guilt-offering for a sin and is informed that he did not commit a sin — [if [this is] before it is slaughtered, it goes forth and pastures in the flock] M. Ker. 6:2B. [If this is] after it is slaughtered, its appearance is allowed to rot, and it is taken forth to the place of burning.

T. 4:3 A beast which is to be stoned, [if] the witnesses against it turn out to be conspirators, is available for benefit. A heifer whose neck is to be broken, [if] the witnesses against it turn out to be conspirators, is available for benefit. Those who owe a heifer whose neck is to be broken, for whom the Day of Atonement passed, are liable to bring it after the Day of Atonement. [If] one found the murderer, one way or the other, they slay him, since it is said, "You shall not thus pollute the land in which you live, for blood pollutes the land, and no expiation can be made for the land, for the blood that is shed in it, except by the blood of him who shed it" (Num. 35:33).

M. 6:4 Those who owe sin offerings and unconditional guilt offerings for whom the Day of Atonement passed [without their making those offerings] are liable to bring [the offerings] after the Day of Atonement. Those who owe suspensive guilt offerings are exempt. [The Day of Atonement has atoned for those transgressions that may or may not have taken place.] He who is subject to a doubt as to whether or not he has committed a transgression on the Day of Atonement, even at twilight, is exempt. For the entire day effects atonement.

M. 6:5 A woman who owes a bird offering as a matter of doubt, for whom the Day of Atonement passed [without her making said bird offering] is liable to bring it after the Day of Atonement. For it renders her fit for eating animal sacrifices [and is not expiatory in character]. A sin offering of fowl which is brought on account of doubt, if after its neck is pinched it is known [that the woman has not actually sinned at all], Lo, this is to be buried.

M. 6:6 He who sets aside two selas [Lev. 5:15] for a guilt offering and purchased with them two rams [at one sela each] for a guilt offering — if one of them [went up in value so that it now] is worth two selas, let it be offered for his guilt offering. And the second, [which is no longer required, the proper value having been attained in the first of the two,] is set out to pasture until it is blemished, then sold, and its proceeds fall [to the Temple treasury] as a freewill offering [M. Tem. 3:3: that is, in the class of a guilt offering, the owners of which have effected atonement]. [If] he [who sets aside two selas for a guilt offering] purchased with them two rams for unconsecrated use, one worth two selas and one worth ten zuz — the one worth two selas is offered for his guilt offering [incurred through the act of sacrilege]. And the second is for restitution for his sacrilege. [If] one was for a guilt offering and one was for unconsecrated purposes, if the one for the guilt offering was worth two selas it is offered for his guilt offering. And the second is for restitution for his sacrilege. And let him bring with it a sela and its added fifth.

T. 4:5 A guilt-offering for thievery, a guilt-offering for sacrilege, a guilt-offering for sexual relations with a betrothed handmaiden, which [offering] one brought at an age of less than thirteen months and one day, not worth [two] silver sheqels, are invalid. [If] one brought them at an age of more than thirteen months and one day, even if they are superannuated, they are valid.

T. 4:6 A guilt-offering of a Nazir and a guilt-offering of a *mesora'* which one brought at an age of more than twelve months are invalid. [If] one brought them at an age of less than twelve months, even on the eighth day [of their life], they are valid. [If] one brought them at the value of a sela, [if] one brought them at the value of a sheqel, [if] one brought them at the value of five denars, they are valid.

T. 4:7 A. He who separates two selas for a guilt-offering land] purchased [M. Ker. 6:6A] with one of them a ram for a guilt-offering — if it was worth two selas, it is to be offered as his guilt-offering. And the [funds for the] second fall to [to the Temple-treasury] as a freewill-offering. If not, let it be put out to pasture until it is blemished and then be and let him bring with its proceeds a guilt-offering worth two selas And as to the second, let it[s proceeds] fall [to the Temple-treasury] [If] he purchased with them [the two selas] two rams for a guilt-offering. If one of them was worth two selas, it is to be offered as his guilt-offering. And the second is to be put out to pasture until it is blemished then is to be sold, and its proceeds are to fall to the Temple-treasury as a freewill offering [M. Ker. 6:6A-D]. If not, then both of them are to be put out to pasture until they are blemished, then they are to be sold, and let him bring with them a guilt-offering worth two selas. And the rest [of the proceeds] fall [to the Temple-treasury] as a freewill-offering.

T. 4:8 [If] he purchased with them two rams for unconsecrated use, one of them worth two selas and one of them worth ten zuz the one which is worth two selas is to be offered as his guilt-offering.

And the second is his restitution for sacrilege. [If] one was for guilt-offering and one for unconsecrated purposes, if the one purchased as a guilt-offering is worth two selas, it is to be offered as his guilt-offering. And the second is for the restitution for sacrilege. Let him [further] bring a sela and its added fifth form his own property [M. Ker. 6:6E-L].

T. 4:9 [If] he purchased one ram for a sela and fattened it up, so that, Lo, it is worth two, it is valid. Let him [however] bring a sela from his own property.

T. 4:10 [If] he separated one ram from his flock, worth, at the time of its being separated, a sela, and at the time of its being offered up, two, it is valid. [If] it was worth two selas at the time of its separation and at the time of its being offered up, one sela, it is invalid.

M. 6:7 He who sets aside his sin offering and dies — his son should not bring it after him [for a sin the son has committed (M. Tem. 4:1)]. Nor should one bring for one sin [a beast set aside in expiation] for another — even [a beast set aside as a sin offering] for forbidden fat which he ate last night should he not bring [as a sin offering] for forbidden fat which he ate today, since it is said, "His offering for his sin" (Lev. 4:28) — that his offering should be for the sake of his [particular] sin.

T. 4:11 A. He who brings a suspensive guilt-offering for a matter of doubt concerning forbidden fat or for a matter of doubt concerning blood, and is informed that he did not commit a sin, [if this happened] before it was slaughtered, it goes forth to pasture in the flock. If this happened] after it was slaughtered, its appearance is allowed to rot and it goes forth to the place of burning.

M. 6:8 [With funds] consecrated [for the purchase of] a female lamb [as a sin offering], they purchase a female goat. [With funds] consecrated [for the purchase of] a female goat [as a sin offering], [they bring] a lamb. [With funds] consecrated [for the purchase of] a female lamb and a female goat [they purchase] turtledoves or young pigeons (Lev. 5:7). [With funds] consecrated [for the purchase of]turtle doves or young pigeons [they purchase] a tenth of an ephah [of fine flour, for a meal offering]. How so? [If] one set aside [funds] for the purchase of a female lamb or a female goat and then grew poor, he may bring a bird. [If] he grew still poorer, he may bring a tenth of an ephah [of flour]. [If] he set aside funds for a tenth of an ephah [of flour] and got rich, he may bring a bird. [If] he got still richer, he may bring a female lamb or a female goat. [If] he set aside a female lamb or a female goat and they were disfigured, if he wants, he may bring a bird with their proceeds. [If] he set aside a bird and it was disfigured, he should not bring a tenth of an ephah with its proceeds, for a bird is not subject to redemption.

T. 4:14 [If] he separated coins for the tenth of an ephah or fine flour and got rich — let him add to them [the coins] and purchase with it [the money] turtle-doves or pigeons. [If] he separated turtle-doves or pigeons and got rich, [if they have] not been expressly designated, let them be left to die, for fowl is not subject to redemption [M. Ker. 6:8L]. [If they have been] expressly designated, that which is the sin-offering is left to die. But that which has been designated as a burnt-offering is offered as a burnt-offering. [If] he set aside coins for turtle-doves and pigeons and got rich, let him add and purchase with them [the whole sum] a female lamb and a female goat [M. Ker. 6:8].

We pursue a question of detail: if a suspensive guilt-offering turns out not to be required, how do we dispose of the animal that has been designated for that purpose? How do we deal with the situation of those obligated to sin- and guilt-offerings whose sin is expiated by the Day of Atonement (M. 6:4)? These and associated questions do not respond to the particular hermeneutics of the category-formation but to the considerations of the generic hermeneutics.

IV. DOCUMENTARY TRAITS

A. THE MISHNAH AND THE TOSEFTA
The familiar relationship persists.

B. THE BAVLI
Beyond its exegetical work, not surveyed here, I see little of importance in the Bavli's presentation of the Halakhic category-formation.

C. THE AGGADAH AND THE HALAKHAH IN THE BAVLI
The free-standing composites are to be taken up one by one, each in its context.[16] What we wish to know is, first, why has the free-standing composite in a Bavli-construction been inserted where it stands? Second, how has the inclusion of the composition affected our understanding of the topic or proposition that defines the primary framework of discussion — Halakhic exposition of the Mishnah and parts of the Tosefta and *baraita*-corpus?

---

[16] I summarize briefly the discussion in my *Rationality and Structure: The Bavli's Anomalous Juxtapositions*. Atlanta, 1997: Scholars Press for South Florida Studies in the History of Judaism, which draws upon my *The Talmud of Babylonia. A Complete Outline*. Atlanta, 1995-6: Scholars Press for *USF Academic Commentary Series*. IV.B. *The Division of Holy Things and Tractate Niddah. Bekhorot through Niddah*.

I.F THE ANOINTING OIL:

The topic is introduced by the immediately-preceding Mishnah-statement. I see no animating proposition in this compilation of topical information.

V.C THE OFFERINGS OF A PROSELYTE:

The reason for the inclusion is obvious: the Mishnah has omitted reference to the proselyte's offerings, and the Talmud has explained why his offerings have been omitted. Then comes a free-standing exposition on the theme. The point is made that the proselyte's offerings really do correspond to the Israelite's. His are different but equivalent, and Scripture is explicit. Just as your forefathers entered the covenant only with circumcision and immersion and sprinkling of blood through the sacrifices, so they [proselytes] will enter the covenant only through circumcision, immersion, and sprinkling of blood on the altar — that is the paramount proposition. The character of the prior list can have left the contrary impression, so a sustained demonstration is required to right matters.

XIII.B A PREGNANT WOMAN OR NURSING MOTHER EATS WHAT OTHERS MAY NOT EAT, BUT ONLY IN LIMITED VOLUME:

The immediately preceding discussion sets forth rules governing the eating, in very small volume, of prohibited food. That may take place over a long period of time, so that the requisite volume of food for which culpability is incurred is not consumed in so brief a period as to warrant being taken into account. We then turn to another case in which forbidden food may be eaten; it is the pregnant woman. To her applies the opposite consideration: she may eat only a limited volume of forbidden food, but there is no restriction that requires her to eat it over a protracted period of time. So she enters the picture in order to give a pertinent, but diametrically opposite, case from the one that has been discussed: now not time but volume matter.

XXVII.B ACQUIRING OWNERSHIP: WHEN DOES THE INITIAL OWNER GIVE UP HOPE OF RECOVERING PROPERTY AND SO RELINQUISH TITLE?

Including this significant discussion makes a profound point. The superficial intersection is topical. In the immediately preceding discussion, we take up the issue of assigning ownership of an abandoned beast. The topic that now comes forward is abandoning ownership of property in general. But the more profound connection is not to be missed. We have been discussing the attitude of a person who dedicates a beast: is it conditional or unconditional? The premise therefore is this: the man's heart is what has moved him, we assume that he has resolved to dedicate the beast unconditionally. That principle calls to mind other ways in which the owner of property gives up his rights of ownership, and, once more, we are reminded, attitude is all. Just as a person may dedicate something to the Temple without condition or qualification, so he may give up ownership of his property through an act of will. That is, he relinquishes ownership of property that he has lost when he gives up hope of recovering it. It goes without saying that that attitude is not subject to qualification or condition. By including what is in fact a free-standing essay, the framer of the large-scale composite has vastly deepened our grasp of the principle operative in his basic Mishnah-commentary, namely, the matter of condition or stipulation as it affects rights of possession and ownership. Seeing the issue of the status of the animal that has been dedicated in this larger context affords us a perspective on what is at stake, and that, is one's attitude towards one's possessions, whether animals given to the Temple or property of which one has lost possession. On the one side, an act of consecration, on the other, an attitude of despair — these form counterparts. Were I a preacher, I would then formulate a sermon based on the contrast between trust in God contained in an act of unconditional consecration, as against the vagaries of trust in property, which we give up by not an act of consecration and hope, but one of despair and renunciation of hope.

XXVIII.D SINS FOR WHICH THE DAY OF ATONEMENT EFFECTS ATONEMENT:

The context is a reasonable one: the kinds of sin for which the Day of Atonement effects atonement. The principal concern of the thematic composite is precisely the opposite: to specify the matters for which the Day of Atonement does not effect atonement at all. And that comes down to a recurrent point, subject to dispute: is uncleanness a matter of sin at all? This is made explicit in the following language: For all your sins..., and not 'for all your occasions of uncleanness,' which are not matters of sin in any event, thus eliminating the sin offering brought by the woman after she has given birth, which is a purification rite. That same matter is systematically demonstrated for other categories. The point then is to differentiate sin from uncleanness and to demonstrate that uncleanness concerns access to the Temple and has little bearing on one's moral condition. That too offers an important theological point, and the contrast between the discussion of sins for which the Day of Atonement effects atonement and other considerations altogether — which the composite draws sharply — then sets forward a most fundamental principle.

XXIX.B ATTAINING ATONEMENT WITH THE INCREASE IN THE VALUE OF CONSECRATED PROPERTY:

This theoretical problem is introduced because the Mishnah-passage provides an illustration of how consecrated property may increase in value and the consequence of such an event. But the theoretical issue is quite distinct from the context in which it is discussed. The issue is framed in this language: can a man attain atonement with the increase in the value of consecrated property? Where his own efforts have led to the increase in value, beyond what is required for the original purpose for which he consecrated a beast, there is a strong case to be made that he may designate that increase in value for some other, also holy purpose, e.g., an offering that he has to make. He has not made secular use of what he consecrated, but he has taken for himself the right to designate, in his own behalf, the particular sacred use to which the increase may be put. The case can also be made that he may not attain atonement with that increase, because the original act of consecration, which has defined the status of the property, e.g., the beast, was not for the purpose that he now has in mind. So, in general terms, the question has been raised: may or may not a person gain atonement through the increase in the value of consecrated property? Introducing the question at just this point is absolutely required, since the Mishnah's case invites precisely this question. But the question is one of theory, and a variety of considerations now enters into the matter: the man's own effort, the conflict between a general act of consecration and an act of consecration for a particular purpose. But the deeper issue circulates throughout: if a person consecrates something, may he make himself a partner with God in the utilization of what he has given to God? Here too, the problem is deepened by what is a theological issue formulated in practical, legal terms of the cult. The problem concerns man's partnership with God in the ownership of the natural world, with special attention to man's right to effect his purposes through what he has donated for God's: is the confluence of interest plausible or inappropriate, sharing or hubris?

XXXII.B ISSACHAR OF KEFAR BARQAI

This singleton has already been dismissed; it is topically relevant but generates no profound thought.

The upshot is simply stated. Most, though not all, of the free-standing topical composites not only make important points of their own but also impart to the context in which they are located a theological dimension that, without them, would be absent. These points emerge.

[1]   The proselyte is fully equivalent to the home-born Israelite. The rules of the cult demonstrate that fact.
[2]   Food that is prohibited may nonetheless be utilized if it affords no ma-

terial benefit, e.g., is eaten over a long period of time, or if it is eaten in such small volume as to provide no nourishment of consequence. Prohibitions, then, are set aside when they mark distinctions between the permitted and the prohibited that really make no difference. Only what makes an important difference, e.g., in sustaining life is subject to the prohibitions of the Torah.

[3] Ownership of property depends upon one's attitude toward the property. If one consecrates the property, God through the Temple becomes the owner. An act of will alienates the rights of ownership. If one relinquishes ownership by reason of despairing of recovering possession of the property, he also loses the rights of ownership. So one may give up property either as a gift to Heaven or as a surrender to bad fortunate. Ownership by itself therefore makes little difference; one's attitude toward one's property, on the one side, and one's disposition of possessions, on the other, govern. One does well, therefore, to hold with open arms; one does better to give up ownership of property to Heaven as an act of donation than relinquish ownership to violence as an act of despair.

[4] Various classifications affect a person, and they are not to be confused with one another. A person finds himself in a variety of grids, each covering a particular territory of life. He may be unclean or clean, with consequences having to do with the Temple. He may do a religious duty or commit a sin, with consequences having to do with the moral life. The rites of the Temple, where they matter, concern not the cultic life of cleanness or uncleanness but the moral life of sin and atonement. The Day of Atonement — the single most consequence exercise of the cult — makes a difference to the moral condition of a human being, not to his cultic classification. The theological statement that morality takes priority over ritual, and that right — forgiveness of sin and atonement — stands above rite will hardly have surprised the prophets.

When we can explain the connections people make, we also can follow the rationality of the conclusions that they draw. The connections between the topic defined in the context of Mishnah-exegesis and that of the free-standing compositions and composites of a topical character yield the conclusions just now set forth. Generalizations about the system that animates the document as a whole will have to await an examination of the entire repertoire of connections between Mishnah-problems and their exegesis and extra-Mishnaic topics and their exposition. The four points we have identified in Bavli tractate Keritot cannot be taken up in isolation from the rest of the document. The demonstration of a single coherent structure imposes its own logic upon the exposition of what may or may not emerge as a cogent and uniform system.

If I had to select a single recurrent problem that attracts the interest of the authors of compositions and compilers of composites, it is the theory of classification, specifically, the subdivision of a genus into species, on the one side, and the way in which Scripture teaches us how to accomplish that generative problem of thought, on the other. This problem is in two parts: how does a given action subdivides into two or more classifications; how do two or more actions coalesce into a single classification. A second problem that occurs wherever relevant concerns the relationship of intentionality and culpability. A third recurrent exercise is to demonstrate the scriptural foundations of Mishnah-propositions. A fourth is the proof that authorities rule in a consistent way, so that their opinions prove harmonious. A fifth is the inquiry into how differences of opinion rest upon reasonable, but conflicting, principles; disputes are not irrational (or personal!) but always involve good reason for each side's ruling. A sixth is the introduction of an abstract, theoretical problem into a concrete case, e.g., may a prohibition apply to what is already prohibited? A sixth is the extension to a variety of concrete problems of a single, encompassing conception, e.g., the sin offering atones for a concrete action, done unwittingly and later found out, and is not generalized but highly particular; the complementary conception that the suspensive guilt offering is governed by the same rule and corresponds, in the case of what may or may not have taken place, to the situation of a sin offering presented when knowledge of what has happened is certain and precise. What we have, in other words, is the application of the generic hermeneutics of the Halakhah.

V. THE HERMENEUTICS OF KERITOT

A. WHAT FUSES THE HALAKHIC DATA INTO A CATEGORY FORMATION?

How the Halakhic data fuse into a category-formation is now self-evident. It is because of the sanction for inadvertent sin, which is an offering. Hence, in the present context, in the Temple, God's abode, man meets God; here the offering is brought that expiates inadvertent sins or crimes. God is party to the transaction, for reasons already spelled out. And, corresponding to the Temple, it is in the course of the Israelite's life that God uniquely intervenes, shortening the years of the deliberate sinner in response to the offense against life represented by deliberate sin or crime of the specified character. And that brings us back to the classes of transgressions that God punishes and man does not punish: sins involving sex, the Temple, and the violation of negative commandments (e.g., not to eat forbidden fat, not to work on the Day of Atonement and the like). None of these represents a social sin, and none endangers the social order. All involve God and principally God, and none encompasses a victim other than God. So the whole holds together.

Where else, if not in the activities subject to extirpation or the sin-offering (and so too with the other offerings treated here) will God's power to know precisely what man intends be better brought to bear? Sins or crimes that affect the social order, that endanger the health of the commonwealth, come to trial in the court conducted by sages and are penalized in palpable and material ways: death, flogging, and the like. Here God does not intervene, because man bears responsibility for this-worldly transactions. But just as man shortens the life of the criminal or sinner in the matters specified in Sanhedrin and exacts physical penalty in the matters covered by Makkot (not to mention Shebuot, where specified), so God shortens the life of the criminal or sinner in matters of particular concern to God. These are matters that, strictly speaking, concern only God and not the Israelite commonwealth at large: sex, food, the Temple and its cult, the laws of proper conduct on specified occasions. Where the community does not and cannot supervise, God takes over, he who knows what man does in private and what animates and motivates his actions. Israel does Israel's business, God does God's. For both the upshot is the same: sin or crime is not indelible. An act of rebellion is expiated through life's breath, an act of inadvertent transgression through the blood of the sacrificial beast, with the same result: all Israel, however they have conducted themselves in their span of time on earth, will enjoy a portion in the world to come: all but the specified handful, enter to eternal life beyond the grave.

That explains what is unique to Keritot and defines its principle of selection and interpretation of its data, which is its distinguishing the unintentional sin, penalized by a sin- or guilt-offering, from the intentional one, penalized by extirpation. The reason that that critical distinction concerns us in the particular Halakhah at hand is self-evident. Here, at the cult, is where God intervenes. He accepts the blood-offering as an act of expiation of the inadvertent sin — or he rejects it, if improperly motivated; and instead he imposes early death. It is God above all who knows what is in man's heart and can differentiate intentional from unintentional actions. And it also is God who has the heaviest stake in the matter of intentional sin, for intentional sin represents rebellion against the Torah and God's rule through the Torah. So the category-formation finds its most appropriate setting in the division devoted to the altar, and it forms the ideal medium for delivering its particular message.

B. THE ACTIVITY OF THE CATEGORY-FORMATION

Made up mainly of lists of sins or crimes expiated by specified offerings, the tractate carries forward the investigation of sin and the penalty thereof, now with special attention to the use of animal offerings to expiate sins committed inadvertently. At issue to begin with is the penalty of extirpation, inflicted by Heaven for deliberately doing the sins specified above, matched by the sin-offering, required when said sins are inadvertent. These fall into three main categories: incest and other forms of improper sexual relationships, blasphemy, and violations of specified negative commandments (not to impart uncleanness to the Temple, not to eat Holy Things and the like). We note that the earthly court penalizes some of these same actions through flogging, as Chapter Three of Makkot indicates. So what we see here is how God's court not only, or in addition to, the earthly court, takes its part in removing the consequences of sin or crime. The tri-partite system of penalties — in the hands of, respectively, God, what we should call civil authorities (sages, king), and priests — functions to express the interests of the three components of the politics of holy Israel, the three agencies that legitimately inflict violence, God, king through sages, and priests.

The second penalty for inadvertent sin is the offering of variable value, and once more, we list those who are required to present such an offering, and special situations in that regard. The third is the suspensive guilt-offering, presented when one has some reason to suppose that he has carried out a sin but lacks adequate, positive grounds for confessing inadvertent commission of a sin. That once more carries us to address cases of doubt and how these are to be resolved. All of this forms a tight fit.

DESIGNATING AN OFFERING FOR A PARTICULAR ACT OF SINFULNESS: Since we are concerned to match the sin or crime with the correct penalty, we cannot find surprising the Halakhic principle that for an animal to serve in expiation of a given sin, it must be correctly designated for that purpose and only for that purpose. That is a point that we meet many times in the Halakhah, e.g., in the presentation of animal and meal offerings. Not only must the punishment fit the crime or sin, but the particular punishment must match the particular criminal or sinner. What that means is that the beast that the inadvertent sinner or criminal designates for the particular sin or crime that he has committed must be offered by the priest for that particular man and (it goes without saying) that sin or crime and no other. The animal designated as a suspensive guilt offering turns out not to be needed, the man having found out he did not commit the act he thought he might have done. That animal can serve some other purpose, since the designation turns out to have been in error; the proceeds of the beast are available for a freewill offering. A different rule responds to the mis-designation of the unconditional guilt offering. Here there was no doubt, at the moment the beast was designated, that the offering was required. It is, then, an act of sanctification carried out in error and is null.

THE SUSPENSIVE GUILT-OFFERING: The affect of the Day of Atonement comes under consideration. It functions as does a suspensive guilt offering, that is, to make atonement in cases where whether the sin has been committed is in doubt. That accounts for the role of the Day of Atonement in the atonement process; it has no bearing on the requirement of sin- or unconditional guilt-offerings; these must be paid for the specified deed.

THE GENERIC HERMENEUTICS OF THE HALAKHAH: It is one thing to define the hermeneutics of the category-formation, quite another to identify the points at which that hermeneutics engages with the data, or at which the category-formation itself transforms the facts into useful knowledge. What I see, in the main, is a composite of inert information, analyzed through the generic hermeneutics, with much attention to the matter of interstitiality.

C. **THE CONSISTENCY OF THE CATEGORY-FORMATION**
The category-formation is economical and internally coherent.

D. **THE GENERATIVITY OF THE CATEGORY-FORMATION**
I see no marks of generativity in the category-formation as I have accounted for it. Once the hypothetical reconstruction of the process of category-formation — comparison of common traits of classifications to constitute a genus, speciation of the classifications by contrasts of where they differ — has done its work, I discern little more than the classification and hierarchization of data. As in the kindred tractates, Sanhedrin-Makkot, so here too, the Halakhah focuses on two matters: the catalogues of sins, the disposition of the offering presented in expiation thereof. The secondary development at unit two — the case of multiple sin offerings, whether a single sin-offering for many sinful actions, or several sin-offerings for a single, complex one — represents the generic hermeneutics, which accounts for the largest part of the category-formation's exegetical activity.

But the failure of the hermeneutics to generate interesting problems and suggestive extensions and amplifications should not surprise us. For the purpose of establishing the category-formations, Keritot and Sanhedrin-Makkot, in the end is to organize data into lists. Once the traits of data for a given list are established, the intellectual task has come to fulfillment, and the scholarly one of data-collection and organization is all that remains. So in Keritot we deal only with crimes or sins that require God's role in the process of saving people from the effects of willful or inadvertent violation of the torah, in Sanhedrin-Makkot with crimes or sins that the expiation of which depends on man's action. The category-formations in both cases lack generativity because they fully respond to their respective hermeneutical programs — selection and interpretation of data — in the construction of their lists. Only where the lists intersect does the hermeneutics come to the fore, and that is only to effect the differentiation of the two category-formations — its sole task.

8.
TRACTATE MEILAH

I. THE DEFINITION OF THE CATEGORY-FORMATION

The category-formation, Meilah, sacrilege, provides the occasion for an exercise in comparison and contrast of what has been sanctified with what is available for secular use. Viewed in broadest terms, the species, sacrilege, encompasses that which man has sanctified to God, which man may not convert to his own use. Then the counterpart species of the common genus can only be, that which belongs to man, which is available for secular and private benefit. But so global a context for analogical-contrastive analysis, — God's versus man's property — hardly illuminates. What suggestive, generative problems can possibly present themselves? So we must immediately limit matters. This the topical program of the category-formation does for us. Its primary (but not sole) focus centers upon sacrilege committed against animal-offerings (and their analogues). Here is the outline of the category-formation:

   I.   SACRILEGE COMMITTED AGAINST SACRIFICES IN PARTICULAR
        A.   When the Laws of Sacrilege Apply to an Offering
        B.   Stages in the status of an offering: the point at which the Laws of sacrilege apply to various offerings
        C.   Cultic Property that is Not Subject to Sacrilege but that also Is Not to be Used for Non-Cultic Purposes

   II. SACRILEGE OF TEMPLE PROPERTY IN GENERAL
        A.   Sacrilege Has Been Committed Only When the Value of a Perutah of Temple Property Has Been Used for Secular Purposes
        B.   Sacrilege Is Defined by the One Who Does It or by the Thing to which It Is Done
        C.   Sacrilege Effects the Secularization of Sacred Property
        D.   Agency in Effecting an Act of Sacrilege

The first unit focuses upon sacrilege committed against animal offerings, and the second, sacrilege defined analogously, now against property devoted to the Temple and its upkeep. Hence, our hypothetical process of comparison and contrast must limit itself to animals that man has designated for the altar as against animals that he has not consecrated. The cognate category-formations are, then, Zebahim and Hullin, each representing a species of the genus before us. But, once defined, the comparison is not the illuminating point, the contrast is. Then how, and to what end, do we contrast the two species of the genus, animals that serve man's purposes, secular and sacred, specifically, animals that man has kept for his own use with animals he has devoted to God?

To address that question, we start with the fundamental method of the hermeneutics of comparison and contrast that I propose has given shape and structure to the Halakhic category-formation. Beginning from the starting point, we therefore have to answer the question, How does the Halakhah ordinarily deal with comparable genera and their species, thus the sacred and the secular species of the same genus? That question, happily, has a definitive answer: in its labor of hierarchical classification, the Halakhah differentiates the species at the higher status, leaving undifferentiated the comparable species at the lower. In the present case then, we have a perfectly familiar exemplification of the analytical rule. Specifically, since in our category-formation we deal with animate beings (and inanimate analogies thereto), we turn to that *other* animate being that defines the very center of things, who is man. If man is the genus, in this system the species can only be, Israel and the nations. And how does the taxonomic process undertake its task of hierarchical classification?

The answer is very simple. The Halakhah performs an acute and detailed taxonomy of Israel, but treats the nations as undifferentiated. Its "they" all look alike, its "we" is infinitely sub-speciated. In that way, the Halakhah gives its signal and accomplishes its goal of hierarchical classification, The higher classification being differentiated, the lower, not, here, the Halakhah discerns in Israel a number of classifications, e.g., priests, Levites, Israelites and so on (as at M. Qid. 4:1ff.), hierarchizing the classes of Israel. But the Halakhah does not differentiate taxa and classify and sub-speciate gentiles, treating all gentiles as a single taxon. Since gentiles by definition bear the uncleanness of corpses, the Halakhah colors them all the color of death, which is white.

That case, with numerous counterparts, guides us in the speciation and subspeciation of sacrilege, in identifying the power of analogy to encompass initially-unrelated data and to establish a structure and a system out of discrete rules. The process of analogical-contrastive analysis thus leads us to anticipate in the Halakhah of Meilah a comparative hermeneutics of differentiation, an explicit classification of stages in the condition of a sanctified beast at which sacrilege and other, comparable considerations pertain. Then what will generate problems for analysis will be a particular hermeneutics of Meilah, on how, in the differentiated chapters of the story of the beast from the act of sanctification to the ultimate disposal or utilization of the carcass, the possibility of sacrilege pertains. The particular hermeneutics of Meilah will extend the selection and interpretation of data to consideration of what other, comparable conditions, besides conversion of the sacred to personal purposes, disqualify the beast or disrupt the realization of the original purpose in sanctifying it. And that hermeneutics is not a matter of abstract theory; it explicitly governs the articulation of the Halakhah by one of the many triumphs of the Rabbinic Halakhic category-formations. Then, to substantiate that claim of mine, here is one case among many of how the hermeneutics of Meilah shapes the data into an explicit account of the classification of stages or conditions, as to sanctification, of the animal that has been sanctified for the altar:

[1] STAGE ONE: SACRILEGE APPLIES: A sin offering, and a guilt offering, and communal sacrifices of peace offerings — the laws of sacrilege apply to them once they have been sanctified.

[2] COMPARABLE RULES PERTAIN, CONCERNING THE CONDUCT OF THE PRIESTHOOD: [When] they have been slaughtered, they are rendered fit to be made invalid by a tebul-yom and by one whose rites of atonement have not yet been completed and by being left overnight.

[2] STAGE TWO. COMPARABLE RULES CONCERNING THE CONDUCT OF THE PRIESTHOOD: [When] their blood has been tossed, they are liable on their account because of violation of the laws of refuse, remnant, and uncleanness.

[1] SACRILEGE NO LONGER APPLIES, THE MEAT HAVING BEEN PERMITTED FOR CONVERSION BY A PRIVATE PARTY (THE PRIEST): The laws of sacrilege do not apply to the meat. Then, for the same reason —

[1] SACRILEGE CONTINUES TO APPLY: THE SACRIFICIAL PORTIONS REMAINING SUBJECT TO PROHIBITION: But the laws of sacrilege apply to the sacrificial parts until they are taken out to the ash heap.

M. 2:5

These and comparable rules yield the following sequence, applicable to a variety of cases, imposing a common structure upon them all:

1. A householder declares a secular beast to be sanctified for a particular purpose, e.g., as a sin-offering. If used for secular purposes, an act of sacrilege has been committed.
2. Once the animal has produced its blood, the animal is subject to the considerations of invalidation represented by the engagement of priests who are have not fully emerged from a cultic uncleanness; or of priests who have the wrong intentionality. The beast remains subject to sacrilege.

3. Once the blood of the animal has been validly tossed, the priests may make use of the meat that is assigned to them; the laws of refuse, remnant, and uncleanness come into play for the priesthood (whose intentionality and activity take effect);
4. And then the laws of sacrilege no longer apply, since what is available for secular use to anyone is not susceptible to sacrilege.
5. In the case of Holy Things, once an act of sacrilege has been committed, the Holy Thing is secular, a further act cannot be committed.
6. The laws of sacrilege continue to apply to what belongs to God until these have been disposed of.

The key rules are Nos. 4 through 6: the laws of sacrilege apply to a sacrifice that has never been subjected to the private use of the priests but has always remained the possession of the altar. Sacrilege ceases to pertain to a sacrifice that at some point has belonged to the priests. Once the priests have tossed the blood of the offering on the altar, they have done their work; they have a right to the meat of offerings other than burnt-offerings. That is the point at which the meat remaining from the offering concomitantly is secularized, available for (some) men's use, not only God's enjoyment.

The upshot may be simply stated. An animal, originally secular, when identified to serve as an offering passes through four stages:

1. It is consecrated, therefore susceptible to sacrilege;
2. It is susceptible to invalidation by a person not wholly in a state of cleanness but also not unclean;
3. It is susceptible to the prohibitions of refuse, remnant and uncleanness;
4. And it is no longer susceptible to sacrilege.

The act of sanctification on its own commences a process, it does not permanently transform what was secular and now has been sanctified, and sanctification is not treated as an indelible substance, inhering in things, only as a status that, in the nature of the process, is transient. The fact that what is sanctified may be resecularized underscores the Halakhic principle that directs attention to matters of attitude and negotiation and away from the working of the sacred *ex opere operato*. Here, as time and again we have seen elsewhere, sanctity is a matter of status and classification, not of substance, tangibility, and actuality. And that expresses in the category-formation the main point of the hierarchical taxonomizing that the Halakhah favors, which here is the variable status of that which has been sanctified.

So much for the structure, what of the system? That is to say, our task now is to identify that which animates, imparts dynamism, to the Halakhic category-formation. With its self-evident focus upon the power of man's will to classify, therefore, to intervene in the hierarchization of things, the hermeneutics of comparison and contrast logically and inevitably identifies as its dynamic the variable intentionality of man. Here that logic comes to a simple equation. Since it is man's intentionality that classifies the beast that he possesses as his own as sacred, man's intentionality cannot also classify the same beast as secular. In a conflict of intentionalities, the one in effect must dominate. Hence the contrary intentionality, to treat the sanctified beast as secular, is null, and the contradictory action of sacrilege can only come about, take effect, unintentionally. Two consequences follow.

First, the act of sacrilege to which the written Torah refers at Lev. 5:15 is unintentional and inadvertent; here Scripture explicitly confirms the inner logic of the matter.

Second, once the unintentional act of sacrilege has taken place, the action nullifies the prior intention, and what has been secularized remains secular.

Thus, the principal problem that occupies the Halakhah is, what is the status of a Holy Thing that has been subjected to sacrilege? The governing theory is, if we punish a person for inadvertently committing sacrilege, we treat as secular what has been subjected to sacrilege.

The definition of matters encompasses a broad range of possibilities, extending far beyond the altar itself. Sacrilege involves any use of Holy Things for private purposes. What is at issue, however, is limited. Once any party, for any reason, has legitimate access to Holy Things, then the classification, sacrilege, no longer pertains, even though the individual Israelite who has unintentionally carried out the act has no right to make use of the Holy Things. A simple case suffices to make the point. Parts of offerings that may be eaten by the priests are not subject to sacrilege, because someone may enjoy them, even if the non-priest may not. Once something is permitted for other than divine use, sacrilege does not pertain.

To state matters concretely, Scripture best serves. What happens when Holy Things unintentionally are used for ordinary purposes, God's property for the common Israelite's benefit? To state that the sacrilege was not deliberate, the value received must be returned, along with a penalty of a fifth more. But in the case of inadvertent sacrilege, no further penalty is imposed. The pertinent verse of Scripture is as follows:

> "If anyone commit a trespass of sacrilege and *sin through error* in the Holy Things of the Lord, then he shall bring his forfeit to the Lord, a ram without blemish for a guilt offering, and he shall make restitution for that which he has done amiss in the holy thing and

add the fifth part thereto."

Lev. 5:15-16

We must lay stress on the phrase, "through error." The Halakhah rests upon the principle that people do not deliberately steal from God. The Halakhah does not conceive "the Holy" to inhere in such a way that sacrilege of an unintended character bears the same dire results as that which is intended. The governing distinction is in line with the principle that sanctification is not a matter of substance but of status. Ordinarily, what happens is, the guilty party restores the value to the sanctuary of what he has misappropriated, including also a heavy fine, but then what has been subjected to sacrilege is treated as secular. So sanctification is not inherent but imputed — a familiar notion in the Halakhah.

II. THE FOUNDATIONS OF THE HALAKHIC CATEGORY-FORMATION

The relevant verse of Scripture has already been cited. While important, it is still a detail within the larger logical unfolding of the whole.

III. THE EXPOSITION OF THE COMPONENTS OF THE GIVEN CATEGORY-FORMATION BY THE MISHNAH-TOSEFTA-YERUSHALMI-BAVLI

I. SACRILEGE COMMITTED AGAINST SACRIFICES IN PARTICULAR

A. WHEN THE LAWS OF SACRILEGE APPLY TO AN OFFERING

M. 1:1 Most Holy Things which one slaughtered in the south [side of the altar, instead of the north side, where the rite is supposed to be carried out] — the laws of sacrilege apply to them. [If] one slaughtered them in the south and received their blood in the north, in the north and received their blood in the south. [if] one slaughtered them by day and tossed the blood by night, by night and tossed the blood by day, or [if] one slaughtered them [with the intention of eating that which is usually eaten or offering up that which is usually offered up] outside of their proper time or outside of their proper place — the laws of sacrilege apply to them. A general principle did R. Joshua state: "Whatever has had a moment of availability to [for use by] the priests — the laws of sacrilege do not apply thereto. And [whatever] has not [yet] had a moment of availability to the priests — the laws of sacrilege do apply thereto." What is that which has had a moment of availability to the priests? That which [after the proper tossing of the blood] has been left overnight, and that which [after the proper tossing of the blood] has been made unclean, and that which [after the proper tossing of the blood] has gone forth [beyond the veils]. And what is that which has not [yet] had a moment of availability to the priests? That which has been slaughtered [with improper intention to eat that which is usually eaten or to offer up that which is usually offered up] outside of its proper time or outside of its proper place. And that, the blood of which invalid men have received or tossed.

T. 1:1 R. Joshua says, "Most Holy Things which one slaughtered at the southern [side of the altar] — the laws of sacrilege apply to them. If one slaughtered them at the south and received their blood at the north, at the north and received their blood at the south, [if] one slaughtered by day and tossed the blood by night, by night and tossed the blood by day, put those drops of blood which are to be put below, above, or those which are to be put above, below, or those which are to be put [on the altar] at the inside, outside, or those which are to be put outside, inside, or one slaughtered them [intending to offer up that which is offered up and to eat that which is eaten] outside of the proper time or outside of the proper place, the laws of sacrilege apply to them."

T. 1:2 A general principle did R. Joshua state: "Whatever has had a moment of availability to the priests — the laws of sacrilege [read: do not] apply thereto. And whatever has not [yet] had a moment of availability to the priests, the laws of sacrilege do apply thereto. As to that which is made refuse in the case of Most Holy Things, the laws of sacrilege apply thereto. But in the case of Lesser Holy Things, the laws of sacrilege do not apply thereto."

T. 1:3 There is remnant [meat left overnight, the blood of the animal from which the meat derives not having been tossed on the altar at the proper time) to which the laws of sacrilege apply, and there is remnant to which the laws of sacrilege do not apply. How so? [If] the meat was left over night before the tossing of the blood, the laws of sacrilege apply to it. [If this happened] after the tossing of the blood, the laws of sacrilege do not apply. But as to that which is unclean, whether it was made unclean before the tossing of the blood or whether it was made unclean after the tossing of the blood, the laws of sacrilege do not apply to it, for the priestly frontlet effects atonement for it.

M. 1:2 The meat of Most Holy Things which went forth [beyond the veils] before the tossing of the blood — R. Eliezer says, "The laws of sacrilege apply to it. And they are not liable on its account because of violation of the laws of refuse, remnant, and uncleanness." R. Aqiba says, "The laws of sacrilege do not apply to it. Truly are they liable on its account because of violation of the laws of refuse, remnant, and uncleanness." Said R. Aqiba, "Now, Lo, he who separates a sin offering which is lost, and separated another in its stead, and afterward the first turns up, and Lo, both of them are available — is it not so that just as its blood exempts its flesh [from the laws of sacrilege], so it exempts the flesh of its fellow? Now if [the proper tossing of] its blood has exempted the flesh of its fellow from being subject to the laws of sacrilege, is it not logical that it should exempt its own flesh?"

M. 1:3 The sacrificial parts of Lesser Holy Things which went forth [beyond the veils] before the tossing of the blood — R. Eliezer says, "The laws of sacrilege do not apply to them. And they are not liable on their account because of violation of the laws of refuse, remnant, and uncleanness." R. Aqiba says, "The laws of sacrilege do apply to them. And they are liable on their account because of violation of the laws of refuse, remnant, and uncleanness."

T. 1:4 The meat of Most Holy Things which went forth [beyond the veils before the tossing of the blood [M. Me. 1:2A], and the blood was tossed in its behalf — R. Eliezer says, "The laws of sacrilege apply to it, and they are not liable on its account because of violation of the laws of refuse, remnant, and uncleanness." R. Aqiba says, "The frontlet [of the high priest] effects atonement for that which goes forth. The laws of sacrilege do not apply to it. Truly are they liable on its account because of violation of the laws of refuse, remnant, and uncleanness."

T. 1:5 Said R. Simeon, "When I passed the Sabbath in Kefar Beth Page a certain one of the disciples of R. Aqiba came upon me and said to me, 'Meat which has gone forth beyond the veils and in behalf of which the blood was tossed has been accepted.' But when I came and laid the matters out before my colleagues in Galilee, they said to me, 'And is it not invalidated? So how [does the frontlet] effect atonement for that which is invalid?' So when I came and laid the matters out before R. Aqiba himself then he said to me, 'Lo, he who separates his sin-offering, which is lost, and separated another in its stead, and afterward the first turns up, and Lo, both are available [M. Me. 1:2D] — the laws of sacrilege apply to both of them. [If] one slaughtered it, and Lo, its blood is setting in cups 'the laws of sacrilege apply to both of them. 'If the blood of one of them is tossed, it has afforded protection for the flesh of its fellow from liability to the laws of sacrilege. 'If it has afforded protection for the flesh of its fellow from liability to the laws of sacrilege, even though it [the fellow] is invalid, it surely is logical that it should afford protection for its own flesh [as well]!'"

T. 1:6 The sacrificial parts of Lesser Holy Things which went forth [beyond the veils] before the tossing of the blood [M. Me. 1:3A], and the blood was tossed in their behalf — R. Eliezer says, "The laws of sacrilege do not apply to them, and they are not liable on their account because of violation of the laws of refuse, remnant, and uncleanness." And R. Aqiba says, "The priestly frontlet effects atonement for that which goes forth. The laws of sacrilege apply to them, and they are liable on their account because of refuse, remnant, and uncleanness" [M. Me. 1:3B, C].

M. 1:2-3 Tossing the blood takes effect even after part of the animal goes forth beyond the veil only if the meat in particular is what has been carried beyond the limits, but if it was part of the blood, then tossing the rest of the blood is null. So too it has been taught on Tannaite authority: If one slaughtered the animal in silence [without voicing an improper intentionality], and the blood of the beast was taken outside of the holy place, even though it was brought back and tossed, the priest has done nothing. In the case of Most Holy Things, the laws of sacrilege apply; and in the case of Lesser Holy Things, the laws of sacrilege do not apply.

M. 1:4 A deed having to do with the blood in the case of Most Holy Things produces a ruling which is lenient and one which is stringent. But in the case of Lesser Holy Things, the whole [tendency] is to impose a stringent ruling. How so? Most Holy Things before the tossing of the blood — the laws of sacrilege apply to the sacrificial parts and to the meat [which is for the priests]. After the tossing of the blood, the laws of sacrilege apply to the sacrificial parts but they do not apply to the flesh. On account of this and on account of that they are liable because of violation of the laws of refuse, remnant, and uncleanness. But in the case of Lesser Holy Things, the whole [tendency] is to impose a stringent ruling — how so? Lesser Holy Things before the tossing of the blood — the laws of sacrilege do not apply either to the sacrificial parts or to the flesh. And they are not liable because of violation of the laws of refuse, remnant, and uncleanness. After the tossing of the blood, the laws of sacrilege apply to the sacrificial parts, but they do not apply to the flesh. On account of this and on account of that they are liable because of violation of the laws of refuse, remnant, and uncleanness. It turns out that a deed having to do with the blood in the case of Most Holy Things produces a ruling which is lenient and one which is stringent, but in the case of Lesser Holy Things, the whole [tendency] is to impose a stringent ruling.

The laws of sacrilege apply to Most Holy Things slaughtered at the altar, even not at the right place, even subject to improper intentionality. That is because the initial act of sanctification governs. But once anyone has had a right to the beast, e.g., the priests once the blood has been tossed, so permitting them to eat their portion of the meat, then the laws of sacrilege no longer pertain. The interstitial issues, e.g., M. 1:2-3, do not change the main point and do flow directly from it. So too, the generative problematic of hierarchical classification, e.g., at M. 1:4, introduces a familiar mode of thought to fresh data. It is simply impossible to conceive of a more cogent and tightly-reasoned composition.

B. STAGES IN THE STATUS OF AN OFFERING: THE POINT AT WHICH THE LAWS OF SACRILEGE APPLY TO VARIOUS OFFERINGS

M. 2:1 The sin offering of fowl — the laws of sacrilege apply to it once it [the bird] has been sanctified [designated as a sin offering]. [When] its head has been severed, it is rendered fit to be made invalid by a tebul-yom and by one whose rites of atonement have not yet been completed and by being left overnight. [When] its blood has been tossed, they are liable on its account because of violation of the laws of refuse, remnant, and uncleanness. And sacrilege does not apply to it [any longer].

M. 2:2 Burnt offering of fowl — the laws of sacrilege apply to it once it has been sanctified. [When] its head has been severed, it is rendered fit to be made invalid by a tebul-yom and by one whose rites of atonement have not yet been completed and by being left overnight. [When] its blood has been squeezed out, they are liable on its account because of violation of the laws of refuse, remnant, and uncleanness. And the laws of sacrilege apply to it until it is taken out to the ash heap.

M. 2:3 Cows which are to be burned and goats which are to be burned — the laws of sacrilege apply to them once they have been sanctified. [When] they have been slaughtered, they are rendered fit to be made invalid by a tebul-yom and by one whose rites of atonement have not yet been completed and by being left overnight. [When] their blood has been tossed, they are liable on their account because of violation of the laws of refuse, remnant, and uncleanness. And the laws of sacrilege apply to them in the ash heap until the meat is reduced to cinders.

M. 2:4 The burnt offering — the laws of sacrilege apply to it once it has been sanctified. [When] it has been slaughtered, it is rendered fit to be made invalid by a tebul-yom and by one whose rites of atonement have not yet been completed and by being left overnight. [When] its blood has been tossed, they are liable on its account because of violation of the laws of refuse, remnant, and uncleanness. And the laws of sacrilege do not apply to its hide. But it will be taken out to the ash heap.

M. 2:5 A sin offering, and a guilt offering, and communal sacrifices of peace offerings — the laws of sacrilege apply to them once they have been sanctified. [When] they have been slaughtered, they are rendered fit to be made invalid by a tebul-yom and by one whose rites of atonement have not yet been completed and by being left overnight. [When] their blood has been tossed, they are liable on their account because of violation of the laws of refuse, remnant, and uncleanness. The laws of sacrilege do not apply to the meat. But the laws of sacrilege apply to the sacrificial parts until they are taken out to the ash heap.

M. 2:6 The Two Loaves — the laws of sacrilege apply to them once they have been sanctified. [When] they have formed a crust in the oven, they have been rendered fit to be made invalid by a tebul-yom and by one whose rites of atonement have not yet been completed and to have slaughtered the animal sacrifice [which pertains to them (Lev. 23:18)] on their account. [When] the blood of the lambs has been tossed, they are liable on their account because of violation of the laws of refuse, remnant, and uncleanness, But sacrilege does not apply to them.

M. 2:7 The show bread — the laws of sacrilege apply to it once it has been sanctified. [When] it has formed a crust in the oven, it has been rendered fit to be made invalid by a tebul-yom and by one whose rites of atonement have not yet been completed and to be laid out on the table. [When] the dishes of incense have been offered, they are liable on its account because of violation of the laws of refuse, remnant, and uncleanness. And sacrilege does not pertain to it [any longer].

M. 2:8 Meal offerings — the laws of sacrilege apply to them once they have been sanctified. [When] they have been sanctified in a utensil, they are rendered fit to be made invalid by a tebul-yom and by one whose rites of atonement have not yet been completed and by being left overnight. [When] the handful [of the meal offering] has been offered, they are liable on their account because of violation of the laws of refuse, remnant, and uncleanness. And the laws of sacrilege do not apply to the residue. But the laws of sacrilege apply to the handful [of the meal offering itself] until it is taken out to the ash heap.

M. 2:9 The handful, the frankincense, the incense, the meal offerings of priests, and the meal offering of the anointed priest, and the meal offering which accompanies drink offerings [M. Zeb. 4:3] — the laws of sacrilege apply to them once they have been sanctified. [When] they have been sanctified in a utensil, they are rendered fit to be made invalid by a tebul-yom and by one whose rites of atonement have not yet been completed and by being left overnight. And they are liable on their account because of violation of the laws of remnant and because of violation of the laws of uncleanness. But the prohibition of refuse does not apply to them.

This is the general principle: For whatever is subject to that which renders the offering permitted [the tossing of the blood for the atonement rite, in the example of the animal offerings] are they not liable on account of violation of the laws of refuse, remnant, and uncleanness until what renders the offering permitted has been properly offered. And for whatever is not subject to that which renders the offering permitted, once it has been sanctified in a utensil are they liable on account of the violation of the laws of remnant, and on account of violation of the laws of uncleanness. But the law of refuse does not apply to it [at all].

T. 1:7 Cows which are to be burned, once one has slaughtered them and tossed their blood — the laws of sacrilege apply to them. "And they are liable on their account because of violation of the laws of refuse, remnant, and uncleanness," the words of R. Meir [M. Me. 2:3D]. And sages say, "The prohibition of refuse does not apply [to offerings on the altar] inside [but only to those made on the outer altar]."

M. 2:2-8 II:1/9B He who derives benefit from money designated for the purchase of an animal for a sin offering or for a guilt offering if he makes restitution prior to the offering his sin offering, he should add a fifth to the original sum and spend the whole on a sin offering; if this was before presenting his guilt offering, he should add a fifth and spend the whole on a guilt offering. But if he makes restitution after he has offered his sin offering [and thus cannot present another], he should take the money set aside for restitution and toss it into the Dead Sea, so that it will never be used for a secular purpose, and if it is after he has offered his guilt offering, the money is to go to the Temple as a votive offering, along these lines: he who derives benefit from Most Holy Things prior to the tossing of the blood, or from the sacrificial limbs of Lesser Holy Things after the tossing of the blood, restitution for the benefit he has enjoyed should go for a votive offering; all restitution for an offering that was to be used for the altar is assigned to buy something for the altar; if it is restitution for money assigned for the upkeep of the Temple house, it is used for that purpose; if it is restitution for funds assigned for an offering for public worship, then the restitution is to go to public freewill offerings.

The triumph of the opening unit is matched by the second, which works out that problematic to which I made reference in section I. The same pattern is applied to successive classifications of offerings, meaning, taxa to which a beast may be sanctified. The laws of sacrilege apply at the point of sanctification until the tossing of the blood, at which the animal is permitted to the priesthood; if the animal is not permitted to the priesthood, e.g., in the case of the burnt offering, the laws of sacrilege pertain throughout. The separate consideration of priestly misconduct, e.g., the possibility of the offering's being made invalid by a priest who awaits sunset for the completion of a purification rite or who has yet to complete the rites of atonement, or if the meat is left overnight, enriches the presentation. I do not believe that the power of the Halakhah, in form and in generative logic, to set forth a coherent statement in line with a cogent hermeneutics, is better illustrated than in this category-formation.

C.   CULTIC PROPERTY THAT IS NOT SUBJECT TO SACRILEGE BUT THAT ALSO IS NOT TO BE USED FOR NON-CULTIC PURPOSES

M. 3:1 (1) The offspring of a sin offering, and (2) the substitute of a sin offering, and (3) a sin offering, the owner of which died, are left to die. [The sin offering] (1) which became superannuated, or (2) which was lost, or (3) which turned out to be blemished, if [this is] after the owner has effected atonement, is left to die, and does not impart the status of substitute [to an animal designated in its stead]. And it is not available for enjoyment but is not subject to the law of sacrilege. And if [this is] before the owner has effected atonement, it is put out to pasture until it suffers a blemish, then is sold, and with its proceeds he [the owner] brings another, and it does impart the status of substitute [to an animal designated in its stead]. And it is subject to the law of sacrilege.

T. 1:8 All sin-offerings which are left to die [M. Me. 3:1A, B-E] — the funds [set aside for their purchase] go to the Salt Sea [M. Me. 3:2F]. They are not available for benefit. But the laws of sacrilege do not apply to them [M. Me. 3:2]. A sin-offering which died of natural causes and a burnt-offering which died of natural causes — the laws of sacrilege do not apply to them. A burnt-offering of fowl, the blood of which one has squeezed out — the down and craw have left the domain of sacrilege. The laws of sacrilege apply to it [the bird itself] until it is taken out to the ash-heap.

M. 3:2 He who sets aside coins for his Nazirite offering[s] [Num. 6:14: a he-lamb as a burnt offering, a ewe-lamb as a sin offering, a ram as a peace offering] — they [the coins] are not available for benefit. But they [the coins] are not subject to the laws of sacrilege, because they [the sacrifices] are appropriate to be offered wholly as peace offerings [Lesser Holy Things, not subject to sacrilege before the blood is tossed]. [If] he died, [if] they were not designated [for their particular, respective purposes], they fall [to the Temple treasury] as a freewill offering. [If] they were designated [for their particular, respective purposes], the money set aside for the sin offering is to go to the Salt Sea. They are not available for benefit, but they are not subject to the laws of sacrilege. [With] the money set aside for the burnt offering, they are to bring a burnt offering. And [with] the money set aside for peace offerings, they are to bring peace offerings. And they are eaten for one day [M. Zeb. 5:6] and do not require bread [Num. 6:19].

T. 1:9 He who sets aside coins for his Nazirite-offering — they [the coins are not available for benefit. But they are not subject to the laws of sacrilege, because they [the animals to be purchased with the coins] are appropriate to be offered wholly as peace-offerings [M. Me. 3:2A-C]. Under what circumstances? When they [the coins] are left undesignated [for the purchase of a particular animal-sacrifice]. But if they were designated [for the purchase of a particular animal sacrifice], the laws of sacrilege apply to the funds set aside for a sin-offering and to the funds set aside for a burnt-offering. But the laws of sacrilege do not apply to the funds set aside for peace-offerings [M. Me. 3:2F]. If it was a beast, the laws of sacrilege apply to the sin-offering and to the guilt-offering, but the laws of sacrilege do not apply to peace-offerings. [If the owner] died, [if] they were undesignated, they fall [to the Temple-treasury] as a free-will offering. [If they were designated [for particular purposes], the funds set aside for the sin-offering go to the Salt Sea. The funds set aside for the burnt-offering and the funds set aside for the peace-offerings are to be spent in the purchase of animals which are to be offered [M. Me. 3:2H, I]. If it [the beast] was [designated as a] sin-offering, it is left to die. [If] it was designated as a burnt-offering or as peace-offerings, it is to be offered.

T. 1:10 [If the owner said], "These [coins] are for my burnt-offering and the rest are for the remainder of my Nazirite-offerings," and then died, [with] the money set aside for the burnt-offering, [the executor] should bring a burnt-offering. The laws of sacrilege apply to it. And the rest of the money falls [to the Temple-treasury] as a free-will-offering. And the laws of sacrilege apply to them [the coins]. [If he said], "These are for my peace-offering, and the rest [of the money] is for the remainder of my Nazirite-sacrifices," and died — with the money set aside for peace-offerings, let him [the executor] bring peace-offerings. The laws of sacrilege [do not] apply to them. And the rest of the money falls [to the Temple-treasury] as a freewill-offering. And the laws of sacrilege do apply to them. [If he said], "These are for my sin-offering, and the rest is for the other Nazirite-offerings," and then died, the money set aside for a sin-offering goes to the Salt Sea [M. Me. 3:2F]. And it is not available for use. But it is not subject to the laws of sacrilege. And the rest of the coins — [if] one wants to bring with them a burnt-offering, he brings a burnt-offering. [If] he wants to bring peace-offerings, he may bring peace-offerings. And the laws of sacrilege apply to all of them [the coins], but the laws of sacrilege do not apply to [making use of] only part of them [the coins].

T. 1:11 [If] one was liable to offer a sin-offering of fowl and said, "Lo, I pledge myself to bring a burnt-offering," and he set aside coins and said, "Lo, these are for [purchasing an animal in fulfillment of] my obligation," [if] he wanted to bring with them a sin-offering of fowl, he may not bring it. [If he wanted to bring with them] a burnt-offering of fowl, he may not bring it with them. And the laws of sacrilege apply to all of them [the coins], and the laws of sacrilege apply to only part of them. [If] he died, the coins go to the Salt Sea, because money set aside for a sin-offering is mixed up among them.

T. 1:12 [If a Nazirite designated], these [coins] for his sin-offering and these for his burnt-offering, and these for his peace-offerings, but then they got mixed up together, Lo, this one purchases with them three beasts, whether in one place or in three places. He declares the money set aside for the sin-offering to be rendered unconsecrated by means of the animal he has purchased for the sin-offering, the money set aside for the burnt-offering, by means of the animal set aside for the burnt-offering and the money set aside for peace-offerings, through the animal set aside as peace-offerings. The laws of sacrilege apply to all of them [the coins], and the laws of sacrilege apply to part of them.

T. 1:13 The Zab, the Zabah, the woman after childbirth, the *mesora'*, and [any one of] all those mentioned in the Torah who are liable to bring bird-offerings, who separated coins, Let him say, "Lo, these are for [the purchase of an animal in fulfillment of] my obligation." [If] he wanted to bring with them a sin-offering of fowl, he may bring [If] he wanted to bring with them a burnt-offering of fowl, let him bring it. The laws of sacrilege apply to all of them [the coins], and the laws of sacrilege apply to part of them. [If] he died, let them fall [to the Temple-treasury] as a freewill-offering. And the laws of sacrilege apply to them.

T. 1:14 [If one said], "A purse among my purses is consecrated," or, "An ox among my oxen is consecrated" — the laws of sacrilege apply to all of them [the coins, the oxen], and the laws of sacrilege apply to any one of them [the coins or oxen]. What is he to do? He brings the largest among them and says, "If this one is consecrated, Lo, it is the consecrated one. If not, then that which is consecrated in every place is to be deemed as unconsecrated in exchange for this one [which is now consecrated]."

T. 1:15 The bones and the sinews and the hooves and the horns which separated from consecrated animals before the tossing of the blood — the laws of sacrilege apply to them. [If they separated] after the tossing of the blood, the laws of sacrilege do not apply to them. But a coal which burst from off the altar, whether before midnight or after midnight, — Lo, this one should not return it. It is not available for benefit, but the laws of sacrilege do not apply to

M. 3:3 R. Simeon says, "Blood is subject to a lenient law at the outset and to a strict law at the end, and the drink offerings are subject to a strict rule at the outset and to a lenient rule at the end. The blood at the outset: the laws of sacrilege do not apply to it. [When] it has gone forth to the Qidron Brook, the laws of sacrilege apply to it. Drink offerings at the outset: the laws of sacrilege apply to them. [When] they have gone forth to the pits, the laws of sacrilege do not apply to them."

T. 1:16 R. Simeon says, "Blood is subject to a lenient law at the outset and to a strict law at the end" [M. Me. 3:3A]. It is mixed together in the gutter and rolls on downward to Qidron Valley and is sold to the farmers for manure. And the laws of sacrilege apply to them [the coins paid]," the words of R. Meir and R. Simeon. And sages say, "Sacrilege does not pertain to the money." And so did R. Simeon say, "He who sanctifies money for the upkeep of the house — "the laws of sacrilege apply to them [the coins]." And drink-offerings are subject to a strict rule at the outset and to a lenient rule at the end [M. Me. 3:3A]. R. Eleazar bar Sadoq says, "There was a little channel between the porch and the altar, at the west of the ramp. Once in every sixty or seventy years, the young priests would go down there and from there collect wine congealed like dried figs. They bring them up and burn them in a state of sanctity since it is said, In the holy place you shall pour out a drink-offering of strong drink to the Lord (Num. 28:7). Just as it is poured out in a state of holiness, so it is burned in a state of cleanness." And it says, "He built a watchtower in the midst of it and hewed out a wine vat in it" (Is. 5:2) — "He built a watchtower" — this is the Hekhal. "He hewed out a wine vat in it" — this is the altar. "And also he hewed out a wine vat in it" — this is the pit.

M. 3:4 The ashes [of the incense] of the inner altar and [of the wicks that remain] of the candelabrum — are not available for benefit, but the laws of sacrilege do not apply. He who sanctifies the ash to begin with — the laws of sacrilege apply to it. (1) Turtledoves which have not yet reached their maturity and (2) pigeons which have become superannuated are not available for benefit, but the laws of sacrilege do not apply. R. Simeon says, "Turtledoves which have not yet reached their maturity — the laws of sacrilege apply to them. But pigeons which have become superannuated are not available for benefit, but the laws of sacrilege do not apply."

M. 3:5 The milk of animal sacrifices and the eggs of turtledoves are not available for benefit, but the laws of sacrilege do not apply to them. Under what circumstances? In the case of what is made holy for the use of the altar. But in the case of what is made holy for the upkeep of the Temple house — [If] one has sanctified a chicken, the laws of sacrilege apply to it and to its egg. [If he sanctified] an ass, the laws of sacrilege apply to it and to its milk.

M. 3:6 Whatever is appropriate for [use on] the altar but not for the upkeep of the house, for the upkeep of the house and not for the altar, not for the altar and not for the upkeep of the house the laws of sacrilege apply thereto. How so? [If] one sanctified (1) a hole full of water [B], (2) a dung heap full of dung [C], (3) a dovecote full of pigeons [A], (4) a tree covered with fruit, (5) a field full of herbs — the laws of sacrilege apply to them and to what is in them. But if he sanctified (1) a hole, and afterward it filled with water, (2) a dung heap, and afterward it was filled with dung, (3) a dovecote, and afterward it was filled with pigeons, (4) a tree and afterward it filled with fruit, (5) a field and afterward it was filled with herbs — "the laws of sacrilege apply to them, but the laws of sacrilege do not apply to what is in them," the words of R. Judah. R. Simeon says, "He who sanctifies a field and a tree — the laws of sacrilege apply to them and to what grows in them, for they are the offspring of that which has been consecrated." The offspring of the tithe of cattle may not suck from [a beast that is] tithe [of cattle]. And others donate [their beasts] thus [on condition that, if the tithe of their cattle should be a female beast, its milk should not be deemed consecrated but should be available for its offspring]. The offspring of a consecrated beast should not suck from consecrated beasts. And others donate their beasts thus. Laborers should not eat of dried figs which have been consecrated. And so: A cow should not eat of vetches which have been consecrated.

T. 1:17 Whatever is appropriate for use on the altar but not for the upkeep of the house, for the upkeep of the house and not for the altar, not for the altar and not for the upkeep of the house — even milk, even cheese, and even brine — the laws of sacrilege apply to them. [If] he consecrated a cow, the laws of sacrilege apply to it, to its offspring, and to its milk. [If he consecrated] an ass, the laws of sacrilege apply to it and to its [If he consecrated] a chicken, the laws of sacrilege apply to it and to its egg.

T. 1:18 The egg of a turtledove [M. Me. 3:5A], the crop of fowl, and the offerings of gentiles are not available for use, but are not subject to the laws of sacrilege. He who sanctifies turtledoves for the upkeep of the house — the laws of sacrilege apply to their eggs [M. Me. 3:5E].

T. 1:19 A dung-heap — the laws of sacrilege apply to it and its dung. A pit — the laws of sacrilege apply to it and to its water. A dovecote — the laws of sacrilege apply to it and to its doves. [If] one sanctified them empty and afterward they were filled up, " The laws of sacrilege apply to them, but the laws of sacrilege do not apply to what is in them" [M. Me. 3:6I], R. Eleazar b. R. Simeon says, "Also: the laws of sacrilege apply to what is in them."

T. 1:20 Said R. Yosé, "I prefer in all cases [of M. Me. 3:6H] the opinion of R. Meir, except for the case of the field and the tree, "because in these cases it is usual for them to be filled up [with herbs or fruit, and hence that was to be expected at the outset]."

T. 1:21 Laborers who work in the sanctuary should not eat dried dates which are consecrated. But others donate for them. And so: A cow which was working in the sanctuary should not eat from vetches which have been consecrated. But others donate for them [M. Me. 3:6P-Q].

T. 1:22 [If] one sanctified a cow, vetches, and sheaves, they do not say, "Let this cow eat the vetches and the sheaves." But others donate for it.

T. 1:23 A laborer who did work [for the sanctuary], whether for a hundred [a maneh] or for two hundred zuz, should not say, "Give me this cow for the maneh [which you owe me] and this cloak for fifty zuz." For that which has been consecrated is not rendered unconsecrated in exchange for an act of labor but only in exchange for money alone. How do they carry out the procedure? They set aside the payment for the craftsmen. They render them [what is set aside] unconsecrated in exchange for the coins of the craftsmen and they give them [the specified objects, now deemed unconsecrated] to the craftsman as their salary. Then they go and take them from the heave-offering Fund of the Chamber. Manure and dung of consecrated animals — Lo, these are prohibited. And funds paid for them fall to the Temple-treasury.

M. 3:7 [If] the roots of a privately owned tree come into consecrated ground, or those of a tree which is consecrated come into privately owned ground, they [the owners of the tree or property, respectively] are not available for enjoyment, but they are not subject to the laws of sacrilege. A well that gushes forth from a field that is consecrated — [the water] is not available for enjoyment, but the laws of sacrilege do not apply. [If] the water went outside of the field, they derive benefit from it. Water that is in a golden jar is not available for benefit but is not subject to the laws of sacrilege. [If] one put it into a glass, the law of sacrilege applies to it. The willow branch [set beside the altar] is not available for benefit but is not subject to the law of sacrilege. R. Eleazar b. R. Sadoq says, "The elders would take some of it for their lulabs."

T. 1:24 That which is located in the shadow of a dovecote or in the shadow of a cave [belonging to the sanctuary] — they are not available for use, but the laws of sacrilege do not apply [M. Me. 3:7A-C]. And that which is on lands [of the Temple] — the laws of sacrilege apply. Water which is in the pitcher — the laws of sacrilege do not apply to it. [When] one poured it into a glass, the laws of sacrilege apply to it [M. Me. 3:7H]. But as to the pitcher and the glass itself, the laws of sacrilege apply to them, because they themselves are consecrated [M. Me. 3:7F-H].

M. 3:8 A nest which is up at the top of a tree which has been consecrated is not available for benefit, but is not subject to the law of sacrilege. And that which is on an asherah tree one may flick it off with a reed. He who sanctifies a forest — the law of sacrilege applies to the whole of it. And the Temple treasurers who bought wood — the laws of sacrilege apply to the wood. But the laws of sacrilege do not apply to the chips and [they do] not [apply] to the foliage.

T. 1:25 He who sanctified a forest for beams [for the Temple] — the laws of sacrilege apply to the beams, and the laws of sacrilege apply to the chips and to the foliage [M. Me. 3:8E-F]. But the Temple-treasurers who purchased a forest for wood — the laws of sacrilege apply to the wood, but the laws of sacrilege do not apply to the chips and to the foliage [M. Me. 3:8G-I].

The particular hermeneutics having come to full expression in the opening two chapters of the Mishnah and its continuator-documents, we come now to the generic hermeneutics of the law. If the category-formation builds upon two classifications, what is subject to the laws of sacrilege and what is available for secular purposes, then the generic hermeneutics can be relied upon to ask about an interstitial category: not subject to sacrilege, not available for secular use. That is the analytical reasoning — the mediation between opposites — that identifies and defines interstitial classification(s). The exposition of the interstitial case, through lists such as those at M. 3:4-5, carry in their wake their own distinctions, e.g., between what is made holy for the use of the altar and what is made holy for the upkeep of the Temple house. This comes to a climax at M. 3:6, with its secondary expansion at M. 3:7.

II. SACRILEGE OF TEMPLE PROPERTY IN GENERAL

A. SACRILEGE HAS BEEN COMMITTED ONLY WHEN THE VALUE OF A PERUTAH OF TEMPLE PROPERTY HAS BEEN USED FOR SECULAR PURPOSES

M. 4:1 Things consecrated for the altar join together with one another [for making up the requisite quantity — a perutah's worth — to be subject to] the law of sacrilege, and to impose liability on their account for transgression of the laws of refuse, remnant and uncleanness. Things consecrated for the upkeep of the house join together with one another [in regard to sacrilege]. Things consecrated for the altar and things consecrated for the upkeep of the house join together [for making up the quantity to be subject to] the law of sacrilege.

M. 4:2 Five components in a burnt offering join together [to form the requisite volume for liability to sacrilege]: (1) the meat, (2) the forbidden fat, (3) the fine flour, (4) the wine, and (5) the oil. And six in the thank offering [join together]: (1) the meat, (2) the forbidden fat, (3) the fine flour, (4) the wine, (5) the oil, and (6) the bread.(1) Heave offering, and (2) heave offering of tithe, and (3) heave offering of tithe of Demai, and (4) dough offering, and (5) first fruits join together to impose a prohibition and to impose liability to the added fifth on their account.

T. 1:28 A half-perutah in value of things consecrated for the altar and a half-perutah in value of things consecrated for the upkeep of the house join together with one another for purposes of sacrilege [M. Me. 4:1D]. A burnt-offering and its sacrificial parts join together with one another [to impose liability for] offering them up outside and to impose liability on their account because of violation of the laws of refuse, remnant, and uncleanness. A burnt-offering and its drink-offerings join together with one another [to impose liability for] offering them up outside and to impose liability on their account because of violation of the laws of refuse, remnant, and uncleanness [M. Me. 4:2A]. A thank-offering and its bread join together with one another [to impose liability for] offering them up outside and to impose liability on their account because of violation of the laws of refuse, remnant, and uncleanness. A half-olive's bulk of meat and a half-olive's bulk of bread join together with one another to impose the status of refuse on the bread, but not on the meat [M. Me. 4:2B]. That which has been rendered refuse in the case of Most Holy Things joins together. That which has been rendered remnant, whether in the case of Most Holy Things or in the case of Lesser Holy Things does not join together.

M. 4:3 All forms of refuse join together. All forms of remnant join together. All forms of carrion join together. All forms of creeping things join together. The blood of a creeping thing and its flesh join together. A general principle did R. Joshua state, "All things that are alike in the [duration of] uncleanness of each and in the requisite measure of each join together. [If they are alike] (1) in [duration of] uncleanness but not in requisite measure, (2) in requisite measure but not in [duration of] uncleanness, (3) neither in [duration of] uncleanness nor in requisite measure, they do not join together [to form the volume that is necessary to convey uncleanness]."

M. 4:4 Refuse and remnant do not join together, because they are of two [different] categories. The creeping thing and carrion, and so too, carrion and the flesh of a corpse — do not join together with one another to impart uncleanness, even in accord with the lesser of the two of them. Food which has been made unclean by a Father of Uncleanness and that which has been made unclean by an Offspring of Uncleanness join together to impart uncleanness in accord with the lesser remove of uncleanness of the two of them.

M. 4:5 All foodstuffs join together — to render the body invalid, at a volume of half a half-loaf of bread; in the case of food, two meals for an erub [M. Erub. 8:21; in the volume of an olive's bulk to impart uncleanness as food, in the volume of a fig's bulk in connection with removal [from one domain to another on] the Sabbath [M. Shab. 7:4], and in the volume of a date's bulk [for the volume prohibited for eating] on the Day of Atonement [M. Yoma 8:2]. All liquids join together — to render the body invalid, at a volume of a quarter-log; and for the mouthful [which it is forbidden to drink] on the Day of Atonement.

M. 4:6 Orlah fruit and diverse kinds of the vineyard join together. R. Simeon says, "They do not join together." Cloth and sacking, sacking and leather, leather and matting join together with one another. R. Simeon says, "That is because they are suitable to be made unclean as that which is used for sitting [with moshab uncleanness]."

T. 1:29 All liquids join together to form a quarter-log [M. Me. 4:5G-H] and pour the measurement of pouring out on the Sabbath. A creeping thing — its blood, its flesh, and its limbs join together to form the requisite volume of a lentil [M. Me. 4:3E]. All those things which are prohibited in the case of a Nazir join together with one another to form the requisite volume of an olive's bulk. A half olive's bulk from a clean beast while it is alive and a half olive's bulk of the same after it has died — Lo, these join together. A half olive's bulk of an unclean beast while it is alive and a half-olive's bulk of an unclean beast after it has died do not join together. A half olive's bulk of a clean beast and a half olive's bulk of an unclean beast, whether alive or dead, do not join together.

T. 1:30 All corpses join together with one another to form the requisite volume of an olive's bulk. A half olive's bulk of flesh and a half olive's bulk of corpse-matter join together with one another [M. Me. 4:3F]. But all other sources of uncleanness in connection with a corpse do not join together with one another, for they are not equivalent in respect to the requisite volume of them required for imparting uncleanness [M. Me. 4:3G]. A half olive's bulk of meat and a half olive's bulk of milk join together to impose liability on their account because of [eating forbidden] food and because of cooking. The stones of a house afflicted by a nega' and its wood and dirt join together with one another. R. Simeon says, " Cloth and sacking and hide and matting join together with one another because their measurement; a handbreadth by a handbreadth, is equivalent on account of being cut off and used for sitting" [M. Me. 4:6C-D].

We move from the particularities that attend to the character of what has been sanctified to the generalizations that cover everything that has been sanctified. The first rule is, the consideration of sacrilege comes into play only for a volume of holy material that to begin with someone would take into account, that is, a volume that would be subject to intentionality. That familiar consideration immediately invokes the matter of mixtures or joining together of diverse classes of holy materials to constitute a sufficient volume to meet the minimum standard, the matter of mixtures of diverse classes of substances of the same genus being a standard of the generic hermeneutics. The elaborate lists then complete the instantiation of the perfectly familiar problem of interstitiality: like and unlike.

    B.   *SACRILEGE IS DEFINED BY THE ONE WHO DOES IT OR BY THE THING TO WHICH IT IS DONE*

M. 5:1 "He who derives benefit to the extent of a perutah's value from that which is consecrated, even though he did not cause deterioration [through use of it], has committed an act of sacrilege," the words of R. Aqiba. And sages say, "Anything which is subject to deterioration through use — he has not committed an act of sacrilege unless he has caused deterioration through use. But anything which is not subject to deterioration through use — once he has derived benefit from it, he has committed an act of sacrilege." How so? [If a woman] put a chain around her neck, a ring on her finger, drank from the cup of gold [M. Tam. 3:4B, used for water for the animal to be offered as the whole offering of the day], once she has derived benefit from it, she has committed an act of sacrilege. [If a man] put on a shirt, covered himself with a cloak, used an ax to split wood — he has not committed sacrilege unless he has caused deterioration through use. [If] he pulled wool out of a sin offering [lamb] when it was alive, he has committed an act of sacrilege only if he has caused deterioration. But if this was after it was dead, once he has made use of it, he has committed an act of sacrilege.

M. 5:2 [If] one derived benefit to the extent of a half-perutah and caused deterioration to the extent of a half-perutah, or [if] he derived benefit to the extent of a perutah from one thing and caused deterioration to the extent of a perutah in some other thing — Lo, this one has not committed an act of sacrilege — until he will derive benefit to the extent of a perutah and [or] cause deterioration to the extent of a perutah in the very same thing.

T. 2:1 He who derives benefit and he who causes deterioration to the extent of a perutah from that which is consecrated commits an act of sacrilege. [If] he derived benefit but did not cause deterioration, caused deterioration but did not derive benefit, Lo, this one has not committed an act of sacrilege — until he will derive benefit and intend to derive benefit, so that his act of deriving benefit and his causing deterioration should be simultaneous, [and should apply] to the case of something which is usually subject to deterioration, and at the time that he has derived benefit, he has caused deterioration, and, in the case of an agent, that he [the agent] has carried out his agency. R. Aqiba says, "If one derived benefit, even though he did not cause deterioration, he has committed an act of sacrilege" [M. Me. 5:1A-C]. R. Aqiba [B. Me. 18a: sages] concedes to sages in respect to things which are not subject to deterioration, for example, bracelets, nose-rings, necklaces, and finger-rings, that if he derived benefit, even though he did not cause deterioration, he has committed an act of sacrilege. Sages [B. Me. 18b: Aqiba] concede to R. Aqiba [sages] in respect to things which are subject to deterioration, that if he derived benefit but did not cause deterioration, he has not committed an act of sacrilege.

T. 2:6 One cannot commit sacrilege after another has committed sacrilege in the same thing in the case of consecrated things, except for a beast [M. Me. 5:3A-B]. R. Nehemiah says, "A beast and a utensil of service." He who derives benefit from a sin-offering while it is alive has committed sacrilege only if he caused deterioration. But if it is dead, once he has derived benefit, he has committed sacrilege [M. Me. 5:1/0-P], for deterioration does not pertain to that which is dead. If he derived benefit but did not cause deterioration, caused deterioration but did not derive benefit, Lo, this one has not committed an act of sacrilege — until he will derive benefit and cause deterioration, and intend to derive benefit, until his deriving benefit and his causing deterioration should be simultaneous, and should pertain to that which is detached from the ground, and in the case of an agent, that the agent should perform his agency. If there is consecrated meat and ordinary meat for guests, and he said to him [the waiter], "Give them each a piece," and he [the waiter] says to them, "Take two each," and they took three each, all of them have committed an act of sacrilege [M. Me. 6J]. But in the case of a burnt-offering, only those who eat have committed an act of sacrilege.

The subtle, interstitial issue that is raised — whether the value of the act of sacrilege is assessed from the perspective of the Holy Thing or the actor — is made explicit in the opening composition.

C. *SACRILEGE EFFECTS THE SECULARIZATION OF SACRED PROPERTY*

M. 5:3 One does not commit sacrilege after another has committed sacrilege [in the same thing] in the case of consecrated things, except for a beast or a utensil or service. How so? [If] he rode on a beast and his fellow came along and rode on it and yet another came and rode on it — drank from the golden cup and his fellow came along and drank from it, and yet a third party came along and drank from it and pulled wool out of a sin offering, and his fellow came along and pulled wool from the sin offering, and yet a third came along and pulled wool from the same sin offering — all of them have committed an act of sacrilege. Rabbi says, "Anything which is not subject to redemption is subject to a case of sacrilege following sacrilege."

M. 5:4 [If] one took a stone or a beam from what is consecrated, lo, this one has not committed an act of sacrilege. [If] he gave it to his fellow, he has committed an act of sacrilege. But his fellow has not committed an act of sacrilege. [If] he built it into the structure of his house, Lo, this one has not committed an act of sacrilege — until he actually will live under it [and enjoys its use] to the extent of a perutah's worth. [If] he took a perutah of consecrated money, Lo, this one has not committed an act of sacrilege. [If] he gave it to his fellow, he has committed an act of sacrilege. But his fellow has not committed an act of sacrilege. [If] he gave it to a bath keeper, even though he did not take a bath, he has committed an act of sacrilege. For he [the bath keeper] says to him, "Lo, the bath is open to you. Go in and take a bath."

M. 5:5 What he has eaten and what his fellow has eaten, what he has used and what his fellow has used, what he has eaten and what his fellow has used, what he has used and what his fellow has eaten join together with one another — and even over an extended period of time.

T. 2:2 [If] one took an ax which had been consecrated and cut wood with it [M. Me. 5:1M], if he derived benefit and caused deterioration to the value of a perutah, he has committed an act of sacrilege. [And] if not, he has not committed an act of sacrilege. [If] his fellow came and cut wood with it, both of them have committed an act of sacrilege. [If] the first took it and gave it to the second, the first party has committed an act of sacrilege, and the second has not committed an act of sacrilege [M. Me. 5:4B-C].

T. 2:3 [If] he took an ass which had been consecrated and rode on it, if he derived benefit and caused deterioration to the extent of the value of a perutah, he has committed an act of sacrilege. And if not, he has not committed an act of sacrilege. [If] his fellow came and rode on it, both of them have committed an act of sacrilege. [If] the first one took it and gave it to the second, the first has committed an act of sacrilege, and the second has not committed an act of sacrilege.

T. 2:4 [If] one took a stone which had been consecrated and built it into his house, a beam and built it into his house, Lo, this one has not committed an act of sacrilege — until he will live under it [and enjoy its use] to the extent of a perutah's worth [M. Me. 5:4D-E].

T. 2:5 If he took a perutah which had been consecrated and said, "Lo, it is mine," he has said nothing — until he spends it for secular purposes. [If] he gave it to a barber, even though he did not cut his hair, he has committed an act of sacrilege. And in the case of a burnt-offering, [if] he gave it to his fellow, and his fellow to his fellow, all of them have committed an act of sacrilege [M. Me. 5:3H].

T. 1:26 He who separates his sheqel and spent it — lo, this one has committed an act of sacrilege. He who separates his sheqel for his fellow [which his fellow spent] — Lo, this one has committed an act of sacrilege. [If] he purchased with it bird offerings for Zabin, bird-offerings for Zabot, and bird-offerings for women who have given birth.

T. 1:27 he who brings his sin-offering or his guilt-offering or his Passover-offering from that [money] which is [already] consecrated — he who pays his sheqel or a zuz form a zuz which he has consecrated — "once he has taken it [for the stated purpose], he has committed an act of sacrilege," the words of R. Simeon. And sages say, "He has committed an act of sacrilege only after the blood [of the sacrifice] has been tossed." On this basis did they say: They do not bring meal-offerings, drink-offerings, meal-offerings of cattle, or the bread of the thank-offerings from that which has not yet been tithed, or from heave-offering, from first tithe from which the heave-offering has not yet been removed, from second tithe and from that which has been sanctified which have not been redeemed, from that which is mixed up with heave-offering or from that which is new [before the 'omer], from fruit which has been grown in the seventh year. But if one brought [meal-offerings] from such sources, he has not committed an act of sacrilege. And one need hardly say, [one should not bring] from 'orlah-fruit and from produce which has grown as mixed seeds in a vineyard [= T. Men. 8:30].

The secularization, by an act of sacrilege, of the Holy Thing simply carries forward the logic of the matter. What is treated as secular indeed is classified as such. So too, the act of sacrilege is deemed effective at the point at which the actor has derived benefit from the action, M. 5:4. The matter of mixtures signals another quite familiar initiative precipitated by the generic hermeneutics; what singles out the presentation before us is the clarity of the issues.

D. *AGENCY IN EFFECTING AN ACT OF SACRILEGE*

M. 6:1 The agent who carried out his errand [and thereby inadvertently committed an act of sacrilege] — the householder [who appointed the agent is responsible and] has committed the act of sacrilege. [If the agent] did not carry out his errand [in committing an act of sacrilege], the agent [is responsible and inadvertently] has committed the act of sacrilege. How so? [If] he said to him, "Give out meat to the guests," but he gave them liver, "Liver," and he gave them meat — the agent has committed the act of sacrilege. [If] he said to them, "Give them one piece each," and he [the agent] said, "Take two each," but they took three each, all of them are guilty of committing an act of sacrilege. [If] he said to him, "Bring [such and such a thing] from the window," or, "From the chest," and he brought it to him, even though the householder said, "I meant only from here," and he brought it from there, the householder has committed the act of sacrilege. But if he said to him, "Bring it to me from the window," and he brought it from the chest, or "From the chest," and he brought it from the window, the agent has committed the act of sacrilege.

M. 6:2 [If] he sent by means of [an agent who was) a deaf-mute, an imbecile, or a minor [to purchase goods with money which unbeknownst to the sender, was consecrated], if they carried out their errand, the householder has committed the act of sacrilege. [If] they did not carry out their errand, the storekeeper has committed the act of sacrilege. [If] he sent something by means of a person of sound senses, and realized before he reached the storekeeper [that the coins are consecrated and, therefore, regretted having sent those coins], the storekeeper will have committed the act of sacrilege when he pays out [the coins]. What should he do? He should take a perutah or a utensil and state, "A perutah which is consecrated, wherever it may be, is made unconsecrated by this." For that which is consecrated is redeemed by money or by something which is worth money.

T. 2:7 [If the father said,] "A perutah which has been consecrated do I have in the window," and the son went and [inadvertently] paid it out — the son has committed an act of sacrilege, and the father has not committed an act of sacrilege. [If] his father said to him, "Go and take it," the father has committed an act of sacrilege, and the son has not committed an act of sacrilege. [If] he gave him a perutah and said to him, "Go and buy me goods from the market," and the householder realized that it had been consecrated but the agent did not realize it, the agent has committed an act of sacrilege. [If] both of them realized, both of them have not committed an act of sacrilege. But the storekeeper will have committed an act of sacrilege when he will pay it out. [If] all three of them realized [that it was consecrated], none of them has committed an act of sacrilege. But the goods belong to the sanctuary. What should he do to remove his fellow from the grip of sacrilege?

T. 2:8 [Let him] take a perutah or a utensil, saying, "The perutah which has been consecrated, wherever it may be, is rendered unconsecrated by means of this sela', or by means of this pitcher, or by means of this cloak." For the status of consecration applies to everything, but it does not apply to slaves, deeds, or real estate.

M. 6:3 [If] he gave him a perutah [and] said to him, "With half of it bring me lamps, and with half of it wicks" and [if] he went and brought back lamps for the whole of it or wicks for the whole of it — or if he said to him, "Bring me lamps for the whole of it," or, "Wicks for the whole of it," and he went and brought him lamps for half of it and wicks for half of it, both of them have not committed an act of sacrilege. But if he said to him, "Bring me lamps for half of it from such-and-such a place, and wicks for half of it from such-and-such a place," and he went and brought for him lamps from the place in which he was supposed to get the wicks, and wicks from the place from which he was supposed to get the lamps, the agent has committed the act of sacrilege.

T. 2:9 [If] one gave him a perutah and said to him, "With half of it bring me lamps, and with half of it wicks," but he went and brought him lamps for the whole of it, [or] wicks for the whole of it, both of them have not committed an act of sacrilege [M. Me. 6:3A-C] — the householder, because his errand has not been carried out; and the agent, because he has not changed the terms of his errand to the value of an entire perutah. But [if] he gave him a hundred pieces of silver and said to him, "With the whole of it bring me lamps," "With the whole of it bring me wicks," and he went and brought him lamps with half of it and wicks with half of it, both of them have committed an act of sacrilege — the householder, for his errand has been carried out to the extent of a perutah of value; and the agent, because he has changed the terms of his errand to the value of a perutah. But if he said to him, "Bring them to me from Joseph['s shop]," and he brought [them to] him from Simeon['s shop], "[Bring me] from Shihin," and he brought him from Sepphoris, it is the agent who has committed an act of sacrilege.

M. 6:4 If he gave him two perutot [and] said to him, "Bring me an etrog," and he went and brought him an etrog for a perutah and a pomegranate for a perutah, both of them have committed the act of sacrilege. R. Judah says, "The householder has not committed an act of sacrilege. For he says to him, 'I wanted a big etrog, and you brought a small and poor one.'" [If] he gave him a golden denar [= six selas] [and] said to him, "Bring me a shirt," and he went and brought him a shirt for three selas and a cloak for three, both of them have committed an act of sacrilege. R. Judah says, "The householder has not committed an act of sacrilege, For he says to him, 'I wanted a large shirt, and you brought me a small and poor one.'"

T. 2:10 [If] one gave him two perutot and said to him, "Bring me an etrog," and he went and brought him an etrog for a perutah and a pomegranate for a perutah, both of them have committed an act of sacrilege. R. Judah says, "The householder has not committed an act of sacrilege, for [he may claim], 'I wanted a large etrog, and you brought me a small, poor one.' If he gave him a golden denar [=six selas] and said to him, "Bring me a shirt," and he went and brought him a shirt for three [selas] and a cloak for three [selas], both of them have committed an act of sacrilege. R. Judah says, "The householder has not committed an act of 'sacrilege, for he may say to him,' I wanted a large shirt, but you brought me a small, poor one"' [M. Me. 6:4]. But R. Judah concedes in the case of pulse, that both of them have committed an act of sacrilege. For pulse which sells for a sela is like pulse which sells for a perutah.

M. 6:5 He who deposits coins with a money changer — if they were bound up, he [the money changer] should not make use of them. Therefore, if he paid [them] out, he has committed an act of sacrilege. If they are loose, he may make use of them. Therefore, if he paid them out, he has not committed an act of sacrilege. [If the owner of the coins] deposited [them] with a householder, one way or the other, he [the householder] should not make use of them. Therefore, if he paid them out, he has committed an act of sacrilege. "A storekeeper is deemed equivalent to a householder," the words of R. Meir. R. Judah says, "He is equivalent to a money changer."

T. 2:11 He who deposits coins with a moneychanger — if they are bound up, he [the money-changer] should not make use of them. Therefore, if he paid them out, he has committed an act of sacrilege. If they are untied, he may make use of them. Therefore if he paid them out, he has not committed an act of sacrilege. [If he deposited them] with a householder, one way or the other, he should not make use of them. Therefore if he paid them out, he has not committed an act of sacrilege. A storekeeper is equivalent to a householder," the words of R. Meir. R. Judah says, "He is equivalent to a money-changer" [M. Me. 6:5].

M. 6:6 **A perutah which has been consecrated, which fell into a purse [containing other money], or if one said, "A perutah in this purse is consecrated"** — **"as soon as one has paid out the first [coin in the purse], "he has committed an act of sacrilege," the words of R. Aqiba. And sages say, "[He has not committed an act of sacrilege] until he has paid out all the money in the purse." And R. Aqiba concedes in the case of one who says, "A perutah in this purse is consecrated," that he goes along and pays out the money [without having committed an act of sacrilege] until he will have paid out all the money which is in the purse.**

T. 3:1 A perutah which has been consecrated which fell into a purse, or he who says, "A perutah in this purse is consecrated," once he has paid out the first [M. Me. 6:6A-C], he brings a suspensive guilt-offering. And once he has paid out the second, he brings an unconditional sin-offering," the words of R. Aqiba. And sages say, "He brings a suspensive guilt-offering only on account of something which is subject to extirpation for the inadvertent doing of which one is liable to a sin-offering."

T. 3:2 To whose benefit does this [money paid] sacrilege fall? He who makes use of a sin-offering or a guilt-offering, Lo, this one adds [the added fifth], bringing [with the funds] another sin-offering or another guilt-offering. [If] his sin-offering already had been offered, then it [the money for the new one] goes to the Salt Sea. [If] his guilt-offering already had been offered, then it [the money] falls to the Temple treasury as a freewill-offering. [If the foregoing pertains to making use of] Most Holy Things before the tossing of the blood, Lesser Holy Things after the tossing of the blood [M. 1:4], a burnt-offering and sacrificial parts, a handful [of the meal-offering] and an incense-offering, the meal-offering of an anointed priest and the meal-offering which accompanies drink-offerings — Let the funds [set aside for that purpose] fall to the Temple treasury. [If the foregoing pertains to making use of] community offerings, let them [the funds] fall to the Temple treasury as a freewill-offering. [If the foregoing applies to making use of] that which is sanctified for the altar, let the coins fall to the benefit of that which is consecrated for the altar. [If the foregoing applies to] that which has been sanctified for the upkeep of the house, let the coins fall to the benefit of that which is sanctified for the upkeep of the house.

If the agent carries out the instructions of the one who sent him, then the one who sent him is responsible for the agent's actions. If he did not do so, then he is responsible for what he has done. That general principle is applied to the category-formation at hand. The generic hermeneutics then takes over and accounts for the entire composite.

IV. DOCUMENTARY TRAITS

A. THE MISHNAH AND THE TOSEFTA

The standard, and huge contribution of the Tosefta to the amplification of the Mishnah's definition of the category-formation wins recognition. But I see no grounds for proposing that the Tosefta reconceptualizes matters to any material extent.

B. THE BAVLI

There is no point in asking how the Bavli has reconfigured the category-formation; it has scarcely contributed to its amplification, except at the level of tertiary exegetics.

V. THE HERMENEUTICS OF MEILAH

A. WHAT FUSES THE HALAKHIC DATA INTO A CATEGORY-FORMATION?

At stake in sacrilege — what unifies the category-formation — are provision for the minimum protection of Holy Things from inadvertent misuse, with appropriate reparation of value to the Temple when required, on the one side, and the maximum instantiation of the conditional, not absolute, status of sanctification, on the other. These quite distinct concerns pervade the whole and accomplish those larger results of analogical-contrastive logic — the detailed subspeciation of the species, the Holy — that I outlined at the opening section. Then balancing sacrilege against sanctification, the Halakhah weighs what is done by inadvertence against what is done with full deliberation. The act of sanctification, an act of intentionality, vastly outweighs the act of sacrilege, an act of inadvertence. That is because by the Written Torah's definition, sacrilege subject to an atoning offering — and that is what is at issue here — takes place by inadvertence, not by an act of will. Sanctification, by contrast, comes about by an act of praiseworthy will. The Halakhah has not only recapitulated the familiar notion of sanctification as a matter that is relative to circumstance, it has also made an eloquent statement indeed that in the cult Israel relates to God in full sincerity. The occasion of unintended sacrilege, its discovery and atonement, match the moment of sanctification: the Halakhah's disposition of both transactions underscore what the Halakhah finds important in the meeting of God and Israel at the altar: Israel's exemplary love and loyalty to God.

The unifying center of the category-formation — ample differentiation having taken place — therefore is reached at the matter of intentionality, just as Scripture specifies. But here the issue is distinct from Scripture's, even when the same consideration governs. In the present category-formation, the hermeneutics selects and interprets data to make one point. That is, what man has by an act of intentionality classified as holy he cannot by a later act of intentionality classify as secular. But if an inadvertent action has contradicted the initial intentionality, man can manifest his correct and consistent attitude toward the thing he has made holy, and all the rest flows from that hermeneutics, deriving from the process of comparison and contrast already outlined.

The governing theory, if we punish a person for inadvertently committing sacrilege, we treat as secular what has been subjected to sacrilege, places narrow limits on the matter of sacrilege. For, the Halakhah holds, once anyone may legitimately use what is God's, then the status of sanctification — what belongs uniquely to God — is suspended. If any person may legitimately utilize for his own benefit a Holy Thing, even a priest, the Holy Thing is no longer subject to sacrilege. So an ordinary Israelite who inadvertently eats meat of an offering that the priests have every right to consume, he is not guilty of sacrilege. Once the meat of a meat offering has been permitted to the priesthood, the blood having been sprinkled on the altar, then the meat that is left for the priests is no longer subject to sacrilege. Since some persons are permitted to enjoy them, anyone who enjoys them is not guilty of sacrilege. So long as there has been a time at which the Holy Thing was permitted, sacrilege is no issue. What belongs wholly to God, by contrast, as a burnt offering, is subject to sacrilege. If this is done inadvertently, one pays the value of what he has used plus an added fifth of the value and also offers a ram of a specified price as a guilt offering; that effects atonement. So much for the particular hermeneutics of the category-formation, which as usual works out its interests in the opening compositions of the composite.

B. THE ACTIVITY OF THE CATEGORY-FORMATION

When it comes to the working of the generic hermeneutics of the Halakhah, we account for the character of a large component of the whole. As usual, the Halakhah makes its contribution by the systematization of the rules, generalizing and classifying data. Scripture's few facts are closely analyzed and logically extended. The generic hermeneutics tends to govern in the later stages of the exposition of the category-formation. What makes Meilah quite remarkable is its inner cogency and compelling harmony. It is the one category-formation that we can cite for the perfection of the match and balance between contributions of the particular and the generic category-formations.

SECULARIZING THE SACRED: SACRILEGE EFFECTS THE SECULARIZATION OF SACRED PROPERTY: In the case of Holy Things, once an act of sacrilege has been committed, the Holy Thing is forthwith reclassified as secular, a further act cannot be committed. But in the case of objects of permanent use, the rule is otherwise. If one rode on a beast that was consecrated, and his fellow came along and rode on it and yet another came and rode on it — drank from the golden cup and his fellow came along and drank from it, and yet a third party came along and drank from it and pulled wool out of a sin offering, and his fellow came along and pulled wool from the sin offering, and yet a third came along and pulled wool from the same sin offering — all of them have committed an act of sacrilege. The act of sacrilege must involve a positive benefit; that may be psychological or material. If he took a perutah of consecrated money, Lo, this one has not committed an act of sacrilege. If he gave it to his fellow, he has committed an act of sacrilege. But his fellow has not committed an act of sacrilege. If he gave it to a bath keeper, even though he did not take a bath, he has committed an act of sacrilege.

SACRILEGE OF SACRIFICES IN PARTICULAR: WHEN DOES THE LAW OF SACRILEGE APPLY: If the blood is properly tossed, the laws of sacrilege no longer apply to that offering, the meat now being available to the priests. But if the blood is not properly tossed, the laws of sacrilege remain in effect for the animal under discussion. That point is made through an elaborate formulation of facts, thus: Most Holy Things which one slaughtered in the south side of the altar, instead of the north side, where the rite is supposed to be carried out — the laws of sacrilege apply to them. If one slaughtered them in the south and received their blood in the north, in the north and received their blood in the south. If one slaughtered them by day and tossed the blood by night, by night and tossed the blood by day, or if one slaughtered them with the intention of eating that which is usually eaten or offering up that which is usually offered up outside of their proper time or outside of their proper place — the laws of sacrilege apply to them. Whatever has had a moment of availability to for use by the priests — the laws of sacrilege do not apply thereto. And whatever has not yet had a moment of availability to the priests — the laws of sacrilege do apply thereto. There is a difference between Most Holy Things and Lesser Holy Things. Most Holy Things before the tossing of the blood — the laws of sacrilege apply to the sacrificial parts and to the meat which is for the priests. After the tossing of the blood, the laws of sacrilege apply to the sacrificial parts but they do not apply to the flesh. Lesser Holy Things before the tossing of the blood — the laws of sacrilege do not apply either to the sacrificial parts or to the flesh. And they are not liable because of violation of the laws of refuse, remnant, and uncleanness. After the tossing of the blood, the laws of sacrilege apply to the sacrificial parts, but they do not apply to the flesh.

The laws of sacrilege apply from the moment a beast or bird has been designated for a sacred use, that is, has been sanctified, and they no longer apply, as we have seen, once the blood has been tossed. When the laws of refuse, remnant, and uncleanness pertain, the laws of sacrilege apply no longer.

So much for the activity of the particular hermeneutics of the category-formation. That carries us to the generic hermeneutics.

CULTIC PROPERTY NOT SUBJECT TO SACRILEGE BUT NOT TO BE USED FOR NON-CULTIC PURPOSES: We come to an interstitial classification of Holy Things, specifically, things that are not subject to the penalties of sacrilege but that nonetheless are reserved for the Temple and its requirements. Whatever is appropriate for use on the altar but not for the upkeep of the house, for the upkeep of the house and not for the altar, not for the altar and not for the upkeep of the house the laws of sacrilege apply thereto. The interstitial status — not subject to sacrilege but not available for secular usage — applies to things that have been sanctified but cannot now serve the purpose for which they were set aside and also cannot serve for any other purpose. Animals sanctified as sin-offerings but the owner of which has died cannot be used for some other purpose, e.g., a sin-offering for some other purpose. Since these animals cannot be offered, they are not subject to the laws of sacrilege. But having been designated as sin-offerings, they retain the status bestowed upon them when they were so designated. They cannot be used in any secular purpose. The same status pertains to what animals designated as holy produce, e.g., milk or eggs. The milk or eggs cannot be used for personal benefit but are not subject to the laws of sacrilege. What is sanctified not for the altar but for the upkeep of the Temple house may be sold and so secularized, the value then applied to the purpose of the donor.

SACRILEGE OF TEMPLE PROPERTY IN GENERAL: Another common focus of the generic hermeneutics, the problem of interstitiality expressed in the matter of mixtures of classes of data that are both alike and unlike, accounts for the next unit. We know that minimum value must be converted for personal use for the act of sacrilege to have been committed. That is because, as I have stressed, sacrilege is a matter of status, not substance. Since sanctification defines the disposition of something but not its intrinsic character or quality, sacrilege pertains to how something is used, meaning, whether or not the benefit the private person has derived deserves consideration or is inconsequential. Here, then, the likely attitude of the person involved comes into play in an important way. If one has derived benefit from a Holy Thing to a value of less than a small coin's worth, the law of sacrilege does not apply. But if one has derived benefit to less than the stated value from a variety of Holy Things, then the cumulative worth registers: Things consecrated for the altar and things consecrated for the upkeep of the house join together for making up the quantity to be subject to the law of sacrilege. The upshot is simple: if the person who inadvertently made use of the Holy Things can have cared about the benefit he derived, then he is subject to a penalty. But if he in no way can have paid attention to the trivial benefit involved, then we take no account of the transaction to begin with. By introducing the criterion of the perutah's value, we explicitly invoke consideration for the attitude of the participant in the action, not merely the deed that he has done.

In regard to sacrilege, we distinguish between deriving benefit from a Holy Thing and causing damage or deterioration to it. Either one or the other imposes liability to sacrilege, for sacrilege depends on the one who does it, not on the thing to which it is done. That principle is qualified, but endorsed by the conflicting one: Anything which is subject to deterioration through use — he has not committed an act of sacrilege unless he has caused deterioration through use. But anything which is not subject to deterioration through use — once he has derived benefit from it, he has committed an act of sacrilege.

RESPONSIBILITY AND AGENCY: A third point of recurrent interest for the generic hermeneutics has to do with problems of causation, in the details of the Halakhah coming to express in assignment of responsibility, that is, who has brought about a given situation and therefore pays the penalties? The definition of sacrilege as an act of inadvertence bears implications for assigning responsibility. Take the matter of agency for example. The agent who carried out his errand and thereby inadvertently committed an act of sacrilege — the householder who appointed the agent is responsible and inadvertently has committed the act of sacrilege. If the agent did not carry out his errand in committing an act of sacrilege, the agent is responsible and inadvertently has committed the act of sacrilege. If he sent by means of an agent who was a deaf-mute, an imbecile, or a minor to purchase goods with money which unbeknownst to the sender, was consecrated, if they carried out their errand, the householder has committed the act of sacrilege. If they did not carry out their errand, the storekeeper has committed the act of sacrilege. If he sent something by means of a person of sound senses, and realized before he reached the storekeeper that the coins are consecrated and, therefore, regretted having sent those coins, the storekeeper will have committed the act of sacrilege when he pays out the coins.

C. THE CONSISTENCY OF THE CATEGORY-FORMATION

Here is a remarkably coherent category-formation, nearly all of the components of which collaborate in setting forth the principal hermeneutical concern that we have identified as critical. The two types of hermeneutics that, in my reconstruction of matters, explain the character of the category-formations, their choice of data and interpretation thereof, account for the character of nearly every line of the category-formation.

D. THE GENERATIVITY OF THE CATEGORY-FORMATION

The category-formation, Meilah, clearly exhibits the power to expand its own limits and to explore what is at best implicit in its initial program. This we see in the second-level consideration of the implications of the notion that sacrilege effects the secularization of sacred property. We immediately ask, is that the case even with what has been sanctified as to value, not corpus, e.g., an ass? Cannot a distinction be drawn between that the corpus of which is suitable for the altar, which is subject to secularization, and that the value of which is sacred, but the corpus of which cannot be? That distinction is drawn, and a whole new range of problems comes into view. A further mark of generativity appears in categorical interstitiality, the recognition of a classification of property that, while not subject to sacrilege, also may not be used for other-than-cultic purposes. The subspeciation of the species, the category-formation, clearly signifies a complex, therefore, dynamic category-formation indeed. The issue of intentionality, third, invites tertiary consideration of matters of minimal value: there is a minimum beneath which, by common consent, no one is going to form an intentionality, that is, beneath consideration altogether. What is not significant also is not subject to sacrilege — the foundation of a rich corpus of inquiries indeed. That too is a subset that flows logically from the main interest of the category-formation in intentionality, a mark of the generativity of the formation. Here, then, is a case in which the particular hermeneutics of the category-formation, and not the generic hermeneutics of the Halakhah, has guided the formation and articulation of nearly the whole of the category-formation.

The hermeneutics — the theory of the category-formation that governs the selection and interpretation of data — of the Halakhah rests on a reading of Israel's proper intentionality. Israelites are assumed not to wish to appropriate for their own use what belongs to God and will not do so. If they do so and realize it, they make amends. In this way they make manifest their correct attitude, they realize and embody what the sacrificial process is meant to nurture: acceptance in full freedom of will of God's dominion. And for his part, God responds to the manifest right thought with its counterpart. That is why he readily gives up what is his; once the priest has a right to part of an offering, God's claim to the offering is set aside, and sacrilege no longer pertains. The upshot is, the act of sanctification effects a change in the status of what is sanctified, but only for a limited period and for a highly restricted purpose. In imposing such a narrow construction to the matter of sacrilege, — inadvertent misuse of what God alone may use — the Halakhah underscores a now-familiar principle. It is that sanctification is relative to Israel's condition, not intrinsic to the condition of what is consecrated. How better say so than by treating as secular what has one time only been subjected to sacrilege or what has to someone, if not the right one, been permitted for personal benefit? From that minor detail, as from many other equally humble rulings, we can in stages reconstruct the hermeneutics that has shaped the entire category-formation. That marks the measure of the intellectual triumph attained at Meilah, one of the Halakhah's many remarkable successes.

WITHDRAWN